THE BIRDS OF THE BRITISH ISLES

VOLUME EIGHT

PHALACROCORACIDAE   DIOMEDEIDAE
SULIDAE   PODICIPEDIDAE
FREGATIDAE   GAVIIDAE
PROCELLARIIDAE   COLUMBIDAE
PTEROCLIDIDAE

THE BIRDS OF THE BRITISH ISLES

BY

DAVID ARMITAGE BANNERMAN

M.B.E., M.A., Sc.D., F.R.S.E.

GOLD MEDALLIST OF THE BRITISH ORNITHOLOGISTS' UNION

HONORARY ASSOCIATE, BRITISH MUSEUM (NATURAL HISTORY). PAST VICE-PRESIDENT
OF THE BRITISH ORNITHOLOGISTS' UNION. HON. FELLOW OF THE AMERICAN
ORNITHOLOGISTS' UNION AND OF THE SOCIÉTÉ ORNITHOLOGIQUE DE FRANCE

ILLUSTRATED BY

GEORGE E. LODGE

PAST VICE-PRESIDENT OF THE
BRITISH ORNITHOLOGISTS' UNION

VOLUME EIGHT

OLIVER AND BOYD

EDINBURGH: TWEEDDALE COURT
LONDON: 39A WELBECK STREET, W.1

FIRST PUBLISHED   1959

PREFACE

HAVING completed the treatment of the *Anatidae* (ducks) with volume VII, the present volume opens with the Order Pelicaniformes, embracing a group of web-footed birds which includes the cormorants, shag, frigate bird, and gannet. Next in sequence, following Hartert's order, are the Tubinares, in which we group the petrels, shearwaters and albatrosses; the first two are well represented on the British List, though few actually breed within our confines. Then follow two Orders of diving birds: the Podicipediformes embracing the grebes of which we have six species, and the Gaviiformes (formerly Columbiformes) embracing the divers of which four species figure on our list. Next in sequence comes the Order Columbiformes in which we find the pigeons and doves, well represented in our islands; and finally Pallas's sandgrouse—the sole representative of the Order Ptericletiformes—which has visited these islands from its home in the desert wastes of Asia.

Nine families are dealt with in sequence, whose names are set out on the cover of this volume.

When discussing the Tubinares some controversial matters are raised. In the arranging of that group I find myself in much closer agreement with those responsible for the A.O.U. Check-List (1957) than with the Check-List issued by the B.O.U. (1952). I have, for instance, retained the genus *Puffinus* for the shearwaters and thoroughly disagree with the grouping (in the British List) proposed for the genus *Bulweria*. Nor do I agree with the B.O.U Committee in dropping the genus *Pterodroma*. I retain it here for the capped petrel.

The retention on the British List of the kermadec petrel (*Pterodroma neglecta*) and the collared petrel (*Pterodroma brevipes*) appears to me to be unjustified; whereas I would give the benefit of the doubt to the Cape " pigeon " (*Daption capense*) as a chance wanderer to British seas. Arguments in support of these decisions will be found in my text. No doubt they will be hotly contested in some quarters but *not* in all.

ACKNOWLEDGMENTS

In this volume I find myself under a deeper debt than ever to the numerous specialists who have devoted their brains and their time to assist me in these essays. To name all in this Preface would be impossible, to many I have made acknowledgment in the text.

Whole essays have been provided by Mr. George Waterston (the gannet), and Dr. Alexander Wetmore (Audubon's shearwater and the black-capped petrel); major contributions have come from Mr. R. M. Lockley on the habits, nesting and migrations of the Manx shearwater; Mr. James Fisher on the fulmar; Mrs. M. K. Rowan and H. F. I. Elliott on the history of the great shearwater on its breeding ground; Dr. L. Harrison Matthews has written a fresh account of the nesting of the black-browed albatross and Dr. Brian Roberts describes for the first time his finding of a colony of the sooty shearwater on Kidney Island, and contributes notes on Wilson's petrel during the voyage of the *Scotia*. Dr. Ian Pennie has brought up to date the distribution of the Slavonian grebe in Scotland; and in particular Mrs. (Cecilia) Knowles, formerly of Dunlichity Lodge, has provided most valuable new field notes on the same species, enabling me to give the most comprehensive review of this grebe ever published, including its courtship. Very important is the long account of the breeding behaviour of the great crested grebe by Mr. Kenneth Simmons, whose work on this subject is already well known, but who brings his researches up to date in the valuable contribution he has now made to this volume. Last, but not least, I must extend my thanks to Mr. I. J. Ferguson-Lees for tracing for me the spread of the collared dove in the British Isles during the last two seasons, and to my old friend Professor Erwin Stresemann for reading the whole of the essay on this dove in the light of the comprehensive survey which he has just published on the spread through Europe of this Asiatic species.

Madame E. Kozlova has again sent in original notes from Russian sources and has helped with notes on the distribution of several species in the U.S.S.R. Similarly, Dr. Gudmundsson of Reykjavik has assisted with field and distributional notes on Iceland birds. Once again I have found Dr. Salomonsen's notes on Greenland birds of very great help when writing my essays.

When tracing the routes taken by wood-pigeons on their migrations in Europe, I have had correspondence with all the ringing stations of note in western Europe: the names of their directors and those who have sent me their ringing returns and other pertinent information, will be found in the main text. To one and all I extend my gratitude for the trouble they have taken on my behalf. I have in earlier volumes paid tribute to the authors of the standard works on the birds of Scotland and the birds of Ireland—how badly we need a similar work on the birds of Wales despite the valuable work being done in the Principality by Mr. Geoffrey C. S. Ingram and Colonel H. Morrey Salmon. I have made constant use of both these works.

The late appearance of this volume has not been the fault of the author, but it may be some satisfaction to those who have had to wait so long for volume VIII to learn that volume IX is well on the way to completion so far as the writer is concerned.   It will begin the huge Order Charadrii-formes, the text of which will fill two volumes.

Throughout the preparation of volume VIII I have been helped in no small measure by my wife ; she has added to my debt to her by reading the whole of the proofs.

David A Bannerman

BORELAND OF SOUTHWICK
By DUMFRIES
April 1959

ERRATA IN EARLIER VOLUMES

Very few other than minor errors have so far been brought to my notice but I have two apologies to make for past sins in the preparation of this work.

In my treatment of the short-toed lark (vol. II, p. 15) ; wagtails *B. feldegg* and *dombrowskii* (vol. II, p. 116), woodwarbler (vol. III, p. 28) and red-rumped swallow (vol. III, p. 380) and " harriers " in Malta (vol. V, p. 176) I attributed to Lt.-Colonel W. A. Payn notes which in point of fact were taken from a paper in the *Ibis* on the birds of Malta by Mr. W. H. Payn. The similarity of their initials caused this confusion. Mr. W. H. Payn's work on the birds of Malta is constantly mentioned in my text under other species but fortunately I there give the credit where it is due. I hope the author of that valuable contribution will forgive me.

The last—and I hope the final—error for which I must apologize is much more serious.   It occurred in vol. V, p. 299 where, under the honey buzzard (*Pernis apivorus*) I quote Colonel Scroope as having written in *Birds of Ireland* (1954) that the bird was formerly " a widespread breeding species " in Ireland.   That, of course, is quite untrue, and Colonel Scroope wrote nothing of the kind.   How this unfortunate mistake arose I am at a loss to explain, but I would ask those in possession of that volume to make the necessary correction—and also in the status as given on p. 298, where the last six words should be erased.   To Ireland the honey buzzard is, as Colonel Scroope correctly wrote : " A very rare passage migrant in summer and autumn."

I have already, through the courtesy of the Editors of the *Irish Bird Report* and of *British Birds*, been able to correct this error ; but I would like again to apologize unreservedly to Colonel Scroope who has taken this unforgivable mistake in such a sporting and generous way.

CONTENTS

In this list when a species is represented by *one race only* the English name is followed immediately by the Latin trinomial, or by the binomial if the species is monotypic.

If more than one race is represented in Britain, the species name is first given binomially, below which the recognized races follow in sequence, each with its English name and Latin trinomial.

As the majority of the species in the British List are illustrated, only a few great rarities not being depicted, a separate list of plates is unnecessary. On the left are given the plate numbers, and on the right the page numbers of the birds described. The plate numbers are placed opposite the *actual races* which are illustrated. As far as practicable the plates have been placed in the text facing the species which they depict.

PLATE				PAGE
	Cormorant	Phalacrocorax carbo		1
1	1. Cormorant	Phalacrocorax carbo carbo		1
	2. Southern Cormorant	Phalacrocorax carbo sinensis		1
2	Shag or Green Cormorant	Phalacrocorax aristotelis aristotelis		13
3	Gannet	Sula bassana		21
	Magnificent Frigate Bird	Fregata magnificens rothschildi		35
4	Stormy Petrel	Hydrobates pelagicus		39
5	Leach's Fork-tailed Petrel	Oceanodroma leucorrhoa leucorrhoa		48
6	Harcourt's or Madeiran Petrel,	Oceanodroma castro		60
6	Wilson's Petrel	Oceanites oceanicus		68
6	White-faced or Frigate Petrel,	Pelagodroma marina hypoleuca		78
	Manx Shearwater	Puffinus puffinus		86
7	1. Manx Shearwater	Puffinus puffinus puffinus		86
	2. Balearic Shearwater	Puffinus puffinus mauretanicus		86
	Little Shearwater	Puffinus baroli		101
8	1. Madeiran Little Shearwater,	Puffinus baroli baroli		101
	2. Alexander's Little Shearwater,	Puffinus baroli boydi		101
	Audubon's Shearwater	Puffinus l'herminieri l'herminieri		108

ix

PLATE			PAGE
9	GREAT SHEARWATER . .	Puffinus gravis	111
	MEDITERRANEAN SHEARWATER .	Puffinus diomedia	123
	1. MEDITERRANEAN SHEARWATER, Puffinus diomedia diomedia . .		123
8	2. CORY'S OR ATLANTIC SHEARWATER, Puffinus diomedia borealis .		123
10	SOOTY SHEARWATER . .	Puffinus griseus	135
	BLACK-CAPPED PETREL . .	Pterodroma hasitata	146

A Discussion as to the advisability of retaining the two Pacific species, the Kermadec Petrel, *Pterodroma neglecta*, and the Collared Petrel, *Pterodroma leucoptera brevipes*, on the British List, and the possible acceptance of the Cape Pigeon, *Daption capensis*, as an accidental wanderer to the British Isles. 150

	[COLLARED PETREL . .	Pterodroma leucoptera brevipes] . . .	155
	[CAPE PETREL OR CAPE PIGEON, Daption capensis]		156
8	BULWER'S PETREL . .	Bulweria bulwerii	161
11	FULMAR PETREL . . .	Fulmarus glacialis glacialis	167
12	BLACK-BROWED ALBATROSS .	Diomedia melanophrys melanophrys . .	188
13	GREAT CRESTED GREBE .	Podiceps cristatus cristatus . . .	200
	RED-NECKED GREBE .	Podiceps griseigena	223
14	1. RED-NECKED GREBE .	Podiceps griseigena griseigena . . .	223
	2. HOLBOELL'S GREBE .	Podiceps griseigena holböllii . . .	223
15	SLAVONIAN OR HORNED GREBE, Podiceps auritus		235
16	BLACK-NECKED GREBE . .	Podiceps caspicus caspicus . . .	250
17	LITTLE GREBE . .	Podiceps ruficollis ruficollis . . .	261
18	GREAT NORTHERN DIVER .	Gavia immer	272
19	WHITE-BILLED NORTHERN DIVER, Gavia adamsii		283
20	BLACK-THROATED DIVER .	Gavia arctica arctica . . .	298
21	RED-THROATED DIVER .	Gavia stellata	312
22	WOOD-PIGEON . .	Columba palumbus palumbus . .	324
23	STOCK-DOVE . .	Columba oenas	338
24	ROCK-DOVE . . .	Columba livia livia . . .	349
25	TURTLE-DOVE . .	Streptopelia turtur turtur . . .	361
	RUFOUS TURTLE-DOVE .	Streptopelia orientalis . . .	373
	COLLARED TURTLE-DOVE .	Streptopelia decaocto decaocto . .	375
26	PALLAS'S SANDGROUSE .	Syrrhaptes paradoxus . . .	388

Order PELECANIFORMES

Sub-order PELECANI

Family PHALACROCORACIDAE

Genus *PHALACROCORAX* Brisson

CORMORANT

Phalacrocorax carbo (Linnaeus)

1. Cormorant   PLATE I

Phalacrocorax carbo carbo (Linnaeus)

A resident species ; partly migratory

2. Southern Cormorant

Phalacrocorax carbo sinensis (Shaw and **Nodder**)

A non-breeding Visitor of which a number have been identified,
mainly on east and south coast, probably more numerous than
recorded specimens indicate

DISTINGUISHING CHARACTERS OF THE TWO RACES : The southern representative (*sinensis*) can be distinguished in the breeding season by the greater area of white on the head and at all seasons, when handled, by the fact that its plumage is glossed with metallic green instead of metallic blue as in the typical subspecies (see also under Identification).

IDENTIFICATION : The whole plumage of the cormorant is black with an oily-blue gloss on the upper and lower parts. The underside is deep blue-black, almost purplish-blue in some reflections. The feathers of the back, scapulars and wings have a bronze lustre. From the eye to the gape there is a whitish or buff patch and the chin is also whitish. The crown feathers are somewhat elongated and form a loose crest. In January there is a very conspicuous white patch on the thighs, which disappears in the early summer. The tail is long and stiff and contains fourteen feathers. The eye is green, the bill brown and the feet black. It is 36 inches in length.

The southern cormorant, sometimes named the lesser cormorant, is slightly smaller than *P. c. carbo* and is greenish-blue, not purplish-blue, on the underparts and oily blue on the upperparts. As well as the white thigh patch, it grows in spring long white feathers on the crown, the sides of the nape, the back of the upper neck and round the upper throat, which give the head a more or less white appearance. All the white head feathers disappear by the end of spring. The immature bird is browner with whitish underparts. Adult plumage is attained by the third year.

THE CHANGES OF PLUMAGE in the cormorant have caused much controversy in the past and for long were little understood. They are described in bewildering detail in *The Handbook*, but much more succinctly by the late W. R. Ogilvie-Grant, one-time keeper of Ornithology in the British Museum. He made a close study of the subject and at a meeting of the British Ornithologists' Club in 1910, at which both George Lodge and myself were also present, he exhibited a series of skins which clearly proved that the white-breasted birds were young of the year, a fact not at that date generally known. The sequence of plumages was described in *Bull. B.O.C.*, xxvii, pp. 22-25, and later appeared with an excellent photograph of the skins in a Country Life publication entitled *Our Common Sea Birds*, by Percy R. Lowe.

There is a good deal of variation in the first-year plumage, generally described as dark brown above, and dull white mottled with pale brown below. Some year-old birds and others still older (about 15 months) are white-breasted. At first the iris is brown, then after the first year pale bluish-green, and when the bird is fully adult emerald green. In the second year the feathers of the back are much like those of the adult, but the feathers of the underparts are glossy black, more or less mottled with white. After the second summer moult the cormorant assumes its adult dress, with the underparts uniform glossy greenish-black. In British specimens the white hair-like feathers of the head and neck and the white flank-patches begin to appear early in January, the perfect breeding plumage being generally assumed by the end of February. The white plumes on the head are retained until the beginning of April when they begin to drop out, and they disappear entirely by the middle of May: the white flank-patches are retained till the middle of June and do not altogether disappear until the end of July.

LOCAL DISTRIBUTION : The typical subspecies breeds on many cliffs around the coasts of Great Britain and Ireland and is fairly generally distributed. There are, however, wide stretches where it does not nest, especially in England where the coast is unsuitable. There are few parts of the coast, however, where it is not to be seen flying over the sea or sitting with wings outstretched on buoys or breakwaters. It nests on numerous islands round the English coast and is common on the Farne Islands off Northumberland and also in the Isle of Man.

The distribution of the cormorant in Scotland since 1684 is given in such detail in *The Birds of Scotland* (1953) that it is unnecessary to repeat it here, except to observe that its stronghold in Scotland appears to be in the Galloway country. Even there it will occasionally shift its quarters, as when the cormorants deserted the Balcary cliffs in favour of these at

Orroland in 1956, as recorded by E. Blezard in the *Scottish Naturalist* for that year. The cliffs of the Mull of Galloway, which the writer visited recently, afford an instance where both cormorants and shags can be seen inhabiting the same cliffs—both birds being plentiful. Cormorants breed sparingly on some of the islands of the Inner Hebrides. It has long been known to breed in Orkney and does so in Shetland where, however, it is greatly outnumbered by the shag. In winter the birds occur in many parts where they do not nest and flocks may be seen in the estuaries and especially in the Firth of Forth.

Similar details of distribution are given by the authors of the new *Birds of Ireland*, in which country it is stated to be generally distributed on all coasts and commonly found inland (as it is in Scotland); on the other hand in some places where sites seem suitable for nesting, the bird is unaccountably absent or breeds sparingly. This remark also applies to the bird's distribution in Scotland where it suffers competition from the shag, especially on the west coast and on the northern isles. Cormorants may frequently be seen far from the sea and delight in fishing in fresh waters, especially where trout are plentiful.

OCCURRENCES OF THE SOUTHERN CORMORANT IN BRITAIN : It is not easy to define the status of *P. c. sinensis* in these islands owing to its similarity to the resident bird. Moreover, although termed the southern cormorant, it is not restricted to southern Europe, but has breeding colonies in Belgium, Holland and northern Germany, from which areas birds may very easily reach our shores. In *The Handbook* Mr. Witherby records ringed examples from the countries mentioned above which have been recovered in Suffolk, Kent, Sussex and Dorset, while there is a Hampshire specimen in the British Museum. One has also been recorded from Jersey, Channel Islands, a bird which had been ringed near Rotterdam. It was recovered in April 1936 and recorded in the *Ibis* the following year. Mr. Witherby was probably correct when he put forward the suggestion that despite the paucity of specimens examined this cormorant occurs fairly frequently. Looking through the records in *British Birds*, vol. xxx, the following returns were noted :

Ringed				*Recovered*				
Rügen	.	.	. 30.5.34	Kent	.	.	.	. 5. 2.35
Rügen	.	.	. 28.5.33	Sussex	.	.	.	. 11. 2.36
Holland	.	.	. 27.6.32	Suffolk	.	.	.	. 11.12.35
Holland	.	.	. 26.5.35	Dorset	.	.	.	. 8. 1.36
Holland	.	.	. 4.6.35	Jersey	.	.	.	. 19. 4.36
Belgium	.	.	. 26.5.37	Kent	.	.	.	. 25. 7.38

Considering the locality of these northern breeding colonies it is not surprising that the continental cormorant's visits to Britain are mainly to the south and east of England. It has apparently never yet found its way to Ireland, for there is no mention of it in the recent work on that country. It is said that birds answering the description of the southern cormorant have been seen in Scotland at the Mull of Galloway, and once on Mochrum Loch in Wigtownshire, but visits to the west of Britain must be very rare indeed.

DISTRIBUTION ABROAD : (1) The northern or common cormorant, as we may term the typical race, inhabits Greenland (rare), Iceland, the Faeroe Islands (once common now very scarce), the British Isles, Scandinavia, and the coasts of northern Russia to the Kola Peninsula. It still breeds also in North America although it can no longer be termed " common ", as was formerly the case on the other side of the Atlantic. Writing in *The Book of Birds*, T. Gilbert Pearson, so well known in Europe for his work on Conservation, describes how at one time the bird bred as far south as Maine ; but at the time he wrote the most southerly colony existed on Cape Breton Island, Nova Scotia, which Pearson visited in 1930, finding " one hundred or more birds " on their nests on a high rocky cliff. The colony is protected and at the time was increasing.

In winter British cormorants travel far afield, birds ringed in Scotland, Ireland, and England having been recovered at points all the way down the west coast of Portugal, while a bird ringed in Wigtownshire has reached Algarve in the extreme south. The northern cormorant has also been recorded in the Atlantic from the Azores, Madeira, and the Canaries, but if any specimens exist they should be re-examined in the light of present-day knowledge of racial forms. It is, however, more likely that stragglers to the Atlantic islands will belong to the typical northern cormorant than to the Moroccan resident race which is most likely a sedentary bird.

(2) The southern cormorant or, as it was formerly termed, the lesser cormorant, breeds sparingly in Holland and Belgium, on the coasts of France and northern Spain, and in the Mediterranean from Sardinia and Italy to Asia Minor and Transcaspia, then eastwards to India and China. There are, or were, breeding colonies in Tunisia but on the Atlantic coast of Morocco its place is taken by another resident race *P. c. moroccanus*. In winter the southern cormorant (*sinensis*) is commonly found in the Suez Canal area and is reported to ascend the Nile as far as the Sudan frontier. It has once wandered as far inland as Biskra in Algeria (Hartert). That it migrates considerable distances, like the typical subspecies, is shown by a bird ringed in July near Rotterdam which was recovered in November of the same year in Minorca.

For many years the cormorant which bred in the Netherlands, Belgium, Denmark, and south Sweden was named *P. c. subcormoranus* Brehm, with type locality Holland, and was considered to be different from the eastern cormorant *sinensis*, type locality China. Only comparatively recently have they been united under the latter name, no grounds being found to keep them separate.

HABITS : The cormorant is such a familiar bird around the coasts of

PLATE I

CORMORANT

Phalacrocorax carbo carbo (Linnaeus)

the British Isles that it is known to most people, though not everyone distinguishes between it and the shag which, though smaller in size and less bulky in appearance, with greener, more glossy, plumage and no white patches on the flanks or cheeks, is so often mistaken for its larger relative. At all ages the cormorant's fourteen tail-feathers as against the shag's twelve are absolutely diagnostic.

Cormorants are sociable birds both in and out of the nesting season. Where one or two are to be seen perched on rocks at the end of a break-water others are pretty sure to be just out of sight, for they are very faithful to the same nesting place and take pleasure in each other's company. Floating buoys have an irresistible attraction for them, and it is no un-common sight to see two or three, with their wings held out as if to dry, on the buoys marking the channels in most harbours. The common cormorant is not so wedded to the sea as is the shag and may often be found on inland lochs and on rivers far from the coast—in fact wherever fish are to be picked up the cormorant may be encountered. Though we associate it with the sea it is not a deep-sea bird like the gannet and seldom goes far out of sight of land.

There has been a good deal of speculation as to the reasons which prompt the cormorant to favour certain parts of our coastline and the shag others, for both take their toll of the sea and their habits are not so very distinct. Both frequent stretches of coast where rocks and cliffs provide roosting places and nesting sites, but it is unusual, though by no means impossible, to find them together. In a book (*Our Common Sea Birds*) published by Country Life some years ago, Dr. Percy Lowe discusses this very point and, after drawing attention to the stretches of coast where one or other species predominates, observes that, generally speaking, where the coastline is especially steep, rugged, and rocky, the shag appears to be more in its element ; while on the contrary the cormorant seems more at home where the coast is lower, with alternating stretches of sand-flats and rocks, or where there are creeks, inlets, marshes, or ancient relics of former marine extensions. Moreover he suggests that these sharply differentiated varieties of coastal features favour the existence of quite different varieties of fish food, in the one case favourable, in the other unfavourable, to either species. Whether that quite reasonable hypothesis is borne out by an analysis of food taken seems open to doubt, for fish of all kinds are consumed by both species, although freshwater fish such as trout do not figure in the diet of the shag and flat fish are more often consumed by cormorants than by shags. It also depends very much on the latitude in which the birds are fishing which species of fish prey pre-dominate. That seems to be borne out by the analysis of stomach contents as quoted in *The Handbook* ; for instance, G. A. Steven, on the basis of 27 cormorants obtained in Cornwall, over half from estuaries, found that 40 per cent. of fishes eaten were flat fish, 10 per cent. marketable fishes, and about 50 per cent. non-marketable fishes. W. E. Collinge came to somewhat different findings from the examination of 43 birds, the stomach contents producing 98·86 per cent. animal food made up of 95·8 per cent. food fishes, 0·75 per cent. crustacea, and 1·14 per cent. vegetable algae. It seems to me that the structure of the coastline has much more influence on the distribution of the two species than the type of animal food predominating in a certain area, but see discussion on food of shag pp. 17-19.

It cannot be said that the cormorant has any graceful movements except when in the water. There is, as T. A. Coward once asserted, much that is ungainly, awkward, and uncouth about it. Its body is heavy and its flight usually low over the waves with the head and neck thrust out and the feet tucked behind. Over land it rises much higher, for it is then more suspicious and keeps well out of gunshot. On a small well-stocked trout loch which we own in Kirkcudbrightshire the visiting cormorants come in at a good height—usually only one at a time—to see if the water is deserted. If a boat is out they seldom venture to descend but fly round a few times and then make off, flying at several hundred feet.

There are several instances of cormorants soaring to spectacular heights, and the conclusion at which B. W. Tucker (who drew attention to the occurrence) arrived, is that such instances have some connexion with a nuptial performance, though as seldom witnessed they may express exceptional exuberance in certain individuals. An early case was recorded in the *Zoologist* of 1875 by Mr. G. E. Mathew, who observed a single bird rise in spirals to a considerable height when it was joined by another bird ; the two continued to wheel upwards round and round each other until they were nearly out of sight and looked mere specks in the clear sky. They amused themselves in this manner for nearly half an hour, when suddenly one of them closed its wings and fell at a tremendous pace through the air for some distance, performing apparently a somersault in its descent ; this manœuvre was immediately followed by its companion and repeated several times in succession until both birds were only a few feet above the surface of the sea.

I am inclined to doubt the performance having any sexual significance in the instance quoted, which took place in November. On the other hand Seton Gordon witnessed similar behaviour on the part of two cormorants on 22nd March 1942 over Broad Water in the Lake District of Cumberland. Many cormorants, so Mr. Gordon remarks, frequent that great sheet of water during the winter and early spring and no less than twenty were seen on the date mentioned in the air at the same time. Then a curious thing happened :

Two birds separated from the flock and for the best part of half an hour flew backwards and forwards overhead, keeping so close together that at times they seemed almost to touch. All the while they gathered altitude until they were perhaps 3000 feet above us and scarcely visible to the unaided eye. They then began to slant earthward at great speed, as a peregrine falcon might do, but checked their descent and continued to fly backwards and forwards and to circle overhead at a great height as before. The sun had already set behind the hills where we stood, but still shone upon the cormorants, and the white thigh-spots on both the birds were visible. It seemed to us that this was a courtship flight.

Mr. Seton Gordon adds that in his experience he had never seen cormorants rise so high, nor remain so long in the air, travelling all the time at their utmost speed. This flight certainly appears to have had some sexual significance and reminds one closely of the courtship flight of the mallard at the same time of year, except for the fact that the ducks do not rise to any great height—speed, and proximity to one another being, in their case, the keynote of the performance.

The dexterity of a cormorant below the surface of the water has to be seen to be believed, especially when in pursuit of live fish. When swimming on the surface the cormorant sinks its body low, and preparatory to diving gives a little leap before disappearing beneath the surface. If alarmed a bird can sink its body, in the manner of a darter, until only its head and neck are visible. There has been some controversy as to whether a cormorant uses its wings under water and, though it is never quite safe to be too dogmatic, the general opinion has been expressed by T. A. Coward when he wrote : " When turning, checking speed or rising to the surface the wings are slightly, very slightly, opened, but after watching the bird in the sea and in tanks, I am convinced that the statements that it uses its wings for swimming under water are erroneous."

All who are familiar with this bird must have noted the characteristic pose it so often indulges in of sitting on rocks or fish-traps with wings wide spread, sometimes gently swaying back and forth, but more often holding them rigidly open, the pinions wide apart. There seems to be no doubt that this is to dry the primaries and, as Tucker has observed in *The Handbook*, it has been suggested by Otto Heinroth that the cormorant's rather large wings are less effectively protected by contour feathers than those of most diving birds, hence the need for drying them after a spell of diving. Tucker did not entirely subscribe to this view, but believed that the cormorant's wing-feathers are less effectively water-proofed than those of other diving species. We have seen a group of griffon vultures drying out their wings in exactly the same manner after a heavy shower of rain in Andalucia. What is much less often seen is the cormorant doing the same thing while sitting or standing on calm water. Several observers wrote to *British Birds* in 1949-50 on the subject giving their experience ; among them Lord Hurcomb, Mr. C. M. Veysey, Mr. K. G. Spencer and Mr. E. G. Richards had all witnessed this singular occurrence on different occasions both on salt and fresh water. In the case of Mr. Veysey's bird, it maintained the drying position between for five and ten minutes before taking flight.

Under the heading Distribution Abroad, mention has been made of the cormorants from British colonies which wend their way south across the Channel and the Bay of Biscay to spend the winter months on the coast of northern Spain and the Atlantic coast of Portugal. Ringed birds have given undisputed evidence that individual birds—by no means all—feel this impulse to travel south every autumn.

In vol. xxv of *British Birds* (1931) Harry Witherby and Miss Leach summarized the movements of cormorants as ascertained by ringing up to that year with the results mentioned above. We have studied the published returns since that date and find that the same general trend of migration is borne out. Among the records there is one of a cormorant ringed as young in Sutherland 27.6.32 recovered three months later 30.9.32 off Finisterre. Another case of interest is a bird ringed in Co. Dublin in 1939 and recovered on the north coast of France in October 1950! Of birds ringed as young in Wales, nearly all in Anglesey, in 1950, thirteen were recovered during the subsequent autumn, winter and spring farther south on the west coast, or on the south coast, or on the east coast as far north as Norfolk. Nine others were recovered on the coasts of France, mainly on the Channel or in Brittany, but in one case a bird had travelled as far as the Gironde. Another record refers to a bird recovered twelve years after it was ringed and within 75 miles of its ringing locality. In the 1934 report the interesting fact emerges that out of some 190 recoveries of cormorants ringed in Britain 41 were reported from abroad, whereas only 2 shags out of 135 were found abroad and these had only travelled a short distance, ample evidence that of these two species the cormorant is much more addicted to leaving its birthplace.

In the latest Report on Bird-Ringing, *i.e.* that for 1957, it is recorded that eight cormorants from Anglesey, Pembroke, Devon and Wigtownshire were recovered in French waters and two off the north coast of Spain, between the months August to February. Eight of these birds were in their first winter, two in their second. Recoveries in home waters during the same year showed movements of up to 260 miles.

I have left till the end reference to the statistics published by Lord David Stuart of the movements of cormorants from the Mochrum cormorant colony on his Wigtownshire estate. The cormorants begin to frequent the colony in March and by the end of September it is quite deserted. Between 1919 and 1939 some 820 nestlings were ringed by J. G. Gordon, Lord Bute and Lord David himself; 172 were recovered and these were closely analysed by Lord David Stuart in *British Birds*, xli, pp. 194-199. He writes :

When one examines the migrations of Mochrum cormorants it appears they disperse all round the British Isles except north of the Caledonian Canal. No observable difference was found between the movements of first year birds and others (as in the case of the gannet in which yearlings tend to move farther to the south than the rest. . . . It seems clear that some birds must fly across Scotland, but whether they do this from the Solway to Berwick or from the Clyde to the Forth is impossible to say at present. My own view is that it is by the latter route.

Lord David illustrated the points of recovery in Britain in a map and on a second map those which were recovered outside the British Isles. Many recoveries were from the Brittany coast around Ushant, others again from Finisterre ; two had reached Portugal, one the extreme south, the other an inland locality not far from the Spanish border. Lord David was astonished at the proportion of these birds which met their death by shooting. Out of the 70 per cent. which died in their first year 67 per cent. were recorded as shot ; in their second year 64 per cent., and in their third year 30 per cent., confirming the supposition that as the birds grow older they learn by experience to avoid danger. The mortality rate in a cormorant colony is very great ; there are not, apparently, sufficient returns of adults to work out how many survive, but from the figures at Lord David's disposal he came to the conclusion that it is impossible for the species to maintain its breeding stock. A similar conclusion was arrived at by Dr. David Lack, *i.e.* that *on paper* sufficient numbers of young and adults do not survive to keep up the average breeding stock : the approximate number of birds in the Mochrum colony is estimated at 200-220 pairs. It is interesting to note that the size of the colony has never varied very much since Lord David can remember, so that here at any rate we have a colony in Britain which seems to be holding its own. Were it to be situated beyond the protection which Lord David affords the birds, it would be another matter. The birds breed on low rocky islands in the Castle Loch in the parish of Mochrum.

BREEDING HABITS : Edmund Selous devoted a whole chapter in his book *Bird Watching* [1] to the cormorant's social behaviour and to that of the guillemot, birds which he considered of particular interest. But it was the cormorant and the shag which really appealed to him most ; the former having, in his opinion, " a winning and amiable character . . . to which scant justice has been done " ; adding, " For whatever the cormorant may look like he is in reality—except from the fish's point of view, which is no doubt a strong one—both a very innocent and . . . a very amiable bird. He shines particularly in scenes of quiet domestic happiness—in the home circle both giving and receiving affection."

Selous then makes it clear that his remarks about the cormorant apply equally to the shag, the social habits of the two birds being almost the same if not quite identical. Of the courtship of the cormorant and of the manner the male makes love to the female he writes as follows :

Either at once from where he stands, or after first waddling a step or two, he

---

[1] Published in 1901, by J. M. Dent and Sons Ltd., to whom my acknowledgments are due.

makes an impressive jump or hop towards her, and stretching his long neck straight up, or even a little backwards, he at the same time throws back his head so that it is in one line with it, and opens his beak rather widely. In a second or so he closes it, and then he opens and shuts it again several times in succession, rather more quickly. Then he sinks forward with his breast on the rock, so that he lies all along it, and fanning out his small, stiff tail, bends it over his back whilst at the same time stretching his head and neck backwards towards it, till with his beak he sometimes seizes, and apparently, plays with the feathers. In this attitude he may remain for some seconds more or less, having all the while a languishing or ecstatic expression, after which he brings his head forward again, and then repeats the performance some three or four or, perhaps, half a dozen times. This would seem to be the full courting display, the complete figure so to speak, but it is not always fully gone through.

Selous completes his picture of the cormorant's love-making by describing a scene " in the dark jaws of that gloom-filled cavern, with the frowning precipice above and the sullen, heaving sea beneath ", in which the birds had made their home :

A nest . . . was on a ledge, and just within the mouth of one of those long, narrowing, throat-like caverns into and out of which the sea with all sort of strange sullen noises licks like a tongue. The bird who had seen me continued for a long time afterwards to crane about its long neck from side to side or up and down over the nest, in doing which it had a very demoniac appearance, suggesting some evil being in its dark abode. . . . Presently the bird's mate came flying in to the cavern, and wheeling up as it entered, alighted on a sloping slab of the rock just opposite to the nest. For a little both birds uttered low, deep, croaking notes in weird unison with the surroundings and the sad sea-dirges, after which they were silent for a considerable time, the one standing, the other sitting on the nest *vis-à-vis* to each other. At length the former, which I have no doubt was the male, hopped across the slight space dividing them, on to the nest, which was a huge mass of seaweed. There were now some more deep sounds and then, bending over the female bird, the male caressed her by passing the hooked tip of his bill through the feathers of her head and neck which she held low down the better to permit of this. Afterwards the two sat side by side together on the nest.

The whole scene was a striking picture of affection between these dark, wild birds in their lonely wave-made home.

Here was love unmistakable between so strange a pair and in so wild a spot. But to them it was the sweetest of bowers. . . .

The male bird now flies out to sea again, and after a time returns carrying a long piece of brown seaweed in his bill. This he delivers to the female, who takes it from him and deposits it on the heap, as she sits. Meanwhile the male flies off again, and again returns with more seaweed, which he delivers as before, and this he does eight times in the space of one hour and forty minutes, diving each time for the seaweed with the true cormorant leap. Sometimes the sitting bird, when she takes the seaweed from her mate, merely lets it drop on the heap, but at others she places and manipulates it with some care. All takes place in silence for the most part, but on some of the visits the heads are thrown up and there are sounds—hoarse and deeply guttural—as of gratulation between the two.

The sexual display has, so Bernard Tucker informed us in *The Handbook of British Birds*, been studied mainly on the Continent where Portielje, Haverschmidt and Heinroth have each published various accounts which have been summarized in the work quoted. There appears to be nothing very exceptional about it. The female, it seems, takes the initiative in "posturing", and has been observed to erect the tail, hold the wings close to the body and repeatedly throw back the head till the crown almost touches the back ; the head is shaken to and fro in this position with the bill half open. The male's reaction to this performance is to raise the feathers of the crown, neck and breast and distend the throat sac. Both birds utter distinctive notes. Coition usually takes place on the nest.

Cormorants are colonial nesters, and though the colonies vary in size 100 to 300 nests is about the limit in the British Isles—the last number referring to a colony on the Farne Is. Jourdain has emphasized that cormorants usually nest apart from shags though their colonies may sometimes adjoin one another on a rocky coastline. There are two or three quite distinctive breeding habitats. The normal situation in which to find the cormorant's nest is on the ledges of the steep face of a cliff falling to the sea ; then again there is the distinctive colony in Wigtownshire on the Castle Loch in the parish of Mochrum where the birds, to the number of about 200 pairs, nest on low rocky islands in the loch. This is an inland nesting place. There are others, but much smaller, in Ireland situated on islets in the small lakes of southern Connemara. A third type of cormorant colony in which the birds nest in trees is instanced by Major Ruttledge in the *Birds of Ireland* (1954) where at Lough Cutra, Co. Galway, about a hundred birds nest in trees on an island. At one time prior to 1904 cormorants nested in high trees on Lough Key in Roscommon, as mentioned by Ussher in 1900. The birds were driven away and have not used it as a nesting place since. I knew of an English locality in east Kent where cormorants have bred in trees but in that case there were only two nests in a dead tree growing out of the water. Mr. T. C. Gregory kindly sent me a photograph of the site in May 1947.

The southern cormorant, *P. c. sinensis*, nests frequently in trees at varying heights, often in company with herons, and also on the ground and on islands in lakes. The colonies of this cormorant are sometimes far larger than any of *P. c. carbo* and are reported to run to two or three *thousand* pairs (Jourdain). Seebohm mentions having seen it nesting in Holland on the bare ground on the flat banks of the Horster mere between Amsterdam and Utrecht, some eight or ten miles from the sea. We have nothing to compare with this in England. The colony consisted of some two hundred nests, many of which touched one another.

There are many cliffs and islands around our own coasts where the cormorant breeds and where the birds can be studied at close quarters by those not possessed of too strong a sense of smell. In her book, *The Farne Islands*, 1951, Miss Grace Watt (Mrs. Hickling) gives a description of what may be encountered :

Not only are the rocks running with limewash, but also the whole area is covered with partially eaten, decaying or regurgitated fish, and the smell is, in consequence, indescribable. Cormorants are sociable birds and their nests may be so close together that they almost touch. The nests are made chiefly of seaweed [on the Farne Is.] together with grass and scurvy grass, and are sometimes piled into mounds which may, in exceptional circumstances, be as high as twenty-three inches. When newly made they look very colourful in the sun, but as time goes on the seaweed dries and blackens and becomes fouled with lime. Cormorants are evidently not entirely lacking in artistic taste, for on May 31, 1945, Goddard found on the North Wamses a nest containing a full clutch of eggs which had a layer of scurvy grass as ornamentation round its edges. Both leaves and flowers were fresh and unwithered and it was obvious that this decoration had only just been added. They use jetsam of all kinds in nest building. . . .

When tree nests are made they are built of sticks and branches roughly put together and unlined. Nests in Britain are repaired or built in March or by the beginning of April, the eggs being laid at the end of April or early in May ; but nesting dates vary much according to locality and naturally show the greatest discrepancy on the Continent. Three to five eggs are usually laid ; they are white with a chalky surface. If the outer deposit is removed the blue undershell is revealed. Jourdain gives the average measurement of 100 British-taken eggs of the cormorant as 65·8 × 40·7 mm. Max. 74 × 41·7 and 68·5 × 44 mm. Min. 57·5 × 39 and 64 × 38 mm. Both parents incubate the eggs. The cormorant nestling is a hideous little creature born blind, " in which condition they remain for ten days or more " (P. R. Lowe). They are also naked, with a black skin. In about three weeks they are beginning to be covered with a thick smoky brown or dull black down. The young are fed by the parents regurgitating the food, the nestling introducing its bill and head, or even a little of its neck, into the gaping bill of the old bird.

Cormorant colonies are kept in control largely by Nature itself, storms early in the year sweeping away nests and eggs, while later the great and lesser black-backed gulls take their toll of the eggs.

Few in this country are likely to relish the idea of cooking a cormorant for dinner, but there is apparently a method of preparing the flesh to which the late W. R. Ogilvie-Grant drew attention in *Country Life* ; he assures us that the dish is " really excellent ". The *modus operandi* is first to bury the cormorant for two or three days ; then, having removed the entrails and substituted a large Portugal onion, to roast or stew it slowly. Before

PLATE 2

SHAG OR GREEN CORMORANT
Phalacrocorax aristotelis aristotelis (Linnaeus)

serving, the onion is removed, and the flesh is then said to be equal to that of the finest wild duck !

REFERENCES : Original Descriptions : 1. Northern Cormorant, *Pelecanus carbo* Linnaeus, *Syst. Nat.*, 10th ed., 1758, p. 133 : Europe, restricted type locality, North Scandinavia. 2. Southern Cormorant, *Pelecanus sinensis*, Shaw and Nodder. *Naturalist's Misc.*, xiii, 1801, Plate 529 : China.

SHAG OR GREEN CORMORANT PLATE 2

Phalacrocorax aristotelis aristotelis (Linnaeus)

A Resident. A very small proportion move south in winter, but not beyond Finisterre apparently

IDENTIFICATION : The shag has deep glossy bronze-green plumage which at a distance appears black. There is no white on the face. The crest in summer is much more in evidence than in the cormorant and is recurved ; in winter it is not seen. It has no white feathers in the breeding season. The gular pouch is bright yellow, and the iris green. The bill varies in colour, sometimes yellow and sometimes mixed with black. There are twelve feathers in the tail. Juveniles are dark brown with occasionally a little white on the breast. The shag is 30 inches in length.

LOCAL DISTRIBUTION : Although the shag is a common breeding bird in these islands its disposition around the coasts and islands is extremely local, and there have always been wide stretches of coastland where, for the obvious reason that the coastline is unsuitable, there is no pair for miles. It is far more numerous in Scotland than south of the Border, and it does not occur anywhere on the eastern coast of England south of the Yorkshire cliffs. Even there no breeding records are substantiated, though Mr. Chislett tells us in *Yorkshire Birds* that visitors have suspected the shag of breeding at Flamborough since 1949 when a party of adults and immature birds were seen on the rocks at the end of June. The birds have certainly not bred in any numbers on the Yorkshire cliffs within the last hundred years, and the numbers which bred there formerly can only be a matter for conjecture.

Mr. Chislett has stated that the shag occurs on the Yorkshire coast only occasionally and inland appearances are rare. Until recently very few shags bred in Northumberland, but now, to quote Mr. Temperley, " there is an increasing colony " on the Farne Islands. Concerning the latter breeding site Grace Watt [1] gives figures to show that the number of breeding pairs increased from one pair in 1931 to fifty-nine pairs in 1950, a number which was exceeded in 1949 when sixty-four pairs were nesting. No shags breed on the south coast of England east of the Isle

[1] *The Farne Islands*, 1951, pp. 97-103.

of Wight.[1] On that island there was a small colony of some eighteen pairs on the Freshwater cliffs in 1946 and also a small colony at Culver cliffs. These were counted by my wife from a boat beneath the cliffs. Mr. Edwin Cohen tells me that in 1954 only a very few bred on Freshwater cliffs. In 1955 there were about ten to twelve pairs at Main Bench. In the winter of 1956 some twenty to thirty—many more than there were cormorants— were identified in Christchurch harbour by Mr. J. V. Boys.[2] It is to be hoped that the shag may increase in the Isle of Wight as a breeding species, for as shown elsewhere it does not injure the edible fish industry as the cormorant does. In Cornwall there is a markedly large shag population compared with the much scarcer cormorant—" common on all coasts suitable for breeding ". It is also a common breeding bird in the Scilly Islands.[3] Many miles of the north coast of Cornwall harbour shags but no cormorants. In Wales the shag is locally distributed where the cliffs are suitable ; many pairs are resident in Pembrokeshire. It is absent from the north-west coast of England but breeds in the Isle of Man, where considerable numbers find suitable breeding places on the precipitous cliffs.

Compared with its status and distribution in England it is very much more numerous in Scotland and is an abundant nesting species. In the islands of western Scotland the shag is still amazingly common, if not perhaps so abundant as when Robert Gray wrote in 1871 that it was found breeding in great numbers in all the caves which intersect the precipitous coasts of Harris and Barra and also on the uninhabited rocks, such as the Haskeir group and other islands lying to the west of North Uist. Very large companies frequented the sounds which separate the islands and in these stations the shags were to be seen daily, at certain states of the tide, fishing in congregations which, in extent, reminded one of a dense colony of guillemots. Late in the afternoon these armies of shags rose in detachments and betook themselves to the caves in which they generally spent the night. One such cave named Liuir on the west side of Harris was estimated to hold not less than two or three hundred " green cormorants " during the breeding season, and at other times of the year gave shelter to the birds when the fury of the winter storms prevented their seaward flight. Gray remarked that in the Inner Hebrides shags were equally common, frequenting similar caves, instancing a number of islands Rum, Skye, Mull, Iona, Staffa, Jura, Islay and Gigha where there were nesting colonies. He remarked its numbers too in the caves along the rocky shores of Ayrshire and Wigtownshire and its frequency especially at the Mull of Galloway and at Burrow Head. For the distribution of the shag in our own time *The Birds of Scotland* can be consulted, the authors having taken pains to set out its breeding haunts in some detail. In

[1] *Handbook of British Birds*, vol. iv, p. 12.
[2] *British Birds*, xxxix, 1946, p. 36.
[3] B. H. Ryves, *Bird Life in Cornwall*, 1948.

southern Scotland the shag's principal nesting place is in the cliffs of the Mull of Galloway, while on the east coast the Berwickshire cliffs have always been a stronghold. In many of the Western Isles, the Outer Hebrides, the Flannans and Fair Isle it has been abundant from time immemorial. Despite a good deal of persecution it is increasing its breeding range on the Scottish mainland, particularly in north-east Scotland.

In Ireland, where it is also a common resident, it breeds abundantly on the precipitous cliffs and marine islands on the north, south, and west coasts, and much less numerously on the east where suitable haunts are limited.[1] Major R. F. Ruttledge adds that on the Great Saltee the shag nests abundantly, and at its many breeding places in Connacht and Antrim it outnumbers the cormorant.

There are a number of instances when shags have been found in inland counties, but such cases are rare. Occasionally it has been known to cross the land but to nothing like the same extent as the cormorant. In winter very large assemblies of shags may be seen. Dr. Baxter and Miss Rintoul record in *The Birds of Scotland* that round most of the coasts and in the sea lochs the shag is very common both in autumn and winter, when it is possible to see hundreds at a time attracted by shoals of fish. Such flocks are especially common among the Northern and Western Isles. The same applies to Ireland.

There is no immigration from abroad so far as we know but there is a tendency for a small proportion of our stock to move south. Up to the year 1934 out of 135 shags ringed in Britain only two were recovered abroad and these had travelled only a short distance. This, as it appears, did not give a true picture, for subsequent reports by the Bird-Ringing Committee showed the following returns :

		Ringed		*Recovered*			
A shag	Lundy Is.	.	3.7.48	Denmark	.	.	.	22.9.48
	Lundy Is.	.	19.7.48	Brittany .	.	.	.	—.10.48
	Farne Is. .	.	23.7.48	Frisian Is.	.	.	.	16.2.49
	Shetland .	.	23.7.50	Norway .	.	.	.	8.3.51
	Farne Is. .	.	26.6.52	Holland .	.	.	.	21.2.53
	Lundy Is.	.	? June 52	Brittany .	.	.	.	—.8.54
4 shags	Lundy Is.	June-Aug. 54		Brittany .	.	.	Dec. 54-Jan. 55
6 shags	Lundy Is.	June-July 55		Brittany .	.	.	Oct.-Nov. 55
	Farne Is. .	.	25.6.54	Pas de Calais .	.	Ca. 23.12.54

Lundy Island shags go farther south than those from any other breeding place. A great many of those which are ringed have been recovered within a short distance of where they were ringed ; some Scottish, Isle of Man and Lundy Is. birds have moved to Ireland. It will be seen from the rather few returns that the shag is a much more stay-at-home species than the cormorant, and even when it does journey south, it does not cover

[1] *Birds of Ireland*, 1954, p. 27.

anything approaching the distance of the larger bird. There have been no returns from the Bay of Biscay, Finistère (Brittany) being the southern-most point from which a British-born shag has been reported.

In the Report on Bird-Ringing for 1957 (published as a Supplement to *British Birds*, 1958, since the above notes were in print) it is stated that thirteen shags ringed in Devon and Cornwall were recovered in French waters, twelve between August and February ; one in May.

DISTRIBUTION ABROAD : The typical subspecies is restricted to the western Palaearctic Region and breeds in Iceland, the Faeroe Islands, Lapland and Norway, south to the coasts of France, western Spain and Portugal. One of the largest breeding places in the latter country is on the rocky Berlengas island where numbers are to be seen. Its southern-most colony is on the islands off the Algarve coast where, however, it was already rare twenty-five years ago and may now be extinct.[1] In the Mediterranean its place is taken by an allied species *P. desmarestii* which ranges east to Cyprus and is the shag which occurs also in the Black and Caspian Seas. Still another race was named by Hartert *P. aristotelis riggenbachii* from the western coast of Morocco where it breeds on Cape Blanco and on the islands off Mogador. The range of this race north and south has never been determined, but Hartert was quite sure of its dis-tinctness from the Mediterranean shag and from the typical European bird. The late Claud Ticehurst and Hugh Whistler pointed out that the Mediterranean shag should be retained as a distinct species and not as a race of our British bird ; with this I agree.

HABITS : When we come to study the habits of the shag we are immediately faced with a comparison with the numerically superior cor-morant, for at first sight their habitat and behaviour and manner of feeding are very much alike. When, however, we look into their respective life-histories more closely we find a number of ways in which the two species differ materially. They are not brought into such close competition with one another as if they had exactly similar tastes, and this applies especially to the type of coast which each bird prefers. Of the two birds, as P. R. Lowe once observed, the green cormorant (or shag) is the more difficult to please, especially in the selection of a breeding site. It loves to choose some inaccessible cave, some isolated island or coastline with plenty of fissures in the rugged cliffs or some ledge of rock protected from the rain, for, as Lowe pointed out, the shag thoroughly dislikes being rained upon. Nor is the shag as sociable a bird as the cormorant, preferring to nest as much alone as possible, so that when no caves are available isolated pairs occupy a small ledge here and there. Shags never nest in trees as does the cormorant in certain places, and in its breeding habits is the more selective of the two birds, showing less inclination to adapt itself to ex-ceptional circumstances.

[1] *Catálogo Sistemático das Aves de Portugal*, 1931, p. 62.

In her book on the Farne Islands Grace Watt gives a description of a communal breeding place as she found it on one of the islands in that group :

Nests are built on rocky ledges and it is probably because of the number of such ledges on Staple Island that the greatest increase has taken place here—indeed in this instance shags seem to be driving out the kittiwakes. Shags make fairly large nests, and as these ledges are comparatively wide, and in places almost terrace-like, this is an ideal communal nesting ground, quite unlike most of the other sites, which are merely isolated ledges or shelves only big enough to hold one nest.

In this same group of islands the cormorant is extremely common and appears to favour islands not chosen by other breeding species. Two of these are the North Wamses and the Little Hascar, rocky islands covered in places with patches of vegetation, mainly coarse grass, scurvy grass, and small clumps of campion. The cormorants nest on these islands in large numbers. I have mentioned them here as affording a good instance of the difficult terrain selected for nesting by shag and cormorant within the same island group. In Cornwall, where it is a plentiful species on all coasts, shags far outnumber cormorants, which breed on widely separated stretches of cliff, mainly in small colonies. The shags in Cornwall breed in colonies on cliff ledges, and also in caves.

The shag and the cormorant were chosen by Dr. Lack to illustrate the ecology of closely related species, and in an analysis of the two birds he stressed the marked difference exhibited in both nesting sites and food.[1] When investigating the bird life of the Orkney Islands Lack had already drawn attention to the breeding place on the Calf of Eday, where both shag and cormorant nest *on the same cliff*; but whereas the cormorants nested on the flat ground on the edge and above the cliffs and on the higher ledges of the cliffs, the shags' nests were all on the lower ledges and consequently there was no overlap in nesting habitat between the two.

Continuing to develop his theme that the two birds are not in violent competition as might at first be supposed, Dr. Lack points to the detailed analysis of the food ascertained by G. A. Steven,[2] which shows that the two species have almost completely different diets and moreover feed mainly in different places. " The cormorant feeds chiefly in the shallow waters of estuaries and harbours, also inland on large rivers and on reservoirs. Only occasionally does it forage farther out at sea. On the other hand the shag feeds mainly out at sea, and seeks food in estuaries and sheltered waters only during stormy weather. Hence the two species rarely feed together." It was found from analysis of the stomach contents of 188 shags and 27 cormorants shot in Cornwall that whereas the staple food

[1] *Journal of Animal Ecology*, xiv, 1945, pp. 12-16.
[2] *Jour. Marine Biology Assoc. U.K.*, xix, 1933, pp. 277-292.

of the shag was sand-eels, that of the cormorant was flat fish and shrimps. A long comparative list of food is given in the paper cited in the footnote. It will be seen from this list that, as Lack points out from the data then available, the shag feeds mainly on free-swimming forms while the cormorant feeds principally on fish which live on or close to the bottom. This general opinion as regards the shag received support in May 1946 when W. H. R. Lumsden and A. J. Haddow [1] of the Marine Station, Millport, published an important paper on the food of the shag in the Clyde sea area. These authors came to the conclusion that *locality* appears to be by far the most important factor in determining the constituents of the diet; moreover of the 900 fishes taken from shag stomachs only 152 (16 per cent.) could be considered as possible food fish, and that, they observe, is a liberal estimate. Their final conclusion is that the shag is *not* a danger to fisheries, however injurious the closely allied cormorant may be. An interesting point emerged from Lumsden and Haddow's investigations :

It was discovered that many of the fish recovered from shags' stomachs belonged to species with well-marked protective adaptations. Among protectively coloured types *Spinachia*, *Cottus*, *Agonus* and *Callionymus* were instanced as examples whose obliterative colouring and patterns appear almost perfect to human eyes. Some species adopting a protective habit occurred also, notably *Syngathus* which is nearly invisible when floating vertically among weed. Powerful defence mechanisms were present in some, such as *Cottus*, whose powerful spines must make it a very difficult fish to swallow. It was interesting also to find fish such as *Centronotus* in the diet, as this species spends much of its time under stones, making only short excursions into the dense weed forests in search of small crustaceans.

During the course of this investigation some highly instructive information was gained as to the feeding habits as well as the food upon which the shag subsists. There is only space to quote a few of the observations here :

When a shag on the water is about to begin fishing it repeatedly dips its head under the surface. . . . The appearance suggests that the bird is looking for fish. When diving the bird springs clear of the water surface and enters head first, making very little splash. Towards the end of the fishing period when loaded with food, it sometimes slides under water in a " seal dive " without the preliminary leap. On favourable ground a shag may complete its meal in one long series of dives. On other occasions, after a run of a few dives, it may fly off and begin elsewhere. . . . Sometimes a bird may be seen to dive repeatedly within one small area, but more frequently it fishes in a zig-zag line, finally turning and traversing back over the same ground to its starting point. . . . Large fish are brought to the surface before being eaten.

Observations proved that small fish were often swallowed under water as shags were frequently seen to surface with the beak empty but gaping

[1] *Journal of Animal Ecology*, xv, 1946, pp. 35-42.

slightly, while a transitory bulge in the neck showed that a fish had been swallowed under water. As an indication of how efficient the shag is as a fisherman Lumsden and Haddow cite an occasion when a shag was seen to bring up six medium-sized fish, thought to be wrasse, in seven dives, and on another three smallish flatfish were brought up in the course of four dives. The longest dives were found to vary in individual cases from only 40 seconds to 1 minute 40 seconds, and the shortest dives from 5 to 35 seconds. Mean resting periods on the surface worked out at 15 seconds but individual maxima varied from 15 to 40 seconds. It was found, too, that the duration of the dives bore no relation to the depth of the water, nor to the preceding and subsequent resting periods. In all cases the time spent under water was considerably greater than that spent resting at the surface. When swimming under water the shag was seen to hold the wings closely pressed to the sides ; the legs are angled outwards and the feet, widely separated, beat simultaneously.

There is a great deal more in the most instructive paper from which these extracts are given, but enough has been quoted to vindicate entirely the shag's character as a potential danger to edible fish.

Col. J. H. Ryves, in his *Bird Life in Cornwall*, gives the following instance of the shag's amazing prowess in swimming and diving. He was watching a shag flying across a narrow inlet when a huge wave broke just above it, enveloping it in a volume of water, and carrying it to the raging sea below. It looked as if the bird must be battered to death against the cliff-foot, but it instantly dived, and shortly afterwards rose to the surface a hundred feet away obviously unscathed. Comparisons perhaps are odious but it is safe to assert that no bird is better equipped to withstand the dangers of a raging sea. As a diving bird it is incomparable.

In the previous essay we drew attention to the cormorant's well-known " wing-drying " posture. The shag has the same habit, though it is less often seen. Notes on the wing-drying of shags were contributed to *British Birds*[1] by M. W. and H. M. Pickering from observations at Arbroath. On one occasion when a shag was swimming with two cormorants not far from the cliffs, it raised its wings and held them in an up-raised, half-spread position for about half a minute while continuing to swim along at the head of the party. Shags often sit, or rather stand, on rocks with their wings open and the observers watched one bird in this position for 32 minutes after they noticed it. It waved its wings to and fro for the first 12 minutes and then held them out motionless ; meanwhile it occasionally ran its bill through its breast feathers.

Another note which appeared in *British Birds* more recently (1957) from C. H. Fry refers to a raft of about 400 shags some 50 yards off shore on a rough sea (wind force 5-6), when about 20 shags had their wings

[1] *British Birds*, xliii, 1950, pp. 378-379.

extended in drying attitudes while others chose an adjacent rock as a vantage point. The incident occurred on 30th September 1956 at Pittenweem on the coast of Fife.

BREEDING HABITS : The preference shown by the green cormorant for nesting in caves when these are available has been stressed in an earlier paragraph, and no more need be said of its choice of nesting sites than has been remarked already. Rock ledges, either in caves or on the open cliffs, are the sites where the shags build their fairly large nests of seaweed and bleached sticks ; coarse grass and heather stems may also be used in the nest construction with " decorations " picked up from the foreshore such as old bits of twine. Green leaves and flowers are also recorded as having been found decorating a nest. When first built the nest appears fresh and clean, the birds taking care not to foul it with their excrement which is deposited on the rocks around. As time goes on the bulky nests of rotting seaweed and matted grasses smell very badly, the remains of putrid fish adding in no small degree to the unpleasant odour of a shag's nesting cave.

In the Balearic Islands Philip Munn records nests of the Mediterranean shag made singly, or a few together, in caverns and holes on the face of the lower parts of the cliffs, the opening of the hole sometimes being decorated with growing clumps of purple stock through which the bird has to push its way on entering or leaving the nest. As a rule the birds roost at their nesting places or on the rocks and cliffs near by.

Three eggs are the usual complement. Jourdain mentions that two and six eggs have been recorded and occasionally four or five. There is a record of seven from an island off Antrim, 29th May 1943, by H. T. Malcolmson, which is mentioned by Major Ruttledge in *Birds of Ireland*, and about which there seems to be no doubt.

The eggs of the shag are chalky-white with a pale blue undershell below the deposit. Measurements by Jourdain are : average of 100 eggs, 62·87 × 38·4 mm. Max. 74·6 × 38 and 60·4 × 41·7 mm. Min. 56·6 × 39·1 and 61·1 × 34·9 mm.

The dates when eggs may be found vary considerably, the latter part of March being an early date ; though as P. R. Lowe has recorded there is a record from the Orkneys of an egg being found on 24th February by H. W. Robinson. In Ireland, 20th March is the earliest date when single eggs have been taken, but owing to various causes, such as storms which sweep away the eggs, fresh layings may be found in late May and even in June. On an average April is probably the most likely month in which to find first clutches. Eggs take twenty-four to twenty-eight days to hatch. The young, which are at first both blind and naked, are tended by both parents and fed in the same manner as young cormorants. During the fledging period the old birds are most devoted in their attentions and are not readily induced to leave their young. Grace Watt has stated that

PLATE 3

GANNET
Sula bassana (Linnaeus)

if an intruder approaches they make curious snake-like darting movements towards him with their heads, at the same time opening and shutting their mouths to show the yellow interior : this movement is copied by the young at an early age. When the young are becoming fledged, both parents may often be seen with them on the nest.

Both in Britain and in the Mediterranean the shag shows little inclination to wander far from its nesting haunts. Norman Ticehurst found that a distance of 300 miles was probably exceptional and many birds undoubtedly remain in their home waters all the year round.

REFERENCES : Original Description. *Pelecanus aristotelis* Linnaeus, *Faun. Svecica, Faunula,* 1761, p. 5 and No. 146, ex. p. 51 : Sweden.

Family SULIDAE

Genus *SULA* Brisson

GANNET   PLATE 3

Sula bassana (Linnaeus)

GEORGE WATERSTON

Resident, breeding in colonies mainly in traditional sites on certain islands, sea-cliffs, and rock stacks around Britain. Immature birds are migratory, but adults are only partially so

IDENTIFICATION : The gannet is our largest and most spectacular British breeding sea-bird, and probably the most easily identified. This big long-winged white sea-bird with black wing-tips, long neck, and pointed bill can be easily picked out far out at sea as it flies along, often in an undulating string of others, in purposeful flight making its way to or from its feeding grounds. Its torpedo-shaped body, long slender wings, and pure white plumage (adult) give it an air and grace quite distinct from any other sea-bird. Its mode of fishing, when it stalls suddenly in mid-air, plunges vertically from a height, and folds its wings just before entering the water, is a magnificent sight.

At close quarters on its breeding grounds, the gannet is a much larger bird than most people might imagine—a fully grown male measures quite three feet from bill to tip of tail, and the wings have an expanse of six feet when fully extended. In the structure of its bill and feet it holds a unique place among British birds. The bill is long (95-110 mm. from the feathers), gently sloping but not hooked, bluish-white in colour with dark slate lines ; the cutting edge is slightly serrated and the ridge of the culmen flattened, and a linear groove runs the whole length of the culmen on either side.

The foot is completely webbed, all four toes being connected, and is brownish-white in colour with pale bluish-green lines. At close range the bifocal eyes, set in a bare patch of slate-grey skin, look cold and cruel— the iris silvery-white or pale yellowish-green. The body plumage is dazzling white including the long cuneate-shaped tail ; but the crown of the head, and to a lesser extent the sides of the head and neck, are yellowish-buff— a feature which can be noted from a considerable distance.

Young gannets may often be seen at sea in company with adults, their blackish-brown plumage flecked with white, or, when more advanced in age, a pied black and white dress which denotes a bird of the second summer. The fully adult plumage is not attained until the fifth or even sixth year. Even in these intermediate plumages, there can be no mistaking the species, for though the bill is then dark, the outline is the same as in the adult, and the unmistakable pointed tail, carriage of the neck, and characteristic rigid wings save it from confusion with any other bird around our coasts.

LOCAL DISTRIBUTION : For a bird that has provided man with food from early historical times at its island stations, it is perhaps not surprising that the gannet should be the best catalogued species in history as far as numbers and breeding haunts are concerned. In a monumental work involving painstaking research in literature, James Fisher and H. G. Vevers [1] have compiled a thorough historical survey of the entire breeding population of the North Atlantic gannet through the ages. In 1939 they organised a count of all the breeding pairs at every known colony on both sides of the North Atlantic, and the results show that the main breeding population is centred around the British Isles. Of a total of 166,000 breeding adults in 22 colonies, about 109,000 were counted in 12 colonies in the British Isles.

In 1949 James Fisher and H. G. Vevers, with the assistance of various helpers, carried out a census of nests on the east side of the Atlantic. As a result of this it was shown [2] that in 1939 " the gannet on the east side of the North Atlantic occupied about seventy thousand nests at seventeen colonies, and in 1949 about eighty-two thousand nests at twenty-three colonies. This represents an increase of 18 per cent. in ten years, and a clear continuation of the steady upward trend in the gannet's population since it was at its lowest on the east side, at under fifty thousand nests, in 1889."

[1] J. Fisher and H. G. Vevers, " The breeding distribution, history and population of the North Atlantic gannet (*Sula bassana*). Part 1. A history of the gannet's colonies and the census in 1939," *J. Anim. Ecol.*, xii, 1943, pp. 173-213. Also " . . . Part 2. The changes in the world numbers of the gannet in a century," *J. Anim. Ecol.*, xiii, 1944, pp. 49-62.

[2] J. Fisher and H. G. Vevers, " The present population of the North Atlantic gannet (*Sula bassana*)," *Proceeds. Xth International Ornithological Congress, Uppsala* (1951), pp. 463-467.

I am very much indebted to James Fisher for the following contribution on gannet colonies in the British Isles, which brings our present knowledge right up to date :

GANNET COLONIES IN THE BRITISH ISLES

COMPILED BY JAMES FISHER

SOUTH-WEST BRITAIN GROUP

Ortac, near Alderney, Channel Isles. Founded in 1940, when one nest; about 250 nests in 1946 ; over 234 in 1948 ; 200 to 250 in 1949 ; 570 in 1950.

Les Etacs, Alderney, Channel Isles. Date of foundation unknown—after 1940 ; but more gannets had been seen about since 1936. About 200 nests in 1946, 200 or more in 1948, 418 in 1949, and 615 in 1950.

Gulland Rock, Cornwall. Breeding *c.* 1468 ; not breeding in recent years.

Gannet Stone, Lundy, Devon. Breeding 1274, 1321, 1325 or 1326, 1631. Not mentioned 1787. Breeding 1829 and 1839. Plentiful, but decreasing through persecution 1871. Persecution continuing ; none reared *c.* 1883 to *c.* 1891 ; 16 nests, none reared 1887 ; nearly 70 nests, none reared 1889. Eggs taken *c.* 70 nests, none reared 1890 ; 30 pairs present 1893. 3 pairs present 1900 ; 7 pairs present 1901 ; no report 1902 ; 5 pairs present, 5 eggs taken 1903 ; no eggs laid 1904 ; 2 pairs failed to breed 1905 ; birds returned, no breeding 1906 and 1907 ; colony extinct 1909. Single bird attempted to build 1922. Attempts at reintroduction unsuccessful 1938 and 1939.

Grassholm, Pembrokeshire. Possibly breeding 1820 ; probably breeding before 1860, " few nests." Certainly breeding 1864 ; 20 nests 1883 ; 250 nests 1886 ; *c.* 225 pairs 1889. Over 200 pairs 1890 ; 240 nests 1893 ; 300 nests and plundering 1895 ; great egg raid 1898. 250-300 pairs 1903 ; under 300 pairs and very few young reared 1905 ; 100-130 young reared 1906 ; *c.* 300 young reared 1907. *c.* 300 pairs up to 1914 ; increase 1919 onwards. 800-1000 pairs 1922 ; 1800-2000 pairs 1924 ; flat ground north side not occupied 1928. 4750 nests 1933 ; one side of island practically covered 1934; *c.* 5000 nests and flat ground on north side occupied 1937 ; 5875 nests in 1939 ; about 6000 in 1946 ; 6100 to 6150 in 1947 ; 7000 in 1948 ; 9050 to 9500 in 1949 ; 10,550 in 1956.

Little Skellig, Kerry, Eire. Breeding 1700 ; an " incredible number " breeding *c.* 1748. Breeding 1828 ; 500 pairs, young eaten 1850 ; young and feathers taken 1869 ; breeding 1870 ; *c.* 30 pairs 1880 ; 150-200 pairs 1882 ; increasing 1884. Several thousand pairs 1890 ; many thousands 1896 ; 15,000-20,000 pairs 1906 and 1908 ; 8000 pairs 1913 ; range extended 1914 ; 10,000 pairs " almost every available ledge occupied " 1930. 9000-10,000 pairs 1938 and about the same number 1939 and 1941 ; about 10,500 nests 1946 ; about 12,000 nests 1949.

Bull Rock, Cork, Eire. Birds first seen on rock 1853 ; first nests found 1856 ; 11 pairs 1858. " Many hundreds " but only few eggs 1868 ; up to 1000 pairs 1884 ; lighthouse built 1884-5 ; possibly 500 pairs 1889 ; 100-110 pairs 1891 ; greatly diminished 1896 ; *c.* 100 pairs 1899 ; *c.* 1000 pairs 1902 ; 300 pairs 1908 ; 250 pairs 1913 ; 400 pairs and birds increasing 1930 ; 2000-3000 pairs (error) 1936 ; *c.* 450 pairs 1937 ; 442-500 pairs 1938 ; 550-600 pairs 1939 ; 270-320 in 1949.

Great Saltee, Wexford, Eire. 2 pairs, 2 eggs, both destroyed 1929 ; 1 pair, no egg seen 1930. 2 pairs, 2 eggs, no young reared 1932 ; 1 pair, young reared 1933 ; 1 pair 1934 ; 1 pair, nest 1935 ; 1 pair 1936 ; 2 pairs, 1 young hatched but not reared 1937 ; 3 pairs,

3 eggs, 1 egg destroyed, 2 young reared 1938. No pair proved to occupy a site 1939, though six birds about; one nest 1942; 2 pairs, 1 egg (destroyed) 1943; one nest 1946 and 1947; two nests 1948 and 1949; four nests 1953; at least four nests 1954; at least 8 pairs bred 1955; at least 7 pairs bred 1956; 12 young reared 1957.

Stags of Broadhaven, Mayo, Eire. Possibly breeding *c.* 1756, *c.* 1823-8, 1836. Not breeding 1873, 1882, 1898, 1911, 1924, 1928-30, 1939 or thereafter.

East Britain Group

Bempton Cliffs, Yorkshire. One pair present 1924-6, 1928-9. One pair present, one egg taken 1937; 2 pairs present, 1 young reared 1938; 4 pairs present, 1 young reared 1939; birds present (? nesting) 1941 through 1947; three nests 1948; two or three nests, 1 young reared 1949; 5 adults about, 1 sitting 1950; 2, possibly 3 young reared 1951; 3 pairs, all reared young 1952 and 1953; 4 pairs, all reared young 1954; 3 or 4 pairs, 3 young reared 1955; 5 or 6 pairs, 2 young reared 1956; 2 pairs, both reared young 1957.

Bass Rock, East Lothian. " Marvellous multitude " 1521; " incredible number " 1526; " could not be easily estimated " 1535; " plenty " 1555; " numbers obscure the sun " 1570; " more abundant than Ailsa Craig " 1578; " abundance, breeding on the sides of the rocks " 1635; grass top entirely covered 1641; " multitudes," " innumerable " 1661; surface almost covered 1693; whole surface covered (also breeding Craigleith, Lamb, Fidra ?) 1710; still multitudes, nesting on the sloping part 1769; still nesting on the summit 1816; 300 nests on gravel slope near landing, estimate *c.* 10,000 pairs 1831; estimate 5000 pairs 1847 or 1848; estimate (based on doubling number of young taken) *c.* 3400 pairs 1850; had not yet abandoned upper slopes 1859; still some nesting on the grassy slopes 1862; nesting well above 1904 limits, estimate *c.* 6000 pairs 1869; estimates (of little value) *c.* 10,000 pairs 1871 and 1872; increasing 1873; less molestation 1885; decrease to 3000 pairs 1904; further protection 1905; increasing 1909; estimate *c.* 3250 pairs 1913; count of 4147 pairs 1929; estimate 4150 pairs 1936; count of 4374 nests 1939; and 4820 nests 1949.

Isle of May, Fife. Before 1850 the gannet used to breed here according to Jardine who writes : " We have shot it there and taken the young from the nest." In 1922 a pair of gannets attempted to nest, but without success.

West Britain Group

Calf of Man, Isle of Man. Possibly breeding 1586, 1648 and 1652. One pair present, not breeding, 1939.

Scar Rocks, Luce Bay, Wigtownshire. 2 nests 1883. 2-6 pairs, 1 nest, 1 young reared 1939. Breeding not proved 1940; breeding not proved, but possibly 10 pairs 1941; *c.* 25 pairs breeding 1942; *c.* 45 pairs 1943; 35-45 nests 1945; at least 28 nests 1946; 90 nests 1948; and 100 nests 1949.

Ailsa Craig, Ayrshire. Breeding first recorded " plente " 1526; abundant 1549; abounds, but not so abundant as at Bass 1578; abundant 1583; many 1587. Abundant, eaten by man 1635; great plenty, eaten by man 1696; mentioned at second hand 1710, 1718, 1722; " filled the air " *c.* 1791; immense flocks 1813; feathers sold commercially. Rent £30 p.a. 1824; rent still derived chiefly from sale of feathers 1837; maximum of 500 young taken a year certainly 1853 to *c.* 1860, possibly up to *c.* 1880, eggs taken later. Estimates *c.* 7500 pairs 1868, *c.* 6000 pairs 1869. Suggestion that ledges were full up, young taken 1871. " Thousands " 1901; possibly *c.* 3250 pairs 1905. Increase 1913; large numbers top ledges 1914; *c.* 4900 pairs 1922;

increases recorded 1923-5 ; Barestack first occupied and estimate *c.* 8000 pairs 1924 ; *c.* 7000 pairs 1929 and eggs probably taken until this date. *c.* 7000 pairs 1935 ; 4800 pairs 1936 and Main Craigs, Far East first found occupied ; *c.* 5945 pairs 1937 ; 5387 pairs 1938 and Main Craigs, East Top first occupied ; 5419 nests 1939 ; 6232 nests 1940 ; 3518 nests 1941 ; 4829 nests 1942 ; 5383 nests 1947 ; 5190 nests 1948 ; 4947 nests 1949 ; 6579 nests 1950 ; 7833 nests 1951 ; 7987 nests 1952 ; 8249 nests 1953 ; 8555 nests 1954 ; 10,402 nests 1955 ; 8063 nests 1956 ; 7742 nests 1957.

Holy Isle, Arran.   3 birds seen 1946 ; birds carrying nesting material 1947 ; about 17 roosting 1948 ; about 12 roosting and carrying nesting material 1949 ; about 25 birds 1950, carrying nesting material ; 6 birds present 1951 ; none present 1952 or since.

Glunimore Island, Kintyre.   In 1941 a pair built a nest, but no egg was laid.

Islay, Argyll.   Doubtfully breeding 1703 ; no modern evidence of breeding.

Eigg, Inner Hebrides.   Possibly breeding 1549 ; no modern evidence of breeding.

Rum, Inner Hebrides.   Possibly breeding 1549, 1597 ; no modern evidence of breeding.

NORTH BRITAIN GROUP

Oigh-sgeir Eagach (Haskeir), Outer Hebrides.   Possibly breeding 19th century ; not breeding 1939, 1942.

Boreray, Stac Lee, and *Stac an Armin*, St Kilda.   1549 : " wyld foullis " paid in duties to owner.   1684 : gannets nesting in the Hebrides.   1696 : at least 800 taken Stac an Armin ;   22,600 (erroneously) said to be eaten in all.   1697 : Stac Lee stated to provide 5000, 6000, or 7000 gannets a year ; Boreray, " solan geese possess it for the most part " ; Stac an Armin, " abounds with Solan Geese." 1758 : eggs taken Boreray and Stac an Armin only, young taken on these and on Stac Lee.   20,000 gannets (erroneously) said to be still taken annually.   *c.* 1786 : 1200 said to be taken in one night.   Up to 1829 : never more than 5000 young taken.   1829-43 : never more than 2000 young taken.   1840 : all stacks occupied, some non-breeders present, *c.* 1600 young taken.   1841 : *c.* 1120-1400 gannets taken ; record of 15,000 gannets taken erroneous.   1847 : 1100 gannets taken in single night.   *c.* 1869 : population estimated (not reliable) *c.* 25,000 pairs.   1875, 1876 : probably very few gannets taken.   1879 : Stac an Armin and Stac Lee covered on slopes, summits, and sides. 1884 : breed in " tens of thousands." 1885 : capture of 660 adults in two nights considered a great success.   1895 : *c.* 3200 birds taken in all.   1902 : only 300 taken, raids fallen into abeyance ; reliable estimate 14,500-15,000 pairs.   1910 : 600 adults taken, young no longer caught.   1930 : man ceased to reside in St. Kilda through the year, as from September.   1931 : estimate *c.* 16,500 pairs.   1939 : count (a quarter estimated) *c.* 16,900 pairs.   1941 : probable increase on all three stacks.   1942 : possible further increase on Stac Lee.   1949 : 17,035 nests ; increases probable 1956 and 1957.

Rockall, North Atlantic.   Present on or near Rockall 1810.   Present on the rock but not breeding 1887, *c.* 1894, 1896 (10 birds), 1921.   Up to 15 near rock, 1941.   12 about, adults carrying nest material, but no nests, 1949.

Sula Sgeir, Outer Hebrides.   Breeding, birds taken by men from Ness 1549 and 1597. Great gannet resort 1819 ; gannets present 1860.   " Several thousand " birds usually killed annually 1869, and ridiculous estimate 150,000 pairs.   Mentioned 1871.   Ness men's raiding boat wrecked in June some years before 1883 ; average 2000-2500 young, maximum 3000, taken annually by 1883.   2800 birds taken in 3 days—population *c.* 7000 pairs, 1884.   Over 5000 pairs, adults taken in June 1887.   " Perhaps twice as many " as on Sule Stack, 1891 ; young taken *c.* 1892 ; 2500 birds taken 1898. Young taken 1911 ; 2200 taken 1912. 1100 young taken 1915 ; numbers deserted owing to gunnery practice 1914-18. 2000 birds killed, unreliable estimate *c.* 9000 adults on rock 1931. *c.* 5000 breeding pairs 1932 ; 2000 birds killed 1933 ; 1400 taken 1934 ; none taken 1935 ; 2060 taken 1936. 1800-2000 killed 1937, 4418 breeding pairs, area occupied smaller than in 1932. *c.* 2000 gannets taken in 1938. Birds taken 1939, 3970 breeding pairs and occupied area still further reduced. 6182 nests in 1949.

North Rona, Outer Hebrides. J. Swinburne, who visited North Rona in 1883, says that gannets are said to have bred there, but there is no further information on the subject. Have certainly not bred since to our knowledge.

Sule Stack, Orkney. First mentioned 1710 ; mentioned again 1776. Raided for young birds from Orkney some time before 1795. Raiding ship wrecked *c.* 1800 ; raid in 1806, when great increase alleged. Mentioned 1860 ; recorded as " large colony " 1869 and population estimated quite erroneously at 25,000 pairs. Mentioned 1871. Summit densely populated 1887, many immature birds, colony still raided (probably from Ness, Lewis) at this period. Large numbers of immature birds present at colony, possibly *c.* 3500 breeding pairs 1890. Rock " simply covered " 1902 ; attempted raid from Ness 1903 or 1904 ; up to 1000 birds taken in some years previous to this. *c.* 4000 pairs estimated *c.* 1904. Young taken 1911 ; *c.* 4000 pairs estimated 1914. 1200 birds said to be taken in some years up to 1932, since when no further raids. 3418 breeding pairs 1937, many immature birds and non-breeders. 3490 nests 1939 ; 2010 nests 1949.

Copinsay, Orkney. Attempt at breeding not proved, 1 pair present 1907 or 1908. Possible attempt at breeding, 1 pair present *c.* 1911. No birds present 1914, 1915, or 1924. Unsuccessful attempt at breeding, 1 pair present 1925 or 1926. No birds present 1927 or thereafter.

Noss, Shetland. No birds present 1909. Birds first showed interest 1911 or 1912 ; one pair bred 1914 ; 4 pairs bred 1915 ; 3 young reared 1918 ; 5 pairs bred 1919 ; 10 pairs bred 1920. *c.* 200 pairs 1930 or 1931 ; *c.* 800 pairs 1934 or 1935 ; birds " like snow " 1936 ; *c.* 913 (+ ?) pairs 1937 ; 1518 pairs 1938 ; 1830 nests 1939 ; about 3230 nests 1945 ; between 2600 and 3775 nests 1946 ; 2100-2300 nests 1949.

Hermaness, Shetland. Not breeding 1874, 1913. Colony established Vesta Skerry 1917. Had spread probably to Burra Stack, at least 109 pairs, by 1920. Estimate 1000 pairs probably too high 1928. Had spread to Humla Houl, the Neap and Neapna Stack by 1932. May have been over 600 pairs in 1934 ; *c.* 1000 pairs 1935. Had spread to Humla Stack, count of 2045 pairs 1938. 2611 nests 1939 ; nearly 4000 in 1945 ; at least 3150 nests estimated 1949.

From a study of the above details, several interesting facts emerge. In the south-western area of the British Isles, Fisher and Vevers [1] noted a steady increase in the total population of the colonies here from about 1859 onwards, largely influenced by the increased numbers on Little Skellig—from 30 pairs in 1880 to perhaps 17,600 in 1906, a period of 26 years. The taking of gannets for feathers and food on Little Skellig stopped some time prior to 1878, and may have resulted in this great increase

[1] J. Fisher and H. G. Vevers, " The changes in the world numbers of the gannet in a century," *J. Anim. Ecol.*, xiii, 1944, pp. 49-62.

in numbers. That the gannet is still increasing in the area is shown by the colonisation of two sites—Les Etats and Ortac in the Channel Isles—about 1945.

On the east coast, the breeding population in the old-established colony on the Bass Rock has remained remarkably steady. Economic exploitation by man ceased by 1885. On the west coast, too, we see a similar state of affairs at Ailsa Craig with perhaps more marked fluctuations during the past hundred years. Man's exploitation of the birds ceased about 1880.

It is in the colonies in the north of the British Isles that we see the most spectacular changes in numbers. As Fisher and Vevers say, " the remarkable development of the two Shetland colonies at Noss and Hermaness from nothing to major size in under 30 years, has been the feature of this group." The great central colony of St. Kilda, the largest in the world since the decline of Bird Rocks in the Gulf of St. Lawrence, has scarcely changed in numbers at all since 1901, the earliest year in which we have a reliable estimate. The Shetland colonies have been steadily colonised since they began in 1914 and 1917; and certainly at Hermaness this increase is still going on.

DISTRIBUTION ABROAD : The gannet is restricted to the North Atlantic Ocean ; and outside the British Isles it is to be found breeding in the Faeroes, Iceland, and the east coast of Canada from the Magdalen Islands in the Gulf of St. Lawrence north to Funk Island in Newfoundland. I am indebted to Fisher and Vevers [1] for the following :

Until the eighties of last century, the colony on the Bird Rocks off the Magdalen Islands was the dominant gannet colony in the world, and by far the largest. In 1833 it held about twice as many gannets as the rest of the world. But the Newfoundland Banks fishermen, and their colleagues, did not harvest its gannets so much as savage them, wantonly, with the result that by 1887 it had become a colony of normal size by the standards of the others (5000 pairs) ; and by 1898 it had become small (750). Protective legislation took about 25 years to come into effect, and robbing went on until at least 1900, though probably not to any significant extent after 1904.

The general trend of the west Atlantic population of the gannet is dominated by the history of the Bird Rocks colony until the end of the nineteenth century, when the total population in this group was at its lowest. But before the end of the century, interesting developments had taken place at other colonies. Between 1870 and 1887, the two colonies in the Bay of Fundy, and the colony in the Perroquet Islands, were extinguished, probably by savage predation by man ; and the colony at Cape St. Mary was established and rapidly colonised. The history of the Bonaventure Island colony is well known only from 1887 and quite unknown before 1860 : it may well have been established after the colony at Bird Rocks had begun seriously to decline. Most interesting of all has been the continued colonisation of

---

[1] Fisher and Vevers, *op. cit.*

Newfoundland after the establishment of the Cape St. Mary colony; in the twentieth century Bacalieu Island had been colonised, and Funk Island recolonised, albeit in small numbers as yet. After a period of rapid colonisation, the colony at Gullcliff Bay, Anticosti, which can reasonably be regarded as an offshoot of the Bird Rocks colony, has remained steady in numbers, with a fairly small population of 500 pairs, for 12 years.

To Dr. Finnur Gudmundsson [1] I am indebted for the following account of gannetries in Iceland:

In Iceland there are at present gannet colonies on four outlying islands (Súlnasker, Hellisey, Geldungur, and Brandur) belonging to the Vestmannaeyjar off the south coast. Other colonies are on the island of Eldey, off Cape Reykjanes, in the south-west; on the headland Raudinúpur in the district of Melrakkaslétta, in the north; and on the island of Skrúdur, off Fáskrúdsfjördur, in the east. The four colonies in the Vestmannaeyjar were already recorded in sources from the beginning of the eighteenth century. . . . Fisher and Vevers in connection with their census of the world gannet population made a count in the year 1939 and again in 1949 of the gannet population in the Vestmannaeyjar colonies and in the Eldey colony. . . . When counted in 1939 the number of nests in the Vestmannaeyjar proved to be 4359, the number having risen to 5534 in 1949. In 1949 the number of nests on Súlnasker proved to be 1918, on Hellisey 2216, on Geldungur 913, and on Brandur 487. The largest gannet colony in Iceland and also one of the largest in the world is the one on the island of Eldey. In 1939 the number of nests there proved to be 9328, and in 1949 at least 11,000. . . . The Raudinúpur colony is of comparatively recent date. The first pair nested there either in the summer of 1944 or 1945. It is thought that 2 pairs nested there in the following summer. In the summer of 1949 the number of breeding pairs had risen to 6. The Skrúdur colony is also of recent date. The first pair nested there in the summer of 1943. Björn Björnsson visited the colony in 1949 and counted 150 gannets in the cliffs and 10-15 on the wing. In view of these figures the number of nests was estimated at 150. In 1952 Thorsteinn Einarsson visited the colony and he arrived at the figure of 134 when counting the nests. . . . Either in 1944 or 1945 gannets (1 or 2 pairs) nested for the first time on the stack Kerling near the island of Drangey in the Skagafjördur in the north. In the summer of 1946 two pairs were found nesting in this locality, but in 1949 only one pair. In the summer of 1953 no gannets bred or were seen there. On the island of Grímsey off the north coast there was formerly the northernmost gannet colony in the world, and the only gannet colony within the Arctic Circle. On Grímsey the gannets originally occupied the stack Hafsúlustapi and the opposite cliff on Grímsey itself. Later on, after Hafsúlustapi had collapsed, all the gannets moved to the cliff of Grímsey itself. According to Faber . . . about 20 pairs were breeding on Grímsey in 1820 and in 1821 Thienemann . . . found about 18 pairs breeding there. Later on the gannet must have increased considerably in numbers on Grímsey, for Hantzsch found 50-70 pairs breeding there in 1903. . . . The size of the Grímsey colony has been subject to considerable fluctuations since that

---

[1] F. Gudmundsson, " Íslenzkir fuglar VII. Súla (*Sula bassana*)," in *Náttúrufraedin-gurinn*, xiii, 1953, pp. 170-7.

time. In June 1934 the colony suffered seriously through dislodgement of material from the cliff face as a result of the Dalvík earthquake. In spite of this 45 nests were found on Grímsey in 1939. . . . After 1939 dislodgement of material from the cliffs occurred repeatedly, and this may be the main reason for the dwindling of the Grímsey colony which continued until only 3 pairs were left there in 1946. Since that time no gannets have bred. . . .

With exception of the small and comparatively recent colony in Raudinúpur all the gannet colonies in Iceland are to be found on uninhabited, remote, and rocky islands. In such places they may occupy the top plateau (cf. Eldey and Súlnasker) or they may breed on ledges or shelves in precipitous cliffs. . . ."

MIGRATION : Although the gannet is found in British waters throughout the year, and some of the breeding stations are said to be " not completely deserted " for more than a few weeks in mid-winter, there is known to be a considerable southward movement in winter. Sir Landsborough Thomson has published [1] a summary of the results achieved by ringing gannets at their breeding stations in the British Isles, and from this some definite deductions can be made. As he points out, the evidence obtained from the recovery of marked birds bears out the winter range as we knew it from observation alone. When the young gannet is fully grown, there is a strong impulse in first-year birds to move south, and this they proceed to do sometimes as early as August.

Mr. G. Theo Kay, in a fascinating study [2] of the movements of young gannets on leaving their nests, has shown that when the young birds reach the water from the ledges of the nesting cliffs of Noss in Shetland, they are completely flightless,[3] and their first instinctive action is to paddle away from the nearest land and make for the open sea. He writes : " Two thousand individuals would be a conservative estimate of the number of young gannets getting to the sea from Noss. The period of their departure from the ledges may be roughly stated as the last three weeks in August and the first three in September, although stragglers may be found into October."

In the above-mentioned paper, and in subsequent correspondence,[4] Mr. G. Theo Kay has shown that young gannets may cover considerable distances on the surface of the sea while still in a flightless state. A bird caught at Fair Isle, 45 miles south of the nearest colony, was found to be in perfect condition although quite unable to fly. It was ringed and released, and was last seen swimming towards the southern horizon.

[1] A. L. Thomson, " The migration of the gannet," in *British Birds*, xxxii, 1939, pp. 282-289.

[2] G. T. Kay, " The young gannet," in *British Birds*, xlii, 1949, pp. 260-263.

[3] James MacGeoch has, however, seen a juvenile launch itself from the top of the Sula Sgeir cliffs and do a long glide of $\frac{1}{4}$ mile before plumping into the sea.

[4] G. T. Kay, " Migratory movements of gannets," in *British Birds*, xliii, 1950, pp. 230-232.

Young gannets, unable to fly, have been seen 7, 12 and 17 miles from the land, swimming towards the open sea.   Mr. Kay poses a question to which as yet no one seems to have supplied a satisfactory answer—how far does the young gannet swim before getting on the wing ?   One young Bass Rock gannet, caught and ringed on the Isle of May on 7th September, was recovered nine days later at Schouwen Island in Holland—a distance as the crow flies of 450 miles.   It is doubtful whether it would have paddled all this distance !

By September, many of the young birds have made their way south of Ushant and a further spread is noticeable in November to the north-west African coast and down the waters which wash the shores of Mauretania. The adult birds, however, linger longer in northern waters, and indeed do not appear to have the same marked migratory urge as the young birds.   Sir Landsborough Thomson (*op. cit.*) has shown from an analysis of the ringing recoveries that young birds in their first year are definitely migratory and may spend their first winter off the west coast of Africa. Subsequently, however, the migratory instinct becomes less year by year and older birds appear to winter in the Bay of Biscay and on the west coast of Portugal.

Dr. David Bannerman tells me that the scarcity of records of three-year or adult birds from semi-tropical waters tends to prove that the southern movement of adult gannets beyond the latitude of the Canary Islands is almost non-existent, but he can affirm from personal experience that adult gannets reach the latitude of Cape Juby.   Sailing down the Moroccan coast on 18th February 1927, he saw hundreds of gannets—both young and old—off Agadir, and for the next twelve hours, as the ship was approaching Cape Juby, lesser numbers were encountered.   The seas off the Rio de Oro coast, and between Agadir and Cape Juby, are famous for the quantities of fish which abound in their waters ; and it is no doubt this attraction which tempts the first-year gannets to spend so much of their early life in these latitudes.   C. G. Bird met with gannets in large numbers between Cape Juby and La Aguera in April and May,[1] and he remarked that all were young birds with one exception.   There are few records from farther south.

Gannets return early in the year to their breeding grounds.   According to James Fisher, to whom I am greatly indebted for much valuable data, the main assembly of adults at most British breeding haunts takes place in January, beginning about 7th January at Ailsa Craig.   Here, and at the Bass Rock, adults are regularly settling on ledges and taking up nest territories in the fourth week in January, and displaying on ledges and on the sea.   At Ailsa, the *full* breeding population is in occupation of nest sites by the last week of March.   This assembly at the breeding place is markedly later at St. Kilda, Shetland, and the Faeroes, where it does

[1] *Ibis*, 1937, p. 725.

not take place (apart from a small number of early prospectors) until the
second half of February or the beginning of March, a full month later
than Ailsa Craig.   In Iceland and in the New World, the assembly is
normally a full month or more later still, at the beginning of April, though
large numbers have been seen on Eldey in Iceland as early as 21st February.

BREEDING : [1] Gannets breed in large colonies, the nests being situated
close together, just out of "pecking" distance of the adult birds.   The
dates of egg-laying tend to follow the pattern of the dates for assemblage
at each colony ; first eggs are laid in April at Ailsa and the Bass, and
mostly in May in Shetland and St. Kilda.   Early egg-dates are the last
week of March (Bass Rock), 8th April (Ailsa Craig), 1st May (St. Kilda),
5th May (Bird Rocks, Gulf of St. Lawrence).   A gannet normally lays
one egg, but if this is destroyed, it lays a replacement up to very late
in the season, and, it is alleged, may lay further replacements after
further mishaps.   Certainly any eggs found in British colonies in July
or August are likely to be replacements, though what were probably
first eggs have been found new-laid on 10th June.   There is evidence
that fertile eggs may hatch up to about 18th August, and Mr. Fred
Marr of North Berwick tells me that in 1958 a young gannet hatched
in the last week in August and did not leave the Bass Rock until
10th November.   This appears to be the latest known date for a young
bird to leave its nest in the British Isles ; but James Fisher records that
on precisely the same date, a young gannet was seen in its nest on Bonaventure Island, Quebec ;   on this date, falling icicles endangered the
young.

The incubation period has only once been determined from direct
field observation; J. M. Campbell found that an egg, laid on the Bass
Rock on 22nd April 1910, hatched on 5th June, after 44 days.   E. T.
Booth, the only person to have bred gannets in captivity, found the
incubation period was 43 to 45 days.   William Evans put gannets' eggs
under domestic hens and found it to be 39 days in one case and 42 days
or more in another.   An excellent observer, Neil Mackenzie, who was
minister on St. Kilda from 1829 to 1843, gives 42 days.

The earliest date on which a newly-hatched gannet has been seen is
10th May (Bass Rock), from an egg laid presumably on or about 29th
March.

On Ailsa Craig and the Bass Rock, the peak period for the laying of
first eggs appears to be from about 29th April to 13th May; the peak
period for hatching is six weeks later, from about 10th to 24th June ; and
the peak period for the young leaving their nests is from about 26th August
to 9th September, eleven weeks after hatching.

Most writers stress the amount of seaweed, particularly *Laminaria*

[1] The writer wishes to acknowledge an immense amount of information kindly made
available to him by James Fisher.

and *Fucus*, with which the gannet makes its nest; but on the Bass and Ailsa, grass is used to a marked extent, as it is on St. Kilda. On all three stations there are favourite places from which the birds collect grass; the St. Kildans complained to their visitor, Martin Martin, in 1697, that the gannets robbed sheep pasture on Boreray of precious grass. Other plants used include the campions *Silene incubalis* and *S. maritima*.

The gannet's egg is faintly green, the green being much obscured by an outer white calcareous layer which in turn is much dirtied by the gannet's feet after it is laid. Its shape is elliptical and its dimensions average exactly 3 inches by 2 inches.

There is no incubation patch and, when sitting, the gannet carefully spreads the web of one foot over the egg, and then the web of the other foot over the first. Both sexes share equally in the building of the nest, in the defence of the site before the egg is laid, in the incubation of the egg, and the management of the young. During the early stages of incubation on Ailsa Craig, a large group of nesting birds averaged five " changes " a day, each accompanied by much barking and " scissoring."

The young gannet, although provided with an egg-tooth, often takes half a day to hatch. When it has done so, it looks very black and reptilian, and it continues so for nearly a week, during which it is incubated much as an egg. On the fourth day, white down begins to be visible, and by the eleventh it is covered with white down. It usually opens its eyes on the eighth day. After about three weeks it loses its egg-tooth and its wing feathers begin to sprout; henceforward it gradually assumes the speckled black-and-white plumage of the immature bird and loses its white down. Throughout, it is fed on partially digested fish by its parents, inserting its head and neck inside its parent's gullet for the purpose.

A visit to a gannet colony at the height of the breeding season is a wonderful experience. The whole scene is one of continuous animation and the noise is terrific. At the beginning of July, a visitor can see eggs still in the nest and young in varying stages of development. On the Bass, the parent birds defend their young courageously from the human intruder and often have to be pushed aside. If there is a good breeze blowing, the gannets soar into it and one often witnesses a steady procession of birds flying round the rock. Displays occur almost right through the breeding season—posturing, facing each other with bills held erect, and that curious behaviour of fencing with their bills or " scissoring " as it is called. Nest material is often stolen should a bird happen to leave a nest unattended. Mr. Fred Marr of North Berwick (who often fishes close to the Bass) tells me that he has seen gannets gathering or carrying seaweed in every month of the year. He has noted that the birds do a " fluttering " dive when gathering seaweed, a shallow or angled dive for sprats, and a vertical " high " dive for mackerel.

Mr. Fred Marr has also drawn my attention to a point which I have not seen noted before, and that is the young gannet's apparent enjoyment of rain. When a shower comes on " all the young birds start to flap with gay abandon." (This may be to shake off the rain drops to prevent the down from becoming sodden.)

HUMAN PREDATION : With the exception of the great skua, Man is the only predator with which the gannet has had to contend. In the early days, nearly all the gannet colonies were raided annually ; they provided food in the form of flesh and eggs, and the down and feathers were also a useful commodity. The earliest record I can find of the exploitation of gannets is in a Papal Bull in the General Register House in Edinburgh [1] dating from the middle of the twelfth century. It includes a reference to a dispute between the nuns of North Berwick and the Laird of the Bass Rock about tithes consisting of so many barrels of fat of the solan geese on the Bass Rock. I have not the space to go into all the details concerning predation by man from that time onwards ; anyone wishing to study this should consult the papers by James Fisher and H. G. Vevers referred to earlier. It is, however, of interest to record that on 5th August 1768, the following advertisement appeared in the *Edinburgh Advertiser* : " There is to be sold, by John Watson, Jnr., at his stand at the Poultry, Edinburgh, all lawful days in the week, wind and weather serving, good and fresh Solan Geese. Any who have occasion for the same may have them at reasonable rates."

Today, the only two places where the North Atlantic gannet is taken for food are Mykines in the Faeroes, and Sula Sgeir which lies 40 miles N.N.E. of the Butt of Lewis in Scotland.

I am very much indebted to my friend James MacGeoch of Inverness for the following account of the raids carried out on the Sula Sgeir gannets annually by the intrepid men of Ness in Lewis.

Tradition has it that for centuries, probably as far back as the twelfth century, men from the district of Ness have gone out annually in the autumn to Sula Sgeir to take a harvest of young gannets, known in Gaelic as " gugas." Sir Donald Munro, High Dean of the Isles, 1549, mentions the practice of the Ness men going to Sula Sgeir (his " Suilskeray ") to take home " wildfowl "—presumably the gannet.

The custom flourishes as strongly as ever, and today two crews from Ness visit the island annually and stay there in rough stone bothies up to three weeks at a time, during which period they catch and salt down on an average some 3000 " gugas." The total fluctuates—depending on weather and whether one or two crews are present. One crew normally charter a seine-net fishing-boat at a cost of £100 for the two-way trip, while the other crew sail in their open boat with inboard engine and haul this boat partly up the steep sixty-foot cliff at the landing place to save it from the seas. In 1958 they went out and failed to land and had to return. They came out a week later by chartered boat. Each crew consists of nine men.

---

[1] W. Forbes Gray, " The Bass Rock in history," in *Trans. East Lothian Antiq. & Field Nat. Socy.*, 1948, p. 51.

Stores cost £80 per boat and the " gugas " are sold ashore locally to defray these costs and give a wage to each man for his period away from home.

The average catch on the 19 raids made since 1919, war and bad weather interrupting, amounts to 2360 young gannets. In 1919 and 1920, the hauls were as low as 1500 and 1600, with only 1800 taken in 1924 after a stay of twenty-eight days. Murdo Campbell, now 76, who took part in the 1919 raid, and a regular visitor to the island on raids up to and including 1954, informed me that the gannets had greatly increased since his first visits. Apparently the birds did not occupy the flats at the summit cairn (229 feet) to the extent that they do today. They had to collect their catch on the great cliffs only. The present-day hunters maintain that the gannets are more plentiful, and point to where the boundary has extended some twenty feet past the marker cairn on the north-west boundary which I erected in 1954. From my own observations, I can say that the gannetry has in no way diminished since my 1954 visit. How long this will continue I hesitate to say, as there is a tendency today to take bigger catches. Fortunately the local market did not come up to expectations in 1958, and the second boat was left with most of its catch on arrival at Ness. They re-salt and sell them during the winter, and of course use some for their own needs. This should help to limit the catches in the future. My own contention is that the Sula Sgeir gannets are augmented by the St. Kilda overspill, and if such is the case, then there should be no fear of the stock decreasing on Sula Sgeir.

I have been six times to the island, and stayed with the gannet hunters for three weeks in 1954, two weeks in 1957, and twelve days in 1958. The other occasions were day visits. The Protection of Birds Act, 1954, prohibited the taking of gannets throughout the British Isles : the Wild Birds (Gannets on Sula Sgeir) Order, 1955, gave the Ness men a reprieve, but confined the taking of gannets to outwith the close season which finishes on 31st August. The situation at present is that the Ness men establish themselves about 29th or 30th August and remain until 11th or 12th September unless bad weather dictates otherwise—as it did in 1957 when the other boat crew were marooned for twenty-one days, nine days overdue.

The birds taken are the fully-fledged juveniles, completely clothed in brown feathering, at the time when they are ready to make off to sea. They do not take the adults or white-coated young. The " gugas " are snared by long bamboo catching-poles to which is fixed a spring device to seize the bird by the throat while another member of the crew despatches it. The two crews combine, using the two most skilled catchers in each crew, as work on the ledges is somewhat confined. The catch is passed to the top of the cliff by hand from man to man, or by rope. It is then divided equally and each crew carry their own birds to the plucking bothy or small stone fank, whichever they use, where the birds are plucked and singed over strong peat fires. Thereafter they are split open, the inside and the remaining outer skin, etc. removed, and are salted and stacked into a large beehive-shaped pile ready to await the arrival of the boat, or for the day when the crew will launch their own boat.

Today, the gannets seem to be on the increase everywhere.

REFERENCES : Original Description : *Pelecanus bassanus* Linnaeus, *Syst. Nat.*, 10th ed., 1758, p. 133 : Scotland.

Family FREGATIDAE

Genus *FREGATA* Lacépède and Daudin

MAGNIFICENT FRIGATE BIRD

Fregata magnificens rothschildi Mathews

An Accidental Visitor

IDENTIFICATION : Frigate birds are easily recognized by their large size—the females noticeably larger than the males—their long pointed wings, the powerful long hooked bill, and especially by the very long scissor-forked tail, the outer feathers being about 18 inches long. The male is remarkable for the naked gular pouch, which can be expanded like a balloon at the time of sexual display. The male is black with a purple gloss above and a brown gloss below. The female has no gular pouch and her breast is white. This plumage is attained early in the third year. The iris, legs, and feet are black. Its approximate length is 36 inches, the wing span 7 feet.

Immature frigate birds in the first year have the head, neck, and underparts white in both sexes, with dusky flanks and occasionally some brown mottling on the head and neck. The immature female captured on Tiree (see next paragraph) had a wing-span of 6 ft. 6 in., and a length of 33 in.

OCCURRENCES IN GREAT BRITAIN : The only British record to date of a specimen captured is of an immature female taken alive in Tiree, W. Scotland. It was recorded in *British Birds*, xlvii, 1954, p. 58, as follows :

On July 10th, 1953, at Loch a' Puill, a freshwater lochan in the south-west corner of the island of Tiree, Inner Hebrides, Mr. John Graham caught in a landing net " a big bird with an all white head and an albatross beak ". He noted that the whole of the back and tail were a brown colour and the tail was deeply forked. There was " quite a lot of white on the underparts and freckled black and white feathers down the legs to the toes ".

It was exhausted when found at 10.30 a.m. (B.S.T.) and died at 8 p.m. The specimen was made into a cabinet skin which is now in the Royal Scottish Museum, Edinburgh. It was identified by Sir Norman Kinnear at the British Museum as an immature female of the Caribbean race, *rothschildi*.

The discovery of this bird was first made known through *The Times* newspaper of 25th July 1953 by Mr. Iolo Williams (on the staff of that paper) to whom Mr. Graham had communicated the fact of its capture. See also *Scottish Naturalist*, lxv, No. 3, 1953, p. 193.

A sight-record of a frigate bird observed off the south-west coast of

Ireland on 25th May 1953 by W. K. Richmond, was published in the *Fair Isle Bird Bulletin*, 1953, Pt. 1, p. 40. Mr. Richmond reckons that the S.S. *Mauretania*, in which he was travelling at the time, was about 150 miles from land, the noon position being Lat. 51° 04′ N., Long. 13° 05′ W. The bird was sighted shortly before 1 p.m. The weather the previous day had been foggy and the ship fog-bound off the Lizard, but the fog cleared later and when the frigate bird was sighted the weather was sunny and calm. It will be noted that this bird was seen off Ireland some seven weeks before one was caught on Tiree.

There are two authentic records of frigate birds caught in France, according to Prof. Berlioz, and a doubtful German record, but to what race these wanderers belonged does not appear to have been ascertained.

DISTRIBUTION ABROAD : The Caribbean race of the magnificent frigate bird breeds (according to the fifth edition of the A.O.U. *Check-List of North American Birds*, 1957) along the Pacific coast from Baja, California south to the Pearl Islands, Panama, and the Gulf of Guayaquil, Ecuador. On the Atlantic coast the range is given in great detail and includes some of the Bahama islands, some of the Lesser Antilles, Cuba, the islands off the coast of Venezuela, coastal islets of Puerto Rico, the Virgin Islands, the Grenadines, Fernando de Noronha and the Abrolhos Islets as well as on islets off Rio de Janeiro and Santos on the coast of Brazil.

The only other race of *Fregata magnificens* in the Atlantic which might some day wander to our shores is the subspecies *F. m. lowei* described by myself [1] from the Cape Verde Islands. Its chief difference from *F. m. rothschildi* is in its enormous bill, which measures from the gape 145 mm. in the male and 151 mm. in the female. The type specimen in the flesh measured 38·5 in. in length. It would naturally be impossible to distinguish the two Atlantic races of the magnificent frigate bird unless specimens were obtained.

Only by the merest chance are we likely to have more records of the frigate bird, for although it travels far over the Atlantic it has no set migrations. The northerly winter limit of *rothschildi* appears to be the coasts of northern Florida and of Louisiana, while to the south it reaches Brazil. Mr. A. C. Bent writes that between nesting seasons it is apt to wander far from home and has often been noted in most unexpected places, even in the interior of " the Continent ".

HABITS : Of all the ocean birds the frigate or man-o'-war bird is the most confined to the air. It has never been recorded on the water in the manner of the shearwaters and petrels but may be encountered hundreds of miles from land. I have myself seen one in mid-Atlantic between the Azores and Barbados and nearer to the Azores. It is, as Mr. W. B.

[1] Bannerman, in *Bull. Brit. Orn. Club*, 1927, p. 12 : Sal Rei, off Boavista, Cape Verde Islands.

Alexander writes in his *Birds of the Ocean*, " perhaps the most easily recognized of all sea-birds, but in ordinary sailing flight the tail is not spread, so that its forked nature is not always apparent ". In A. C. Bent's *Life Histories of North American Shore Birds* [1] is an excellent description of the behaviour of these man-o'-war birds from which I have taken the following passages, though not verbatim.

While soaring, either in a calm or in the teeth of a howling gale, the long tail-feathers are held parallel and close together, and are moved only slightly to steer or balance the bird, but when fighting in the air, as the males often do, or when courting or playing, they are frequently opened and closed like a pair of scissors. In contrast to the long powerful wings the feet of the frigate bird are very weak ; it can barely stand upon them and can hardly walk. It never dives and is helpless in the water, its plumage becoming wet and draggled, preventing it from rising.

Its food consists largely of fish and of the disgorged fare of boobies, pelicans, gulls, and terns which, in the manner of the parasitic skuas, it forces its victims to give up. It is greatly dreaded on that account by other birds of the ocean but it is not entirely dependent on robbery to obtain its food. Bent observes that while floating high in the air, almost out of sight, its keen eye detects some morsel of food in the water below it ; with wings half closed it shoots downwards like a meteor, and so accurately does it gauge its speed and distance that, just as it seems as if it must plunge like a falling arrow into the water, it checks its momentum with a marvellous twist of its great wings and lightly picks up the morsel from the surface with its bill without wetting a feather.

When the males indulge in fighting they utter harsh grating notes ; normally they are silent but in the breeding season they make clucking noises.

Despite the ferocity with which it attacks other birds in the air it shows quite another side to its nature should misfortune befall one of its own species. A frigate bird with a withered wing was found to be in excellent plump condition, the inference being—and no other explanation seems possible in the circumstances related—that the cripple had been fed for some considerable time by birds of its own species which, realizing that it had lost the power of flight and therefore of the means to secure its own food, had continued to supply it from their own larder ; it was evident, as Mr. Bent proclaims, that " even in that busy community of thousands some of them found time to feed the unfortunate ".

Of its behaviour in winter Mr. Bent writes :

The man-o'-war bird is not a migratory species and is practically a resident throughout the year in the general vicinity of its breeding range. During the

---

[1] Bulletin 121 of the United States National Museum, to the authorities of which and to the late author my full acknowledgment is made for having made some extracts from the text.

summer, fall and winter it is often as gregarious as during the breeding season, especially in its roosts at night, when it gathers in enormous rookeries, frequenting the same roost regularly. Large flocks of man-o'-war birds may often be seen resting on the mangroves during the daytime, in company with pelicans, cormorants and other water birds. It is also a common sight to see them perched in flocks on sand bars, coral reefs, old wrecks, or abandoned structures, lazily digesting their food or waiting for another meal.

When the period for courtship arrives the frigate bird indulges in " startling, playful antics in the air ", and performs much of its courtship on the wing caressing its mate as gracefully in mid-air as on the ground. During the courtship period the gular pouch of the male is enlarged and can be inflated to a large size. The pouch becomes a bright red and the bird appears to have a balloon attached to its throat. This inflated air-sac varies from crimson to carmine. A male frigate will sit on the nest with the sac blown out to such a size as to obscure the whole front of the sitting bird. This " ornament " is obviously intended to attract the female and when at the same time the male erects its long greenish scapulars it presents a most peculiar appearance.

Frigate birds nest in large colonies and the nests may be placed on the tops of prickly pears, on sea-grapes and in mangroves. The nests are frail, open-worked, slightly hollowed platforms of small sticks and twigs, and are usually from two to four feet from the ground. Several nests may be in the same bush. Only one egg is laid, pure white and elliptical ovate in shape. The shell is thin, smooth and without gloss. Mr. Bent gives the measurements of fifty eggs as averaging 68·4 × 46·5 mm.

The young are born naked but eventually are covered with white down. Even at that early stage their wings seem to be too big for their bodies. The plumage development is puzzling but the sequences are well described in Mr. Bent's thorough manner. The full plumage of the adult is not acquired until after the second post-nuptial moult when the bird is in its third year.

When fully grown the frigate bird is probably the most wonderful exponent of flight in the world ; and as A. C. Bent has expressed it, " the most marvellous and most perfect flying machine that has ever been produced, with 7 or 8 feet of alar expanse supporting a 4 lb. body, steered by a long scissor-like tail ".

REFERENCES : Original Description. *Fregata magnificens rothschildi* Mathews, *Birds of Australia*, iv, 1915, p. 280 : Aruba, West Indies.

PLATE 4

STORMY PETREL
Hydrobates pelagicus (Linnaeus)

Order TUBINARES

Family PROCELLARIIDAE

Genus *HYDROBATES* Boie

STORMY PETREL   PLATE 4

Hydrobates pelagicus (Linnaeus)

Summer Resident, partially migratory

IDENTIFICATION : The upperparts of the stormy petrel are sooty black, the major wing-coverts narrowly tipped with white. The rump is white and very conspicuous on this black little bird. The upper tail-coverts are white, tipped with black. The square tail is black. The underparts are sooty brown, the axillaries tipped with white. The thighs are brown and white. The under tail-coverts are mainly white, tipped with black. The eye is brown. The bill, legs, and feet are black. It is 6 inches in length.

The diminutive size of this petrel, no bigger than a house martin, though with a wider wing-spread of fourteen inches, its white rump and squared tail, all make it easy to identify from the deck of a steamer. It is frequently to be seen in the wake of a big ship and often dangles its feet just above the water. If the black feet are seen, they will also help as an identification, as the rather similar Wilson's petrel has yellow webs to its feet.

LOCAL DISTRIBUTION : The stormy petrel breeds locally round the British and Irish coasts but mainly on islands ; mainland breeding places are exceedingly uncommon. In England the largest colonies are to be found on the Scilly Isles and on the islands of Skokholm and Skomer off the Welsh coast. It does not breed on the Farne Islands but has once been recorded as nesting (1904) on the Bass Rock.

In Scotland it breeds on many of the islands off the west coast, the smaller islands being more favoured than the larger ones. There is said to be no record for Skye though it breeds on small isles off that coast. It has been recorded as breeding in the St. Kilda group since 1697 and has many colonies in the Outer Hebrides, the Orkneys, and Shetlands. Dr. Baxter and Miss Rintoul in their *Birds of Scotland* give a list of many islands in which the stormy petrel is reported to breed or to have bred in the past, but they confess that the information regarding the nesting places on the islands is not up to date. It is said that there is no known case of it breeding on the Scottish mainland.

In Ireland the stormy petrel breeds abundantly on numerous islands off the north and west coasts, for the details of which I refer the reader to Major Ruttledge's account in the *Birds of Ireland* (1954). On the Great Skellig Rock off Kerry their numbers are computed as " enormous " by the various lightkeepers who have been stationed there, while another vast breeding place is to be found rather farther north on Inishtearaght Island. On the Saltee Islands off Wexford none have been proved to breed.

After the breeding season is over the stormy petrel wanders far afield.

DISTRIBUTION ABROAD : The stormy petrel has many breeding places from the Westmann islands and the Faeroes in the north to the Canary Islands and the Mediterranean in the south, and has once been recorded as breeding on the Desertas off Madeira. There are breeding places in the Channel Islands and on the Brittany coast,[1] as well as on the coast of Spain. There is no breeding record from the Azores. The statement of its nesting on the Desertas rests on three eggs in the collection of the British Museum (Nat. Hist.) taken in 1849, probably by Dr. Frere ; but it has never been taken in that group since, and doubt has always been thrown on the authenticity of the record quoted. There is no doubt, however, about the nestling from the Canary Islands [2] and it is therefore just as likely to nest spasmodically on some outlying islands of the Madeira group which are very seldom visited by ornithologists.

The discovery by Dr. Hugh Cott of a nestling on an outlying rock of the eastern Canary Islands had been foreshadowed by my own discovery in a sea cave in the same group of an adult male with its sex organs greatly enlarged in June 1913. This pointed to its breeding in the Canaries, but it was not for some years afterwards that actual proof came to hand.

I had also suspected that it would nest on the Berlenga islands off the Portuguese coast, but that has not turned out to be the case. In the Mediterranean Sea it has a breeding place on the Isle de Riou near Marseilles [3] and has been reported to have nested on Corsica, Sardinia, Elba and Malta as well as off the east Spanish coast on the Hormigas,[4] and on Pityusae in the Balearic group where Claud Ticehurst and Hugh Whistler discovered a colony in 1930. The above is a very brief survey of its various breeding places ; it is not exhaustive and there are sure to be other undiscovered sites on seldom visited islets or outlying uninhabited rocks.

HABITS : Of the large number of petrels and shearwaters which frequent the oceans of the world, the little storm petrel, or " Mother Carey's chicken " as sailors name it, is to British observers the best known. There are localities around our coasts, all on outlying islets—often uninhabited save perhaps for a lighthouse—where the storm petrel can only be described as an abundant species ; but this is only during the period of nesting, when it comes to land to lay its egg and tend its young. At other seasons

[1] *Alauda*, 1941, pp. 23-26.   [2] *Bull. B.O.C.*, lix, 1939, pp. 142-145.
[3] *Rev. Fr. d'Orn.*, 1918, pp. 305-309.   [4] Off the Province of Murcia.

of the year its home is the ocean, and only those whose business takes them upon the sea are likely to encounter it. Ocean travellers will be familiar with its sprightly little form flitting backwards and forwards as it follows in the wake of a vessel ploughing its way through the waves. It was believed at one time that the birds were on the look-out for any oily substance thrown over the ship's side, but that was evidently a fallacy, for as P. R. Lowe wrote in an account of the species :

Almost certainly the reason which induces the storm petrel to follow a ship so persistently is because the screw or the plunging of the vessel churns up the water and kills or injures myriads of minute marine animals and animalcules, which float up to the surface to drift helplessly in its wake. Almost every minute one may observe one of the pursuing birds pause in its flight, hover over the water with legs let down and half pattering on the surface ; while at the same time the bird bends forward and picks some invisible speck from the water.

Dr. Percy Lowe had exceptional opportunities of observing the manner of feeding of this and other members of the petrel family when serving as private physician to Sir Frederick Johnstone on his yacht, in which he made six voyages to the West Indies and others to the Azores, Canaries, and Cape Verdes to which hundreds of petrels and shearwaters come every year to breed. One other petrel to be seen in northern waters has this same habit of following vessels at sea—Wilson's petrel, a bird which closely resembles the storm petrel but which may be distinguished, apart from its slightly larger size, by the long legs with yellow webs to its feet.

The stormy petrel—to use its old familiar ungrammatical name—is the smallest known bird with webbed feet, its body no bigger than that of a sparrow and—as already noted—with a striking resemblance at first sight to a house martin—the white rump, narrow wings and dark body-plumage helping to that end.

There has always been speculation regarding the thick orange-yellow oily matter found upon dissection in the stomach of the storm petrel, and various improbable suggestions have been put forward to account for it. A more likely explanation may be found as the result of Mourgue's experiments [1] in which the contents of stomachs of storm petrels captured on Ile Plane near Marseilles in April 1920 were analysed. M. Mourgue separated the contents and found, among various indeterminable débris, clear remains of *Heliozoum*, and as these organisms are known to contain a drop of oil, it is suggested that the petrel is not merely content to take in quantities of these animals, which are microscopic in any case, but it also feeds on their decaying corpses with their covering of oil. M. Mourgue did not assert that this is the sole source of their food supply, but rightly considered the results of his laboratory tests of sufficient importance to give

[1] Mourgue in *Rev. Fr. d'Orn.*, 1920, p. 126.

to his brother ornithologists. In *The Handbook of British Birds* the food of *Hydrobates pelagicus* is discussed by F. C. R. Jourdain, who observes that there is " little direct evidence, but probably derived from plankton or floating oil. Thick orange-yellow oily matter in stomach, and pieces of fish-liver, otoliths, fragments of fish, small Mollusca and Crustacea, also apparently fragments of green seaweed and minute seeds have been recorded, and insects by birds driven inland by stress of weather." Jourdain makes no reference to Mourgue's experiment which he may have over-looked, though from long experience of F. C. R. Jourdain I think that is extremely unlikely. Jourdain did not miss much ! It looks very much as if " F. C. R. J." took his account closely from that of the great Scottish ornithologist Macgillivray (1852 !), who wrote : " The food of this species —the storm petrel—is said by authors to consist of oily and fatty substances, small crustacea and mollusca, fishes, animal matter of any kind, garbage thrown from ships and even seaweeds . . . generally its stomach and gullet are found to contain oily matter, which, on being seized, it vomits like the other species of its family ". F. Du Cane Godman, in his *Mono-graph of the Petrels*, records that he has himself seen them feeding on the carcase of a dead whale. That they are attracted by any oily substance seems to be generally recognized.

It was Macgillivray again who gave a description of their flight, long before present-day naturalists were born or thought of. " Their manner of flying ", wrote the old naturalist, " is similar to that of the smaller gulls ; that is, they glide lightly along with expanded wings, sailing or gliding at intervals and then plying their feathery oars. It is only when picking up their food that, with upraised wings they hover over the spot, and pat the water with their feet ; although many persons have described this as their ordinary mode of progression. In calm weather when the sea is smooth, they hover, skim, and wheel around much in the manner of swallows, though with less velocity."

Robert Gray has recounted how on a stormy trip from Ailsa Craig the fishing craft in which he was travelling was followed to within a mile of the mainland by three or four storm petrels : " The birds did not appear to pick up anything, but untiringly followed the rising and falling of the water—now going down into a hollow, and now rising with the wave until the edge broke and curled over, when the little feet were let down with a gentle tripping movement as if trying to get a footing on the treacherous deep. Sometimes as one of them remained in the trough of the sea, until the wave seemed ready to engulph the little creature, it mounted sideways to let it pass, and down it went on the other side with contemptuous celerity."

In the winter gales which lash our coasts storm petrels may be driven far inland and the poor birds have been picked up in many curious places. Thick fog sometimes has a similar consequence, but except through mis-chance of this nature they never willingly come to land until darkness has fallen. How they find their way from far beyond sight of land to the island which they forsook before dawn and then to their own particular nest-hole amid a mass of fallen rocks and immense boulders, to our eyes appearing exactly alike, is a problem which has baffled many minds before mine; but that they return unfailingly is a matter of common knowledge.

When not nesting, for which purpose the petrels come to land after darkness has fallen, they remain far out at sea. Their energy appears inexhaustible and all day long they skim backwards and forwards just clear of the water, for all the world, as Percy Lowe wrote, as if they were catching flies as martins sometimes do close to the flat surface of a lawn or meadow. " This they will do from the very first hour of daylight until dark, flitting continually here, there and everywhere in tireless flight." They can, of course, rest upon the water as all of their kind, but it is extraordinarily seldom that one sees them thus engaged, though as Professor Wynne-Edwards and others have noted, the storm petrel occasionally settles on water and floats buoyantly. I have come across very large numbers off the African coast in winter : on one occasion, in February, the ship in which I was travelling passed close to a hundred or more between Cape Blanco and Cape Verde, restlessly flying to and fro over the calm sea.

Storm petrels ringed in the British Isles have seldom been recovered away from their nesting burrows. Indeed, when the 1939 edition of *The Handbook* was issued, Dr. Norman Ticehurst wrote that " no ringed birds have yet been recovered elsewhere than at breeding places ". Since then a few have been captured on the high seas, *i.e.* :

	Ringed		*Recovered*	
Skokholm Is.	. . 16.6.49	at sea, 50° 40′ N., 6° W.	.	1.7.51
Skokholm Is.	. . . 16.6.49	10 miles north of Land's End	. . . .	18.6.52
Kerry	. . . . 10.7.55	off Mauretania	. .	28.1.56
Skokholm Is.	. . . 16.9.56	Morbihan, France, end of Dec. 1956		

We are still very much in the dark as regards the distances which our home-bred birds travel in the winter. There are no *regular* breeding places to my knowledge south of the Mediterranean, but large numbers pass down the coast of West Africa and I have numerous records of their being seen at sea—mainly in January and February, off the coast of Mauretania, Rio de Oro (April), Liberia, Sierra Leone, Gold Coast, and the Gulf of Guinea, and from thirty miles north of the equator. Charles Bird, who recorded it from Rio de Oro, wrote that it is one of the characteristic sea-birds of those waters : " one sees them in large numbers everywhere along the coast ". It seems most likely that such large numbers as appear off the African mainland come from the large colonies such as we know to exist in south-west Ireland. The numbers which have nesting places south of the Bay of Biscay are really insignificant in comparison, and no very large colonies have been found in the Mediterranean. Where else then can such large concentrations come from ? In the British Museum there are eight specimens from African waters. It is recorded too from Table Bay. F. du Cane Godman, that great authority on the Tubinares, observes that it not only reaches the Cape but extends its wanderings up the East African coast to the latitude of Zanzibar, but I know not on what he based that statement. It has definitely been seen by Dr. G. J. Van Oordt some hundreds of miles south of the Cape of Good Hope in 1953. On the other side of Africa the storm petrel has been recorded by Von Heuglin from the southern Red Sea but these examples would perhaps be from the Mediterranean colonies. How far—if at all—they may wander in the Indian Ocean and down the coasts of north-east Africa has never been determined. It was suggested many years ago that the western Mediterranean population of this petrel was distinct from the typical subspecies, but subsequent examination of specimens has not borne it out.

It seems to have been assumed by older writers that this petrel winters to a great extent in the north Atlantic. Norman Ticehurst observes in *The Handbook* that most leave immediate British waters by the end of November and have *spread farther out into the Atlantic*. If they spread out westwards of their breeding stations after the end of the nesting season, how is it that in their twenty-eight crossings of the north Atlantic in 1943-44 Messrs. Neal Rankin and Eric Duffey only definitely met with *H. pelagicus* on one occasion, and that on 9th June in 50° N., 25° W., when a number suddenly appeared around the ship and were common for an hour and a half ? " They did not follow the ship but flew leisurely northwards ". In their report, *Bird Life of the North Atlantic*,[1] the authors were puzzled that they did not come across this petrel more often, as they expected to see it in appreciable numbers. Dr. Ticehurst certainly implies that these petrels take a south-westerly direction in their wanderings, as he remarks that as early as 21st-23rd September examples have been met with 470 miles south-west of Plymouth. I suggest that they avoid the turbulent North Atlantic purposely and that, as existing sight-records indicate, in the months from January to April the storm petrel is regularly to be found off the west coast of Africa. The numbers are greatest north of the equator, but as already mentioned they reach the Cape and beyond. The parties which Charles Bird encountered off the coast of Rio de Oro in April would be on their leisurely journey north to their breeding grounds, where the bulk of the population arrive from mid-May onwards in the British Isles.

BREEDING HABITS : There have been many excellent accounts published in *British Birds* and elsewhere on the nesting of this species, the latest of which has just appeared (vol. l) in time for me to consult it. Most of the observations by R. M. Lockley and others have naturally been made

[1] *British Birds*, xli, 1948, Supplement, p. 6.

on Skokholm off the Pembrokeshire coast, but I will open this account by quoting some remarks by my old friend Eagle Clarke [1] of the Royal Scottish Museum when he visited the Flannan Islands over fifty years ago, for it is naturalists like him who paved the way to our knowledge to-day. We should not lose sight of their names.

The storm petrel is very numerous during the summer when they fly noisily about the islands during the night time. They breed on Eilean Mhor, and probably on the other islands, in abundance. Many chicks, some of them quite recently hatched, were found during our visit in September, and we saw young ones in every stage from a few hours old (tiny balls of pretty lavender-grey down) to birds full grown and fully feathered, except that they had a bunch of down still present on the lower part of the abdomen. The old birds are entirely absent during the day time, leaving even the small chicks to take care of themselves, and do not return until darkness sets in, when they tend their young and depart again early in the morning, probably to spend the day far out at sea in search of food. We opened out a number of their nesting holes at all hours of the day, but the old birds were always absent, except in one instance, when the young had only recently emerged from the egg. Occasionally they visited the lantern. They nest in the remains of the old building, in holes in turf, and under stones among grass. The nest is a mere mat composed of dry roots, grass, etc. I received a young one in full down which had been taken on 3rd October ; probably the first egg of this pair had been taken or destroyed.

In a few words Eagle Clarke gives a brief picture of the stormy petrels' home in the Flannan Isles as he found them, and nothing has occurred to alter the scene to-day. The details have been filled in by both Mr. and Mrs. Seton Gordon [2] in the Hebrides, by Lockley at Skokholm, and now a final analysis has appeared by Peter Davies. It is to this band of observers, and especially the last-named, that I am indebted for the notes which follow. The more detailed observations were carried out at Skokholm.

The petrels are remarkably punctual when returning to their nesting-holes, their first evening visit being recorded, over a number of burrows selected to be watched (eleven in 1955, fourteen in 1956), between 24th April and 29th May in 1955 and 30th April and 16th May in 1956. The first eggs were found between 12th June and 4th July 1955, and between 8th June and 2nd July 1956. Mr. Davies, from whose investigation these figures are taken, suggests that very late eggs and chicks which are recorded from time to time can be accounted for by an old-established breeder having lost its first mate ; by the time a new mate is found it may be thirty days before eggs are laid, which can account for eggs having been found at the end of July or even in the third week of August. Many years earlier (1928-31) Lockley found that the first adults arrived on Skokholm between

---

[1] " Birds of the Flannan Islands ", in *Annals of Scottish Natural History*, 1905.

[2] Audrey Gordon in *British Birds*, xiii, 1920, pp. 232-234, and xiv, 1921, p. 175 ; Seton Gordon, *op. cit.*, xxiv, 1931, pp. 245-248 ; R. M. Lockley, *op. cit.*, xxv, 1932, pp. 206-211 ; Peter Davies, *op. cit.*, l, 1957, pp. 85-101.

26th and 30th April, the birds becoming numerous by 10th to 16th May and the first eggs laid between 28th May and 5th June. In these years laying appears to have begun rather earlier than in 1955-56.

The presence of the birds is made known immediately they arrive in their nest-holes by the crooning notes which they utter towards evening and throughout the night up to two hours before sunset.

To judge from Mr. Davies's figures and those of earlier investigators, the number of petrels is fairly low until the middle of May, the bulk of the population returning in the second half of that month. It was found that most of the non-breeding birds arrived towards the end of May and early June, at which time the number of strange visitors to the burrows increased sharply. The population is at its highest level until late July or early August. The first birds to arrive at their nest-holes were all found to be experienced breeders, many of which had been taken in the same burrows on a previous occasion.

The nesting places show a wide variety of sites, and on Skokholm, where there may be a population of 1500 birds or more, the greater number were in natural crevices—among boulders above high-water mark, under slabs of sandstone broken from the cliffs or in fissures of the solid rock. The remainder, probably half, were either in the hedge banks of the old fields, a few in dry-stone walls or in the burrows of rabbits, shearwaters, and puffins in more open country. Exceptionally nests may be found under wood piles or wooden huts. Many of the burrows are excavated by the birds themselves, which loosen the earth with the bill and throw it back with the feet. The average nest scrape is, on Mr. Davies's showing, two feet six inches from the entrance, but may be anything from four inches to eight feet. Most nests are in complete darkness but a few are exposed to sunlight. " The nest itself is usually just a shallow depression, about 3 inches in diameter, in dry earth or fragments of stone. A few short pieces of bracken and other dry vegetation are very occasionally present. . . . Many nests acquire contour feathers from the sitting bird when the body moult takes place in July and August." Mrs. Seton Gordon found in the Hebrides that a rough nest was often made in shallow holes where material was at hand, and it is probable that on occasions the stormy petrel will construct a nest as Wilson's petrel is known to do at times. Before the egg is laid the old birds spend roughly one day in three at the nest, remaining about twenty-four hours. Egg-laying takes place over a long period : the earliest egg-date for Skokholm is 28th May over several years, the latest 20th August. Most of the eggs are produced in the second half of June and the first few days of July. Only one egg is laid. The egg is pure white often with a few reddish-brown speckles at the larger end. Jourdain's measurements, reproduced from *The Handbook*, are : average of 100 British-taken eggs 27·97 × 21·19 mm. Max. 30·7 × 22·4 mm. Min. 25·3 × 19·5 and 27 × 19·1 mm.

The incubation period is thirty-eight to forty days; the fledging period shows wide variation but averages sixty-one days.

Both Mr. Davies, and Mr. Lockley before him, were able to make a number of more general observations on this species and these may be recounted here. It was found that the storm petrel is extremely active in all its movements at night. It can run along flat and perpendicular surfaces with the greatest ease and with some speed, beating its wings rapidly to help its progression. In this manner it has been seen actually to negotiate the surface of an overhanging cliff, the beak being used when necessary. R. M. Lockley was the first to remark the courtship flight of the storm petrel and frequently noticed that a pair would fly round in a circle near or above the site of the nest, one apparently pursuing the other. They kept fairly strictly to the same circle and continued to fly steadily for several minutes. This display may be witnessed in May, June, or July and can often be watched by moonlight. Mr. Davies, who has also witnessed this flight, observes that a loud call which he interprets as " terr-*chick* " is given at intervals. If a third bird joins in and the excitement mounts snatches of a purring song are given and sometimes, though rarely, a very rapid " wick-wick-wick ". Charles Oldham, a first-rate field naturalist in many spheres, described the usual notes of the storm petrel as " a not loud but penetrating sound consisting of a harsh uneven purring urr-r-r-r-r long sustained, ending in a hiccough like a fairy being sick " (!), a description which Mr. Davies endorses. Those who have a liking for tables and graphs will find plenty to satisfy them in Mr. Peter Davies's paper, but unlike many of our present-day naturalists he does not rely on this mode of expression, and explains very clearly in Queen's English the many interesting points he discusses, making his investigations easy to quote in a work such as this. I take this opportunity to acknowledge my indebtedness to him and the other able naturalists who have unknowingly contributed to this essay.

REFERENCES : Original Description. *Procellaria pelagica* Linnaeus, *Syst Nat.*, 10th ed., 1758, p. 131 : Habitat *in alto Oceano*. Restricted type locality : coast of Sweden.

Genus *OCEANODROMA* Reichenbach

PLATE 5   **LEACH'S FORK-TAILED PETREL**

Oceanodroma leucorrhoa leucorrhoa (Vieillot)

Resident and breeding in four outlying Scottish islets, and formerly
on isolated islets off the Irish coast. Some evidence of migration off
west coast of Ireland, otherwise visits to British coasts are irregular

IDENTIFICATION : Leach's fork-tailed petrel is in general colour dark
brown with a slight greyish wash on the upperparts. The wings and tail
are blackish, the wing-coverts greyish, and the scapulars tipped with white,
forming a definite light band across the wing. The upper tail-coverts are
white and very long, some streaked with brown. The white thigh feathers
are also streaked with brown. The black bill is comparatively heavy,
with the nostrils much raised ; the legs, feet, and webs are also black.
Its length is 8½ inches.

In flight this is a dark brown bird with white on the rump and with a
light conspicuous band across the base of the long pointed wings. The
tail is acutely forked, which distinguishes it from Wilson's petrel and the
Madeiran petrel when this feature can be seen. The body is about the
size of a starling's. Leach's petrel, unlike the smaller storm petrel, does
not follow ships. Its flight is distinctive, constantly changing speed and
direction. Writing on the *Bird Life of the North Atlantic* Neal Rankin
and Eric Duffey observe that this is a most delightful bird to watch, as it
dances amongst the waves with what seem excessively large wings. These
authors emphasize that the forked tail is difficult to note at sea and should
not be relied upon for identification. They never saw it following in the
wake of vessels but on two occasions it came to refuse thrown overboard.

Dr. R. C. Murphy is emphatic that Wilson's petrel and Leach's petrel
can be distinguished by their flight " almost as far away as the birds can
be seen ". Leach's flies with rapid leaping strokes quite unlike the alterna-
tions of gliding and synchronous flutters which characterize the flight of
Wilson's petrel ; the difference in their flight is very striking if the two
species are seen together. Wynne-Edwards writes that Leach's petrel
" springs and bounds through the air in the strangest erratic manner, now
gliding like a miniature shearwater, now beating on buoyant wings like a
nightjar, or turning with incredible swiftness as it is caught and borne
on a stronger gust down the breeze. Only in the calmest weather does its
flight approach the monotony of that of *Hydrobates*."

LOCAL DISTRIBUTION : Few breeding places of Leach's petrel remain
to-day in the British Isles. It still nests on a few of the most inaccessible
islets off the coast of Scotland—St. Kilda (Dun), the Flannans (Eilean
Mor, Eilean Tigh), North Rona, and Sula Sgeir. The history of its

PLATE 5

LEACH'S FORK-TAILED PETREL

Oceanodroma leucorrhoa leucorrhoa (Vieillot)

PLATE 5

LEACH'S FORK-TAILED PETREL

Oceanodroma leucorhoa leucorhoa (Vieillot)

breeding in these four colonies has been traced by Dr. Evelyn Baxter and Miss Rintoul in their *Birds of Scotland* (1953), in which some other reported breeding records, not properly established, are mentioned.

In Ireland it is known to have bred on two islands off the Kerry coast between 1886 and 1889. Breeding was established in 1886, 1887, and 1888 on Inishtearaght, and in 1889 on Inishnabro. In the same year an egg was taken on Blackrock off the Mayo coast and in 1906 three eggs were taken on Duvillaun Beg not far from Blackrock. Since then no proof of breeding on the Irish coasts exists. In spite of intensive searches in likely places Major Ruttledge and his collaborators have failed to find any sign of the bird nesting either in its old haunts or on other islets examined. "It seems quite certain," writes Major Ruttledge in *Birds of Ireland* (1954), " that no colony exists anywhere on our coast and that cases of breeding have been and may still be entirely sporadic." He adds that evidence of a migratory movement along the *west coast* of Ireland is supported by specimens from lighthouses under weather conditions which make it impossible that they have been storm-driven.

A review [1] of the breeding status of Leach's petrel in Britain by Robert Atkinson and John A. Ainslie in 1940 gives the latest information available at that date in some detail. During the first week of August 1951 the remains of what appeared to be two Leach's petrels were found by Mr. Samuel Bruce on Whalsay island, Shetland, the birds having apparently been eaten by cats which prey largely on the storm petrels on that island. No trace ofnesting was found, however,[2] nor has the species ever been known to have bred in the Shetland islands.

DISTRIBUTION ABROAD: Although Leach's petrel has a wide distribution in the sense that the typical subspecies breeds on both sides of the Atlantic and also in the Pacific Ocean it is, in another sense, very restricted, for on the eastern side of the Atlantic it breeds, in addition to the islands enumerated in Britain, only on the Faeroes (West Mykines and Mykineshólmur) and Iceland. On the western Atlantic seaboard we find it breeding in southern Greenland, ranging south on the American coast to about the latitude of Massachusetts, but especially on the coasts of Labrador and Maine. In winter this large population migrates south to reach the coasts of Brazil and perhaps beyond. There are other colonies of *Oceanodroma leucorrhoa* in the Pacific Ocean—in Japan, the Aleutian, Commanders, Kurile, and Copper Islands. Subspecies have been described from western North America mainly on account of their smaller size.

It cannot be too strongly emphasized that by far the greater proportion of the Atlantic population of Leach's petrel inhabits the islands off the coasts of eastern and north America, from south Labrador and Newfoundland to Nova Scotia and Maine. In an important contribution to

[1] *British Birds*, xxxiv, 1940, pp. 50-55.
[2] *British Birds*, 1952, p. 421.

the literature of this species (*Auk*, lii, 1953, pp. 382-399), A. O. Gross estimates the breeding population on five small islands at the entrance to the Bay of Fundy alone, as over 27,000 pairs. Therefore when exceptional numbers are found in the eastern Atlantic the birds have drifted far from their usual haunts for some reason over which they have no control. It is when westerly gales are persistent that the greatest dislocation is caused, the small birds being steadily forced before the wind. When, as in October 1952, these conditions begin a month earlier than usual and persist, the consequences may be disastrous, as will be shown later in this essay. Under normal conditions, by the end of September or October the breeding birds and young have gone out to sea, and by the end of the latter month the petrels mostly depart for the tropical South Atlantic where they spend the northern winter and so escape the worst of the North Atlantic storms.

I have received records of Leach's petrel from various localities off the West African coast—Liberia, the Gold Coast, the Cape Verde Islands, and Ascension Island, while Austin Roberts includes it in his *Birds of South Africa* without stating localities.

In 1952 Professor G. J. Van Oordt and Mr. J. P. Kruijt,[1] when voyaging in the Southern Ocean, saw several Leach's fork-tailed petrels in the South Atlantic north-west of the Cape from 12th to 15th January and again from 26th to 29th March. They remark that the species was especially numerous on 13th January, fifteen birds being counted ; the ship's noon position was 30° 45′ S., 5° 48′ E. Numerous examples were seen on the other side of the Atlantic off the coasts of Brazil.

If in fact Dr. R. C. Murphy was correct, as I have no doubt he was, in stating in 1932 from existing records that " in winter it migrates to the equator ", the birds would appear to range farther south on the African than the South American side of the Atlantic. It must be remembered, however, that much information regarding the distribution of petrels and shearwaters has been obtained since he wrote and there was little then to indicate that Leach's petrel ever proceeded south of St. Paul's rocks where Michael Nicoll recorded seeing it between those rocks and Bahia when naturalist on Lord Crawford's yacht *Valhalla*. On another voyage between Tenerife and the Cape it followed the yacht[2] to a little south of the line. Godman, in his *Monograph of the Petrels*, evidently considered St. Paul's rocks to be as far south as Leach's petrel occurred, and he threw doubt on the correctness of the label of the specimen (now in the British Museum), which Sir Andrew Smith collected " in the Cape Seas ". Professor Van Oordt's records throw a very different light on the subject.

Regarding its spasmodic occurrence in the Mediterranean there are several instances on record of birds seen or obtained off Italy, Sardinia, Sicily, and Algeria. M. J. Nicoll saw it two days out from Port Said

---

[1] *Ardea*, xlii, 1954, p. 270.
[2] Leach's petrel does *not* usually follow shipping but Nicoll was a careful observer.

when steaming to Gibraltar; R. C. Murphy obtained one fifty-three nautical miles west-north-west of Minorca; Philip Munn saw it in the Bay of Alcudia, Majorca, on 11th June 1924 and 28th August 1925; Col. Irby records it from Malaga while Favier picked up nine on the Tangier side of the Straits of Gibraltar, but no dates, only years, are given.

More remarkable still is this bird's occurrence as a vagrant in Finland and the Baltic, while there are records from most other European coasts including Denmark, Norway, and Heligoland, and even Switzerland where a single bird was picked up at Basle on 8th November 1952.

Mr. Spencer[1] has recorded that of 233 Leach's petrels ringed in Britain not one has been recovered up to 31st December 1955. In comparison there were ringed 2,372 storm petrels, the grand total of recoveries amounting to five only. Of 60,502 Manx shearwaters ringed in Britain, 635 have been recovered up to the end of 1955, for details of which see that species.

HABITS: Of the various petrels and shearwaters which occur in the North Atlantic Leach's fork-tailed petrel has had more attention paid to it than almost any other. It is one of the very few which we can claim as a breeding species, although, as Mr. Robert Atkinson has reminded us in an excellent article in *The New Naturalist*, " the species but brushes a wing-tip at the British Isles ". Of the small band of naturalists who have set foot on its breeding grounds—in particular the most inaccessible of all— Mr. Atkinson has had exceptional experiences and he will, I am sure, allow me to quote from his writings and make use in this essay of his notes. He reminds us that it is known in two islands—North Rona and Sula Sgeir—and in two groups of islands—St. Kilda and the Flannans. It seems that he has visited them all, for he writes with the authority of the man who knows. He computes the total population of Leach's petrel on these islands as " something of the order of 2,000 pairs. Even in the Flannans, where probably at least 200 pairs nest within a surface area of only some 40 acres, there is in day-time literally no sign or sound of petrel habitation. The burrow entrances are tiny in the broken ground, usually overgrown with chickweed, mayweed, or thrift, and even when discovered commonly show no signs of use ". On this group of islands the petrels still breed in ground swept by stray beams from the lighthouse, and a few yards from the lighthouse compound one is in the midst of their strange night flighting. By a coincidence, two days before beginning this essay the present writer was in the lighthouse at the tip of the Mull of Galloway. The head keeper there, with whom we were in conversation about the birds, had had his share of duty on the Flannans and was speaking of the petrels which lived almost at his front door. They seem to have compensated to some extent for his sojourn on what must be one of the loneliest light stations in the whole of the British Isles.

When on 3rd August 1939 Mr. Atkinson landed on Sula Sgeir, he

[1] Director of the British Bird-ringing investigations, British Museum (Nat. Hist.).

was accompanied by Mr. John Ainslie, another naturalist who has now had wide experience of this petrel. Although they worked hard and heaved up many boulders only three nestlings of Leach's petrel came to light, but as darkness covered the island the night air became alive with petrels and they guessed that 400 pairs were in possession, as many, in fact, as in the colony on North Rona, where the green walls of the old half-underground village are riddled with petrel's holes. How well I know the transformation which takes place on a petrel island when night falls. Many of the birds on Sula Sgeir were nesting in and below the walls of the few dry-stone bothies on the rock, which are still used by the men who come to gather the young gannets every autumn. Mr. Atkinson reminds us how easily petrels' nesting burrows may be overlooked. He instances the disappoint-ment of Macgillivray at not finding Leach's petrel breeding on Dun in 1840 and Elwes's similar failure in 1868,[1] for as he observes the birds must certainly have been there. Mr. Atkinson states that in 1948 (when his article appeared), the number of Leach's petrel breeding on Dun in the St. Kilda group was quite unknown; but it has always been assumed by Eagle Clarke and other fine naturalists of days gone by that St. Kilda was in fact the headquarters of the fork-tailed petrel in Britain and their numbers can hardly have waned, though no census has been attempted. The new warden of St. Kilda—Mr. Kenneth Williamson—may have a chance to form a definite opinion.

Just what has happened to some of the old nesting haunts described in 1871 by Robert Gray in *Birds of the West of Scotland* we shall never know, but Gray's account is worth quoting. After reminding his readers that Leach's petrel was discovered on the island of St. Kilda in 1818 by Mr. Bullock, and mentioning the newly-discovered colony on Dun " under the loose rocks near the summit ", he observes that it is also known to frequent the island of Mingalay in Barra, " where a few pairs incubate every year " in company with the storm petrel. He continues : " There is a more extensive breeding place in the island of Rum, situated on rough stony ground at the north-west side at a place called Braedinach. Having repeatedly obtained specimens within the parish of the ' small isles ', I some years ago instituted inquiries which resulted in the discovery of this additional nursery." At that time Gray considered its numbers to be equal to those of the storm petrel. He ends by drawing attention to the birds which are driven inland during stormy weather, observing that it seems unable to withstand the force of the blasts which frequently occur in the vicinity of our mountain ranges ; a subject about which more will be said later in this essay.

Naturalists who have lived on islands where Leach's petrel breeds have left striking accounts of the remarkable night flying in which this species in particular indulges, though all members of the Order to which

[1] " Bird Stations of the Outer Hebrides ", in *Ibis*, v, 1869, pp. 20-37.

it belongs are largely nocturnal. When living on North Rona Dr. Fraser Darling was greatly impressed by this phenomenon, which he describes with his customary facility :

Several were flitting about by half past twelve, then more came in rapid succession, and these already in their burrows in their dry-stone walls began to sing in an ascending trill most pleasant to hear. It seemed to me that more petrels gathered near the place immediately after these trillings. Soon the birds in the air began to scream, but this was no unpleasant sound like that of the Manx shearwaters. It was a succession of eight or ten notes in a definite cadence and of varying pitch, rather like a staccato, musical laugh. The swift-flying shapes increased in number and the volume of sound grew. We could feel the excitement waxing in this community of little black birds. Their flight is erratic and swift, and when two or three hundred are flying in this way within a restricted space collisions are common. Our faces were brushed by the soft wings smelling strongly of the characteristic petrel musk. A pitch of excitement is reached after one o'clock in the morning, and the laughter and erratic movements wane before dawn.

Mr. Atkinson has given an even fuller account of the night life of Leach's petrel from which we can visualize the excitement which prevails as the night draws on :

The first birds begin to arrive soon after dark—a shadowy brushing of wings. They fly in silence. When a company has gathered the staccato calling begins, and soon works up to a pitch. The cries are loud and outlandish ; the flight is headlong, at breakneck speed in the darkness. There are collisions—birds tumble to the ground. They plump down and shuffle underground to visit their young, and there feed them with oily regurgitations. Others are digging at their burrows—this continues even late in the season. They scuffle and call from underground as loudly as from the air and the excited peeping of the chicks adds to the noise. The impression of the night flying—for which no particular reason has been suggested —is of unbounded excitement and urgency, energy unleashed. It goes on without flagging all night until with the first sign of dawn, the activity gradually runs down; the birds go back to sea or, if they have eggs or newly-hatched chicks, remain quietly below ground all day.

It is well known that Leach's petrel is strongly attracted by light and, as Dr. Evelyn Baxter tells us, it is often recorded from lighthouse lanterns, chiefly in September and October, but also occasionally in August and May. It is not only to such powerful lights that the birds are drawn. When Dr. P. R. Lowe of the British Museum was yachting in 1906, within one day's sail of St. Vincent, Cape Verde Islands, on 13th January, an entry in his private note-book records that the yacht was passing through an increasing crowd of petrels ; after dark four fell on the deck, attracted by the lights of the yacht ; all were *O. leucorrhoa*. During the night twenty or more petrels boarded the yacht as it sailed through the archipelago. Fifty miles south of St. Vincent a single specimen of *O. castro* was taken on board.

Professor Wynne-Edwards has stated [1] that like the fulmar many Leach's petrels pass the entire summer at sea without breeding. There is, as Niall Rankin and Eric Duffey [2] have shown, an immense concentration of Leach's petrels in a well-defined area about 500 miles wide between the American coast and lat. 37° W. These authors saw many birds in the southern part of the area in April and May and they continued abundant throughout June to September. By October the movement away from the coast was in full swing. Rankin and Duffey suggest that the birds probably gather off shore before the general movement southwards takes place.

The effect of severe gales on Leach's petrel is emphasized by Rankin and Duffey who observe :

During our months at sea the behaviour of several species under severe weather conditions was occasionally seen and it is interesting to note that this small bird [O. leucorrhoa] was the only one to show actual distress and inability to combat the conditions imposed upon it. On 19th October 1944, in mid-ocean, we experienced a gale of 80-90 knots windspeed. We did not expect to see any birds in such terrible weather, but somehow this species and three others had been caught in the worst part of a very large gale area. The Leach's petrels endeavoured to use the ship's lee-side for shelter and it was remarkable to see such small birds often holding their own against such powerful forces. They kept very close to the sea, hugging the wave-hollows but all the time losing ground. As long as they were able to elude the main draught they could control their movements sufficiently well to avoid disaster, but every now and again, through fatigue or just bad luck, some were caught by the gale and whisked away like feathers in a hurricane at an incredible rate. Several hit the ship's side disintegrating in a puff of feathers.

The larger shearwaters present, the great and the North Atlantic, showed no apparent discomfort and at times were even flying well above the wave tops.

In Great Britain we have had two devastating examples of the dangers which beset this small sea bird quite apart from a number of minor instances. Owing no doubt to the greater interest taken at the present time in bird life, the disaster which overtook Leach's petrel in the autumn of 1952 in these islands was recorded in great detail for the whole of Britain except Scotland by Hugh Boyd, [3] and for Scotland by Wynne-Edwards, [4] from whose reports all the information on this subject is gathered.

Wynne-Edwards opens his statement by noting the time of year, between 25th September and 25th November, when Leach's petrels have been driven ashore and have perished in considerable numbers in the British Isles and in other countries of Western Europe. The most severe of these disasters prior to that of 1952 took place in the days following

[1] *Proc. Boston Soc. Nat. Hist.*, 1935, p. 280.
[2] *British Birds*, xli, 1948, Supplement, pp. 6-8.
[3] *British Birds*, xlvii, 1954, pp. 137-163.
[4] *Scottish Naturalist*, lxv, 1953, pp. 167-189.

26th September 1891, when birds were reported from eighteen counties of Ireland [1] and in Scotland from a broad belt extending from the Borders to Mull and Angus.[2] All previous records, however, were surpassed by the great "wreck" of 1952. In Scotland alone Leach's petrels were picked up dead or alive in twenty-four of the thirty-three counties of Scotland and were just as widespread and even more numerous in Ireland, England, and Wales. At the same time reports of similar small-scale disasters were received from areas south of the Pyrenees, the Rhine Valley, and Switzerland; but the numbers on the Continent were everywhere small. From Scotland alone 500 birds were accounted for and, as Dr. Wynne-Edwards points out, for every petrel found there must have been many others which perished and lay unseen, in heather, woods, and bracken.

The meteorological charts in the latter half of October 1952 showed an almost uninterrupted series of westerly gales over the whole area, supporting the view that Leach's petrels were driven eastward from the entire width of the North Atlantic. They appeared first on the coasts of southern Ireland on 24th October or even a day or so earlier. In Scotland they were seen in a strong gale on 26th and on the three following days were scattered across the country from Shetland to Berwickshire, appearing even on the east coast. The dispersal of the birds over Scotland was not uniform. They were driven on to the west coast chiefly between Galloway and Mull, the largest numbers appearing in Ayrshire and Argyll. No bird was found higher than 1700 feet. Those which were found alive were all at the point of exhaustion. A number of the unfortunate birds were pursued by rooks and jackdaws which, however, did not appear to attack them once the petrels came to ground.

Petrels were found in every English county except Rutland, in every county in Wales, and in twenty-nine of the thirty-two Irish counties, About one-third of the reported casualties were found in Bridgwater Bay, Somerset. Mr. Boyd concluded that the total number of Leach's petrels dying in Britain in 1952 was certainly not less than 2600 and probably very much more. He even mentions the figure 6700 which includes " estimated numbers " where the petrels seen were very numerous. His paper in *British Birds* should be consulted for the details.

Mr. Boyd mentions various causes which may have contributed to the disaster described, such as that the moult may have reduced the capacity of the petrels to withstand strong winds, or that the presence of young birds in the population at the end of October may have affected the number of casualties; that the birds may have suffered from some epizootic disease or poisoning (though there was no evidence in support), or again that the birds may have been induced to undertake abnormal movements through

[1] E. Williams in *Zoologist*, 1891, p. 469.
[2] W. Evans in *Ann. Scot. Nat. Hist.*, 1892, p. 74.

scarcity of their food supply, as many people finding dead birds noted their emaciation. Over a hundred specimens picked up at Brean Down by N. W. Moore revealed the absence of dermal fat and of recently ingested suitable food ; extensive wasting of the muscles was also apparent. Wasting of muscles would certainly take place in birds subjected to long buffetings by storms and the same cause would account for empty stomachs. It seems, taking all these things into consideration, that the persistent gales were the primary cause of this " wreck ", the birds being driven against a lee shore at a time when they must have been greatly weakened by their continuous efforts to battle against the storm and their consequent inability to find suitable food. Weather charts showed that this wind of exceptional velocity had its origin in the western Atlantic.

That our islands are not alone in suffering such disasters is apparent from an editorial note in the *Auk* of 1934, where we read that the great gale of 21st-23rd August, which reached hurricane proportions along the American Atlantic seaboard, brought numbers of Leach's petrels from the open ocean to the sea beaches and carried many to points far inland. In New Jersey, where the storm was perhaps more severe than elsewhere, numbers of these petrels were seen all along the ocean front and flying over the inundated streets and driveways. Although evidently the loss of life here recorded was infinitesimal compared to what occurred recently in Britain, it does point to Leach's petrel being especially vulnerable to inclement weather on both sides of the Atlantic.

Although it barely comes under the heading of Habits or Behaviour, it may be mentioned that, as with our Manx shearwater, the subject of this essay also lends itself to homing experiments ; and although we may be glad that our small population in Britain has not been subjected to these tests, it is not without interest to learn what has been accomplished on the other side of the Atlantic. For the experiments a number of fork-tailed petrels nesting on the outer sea islands of the Bay of Fundy were selected and the results communicated to the *Auk* (the Journal of the A.O.U.) by Mr. Donald R. Griffin [1] who instituted the enquiry. The first week of July was chosen as the birds were less likely to desert their nests at that time. Birds were taken considerable distances before being released, and a large percentage returned from distances up to 360 miles from the nearest land and 470 miles from their nests. Several birds appear to have flown over at least eighteen miles of high wooded land rather than follow the coastline round Nova Scotia.

BREEDING HABITS : In the year 1940, when the last estimate appeared of the minimum number of Leach's petrel nesting on British islands, the figure of 2000 pairs was suggested, evenly distributed among the four remote breeding places. The status of the birds was investigated by

[1] *Auk*, 1940, pp. 61-74.

Robert Atkinson and John A. Ainslie and it is from the excellent report [1] of these two naturalists and their earlier work on the breeding habits of this petrel on North Rona [2] that, unless otherwise stated, I have compiled the following account. All four of the island groups were visited. The nesting population was computed to be as follows : North Rona (1936), 380 nesting pairs ; Eilean Mor, Flannan Isles (1937), *circa* 200 pairs ; Sula Sgeir (1939), *circa* 400 pairs ; St. Kilda group, colonies on Dun, Boreray, Soay, Levenish, and Hirta, numbers estimated in 1931 by T. H. Harrisson as at least 1000 pairs. There appears to be no recent estimate for the St. Kilda population.

There are quite a number of other likely breeding places on well-nigh inaccessible islands, but the difficulty of landing on small storm-swept islets has made it impossible to prove. One of the chief difficulties to be overcome is the spending of a night on one of these islets or exposed rocks, for even if a landing is accomplished it may be impossible to leave the next day, and the possibility of being stranded indefinitely on a waterless island is enough to deter the most venturesome naturalist from making the attempt —even if a boatman can be found to risk his vessel ! The writer once spent a week on one such uninhabited island, though not in the British Isles, and has some knowledge of what it means.

The islands suggested by Atkinson and Ainslie as a possible breeding place of Leach's petrel, either now (in cases where no one has yet spent a night) or in the future, are as follows : Sule Skerry ; Eilean Tighe, Soray, Roareim, and Eilean à Ghobha in the Flannans ; Gasker ; Haskeir and satellites ; the Monach Isles, Vetersay, Sandray, Pabbay, Mingulay, and Berneray ; and any islands outlying from the west coast of Ireland. Of these Haskeir seems the most likely as a petrel was found there in a hole in the nesting season, and also Mingulay, from which it was reported by Robert Gray and Elwes.

Nesting colonies of Leach's petrel on the Flannan islands were visited by Dr. Eagle Clarke [3] in 1904, when he spent sixteen days on Eilean Mor from 6th to 21st September. He was mainly, of course, concerned with migration ; but with time on his hands he was able to examine the nesting places of Leach's petrel and has left notes of what he found. Eagle Clarke, who had the widest experience of remote Scottish islands in his time, considered that in those days Eilean Mor was one of the chief breeding stations of Leach's petrel in the British Isles, and he expected it to remain so, thanks to its inaccessibility. He found them to be abundant, more so than

[1] " The British breeding status of Leach's Fork-tailed Petrel ", in *British Birds*, xxxiv, 1940, pp. 50-55.

[2] " On the breeding habits of Leach's Fork-tailed Petrel ", in *British Birds*, xxx, 1937, pp. 234-247.

[3] *Annals of Scot. Nat. Hist.*, liii, pp. 8-19, and liv, 1905, pp. 80-86 ; *Studies in Bird Migration*, vol. ii, 1912, pp. 250-285.

the storm petrels, and like the latter they flew noisily over the island on the short summer nights. The earliest date for their eggs he recorded was 29th May. He found the nurseries under stones among turf, in holes in turf overgrown with grass yet showing not the slightest signs of the incomings or outgoings of their occupants, and in the walls of the old buildings. In some of the burrows the mat-like cradles of roots and fibrous vegetable matter were placed several feet from the entrance. At the time of Eagle Clarke's visit the burrows were occupied by young of various ages. The chicks, sooty black in colour, were darker than those of the storm petrel and were more advanced, but youngsters only a few days old were found in the early days of the visit, *i.e.* after 6th September. Others were in every stage of development up to some almost ready to fly. The old birds were entirely absent during the daytime.

In contrast to the nests described by Eagle Clarke, in which a cradle of nest material was used, the burrows made by this petrel in the islands of the Bay of Fundy are described by W. A. O. Gross[1] as containing little or no nesting material—a feather or a twig or two generally sufficing. About three days were taken in building the burrow which is prepared by the male using both feet and beak when excavating. During the first evening the site is chosen and the entrance way constructed, the second night the burrow is half completed and the bird remains digging the following day instead of going out to sea. After three days the nest is completed and the birds were found mating by Mr. Gross that same night. During the court-ship period the females flutter over the breeding colony and the males call from their burrows ; the females reply and by these calls the birds are mutually attracted and finally mating takes place to the tune of a rhythmic series of notes with a short break in the middle. The nests were found by Mr. Gross to be deserted during the day following, after which the female lays her egg. In his paper Mr. Gross makes a suggestion which I have never heard before, *i.e.* that the musk smell, which we associate with all petrels, may be a highly differentiated characteristic of the individual, which if true would explain the bird's ability to single out its mate in the dead of night.

North Rona, which consists of some 300 acres of rough grass and sedge, lies some 40 miles north-west of Cape Wrath and has been un-inhabited for a great many years. It was visited by several naturalists in the past, the most fruitful visit being that by T. H. Harrisson (28th August to 3rd September 1931), who estimated the numbers of Leach's petrel to be about 120 pairs.[2] North Rona had also been visited by the Duchess of Bedford in her yacht. John Ainslie and Robert Atkinson spent twenty-seven days and nights on the island from 16th July to 12th

---

[1] " Life cycle of Leach's petrel on the outer sea island of the Bay of Fundy ", *Auk*, lii, No. 4, 1935, pp. 382-399.

[2] *Ibis*, 1932, pp. 441-457.

August 1936 in an attempt to learn more of the life history of the fork-tailed petrel than had ever been possible before.

In this they were successful as the following notes on the bird's breeding biology will show. They found the thrift-grown banks and tumbled walls of the village area riddled with nesting burrows of this petrel, and as many of the burrows followed more or less natural tunnels between stones they showed great variety in shape and size. Away from the banks and walls, on flat ground, the burrows are commonly excavated beneath large stones. The most usual type was a straight or winding burrow in a bank of thrift, ending in a rounded nesting chamber; the shortest measured two feet from the entrance to the nest, the longest four feet. From one to four " lay-bys ", as we may term them, up to eight inches long led off the main tunnel and were used when two birds were in the tunnel at the same time—one bird would remain in the tunnel or in one of the sidings and call to its mate on the nest. Not infrequently a single nest was found to have two entrances, and tunnels within the stone walls often communicated. All burrows were obviously excavated by the birds themselves in the manner already described by Mr. Gross, but usually only the feet were used and the earth was thrown backwards as far as eight inches behind the burrowing bird. A number of half-excavated burrows were found and work was going on in these spasmodically as late as August, but so far as could be seen they were never completed. The nest chambers examined varied from a loose mat of thrift rootlets to quite a substantial pad of dead grass, moss, lichen, and occasionally sheep's wool. This is very different from the nests on the Bay of Fundy islands described above.

Leach's petrel begins to lay earlier than the storm petrel on North Rona. It will be remembered that Eagle Clarke's earliest date for an egg on the Flannans was 29th May; Jourdain in *The Handbook* gives the breeding season from early June, and mentions an egg taken on St. Kilda on 28th May. Mr. and Mrs. Seton Gordon record that in a colony in the Hebrides most of the birds had laid by 15th July, while on 23rd August two chicks were found approximately one and two weeks old respectively. On North Rona young petrels at least a week old were found on 16th July, and by 12th August all fertile eggs had hatched, whereas on that date the storm petrels were still brooding. Messrs. Ainslie and Atkinson found that both parents brooded the young, apparently in stretches of a few days each; the sitting bird was visited by its mate at night and was, presumably, fed. Birds which had been incubating, without relief, for several days and which had not been fed for at least one night, left their burrows at dawn and flew straight out to sea.

Leach's petrel feeds on plankton, floating organisms which occur in their greatest density in the North Atlantic within which area the birds have their breeding places on both sides of the Atlantic. The young are presumably fed by the parents by regurgitation on the same organisms, but, as Atkinson and Ainslie have shown, at very irregular intervals. It was found, too, that when fledged the young were intentionally starved, presumably with the intention of forcing them to take to the sea and find their own living. The fledging period is not exactly known, but is well over fifty days. The egg of Leach's petrel can be distinguished from that of the storm petrel by its larger size. Jourdain has given the average of 91 eggs of British origin as 32·76 × 23·85 mm. Max. 35·3 × 24 and 33·4 × 25·4 mm. Min. 30·2 × 24 and 30·4 × 22·4 mm. The egg is dull white, usually with a zone of fine reddish spots.

Probably by far the greatest danger to old and especially to the young when they first emerge from their burrows are the black-backed gulls *Larus marinus*—birds which it would be wise for the Nature Conservancy on St. Kilda to keep under strict control if the fork-tailed petrel colonies are to thrive as we may hope. These little petrels have all they can do to sustain life against the elements alone and anything we can do to ease their life on the remote islands where they attempt to rear their young should be done. They are dwindling British breeding birds and need our protection.

REFERENCES : Original Description : *Procellaria leucorrhoa* Vieillot, *Nouv. Dict. d'Hist. Nat.*, new ed., vol. xxv, 1817, p. 422 : Picardy in France.

PLATE 6 **HARCOURT'S OR MADEIRAN PETREL**

Oceanodroma castro (Harcourt)

Accidental Visitor

IDENTIFICATION : Harcourt's petrel has brown upperparts washed with grey, particularly on the face and chin. The upper tail-coverts are white, broadly tipped with black. The wings are black with light brown coverts forming a pale bar. The underparts are brown, the thighs white tipped with brown. The black tail is slightly forked, definitely less than in Leach's fork-tailed petrel. The bill, legs, feet, and webs are black, the tarsus rather short. Its length is 8 inches.

Seen at sea, this petrel can only be distinguished from Leach's, which it closely resembles, by the *slightly* forked tail (nearly square) and the very inconspicuous wing-bar. The white rump is neater in appearance and not as ragged as in Leach's, but these are very poor characters upon which to rely for recognition when the bird is seen from the deck of a steamer. If handled there is less chance of confusion with any other species, for Harcourt's petrel has the white upper tail-coverts tipped conspicuously with black, whereas in Leach's petrel these feathers are white without black tips.

Dr. W. R. P. Bourne, who has studied this petrel in the Cape Verde Islands, considers that it can best be recognized by the style of its flight.

PLATE 6

WILSON'S PETREL
Oceanites oceanicus (Kuhl)

HARCOURT'S OR MADEIRAN PETREL
Oceanodroma castro (Harcourt)

WHITE-FACED OR FRIGATE PETREL
Pelagodroma marina hypoleuca (Webb, Berthelot and Moquin-Tandon)

Under Habits I have quoted Dr. Bourne's notes more fully, especially the comparison which he draws between this bird, Leach's, and Wilson's petrels.

OCCURRENCES IN GREAT BRITAIN : Only four or five examples have been found within our limits.   One at Littlestone, Kent, found dead on 5th December 1895, one shot near Hythe, Kent, 8th November 1906, another picked up dead, Milford, Hampshire, 19th November 1911, and one in Ireland obtained at Blackrock Lighthouse, Co. Mayo, on 18th October 1931.   Of these there is no dispute.   I can only guess on what grounds H. F. Witherby considered a specimen said to have been picked up by a police officer at St. Leonards, Sussex, on the night of 26th November 1905 " insufficiently authenticated ".   He must have been aware of the history of this specimen as set out by J. Walpole-Bond in his *History of Sussex Birds*, vol. iii, p. 61, as his firm were the publishers of that book in 1938. He evidently had grounds for rejecting it, but gives no reason.   The bird in question is in the Booth Museum, Brighton.   I do not accept Mr. Walpole-Bond's reason for the omission of this record from *A Practical Handbook of British Birds* (1924), considering it to be too improbable.

DISTRIBUTION ABROAD :   the typical race of this shearwater was described from the Desertas, by Vernon Harcourt in *Sketch of Madeira*, 1851, and some years afterwards, in 1882, Professor Ridgeway described what has proved to be the same species from the Hawaiian Islands, naming it *cryptoleucura*, a name which for long was used for the Madeiran birds as well, until Godman in his *Monograph of the Petrels* (1907-10) put the matter in the right perspective and showed that Harcourt's name must have precedence.

The range of the species (if we accept the fact, which some dispute, that the Atlantic and Pacific populations are indistinguishable) is as follows : it is to be found breeding in the Azores, Madeira, Desertas, Porto Santo, Salvages, and the Cape Verde Islands in the Atlantic.   It does not occur as a nesting species in the Canaries, to which group it is a rare straggler. It has been said to nest on St. Helena and Ascension.   In the Pacific it has two main breeding places—the Galapagos islands, where it has been given the name *O. castro bangsi*, and the Hawaiian islands from which comes the type of *O. castro cryptoleucura*.   These are very doubtfully distinct from the Atlantic birds.

The notes which follow will be mainly concerned with the Atlantic breeding places as it would naturally be from that ocean that British-taken specimens must have come.

As a vagrant this petrel has reached Ontario. [1] The example reported to have been taken in Germany and so recorded, was wrongly identified and is a specimen of *O. leucorrhoa*.[2]

[1] P. A. Taverner in *Auk*, 1934, p. 77.
[2] E. Stresemann in *Orn. Monatsber.*, 1925, p. 90.

HABITS AND BREEDING : When Godman wrote his great *Monograph of the Petrels* over fifty years ago he was able to publish very little about the habits of this bird, and even Cleveland Bent, writing in 1922, had to confess that he was not much better placed with regard to its life history. Its close resemblance to Leach's petrel caused the two birds to be confused for a long time. Godman himself paid a visit to Châo in the Desertas group in the spring of 1871 but did not meet with this petrel and failed, owing to rough seas, to land on Deserta Grande. It was not therefore until W. R. Ogilvie-Grant of the British Museum made his expedition to the Salvage Islands in 1895 that anything was known about it, though eggs had been taken on Porto Santo some years earlier. To Padre Schmitz of Madeira, more than to anyone else, are we indebted for notes of its breeding. It was Ogilvie-Grant again who records this petrel from the Azores, to which group he made an expedition in 1903, but although he identified a specimen in the Ponta Delgada Museum labelled " San Miguel ", and obtained a single bird in a hole in the rocks on Praya island on 25th April and picked up a dead one on Villa Islet, Santa Maria, on 1st June, he was able to learn nothing of its nesting habits as the birds had not yet commenced to breed and their nest-holes were empty. It seems that September is the month when they come to land for that purpose in the Azores. Even to-day it is not possible to say whether Harcourt's petrel breeds in the spring in this group but it is worth recording that Dr. Percy Lowe met with numbers within sight of Ponta Dalgada on 22nd and 23rd May 1907.

Harcourt's petrel breeds in all the islands of the Madeira group without exception, the island of Porto Santo being the most favoured. It was to that island that Padre Schmitz paid most attention, visiting it many times between 1893 and 1910. At first sight it appeared (as I wrote in 1914) [1] as if the bird has no particular breeding season in the Madeira group for it is a fact that eggs or young in down have been taken in practically every month except May. If two " seasons " can be recognized the first is in June, when nesting has become general, and the second in October when any number of fresh eggs have been taken ; probably quite different populations are then engaged. Even in December some birds have eggs, which accounts for young in down being found occasionally in February and March. In 1899 Padre Schmitz suggested that this petrel has no fixed season at all, but I disagreed with him in my paper written in 1914 and suggested that the first period commenced in June and extended through July, August, and September, and the second began in October, lasting through November and December—the late birds of the first season overlapping the early ones of the second. I do not believe the same individuals ever nest twice, but that the different colonies have quite different

[1] " On the distribution and nidification of the Tubinares in the North Atlantic Islands ", *Ibis*, 1914, pp. 438-494.

nesting dates. I have seen nothing written or produced since the first World War to make me alter that opinion.

The last naturalist to visit the haunts of Harcourt's petrel in the Desertas and Salvage islands was Ronald Lockley, who was on Châo Deserta on 10th July 1939. There he found numbers of the birds flying about the island after dusk, calling with a soft squeaky note " exactly like a finger rubbed hard on a window pane ", and thus not unlike the flight call of the stormy petrel (*H. pelagica*) which, however, Mr. Lockley states is much softer. A bird caught in its hole made a noise not unlike the purring note of the storm petrel ; the nest was in the rocks of an old boundary wall typical of a storm petrel site. A bird caught on 13th July and released in daylight flew with a snipe-like zig-zagging flight to the sea, the pale fringes to its secondaries making it appear as if it had a bar on the wing. This bar was also noticeable in birds encountered at sea between Madeira and Lisbon, but it otherwise looks completely black, except for the white rump. The scarcely forked tail appears blunt and square in flight. Mr. Lockley thought that about this time the numbers calling increased, as if the breeding season was nearer. It was observed that in passing over the island they flew higher than Bulwer's petrel, up to probably 100 feet above the ground. The birds called excitedly and Mr. Lockley suggests that these high flights may be connected with their courtship. On Deserta Grande these petrels were heard calling up to about 1300 feet but none were heard underground among the numerous stone walls and debris. When Mr. Lockley reached Great Salvage on 16th July Harcourt's petrel was nesting, and several adults and a few crushed eggs were turned out by the guano-diggers. One undamaged egg was well incubated ; it was a little larger than a storm petrel's egg, with a similar faint zone of spots just above the greatest circumference.

In the days, now long past, when the present writer was exploring the Canary Islands a special look-out was kept for this petrel on the outlying islands and rock groups off the eastern islands, Fuerteventura and Lanzarote and their satellites, but not once was it seen. Michael Nicoll states that when on the yacht *Valhalla* he saw large numbers on 12th November just before reaching Grand Canary ; unfortunately none were procured. Harcourts' petrel is so very difficult to distinguish unless one knows their individual flight. Off and on I spent some eight years exploring these islands and camped on those which were uninhabited for weeks at a time when the other petrels were breeding. Moreover, this group has been very thoroughly worked by able German and Austrian ornithologists as well as by several British ornithologists of standing. They would surely have found it, had it occurred.

We must turn therefore to the Cape Verde Islands in which group Harcourt's petrel has been known to breed since 1897 when the late Captain Boyd Alexander discovered it on the Rombos islands—a group of uninhabited islets five miles north of Brava ; and later on Branca, another island of the group. Alexander was an able observer and writer and his account of Harcourt's petrel as he found it is worth repeating again, though written so long ago.[1] It was on 13th March 1897 that Alexander and his companions set out to explore the Rombos islands—" a small group, three in number, uninhabited and devoid of water . . . their sandy-brown appearance, unrelieved by any growth, affording a striking contrast to the deep blue of a southern sea ". His attempt failed owing to the heavy sea, but two days later he set foot on the largest of the three islands, barely two square miles in extent. Its general character he described as flat, save for a lofty hill of sugar-loaf shape that rises up about its centre, while creeks and small bays indent the coastline. In many places its surface was strewn with ironstone, while there are several creeks that hold nickel and copper. The petrels which used to breed here had been driven away by the descendant of a pair of cats brought over from the mainland. Alexander's hopes were then centred on the remaining island of the group and he was not doomed to be disappointed. He may now take up the tale :

On the Brava side this island culminates in a rocky headland of considerable altitude, serving as a screen to hide from view the low, flat, gravelly land directly behind it, in length about two miles and one [mile] in width at its broadest part. This portion was literally honeycombed by petrels, causing the ground to give way at nearly every tread. The first species discovered was the elegant white-breasted petrel *Pelagodroma marina*. We found it breeding in considerable numbers. . . . The nest-holes had an average depth of 8 inches and a length of 2 feet. . . . In unearthing these petrels several managed to escape. They ran along the ground in a dazed condition and before we could rescue them they were pounced upon and carried off by kites. In close proximity to *Pelagodroma marina* was a colony of *Oceanodroma cryptoleucura* [the name by which Harcourt's petrel *O. castro* was then known], the burrows of which, however, ran farther into the ground, besides being more tortuous. Many had young, while most of the eggs were well incubated. Farther up the island and towards the rocky headland we discovered *Puffinus assimilis* breeding, not only in holes, but many beneath rocky boulders and in small clefts and overhanging rocks, while in one instance a bird had made its nest beneath the boards of a tumble-down hut. . . .

When the night shadows began to brood vaguely over this lone waste of an island, the petrels came abroad and filled the still air with their weird cries. They mustered strongly, flitting to and fro over the low-lying ground in hundreds. Among the number the most noticeable was *Puffinus assimilis*, as it glided like some large soft-winged bat over the small sand hills, and even sometimes brushing past our camp fire, for ever uttering its weird cry " *karki-karrou, karki karrow, karki-karrou* " while amid these a similar but softer one would often strike fitfully upon

[1] *Ibis*, 1898, pp. 94-97. It will be noted that all three petrels mentioned by Alexander in the account quoted figure on the British list and are dealt with in turn in this volume ; *i.e.* Harcourt's petrel, the frigate petrel, and the little shearwater of the Cape Verde Islands.

the ear, coming from *Oceanodroma cryptoleucura* [i.e. *castro*] as it flitted over the island, crying to its white-breasted relation " I'm a nigger, I'm a nigger, I'm a nigger ". And the white-breasted petrel (*Pelagodroma marina*) replied by uttering grating notes like those of a pair of rusty springs set in motion.

As the night wore on, the cries of these petrels died away, only to recommence, however, with redoubled energy just as dawn arrived, and then, as soon as the dusky light waxed clear, these voices ceased as suddenly as they had commenced, indicating that their owners had crept noiselessly into their dark retreats, there to remain till the heat had once more abated.

We know that Harcourt's petrel breeds too on Raza for that is the type locality of *Thalassidroma jabe-jabe* Bocage [1] (=*Oceanodroma castro*). The type specimen is, or was, in the Bocage Museum, Lisbon, if it did not perish in the disastrous fire in which so much of that valuable collection was lost. Alexander did not find it on Raza [2] when he landed there in 1897. He did find it on Branca, which he described as nothing more than a small irregular chain of lofty, craggy hills rising up from the sea with extraordinary abruptness on its north side, with an almost glacis-like slope to the sea from about half-way down. This slope he found to be honey-combed with petrels, the same three species as he found on the Rombos isles. He obtained specimens and the young of all three and five eggs of the subject of this essay, *O. castro*. The islands were not visited again until 1922 when Mr. José Correia made an expedition there on behalf of the American Museum of Natural History. Correia's visit was not long enough for his observations to cover more than a few days on each island. He was on Raza between 17th and 26th May and on the Rombos Is. (Cima) between 17th and 29th June. On Raza he took three eggs of *O. castro* which measured 24 × 31 and 23·6 × 31 mm. There were two quite distinct nesting sites used. At Raza, where the ground is stony, these petrels do not burrow to make a nest but seek the shelter of projecting slabs of rock, beneath which they brood their single egg. At Cima, however, Mr. Correia found them breeding only in burrows and in soft soil. He describes the nest-hole as about two inches in diameter and from six inches to a foot in depth, from where it may extend laterally two feet or more. The islands were next visited in 1923-24 by a party collecting for the Cleveland Museum of Natural History, U.S.A. No report on this expedition in the sailing vessel *Blossom* was published, although a large collection was made. Fortunately Dr. W. R. P. Bourne, who visited the group in the summer of 1951, was able to secure a list of the specimens obtained by the *Blossom* expedition and these he incorporated with some notes in the valuable paper he wrote on his return home.[3]

[1] Bocage, *Jorn. Sci. Math. Phys. Nat. Lisboa*, v, 1875, p. 120 : Raza, Cape Verde Islands.

[2] The Italian collector L. Fea met with it on Raza between 1st and 6th November and obtained ten specimens, but the birds were not then breeding.

[3] *Ibis*, 1955, pp. 508-556.

Dr. Bourne's remarks on Harcourt's petrel, *O. castro*, relate to its field identification and to its breeding. He agreed with Dr. Bierman[1] who has stated that only exceptionally does it resemble Leach's petrel in the field, equally often resembling Wilson's petrel or especially the British storm petrel. He further remarked that it had a characteristic fluttering flight rather resembling that of *H. pelagicus*, though it sometimes patters over the waves like *O. oceanicus* or swoops like *O. leucorrhoa*. He was unable to discern the forked tail or the absence of markings on the rump in the field, but the white rump seemed more prominent and the legs were seen more often than in *O. leucorrhoa*, while the wings seemed longer, the feet extending beyond the tail much less than in *O. oceanicus*. It was noticeably larger and longer winged than *H. pelagicus*, but otherwise similar. It looked slightly browner than the other storm petrels.

Dr. Bourne notes that it is absent from the Cape Verde Islands from July to September and returns about 11th October. It must start laying by January as Alexander found young by mid-March. Eggs have been taken on many dates till mid-May, and the *Blossom* naturalists took young on Cima, Rombos Is., in April. As I pointed out myself many years ago[2] Harcourt's petrel has a prolonged breeding season in the autumn. In St. Helena it is said to lay its eggs in November.[3] Dr. Bourne would explain the remarkable discrepancy in breeding dates, which I had shown in 1914 to exist in the petrels of the North Atlantic islands, to a desire on the part of the birds to avoid competition for food ; thus they choose to nest at different seasons. He does not accept my own or Mr. R. M. Lockley's suggestions that competition for breeding sites is the principal cause. It is a suggestion, however, which may well apply in certain cases and always to very small islands but I must agree with Dr. Bourne that in the Salvage Islands there should be nesting sites and to spare for all the petrels and shearwaters which select that wild group upon which to rear their young. The suggestion put forward that the reason is to secure for each breeding colony a sufficiency of food at the time when the young are being tended merits consideration, but will be a very difficult point to prove. For my part I should have thought there is food and to spare for all. Probably we are all three to some extent correct in the suggestions we have made. I will conclude this essay by reprinting from the *Ibis*, 1914, pp. 454-455, the dated records connected with the breeding season and distribution of *Oceanodroma castro* in the North Atlantic islands. It shows more plainly than in any other way the wide variation exhibited. I have taken the opportunity of incorporating any additional information which has come to hand in the intervening years.

[1] W. H. Bierman and K. H. Voous in *Ardea*, 1950, Supplement.
[2] *Ibis*, 1914.
[3] E. L. Haydock in *Ostrich*, xxv, 1954, p. 62.

RECORDS CONCERNED WITH THE RANGE AND
BREEDING SEASONS OF HARCOURT'S PETREL
IN THE ATLANTIC ISLANDS [1]

January	14	Two adults boarded yacht 50 miles S.E. of St. Vincent, Cape Verde Is. : Percy Lowe.
	29	Two down-covered young taken, Madeira group : Schmitz.
February	13	Down-covered young, Porto Santo : Schmitz. One egg obtained, Desertas : Dalgleish.
	24	Three young obtained, one just hatched, Porto Santo : Schmitz.
March	16	Ten adults, four young in down, seven eggs collected on Rombos Is., Cape Verde Is. : Boyd Alexander.
	25	One down-covered young, Madeira group : Schmitz.
April	6	One almost fledged young, Madeira group : Schmitz.
	21	One adult obtained, birds not yet breeding, Great Salvage Is. : Ogilvie-Grant.
	—	Young birds collected on Cima Is., Rombos group, Cape Verde Is. : naturalists of the *Blossom* Expedition.
May	5	Adults, young and eggs collected, Branca, Cape Verde Is. : Boyd Alexander.
	1-29	None met with on Azores : Ogilvie-Grant.
	18-20	None seen on the Desertas, Madeira group, or at sea : R. Meinertzhagen.
	22-23	Numbers seen as nearing S. Miguel, Azores : Percy Lowe.
June	1	Birds not yet breeding, one adult picked up dead, Villa Islet, Azores : Ogilvie-Grant.
	6	Two fresh eggs obtained, Madeira group : Schmitz.
	13	Two fresh eggs obtained, Madeira group : Schmitz.
Mid-June		Fifteen eggs, well incubated, Baixo Is., Porto Santo : Schmitz.
	18	One egg, Porto Santo : Schmitz.
	21	Few eggs taken, mostly incubated, Madeira group : Schmitz.
	23	One egg taken, Baixo Is., Porto Santo : Schmitz.
	24	Two eggs taken, Porto Santo : Schmitz.
	25	Four eggs obtained, Desertas, Madeira group : Schmitz.
	26	Birds breeding, Madeira : Schmitz. [It is doubtful if Padre Schmitz intended the main island.]
July	10-15	Numbers calling Deserta Grand and Châo Deserta, Madeira group, suggesting proximity breeding season. High flights over island believed to be courting flight. Birds in holes in rocks but no eggs to date : R. M. Lockley.
	16	Found nesting, Great Salvage Is., several eggs unearthed by guano-diggers, one undamaged was well incubated : R. M. Lockley.
	17	Two birds obtained, Porto Santo : Schmitz.
	23-24	Frequently heard calling during night but none found in rocks owing limited time, Baixo Is., Porto Santo : R. M. Lockley.
August	1	One fresh and one incubated egg taken, Madeira group : Schmitz.
	17	Adults obtained, Madeira : Schmitz.
	22	One young in down obtained, Desertas : Schmitz.

---

[1] Azores, Madeira, Desertas, Baixo Island, Porto Santo, Salvages, and Rombos group, Cape Verde Islands.

September	1	Young in down obtained, Porto Santo : Schmitz.
	12	More birds obtained, Porto Santo : Schmitz.
	12	Adults come ashore to breed, Villa islet, Santa Maria, Azores : Ogilvie-Grant and Camara.
	21	Seen at sea between Lisbon and Madeira : Schmitz.
October	—	" The first eggs collected ", Porto Santo : Schmitz. (Presumably Schmitz intended the first eggs of the month, he had obtained young in down on 1st September.)
	11	Two adults taken on Raza, Cape Verde Is. : Boyd Alexander.
End of month		Not breeding but abundant on Raza, Cape Verde Is. : Fea.
November	1-6	Ten adults obtained, Raza, Cape Verde Is. : Fea.
	—	Eggs more or less incubated, Porto Santo : Schmitz.
	27	A very few seen at sea nearing Desertas : Percy Lowe.
End of month		" This is the time recommended for egg hunting in Madeira group of islands " : Schmitz.
December	13	Downy young and eggs, Cima Is., Porto Santo : Schmitz.
	20	One egg taken, Porto Santo : Schmitz.
	23	Thirteen eggs obtained, slightly incubated, Porto Santo : Schmitz.

REFERENCES : Original Description. *Thalassidroma castro* Harcourt, *Sketch of Madeira*, 1851, p. 123 : Desertas off Madeira.

Genus *OCEANITES* Keyserling and Blasius

PLATE 6   **WILSON'S PETREL**

Oceanites oceanicus [1] (Kuhl)

A Rare Visitor

IDENTIFICATION : The entire upperparts, wings, and tail of this petrel are blackish except for the upper tail-coverts which are white, and the major wing-coverts which are brown, tipped with white in the new feathers. The underparts are sooty-brown. The thighs are white, sometimes streaked with brown. The bill, legs, and toes are black. The webs of the feet orange-yellow, black at the extremity. It is 7¾ inches in length.

Wilson's petrel, like the smaller storm petrel, can often be seen over the wake of a ship with the rather long legs dangling, and the yellow feet are then conspicuous. It looks quite black above with a white rump and square tail. The white wing-coverts soon become abraded and do not then form the conspicuous white band of the fresh plumage. The wings appear more rounded in flight than is apparent when handling a skin. The body is starling-sized.

Wilson's petrel, though easily distinguishable with a little care, has

[1] Unless captured on their breeding grounds the described races of Wilson's petrel cannot be determined with absolute certainty. Therefore I name specimens captured in British seas binomially. D. A. B.

frequently been confused with Leach's petrel. The most diagnostic feature was pointed out by Wilson himself—the fact that the feet and yellow webs extend beyond the tail, whereas in Leach's petrel the short, black-webbed feet are concealed beneath the tail.

For additional field notes which may aid in identification see under " Habits ", especially the excellent account written by Dr. B. B. Roberts from which I shall have much to quote. In their study of the bird life of the North Atlantic, Neal Rankin and Eric Duffey stress the " weak gentle flight, and the more conspicuous white rump as compared with Leach's petrel ". The square-cut tail is only evident at close quarters.

OCCURRENCES IN THE BRITISH ISLES : The oft-quoted observation by Gould that he saw this petrel in abundance off Land's End in May 1838 has met with considerable doubt as to whether it was a case of mistaken identity. Wynne-Edwards in his *Birds of the North Atlantic* refers to this as " a highly abnormal circumstance which has never recurred in the intervening century "—or since, we may add. The British Isles are quite obviously beyond the normal range of any flocks and all that we can hope to see off the south-west coast of England or Ireland are occasional birds. Professor Wynne-Edwards in his masterly review of the summer range of this petrel in the North Atlantic, both on the American and eastern side, has made that perfectly clear. To tabulate the specific records when birds have been captured in British waters is not then so very difficult. The dates and places of occurrence have already been clearly set out by Eagle Clarke and by Witherby in their respective works as follows : Leaving aside Gould's 1838 record, an example of Wilson's petrel was found dead near Polperro, Cornwall, in November [1] of that year, and from that date we have the following recorded examples the authenticity of which has been proved : 1849, November, Wiltshire ; 1863, November, Isle of Wight ; 1874, November, Yorkshire ; 1881, Cumberland ; 1888, autumn, Isle of Wight ; 1890, November, Lancashire ; 1891, 1st October, Jura, Inner Hebrides (found alive) ; 1891, 1st October, Lough Erne, Ireland ; 1891, 2nd October, Mossvale, Co. Down, Ireland ; 1914, December, Sussex.

Mr. Witherby refers to four other examples with the identification or authenticity of which he was dissatisfied, and as he doubtless went into the question most carefully at the time we had better leave past records to his judgment, which invariably erred on the side of caution. Eagle Clarke, in the third edition of Howard Saunders's *Manual of British Birds*, accepts two records instead of one for Sussex, and three instead of one for Cumberland. The several November dates when these petrels were taken in British seas is surely very curious. By the end of that month they should be back in the Antarctic.

[1] Both Yarrell (1885) and Howard Saunders give the month as November. Witherby in *The Handbook* gives mid-August as the month, if referring to the same record.

BREEDING DISTRIBUTION : The life cycle of Wilson's petrel has been the subject of a meticulous survey by Dr. Brian Roberts of the Scott Polar Research Institute on his return from the British Graham Land Expedition, 1934-37, on which he served as ornithologist. In this essay Dr. Roberts's work will constantly be quoted. His summary of the breeding localities of Wilson's petrel is set out in detail in his report.[1] The lands and islands in which it had been found nesting up to 1940 were : South Victoria Land, Adélie Land, Queen Mary Land, MacRobertson Land, Kaiser Wilhelm II Land, Enderby Land, Graham Land, South Shetland Islands, South Orkney Islands, South Georgia, Falkland Islands, Tierra del Fuego, and Kerguelen Island. The above are localities in which breeding has been proved, but in addition there are many other localities at which breeding has been suspected. Dr. Roberts states that it is probably true to say that almost every suitable exposed rock area of the coast of the Antarctic continent is a breeding place of the species and we may expect the same of the majority of off-lying islands.

Dr. Roberts recognizes four distinct populations which can only be distinguished by their measurements. These he lists as follows :

1. *Oceanites oceanicus oceanicus* (Kuhl) : South Georgia designation as nesting station by R. C. Murphy, but type obtained in South Atlantic ocean off the mouth of the Rio de la Plata.
2. *Oceanites oceanicus exasperatus* Mathews : Graham Land, South Shetlands, Queen Mary Land, Adélie Land, South Victoria Land.
3. *Oceanites oceanicus parvus* Falla : Kerguelen Islands.
4. *Oceanites oceanicus magellanicus* Roberts : Falkland Islands, Tierra del Fuego.

He suggests that a binomial only should be used to denote birds captured at sea, as owing to the overlapping of measurements the identity of individual birds cannot be determined with absolute certainty.

The birds return to their Antarctic breeding grounds in November or December and leave them again in March or April. As soon as breeding is done they migrate rapidly northwards and are to be found generally distributed over the whole ocean to 30° N.

A detailed study of the Atlantic *Oceanites*, in which the plumages and moults of Wilson's petrel are fully described, is given by Dr. R. C. Murphy in the *Bulletin of the American Museum of Natural History*, 1918 —an admirable review, of which Dr. Roberts made full use in his own study.

LIFE CYCLE (after Brian Roberts) : In his report Dr. Roberts discusses the movements of Wilson's petrel in the Atlantic ocean month by month,

[1] *British Graham Land Expedition*, 1934-37. *Scientific Reports*, 1940-41, British Museum (Nat. Hist.). See pp. 141-194.

giving very fully the data upon which he bases his general conclusions. Very briefly this is what happens :

January : Wilson's petrel is confined almost exclusively to the region south of 50° S. Birds occur sparsely to 30° S. but only close to the South American coast.

February and March : Distribution is about the same as in January but South American records extend some 10° farther north.

April : After breeding the birds migrate rapidly north.

May : Migration continues through tropical and American waters : there is an absence of records from the central parts of both the North and South Atlantic.

June : It is completely absent from the Atlantic south of the equator.

July and August : The birds chiefly concentrate along the Gulf Stream off the American coast. Apart from two important records they appear to be absent from the region between 30° and 60° W., and there is no reliable evidence of their presence in American waters north of latitude 52° 30'. Off Nova Scotia and to the south they occur in great numbers. On the eastern side of the Atlantic the range of Wilson's petrel extends as far north as the Bay of Biscay, beyond which it is very rare, as has been shown by the paucity of records for the British Isles. There are several Mediterranean records, as far at any rate as the coast of Provence and Sardinia.

September : The return migration has begun. Some birds linger off Long Island and off the Spanish coast but the majority have already left northern waters and are to be found scattered as far south as the Falkland Islands and South Africa.

October : Migration is in full swing. Observations for this month and September suggest the possibility of a movement from west to east in the North Atlantic at this time. The American coast is evacuated before Africo-European waters. The main passage route in the southern hemisphere appears to follow the South American coast. There are a large number of records from the shipping routes on the west side of the Atlantic and a complete absence from these in the east.

November : The foremost birds have already reached their breeding grounds in west Antarctica. There are no records in this month from north of the equator.

December : Apart from exceptional records none have been seen north of 30° S. The concentration is again mainly in the western part of the South Atlantic.

Attention is drawn to the fact that even in the non-breeding season birds are dispersed over the southern ocean, and an occasional Wilson's petrel may be seen in tropical waters throughout the whole year. Dr. Roberts considers it almost certain that juvenile birds do not breed until they are two years old, and that the whole of this period must be spent at sea ; therein lies the probable explanation of the occurrence of the species in the tropical Atlantic during the southern summer. It is certain that there is a definite north and south migration of these non-breeding birds but it is much less extensive than that undertaken by the adult.

Dr. Roberts goes on to describe similar movements in the Pacific and Indian Oceans, which follow much the same general trend as those in the Atlantic. Migration north begins in March and is in full swing in May. It is remarkable that with few exceptions all the records for the next four months, June to September inclusive, are from the Arabian Sea and the Red Sea : there is in fact a concentration in that region analagous to the concentration in the Atlantic on the eastern seaboard of the United States. On the advent of October the southward migration begins and is continued through November : in the latter month the main body of the migrants have passed south of 50° S.

Summarizing these movements in the Atlantic and Pacific Oceans which he has expounded so clearly, Dr. Brian Roberts concludes :

The migration of Wilson's petrel is one of the longest and perhaps the most remarkable of any known bird. From their antarctic breeding grounds they fly northwards every year, extending to Newfoundland and the British Isles in the Atlantic, to the Red Sea and Persian Gulf in the Indian Ocean, to New Guinea and northern Peru in the Pacific. In a straight line the Atlantic migration is about 7000 miles in each direction, yet the flight throughout is indirect and quite unlike that of land birds crossing the sea. For the greater part of eight months most of them probably never come within sight of a landmark, yet they return at almost the same date each year to the same burrow and mate. Oceanic migration of this type provides a noteworthy example of powers of endurance, and it also raises the problem of orientation in its most difficult form.

When writing of the distribution of Wilson's petrel in the North Atlantic Dr. Roberts had the advantage of having read Professor Wynne-Edwards's exhaustive paper in the *Proceedings of the Boston Society of Natural History* (1935) on the birds of the North Atlantic. This British author—especially well known to Scottish ornithologists—devotes several pages to *Oceanites oceanicus* and his findings have evidently been embodied in Dr. Roberts's report. Two points, however, caught my eye ; the facts that in summer Wilson's petrel is, on the eastern side of the Atlantic, most abundant off the coast of Portugal, and that it is fairly numerous off the West African coasts and islands until December or even January. Dr. Wynne-Edwards was the first to prove that Wilson's petrel does not range as far north as had been stated by most writers before his treatise appeared.

In a footnote to yet another contribution [1] on North Atlantic birds

[1] *A Study of the Bird Life of the North Atlantic, British Birds*, 1948, Supplement to vol. xli.

by Neal Rankin and Eric Duffey, Wynne-Edwards suggests that the northern limit of Wilson's petrel evidently varies considerably from year to year. He remarks that he had himself seen them north to the Straits of Belle Isle, and that in May 1945 he found them in fair numbers north of the Azores east to 46° N., 18° W.

An important point to remember in the life history of Wilson's petrel compared to those of the stormy petrel, *H. pelagicus*, and Leach's petrel, *Oceanodroma leucorrhoa*, is the advantage which Wilson's petrel holds over these two northern breeders in having to return south to the southern summer to breed, before the winter storms of the North Atlantic are let loose with all their devastating ferocity, which leads occasionally to the " wreck " on our shores of the other two birds. Wynne-Edwards pointed out this advantage, and also the fact that even in the northern summer it never extends quite as far north as the others. It is significant also that the storm of 26th September 1891 and the following days brought to Scotland and Ireland among the wreck of Leach's petrels the only examples of Wilson's petrel which have been recorded from those countries.[1] This storm was rather earlier than usual and occurred while some Wilson's petrels still lingered in northern waters. In the storms of October and November 1952, which caused such havoc to Leach's petrel, no Wilson's petrels were among the wreck, the extra month having given them time to get beyond the radius of the storm.

HABITS : This heading might equally be employed for the information already given under " Life Cycle ", for so much of the life history and habits of Wilson's petrel is bound up with its migrations, which have already been discussed rather fully. Reference was made in one paragraph to an apparent concentration of this petrel in the Arabian Sea and this led me to consult Sir Geoffrey Archer's work *Birds of Somaliland*, to which Dr. Roberts had already made brief reference. Geoffrey Archer writes well, and his field observations always merit attention. He describes how on several occasions he met with petrels, which at first he believed to be *Hydrobates pelagicus*, in flights of twenty or thirty individuals on the crossing between Berbera and Aden, generally closer to the Arabian than the Somali coast :

Their flight and habits were typical. They came skimming along scarcely a foot above the ocean-wave in the manner of swallows hawking for insects over placid waters inland. They flew very quickly, passing and repassing the ship on the leeward side, twisting and circling, rising just sufficiently to cap the crest of the billows and dipping to the trough, and every now and again for a brief space hovering over the surface with suspended feet or making contact with the waters to scoop up some delectable ocean mite. For a full hour they would accompany us thus on our voyage and then pass out of sight. . . . I was under the impression that the

---

[1] *Scottish Naturalist*, 1953, p. 169.

petrels here seen belonged to the northern genus *Hydrobates*. But I have since had cause to change my mind.

A unique opportunity to observe storm petrels in the Gulf of Aden presented itself more recently. As we passed out of Aden harbour in the early morning of 5th September on a northward bound P. & O. steamer we met with these birds in incredible numbers. They were scattered over the sea in every direction as far as the eye, aided by binoculars, could reach; and there was no abatement in their numbers till the Straits of Bab-el-Mandeb were left behind after a run of 100 miles. Certainly *many, many thousands* were seen, and they were clearly on passage. They were disporting themselves over a glassy sea, some settled and bunched like phalaropes, many tripping merrily along the surface touching or treading water, most skimming low over the sea as they flitted hither and thither, and seemingly all going north. . . . Though I watched continuously for a full two hours the character of the yellow webs could not be distinguished, yet [for various reasons which he gives] there was no doubt left in my mind that the birds we were watching were not the British storm petrel but Wilson's petrel assembled about the northern limit of its range. And this view was shared by an experienced American naturalist who happened to be a fellow passenger and joined me in my observation.

It has fallen to few naturalists to see Wilson's petrel in such numbers so far from its Antarctic home but there seems little doubt that it was this bird, congregating in its thousands, which Sir Geoffrey Archer observed and of which he has left so graphic a description.

The notes from the observations of well-known naturalists which I have consulted about the flight of Wilson's petrel seemed to me slightly contradictory and it was with interest that I turned to Dr. Brian Roberts's observations on this subject for no one can be more familiar with it than the ornithologist of the *Penola*, who wrote as follows :

No one who has watched Wilson's petrel at sea can fail to be impressed by their wonderful adaptation to the environment. Often they follow a ship for hours on end, coursing back and forth, dipping and rising with the undulations of the sea, crossing and re-crossing the wake. Their flight seems almost effortless ; the feet are held together, extended beyond the tail with the webs closed. The feet are dropped only when the bird stalls or approaches the water closely, and they appear to lift the bird off the surface, steadying it and helping it along. As this downward beat of the feet occurs, the webs are spread out, and the bright yellow coloration becomes visible. Wilson's petrels do not " walk " on the water, but rather " patter " on it, lowering both feet simultaneously, three or four times in quick succession, between each short stretch of gliding. When they touch the water with their feet they do not necessarily pick up food ; they pause for a moment with body sloping upwards at about 45°, wings fully extended, and head turned down, presumably searching the surface for food. They very rarely settle on the water but when they do so they float buoyantly in a manner very reminiscent of *Phalaropus*. They are capable of diving, but I have only once seen a bird do this in order to obtain particles of food.

In rough weather they take advantage of the shelter afforded by the troughs between the waves or swell. . . . Even with a strong gale blowing and a heavy swell there is a comparatively undisturbed surface of water on the windward slope of each trough. The birds follow along these windward slopes, keeping within a few inches of the surface and taking advantage of the air currents which are deflected upwards from them. . . . If the birds rise more than a few inches from the water they are instantly blown away down wind.

Dr. Roberts concludes some further remarks on this subject by pointing to the interesting problem which is raised by the inference that Wilson's petrel seldom, if ever, has the opportunity to sleep at any time between March and November.

Investigation of the stomach contents of Wilson's petrel points to the crustacean *Euphasia superba* being the principal food throughout the Antarctic breeding areas, while an amphipod, *Euthemisto*, was found by Falla to be the main food consumed by these petrels at Kerguelen ; small cephalopods are also eaten. Oil or fat of any sort on the water will attract them and huge numbers have been seen gathered round dead whales. From February to May huge flocks come into South Georgia whaling stations to feed, and as many as five or six thousand were in attendance on the factory ship *New Sevilla* in February 1931 in 67° 10′ S., 74° 28′ E., but such numbers are reported to be unusual.

When they migrate northwards in the southern winter the scattered petrels are attracted all along the east coast of North America by the refuse thrown overboard from the fishing boats, but it is presumed that they feed on crustaceans as well. Dr. Roberts records that they are so tame that it is quite easy to watch them at close quarters as they feed on globules of oil or fat on the surface of the water : " While feeding, they flutter their wings and tread water ; their legs are partially immersed but the feathers do not get wet. They remain, however, hovering for three or four seconds in this position, and it is possible to see the oil globules decrease in size and disappear as they are sucked up."

Except at its breeding station Wilson's petrel is usually silent, but when feeding at sea they have been heard by Roberts to utter a querulous chattering, not unlike that of a common sparrow, which is repeated more rapidly when the birds become excited at the abundance of food.

BREEDING HABITS : The following account of the courting and nesting habits of Wilson's petrel is taken entirely from Dr. Brian Roberts's report of his investigations during the British Graham Land Expedition, and all acknowledgment should be given to him for the observations which follow. I have not quoted his account verbatim as it is far too long and exhaustive for my purpose, but it should be consulted by anyone in a position to do so.

Wilson's petrel is very punctual arriving at its particular breeding station but the dates of its appearance vary in the different colonies. For instance, birds were first seen on Argentine Is. on 24th November, while on Debenham Is. their first arrival was noted on 13th December in two consecutive years. November 7th is the earliest date recorded, mid-December the latest. Between these dates all the breeding stations listed in Dr. Roberts's report—eighteen localities are mentioned—are occupied by the birds returning to their nests. Egg-laying varies between 11th December and 3rd February. A period of three to four weeks elapses between the date of arrival and the appearance of the first eggs.

On the Argentine Islands, where Dr. Roberts carried out most of his own work, Wilson's petrel was seen for the first time about a week after the colony had become clear of snow. From then on birds were seen flying round the colony every evening, but they were not seen to visit their nesting places immediately on arrival. Not in fact until the night of 1st-2nd December did the petrels which had arrived on 24th November enter their old holes. After 10th December it was not uncommon to find a pair together but more often single birds of either sex were found in the nest during the day.

According to the reports of naturalists published over the years, the most usual nesting site is in a cavity under loose pieces of rock, sometimes a long way in and quite inaccessible. When there is any soil the birds are often found in burrows. On Kerguelen, Hall found that nests are often made of small stalks, chiefly of *Azorella*, in shallow indentations beneath stones or in any suitable chinks or crevices in slopes of shattered rock. In the Cape Horn area Reynolds found this petrel nesting in burrows or natural holes in damp peaty soil, with a covering of *Azorella* and *Empetrum*. In the South Orkneys Ardley excavated six nests " actually made in blocks of ice which had evidently formed among the rocks during the winter ". E. A. Wilson described a burrow at Cape Adare in which the floor of the tunnel was smooth ice and the nest cavity was lined with feathers of the Adélie penguin. Hunter found nests on Macquarie Island which were also formed largely of penguin's feathers. In the Graham Land peninsula and South Shetland Islands Brian Roberts himself found the nests commonly among shattered rocks, but he also discovered them in sloping moss patches where the soil enabled the birds to make burrows. These usually led in horizontally from the bottoms of small cavities between the bright green moss hummocks; many were in natural moss cavities but the majority must have been excavated by the birds themselves. The inner end, about 40 cm. from the entrance, opened out into a small chamber containing the nest—a shallow depression in a collection of small moss root fragments. It was found that the same burrows are used year after year, new material being placed on top of the old nest.

Wilson's petrels were seldom seen flying round the colony during the day. They came in from the sea each evening and flew up and down above the colony. Dr. Roberts believed this night flying to be an important part of their courtship activities. If one bird of a pair was in the burrow it was common for its mate to alight repeatedly at the entrance and utter its chattering call which would be answered immediately from within. This call is described as a rapid succession of short, high-pitched " peeps ". Frequently one bird would chase another, both following the same zig-zag course at high speed. At these times it was observed how strikingly conspicuous is the white bar at the base of the tail. Apart from this night flighting, courtship goes on in the burrow. Courtship, which was mutual as regards the sexes, consists mainly of preening one another's feathers and running the bill with a vibrating motion over each other's heads, and finally one would firmly grasp the bill of its mate and do a quick vibrating movement during which both birds would utter their harsh chattering call.

Only one egg is laid and if that is removed the bird does not lay again. The egg is white and thin-shelled. Dr. Roberts gives the average measurement of twenty eggs as 33·4 × 24·2 mm. Incubation starts with laying and is shared by both sexes. The change-over always takes place at night. The incubation period varied, in nine nests kept under constant observation, between thirty-nine and forty-seven days, which shows a very marked variation; the average was forty-three days. Dr. Roberts believed that the shortest time was nearer the true period, as in this case the minimum of disturbance was experienced.

The fledging period was subject to considerable variation due to various causes, chiefly interruption in feeding due to the blocking of burrows by snow and the difficulty experienced by the parents in finding food for their chicks during bad weather. In quite a number of cases investigated by Dr. Roberts, parents had attempted to reach their chicks and had failed—chicks consequently are exposed to periods of starvation. It was found that owing to this long incubation period the chicks in Graham Land do not leave their nests until over a month later than the young of any other species. In consequence the short Antarctic summer is only just long enough for the breeding cycle to be completed if the birds start nesting immediately the ground is clear of snow.

REFERENCES : Original Description. *Procellaria oceanica* Kuhl, *Beiträge Z. Zool.*, 1820, p. 136, Pl. 10, fig. 1 : " Southern Oceans ", restricted type loc. South Atlantic east of La Plata. This covers birds from South Georgia.

Genus *PELAGODROMA* Reichenbach

PLATE 6 **WHITE-FACED OR FRIGATE PETREL**

Pelagodroma marina hypoleuca (Webb, Berthelot and Moquin-Tandon).

Accidental Visitor

IDENTIFICATION : The forehead, the superciliary stripe, and the entire underparts are white ; the head, the upperside of the wings and the tail are blackish. The mantle is grey, the wing-coverts and rump brown, the upper tail-coverts light grey. A very important point to note when the bird is in flight is the fact that the under-side of the wing is pure white— a noticeable feature. Some white feathers may also be seen on either side of the grey upper tail-coverts. The bill, legs, and toes are black, the webs orange-yellow. The tarsus and middle toe are nearly $3\frac{1}{4}$ inches long. The length is 8 inches.

This petrel is easily recognized at sea by its colour pattern, the black head, wings, and tail contrasting with the grey mantle and rump. The white forehead, cheeks, broad eye-streak, and underparts are conspicuous, and when pendant the long black legs and the orange webbed feet are very noticeable as is the fluttering flight with legs dangling. When tucked up in flight, the feet extend $1\frac{1}{2}$ inches beyond the tail. The body is about the size of a song thrush.

OCCURRENCES IN BRITAIN : There are two valid records of the frigate petrel from these islands. The first example was picked up dead on Walney Island, Lancashire, in November 1890, washed up with a number of other sea birds. The second was captured alive on 1st January 1897 on the west side of the island of Colonsay and was forwarded in the flesh to the Royal Scottish Museum. Heavy south-westerly gales had been blowing at the time.

DISTRIBUTION ABROAD : The breeding range of *Pelagodroma marina* in the North Atlantic is confined to a very few islands—the Salvage Islands and the Cape Verde Islands. It occurs accidentally only in the Madeira group, the Azores, and the Canaries.[1]

The species *P. marina marina* inhabits the Tristan da Cunha group in the South Atlantic, while other subspecies have been described from the seas of Australia and New Zealand. It is therefore a bird of very extensive but very local distribution. Even in the island groups in which it breeds

[1] In *British Birds*, li, 1958, p. 270, the erroneous statement is made that the frigate petrel breeds in Madeira and the Canary Islands. On my pointing out the mistake (*op. cit.*, p. 447) the author of the article courteously withdrew the statement in a letter published in the same number. Mr. J. Warham's article on this species is based on his knowledge of the bird in Australia and New Zealand and is full of interesting details of its nesting. It appeared after my own notes were already in type and too late for extracts to appear in this essay.

it is very local, and in the Cape Verde Archipelago it is confined to the Rombos islands and to Branca.

How far the North Atlantic population travels over the ocean in the season when it is not nesting is very difficult to determine. A record of great interest was furnished by Neal Rankin and Eric Duffey [1] who saw frigate petrels round the ship from 45° to 37° W., 45° to 46° N. on 16th and 17th October 1944. The birds were in small numbers, being considerably more numerous on the first day. Little attention was paid to the ship's wake but occasionally the same bird would circle round two or three times near the ship's side before moving on. Next day, when only a few were seen, the wind was blowing at gale force and a heavy sea was running. The observers only caught glimpses of the birds but noted that they seemed well able to hold their own. For three days afterwards an extremely severe storm was experienced. When reporting on this experience the authors point to R. C. Murphy's [2] discussion of the effect of hurricanes on birds, in which he suggests that many sea birds are carried along in the calm centre of a disturbance, as was the case with the birds just mentioned, and are unable to free themselves because of strong peripheral winds. This would explain, as they point out, how these frigate petrels were transported so far from their home waters; for many storms originate off the west coast of North Africa, in the area which includes the breeding haunts of P. m. hypoleuca, and sweeping across the Atlantic turn north-east off the American coast, while some may even reach the British Isles.

Messrs. Rankin and Duffey accept this explanation as fitting their experience, believing that the only way the frigate petrels could have wandered so far out of their range was with the assistance of some powerful force over which they had no control. They were amazed that under the circumstances the petrels showed no sign of exhaustion or weakness. They suggest that this is a new record for the temperate North Atlantic.

A second occurrence is recorded by H. G. Alexander who met with the frigate petrel in 41° 44′ N., 51° 58′ W. on 25th August 1945. During the second World War some records were sent me by naval officers serving afloat. In particular Mr. Anthony Mayo wrote that he saw frigate petrels in March 230 miles north-west of Bathurst and others in August between the Cape Verde Islands and the mainland. The birds were observed to flutter along just clear of the water but with legs dangling and dipping into the waves at frequent intervals. The most southerly record was of one seen in latitude 3° 6′ S. in December; the farthest position north is given as 16° N., 21° W.

The population from the islands of Branco and Cima in the Cape Verde Islands have recently been separated by Dr. Bourne as distinct from the Salvage Islands birds and have been given the name *Pelagodroma*

[1] *Bird Life of the North Atlantic, British Birds*, xli, Supplement, 1948, pp. 9-10.
[2] *Oceanic Birds of South America*, New York.

marina eadesi. The Salvage Islands birds are *P. marina hypoleuca,* described from a bird which was taken off Tenerife, Canary Islands, to which group the species is only a non-breeding visitor. The typical race of this petrel, as already recorded, inhabits the southern Atlantic. It should be noted that the first to point out the probable differences between the Salvage Islands frigate petrels and those from the Cape Verde archipelago was R. C. Murphy,[1] but he did not give the latter bird a name.

HABITS : The first account of these frigate petrels (as Latham termed the white-faced petrel) from the Salvages is by W. R. Ogilvie-Grant, who made an expedition to that group of islands in the spring of 1895. The Salvages consist of three barren, storm-swept islands—Ilha Grande or Great Salvage, the Great Piton and the so-called Little Piton—together with a number of isolated rocks. They are situated almost mid-way between Madeira and Grand Canary, rather nearer the latter. Great Salvage lies in latitude 30° 8′ N., longitude 15° 55′ W., and is of very irregular shape with a number of rocks within the distance of a mile. It is much intersected and has several deep inlets. The *North Atlantic Pilot* warns navigators that it is surrounded on all sides with dangers, most of which show but some do not. Great caution is required when approaching. The Great Piton lies eight and a quarter miles west-south-west, three-quarters west from Ilha Grande. The Little Piton lies a mile from the western side of the Great Piton. These isles, states the *Pilot,* are seated upon and surrounded by one dangerous rocky bank.

Ogilvie-Grant was accompanied on his trip [2] by Henrik Grönvold, the well-known bird artist who was also a skilled taxidermist, and by the Hon. Cecil Baring. They made their headquarters on Great Salvage, a volcanic mass rising from the sea to a height of from one to three hundred feet. Above the precipices the top of the island is comparatively flat and mostly strewn with sharp loose stones and volcanic debris which cut ordinary shooting-boots to pieces. The highest point is two conspicuous hillocks which rise to a height of about 450 feet. The most striking plants were the wild tomato with pretty yellow flowers and small scarlet fruits, the ice-plant with lovely white star-like flowers, and the asparagus which grew to a considerable size, some of the bushes being several feet high and forming excellent cover for the rabbits which swarmed everywhere. Of the five or six petrels and shearwaters which nest on the Salvages the beautiful frigate petrel is certainly the most graceful. They were first seen as the steam-tug *Pedro* neared the islands, when numbers were flitting along close to the surface of the sea, with their long legs dangling beneath them and just touching the water. " Now ", wrote Ogilvie-Grant, " they

---

[1] *The Marine Ornithology of the Cape Verde Islands, Bull. U.S. Mus. Nat. Hist.,* 1, 1924, pp. 211-278. Cf. p. 234.

[2] A full account appeared in the *Zoologist,* 1895, pp. 401-417, reprinted from the *Field,* 21st and 28th September 1895. See also *Ibis,* 1896, pp. 41-55.

would be lost sight of in the hollows between the huge Atlantic rollers, now reappear, closely following the undulating waters with their graceful easy flight." On Great Salvage the frigate petrels were breeding in large colonies on the flat top of the island, in burrows dug out in the sandy ground and partly concealed by the close-growing ice-plant, *Mesembryanthemum crystallinum*. The breeding-ground occupied a considerable area and the earth was honeycombed with burrows in every direction. The birds were inhabiting their burrows and it was found that both sexes were taking part in incubating the single egg. Most of the eggs were white, more or less finely spotted, and often zoned towards the larger end, with dark red and purplish dots ; but some few were equally spotted all over the shell, while one was almost entirely devoid of markings. In shape the eggs varied considerably, some being perfect ovals equally round at both ends while others were slightly pointed at the one end.

The specimens collected on this expedition, both birds and eggs, are to be seen in the collection of the British Museum where the writer has often examined them. The eggs were measured by Jourdain who gives the average of twenty-five eggs from the Salvages and Cape Verde Islands as $36\cdot11 \times 26\cdot53$ mm. Max. $37\cdot3 \times 26\cdot7$ and $36\cdot9 \times 27\cdot4$ mm. Min. $33\cdot8 \times 25\cdot7$ and $37 \times 25\cdot4$ mm., two subspecies being included in these measurements.

Ogilvie-Grant discovered the curious fact that quite a number of the frigate petrels had been killed in their burrows and their eggs sucked. This was put down to mice, whose droppings were all over the burrows, while unmistakable teeth-marks were found on the shells of the eggs. The birds had been done to death by being bitten at the nape of the neck, and in some cases part of the brain had been eaten. Several were still quite fresh and almost untouched.

It was found that the most advanced eggs were but half incubated on 27th April. A number of birds were seen flying over the sea in the daytime but no note was ever heard from them. When caught on their egg they uttered a short grunting note. A number are said to breed on the Little Piton where there are neither rats nor mice to interfere with them unless these pests have gained a footing on the island since Ogilvie-Grant's expedition some sixty-five years ago. He spent eight days on the Salvages from 23rd April 1895.

I had always hoped to visit the Salvages, as I have passed within easy sight of them and have seen these white-faced storm petrels dancing on the waves as Ogilvie-Grant has described. It was with very great interest that I read in the *Ibis*, 1952, a description by R. M. Lockley of his visit to Great Salvage on 16th-17th July 1939 and of the field observations he was able to make in that short time. Forty-four years had elapsed since Ogilvie-Grant's visit, which was primarily a collecting trip. Lockley's visit had a wider object, and not having to spend time on taxidermy he was able to devote himself to the breeding biology of the petrels he encountered. Of the frigate he has this to say :

Nesting in considerable numbers in the phosphatic soil on top of the island. The light of the torch showed adults flying like huge long-legged flies over the ground in company with little shearwaters and Madeiran petrels. The burrows were occupied by the three species, but most numerously by the frigate petrels ; they were shallow (the soil being very hard, at any rate at this time of year), about three to nine inches from the surface ; and one's foot constantly trod through into these burrows. Part of the area was covered with the white, red-rimmed flowers of *Mesembryanthemum crystallinum* and here and there the rods and branches of *Nicotiana glauca* rose up thickly, forming groves in which the frigate petrels would become momentarily entangled. All the burrows opened contained well-advanced young [recollect that the date is 16th July]. It is likely that (as in other species of the Procellariiformes) the young are deserted by the parents towards the end of the fledging period ; several youngsters with little down left were found crawling about rather helplessly over the ground in the night, unattended and presumably exercising or making their way to the sea. During the day a number of these fledglings were thrown out of their burrows during the excavations of the guano workers, and were left to crawl into holes or to be devoured by gulls. Adults appeared to be absent by day, further evidence that the end of the breeding season was at hand. But a number of adult Madeiran petrels (*O. castro*) and little shearwaters (*P. assimilis baroli*) were dug out at the same time and evidently this was for these two latter species the commencement of their breeding season, following the vacation of their burrows by the frigate petrels.

The call of the frigate petrel at night was very faint, and not unlike that of a redshank *Totanus totanus* heard at some distance.

It seems from Mr. Lockley's account (which I have quoted in full) that the haunts of the petrel on Great Salvage have changed very little in the last fifty years.

When discussing the breeding places of Harcourt's petrel *Oceanodroma castro* in the Cape Verde Islands I mentioned Boyd Alexander's discovery of a large colony of the frigate petrel on the Rombos Isles during his expedition in 1897. It was breeding on Cima Island (one of the Rombos group) on 15th March when the eggs were in an advanced stage of incubation. During the same expedition Alexander found these petrels on Branca where all the birds had young in the first week of May. No eggs were obtained or found on Branca, all having hatched. Alexander concluded that the birds began breeding on Cima Island and on Branca (which lie some distance from one another) about the same time, *i.e.* early in March, a fact worth remarking considering how late in their laying are some birds of this species in the Salvage group. When Signor Fea landed on Cima island a few years later in August and September the birds were not breeding. His brief field notes read as follows :

This bird remains in holes in the earth or crevices in rocks during the day and is difficult to discover ; only if some lizard or other undesired guest penetrates its hiding-place does it reveal its hiding-place by emitting weak cries. A little after sunset, especially on moonless nights, its strange cry can be heard with frequency ; on San Nicolao they call it Gieb-gieb.[1]

In the second half of June 1922 Correia, collecting for the American Museum, explored Cima and Branca, and though he was too late to find eggs he left a brief description of *O. castro's* breeding-ground (already quoted here under Harcourt's petrel), and made some interesting observations on the white-faced petrel which first appeared in Dr. Murphy's *Marine Ornithology of the Cape Verde Islands* :

I found the *pedreiro azul* [blue stone-mason] chiefly in the vicinity of the Rombos Islets, but also saw two east of Sâo Vicente. This bird flies very close to the water, frequently dragging its feet as though about to alight. It often travels by leaps from wave to wave, striking the water vigorously with its webs. When stopping to feed, it stands upon the surface as though the ocean were stone, the body being held lightly above by the extended wings. I did not discover the particular nature of its food, for the stomachs of the birds examined contained only a black oil.

On the Rombos Islet where this species nests, it seeks places in which the ground can be readily drilled, and then digs nearly straight down for three or four inches before beginning the lateral tunnel which may be a yard or more in length. The nest is unlined. The breeding birds are much persecuted by a kind of crab [2] which kills and eats them in their burrows. This enemy is a sand-crab of light colour, which carries itself well above the ground, and which is found not on the rocks but upon sand or earth. Indeed, it occurs only on islands which have sandy beaches and not at all upon those of sheer rock. When they are at rest the crabs excavate pits in the soil and disappear from view. These crabs seem to subsist mostly upon the flesh of petrels, which they hunt in their holes at night. I found many birds torn to pieces in the nest-chambers, and afterwards I saw crabs picking birds' bones, or dragging out fresh victims that they had captured. This caused me to observe more closely, and I noticed that the crabs regularly introduced themselves into the burrows at evening, leaving at once and moving to another nest if their search was not rewarded. Sometimes they would spend a whole night hunting in this way, often gathering a rich harvest.

It is very sad that in both of its breeding places in the Cape Verde Islands and in the Salvages this most attractive species is subject to so much persecution—mice, cats, and crabs—for its colonies in the Atlantic islands are as nothing when we compare the numbers of individual birds with the enormous numbers which breed in the Australian and New Zealand seas.

Gregory Mathews, in his great work *The Birds of Australia*,[3] gives an account of the frigate petrels which range those seas and quotes from

[1] T. Salvadori, " Uccelli delle Isole del Capo Verde ", in *Ann. Mus. Civ. Genova*, 1899, p. 301.

[2] Bird-eating crabs brought home by Mr. Correia proved to be *Ocypode ippeus*, a widely-distributed North African and southern Mediterranean crustacean.—R. C. M.

[3] Vol. ii, 1912-1913, pp. 19-30, esp. pp. 26-30.

some excellent field notes made during a two-week visit to Ninth Island on the north-east coast of Tasmania by Mr. Frank Littler. So rare are field notes on the petrels as a whole that I have repeated a number of Mr. Littler's observations in this essay, for there is a striking similarity in the breeding-ground of the species at opposite ends of the earth as described by Boyd Alexander and Frank Littler. On Ninth Island the burrows of the frigate petrels were not only driven under the tussock-grass almost everywhere, but also in the soft soil on the top and sides of the island. An investigation of these burrows showed that they were from 2 feet 6 inches to 3 feet in length and that many were curved, some almost forming the letter L. The nest-chamber itself was some 6 inches in diameter, with a few fragments of vegetable debris on the floor. Mr. Littler was unable to form any estimate of the numbers present in the various rookeries beyond the fact that the figure must have run into some thousands. Observation was kept on the rookeries at night by means of a powerful acetylene lamp, and by moving slowly about it was possible to watch the petrels cleaning out their burrows, courting, and fighting. The first petrels arrived each evening punctually at 6.50 p.m. By 8 p.m. the majority had arrived and were in their burrows hard at work " spring-cleaning ". His account continues :

It was a very pretty sight watching them alight and seek out their homes ; they cannot walk after the manner of ordinary birds, but flit over the ground, just tipping it with their toes. They gave one the impression of being full of springs. As soon as a bird arrived at the entrance of its burrow it would come to a stop and dart suddenly out of sight. Even with hundreds of birds of this species around, not a sound was heard while they were on the wing, but when in their burrows a mouse-like squeaking, only slightly louder, could be heard. With many hundreds of birds underground the noise was distinctly audible. From the 22nd to the 25th [September] storm petrels were only fairly numerous ; then a curious thing occurred—not a single bird put in an appearance for three nights. On the 29th they reappeared in vast numbers, and continued every night while I was on the island. . . . Not all the birds left at dawn, for in several instances pairs were found in their burrows during the day.

Frank Littler ends this excellent account of his experiences on Ninth Island with an appreciation of what he encountered :

No prettier sight can be imagined than hundreds, perhaps thousands of these dainty creatures passing and repassing in the rays of the lamp, coming from darkness into light and disappearing again into darkness as they flitted over the rookeries. They looked for all the world like giant moths, and appeared as thick as flakes in a snow shower on a calm day.

In this far-away islet off the Tasmania coast the " white-faced petrels " are not free from danger from the moment they come ashore to rear their young until their final departure. They seem to encounter fewer perils from ocean storms and tempests than from marauding creatures on shore.

On Ninth Island scores and scores of dead frigate petrels in various stages of disintegration were scattered about the rookeries, and in several places among the rocks on the hill-side were heaps of bones and feathers. In addition to a couple of cats running wild on this island " in high condition ", the unfortunate birds had to contend with Pacific gulls ; while penguins also accounted for a number—for they peck them as they search for their burrows, and one peck means death. If this is a question of the balance of Nature keeping the numbers to the right proportion to enable the rookeries to survive, it would appear that on Ninth Island the cats had upset the balance.

It was believed by Mr. S. P. Townsend, who made observations on Mud Island off Victoria, that when the frigate petrels came ashore they merely stayed in the burrows long enough to feed the young ones and then flew away to sea. That may be so when the young are fledging but it cannot be said to be a general rule. The young were fed on a pasty substance which looked and smelt not unlike the bloater paste of commerce. A young bird which Townsend dissected had its stomach abnormally extended with this substance ; the only solid portion of the stomach content was a part of a small shrimp.

REFERENCES : Original Description : *Thalassidroma hypoleuca* Webb, Berthelot and Moquin-Tandon, *Hist. Nat. Iles Canaries*, 1841, p. 45 : Tenerife, described from a specimen evidently having wandered from the Salvage Is. It does not nest in the Canary archipelago, though it is often quoted as doing so.

Genus *PUFFINUS* Brisson

The genus *Puffinus* is here used with intent *for all the shearwaters*, notwithstanding the decision of the B.O.U. List Committee to unite *Puffinus* of Brisson 1760 with *Procellaria* of Linnaeus 1758. I entirely disagree with their ruling and have no intention of following their example.

MANX SHEARWATER[1]

Puffinus puffinus

PLATE 7
1. Manx Shearwater

Puffinus puffinus puffinus Brünnich

Resident ; breeds in considerable numbers

2. Balearic Shearwater

Puffinus puffinus mauretanicus P. R. Lowe

Accidental, of irregular occurrence

DISTINGUISHING CHARACTERS OF THE RACES : The Balearic race *Puffinus puffinus mauretanicus* differs from the typical Manx shearwater in its coloration. It is browner above and below ; the under tail-coverts, the flanks and axillaries are uniformly smoky brown ; some individuals have much darker underparts. It is more uniform in colour than the Manx. It can be distinguished from the sooty shearwater by its smaller size—it is 14 inches in length. In the abnormally dark specimens which occur in the Balearic race the entire underparts may, as Nicholson has stressed, appear pale sooty-brown, " extreme individuals appearing as nearly uniform above and below as a young starling when flying above water ". These dark birds are not common but occasionally several may be seen in company.

The third race of *Puffinus puffinus* is almost as well known to travellers in the Middle East as our bird at home. This is the Levantine shearwater *Puffinus puffinus yelkouan* (Acerbi). It has not yet been recognized in British waters and probably seldom if ever passes the Straits of Gibraltar, being found in the eastern two-thirds of the Mediterranean, the Aegean, the Dardanelles, the Sea of Marmora, the Bosphorus, and the Black Sea. In plumage it is browner than *P. puffinus puffinus* and in this it approaches *mauretanicus*. The flanks are sooty-brown, the axillaries have longer brown tips, and the under tail-coverts are browner than in the Manx.

The Manx is much blacker above, and the demarcation line between the upper side of the body and the white underparts is much more apparent than in either of the Mediterranean races.

[1] I am under a great debt to Mr. R. M. Lockley for having read the whole of this essay, and for his own special contribution beginning on page 92.

When Dr. Percy Lowe first described *mauretanicus* he compared it with *yelkouan*, the race found breeding in the eastern Mediterranean, observing that it was similar to *yelkouan* " but with under tail-coverts, feathers of the crissum, flanks and axillaries entirely and uniformly smoky-brown ". He pointed out that " in the cervical region the smoky-greyish-brown coloration extends well forward from the sides towards the mid-line in front, and also from the flanks across the lower abdomen ". He failed, however, to stress the white underparts of *yelkouan* sufficiently. The distinctions which he pointed out (*Bull. B.O.C.*, 1921, p. 140) were at once recognized, but even to-day the winter ranges of these two races are not very clear, though we have heard much more of *P. p. mauretanicus* since its distinctions became known. Witherby gave the range of *P. p. yelkouan* as the Mediterranean from Marseilles eastwards, presumably therefore including Corsica and Sardinia ; the whole area to the east comes within the range of *yelkouan*. Incidentally all specimens collected by myself and W. P. Lowe off the north Tunisian coast proved to be *yelkouan* and I have little doubt that these were from the breeding population of Galita Island, around which I have seen them in swarms in the early spring months. The description which follows applies to the birds which *breed around the coasts of Britain* (*P. puffinus puffinus*).

IDENTIFICATION OF MANX SHEARWATER : The entire upperparts from the crown to the tail are blackish ; the lores are speckled grey and white and the sides of the neck have a distinct mottling. The underparts are pure white. The axillaries are subterminally barred with brown and the outer web of most of the under tail-coverts are marked with brown. The iris and bill are black, the legs and feet are lead-coloured with pink flush and black streaks (appearing black at a distance in the field). The outermost toe brownish-black. A narrow line of the same colour continues up the back of the tarsus, the webs are ochre. At sea the appearance is of a clean, sharply-defined black and white bird. Its length is 14 inches.

The rather long fine bill, the black upperparts and white underparts, are clearly seen as the bird soars with stiff wings, veering and following the waves. It is seen in scattered groups at sea and does not follow ships, although a party may be seen around for some time. Near the breeding quarters they settle on the sea in large rafts after feeding, particularly at dusk, waiting for night before they visit their nests.

LOCAL DISTRIBUTION : The typical race of the Manx shearwater, which appears to have ceased to breed in the Isle of Man between 1785 and 1790, has many other breeding stations round the coasts of the British Isles. Although Dr. Lack and Mr. W. B. Alexander remarked in 1945 that many of the old colonies were reduced or had become extinct, they were, when estimating its status in that year, able to prove that in other colonies such as the one on Skokholm the birds were in a flourishing position.

When giving its distribution in England and Wales in *The Handbook*, H. F. Witherby records nesting colonies on the Scilly Isles, Skokholm, Skomer, Bardsey, and St. Tudwal off the coast of Wales, remarking that occasional pairs probably resort to the mainland counties of Pembroke and Caernarvon. Many west coast cliffs are visited in the breeding season, R. M. Lockley recording it from Pembroke and Carmarthen, J. H. Salter from Cardigan, and H. M. Salmon from Gower where breeding is believed to be sporadic. *The Handbook* (1940) omitted to mention Lundy Island off the north Devon coast, but eggs of the Manx shearwater were taken there by Captain Lewis R. W. Lloyd in 1922. Captain Lloyd informed me in 1944 that Jourdain had actually handled the eggs. It was shown later by Tucker and Southern [1] that the Lundy colony has been in existence for many years, but there is no evidence that it has ever been large. It is feared that the birds are preyed upon by brown rats which keep the numbers of nestlings which grow to maturity very low. Richard Perry's [2] estimate of the breeding Manx shearwaters on Lundy Isle is stated by Tucker and Southern to be erroneous and very wide of the mark.

On the east coast of England an isolated attempted breeding was reported by Dr. H. M. S. Blair,[3] when Mr. W. Robson of South Shields scaled the dangerous Marsden Rock off the Durham coast in the summer of 1939 and found an egg of *P. puffinus* " well in under an overhanging rocky outcrop covered with grass " on the summit of the rock. Referring to this incident in his *History of the Birds of Durham* (1951) [4] Mr. G. W. Temperley observes that " Marsden Rock is a detached stack, now only accessible to the most daring or foolhardy climber. The summit is so rarely reached that shearwaters could breed there unmolested and un-recognized for years—and may have done so." Be that as it may there has been no further evidence of breeding in this area and it remains to date the sole attempted breeding of the Manx shearwater on the east coast of Britain that has come to notice.

In Scotland it breeds on certain islands of the Inner and Outer Hebrides extending from the Clyde area (Glunimore Island, where Dr. Gibson [5] found it nesting in 1955) to St. Kilda, Eigg, Rhum, and Canna—these last four long-established and apparently flourishing colonies, and in Orkney and Shetland. In *The Birds of Scotland* Dr. Baxter and Miss Rintoul give a long list of islands where breeding took place in the past but which are now deserted ; but they mention other islands in which the shearwater still nests, including Lunga, one of the Treshnish Isles (Fraser

---

[1] *British Birds*, 1944, pp. 122-129.

[2] *Lundy, Isle of Puffins*, 1940.

[3] Dr. H. M. S. Blair, *British Birds*, xxxviii, 1945, p. 276.

[4] *Transactions Nat. Hist. Soc. Northumberland, Durham and Newcastle upon Tyne*, new series, vol. ix.

[5] *Scottish Naturalist*, 1957, p. 53.

Darling), some small islets off Skye (Seton Gordon and Prideaux), an islet near Mingulay, and on the Shiants (Fraser Darling). In their history of the colonies in Orkney and Shetland it is not easy to disentangle those colonies which now exist from those which are extinct—but the reader may be referred to *The Birds of Scotland* for details of both. It seems that the species has never nested on Fair Isle and that there is no record of breeding from the mainland.

In *Birds of Ireland* Major Ruttledge is more concise, observing that this shearwater is found off the coasts throughout the summer, breeding locally on marine islands and on a few promontories. The following are mentioned : the Skelligs off Kerry (large numbers) ; Little Saltee off Wexford (very small colony) ; on Lambay and Howth Head, Co. Dublin (fewer than ten pairs) ; Ireland's Eye (several pairs) ; Copeland Islands off Co. Down ; Rathus Island, Co. Antrim ; Tory Island (a few reported) ; Aranmar, Co. Donegal ; and found on Roaninish ; Kid Island and Inishturk, Co. Mayo ; and breeding suspected on a stack near Porturlin and on nearby cliffs. Inishbofin and Inishshark off Galway hold a few pairs and High Island a fair number. A few breed on Illaunimul but none on Inishmore in the Aran Islands. Major Ruttledge and his collaborators must be congratulated on the success which has attained their efforts to bring our knowledge of the distribution of the Manx shearwater in Ireland so well up to date ; a much clearer picture is required to-day of the breeding colonies which exist in the Scottish Isles—admittedly a difficult proposition but one which the Scottish Ornithologists' Club might profitably undertake.

The movements of the Manx shearwater, when breeding has been completed, will be discussed under " Habits ". The recovery of quite a number of ringed birds from the coasts of Brazil has opened our eyes to the immense distances which some of our British population travel. A spectacular journey has recently been accomplished by a bird ringed in Co. Down, Ireland, 25.8.56, recovered Rio Grande do Sol, Brazil, 21.12.56. There is only one more southerly record.

BREEDING RANGE OF THE MANX SHEARWATER BEYOND OUR SHORES : The most northerly colonies are situated in the Westmann Islands off Iceland, and on the Faeroes where the Manx shearwater is said to nest on most of the islands in the group (Williamson) ; we find it again on various islands off the coast of Brittany (Les Sept Iles, Iles d'Oessant, etc.). It has been found nesting sparingly on Corvo in the Azores [1] (June 1929 and May 1933 by Colonel Agostinho). It breeds—or has bred—in the Atlantic islands on Madeira, the Desertas, and Porto Santo (all on the authority of the late Padre Schmitz.[2] Cf. also Bannerman, *Ibis*, 1914, pp. 472-477.) There is no recent record from the Salvages and it does

---

[1] *Alauda*, 1931, pp. 230-249 ; and *Ibis*, 1938, p. 344.
[2] For a list of his publications see *Ibis*, 1914, p. 448.

not nest on any of the Canary Islands. In its wanderings in the Atlantic it has reached Brazil, the Argentine, and the United States (New York and Maine). Its reputed nesting in Bermuda is very doubtful.

DISTRIBUTION OF THE BALEARIC SHEARWATER : This race has, so far as we know, a very restricted breeding range, the headquarters of which are the Balearic and Pityusae Islands in the western Mediterranean. When Lowe separated this race from *yelkouan* its breeding place was unknown, and he suggested that it would be found in Alboran and Habbas Island, the former nearly midway between Melilla and Almeria in mid-Mediterranean, the latter just off Oran in Algeria. Lowe may well have guessed correctly, but these islets are unknown from the point of view of their bird life. As his type he selected a specimen in the British Museum which had been obtained off Algiers, and mentions Malaga as a second locality, from which there is a skin in the National Collection.

These shearwaters have been constantly reported off the French coast and as E. M. Nicholson observed [1] when summing up his experiences in the English Channel, after several cruises in search of *Puffinus*, this very distinct form is present in substantial numbers annually and is readily separated in the field from the British breeding race. In a later paragraph he draws attention to the fact that *mauretanicus* is known to occur in some numbers regularly between June and September along most of the French Channel coast from Crotoy (Somme) westwards, and the evidence of sight records indicates that, at least in some autumns, plenty move across within easy distance of the Cornish and Devon coasts. The status of *mauretanicus* in the North Sea is even more obscure. There are records from the Danish and from the Dutch coasts and, as Ralph Chislett mentions,[2] of seven shearwaters that passed through the hands of W. J. Clarke on various dates in the September of 1907 and 1908, four were available for re-examination and proved to be *mauretanicus*—as also did one shot from a boat off Scarborough on 3rd September 1912. In his recent review entitled " Shearwaters in the English Channel ", E. Max Nicholson draws attention to one other record from the east coast, a bird shot off North Bamburgh, Northumberland, on 8th September 1921, tangible evidence that the movement which Mayaud has traced up the northern coast of France may continue up the east coast of Britain to the waters of Yorkshire, Durham, and Northumberland as Nicholson suggests.

The last five volumes of *British Birds* (1952-57) contain a small number of sight-records of the Balearic shearwater on evidence which the editors presumably considered as well authenticated as sight-records can ever be : there is always in the case of petrels seen at sea some degree of uncertainty. Anyway we are fortunate in having some of these and other records summed up and analyzed by Messrs. J. S. Ash and K. B. Rooke

[1] *British Birds*, 1952, pp. 43-47.
[2] *Yorkshire Birds*, pp. 208-209. (The volume bears no publication date !)

in a paper entitled " Balearic Shearwaters off the Dorset Coast in 1953 ".[1] They state that the number of Balearic shearwaters seen from Portland Bill between 20th August and 2nd October, with a peak on 13th September, far exceeded any previously recorded close to the British coastline, but whether this was an abnormal or a regular movement must remain to be proved. Balearic shearwaters have now been recognized (nearly all between the beginning of August and the end of October) off Devon, Cornwall, Dorset, Sussex, Kent, and Norfolk in addition to those seen on the north-east coast of England ; also in the entrance to the Channel. But it is instructive to note that in forty trips from July to mid-September, between Penzance and the Scilly Isles, Mr. A. G. Parsons failed to recognize a single *mauretanicus* among the many *P. puffinus puffinus* which he observed from his ship—negative evidence of some importance which suggests that on its migrations the Balearic shearwater enters the English Channel probably keeping nearer the French than the British coast or perhaps to mid-Channel, but that it does not pass into the Irish Sea during its normal migration.

Nicholson made a wise suggestion that a look-out should be kept for its passage in the neighbourhood of Gibraltar, when it might be possible to see movements similar to those of the Levantine shearwater which travellers may witness in the Dardanelles and the Bosphorus. Tarifa Point would be the ideal place and Algeciras an excellent headquarters ; Cape Spartel on the Tangier coast is another vantage point from which a wonderful panorama of the Straits can be obtained, though, as I know from experience, looking *down* on flocks of shearwaters, flying in bunched formation as they do in the Dardanelles, is not the ideal angle at which to identify them. Even so, if they come reasonably near the land the species at least should be recognized. How rewarding it would be to see the Balearic shearwaters passing the headlands of Tarifa Point and Cape St. Vincent on what Lockley terms their " moulting flight " between June and October up the coasts of Portugal and France to feeding grounds in the region of Finisterre, the Roches Douvres, and Gulf of St. Malo off the coasts of Brittany and Normandy.

In our islands the Manx shearwater is so intimately connected with the name of Ronald Lockley that to write of any aspect of its life needs constant reference to his work ; while his name again conjures up memories of the Eighth International Congress when, on board two of H.M. destroyers, the leading ornithologists of the world paid a visit to Skokholm Island, the home of countless numbers of Manx shearwaters and—at the date of our visit—of their custodian. Mr. Lockley has made known to us the fascinating life-history of the Manx shearwater in his books [2] and in his several contributions to ornithological publications,[3] the most important

[1] *British Birds*, 1954, pp. 291-292.   [2] *Shearwaters*, London, 1942.
[3] *British Birds*, xxiii, 1930, pp. 202-218 ; xlvi, 1953, Supplementary Number, pp. 1-48.

of which are cited below. He has in fact spent a lifetime in studying petrels and in particular the subject of this essay, following it from Rockall to Porto Santo and visiting many of its almost inaccessible breeding colonies in the British and Atlantic islands.

It was therefore with the greatest satisfaction that I received his promise to contribute the major part of this essay which now follows :

HABITS, NESTING, AND MIGRATIONS OF THE MANX SHEARWATER

R. M. LOCKLEY [1]

The Manx shearwater exhibits at sea that perfection of flight characteristic of the largest petrels, the albatrosses. The wings are long and slender with powerful bones and muscles, and strong stiff primaries. Progression is less by wing-beating than by gliding, sailing, and soaring. Turning at the end of a glide it loses momentum unless the wind be strong, beats the wings a few times and, gaining height, careens on the other tack and glides forward at speed, perhaps shooting low in the trough of the sea to catch the powerful air lift at the crest of the next wave. One wing-tip seems to touch—but never quite—the water. The mastery of the shearwater's flight is marvellous to see ; it is at its best in a gale, for then the wind sustains it effortlessly.

In my book *Shearwaters*, published in 1942, I described the nesting habits and migrations of the Manx shearwater as then known. I was able to study this bird rather fully from the circumstance of living on the remote 240-acre island of Skokholm off the coast of Pembrokeshire, where I estimated that something like 10,000 pairs were breeding. Some of these birds actually nested a few paces from the back door of the old farmhouse in which I lived on the island. My opportunities were too good to be missed. Yet looking back I could wish I had paid more attention to these shearwaters ; at that time, however, I was much preoccupied with getting my living from the island—shepherding my sheep and lobster-fishing in the summer swiftly sped away the months during which the shearwaters were nesting. I had to confine myself at first to studying at intervals the few pairs which nested in burrows in the shallow turf between the back door and a rocky mound which we called the Knoll. Subsequently many friends came to help me to ring thousands of these shearwaters, which must by now be the most ringed sea-birds in the British Isles.

The shearwaters advertised their presence in no uncertain terms, often landing on our roof and sliding down the slates, screaming out their extraordinary cry. This is difficult to put down on paper. I consider it resembles the efforts of a young cockerel to begin crowing—dying away suddenly

[1] Received from Mr. Lockley in March 1958.

as if the young cockerel's head had been cut off half-way through ! Perhaps that is too drastic a description, but the noise, now captured on sound records and often broadcast on B.B.C. nature programmes, is raucous enough. Part or all of this " song " is used to signify any and all emotions and moods of the bird. It does not vary much ; it can be in a higher or lower key, and often it has a definite crooning or cooing quality. Generally it can be described as first a staccato cackle, then a crooning caw, followed by a brief harsh indrawing of air : *Cack-cack-cack-carr-hoo* ! Enough said !

The shearwaters arrive on Skokholm in late February if the weather is mild, but cold frosty weather with northerly winds temporarily drives them away. By the middle of March they are back in force. Always they arrive on the island by night, first assembling in huge rafts lying off the two islands of Skomer and Skokholm, where altogether probably close upon 50,000 breeding pairs nest. This nocturnal habit is most satisfactorily explained by saying it has evolved through the comparative helplessness of the shearwater while on land, making it in daylight the easy prey of diurnal animals, including man, and particularly the larger gulls, buzzards, and raptorial birds. The long narrow wings of this little albatross, for such the shearwater is, are ill-adapted for taking off on land, while its slender feet are better for swimming than for progress ashore. It has difficulty in standing upright, and can only make short runs before falling forward on its breast. In windless weather it is very easily caught on the surface of the island. On windless nights, once it has landed and is ready to leave again, it will scramble to some rocky outcrop, or rising land, or cliff-edge, to gain height before taking wing.

So the shearwaters fly in after dark, seldom before two hours after sunset, and, except for those individuals which remain in the burrows, they depart before dawn. This means that at midsummer they are above ground for two or three hours only, during which they are extremely active in or near the burrows. Evidence is accumulating that the male is the first to return and occupy the old nesting recess, doubtless because of his strong desire to mate.

By ringing all the shearwaters in or near the dozen burrows of the Knoll, it was possible to establish during ten years of observation that the majority of birds remained faithful to the burrow used the year before. The burrow with its nest is the meeting and mating place of the pair. I feel it is unlikely, because too difficult, that these small birds keep together at sea during the long storms and voyages of winter. They are in fact to my knowledge seldom close together in their lives except at the nest, where they mate and take turns to incubate the one white egg. But some of my marked birds returned faithfully for up to ten years, in fact until the war came and my study had to be abandoned.

Egg-laying begins at the end of April and is general early in May.

Before this, in the long period from the end of February, the pair visit the nest only at intervals, but fortunately for the human observer engaged in recording their visits, they often stay for twenty-four hours or more ashore, love-making, mating, and preparing the burrow. During this stage the birds are noisy underground at night, calling to each other, or if there is only one bird in the burrow it will call at intervals as if expecting its mate, which answers as it flies in from the sea. Mate recognition is by voice in this species, since in the utter darkness of the burrow there is nothing else to recognize the partner by, save scent. (It is possible, of course, that scent is a means of identification in the darkness. All shearwaters have a strong musky smell. Possibly, too, the young bird in the burrow—as well as the stink of the burrow itself—is recognized by its parents by its individual smell ?)

Usually the mated pair keep to their own burrow. Unattached birds and newcomers to the colony (identified by ring numbers) may wander in and out of burrows. These are evidently seeking to establish a home or find a mate. This " visiting " has been recorded of most other shearwaters and petrels. It leads to a certain amount of skirmishing and territorial defence ; but the pair in lawful possession seem able to drive out interlopers, whether visitors or strangers found by the pair returning home from sea.

Territorial battles are noisy but brief. The long hooked beak can draw blood from the human hand. Rabbits retreat when attacked by the shearwater. Almost as many puffins as shearwaters used to nest on Skokholm, and if the shearwaters have a territorial advantage in the fact that they arrive on the island first, the puffin is physically more powerful with its very strong parrot bill. However, I did not often see the two species fighting ; they seemed to have arrived at a satisfactory share-out of the available burrows on the island, the puffins occupying most but not all of those on the cliff slopes, and the shearwaters nearly all of the more inland burrows. There is probably a good biological reason for this : the puffins, being diurnal, like to be near the sea for a quick take-off in case of attack by gulls ; they are poor fliers and when surprised far inland by a gull in calm weather their chances of escape are not very good.

Shearwaters and puffins are quite capable of digging their own burrows, as on those islands where there are no rabbits to do the work for them — like on St. Kilda and Rhum. They do, however, freely use burrows excavated by rabbits, improving and enlarging them to suit their taste, digging with the hooked bill and scratching the loose earth backwards with the webbed feet. Burrows are made in soft peaty turf, but also over the years even in hard subsoil. Some burrows are much too deep, branched and tortuous to be useful for human observation. Fortunately on Skokholm Knoll the soil was shallow over the red sandstone rock and it was easy for me in the first year of observation to follow the tunnels to the nesting chamber, and to cut out a sod of grass immediately above for an inspection lid. In subsequent years I found it convenient to sink a box in the ground (and put a wooden lid on it) covering the nesting chamber at the end of each burrow ; the shearwaters immediately adopted this artificially walled recess.

The nest is usually lined with scraps of bracken, grass, bluebell bulbs, feathers, etc.—in fact anything handy lying near the burrow or found (bluebells) during excavation. If the egg is lost, a replacement is not laid that season, but the bereaved pair will haunt the burrow at intervals during the summer.

The incubation period proved to be fifty to fifty-four days, and this has since been confirmed by recent records at Skokholm (now established as a permanently staffed bird observatory). The male and female take approximately equal turns at the nest, each sitting for one or more days at a time. This unusual procedure has now been found to be common to all species of the petrel family so far studied ; it is associated with the wide-ranging habits of this pelagic family. At first I supposed that the irregular shifts of from one to six days, and sometimes longer, during which one bird remained fasting at the nest, was due to the fact that, during moonlit nights, very few shearwaters appeared to come in from the sea. These moonlit nights are contrastingly quiet, and walking over the island at midnight one can hear only an occasional shearwater underground, or the cries of the gulls disturbed at their nests. The gulls indeed provide the explanation : they can see the shearwaters on a moonlit night, and the shearwaters wisely keep away—those that failed to do so in the past were eliminated by the gulls. While this is still substantially true, one of the main reasons for the long spell of incubation at the nest by one bird is due to the fact that its mate has probably travelled several hundred miles in search of its favourite food of small fishes and cannot always return each night.

Since I began the study of the Manx shearwater thirty years ago over 65,579 shearwaters have been ringed, of which probably more than 90 per cent. have been ringed at Skokholm. From this enormous mass of ringing data, providing as it does several thousand recoveries at home and abroad, it has now become clear that this shearwater can and does travel from the nest during the incubation and rearing season as far south as the southern end of the Bay of Biscay 600 miles away. One bird remains to incubate for several days while the other is away " on holiday " feeding and recuperating after its fast while on duty on the egg. A preliminary analysis of the recoveries up to 1952 showed me that the Manx shearwater is extensively killed in the Bay of Biscay by sardine fishermen, who open it to see if it has been feeding on sardines, when they set their nets accordingly ; these fishermen also eat shearwaters, which are considered a delicacy— they are in fact as tasty as the mutton bird (another shearwater) of New Zealand.

Sardines are a favourite food of this shearwater which assembles in large flocks on the migratory shoals, following them when they move north in the summer towards the Brittany coast and the English Channel. A comparison with the movements of Biscay sardines (*British Birds*, special supplement to Vol. xlvi, 1953) showed that Skokholm-ringed shearwaters were numerous from March to May over the main nursery of the sardines in the corner of the Bay close to St. Jean de Luz. In April and May the older sardines move up towards Brittany and here numbers of ringed shearwaters also have been shot in these months. In June, July, and August many shearwaters are shot or taken in the nets of the sardine fishermen along the coast of southern Brittany. Then in September, October, and November, with the return of the sardines towards the south-east corner of Biscay, the shearwaters move in that direction ; a smaller number are recovered thus far south. During the early winter months, late October to December, the shearwaters disappear and evidently move far to the south ; each year interesting recoveries of British-ringed individuals (chiefly from Skokholm) have come to hand along the coast of Brazil and Argentine.

The shearwaters follow the sun and live in perpetual summer.

After the long incubation period it is rather surprising that the chick is such a feeble creature. It is covered with a grey down and, safe and warm underground, does not need much parental attention—in fact it is not brooded after the first week. The procedure of irregular visits by one or both parents is recommenced after this initial week of brooding. On some nights neither parent may turn up. They have been far away at sea all day, and perhaps for several days and nights, feeding themselves and collecting food. The sardine and small fish food is retained in the large proventriculus or stomach (lined with oil-producing cells) and on arrival at the nest the engorged parent opens its beak, across and into which the chick places its bill, uttering a piping cry. The adult pumps the oily semi-liquid semi-digested fish pulp towards the mouth ; it trickles through the narrow parental gullet into the crosswise-held bill of the chick, and so flows into the capacious stomach of the young bird. Regurgitation is the normal method of feeding in the petrel family. If both parents bring food on the same night, the chick may double its weight temporarily ; it often puts on half its own weight overnight. Thus it grows, alternating between fasting and feeding. It takes some two months to acquire its first full plumage. The first down, which has grown about an inch long, is pushed out but remains attached to the second down, until at two months the young bird looks like an enormous powderpuff, and when asleep with head drawn in it is almost completely hidden by this long thick down.

The visits of the parents begin to slacken off when the chick is two months old. At the same time the food supply, delivered at longer intervals, has grown in volume, perhaps partly because the sardines and other small fish collected from the sea have also grown in size through the warm months

PLATE 7

MANX SHEARWATER
Puffinus puffinus puffinus Brünnich

of summer. The parents are now approaching the period of moult ; the edges of their feathers are ragged and the colour faded a good deal. When the chick is some sixty days old the adults finally cease to visit the island. The chick, which is enormously fat and weighs as much if not more than the adult (up to 18 oz.), remains for two or three days alone in the burrow. Then at night only, protected from gulls by the darkness, it comes to the mouth of the burrow and exercises its wings. This it does for several more nights, until at last, about the seventieth day, it starts off towards the sea alone. It scrambles over the surface until it finally flaps down into the water. Many fail to reach the sea at the first attempt and are surprised by dawn, and killed and eaten by gulls and other predators. The islands of Skomer and Skokholm are littered with the remains of young shearwaters in late August and early September.

At this age it cannot fly properly, and unless borne up by a strong headwind the fledgling falls clumsily into the sea. It swims well and if attacked by a gull escapes by diving and swimming far under water with half-opened wings. It moves hastily away from the land, as well it might do, since the heavy onshore equinoctial gales at this time of year (it is often September before the young shearwater reaches the sea) can result in severe " wrecks " of these and other tender newly-fledged sea-birds. Many in fact are blown inland at this age, so many that the late T. A. Coward supposed that the records indicated a regular migration. Just before Coward died I wrote to him on the subject and pointed out that all the inland records of shearwaters in the autumn were the result of storms which, as meteorological records proved, occurred just before.

The adult shearwaters in late autumn travel far south into the open Atlantic, and eventually many of them reach the coast of South America. It is a striking fact that as in other species of sea-birds such as puffins (as well as many land-birds) the young ones follow of their own volition, and, without guidance from and far behind the adults, they yet reach the same traditional winter quarters of the species, many hundreds—and in the case of this shearwater many thousands—of miles from the nesting site where they were born.

The marvellous powers of flight of this shearwater, and the ease with which it can be taken and re-taken at the nest at Skokholm, make it an ideal subject for homing experiments. A series of these was carried out from Skokholm. Shearwaters were sent long distances where possible by aeroplane, so as to minimize inconvenience to the birds. Of two which were sent to Venice, one on release was observed to spiral up into the sky and instead of flying south-east towards the open Adriatic (as was expected of this oceanic bird), it flew directly inland north-west towards the Bay of Biscay, heading high across the huge land mass of the Italian Alps. This bird got home safely within a fortnight. Other birds returned from nearer home and from the Faeroe Islands. The first series of homing experiments took place before the Second World War ; afterwards a second series was carried out by G. V. T. Matthews, who confirmed the astonishing homing ability of this bird and carried the study of bird navigation further. His releases included some from the tops of buildings in Cambridge ; he found that in bright weather the majority headed straight for Skokholm, that is, westwards, although the nearest sea was eastwards. But in misty weather the birds circled round uncertainly and disappeared without necessarily taking a westerly direction ; and these birds returned home later than those released in bright sunlight.

Experiments by other workers, notably Kramer in Germany, and further observation by Matthews, indicate that birds home by the sun— that is that they have a strong navigational sense, and can distinguish the points of the compass (although not of course exactly as man does by instrumental help). Birds normally start their migrations when the sun or other heavenly signs are visible ; they run into difficulties when cloud or mist obscures the heavenly bodies. Nor do they fly at great speeds : Manx shearwaters I have timed fly at between 25 and 35 miles per hour. Meinertz-hagen recorded a similar speed when timing this species at Ushant Island in Brittany.

The mechanism or physical instrument by which birds are able to orientate is not known. Still more difficult to understand is the apparent ability of the sea-bird to be constantly aware of its position on the face of the earth relative to its breeding quarters, or to its winter habitat thousands of miles away. One of the most astonishing homing feats performed by a bird was that of the Manx shearwater which I persuaded my friend Rosario Mazzeo to take home with him by air from Skokholm to Boston in the summer of 1952. This bird returned to Skokholm (where Matthews recovered it) in twelve days, a distance of over 3000 land miles. Allowing for periods of feeding by day and resting by night, and normal deviation in flight, the average mileage accomplished each day must have been very high, although probably not more than normal in a bird knowing the way home and anxious to return there. This experiment seemed to prove that the shearwater knew in what direction Skokholm lay, 3000 miles from Boston, despite the fact that this shearwater never normally migrates to the coast of North America. There was no time for it to find its way back by random searching, nor could it have been mere coincidence that it found its way straight to Skokholm in such a short time.

I have already said that this shearwater flies as far as the south coast of Brazil and the coast of Argentina ; new records are coming in from the great numbers annually ringed at Skokholm to-day, and I have just read in the latest published returns of more occurrences of Skokholm birds on this coast, both adult and young. It is not known what proportion of these Skokholm shearwaters move so far south but it seems that the great majority do. They must return soon after the beginning of the New Year since the older adults arrive at Skokholm in February. In the four months of journeying between Wales and South America some 12,000 miles are travelled, and ringing dates and recovery dates between them indicate that an average surface speed or travel distance of 100 miles each day is accomplished by this powerful flier.

One of the largest colonies of Manx shearwaters, possibly the largest in the world, is found in the 2000-ft. high mountain-tops of the Inner Hebridean island of Rhum, now fortunately a national reserve under the Nature Conservancy. Mountain-breeding shearwaters have been little studied, but no doubt their habits resemble those breeding in the more interior parts of islands such as Skokholm and Skomer where there are ragged masses of rock, up which the birds climb and take off into the wind. I remember roaming about the mountain tops of Madeira in 1939 while searching for Manx shearwaters which have been recorded as breeding there; although I did not find any, it was easy for me to imagine that shearwaters could breed successfully on these windy barren heights. The constant breeze would aid them on taking off, and the great height would be an advantage when the young birds finally left home in the autumn and made a long glide of several thousand feet down to the sea, over the lower cultivated land (where if they happened to fall by the way they would be in great danger from man and predatory animals). On the mountains of Rhum, where the birds will be protected at least from man, conditions may well be ideal for this shearwater.

How closely the shearwaters breeding on the several islands off British coasts, mentioned by Bannerman above, intermingle at sea is not known, and may never be known, unless there is extensive ringing on Rhum and the other breeding islands. But we do know that ringed shearwaters from Skokholm, especially young birds in subsequent years, visit other breeding-grounds, particularly of course Skomer (two miles to the north), but also Bardsey, Lundy Island, Great Saltee, and the Copeland Islands off Ireland, and Brittany. When in 1952 I wrote the special supplement to *British Birds* on the Manx shearwater I suggested that the Skomer-Skokholm colony might be more or less self-contained, as a south-western group, one of a series of subspecific groups of *Puffinus puffinus* shearwaters, of which the others were a northern group (Iceland, Faeroes, Hebrides, and Shetland); Atlantis group (Azores and Madeira); Western Mediterranean group (the subspecies *mauretanicus*); and Eastern Mediterranean group (*yelkouan*). Nothing published since then has since proved that these groups do not exist as entities, even if they mix on migration. However, the recovery of a ringed Manx shearwater from Skokholm on the borderland between the Northern and South-western group, on the Copeland Islands in the North Channel, may be a pointer towards an exchange of individuals which might upset my tentative divisions. All this is, however, speculative. Bannerman has pointed out that *mauretanicus* migrates into the summer breeding and feeding distribution area of our *puffinus*, and I have seen both subspecies feeding together in the English Channel on several occasions.

After its first winter the young shearwater may not return immediately to any nesting grounds ; it is possible that many juveniles spend their first summer, when they are only a year old, at sea. Ringing has proved, however, that a few may return when they are just over one year out of the egg, and many do so when two years old. They are not sufficiently developed sexually to breed, but they may begin to make themselves familiar with a breeding-ground by arriving at midsummer and setting up temporary homes for the night in a burrow, often singly, but more often in pairs. These adolescent birds may not stay long at night in June and July ; they call a good deal, and scratch and improve burrows—often inadequate sites, since the best burrows are already occupied by experienced breeders. This adolescent behaviour is, of course, biologically important since it prepares the young shearwater for breeding in the future by staking a claim to a site, and at least by its third summer it is capable of a fertile mating. Then the amateurishly prepared site of the previous year will be occupied and improved or a vacant one in the main colony seized upon.

The evidence of ringing suggests that it is the young shearwater which is the colonist, the bird which under pressure of population goes forth and establishes a new colony. Few old breeding birds have been recovered at breeding sites away from the island where they were ringed, but many birds ringed as nestlings have. There is evidently a surplus of Manx shearwaters at present and in spite of the considerable predation of gulls and other birds, and the fact that it lays only one egg, this species is evidently still successful or at least more successful than the puffin, razorbill, and guillemot which are declining at a considerable rate in the same breeding islands. It is believed that this decline is due to their vulnerability, as surface swimmers, to the sheets of tarry bilge oil and oil bunker cleanings dumped by oil-burning ships at sea. The shearwater, however, spends almost its whole life on the wing, and may be able to see and avoid waste oil—certainly it is rarely recorded among oil casualties, a fortunate circumstance in this oil-dominated moment of history.

REFERENCES : Original Descriptions : 1. *Procellaria puffinus* Brünnich, *Orn. Borealis*, 1764, p. 29 : Faeroe Islands. 2. *Puffinus puffinus mauretanicus* P. R. Lowe, *Bull. Brit. Orn. Club*, xli, 1921, p. 140 : western Mediterranean. 3. *Procellaria yelkouan* Acerbi, *Bibl. Ital.*, cxl, Taf. xlvii, 1827, p. 297 : Mediterranean.

MADEIRAN LITTLE SHEARWATER
Puffinus baroli, baroli Bonaparte

BULWER'S PETREL
Bulweria bulweri (Jardine and Selby)

CORY'S OR ATLANTIC SHEARWATER
Puffinus diomedia borealis Cory

PLATE 8

MADEIRAN LITTLE SHEARWATER
Puffinus baroli baroli Bonaparte

BULWER'S PETREL
Bulweria bulwerii (Jardine and Selby)

CORY'S OR ATLANTIC SHEARWATER
Puffinus diomedia borealis Cory

LITTLE SHEARWATER

Puffinus baroli Bonaparte

1. Madeiran Little Shearwater

PLATE 8

Puffinus baroli baroli Bonaparte

Accidental Visitor

2. Alexander's Little Shearwater [1]

Puffinus baroli boydi (Mathews)

Accidental Visitor

DISTINGUISHING CHARACTERS OF THE TWO RACES: Compared with the Madeiran race, which has the upperside blue-black and a white lining to the underside of the quills, the bird from the Cape Verde Is., *P. b. boydi*, may be distinguished by the very dark brown upperparts and by the quill-lining being dusky. The latter character can, of course, only be seen when the bird is handled. In every other respect they are alike and, when seen at sea, the geographical area in which these shearwaters are encountered is the only lead to identifying the species; this is not, of course, infallible, as the Cape Verde little shearwater, like the Madeiran, does wander on occasion far from its own islands.

IDENTIFICATION OF THE MADEIRAN RACE: The entire upperparts from crown to tail are blue-black with a decided grey "bloom" on the features when freshly moulted, but wearing browner later in the season. The major coverts are narrowly fringed with white and the inner lining of the quills is white not dusky; this, however, can only be seen when the bird is handled. The sides of the neck and the cheeks are white mottled with grey, and the underparts are white except for some grey streaks on the flanks and under tail-coverts. The bill is lead-colour with a black ridge, the eye hazel. Its length is $11\frac{1}{2}$ inches. Lockley describes the feet in life as leaden-blue with a pinkish tinge, not yellowish as in museum specimens.

It should not be difficult to recognize this small shearwater. Its relative the Manx shearwater is black above and larger. The blue-black upperparts and wings of the little shearwater are uniform in colour, and the underparts white. The short legs and feet do not protrude beyond the tail. The rather short bill is slender. The wings are long and narrow but the body is only about the size of a mistle thrush.

---

[1] This shearwater was named in honour of Captain Boyd Alexander who was the first to explore the Cape Verde Islands and to bring home specimens. It is a shorter and less clumsy name than the Cape Verde Little Shearwater as used in *The Handbook of British Birds* and also perpetuates the name of a distinguished explorer and ornithologist.

The slight differences in the colour of the upperparts and of the quill-lining between this and the bird from farther south (Cape Verde Is.) have been given in the first paragraph.

OCCURRENCES IN THE BRITISH ISLES : *The Madeiran race* has been obtained on nine occasions (8 England, 1 Ireland) and there is one sight-record from Wales. The first example to be obtained flew on board a sloop off the extreme west coast of Cork off the Bull Rock on 6th May 1853 and is preserved in the Dublin Museum. Since that date the following have occurred in England :

About 10th April 1858. One found dead near Bungay, Suffolk (Evesham Hall).

28th December 1900. One picked up near Bexhill, Sussex.

27th November 1905. One captured near Lydd, Kent.

27th October 1911. One picked up dead at St. Leonards, Sussex.

15th November 1911. One found dead at Pevensey, Sussex.

20th August 1912. One found exhausted at Welling, Kent.

27th December 1913. One shot near Lydd, Kent.

11th May 1929. One picked up dead at Blakeney Point, Norfolk.

7th May 1951. One seen at Aberdaron, Caernarvonshire.

A little shearwater *Puffinus baroli*, identified as of the Madeiran race by Mr. Alfred Hazelwood of the Bolton Museum where the skin is preserved, was found alive on 10th May 1958 by school children in a field near Stockport, Cheshire, and eventually came into the hands of Mr. C. G. Bennett, who recorded it in *British Birds*, li, p. 354. It is noteworthy as being only the third specimen of this shearwater to have been taken in the spring months, all the others being recorded between August and December.

The Caernarvonshire occurrence seems from the detailed description given in *British Birds*, xlv, p. 222, almost certainly to belong to *P. b. baroli*, the blackish upperparts with slaty tinge and the white under tail-coverts pointing to this race rather than to *P. b. boydi*. The observers were R. H. Ryall and Miss W. Allum ; they watched the bird for over an hour at ranges from " a few yards " from the beach with a powerful glass. Although the bird raised its wings the colour of the quill-lining was not apparently noted : it is an important racial character.

The Cape Verde Islands race has been obtained on two occasions as follows : both in England—

4th December 1914. One picked up at Pevensey, Sussex.

2nd January 1915. One captured at West St. Leonards, Sussex.

DISTRIBUTION ABROAD : The breeding range of the two races of the little petrel has not altered since I summarized the facts in *Ibis*, 1914.

P. baroli baroli has not apparently been found breeding in the Azores as Godman believed to be the case : we still lack proof that it does so, but it must be remembered that Major Chares (who knew his island birds) told Ogilvie-Grant when the latter was searching for petrels between 26th February and 2nd June, visiting all the islands, that the little shearwater was not an uncommon bird around the islands. In their observations on the birds of this archipelago in *Alauda*, 1932, Chavigny and Mayaud make no mention of the species. The fact that none of these gentlemen could find it breeding does not rule out the possibility that it does so. I am aware from personal experience of the species how easily a colony may be overlooked.

It breeds regularly in Madeira, the Desertas, Porto Santo, and the Canary Islands and sparingly in the Salvage Islands. Little shearwaters of the Madeiran race have been recorded from as far afield as Sardinia and Italy and the Skagerrack, Britain, and the coasts of Spain and France.

Farther south its place is taken by *P. baroli boydi*, which breeds in the Cape Verde Islands. It is recorded as nesting from Branca, Brava, and Cima in the Rombos group and may do so on other islands as Fea met it on St. Iago, Raza, and Fogo.

HABITS OF MADEIRAN LITTLE SHEARWATER : This is one of the Atlantic islands' petrels of which I can write from personal experience, for I found it nesting on one of the uninhabited islands of the Canary group upon which I lived for a week. In that archipelago it has been found breeding on Tenerife, Grand Canary, Graciosa, and Montaña Clara ; it was on the last-named that I made its acquaintance in 1913. Considering that many fresh eggs were taken in Porto Santo in February I was astonished to find so many nestlings on Montaña Clara between 7th and 14th June. I collected ten specimens from the fluffy nestling to the almost adult with a few downy filaments adhering to the flanks—the only indication that the bird was but recently fledged. Only two eggs were found at this date. I had learned on good authority—when on the nearby island of Graciosa, that the little shearwater colony had all departed by 27th May, young and old together ; and on Tenerife Meade-Waldo had already recorded the finding of young birds on 26th April. These records indicate that even within the limits of the archipelago the breeding seasons were not the same on the various islands. It may be remarked that Graciosa and Montaña Clara are only separated from one another by a narrow neck of the sea.

On Montaña Clara on 7th June I discovered only one colony of these birds, and that was thanks to the Canarian boatman who remained on the island with me ; it was in an almost inaccessible spot and could not have been reached after dark. The island had already been raided once by Spanish fishermen who collect the young of the Atlantic shearwaters and the smaller birds would naturally have been secured also had any been found. To reach the colony, which may have been the only one on this tiny island, it was necessary to descend within the crater, the walls of which were almost perpendicular, to gain the floor beneath. In this basin, one side of which lay open to the sea as the crater walls had crumbled away, the floor was covered with immense boulders fallen from above or from the broken wall. Under the boulders the *Tahoces*, as the little shearwaters were named, were nesting in holes and crevices, and we were able to pull them out. In this way a valuable series was obtained which is now in the British Museum. None of the old birds were "at home" and even the "nests" which contained an egg were not tenanted. These eggs were almost fresh on 8th June.

From the few definite dates of breeding in the various islands of the Canaries, it is apparent that the members of the various colonies nest independently of one another.

Much the same thing occurs on the various islands of the Madeira group : when Ogilvie-Grant visited Deserta Grande on 4th May he found that these shearwaters had not yet bred ; on Great Salvage downy young in various stages and one fresh egg were found between 24th and 29th April, while at Porto Santo on 7th May the birds had already bred and many young were found, some in almost adult plumage. The breeding season on Porto Santo appears to be a prolonged affair for Padre Schmitz has records of many fresh eggs being obtained there between 9th and 20th February and down-covered young in April. The latest date when down-covered young were found on Baixo Island, Porto Santo, is 29th July. I can find no records for August by which time the birds, or most of them, seem to have disappeared from the Madeira group not to return until the erratic breeding season comes round once more.

In the *Ibis*, 1914, pp. 478-479, I published a chronological record of dates when the birds were first seen in the year, and when eggs and young were taken in the various islands of Porto Santo and the Salvages, the Desertas, Madeira, and the Canaries, but I found it very difficult to come to any conclusion as to the normal nesting dates, so erratic did the species appear to be, especially in the islands of the Madeira-Salvage group. Since 1914, when that table was prepared, the islands have been visited by Meinertzhagen in May 1925, and Lockley in July 1939. Meinertzhagen, who was on the Desertas from 18th to 20th May, reported seeing no little shearwaters on their breeding-grounds and only three birds at sea on 19th May off the islands. Lockley saw none on the Desertas from 10th to 15th July ; on Porto Santo (Baixo Island), visited by Lockley 23rd to 24th July, Bulwers' petrel was in possession of the breeding holes, and the lime-stone workers assured him that the little shearwater did not breed there until September. On the Salvage Islands Lockley found that the birds had already arrived on Great Salvage on the 16th July ; a number were seen flying at night and were found cooing and courting in rock crevices —three were found in one hole. No eggs or chicks were discovered and it seems the birds had but recently come ashore. A few adults were dug out of their holes by the phosphate workers. From statistics which he worked out Mr. Lockley came to the conclusion that the little shearwater—or at any rate the majority of the birds—are forced to breed at a season when the burrows on Great Salvage are not occupied by the main body of breeding *P. marina* and *O. castro*. This, he observes, would limit the main breeding season of *P. assimilis* (=*P. baroli*) on this island to the six winter months. But in making this observation Mr. Lockley perhaps overlooked the fact that in the spring of 1895 Ogilvie-Grant had found "downy young in various stages", and what he described as one late egg, almost fresh. Ogilvie-Grant's visit to Great Salvage took place from 23rd to 28th April, which does not point to the little petrel always having to breed " during the six winter months " even if it does sometimes.

Some of these little petrels on Great Salvage were occupying the deserted burrows of the frigate petrel. I would suggest that the burrows are only used when the more normal nesting sites in caves and crevices and under fallen boulders are not available or are all occupied by some other species. The burrows on Great Salvage must have been excavated by frigate petrels and would naturally prove attractive to other small petrels in search of a likely hole. Doubtless the little petrels on Montaña Clara would also be glad to find ready-made burrows ; but there are no frigate petrels in the Canaries, and if there were I doubt if they would choose Montaña Clara upon which to attempt excavations, owing to the extreme hardness of the surface.

The eggs of the Madeiran little shearwater were measured by F. C. R. Jourdain who found that thirty-seven eggs averaged 50·2 × 34·6 mm. Max. 54·2 × 35·5 and 50·5 × 37·5 mm. Min. 45 × 34 and 51 × 32·5 mm.

Mr. Lockley, whose notes I have quoted so fully, was greatly attracted by the charm of the little petrel, which in many ways appeared to be a miniature of the Manx shearwater, but seemingly with a larger eye which gives it an alert appearance in the hand where it struggles animatedly. He describes its note as similar to that of the Manx shearwater but higher and weaker, rising generally to an excited wheezy whistling finish, " phwee-her-her-her-wher ", but flying birds uttered with many variations. The evening flight takes place after dark.

When these petrels leave the islands after the breeding season they probably stay at sea and may wander a long way from their breeding place. We know very little about this period, but as noted under " Distribution " individual birds turn up in the most unexpected places. The main body are not likely to go so far away and it seems probable that the flocks from the various colonies will remain together when at sea.

HABITS OF ALEXANDER'S LITTLE SHEARWATER : Boyd Alexander obtained a series of specimens and five eggs of this shearwater on Cima, one of the small Rombos islands of the Cape Verde archipelago, on 16th March and following days. Two other species of petrel were nesting on the island—the Madeiran petrel and the frigate petrel—and all three species had eggs at the same time. The Madeiran and the frigate petrels were nesting in burrows which they had presumably excavated (in fact the frigate is not known to nest anywhere except in burrows), and these birds occupied low, flat, gravelly land in which they evidently found it possible to excavate tunnels into the earth. The colonies of the Madeiran petrel (*O. castro*), and frigate petrel (*P. marina*) were in close proximity to one another. Farther up the island and towards the rocky headland Alexander discovered the little petrels (*P. baroli boydi*) breeding, not only in holes, but many beneath rocky boulders and in small clefts and overhanging rocks, while in one instance a bird had made its nest beneath the boards of a tumbledown hut. In this last case the nest contained a quantity of dry grass.

Boyd Alexander's description of the night-scene on Cima island at the time of his discovery of the little petrel sixty and more years ago, has already been quoted in my account of Harcourt's petrel (see p. 64), a species which was nesting in an adjoining colony.

Alexander was to meet with it again on the island of Branca, which he described as nothing more than a small irregular chain of lofty, craggy hills, rising up from the sea with extraordinary abruptness on its north side, with an almost glacis-like slope down to the sea from about half-way down. This slope was honeycombed with petrels at the time of his visit during the first week of May. While on the island he obtained specimens, including the young, of the same three petrels as he had met on the Rombos Isles. The birds are troubled in their nest-holes by a species of skink which, in Alexander's view, had been responsible for driving the petrels away from Raza where they formerly bred. Out at sea numbers of little petrels were to be seen and at intervals one of them would disappear and swim after some small fish just beneath the surface of the water, after the manner of a penguin. Yet another species of petrel, the soft-plumaged petrel (*Pterodroma mollis feae*), breeds on Branca on the higher inland precipices.

The islands where Alexander's shearwater breeds were in later years investigated by José Correia who was collecting in the spring and summer of 1922 for the American Museum, and independently in the summer of 1951 by W. R. P. Bourne. Correia saw the little shearwater about many of the Cape Verdes, but never in large flocks like those of some other petrels. He described their flight as exceedingly rapid and always close to the surface of the sea. When feeding they were seen to spend much time below the surface, sometimes emerging at a great distance from the spot at which they had disappeared. In May 1922 the island of Raza had a great population of them and the fishermen affirmed that there were also many at Branca. Every night at Raza these birds fluttered and criss-crossed over their breeding grounds, chattering continually. Most of the chicks in the nests had already assumed feathers in May and were just about ready to fly. Correia remarked, as others have done, on the different breeding sites selected, noting that at Raza they nested under fragments of stone but at the Rombos Isles (Cima) they lived in burrows. They were observed to feed on small fish.

Quite recently Dr. Bourne has reported on these same colonies and writes of Alexander's little shearwater that in its " notes, breeding season, habits, behaviour [how does behaviour differ from habits ?], markings, dimensions, the colour of its legs and the markings of its young it resembles temperate *Puffinus baroli* rather than tropical *Puffinus l'herminieri*, and its superficial similarity to that species must be a result of convergence in related forms ".[1]

Dr. Bourne was on Cima island from 28th to 30th August, after the breeding season was over, and remarked that " several dozen birds " visited the island after dark. They circled low over the island, using the *karki-karrou* call described by Alexander, and later were found in pairs in old nest-sites containing egg-shells beneath the tussocks of the plateau and in holes in the rocks ; they never entered the burrows (it will be remembered that Correia states they *lived* in burrows). In the nest they used a low harsh squalling note which broke into *karki-karous* as they became excited ; up to seven gathered on exposed mounds to display. Dr. Bourne was shown nests in the cliffs of Brava several hundred feet above sea-level and remarks that they nest throughout the cliffs of the islands up to at least a mile inland.

It seems to be perfectly true that this little shearwater lives principally upon fish as Correia has stated. The birds dissected by Bourne held remains of fish and cephalopods up to 3 inches long in the stomach, and in two cases an amorphous yellowish-green mass.

REFERENCES : Original Descriptions : 1. *Procellaria baroli* Bonaparte, *Conspectus Gen. Av.*, xi, 1857, p. 204 : Desertas (Madeira) ; 2. *Puffinus l'herminieri boydi* Mathews, *Birds of Australia*, ii, 1912, p. 70 : Cape Verde Islands.

---

[1] The writer had in earlier literature made *boydi* a race of *l'herminieri* for the reasons stated in *Ibis*, 1914, p. 484, following Mathews, but R. C. Murphy disagreed with us and united *boydi* as a race of the Madeiran bird. This has now been accepted.

AUDUBON'S SHEARWATER

Puffinus l'herminieri l'herminieri Lesson

An Accidental Visitor; found once at Bexhill-on-Sea, Sussex

Dr. Alexander Wetmore, Hon. Fellow b.o.u.
(Research Associate Smithsonian Institute)

IDENTIFICATION : In colour and colour pattern Audubon's shearwater is similar to the Manx shearwater, among those species of this group of sea birds that reach the shores of Britain. It may be distinguished by smaller size and less robust bill, the wing measuring 205 mm. or slightly less, compared to 225 mm., or a little more, in the Manx shearwater. The difference in length of bill is slight, this being 30 mm. or less in Audubon's shearwater and 33 mm. or more in the other species, but in the latter the bill is much heavier. The little shearwater, reported several times as a straggler within our limits, also is small, being, in fact, slightly less in size than the Audubon's, but is deeper black above. It will be obvious that the distinctions between the three species here discussed may be seen only with specimens in hand for close examination.

Audubon's shearwater, like the Manx shearwater, is black with a faint brownish cast over the entire upper surface, and pure white below, except for the under tail-coverts, which are dark laterally like the back.

The latest edition of the *Check-list of North American Birds*, published in 1957, recognizes a distinct genus, *Puffinus*, for the shearwaters,[1] including the present bird, which is listed there as *Puffinus l'herminieri l'herminieri.*

As Audubon's shearwater may conceivably wander again to British waters I have, at Dr. Bannerman's request, included a detailed description of this bird taken with permission from Dr. Murphy's *Oceanic Birds of South America* which reads as follows :

Sexes alike : upper surface blackish-brown, almost black on the outer webs of the wing quills and the primary coverts ; concealed inner webs of wing quills much paler ; lower half of lores white, the line of demarcation between dorsal and ventral plumage being mottled under and behind the eye, and along the cheeks and sides of neck, through a variable mingling of the dark and white feathers ; a faint white stripe on the lower eyelid ; flanks splashed with sooty or greyish-brown, which appears variously as splotches, mottlings, or shaft-streaking on otherwise white feathers ; at the sides of chest this dark colour sometimes extends slightly towards the mid-line, the dark feathers in this region being mostly narrowly edged with whitish. Ventral surface from chin to crissum, including the axillaries, and the wing-lining except along its anterior border, white ; lower aspect of wing and tail quills dark neutral grey, when fresh ; longest

---

[1] This is a decision with which I entirely agree.--D. A. B.

under tail-coverts blackish-brown, the shorter coverts dark mouse-grey and white, some being one or the other, some parti-coloured. Iris brown, bill black, bluish on the mandible and toward the base of the culminicorn; feet and legs flesh-colour, with the outer toe and outer side of tarsus blackish.

Wing measurements 200-216 mm., tail 82-94 mm., exposed culmen 26-32 mm. Total length twelve inches.

OCCURRENCE IN GREAT BRITAIN: The only valid record of the Audubon's shearwater is that reported by James M. Harrison in *British Birds*, vol. xxx, July 1936, pp. 48-49. According to Dr. Harrison's account, one was found on 7th January 1936 on the beach at Galley Hill, Bexhill-on-Sea, Sussex, by Mr. W. E. Dance of Pebsham. The shearwater was rescued from gulls that were molesting it, but seemed unable to fly and died within a short time. Fortunately it was taken to Mr. G. Bristow of St. Leonards for preparation, and came then to Dr. Harrison, who was able to ascertain the full details concerning its finding. (It should be mentioned that there is another specimen of Audubon's shearwater in the British Museum (Natural History) from the Gould collection that bears on the label the statement written by Gould, " said to have been killed in Devonshire, Mr. Whitely ". The record, however, has never been confirmed and is not accepted currently. Its history has been reviewed by H. F. Witherby in *British Birds*, ix, January 1916, p. 203.) Oddly enough this supposed occurrence is not even mentioned in Gould's *Birds of Great Britain*, a point to which Howard Saunders had already drawn attention in his *Manual of British Birds*.

DISTRIBUTION ABROAD: The typical subspecies of the Audubon's shearwater, with which we are concerned, nests on the Bermudas, on Mona Island west of Puerto Rico, and on islets near St. Thomas in the Greater Antilles, at many points in the Lesser Antilles from St. Martin south to the Grenadines and Barbados, and on islets adjacent to Tobago, near Trinidad. Outside the breeding season it wanders through the western Atlantic Ocean regularly north to the latitude of North Carolina, casually as far as Massachusetts, while to the south it is found near South America as far as off the coast of British Guiana. It is to be encountered also off the north coast of Cuba, near Beata and Navassa Islands adjacent to Hispaniola and even in the Gulf of Mexico as far as the coast of Texas. The birds are seen most often, however, near their nesting grounds where some appear to remain throughout the year. The extent of their wanderings eastward over the Atlantic is not known.

DISCOVERY AND HABITS: Audubon—the pioneer ornithologist of America—encountered the shearwater which now bears his name near the southern tip of Florida, and in *The Birds of America*, 1840-44, wrote of his meeting with the species as follows:

On the 26th of June, 1826, while becalmed on the Gulf of Mexico, off the western shores of Florida, I observed that the birds of this species, of which some had been seen daily since we left the mouth of the Mississippi, had become very numerous. The mate of the vessel killed four at one shot, and at my request brought them on board. From one of them I drew the figure which has been engraved. The notes made at the time are now before me and afford me the means of presenting you with a short account of the habits of this bird.

Audubon goes on to describe how they skim low over the water near bunches of Gulf weeds :

Flap their wings six or seven times in succession and then sail for three or four seconds with great ease, having their tail much spread and their long wings extended at right angles with the body. On approaching a mass of weeds they raise their wings obliquely, drop their legs and feet, run as it were on the water, and at length alight in the sea, where they swim with as much ease as ducks, and dive freely, at times passing several feet under the surface in pursuit of fishes which, on perceiving their enemy, swim off, but are frequently seized with great agility. Four or five, some- times fifteen or twenty, of these birds will thus alight, and during their stay about the weeds, dive, flutter and swim with all the gaiety of a flock of ducks, newly alighted in a pond. . . . At times, as if by way of resting themselves, they alighted, swam lightly, and dipped their bills frequently in the water, in the manner of mergansers.

Where their island homes offer exposures of limestone, Audubon's shearwaters nest in the abundant cavities common in such formations. Elsewhere they dig shallow burrows in loose soil. The single egg may be placed on the bare earth or rock, or there may be a slight nest loosely put together from whatever grass and small twigs may be available close at hand. While the nest cavity is sheltered it is not placed far from the surface. The egg is dull white, with an average size of 52·5 × 37 mm. Male and female shearwaters are said to share the duties of incubation. The young on hatching are covered with dusky grey down, becoming whitish on the abdomen. As they grow they change to a firm plumage that is coloured like that of the adult. Movement in and out of the nesting grounds is wholly nocturnal, accompanied by curious cries that are described as strange and mournful, as is usual among shearwaters. The young have a plaintive chirruping call. During the day those adults not on nest duty are found far from the islands where they breed, often resting on the sea in flocks. Eggs are reported from January to May, with young in the burrows often until July.

In steamer or schooner travel past the Bahamas and the more southern Lesser Antilles, particularly near the Grenadines, it is common to see Audubon's shearwaters, usually in early morning, flying with steadily beating wings or scaling low over the water.

From the early days of human colonization fat young shearwaters, when sufficiently grown, have been gathered, salted, dried, and sold in the local markets for food. In spite of this the species seems to maintain a fair number, due mainly to the widely scattered small colonies in which they breed, and the isolation of these from centres of human habitation.

REFERENCES : Original Description : *Puffinus l'herminieri* Lesson, *Rev. Zool.*, 1839, p. 102. Type locality ad ripas Antillarum, *i.e.* Straits of Florida.

GREAT SHEARWATER PLATE 9

Puffinus gravis (O'Reilly)

A regular Visitor in autumn to British waters. Sometimes in early summer, very occasionally in the Channel, more commonly reported off S.W. Ireland and Outer Hebrides. Breeds in South Atlantic.

IDENTIFICATION : The great shearwater has a clearly defined brown cap on the crown ; the upperparts are brown with paler fringes to the feathers after the moult. The sides of the face, throat, and underparts are pure white save for some brown feathers down the middle of the belly which form an irregular patch. There is a narrow white " V " at the base of the tail which is a prominent field mark at a distance. Moulting birds show a definite white line along the wing. The bill is blackish, and the legs and feet pale flesh, except for the outer tarsus and outer toe which are dark brown. The toes are brown. The inside of the tarsus, the two inner toes except for a small patch on the joints and the webs (but not the edges) are said by H. F. I. Elliott to vary in intensity from almost white to the very brightest pink. It is 18 inches in length.

Mr. Elliott has stated that the brown ventral patch on the belly of this shearwater is one of the best possible field characters to observers when it is possible to obtain a view of the underside. Mr. Elliott writes that during three years spent in the vicinity of the main breeding colonies of the great shearwater, with frequent opportunities of observing well over a million pairs of this species, he never saw a bird in which the ventral patch was not perfectly visible in the field. He concludes : " there is in fact the strongest possible presumption that a shearwater observed in conditions which permit a good view of the underside and seen to lack a dark patch on the belly is *not* a great shearwater ". This would of course apply to the Mediterranean and Cory's shearwaters which are much the same size as *Puffinus gravis*, but lack the dark cap of that species. Mr. H. G. Alexander has remarked that *P. gravis* and *P. kuhli* are readily identifiable if a side view can be obtained.

OCCURRENCES IN BRITISH WATERS : There seems to be no shadow of doubt that the great shearwater is a regular visitor to the western end of the English Channel, most often in August, September, and October, and that occasionally it finds its way as far as the Straits of Dover.   Mr. Dorrien-Smith has a specimen taken off the Scilly Isles on 9th August 1899 and another on 24th August 1939 near the Bishop Rock Lighthouse, and saw others in the vicinity.   On 19th September 1934 the Rev. P. H. T. Hartley saw a number—about forty—when trawling near the Eddystone.   It will be remembered that the late Dr. Eagle Clarke, who spent a month in the Eddystone between 19th September and 19th October 1901, saw great shearwaters " almost daily " and often in considerable numbers.   Mr. Witherby reminds us that two were found dead in Kent and Sussex in November 1938 and that there is plenty of evidence of the great shearwater's presence off the coast of south-west England.   Its occurrence on the east coast is decidedly rare but there have been several reliable records from both Norfolk and Suffolk as reported by Riviere and Claud Ticehurst in their county works.   There are also sight records from the Yorkshire coast and a specimen, according to Mr. Ralph Chislett, was formerly in the Hull Museum.

Of its status in Irish waters Major Ruttledge states [1] that its visits take place only rarely in summer ; but in autumn, though uncertain in its appearances, it is more frequent.   It is met with singly, in small parties and occasionally in flocks, but seldom comes very close to the mainland.   In 1854 " thousands " were said to have invaded Dingle Bay from September to November.   There are quite a number of records for June and July, as well as for the autumn months.   The most recent at the time of writing is one seen 400 yards from Inishtrahull Island, Co. Donegal, on 10th September 1953 and three birds on 18th September in the same area ; two others were off Malin Head on 11th September and were recorded by Messrs. Gibbs, Nisbet, and Redman in their account of " Birds of North Donegal " in autumn 1953 (*British Birds*, xlvii).

In Scottish waters we learn from Dr. Evelyn Baxter [2] and the late Miss Rintoul that the great shearwater is commoner in the Hebridean seas in summer and autumn than in any other part of Scotland, but it has been reliably recorded from many other localities though not often from the Inner Hebrides.   Of its occurrences around the Outer Hebrides these authors write of " considerable numbers " especially about St. Kilda and North Rona.   Most of the records come from the second half of June to October.   In June 1914 the Duchess of Bedford came upon a number off Sule Stack.   On the east coast of Scotland it must be decidedly rare. The authors of *The Birds of Scotland* recorded one from the Isle of May on 1st September 1933.   There appears to be only one old record for Shetland (Saxby)—others reported may have been Atlantic shearwaters. It has once, at any rate, been recorded from Holland.[3]

[1] *Birds of Ireland*, 1954, p. 19.
[2] *The Birds of Scotland*, 1953, pp. 483-485.
[3] E. D. Van Oort, *Ardea*, 1915.

PLATE 9

GREAT SHEARWATER
Puffinus gravis (O'Reilly)

Breeding Distribution Abroad : The great shearwater has one of the most restricted habitats during the breeding season of all the large family to which it belongs, for so far as we know it nests on only three islands : Nightingale Island and Inaccessible Island, both in the south Atlantic, and also to a much smaller extent apparently, on Gough Island.[1] There have been unconfirmed reports of nesting on Tristan da Cunha (to which group the first two mentioned belong) " at the western sea-level plateau called Anchorstack ", but it is doubtful whether even a few pairs have nested on Tristan itself[2] : most of the older inhabitants declare that it has not done so within their memories or the memories of their parents. When, in a later paragraph, the habits of this petrel are discussed, Mrs. M. K. Rowan's description of its two principal habitats will be quoted. Great shearwaters arrive on their breeding grounds during late August and September. Nesting takes place in November, laying commencing about the 10th of that month, as Brian Roberts has stated. Details will be given hereafter. In the month of April a large proportion of the breeding population begins to depart north, the old birds leaving, it appears, in large parties but not all at once ; the birds of the year making their departure more gradually as soon as they are ready to fly. It has been found that the birds travel rapidly northwards along the west side of the Atlantic during April and May, spreading north-eastwards towards the coasts of Europe when they have reached the vicinity of 45° N. The suggestion has been put forward by Wynne-Edwards, supported by data, that the return to the south is concentrated mainly on the east side of the Atlantic, but this was disputed by Rankin and Duffey who were the first to suggest that the southerly migration at first took place in mid-ocean and later on via the *west* side of the Atlantic. This suggestion is supported by Mrs. M. K. Rowan[3] in her very able summing up of the conflicting opinions expressed.

Mrs. Rowan believes that a part of the great shearwater population fails to breed each year and that this explains the presence of great shearwaters in the eastern Atlantic during September, October, and November, months when they are reported to be relatively abundant in the vicinity of the Outer Hebrides. Those birds which are still in the north Atlantic in October and November could not possibly, in Mrs. Rowan's opinion, return to Nightingale or Inaccessible in time to rear their young, and even the September birds would, if they arrived on their breeding ground in time, have difficulty at this late date in finding burrows in which to produce their offspring. It has been shown that in the middle of the Atlantic the greater shearwater reaches its highest concentration in June, July, and August, pointing to the fact that these birds represent the bulk of the

[1] H. F. I. Elliott in *Ibis*, 1957, p. 560.
[2] M. K. Rowan (Mrs. Rowan) in *Ibis*, 1952, p. 97.
[3] *Ibis*, 1952, p. 113.

breeding population on their way south. Only after perusal of Mrs. Rowan's paper has the writer found the explanation of why great shearwaters regularly appear in the late autumn off the western coasts of Britain and in the Bay of Biscay at a time when we should expect them to be in occupation of their nesting holes in the south Atlantic. I have seen them in the Bay when on late autumn voyages and know well the distinctions between this and Cory's shearwater. Mrs. Rowan asks one pertinent question when she observes, " Where are the non-breeding birds of any one year during the later months of the breeding season ? Some certainly remain in the North Atlantic as shown by records made between Europe and America in the months December to March. But it would be interesting to know whether the birds, seen off the coasts of Europe and America from September to November, are on their way south, whether they come to the breeding grounds at all and, if so, where they make the crossing from coastal waters to the Tristan group ? " That is one of the questions we still have to answer.

HABITS : There is something romantic about this ocean bird which annually makes such a striking migration from the two small islands in the South Atlantic to appear with some regularity off our own coasts as the year is drawing to a close, and even in our early summer it is sometimes to be seen in considerable numbers west of the Outer Hebrides. The North Atlantic is its home at that season of the year and it is there that it undergoes the moult. Professor Wynne-Edwards, who has studied this phase in its life history, tells us that the plumage is lost exceedingly quickly, although the birds are never actually deprived of flight. He observes that on 5th June he first noticed many with the whitish bases of the quills exposed, owing to an almost simultaneous moult of the greater coverts, producing an irregular light band along the whole length of the wing. This is so conspicuous that anyone seeing the bird for the first time might be mystified in identifying it, because no mention is made of this singular circumstance in recognized handbooks. He found that for " immense areas " the water was strewn with countless floating feathers. On 23rd June, on another crossing of the Atlantic, he noted enormous numbers of floating feathers in the calm water, both quills and contour feathers. By 31st July the moult is all over and done with, at any rate that part of it which is visible to the field observer. But even before that date there appears to be a gradual move eastwards which brings some of the great shearwaters within sight of the Irish coast and of the Outer Hebrides in the month of June.

Only thirty years ago (I write in July 1957) very little was really known about the great shearwater. Dr. Eagle Clarke was able to write in the third edition of Howard Saunders's *Manual of British Birds*, which he edited and revised : " According to present knowledge the breeding haunts of this species are in the Tristan da Cunha archipelago, but it doubtless has other nesting stations in the southern Atlantic. Nothing is known of the nidification of the great shearwater except that four eggs were taken on Inaccessible Island, one of the Tristan da Cunha group, in 1908. . . ."

How different is our knowledge to-day when Mrs. M. K. Rowan [1] can publish an almost complete history of the breeding cycle, and of the bird's life and habits during the nesting season, and when Professor V. C. Wynne-Edwards [2] can complete the picture—or nearly so—in his study of the birds in their winter quarters (our summer) in the North Atlantic. The finishing touches to the story have been added by Niall Rankin and Eric Duffey [3] in their study of bird life in the North Atlantic to which attention has already been drawn.

Mrs. Rowan opens her study of the great shearwater at its breeding quarters with a description of the two islands in the Tristan da Cunha archipelago where it comes during the last days of August to lay its eggs :

Nightingale, where the bulk of the shearwaters breed, is the smallest of the three islands, lying 26 miles south-west of Tristan. It is uninhabited, supports no domestic animals and so far has escaped invasion by the rats and mice, which have become a major pest on the main island. The low seaward cliffs rise gradually to a central plateau (700-800 ft.), which is much broken up into small hills and swampy valleys. A deep valley, which cuts right across the island, separates the central plateau from the High Ridge, an elongated peak which rises steeply in the east.

Mrs. Rowan estimated that Nightingale comprises between 600 and 700 acres of land, by far the greater part of which (400-500 acres) is covered by a dense mantle of tussock grass which grows to a height of 6 or 8 feet in the rich peaty soil. In places the tussock grass gives way to grass clearings, to marshes overgrown with sedge, and to groves of the island tree *Phylica nitida*. The woods, marshes, and meadows are particularly characteristic of the central plateau, where they tend to replace the tussock jungle which invests the rest of the island. Mrs. Rowan states that the burrows of the great shearwater are to be found in almost every sort of habitat that Nightingale affords :

They occur in the meadows, woods and tussock slopes, from the edges of the low cliffs to the summit of the central plateau, and on the highest slopes of the High Ridge. Almost the entire surface of the island is riddled with their tunnels, so that the soil is liable to subside beneath one's weight at every step. Amongst the crags of the High Ridge and outcrops of stone on the lower slopes the shearwaters make use of every crevice large enough to house a nest. . . . The shearwaters are not absolutely excluded from the penguin rookeries, but their nests are relatively sparse in this area.

---

[1] " The Greater Shearwater, *Puffinus gravis*, at its breeding grounds ", in *Ibis*, 1952, pp. 97-121.

[2] *Proc. Boston. Soc. Nat. Hist.*, xl, 1935, pp. 247-260.

[3] *British Birds*, 1948, Supplement.

Lying close to the north side of Nightingale are two small islets—Alex or Middle Island and Stoltenhoff—of which little is known. Alex is one vast penguin rookery and so houses few shearwaters, but according to the Tristan islanders Stoltenhoff is just as densely populated by the shearwaters as Nightingale itself. Mrs. Rowan goes on to describe Inaccessible as roughly seven times the size of Nightingale, but owing to the less suitable terrain it does not support proportionately as many shearwaters. The central plateau of Inaccessible is very marshy, and is largely overgrown with a small tree-fern. Shearwaters' nests are only sparsely distributed throughout the interior of the island, but occur in fair numbers in a narrow belt around the edges of the plateau and in the tussock-covered slopes at sea-level. Eleven other species of sea birds nest on Nightingale during the southern summer of which no less than seven are members of the same family as the great shearwater. Mrs. Rowan observes that almost the same list of nesting species applies to Inaccessible. One can imagine the competition there must be on these islands for nesting places and that any birds late in arriving must find it well-nigh impossible to find an unoccupied nook or cranny. The only predator appears to be the skua, *Catharacta skua*, commonly called the seahen. It does not attack adult shearwaters but is very destructive towards the end of the breeding season when juvenile shearwaters emerge from the burrows and start to fly.

Mrs. Rowan has attempted to estimate the number of breeding petrels at Nightingale. She worked out the area which is available to nesting shearwaters as at least 2,000,000 square yards and as there is, on the average, one nest to every square yard and every nest is occupied during the breeding season, she arrived at the gigantic figure of 4,000,000 greater shearwaters on Nightingale during the southern summer, and believed it to be an underestimate.

The population on Inaccessible was estimated by Mr. H. F. I. Elliott to be not less than 300,000 birds. The total breeding population in the Tristan archipelago would therefore be between four and five million great shearwaters—a figure which Mrs. M. K. Rowan has no doubt is a low rather than a high estimate. This figure takes no account of the first-year or non-breeding birds whose numbers must again reach a high figure. We can but trust that no endemic disease, such as that which presumably wiped out the passenger pigeon, makes itself felt on the great shearwater population which in such circumscribed quarters would have small chance of survival.

The shearwater's eggs and young are naturally exploited by the Tristan islanders, and in her long account of the species Mrs. Rowan devotes much space to the methods employed. The journey is made from Tristan in open canvas boats under sail without centre-boards. The first trip takes place in November and fresh eggs are collected to the number of about 15,000 in a normal year; a second expedition from Tristan—which she describes as the " fat trip "—takes place any time between the middle of March and the beginning of May. The chicks are then collected from the same burrows as those from which eggs had been secured earlier in the season ; Mrs. Rowan does not think that this points to a second laying but more probably indicates that when the burrows have been robbed of their eggs another pair of shearwaters, unable till then to find a vacant burrow, take possession and it is *their* chick which falls victim to the " fat hunters " when it has put on sufficient weight and fat to be worth taking. It was not easy to discover how many birds were taken on this second trip, but it was estimated by Mr. Lawrence that 20,000 great shearwater chicks were taken for fat in one year. Fears have been expressed by Gregory Mathews and by R. C. Murphy, among others, that this systematic plundering of the eggs and young may result in the eventual extermination of a species with such a circumscribed breeding area, but if Mrs. Rowan's figures are correct the total depletion works out at less than 1 per cent. of the Nightingale population. Mrs. Rowan herself considers such fears to-day to be groundless except in the case of *Diomedia exulans*, which species still has a few pairs breeding on Inaccessible.

Mrs. Rowan made some interesting observations on the flight of the great shearwater. She was struck by the fact that this bird, with such marvellous powers of flight as we know it to possess, is singularly clumsy at landing and launching itself into the air. Thus :

Incoming shearwaters approach the land at heights varying from a few feet to a thousand feet above sea-level. They circle once or twice before alighting, and they reduce speed in the usual way, with tail fanned, feet outspread and the whole body tilted slightly upwards. In spite of these precautions the landing speed is still remarkably high. This is no particular handicap on water, but on land the length of the legs and their position well behind the body's centre of gravity, greatly add to the difficulties of a high landing speed. A bird alighting in the open topples forward on breast and beak, and frequently turns one or more complete somersaults before coming to a standstill. A bird coming down in the tussock is a slightly better case, as it plummets straight into the tall grass, which serves to stop it and break its fall. The bird tumbles through the tangled stems and thuds to the ground, usually breast first. Shearwaters were frequently seen alighting in trees, a particularly hazardous landing, which suggests a possible reason for the comparative sparsity of nests in woodland. The bird flies straight into the foliage, which affords less support than the densely ranked stems of the tussock, and it crashes through the bare branches below the leaves sustaining a fall of six to ten feet.

The surprising speed and success with which an alighting bird re-orientates itself and locates the correct burrow after these difficult landings was always a matter of astonishment to the observers. On the tussock-covered slopes of Nightingale, which to the human eye appear monotonously similar, the shearwaters were able to locate their burrows without difficulty ; alighting birds nearly always landed within a few feet of their nests and scuttled with astonishing speed and no apparent hesitation towards their homes. It was found that the birds were capable of moving, or rather running, as fast as a man over the ground, although the bird's body was not supported on fully extended legs but was held only an inch or so above ground. Mrs. Rowan observed that in their efforts to scramble up to some elevation before taking flight, the birds had left their marks on the soft rocks of Nightingale, many of which were deeply scored and grooved by the claws of generations of shearwaters scrambling up their sides. Wings, beak, and feet were all used in the struggle up almost vertical rock-faces. Once on the summit the bird faces the wind and beats rapidly with its wings for a few seconds, it then literally jumps into the air and flaps hard until it becomes airborne. Once the bird rises above the height of the surrounding tussocks into whatever air-currents are flowing the difficulties of the take-off are over, and it can manœuvre with skill.

I have quoted so much from Mrs. M. K. Rowan because in her very able treatise in the *Ibis* she acknowledged having incorporated the work of a number of other naturalists who had visited the Tristan da Cunha archipelago before and during her own visit, which lasted from January 1949 to June 1950, a period covering the greater part of two breeding seasons. She also used facts and material collected by the Rev. C. P. Lawrence, Mr. H. F. I. Elliott, and Mr. A. N. Rowan on both Nightingale and Inaccessible. In a letter to *British Birds* magazine in 1953 Mr. Elliott wrote that he spent *three years* in the vicinity of the main breeding colonies of the great shearwater, with frequent opportunities of observing well over a million pairs of that species. Mr. Lawrence had himself spent two years on Tristan. With such a wealth of ornithological talent upon which to draw it is not surprising that Mrs. Rowan has been able to add so much to our knowledge of the great shearwater.

Before continuing to deal with the bird's breeding biology I would mention two others who have visited the islands where this bird breeds and have left us accounts of what they found. First of these was Sir Hubert Wilkins, the well-known Antarctic explorer, who visited both Nightingale and Inaccessible when acting as naturalist on the *Quest* (Shackleton-Rowett expedition to the southern Antarctic). Wilkins, who was well known by the writer, was in the Tristan group from 9th to 25th May 1922—the tail-end of the shearwater's breeding season. In the report of his visit he mentions how the shearwaters flock in at night by the hundred, but as the landing party returned to their ship before dusk they missed the wonderful sight which can be witnessed at the height of the breeding season when the birds come in in their thousands and fill the air with their cries. Wilkins and his companions dug out many burrows without finding any trace of a nest, but it seems they were unaware when the birds breed, for their lack of success in finding eggs or young is hardly surprising when we remember that the Tristan islanders collect the young between the middle of March and the beginning of May. Any young which the *Quest* party might have found would probably have been full winged by the date of their visit late in May and difficult to distinguish from the parents. When the *Quest* left the islands on 25th May *en route* for the Azores and England the great shearwaters were seen throughout a great part of the voyage. Having bred and reared their young they would then be on their way to the North Atlantic to spend the northern summer months. Whether any shearwaters remain on their nesting grounds in June, July, and August when the bulk of the population has gone north, has yet to be demonstrated.

Another all too brief visit, but one which was rather more fruitful, was that of Dr. G. J. Broekhuysen[1] of Cape Town University who landed on Nightingale on 16th February 1948. The expedition, led by the Rev. C. P. Lawrence, was mainly to investigate some of the marine-biological and agricultural problems of the Tristan da Cunha group. Dr. Broekhuysen only spent one night on the island, but returned again on 4th March with Mr. W. Macnae; Inaccessible was visited on 17th February and 5th March, but in each case only for a few hours. Between these islands and Tristan there was an abundance of great shearwaters over the whole stretch of ocean. On 28th February the ship, the M.V. *Pequena*, visited Gough Island some 200 miles south of Tristan, which afforded Dr. Broekhuysen a further opportunity to meet with the great shearwater. When he first arrived on Nightingale the young were all fairly large and completely covered with blue-grey down, which was lighter on the breast and ventral part of the neck. It was observed that the old birds spent most of the daytime out at sea, where they were often seen from the ship during her cruises among the islands. They were usually in fairly large flocks, all sitting on the water. During the morning and early afternoon very few birds were noticed on the island, but after 4 p.m. the shearwaters began to come back. By 6 p.m. the air above Nightingale became thick with the thousands of shearwaters which were wheeling around before plunging down into the tussock jungle to seek their burrows. Dr. Broekhuysen continues: " It was a most fascinating sight. The noise was terrific. The perfectly symmetrical cone of Tristan da Cunha silhouetted against the soft pink evening sky in the distance made the picture superb." Lawrence, Macnae, and Broekhuysen traversed the tussock jungle until they reached some projecting rocks just on the fringe of the plateau and then sat among the wheeling, croaking birds, drinking in the unique scene. Some of the shearwaters came so close that they could be photographed with flashlight. The croaking noises uttered by the birds were most peculiar and were strangely reminiscent of the noise made by the old-fashioned hooters of early motor-cars. The air remained thick with wheeling birds until 8 p.m.

When anchored in a small bay off Gough Island on 28th February

[1] He gave an account of his visit in *British Birds*, xli, 1948, pp. 338-341.

there were further opportunities of watching great shearwaters among the thousands of birds—petrels, terns, and sooty albatrosses—which were feeding close to the ship. A strong northerly wind was blowing and the birds were feeding in the shelter of the bay.

Courtship is carried on at any time of the day or night, both inside and outside the burrows. In this connection Mrs. Rowan emphasizes that the great shearwater is by no means wholly nocturnal ; a large proportion of the population spends a day at sea during the early part of the breeding season but thousands of birds remain on land, courting and burrowing throughout the day. Moreover, feeding adults come in to land at all hours of the day and night.

During courtship the birds lie side by side and the courtship is punctuated by intervals of rest and silence. Courting consists of rubbing bills, preening each other and nibbling the feathers of the neck. Quivering and calling works up to a high pitch of noise and excitement followed by a quiet period, when the whole procedure starts over again. As soon as one voice is raised in the characteristic call it is joined by hundreds of others ; similarly all the birds leave off calling at the same time, the screaming cacophony giving way to sudden silence. The result is very noticeable at night as the noise comes first from one quarter and then from another. Mrs. Rowan points out the unmistakable communal nature of the ceremonies which she has described.

Although the weather was appalling with frequent squalls Dr. Broekhuysen had a perfect opportunity of comparing the different ways of feeding of the various species. The great shearwaters were flying slowly just above the water, looking down into it and frequently alighting horizontally. Food was then caught by dipping the bill into the water. On some occasions they dived just underneath the surface for a very short time, after which they took to flight again to repeat the procedure. As no birds were shot the nature of the food taken cannot be certain, but samples of plankton showed an abundance of a certain pteropod and it was possible that it was upon this the birds were feeding. Owing to the awful weather it was not possible for Dr. Broekhuysen to verify the statements of previous naturalists that the great shearwater does not nest on Gough Island but they were certainly very abundant in the surrounding waters.

It has since been *proved* by Mr. Hugh Elliott to nest on Gough Island. He found a nestling in a burrow on the south plateau on 25th February 1952. Mr. Elliott inclines to the view that colonization of Gough Island is quite recent.

COURTING AND NESTING : To complete the life story of this interesting bird we must return to Mrs. Rowan's exhaustive field work from which the following facts emerge. It seems from all the data available that although the great shearwaters begin to return to Nightingale and Inaccessible in the latter part of August, birds may still be arriving in October the inference being that the parties returning from the North Atlantic do not all come south at once but over an extended period. Mrs. Rowan has shown that shearwaters may be present on their breeding grounds at least one and a half months before the laying season.

Commenting (in *Ibis*, 1957) on Mrs. Rowan's description of the courtship Mr. Hugh Elliott observes :

Bird voices so dissonant as that of the great shearwater are difficult to describe, but neither Hagen nor Mrs. Rowan do full justice to the courtship vocabulary. Its basis is an explosive bleating—a " teddy-bear " squeak—in making which the bird seems to inflate itself. This is lengthened into a braying which often reaches a pitch of screeching hysteria : " ay-*yeeer*-kuk, coo-*ow*, hoo-*rrooo*-fu, aarrrgh-*yeeee*-ow ", and so on. Another distinct call is the food clamour of the chick, a hysterical gurgling " chwuck, chwuk, uk-zeek, uk-uk, chwuck ", etc.

The date of egg-laying is remarkably regular from year to year, and takes place during the second week of November, the chicks hatching early in January. Lawrence, who accompanied the Tristan islanders in their egg-collecting expeditions on two occasions, confirms that laying seldom starts before 9th November and may be as late as 12th or 13th in some years. The breeding grounds at this season are so over-crowded that hundreds of birds unable to find burrows deposit their eggs on the surface of the soil. These eggs fall prey to the islanders, to a species of *Nesocichla* and to the skuas, the parent bird seldom attempting to incubate.

The average nest burrow is about three feet in length ; the entrance tunnel is sometimes nearly horizontal (on steep slopes), or slants downwards at an angle of seventy degrees. The nest-chamber is about twelve to eighteen inches below the surface. On the tussock slopes the nests are apt to be made beneath the roots of the grass clumps and bits of tussock grass are often drawn into the entrances. Where tumbled heaps of boulders overlie the soft soil burrowing is impossible, but every crevice among the rocks is used as a nest. Every burrow examined was occupied at the end of September.

The egg is white with a smooth shell. Eleven eggs measured by Jourdain averaged 78.4×49.3 mm. Seventy-eight measured by Elliott averaged 80×51.5 mm.

Mrs. Rowan was not able personally to study the bird's habits during incubation but Mr. Elliott's observations tended to show that one bird remains during the day in the burrow while its mate feeds. Towards dusk vast numbers of shearwaters came swarming in to land and enter the burrows where they remained in pairs through the night, bickering and croaking. Shortly after dawn a huge pack of birds, representing half the shearwater population, flew off to sea again. Mr. Elliott considered it probable that male and female shared incubation. By the end of March the chicks had grown to the size of their parents though they retained the downy covering ; by the end of April all but a few chicks were in full plumage and the juveniles start flying during May. Mrs. Rowan describes in detail the method of feeding, the chick nibbling at the feathers of its parent's neck and breast to encourage the adult to disgorge, which it does when ready, opening its beak wide while the chick thrusts its open bill at right angles across the parent's gape, when it is fed at intervals. Close observation in March and April showed that some of the chicks were not being fed by their parents and ample evidence accumulated that this starving process of the young was taking place all over the island. Towards the middle of April many young birds which the islanders from Tristan had collected were dissected and their stomachs were found to contain grass and soil or to be empty. At this time there was a noticeable change in the behaviour of the chicks. Instead of remaining in their burrows they began to come out and squat in the open, nibbling at the grass and probing the soil with their beaks. The grass and soil eating was probably an attempt to fill their stomachs after the parents had deserted. The young birds remained at least a month on the breeding grounds after the departure of the adults. On 5th May young birds were seen making their first attempts at flight, launching themselves from the summit of a rock. Others were seen to emerge from their burrows in the late afternoon and at night when they wandered about croaking incessantly. It was plain to Mrs. Rowan and Mr. Elliott that the young did not leave the island immediately after their initial flight as there was a good deal of coming and going, but from 10th May onwards birds could be seen at all times of the day or night waddling towards the sea. Those from burrows at sea-level entered the sea before taking flight and experienced some difficulty in the surf. At this period of their lives large numbers are killed by skuas. In face of the twice-yearly expeditions of the Tristan islanders and the dangers which the juvenile population have later to face from forced starvation and then from predators, it is truly astonishing that the numbers of breeding birds on Nightingale and Inaccessible are apparently kept up. As the birds have such difficulty in finding space on these two islands in which to rear their young, it is a matter for wonder that they have not attempted to colonize any other island.

I cannot end this essay without expressing my admiration for the work which Mrs. Rowan and her companions, especially Mr. Elliott, have accomplished on this recently little known species. I am grateful to them for having made it possible to give such a full life history of *Puffinus gravis* in my book. Prior to their investigations this would have been quite impossible. I am grateful too for their permission to quote so generously from their published work.

REFERENCES : Original Description : *Procellaria gravis* O'Reilly, *Voyage Greenland and Adjacent Seas*, etc., 1818, p. 140, pl. 12, fig. 1 : Cape Farewell and Staten Hook to Newfoundland.

MEDITERRANEAN SHEARWATER

Puffinus diomedia [1] (Scopoli)

(*Puffinus kuhlii* Boie auctorum)

1. Mediterranean Shearwater

Puffinus diomedia diomedia (Scopoli)

An Accidental Visitor, obtained once only

2. Cory's or Atlantic Shearwater   PLATE 8

Puffinus diomedia borealis Cory

An Occasional Visitor, sometimes in flocks off south coast ; usually seen in autumn

DISTINGUISHING CHARACTERS OF THE TWO RACES : The chief distinction between these two is to be found in the bill, that of *borealis* being markedly deeper and heavier than in the typical *diomedia*. Measurements of the Atlantic race are also larger than those of the Mediterranean race, thus : *borealis* wing ♂ 350-378 mm., ♀ 335-368 mm. ; *diomedia* wing ♂ 335-360 mm., ♀ 325-355 mm., though overlapping.

IDENTIFICATION : This is one of the largest of the shearwaters. The crown and mantle are grey-brown merging gradually into the browner back, rump, and upper tail-coverts. The tail-coverts are margined with white. There is a white eyebrow and a white line beneath the eye. The cheeks and the sides of the breast are white, strongly marked with grey, as are the flanks. The rest of the underparts from chin to under tail-coverts are pure white. The wings and tail are very dark brown. The bill is pale yellowish-horn, the eye dark hazel. The feet are pale flesh. The outer toe and web dusky. The female has a smaller, finer bill and a more slender tarsus. Its length is 20 inches.

This shearwater can be identified at sea by its grey-brown upperparts and white underparts, and by the fact that it has no distinctive cap or patch on the belly (as has the great shearwater). It planes with motionless outstretched wings. The short legs are invisible in flight, but the strong hooked bill can be seen with field-glasses. Its large size separates it at once from all but a very few species.

[1] The List Committee of the B.O.U. of which the writer was at the time a member, discussed at their meeting of 19th June 1946 at the British Museum, the very complicated question of the correct name to be applied to this shearwater. Mr. Gregory Mathews gave reasons why Scopoli's name *diomedia* (1769) with type locality Trimiti Islands, Adriatic, should be accepted for the Mediterranean shearwater, hitherto known as *Puffinus kuhlii* Boie (1838 : Corsica). A former List Committee had rejected *diomedia* on the grounds that the name was indeterminate. Their decision was reversed, but with very great regret so far as the present writer is concerned, who never felt happy about the decision to adopt Scopoli's name in place of Boie's. Cf. especially *Ibis*, 1933, p. 347, and 1946, p. 534, where the matter is discussed.

OCCURRENCES IN GREAT BRITAIN : *Puffinus diomedia diomedia* has been obtained on one occasion only—a female picked up on Pevensey beach, Sussex, on 21st February 1906.

Puffinus diomedia borealis has been *obtained* on two occasions—a female washed ashore alive at Dungeness, Kent, on 21st January 1901, now mounted in the Tring Museum ; and a male picked up at West St. Leonards, Sussex, on 14th March 1914. The first of these specimens for long remained in obscurity, having been wrongly named, but it was re-examined by Mr. J. E. Dandy and Mr. W. E. Glegg and the correct identification communicated to *British Birds*, xxxix, 1946, p. 56. The name " R. Johnson " appeared on the original label, presumably the person who was responsible for finding and preserving it.

Although these are the only specimens to have been obtained the species has been recognized on a number of occasions by competent observers ; but there is absolutely no means of distinguishing the Mediterranean from the Atlantic race unless the bird is handled. Taking into consideration the respective range of these two races it has been presumed, and no doubt correctly, that the flocks which have been seen from time to time off our coasts are of the Atlantic race. In *The Handbook* Mr. Witherby enumerated some of the occasions upon which *P. diomedia* has been seen. These are as follows :

10.9.33. Flocks totalling about 60 birds between Casquets and Devon, 23 miles off Prawle Point (Wynne-Edwards).
21.9.36. One off Newhaven, Sussex (C. M. N. White).
23.8.38. Several, probably this species, between Cornwall and Scilly Is. (A. Farrant).
5.9.38. Several, probably this species, between Cornwall and Scilly Is. (R. S. R. Fitter).
10.9.38. Three or four, probably this species, between Cornwall and Scilly Is. (R. S. R. Fitter).

Mr. Witherby dealt with these records individually in *British Birds*, xxxiii, 1940, p. 249. There is, of course, no means of saying to which race the above records belonged but we can assume that they were probably *P. d. borealis*.

Since 1940, the following records have appeared in *British Birds*, up to midsummer of 1957 :

10.9.47. At sea 1½ miles north of Aberdeen (R. N. Winnall).
15.10.48. Off Langney Point, Sussex (D. D. Harber).
19.11.50. Off Langney Point, Sussex (D. D. Harber).
—.8.51. Between Cornwall and Scilly Is. (Cornwall Bird Watching Soc.).
—.9.51. Between Cornwall and Scilly Is. (Cornwall Bird Watching Soc.).
18.9.53. Within 2 miles of Inishtrahull Is., N. Donegal, recorded in square brackets (I. C. T. Nisbet).
11.53. Two seen 150 yds. off Isle of Sheppey (Kent Bird Report).

As no specimens were secured we can but name them binomially, but again presume them to represent the Atlantic race.

BREEDING DISTRIBUTION : The two races of *P. diomedia* which have found a place on the British list as rare or irregular visitors have a very different breeding range. The typical *P. diomedia diomedia* nests throughout the greater part of the Mediterranean from the southern coast of Spain (east of the Straits of Gibraltar) to ?Asia Minor, the Aegean and Ionian Islands, and also in most of the other Mediterranean islands—Corsica, Sardinia, the Balearic islands, Malta, Filfola Is., and on Grampusa Agria off Crete ; also commonly on islands off the coasts of Italy.

It does *not* breed on Cyprus so far as I can discover, but nests on most of the rocky islands off the coast of North Africa west of Tripoli. It is especially numerous on the small islands off the Tunisian coast such as Ile Pilau off Bizerta. In February and March 1925 we saw them daily off the north Tunisian coast and when passing close by Galita Island in April 1956 the sea around was alive with them. I have no knowledge of its nesting in the eastern Mediterranean other than where specified. To Egyptian waters it is reported to be " a mere vagrant ". It is not included in the Turkish list but Jourdain includes Asia Minor in its breeding range in *The Handbook*. The type locality of *P. diomedia* is the Tremite Islands in the Adriatic, that of *P. kuhlii*, Corsica. It is unfortunately not possible to say whether this race of *P. diomedia* passes through the Straits of Gibraltar in any numbers when the breeding season is over, but it probably does so. That some undoubtedly enter the Atlantic is proved by records of it having been taken in north and west France, Germany, Switzerland, and Czechoslovakia ; once in the Faeroe Islands and at least twice off Long Island, New York. It certainly disappears from the Mediterranean in the winter months.

The Atlantic race *P. diomedia borealis*, which was named *Puffinus borealis* by Cory from a specimen obtained off the eastern American coast " near Chatham Island, Cape Cod, Mass." and named by the present writer *Puffinus kuhli fortunatus* from the Canary Islands (being unaware at the time that the American birds were the same), has a breeding range restricted to the islands off the coasts of north-west Africa, the Azores, and the Portuguese Berlenga Islands. In *Ibis* of 1914 I was able to show that Cory's shearwater nests on the Azores, Desertas, Madeira, Porto Santo, the Salvages and the Canary Islands, but at that date it was not realized that it bred on the Berlengas.

When the nesting season is over the whole population of *P. d. borealis* begins to disperse over the ocean ; by the end of October the colonies which I knew so well in the Canaries are deserted and all the birds have gone to sea. That they disperse widely is evident from the numbers which occur off Long Island and the coast of North America from Cape Cod to Cape Hatteras. It was unhappily one of these visiting birds upon which

Cory bestowed the name which the Atlantic race has to bear. The type locality would have been better in one of the archipelagos where it breeds.

From my experience of breeding petrels I would suspect that the populations from the various groups of islands would not all vacate their breeding places at the same time. For instance, the birds from the Azores may begin to disperse a month earlier than those from the Canaries. December and January are the months when they may be looked for in the North Atlantic in greatest numbers, but from August onwards they may be found already hundreds of miles from their breeding grounds. The species has been reported from the Saragossa Sea, in a position more than a thousand miles west of the Azores, as early as 29th July (Nicholson), and in the preceding few days it was to be seen from the Azores to the edge of the continental shelf off the mouth of the English Channel. By September, as Wynne-Edwards has recorded, they are plentiful between Brittany and the coasts of Devon and Cornwall. He concluded that it reached the northern limit of its dispersal at about the fiftieth parallel in August and September. In October the birds begin working south. Professor Wynne-Edwards considered the northern limit of Cory's shearwater in August to be almost the same as the southern limit of the great shearwater. The destination of the various populations of this shearwater after the breeding season is little more than guesswork for no ringing has been done and if the Mediterranean birds do in fact enter the Atlantic in any numbers, they can only add to the confusion.

The recent discovery (in 1946) by Drs. Bierman and Voous [1] that *P. diomedia* is present at the end of December in large flocks in the seas off the Cape of Good Hope has entirely upset our former conceptions regarding the range of these birds. That this was not any exceptional movement has been confirmed by Professor G. J. Van Oordt and Dr. J. P. Kruijt [2] during a voyage in the South Atlantic in 1951-52. They found the species to be numerous on 17th January 1952 south-east of the Cape and again between the 19th and 24th March it was very numerous near and north of Cape Town. Reporting this occurrence they observe : " From where these Cape sea birds came is not known ". After discussing the distribution of these and other petrels which they encountered on their voyage they observe : " The remaining problem is where the Cape shearwaters breed ". They suggest that they may be North Atlantic breeding birds, i.e. *P. d. borealis*, a view supported by their observation that the large flocks—numbering more than 250 birds—seen on 24th March 1952 had a tendency to fly in a northerly direction.

It seems to the writer that it is completely useless to indulge in speculation as to the origin of these birds until specimens of *P. diomedia* from the Cape Seas can be collected and compared with the known racial forms.

[1] Bierman and Voous in *Ardea*, xxxvii (Supplement), 1950, p. 81.
[2] Van Oordt and Kruijt in *Ibis*, xcv, 1953, p. 626 ; *Ardea*, 1954, p. 263.

To state, as Dr. W. R. P. Bourne has done,[1] " that there can be no doubt that like the Manx shearwater, *Puffinus diomedia* is a northern trans-equatorial migrant with no southern race ", is a premature conclusion to say the least of it, until there are specimens which we can actually handle. Moreover, Dr. Bourne is surely mistaken when he states that the two specimens in the British Museum named " *Procellaria flavirostris* Gould " are " completely indistinguishable from specimens from the Mediter-ranean ". The specimens in the British Museum collected by the *Challenger* Expedition erroneously labelled " Kerguelen Land " have been proved since not to occur there, and their place of origin is obscure, but what is more likely than that they were obtained off the Cape of Good Hope? The type of *Procellaria flavirostris* was obtained by Governor Grey in latitude 30° 39' S., longitude 10° 3' E., that is to say south of the Cape of Good Hope. I had good reason then, in 1915 (*Bull. B.O.C.*, xxxv), for considering the two *Challenger* specimens to be examples of Gould's *flavirostris*, a name which up to that time had been universally but in-correctly applied to the shearwaters we now name *borealis* from the Atlantic islands.

As the two *Challenger* Expedition specimens had obviously much finer bills than birds collected in the North Atlantic islands, I was perfectly justified in giving a new name to the latter birds. This I did in 1915, naming them *Puffinus kuhli fortunatus*, a name which would have been tenable to-day had it not been that Cory had already bestowed the name *borealis* on a bird taken off the eastern coast of North America which proved to be the same. The name *fortunatus* therefore becomes a synonym of *borealis* which has been used ever since for the Atlantic islands' birds, excepting the Cape Verde Islands. In the *Bulletin of the British Orni-thologists' Club* cited I went so far as to figure the bill of one of the specimens brought home by the *Challenger* side by side with a bill of the Atlantic islands' shearwater ♀, in which the distinctions are well brought out by the draughtsman, Mr. Grönvold.

Among the distant localities from which *P. diomedia borealis* has been recorded are Newfoundland, Massachusetts, Rhode Island, Long Island, Bahia (Brazil), and the English Channel and Germany, while it has occurred apparently in New Zealand.[2]

HABITS : Cory's shearwater—to use the name in its specific sense—is a bird with which the writer is familiar, having first made its acquaintance in the Madeira group in 1904 and having spent some weeks on uninhabited islands in the Canary archipelago practically alone with hundreds of them during the height of the breeding season.[3] It is not possible to sail far

[1] *Ibis*, 1955, pp. 145-149. Dr. Bourne has also overlooked my remarks on *P. flavirostris* in *Bull. B.O.C.*, xxxv, 1915, pp. 118-121.

[2] W. R. B. Oliver in *Emu*, 1934, pp. 23-24.

[3] *Ibis*, 1914, pp. 66-70, 80, 267, 268.

among the Atlantic islands in the spring or summer without encountering any number of them and the same applies to the Mediterranean, where their numbers reach high figures in the vicinity of those islands where they come ashore to rear their young. The last time that we encountered it in abundance was in the vicinity of the island of Galita off the north Tunisian coast—an island, incidentally, which would well repay a visit as the probable nesting place of Audouin's gull, in addition to the hundreds of petrels and shearwaters which swarm around its rocky shores. We passed the island on 3rd April 1956, when the surrounding waters appeared to be alive with sea birds, but it was the large shearwater—the subject of this essay—which predominated. As my longest experience has been with the Atlantic race *borealis*, with which I lived in terms of almost too close intimacy on Montaña Clara in the Canaries, most of the field notes in this essay will be of this race but equally applicable to the Mediterranean bird, except, perhaps, as regards the dates of breeding in the various islands.

Cory's shearwater nests in hundreds in the Canary archipelago probably on all the islands, but in greatest abundance on the outlying islands of the eastern group—Graciosa, Montaña Clara, Allegranza, and some smaller islets. The main body of shearwaters arrive in the Canaries at the beginning of March (Savile Reid noted hundreds off Tenerife on 19th), but they do not begin nesting in this month or even in the next. E. G. B. Meade-Waldo, who visited Graciosa on 6th April 1890, reported that the shearwaters had not yet arrived in their breeding holes, and many years after his visit when I landed on Graciosa the fishermen assured me that the *pardelas* arrived during the latter part of April and beginning of May "to clean their nests". It was not until the last week of May that the birds were regularly in their nest holes in pairs but no eggs were laid in that year until the first week of June; by the second week all the birds were sitting on eggs. The young are hatched in July and when they have reached the proportions of their parents but are still covered with down large numbers are collected by the islanders from Lanzarote, who carry away boatloads to boil down for fat. At the end of September the shearwaters begin to leave their nesting places and take themselves to the sea, the main body finally leaving the Canary Islands in November. Some authorities have stated that they left the *islands* in September and it may be that some of the breeding colonies in the western islands—Tenerife, Grand Canary, Palma, Gomera, and Hierro—nest earlier than those on the outer islets of the eastern group and consequently vacate their breeding places at an earlier date. Between 1st October and 17th November I have seen many at sea off Grand Canary. After November the birds are very seldom seen until the end of February when the first-comers appear again in the vicinity of their nesting colonies.

In 1914 the writer made a study of all the petrels and shearwaters which frequented the North Atlantic islands, publishing the results in the

Ibis for that year. The dates of arrival in the various groups of islands, the dates of egg-laying, and the approximate date of departure of old and young is thus given in some detail for each separate group (Azores, Madeira Is., Desertas, Salvages, Porto Santo, and Canaries) in which Cory's shearwater breeds, and this paper is still the only one to have been compiled from existing data. Not much work has been done on these islands among the petrels since I wrote nearly forty-five years ago, except in the Cape Verde archipelago, which I also included in my survey. Reference to this paper will show that in the case of Cory's shearwater there is not much difference in the arrival or breeding dates in the various islands. Padre Schmitz of Madeira, who worked that island, the Desertas, and Porto Santo so thoroughly for many years prior to 1914, found that the birds behaved just as I have described for the Canary population—the birds had all left the islands by the 25th November, and returned on much the same date.

One of the more recent visitors to the Desertas who has left an account of his experiences was Colonel Richard Meinertzhagen, who landed there with his wife on 18th May 1925 and spent two nights on these deserted islets. Cory's shearwater had then not yet begun to lay or even to sit in their holes in any numbers. Many hundreds were seen at sea, some singly but mostly in flocks of from ten to three hundred. It was observed that when they rose from the water they simply opened their wings and glided. Not one was even seen to flap when taking the air as a gull will invariably do. They would, however, need to use their wings in absolutely still air. They normally fed by skimming but on several occasions they were seen to dive from a height of ten to fifteen feet, completely submerging after hitting the water. The seas around the Desertas are nearly always rough and for days on end it is impossible to land. Meinertzhagen was surprised to find that the shearwaters almost invariably chose the roughest and choppiest part of the sea when they wished to rest and they would go to sleep with their head tucked under their wing. When the boat passed through a flock asleep the birds did not awake until it almost touched them. In the stomachs of three obtained were small fish not exceeding an inch in length.

When more recently R. M. Lockley was on the Desertas from 10th to 15th July 1939 he found the large shearwaters very thinly distributed both on Chão and Deserta Grande and very few birds at home though large rafts of 300 birds or so were seen floating off the islands. It seemed that these were breeding in the more inaccessible cliffs and that the toll taken by the fishermen who regularly raid these birds is making itself felt. When Lockley landed on Great Salvage on 16th July he found the whole island alive with " cagarras ", as the Portuguese fishermen name Cory's shearwater : " a real shearwater hubbub filled the air ". Every kind of hole was utilized by the birds, especially the abundant little caves and cracks in the igneous rock and gaps in the several walls built across the island. Even quite slight holes which leave the bird partly in the open were used. At this date most of the birds had eggs which were well incubated, but none had hatched. Small stones had been used extensively with which to line the nests and the accumulation of years resulted in quite an elevated platform or dais in some nest sites. The writer never saw this in the Canaries. Incubation is by both sexes and Lockley found that one bird may stay on the nest for more than twenty-four hours at a time. As the courtship of this bird had never been properly described I give Mr. Lockley's notes in full—it is important in this connection to remember the date when he was on the Salvages—the second week of July:

Much courtship was being conducted, with occasional successful coition. Courting birds sat facing each other, but sometimes at an angle, and appeared to fondle and nibble each others' head and bill. . . . During coition it was observed that the male uttered harshly and continuously "*ka-ka-ka-ka*". Afterwards the female nibbled the male's tail and stern as if fondly inviting more attention. Ten minutes later the male nibbled the head of the female who bowed in submission willingly . . . she then turned and nibbled and preened his head and neck gently and invitingly. When after a long pause they neither of them moved we picked up the male who screamed *ka-ka-ka-ka* a much harsher note than the comparatively soft notes of the female. [Lockley continues.] With the break of dawn many birds were still sailing over the island. There appeared to be no hurry about leaving, and we enjoyed watching great numbers still flying over the dry dusty rocky plateau, with the sun showing on the horizon. One or two individuals might be seen thereafter skimming overhead or along the slopes of the cliffs during the rest of the morning. From noon onwards the numbers in the air increased until by 16.00 hours B.S.T. small flocks were ranging above. As the sun sank to the sea in the cloudy north-west, hundreds of Cagarras filled the air, and thousands more skimmed along under the cliffs, or floated in great rafts off shore. Calling began at least two hours before sunset, in contrast with the behaviour of the birds on the Berlengas and Desertas. The confused babel of cries merged into one grand nocturnal roar as dusk swiftly fell; and the fainter cries of the little shearwater, the Madeiran petrel and, the frigate petrel were added—but as voices only to be heard when these smaller birds passed close to us. . . . It appears that *P. k. borealis* is active diurnally to some degree only on the Salvages. At all other breeding grounds, including the Canaries (Bannerman, 1922), it appears to be nocturnal while on land.

In an account of his visit to the Berlengas Islands off the Portuguese coast from 20th to 24th June Mr. Lockley observed that the aerial activity of Cory's shearwater is strictly nocturnal, the adults gathering on the sea near the island in small bands before sunset and coming in over the island about two hours after sunset. Some birds had eggs at this date but many others were found at night sitting about in pairs both inside the rock débris and outside in the open. They appeared by the amount of calling and caterwauling to be courting but close observation was impossible owing to the darkness of the night. Examination of a small nesting cave showed that several birds were sitting ; five had eggs placed on " nest-platforms " of small stones. These stone platforms were deliberately built since Mr. Lockley saw in the light of his torch one bird in the act of carrying a stone. The sitting birds were silent or almost so, and squawked only when handled. The cries are uttered by birds on the wing. Mr. Lockley remarked that when the calling bird passes close over the observer uttering its rasping cry *kaa-ough* or sometimes *koo-ough*, three or four times in leisurely succession, a distinct sighing note can be heard after each loud double note. It seemed to be caused by the indrawing of breath. When I was living among these birds on Montaña Clara and at other breeding places the males used to utter long-drawn-out wailing notes which were answered by a purring sound from the ground, presumably by the female.

More than one observer has mentioned what I have never seen myself, birds diving from an elevation sufficiently high to cause them to immerse in an attempt, apparently often successful, to catch small fish. Writing of its feeding habits as observed near the Azores in August Mr. G. Beven remarked that they were seen to flutter and hover and then drop onto the surface of the sea to take fish from the water. Many fish were jumping from the water and the birds were seen to take some of these while actually in the air ; the fish were assumed to be flying fish as their actions appeared similar to many which were constantly observed in the neighbourhood. Mr. Beven was at too great a distance to be sure of the species but several birds were seen with a fish in the bill. It was remarked that when so engaged the motions of the shearwaters appeared very different from their usual swift gliding turning flight, skimming the surface of the waves.[1] The usual flight of Cory's shearwater was the subject of a note in *British Birds* [2] from Mr. E. Gathorne-Hardy, who when off Cape Matapan and elsewhere was able to observe its flight actions very closely both in light and strong breezes. He noted that in light breezes the flight was of remarkable regularity, four wing beats occupying two to three seconds followed by a glide of six to seven seconds, regularly repeated. The glide shaved the water so closely that from the deck of the ship it looked as if it would be difficult to slip a soup-plate between the breast of the bird and the water. Later, in the Aegean, when the wind had freshened exactly the same pattern was followed. Mr. Gathorne-Hardy emphasizes that there was no question of " half mile glides " as recorded of the great shearwater in *The Handbook*, which compares the flight of the two birds.

BREEDING HABITS : Much of what has been written already in this essay could be placed under this heading, for the nesting habits take up practically the whole of the time which the shearwater spends ashore ; when at the close of the breeding season it takes to the open sea with its young—not apparently in company—its life is on the ocean and we are

[1] *British Birds*, xxxix, 1946, pp. 122-123.
[2] *British Birds*, xliii, 1950, pp. 404-405.

only permitted to catch glimpses of it as with majestic flight, now gliding, now two or three wing beats and another glide, tilting gracefully from side to side, it literally shears the waves. No one who has seen Cory's shear-water on a rough day in the Atlantic or the Bay of Biscay, as the writer has done scores of times, can fail to admire the grace of its movements, now deep in the trough of a huge Atlantic roller, now mounting to the crest and down again, but never more than a few inches above the surface and never caught by a broken surface, though the spume may be flying from every crest.

But it is of its time ashore that I must write now, and as the events which I shall describe took place more years ago than I care to remember, the reader must forgive me if I take my notes from the book which I wrote on the Canary Islands—their History, Natural History, and Scenery—which was published in 1922. My expedition to the eastern Canary Islands on behalf of the British Museum, accompanied as I was by an excellent taxidermist, Mr. A. H. Bishop, brought me into close touch with Cory's shearwater in the early summer of 1913 when the birds came to the outlying small islands of this group to lay their eggs. The first islet we explored was low and sandy, but with four extinct volcanoes whose crumbling walls are full of holes and crevices which sometimes lead to good-sized caves. Our first meeting with the petrels was just above high-water mark, where a mass of huge boulders was piled up one upon another, over which volcanic sand had blown which made an ideal bed for some scrubby plants, their roots binding the sand together. Small gaps between the boulders led to low caves into which we had to crawl on hands and knees and from which a network of passages led in all directions. In these dark recesses, abound-ing in nooks and crannies, the shearwaters were sitting. The electric torch flashed upon them dazzled their eyes and though they uttered no vocal protest, unless touched, they shuffled farther into the recesses and squeezed behind loose rocks in their attempt to escape the unwelcome glare. In this particular cave no nest of any description had been attempted, although the date was late in May.

Another nest site was in some rugged cliffs of black jagged lava, among the crevices of which large numbers were already nesting. Another colony on Graciosa had chosen to make burrows in the earth which was so hard that it resisted all attempts to dig them out. We only found one other colony in which the birds were breeding in burrows in equally hard earth. We presumed the birds had somehow dug out these holes with claws and bill as there were no rabbits or other rodents on Graciosa, but how this had been accomplished in ground which broke our tent pegs we could never imagine.

Not content with nesting round the coasts the shearwaters had resorted in some numbers to two of the volcanoes—a few were sitting amongst the lumps of loose lava on the summit of Montaña Bermeja at 550 feet, but a much larger colony was found on the slopes of the big central volcano. From 300 to 600 feet the sides of the old crater were honeycombed with holes, in almost all of which shearwaters were nesting. I explored one of the caves with a lad from the fishing village as my guide, without whose help I should never have known a cave to exist. The entrance was by a tunnel through which we squeezed with difficulty—a feat I could not accomplish so easily to-day ! The outer cave (6 × 3 feet) gave no indication of what we found later, but by dint of crawling and wriggling through a further tunnel which ran straight into the heart of the mountain we at last found ourselves in another small cave, with still another passage leading out of it. This tunnel was rather wider but twisted and turned in a bewildering manner and I began to think I should never get out alive. There was no turning back at this stage, but at last we emerged into quite a large cavern which must have been some twenty yards from the entrance. The smell of petrels in this cave was quite intoxicating. The floor of the cave was covered with feathers and in every hole and crevice of the walls the shearwaters had been sitting. It amazed me that they had penetrated so far into the wall of the old volcano. The cave was almost empty of birds but the atmosphere was such that we dared not remain till the birds returned. None had yet laid an egg but it was obvious that at night the occupants would be there in full force. Never once did these shearwaters on Graciosa come to their holes until darkness had fallen. Laying had not become general until after we left the island on 7th June, though we obtained a good series of specimens and a number of eggs. At this stage the majority of the birds would leave their nests before dawn had broken to spend the whole day at sea. How the birds in these inner caves knew that the day was approaching we could never understand, but they were away with the others and not till an hour after darkness had fallen did they return to their holes.

As soon as they began to come in they began calling—a long wailing cry answered from the ground by the mate who had already got home. Before alighting the birds would fly round over their holes or burrows with lessening circles, close above the rocks, to settle eventually close to the entrance to their abode. The boys with me caught a few birds on the rocks before they went into their holes, for once on terra firma they are clumsy creatures and cannot easily launch themselves into the air. On 7th June, the day we left the island, nearly all the birds had laid their egg. A short trip in a fishing boat manned by eight sturdy islanders—all members of one family—took us to Montaña Clara, where one of the men and I were landed while Mr. Bishop was taken on to Allegranza as our time was getting short. The eight days on Montaña Clara taught me more about the petrels than I ever knew before. The tent was struck literally on top of some nest-holes which I did not discover until dark, when the wailing of the rightful owners became louder as the night wore on. The constant roar of the breakers on this rocky islet and the weird cries of the petrels as they circled over my tent was an introduction to Montaña Clara that I shall never forget.   That night I was puzzled by the cries, but I was to learn that no less than four species of petrels and shearwaters were sharing with me this tiny islet, little more than the broken lip of a crater reared above the waves without a tree or water, rising on one side to 700 feet with a sheer drop to the sea.   Three of them were on their breeding ground.[1]   At that time I did not know their calls, but one was a musical pleasant note and I have learned that this was made by Bulwer's petrel, the most delightful of all my companions.   The ugly cries of the " pardelas " drowned even the noise made by a flapping tent, for the wind had risen and so had the sea and my thoughts turned to how I should ever get away if these conditions continued when my eight days were up.   On this island the large shearwaters were as plentiful or more so than on Graciosa.   They were nesting under the shelving strata just beyond high-water mark, in burrows in the only sandhills, under lumps of lava on the mountain side at 600 feet and again in burrows on a plateau even higher up.   They called at all hours of the night but seemed noisiest at 3 a.m., at which hour I believe many went out to sea.   I was sure that both sexes incubated, the male coming in to sit while the hen went out to feed.   If pulled from their holes in the day-time they were completely dazed.   Some would waddle in the direction of the sea, continually catching their wings in bushes and stones and tumbling about in the most grotesque manner as if they were intoxicated. If thrown in the air some would gain their senses, spread their wings and glide out to sea ; others seemed petrified and came down plump on the rocks, whence they made for a rock from which they could launch themselves into space.

The sand on which these shearwaters had burrowed on Montaña Clara was much softer than on Graciosa and I dug out a number of holes. They appeared very like rabbit holes, if anything rather larger in circumference (there are no rabbits on the island).   The entrances measured about 6 × 11 inches and often led 7 feet into the ground.   The egg lay in a scraping about a foot from the end, a few feathers and scraps of seaweed doing duty for a nest.   The passage was generally winding and at times branched at right angles.   In contrast to these long burrows I found birds sitting on their eggs in full daylight, having deposited them in crevices of the cliff, not twelve inches from the entrance, where the sun's rays could fall full upon it.   I did not realize it at the time but these were probably birds which had arrived too late to find a hole or niche unoccupied, and were forced to lay their single egg in an exposed position though never entirely in the open.   The egg is dull white when fresh.   Seventy eggs measured by Jourdain, many of my own taking, averaged in size 73·3 × 50 mm.

[1] *Puffinus diomedia borealis, Bulweria bulwerii, P. assimilis baroli*, and, strangest of all, *Procellaria pelagica*, the last of which we caught in a cave.

PLATE 10

SOOTY SHEARWATER
Puffinus griseus (Gmelin)

Max. 82·5 × 51 and 75 × 53 mm. Min. 68·6 × 46·8 and 73·5 × 45 mm. According to the local fishermen young are not hatched before early July, which would give an incubation period of at least six weeks, but there is no definite information. Although we had come too early to find any nestlings we discovered the young of the little Madeiran shearwater almost ready to fly and also fresh eggs. Bulwer's petrel had fresh eggs but no young by the time we left the island.

The Lanzarote fishermen visit Montaña Clara about 5th August to collect the young " pardelas " for eating purposes while a further visit takes place in September when the young are then very fat, and are boiled down for oil. In the neighbouring island of Allegranza hundreds of adults were captured and killed for the sake of their feathers which are reported to fetch a good price in Las Palmas. Whether this trade still exists I do not know. All reports agreed that young and old together vacated the islands in November and go out to sea.

REFERENCES : Original Descriptions : 1. Mediterranean race : *Procellaria diomedia* Scopoli, *Ann. 1. Hist. Nat.*, 1769, p. 74 : Tremiti Islands, Adriatic. Synonym : *Procellaria kuhlii* Boie, *Isis*, 1835, p. 257 : Corsica. 2. Atlantic race : *Puffinus borealis* Cory, *Nuttall Orn. Club*, vi, 1881, p. 84 : near Chatham Island, Cape Cod, Mass. Syn. : *Puffinus kuhli fortunatus* Bannerman, *Bull. Brit. Orn. Club*, xxxv, 1915, p. 120 : Canary Islands.

SOOTY SHEARWATER

PLATE 10

Puffinus griseus (Gmelin)

A fairly regular Visitor to British seas mainly in autumn ; sometimes numerous off S.W. Ireland

IDENTIFICATION : The sooty shearwater has dark brown head, neck, and upperparts. The scapulars are darker, almost blackish at their ends, and the wing-coverts are more blackish-brown than the back. The quills are black, paler on the inner webs. The lower back, rump and upper tail-coverts are darker than the back. The tail-feathers are black. The sides of the face are paler than the black back and the lower edge of the eyelid is white. The entire underparts are dusky brown with darker sooty-brown axillaries. The under wing-coverts are ashy white with blackish shaftlines, and are mottled with ashy brown towards the ends. The coverts round the edge of the wing are more brown. The bill is a dull greyish-black, the ridge yellowish-brown. The tarsus and toes are bluish-grey, the webs yellowish. The iris is black. The male is 17½ inches in length, the female 16 inches.

The sooty shearwater is often seen at sea with the great shearwater. Both glide close to the waves. Other similar dark birds are the dark phase of the Balearic shearwater, and the dark phase of the fulmar. Wynne-Edwards in his *Birds of the North Atlantic* gave some leading characters of the sooty shearwater, likening it in size and flight to the greater shearwater,[1] though he considered it to be rather heavier in the body and narrower in the wings. Its sooty-black colouring is relieved only by the somewhat paler bases of the quills, while a paler tract along the middle of the underside of the wing helps to distinguish it from all other species in the North Atlantic. That these field characters still hold good Professor Wynne-Edwards was able to demonstrate in late August 1955 when he encountered sooty shearwaters during a crossing from Orkney to Caithness : the birds paid no attention to the ship but continued on their way.

Mr. A. G. Parsons[2] considers the shape of the wing diagnostic, " like the blade of a ham-knife, only pointed ". He further remarks that any shearwater which appears to be " bounding " more than the rest deserves close scrutiny. It has been pointed out by I. C. I. Nisbet[3] that the pale tract on the underwing is not necessarily visible or obvious even at close range and that it should only be considered a subsidiary character—the size, wing-shape, general coloration, and *style of flight* being the first points to look for. In a later communication he and others criticize the sketch in *British Birds*, xlv, p. 49, describing it as misleading, especially if importance is attached to the pattern of the underside of the wing. Nisbet's description of this feature would be : " underwing paler, often noticeably so, grading to whitish or silvery in the centre ".

E. M. Nicholson,[4] writing of the shearwaters to be observed in the English Channel, issues a warning against accepting sight records too easily owing to possible confusion with *Puffinus puffinus mauretanicus*, but anyone familiar with the Manx should spot the difference in size without much difficulty, the sooty being so much larger. In the *Birds of Tropical West Africa* I likened its size to the Cape Verde Island shearwater (*edwardsii*), that species being a distinctly smaller edition of *Puffinus diomedia borealis*.

OCCURRENCES IN BRITISH WATERS : Witherby described this bird in 1940 as a rather scarce autumn visitor and nothing has occurred in the last eighteen years to alter that statement as applied to England and Wales. It has been recorded all around our coasts. We hear of it recently following fishing trawlers off the Shetlands[5] and as early as 22nd August in the Pentland Firth.

Whether it be due to closer observation or not, it appears to be of more general occurrence off the coast of Scotland, particularly in the far

[1] I should personally describe it as distinctly smaller.
[2] *British Birds*, 1953, p. 120.
[3] *British Birds*, 1954, p. 169.
[4] *British Birds*, 1952, p. 53.
[5] G. T. Kay, in *Scot. Nat.*, 1953, p. 51.

north. Dr. Baxter and Miss Rintoul would describe it as occurring " with tolerable regularity in Autumn in the Hebridean seas ", and quote Mr. MacRae as giving many records between 16th July and 17th September in Outer Hebridean waters. Referring to their own observations they record that when the great rollers come in before a north-easterly gale they have watched them from the Isle of May in September and October skimming close over the sea, sometimes being lost to sight in the trough of the waves, only to emerge with their effortless flight. They draw attention to observations made during the 1914-18 war by Commander Hughes Onslow who found sooty shearwaters to be regular autumn visitors, in small numbers, down the east coast of the Scottish mainland ; and we already know that the Firth of Forth is one of its chosen resorts. Records from the Western Islands show that it is more than a chance vagrant and even the term " Irregular Visitor " as employed in the new B.O.U. List is somewhat grudging when all the facts are surveyed.

Major Ruttledge has shown in *Birds of Ireland* that although formerly considered a rare accidental visitor there have been occasions when it appears in some numbers. In 1899 it was found to be frequent— chiefly in August and September—off the south-west coast, while in 1900 Becker [1] found the sooty shearwater " in surprisingly large numbers off the coasts of Kerry, Cork, Waterford, and the south coast of Wexford ". Apart from the southern coast most records have been obtained off Mayo. The late Duchess of Bedford encountered a large number on 17th August 1911 off the Mullet. Major Ruttledge states that records elsewhere are less frequent. It is worth noting that there have been occurrences off the Irish coast on 22nd May, 23rd May, 18th June, and 5th July in addition to the autumn records.

To remind us that considerable flights may be seen even to-day off the shores of Ireland we have the recent experience of Messrs. Gibbs, Nisbet and Redman [2] off North Donegal when a flight of " at least 137 birds off Malin Head during five and a half hours' observation on 9th September 1953 were of this species ; some were in small scattered parties, the largest numbers together being twelve, eleven and nine ". The authors point out that these numbers must be considered exceptional, though the observations of R. M. Lockley [3] and Stephen Marchant suggest there may be a small concentration on the Rockall Banks in summer.

BREEDING DISTRIBUTION : The breeding range of the sooty shearwater is restricted to the southern hemisphere. It breeds on various islands in the New Zealand seas, including Auckland and Chatham Islands ; one of its best-known breeding haunts is the Cape Horn group of islands of

---

[1] *Irish Naturalist*, x, p. 42.

[2] *British Birds*, 1954, p. 221. The editors in a footnote point out that the authors of this statement must alone be held responsible for the identification.

[3] " A midsummer visit to Rockall ", in *British Birds*, 1951, pp. 373-383.

which Wollaston Island and Hermite are the two largest; and also the islands along the coast of Chile and the Falkland Islands.

Three races of this bird have been described. *P. griseus* of Gmelin, for which in his *Birds of Australia* Mathews designated New Zealand as the type locality; *P. griseus chilensis* Bonaparte: West American coasts; and *P. griseus stricklandi* Ridgeway: Atlantic seas. Mathews wrote (p. 97): "Whether Bonaparte's name should be used for the Atlantic form of *P. griseus* or not seems open to doubt. Ridgeway[1] proposed for the Atlantic form the name of *P. stricklandi*, and it would be the wisest course to accept Ridgeway's name."

I adopted this course in my *Birds of Tropical West Africa*, vol. i, when referring to specimens of the sooty shearwater which had wandered to West African seas, but, as Witherby points out, the distinctions between the races are so fine that they have not been generally recognized. In this work I name the bird binomially as I am not now in a position to review again the races critically.[2] I agree with Mathews that if the Atlantic birds can be separated from those from New Zealand, then *stricklandi* must be used for the sooty shearwater which reaches the coasts of Britain.

DISTRIBUTION AND MIGRATIONS OUT OF THE BREEDING SEASON: We have, as already mentioned, three more or less distinct breeding populations of the sooty shearwater to consider in relation to the bird's migrations. The opinion was generally held, or so it appears from the literature I have consulted, that the sooty shearwaters which appear in the North Atlantic from May onwards would almost certainly be restricted to those birds which have their breeding stations in the Cape Horn Islands and in the Falklands. The large numbers which visit the Pacific coast of North America—the main concentration being off the Californian coast—are believed to come from the breeding population on the islands off the coast of Chile; while those which reach the Kurile and Aleutian Islands would have bred in the New Zealand seas. On the face of it, this explanation of the movements of the sooty shearwater fitted in fairly well with the facts as we knew them, for it was realized that it makes one of the longest migrations from its breeding places in the southern hemisphere to winter over a very wide extent of the Atlantic and Pacific Oceans.

A new light was thrown upon this shearwater's movements after the breeding season is over by the observations of van Oordt and Kruijt when on their voyage in the Atlantic and Southern Oceans in the Dutch tanker *Barendrecht* in 1951-52. From Cape Town course was set on 16th January 1952 in a south-easterly direction towards the Antarctic continent, which was reached at about 70° E., 62° S. on 28th January. From there the tanker followed approximately the sixty-third or sixty-fourth parallel as

[1] *Water Birds of North America*, vol. ii, 1884, p. 390.
[2] In the Fifth Edition of the A.O.U. *Check-List of North American Birds*, 1957, no subspecies are recognized.

far as the Balleny Islands at the western end of the Ross Sea. She steamed rather far from the continent to avoid the pack ice. It must be emphasized that Professor van Oordt and Dr. Kruijt had made this voyage for the express purpose of making ornithological observations and throughout the voyage one or both of them were constantly on the look-out. Their account [1] makes fascinating reading.

The sooty shearwater—the subject of this essay—was encountered first a day after leaving Cape Town on the outward voyage when twenty or thirty appeared ; and when the Antarctic Ocean was reached, south of Australia and south-west of New Zealand, large migratory movements of the species were seen. This confirmed the earlier observations of Falla,[2] who encountered large numbers of *P. griseus* flying in a westerly direction in the Antarctic Ocean between 160° and 60° E.

The observers on the *Barendrecht* shall now take up the tale : [3]

In the morning of 3rd February 1952, a beautiful calm day (noon position 63° 47′ S., 120° 13′ E.), we saw the sooty shearwater for the first time in real Antarctic waters, about 1000, forming two large groups on the ocean's surface. Later in the day many big flocks were seen, bringing the total number to about 2000. On the following days (4th-6th February 1952) very large flocks were recorded—many consisting of hundreds of birds—all flying north-west, south-west, or sometimes due west, *i.e.* as much as possible across the direction of the wind. During about eight hours of observation on 4th, 5th and 6th February totals of about 2000, 425 and 5000 respectively were seen. Of these, 4800 passed our ship in the morning, during not more than four hours of observation ! On 7th and 8th February, however, there were 16-20 and 4-5 *griseus* respectively. As no specimens were seen flying in easterly directions, all sooty shearwaters observed must have been migratory birds.

During the homeward voyage towards the end of February, at about the same latitude, these migratory movements were still going on. The first flock was seen, 15-20 examples, at 150° E. On the next day large movements of 3000 individuals were recorded, mainly in a south or south-westerly direction. On 26th February more than 1800 were counted, flying around or swimming ; numbers fell on 27th, but on 28th February the migratory movements were distinct again, with large flocks totalling about 2000. After that date the shearwaters became scarcer.

Professor van Oordt and Dr. Kruijt then continue :

Our observations, as well as those of Falla and possibly also of Routh, stress the fact that in late summer large migratory movements of *Puffinus griseus* take place over the Antarctic Ocean, in the Australian as well as in the eastern part of the Indian sector. The total number of these birds migrating westwards in a single day must be very high, as we only saw a very small part of the ocean and as it is highly possible that these movements take place on a broad front. The question

---

[1] *Ibis*, xcv, 1953, pp. 615-637, esp. p. 624 ; also *Ardea*, 1954, pp. 245-280.

[2] R. A. Falla, *British-Australian-New Zealand Antarctic Research Expedition*, 1929-1931. Ser. 13, ii, *Birds*, Adelaide 1937.

[3] With their permission and that of the editor of the *Ibis*.

whereto these birds fly is still unanswered ; consequently we do not know whether these sooty shearwaters were about to winter in the Atlantic Ocean or would fly along the west coast of Australia to the Pacific. The fact that we did not encounter *Puffinus griseus* in large numbers east of 150° E. leads us to suppose that *griseus* leaves its breeding grounds in New Zealand waters in a westerly direction, without first spreading in different directions over the Southern Seas.

In relation to these migratory movements our observation of relatively large numbers of *Puffinus griseus* near the southern part of South Africa in the second part of March 1952—200-300 birds on 19th March and 75-100 on 23rd March— is in favour of the supposition that at least a large percentage of the New Zealand population of sooty shearwaters winters in the Atlantic.

The New Zealand population must be very large, far larger than that from the Falklands and Cape Horn Islands, for it is reported to nest not only in New Zealand itself but on Norfolk, Stewart's, Kapiti, Snares, St. Stephens, Auckland, Chatham, and probably many other islands in the neighbouring seas. It appears from the observations I have quoted from van Oordt and Kruijt that we may have to alter our previous view that the sooty shearwaters which reach our shores necessarily must come from the Cape Horn or Falkland Islands. By their observations around the Cape of Good Hope our Dutch colleagues have put rather a different complexion on the theories formerly propounded. In support of the theory that some birds may pass via the Cape up the African side of the Atlantic, we may mention this shearwater's occurrence off the coast of Angola and again in the Gulf of Guinea.[1] Boyd Alexander shot one on 8th January off Fernando Po, and Bocage recorded it from the seas off Annobon. The date when the Fernando Po bird was taken certainly does not fit in with any migration as at that date the Cape Horn islands' population should be in the middle of breeding.

In the course of his remarks on the sea birds of the North Atlantic Professor Wynne-Edwards mentions numerous dates when he himself has seen the sooty shearwater during Atlantic crossings. These seventeen observations fall between 7th June and 15th September : fewer were seen in June than in September and they were always more common on the American side ; the area of observation lay between latitude 47° 0′ and 53° 30′ N. There are a number of other sight records available. The British records, as already noted, fall mainly between August and October. There is also one old August record from the Faeroe Islands and others from Norway and Iceland ; but these records for long-distance travel have now been eclipsed by a bird said to have been seen in the Barents Sea on 11th August 1950, twenty-five miles due west of Bear Island in 70° 40′ N., 19° W. Mr. E. Duffey, who reported the occurrence,[2] had the bird under

---

[1] Bannerman, *Birds of Tropical West Africa*, vol. i, 1930, p. 23 : recorded under *Neonectris griseus stricklandi*.

[2] *British Birds*, 1951, p. 179.

observation for two hours. He suggests that this may constitute the longest recorded distance for a migrating bird from its nearest possible place of birth : supposing that it was from one of the Cape Horn islands, it must have travelled some 9500 miles, even by the shortest sea route. This particular bird was seen among a large flock of fulmars which were feeding on discarded remains. It was noted that the fulmars would not tolerate the shearwater and made frequent lunges at it.

On the American side of the Atlantic the sooty shearwater reaches the Massachusetts coast towards the end of May ; it has been reported, among other localities, from off Newfoundland and Labrador, and once from south of Cape Farewell, Greenland, and on our side from Iceland.

HABITS : In his delightful essay on this bird, with which he must have been very familiar, Arthur Cleveland Bent pertinently observes that these ocean wanderers from Antarctic seas which spend their winter off the American coasts are better known to fishermen than to ornithologists, who have long remained in ignorance of the habits of the living bird. For many years they were presumed to breed in the far north but thanks to a small band of explorers we can now write with knowledge not only of its breeding habits in islands of the southern oceans but also of its stupendous migrations along the shores of the Antarctic. Bent describes the flight of the sooty shearwater as swift, graceful and strong, and like other species of its genus it can sail for long distances on its long, stiff wings without even a tremor except to adjust them slightly to the wind, rising at will over the crests of the waves or gliding down into the valleys between them, turning like the albatrosses by lowering the wing on the inner side of the curve and raising the wing on the outer side, holding both in a straight line. It frequently flaps its wings when occasion requires and uses them freely in its squabbles for food. Mr. Bent adds that it swims lightly and swiftly on the surface and dives below it occasionally in pursuit of food, using its wings freely under water, as evidenced by the number caught on the trawl hooks of the cod fishermen. At sea it is a silent bird. Bent quotes Loomis as having seen off the Massachusetts coast on a certain 5th September 275 shearwaters—only a dozen of which were Cory's and all the rest sooty— which had been driven close in-shore by thick and stormy weather outside. He quotes this as an instance of the effect which fog may have on such a pelagic species : usually sooty shearwaters keep well away from the coast. Wynne-Edwards reminds us that it is known to the fisherman as the hagdown or black hagdon—not a very engaging name. When having under observation at the same time the greater, the sooty, and Cory's shearwaters Mr. Bent was always able to recognize the dark-bodied and still darker-winged sooty at any distance.

Regarding food, the sooty shearwater is reported to live largely upon squid, which it catches near or at the surface of the water ; but it is attracted by any oily food such as the livers of soft fish, which it devours greedily.

So fearless do they become when such titbiis are thrown to them that they are easily captured by fishermen with hook and line.

The birds begin to leave the North Atlantic in September to make the long journey to their breeding grounds, and they are found in diminishing numbers in October and November. This applies not only to both sides of the Atlantic but also to the Pacific coast of America, where they depart south at the same time. This, as Bent points out, is really its " spring " migration. I have not consulted the dates when the birds reach the islands in the New Zealand seas. They remain, as we have seen, in the Cape Horn islands until the northern spring is well on the way, but breeding is presumably at its height in November, December, and January. They need not be looked for north of the equator before May ; but there are always exceptions to every rule and we have seen that on the Pacific coast of America they have been reported in every month of the year.

BREEDING HABITS : As we have seen, the sooty shearwater's nearest nesting place to Great Britain is in the islands off Cape Horn in South America, and in the Falkland group. Some of the former islands, particularly Wollaston, Deceit and Barnevelt, were investigated in December 1932 by Mr. P. W. Reynolds, who was a regular visitor on his leaves to the " Bird Room " of the British Museum. Mr. Reynolds at that time was living in Tierra del Fuego, a handy locality for expeditions to the Cape Horn and Chilean islands, which are the breeding places of countless petrels. The following brief description of the islands is taken from the account of his expedition : [1]

The Wollaston and Hermite islands together constitute the group of which Cape Horn is the most southerly point. The Wollastons consist of four major islands : Grévy, Bayly, Wollaston, and Freycinet, besides various islets and rocks. Grévy and part of Bayly are comparatively flat with much peaty ground similar to parts of the Falklands. At Cape Hall and the tussock-covered Daedelus Islands are monumental cliffs composed of square pillars of basalt. Wollaston itself is a large rugged island with a northern peninsula almost severed at Hately Bay. . . .

The Hermite group comprises six large islands—Hermite, Jerdan, Hall, Herschel, Horn and Deceit—besides various smaller islands and rocks. These islands are high and rugged, with numerous peaks and occasional patches of old snow persisting in mid-summer at 1000 feet.

The climate is so consistently wet, with accompanying high wind, that there has been no inducement to settlement on the islands, and one cannot help pitying the unfortunate savages who once lived there. The islands are now uninhabited, but are visited occasionally by otter hunters.

It is amidst such inhospitable surroundings that the sooty shearwater elects to rear its young. Mr. Reynolds' account continues :

The nights we spent at Deceit and Wollaston were made hideous with the

---

[1] " On the birds of Cape Horn ", in *Ibis*, 1935, pp. 65-101.

noise of petrels passing overhead. I attribute the most ghastly sounds to this species [sooty shearwater], although it was always too dark to make certain.

Quoting from his diary of 22nd December at Wollaston he likens the noises made by these petrels to choking cats :

" Cha-whee-whoo ", grating and choking with noise like gurgling intake of breath working often to a climax. The sound is not altogether unpleasant at a distance, but uttered by these birds passing at close quarters it is appalling.

During the crossing to Barnevelt and back great flocks were passing towards Cape Horn, and late in the evening between Deceit and Herschel towards Wollaston. On Deceit in spite of the noise at night we searched unsuccessfully for the nests. . . . On Wollaston we used the dog and took four setts of eggs 2/2[1] and 2/1 ; the eggs were hard set except in the supposed clutches of two. Two more clutches were taken on Bayly island : eggs white, thick shelled with a slight chalky coating and distinct pores. Average of seven eggs 73·4 × 47·7 mm. Max. 81 × 45 and 70·75 × 50·25 mm. Min. 67·25 × 44·25 mm.

This shearwater breeds on steep ground at a height of 500 feet or more. The burrows vary from three feet to several yards in depth, and are well hidden under stunted trees growing about outcropping rock, and in much drier places than the holes of *Oceanites*. The nesting grounds, similarly to these of the storm petrel [*O. oceanicus*], are extremely difficult to detect. The burrows frequently run beneath the roots of the evergreen beech.

Mr. Reynolds adds that both shearwater and Wilson's storm petrel are probably common breeding species in the Wollaston and Hermite groups of islands.

In the Falkland Islands two specimens of the sooty shearwater were captured near Stanley on 10th-11th May 1919 and are preserved in the Stanley Museum as first recorded by Mr. A. G. Bennett in the *Ibis*, 1926, where he observes that since then one or two have been taken from nesting burrows on islands covered with tussock grass, but so far without eggs. Mr. Bennett then states : " They undoubtedly do breed in the Falklands ". No definite proof of this was forthcoming until Dr. Brian Roberts, now of the Scott Polar Institute at Cambridge, made the discovery of a nesting colony on Kidney Island, East Falkland, during a week which he spent on the island from 28th November to 3rd December 1936—of this more anon.

The only breeding evidence which Dr. Roberts was able to gather during his *first* visit to the Falkland Islands in December 1934, was supplied by one rotten egg taken on Kidney Island by A. G. Bennett on 21st December 1933 and broken. This egg measured 2¾ × 2 in. (51 × 70 mm.) ; it was typically petrel in shape and texture but so rotten as to be quite unpreservable. Bennett dug into several holes but found no birds. Dr. Roberts saw no sooty shearwaters on Kidney Island in

---

[1] Normally only one egg is laid. If these paired eggs were laid by one bird it is most unusual.

1934 but they were heard calling—a cry very similar to that of the Manx shearwater.

On 11th April 1936 a dead sooty shearwater was found on the western end of Kidney Island, at which point there were, so Dr. Roberts discovered, numerous promising burrows which were too small to be those of Jackass penguins or Cape hens.

A letter from George Scott to Dr. Roberts in 1936 informed him that a few sooty shearwaters breed on New Island and that he had in his possession an egg taken from a burrow there.

That was the fragmentary evidence available when Dr. Roberts landed on Kidney Island for the second time. The following, taken from his diary, shall tell of his discovery in his own words. These notes have never before been published as Dr. Roberts's work on the Falkland petrels was interrupted by the war and has never been completed. He has most kindly allowed me to publish them in this volume :

BREEDING IN THE FALKLAND ISLANDS

Dr. Brian Roberts (Scott Polar Institute)

DISCOVERY OF NESTING COLONY

(Notes made during a week's stay on Kidney Island,
28th November-3rd December 1936)

28th November 1936. While searching in the place mentioned above where a dead bird had been found, I put my foot through the roof of a burrow which contained an incubating bird. This proved to be a ♂ (No. 432), but unfortunately the egg, which was quite fresh, was smashed.

This is the first authentic record of breeding in the Falkland Islands. Excavations in the vicinity later disclosed four more birds—two ♂♂ sitting on fresh eggs, a ♂ in an empty nest and a ♀ incubating (eggs Nos. 433, 434, and 435 respectively).

The colony is on a precipitous cliff face, grown over with big tussock clumps, at the south-west end of the island. The burrows averaged about three feet long. Most of them had two or more entrances, and seemed almost invariably to curve back on themselves so that the nest cavity was below and in front of the entrance. They were all thickly lined with small bits of dry tussock grass.

During this visit to Kidney Island I found three distinct colonies of sooty shearwaters. It is noteworthy that nearly every burrow was on a steep cliff face. The species is, in fact, quite common.

At night one occasionally hears them calling as they fly overhead ; a sound which is almost identical with that of the Manx shearwater, but slightly more mellow.

Owing to the difficulty of cliff climbing in the dark, I only made one late visit to a breeding place, between 10.30 and 11.30 p.m. on 29th November. There was little to be seen except occasional birds flying round very swiftly with rapid wing beats.

The first birds to come in from the sea arrived each night about the same time as the Cape hens, *e.g.* 1¼ hours after sunset.

Later, they were to be found sitting about aimlessly in the runways between the tussock clumps or at the entrances to their burrows. I saw no signs of courtship.

Five adults were skinned and two more killed for examination.

No.	Sex	Weight
432	♂	34 oz.
433	♂	30 oz.
434	♂	28 oz.
435	♂	28 oz.
436	♀	32 oz.
—	♀	31 oz.
—	♂	29 oz.

The stomachs of all seven specimens contained (exclusively) small cephalopod beaks. Two of the birds carried mallophaga under the wing.

In December 1934 Dr. Roberts examined the two specimens (already mentioned) in Port Stanley Museum. If more than one race is recognized the Falkland Islands' birds would bear the name *Puffinus griseus chilensis*, which is the name used by Dr. Roberts in his note-book when referring to the sooty shearwater. The two examples in the museum showed the following measurements which Dr. Roberts took on the spot :

No.	Sex	Locality	Date	Wing	Tar-sus	Bill greatest width	Length of ex-posed culmen	Middle toe and claw
71	♂	Killed by striking Cape Pembroke Lighthouse	9.5.18	319	56	14	45	65
72	♀ juv.? *	Found wounded on Port Stanley Common	11.5.19	287	52	13	39	63

* The bill of No. 72 is considerably smaller than that of No. 71. The tip plates are much lighter and less developed ; presumably juvenile.

REFERENCES : Original Description : *Procellaria grisea* Gmelin, *Syst. Nat.*, vol. i, pt. 2, 1789, p. 564, based on the grey petrel of Latham, *Gen. Syst.*, vol. 3, pt. 2, p. 399, " in hemisphaerio australi inter 35° et 50° " = New Zealand. Cf. A.O.U. Check List, 5th ed., 1957, p. 15.

Genus *PTERODROMA* [1] Bonaparte

BLACK-CAPPED PETREL

Pterodroma hasitata (Kuhl)

ALEXANDER WETMORE, D.SC.
(Research Associate, Smithsonian Institute)

An Accidental Visitor, which has been obtained once near Swaffham,
in Norfolk

IDENTIFICATION : The white under-surface and dark back identify this bird immediately from two of the other three species of the gadfly petrel group that have come as vagrants to the British Islands, since these others, the Kermadec [2] and Bulwer's petrels, have the plumage dark throughout. The third, the white-winged petrel, is so much smaller, with the wing less than 250 mm. and the bill more slender and delicate, that it may be recognized immediately should there be any necessity of checking identity of a specimen in this group of birds. The black-capped petrel, in addition to the general style of coloration mentioned, has the rump and upper tail-coverts and the forehead white. There is also slight indication of a whitish band across the back of the neck.

A related species, called locally the " Blue Mountain Duck " that nested formerly in the Blue Mountains of Jamaica, described under the name *caribbea* by Carte in the *Proceedings* of the Zoological Society of London in 1866, is blackish-grey throughout, being only slightly paler on the under-surface than on the back. In a study of these petrels published in the *Proceedings* of the California Academy of Sciences in 1918 Leverett M. Loomis suggested that the white-breasted (*hasitata*) and dark-breasted (*caribbea*) birds might be merely colour phases of a single species. This proposal Robert Cushman Murphy believed " highly probable " in 1936 and it has been accepted by James Bond in his *Check-List of the Birds of the West Indies*. The discussion and action described are interesting and suggestive but seem to require further study, a matter of some difficulty since the bird of Jamaica appears to have been exterminated years ago by the introduced mongoose. W. E. D. Scott in 1891 had report of two killed

[1] The black-capped petrel and its allies are here retained in the genus *Pterodroma* in which the authors of *The Handbook of British Birds*, following Hartert, quite properly placed them. The present author takes the gravest exception to the juggling of genera in the British Procellariiformes, as instanced in the recently issued *Check-List of the Birds of Great Britain and Ireland* (1952) by a sub-committee of the B.O.U. Although an original member of the List Committee, 1946-48, and later again co-opted, for a specific purpose, the writer had no part in the final decisions as regards the nomenclature employed, and dissociates himself from the Committee's findings in this respect. D. A. B.

[2] The advisability of dropping the Kermadec petrel from the British List is discussed in the next section (see p. 150).

by a hunter a short time previous, which seems to be the last recorded occurrence. Two specimens in the U.S. National Museum were secured by Edward Newton in St. Andrews, Jamaica, on 17th November 1879, and other available specimens seem to be equally old.

American ornithologists place the black-capped petrel and its close relatives in a separate genus, *Pterodroma*, calling it *Pterodroma hasitata*. It is so listed in the *Check-List of North American Birds* of the American Ornithologists' Union, in which decision Dr. Bannerman agrees with us.

OCCURRENCE IN GREAT BRITAIN : The inclusion of the black-capped petrel in the British list is based on a wanderer, captured in Norfolk at Southacre near Swaffham, in March or April 1850. The bird was caught alive in a furze bush by a boy who killed it when it bit his hand, but fortunately retained it. The falconer of Mr. Edward Clough Newcome of Hockwald Hall, near Brandon, who by chance was hawking in the neighbourhood, saw the petrel in the boy's possession and brought it to his employer. Mr. Newcome, recognizing the bird to be peculiar, mounted the specimen, which proved to be a female, and placed it in his collection. Here it came to the attention of Alfred Newton, who published a detailed account of it in the *Zoologist*, vol. x, 1852, pp. 3691-3698, including two sketches by Wolf, one depicting the bird standing erect like a gull, a position impossible for a petrel. Thomas Southwell, in Henry Stevenson's *Birds of Norfolk*, vol. iii, 1890, pp. 361-364, referred to the specimen as " still the chief attraction in the Newcome collection ". He stated further that the bird had been remounted and included a coloured plate, also by Wolf, showing the petrel at rest on extended legs in a natural attitude. Subsequently the specimen came into the possession of Lieutenant-Colonel T. S. N. Hardinge by whom it was presented in 1949 to the Norwich Castle Museum. There it is (1957) on exhibition in the Bird Gallery as I learn from Miss Ruth Barnes, Keeper of Natural History.

DISTRIBUTION ABROAD : The black-capped petrel, described scientifically by Heinrich Kuhl in 1820 from a bird now in the Leiden Museum, was recorded originally only as from the " Mer de l'Inde ". There are four specimens in the Museum of Comparative Zoology at Harvard University, obtained on the Island of Guadeloupe in the Lesser Antilles by the naturalist L'Herminier in 1842. Two others, from Dominica, are preserved in the local museum on that island. Aside from this the bird has been reported in life from a number of wanderers similar to the one recorded from Norfolk. One of these is a specimen reported from the Museum of Boulogne-sur-Mer in France, supposed to have been obtained nearby, but with no certainty that this was true. From eastern North America records are more numerous, as birds, supposedly storm-blown, have been obtained in inland localities in Ontario, New Hampshire, Connecticut, New York, Ohio, Kentucky and Virginia, and near the sea-coast in eastern Florida. A number also have been recorded on the island of

Hispaniola in the Greater Antilles, both in Haiti and the Dominican Republic, lending basis to the belief that the species may nest somewhere in the inland mountains of that great island. In addition I have identified a bone, a broken humerus, obtained in a Carib Indian midden of pre-Columbian age at Paquemar, near Vauclin, on the island of Martinique, the only record for that island.

There have been a number of reports of living black-capped petrels seen at sea in the past thirty years at localities ranging from 250 miles east of Savannah, Georgia, and 100 miles west of the Azores, to a point south-east of Bermuda. It must be pointed out, however, that possibly some of these sight-records may refer to the nearly extinct Cahow or Bermuda petrel of the Bermudas which is distinguished mainly by its somewhat shorter wing, greyish rather than white rump, and smaller bill—differences that seldom would be noted in birds in flight.

HABITS : Available information on the life history of the black-capped petrel comes from ancient accounts of travellers in Dominica and Guadeloupe in the Lesser Antilles where the bird, known as the diablotin, was hunted for food in the mountain heights to which it resorted to nest.

Père Jean Baptiste du Tertre in 1654 was told by hunters that this petrel, whose meat was highly prized, nested in burrows in the highest mountains, appearing in lowland areas only at night. Père Jean Baptiste Labat, an early missionary, gives a long account of an overnight trip with four black hunters and a young creole in March 1696, to the high slopes of the Soufrière on Guadeloupe where the diablotins were nesting. He mentions especially the considerable noise made during the night by birds passing to and from the distant sea to feed. They nested in burrows in the ground, described as being like those of rabbits, and they were hunted with dogs, trained to bark when they found occupied holes. The petrels then were pulled out by means of poles with a hook at the end. The six men by midday had secured 198 birds, some of which were eaten immediately and the remainder carried down the mountain. Labat describes a second hunting trip that he made in early April, being careful to explain that the missionaries had decided that diablotins and lizards were of a nature that might be eaten by the religious at any time, even during Lent. Down-covered young, very fat, were found in March and were said to be ready to fly in May. Observations made on Dominica also are included.

The name diablotin, sometimes modified to diable, was given for superstitious reasons because of the nocturnal flights and calls of the petrels, though there seemed to be no fear of them on the part of the hunters.

The statements of Labat, other than his story of the hunting trip, have various discrepancies which indicate that his account, published in 1722, may have been written partly from memory. He described the young as clothed in yellow down like goslings, whereas the downy young of petrels of this group, so far as known, are dark grey, sometimes with a white breast. Also he says that each female was accompanied in the burrow by two young, though in the petrel family a single egg is the rule. His description and figure of the birds as black, one basis for the belief that the black-capped petrel may have two colour phases, one light and one dark, in view of what has been said above, may well be questioned, especially since the missionary was not a scientist.

Since these early days a number of competent field men have sought the nesting places of the diablotin without success. On Dominica, F. A. Ober in 1877 was unable to find any, though he was told that twenty years previously the birds had been abundant. They were said to have come from the sea to the tops of the highest mountains to nest. Colonel H. W. Feilden, writing in 1890, tells of an expedition to the Morne au Diable of Dominica that likewise was unsuccessful. The latest actual record for that island is of one found alive in Roseau on 2nd May 1932, that lived as a captive until 26th May. When it died it was prepared as a study skin for the local museum.

News of this capture was sent by Sir Charles Belcher who happened to be in the island at the time to Mr. C. W. Hobley, Secretary of the Society for the Preservation of the Fauna of the Empire, who communicated the facts to Dr. Bannerman at the British Museum. Photographs of the bird when still alive were sent at the same time. An account of the species and its past curious history was published by Dr. Bannerman in the British scientific magazine *Discovery* in the November number, 1932, with further details of the diablotin's re-discovery in Dominica and photographs of the living bird.

On Guadeloupe G. K. Noble in 1914 was told that the diablotin had nested formerly on the north and north-east slopes of Nez Cassé on the Soufrière, where the birds arrived in late September for a breeding season that extended until the following March. An ancient hunter whom he visited claimed that the whole side of the mountain where the birds had their nesting burrows had collapsed in a great earthquake in 1847, and that the petrels since then had not been seen. James Bond in recent years likewise has been unable to locate them. It seems definite, however, that a few still remain, so that there is still the possibility that their nesting-ground may be found somewhere in the rough, elevated terrain in the little-known interior mountains.

From 1st to 3rd June 1920, while I was at sea a short distance south-east of the Bermudas, *en route* from New York to Buenos Aires, I had excellent views of several of these petrels. While the smaller kinds followed the wake of the ship, these larger birds paid no attention to it but circled back and forth far at the side occasionally crossing before the bow of the steamer. Frequently on such occasions they passed within thirty or forty feet of me, and once I had three in view at once in my binoculars. The sailing flight was fairly swift, performed with stiffly spread wings which were stroked seldom though the course was changed frequently.   Usually they remained within ten feet of the surface of the water.   It is barely possible that some of these were the nearly extinct Bermuda petrel but I was certain at the time that the black-capped petrel was the one concerned.

REFERENCES : Original Description : *Procellaria hasitata* Kuhl, *Beitr. Zool.*, pt. ii, 1820, p. 142.   Type locality : Guadaloupe, West Indies.

A DISCUSSION

On the inexpediency of retaining the two Pacific species, the KERMADEC PETREL, *Pterodroma neglecta*, and the COLLARED PETREL, *Pterodroma leucoptera brevipes*, on the British List, and the possible acceptance of the CAPE PIGEON, *Daption capensis*, as an accidental wanderer to the British Isles.

My doubts as to the wisdom of retaining the first two species mentioned above on the list of genuine vagrants to the British Isles are of long standing, just as surely as my conviction that the cape pigeon should be mentioned—at any rate in square brackets.

My interest in this matter dates from 1913, when I was engaged upon a survey of the breeding dates and the distribution of the petrels and shearwaters of the North Atlantic islands, culminating in a lengthy paper in the *Ibis*, 1914, pp. 438-494.   Much extraneous matter then came under review.   About that time Gregory Mathews and Tom Iredale were engaged on the second volume of *The Birds of Australia*, and as we were all working in the Bird Room of the British Museum (Nat. Hist.) many questions relating to the life histories and status of the TUBINARES in various parts of the world were discussed between us.   I had recently been investigating the breeding petrels and shearwaters of the eastern Canaries, and had spent some months on these outlying islands and rocks.   My interest in the petrel family was greatly stimulated by my contacts with Mathews and Iredale, and although I have since had little opportunity to study these birds in the field my interest in them has never waned.

Mathews paid me the signal compliment of naming a genus of the petrel family in my honour and also a species, and though like several Mathews genera " Bannermania " for *B. hornbyi* has fallen by the way, *Puffinus bannermani* from Bonin Island has retained its status.   Tom Iredale in particular was an expert on petrels and his knowledge of the literature of the group was probably unrivalled.   It was about this time that the species then known as *Œstrelata neglecta* came under review and I well remember the discussion which took place as to whether the specimen upon which the British record rests had been correctly identified.   At Iredale's instance the bird in question was re-examined by W. R. Ogilvie-Grant,[1] then in charge of the Bird Department of the British Museum.

[1] *Bull. Brit. Orn. Club*, xxxiii, 1914, p. 124.

Ogilvie-Grant was sure from examination of the bird's primaries, which had white shafts, that the specimen was of the Kermadec Islands petrel, then known as Schlegel's petrel, but his decision was not acceptable to Iredale, an Australian, with very forthright views on life and people. He was absolutely convinced that no petrel from the Kermadec Islands could reach the British Isles ; he knew the species well in the field, having spent over ten months in their midst on Sunday Island, where thousands of *Œstrelata neglecta* (as they were then discovered to be) breed. He declared that they were not particularly strong fliers and that, unlike some others which wander far afield, the Kermadec petrel was a stay-at-home bird.

In 1914—the year that the First World War broke out—both Iredale and I published our respective petrel papers in the July number of the *Ibis*. Iredale's dealt with the surface-breeding petrels of the Kermadec Group, and in particular with the much-debated question as to whether Sunday Island and Meyer Island were inhabited by one species showing remarkable diversity in plumage, or by three incipient species as at least one ornithologist had suggested. Salvin was already of the opinion that the very light as well as the uniform dark birds were only colour variations of one very variable species—*Pterodroma neglecta*.

Iredale landed on Sunday Island on 31st December 1907 and left on 10th November 1908. The Kermadecs are completely isolated, 600 miles from the nearest land point, and at the time of his visit communication with the islands took place only once a year. Iredale remained for ten months, during which time he surveyed the breeding population very thoroughly and actually handled " thousands " of petrels. As a result of the investigation he rejected the " incipient species " theory in connection with the Sunday Island birds : " Every degree of coloration was met with in every location and there seemed no means of distinguishing any forms ". In his article he went on to enumerate the almost countless varieties encountered during a three-day tour of the island ; the birds fell into three classes, dark, light, and medium, about 40 per cent. being dark, 40 per cent. light, and 20 per cent. medium. He concluded by stating his considered opinion that only one species was present—a conclusion which, so it happened, was anticipated by Godman whose *Monograph of the Petrels* was published when Tom Iredale was actually on the Kermadecs. Iredale emphasized that Sunday Island (or Raoul Island) is situated on the 180th meridian of longitude and about latitude 28° S. and is approximately the farthest point east or west of Greenwich that it is possible to reach—a fact which the reader is asked to bear in mind.

Sunday Island—simply the rim of a volcanic crater—is some 7000 acres in extent. Three-quarters of a mile distant lies Meyer Island, a double-humped rocky isle only about 40 acres in extent and rising about 400 feet. Through stress of weather Meyer Island could not be explored as thoroughly as Sunday, but the birds there exhibited every style and combination of coloration although the extremes were much rarer than on Sunday. Iredale could find no detail where the Meyer Island petrels could be separated from those of Sunday Island, despite the fact that the breeding times of the two populations were so different.

Such then is the home of the Kermadec petrel which for fifty years has remained on the British List on the strength of a bird found dead near Tarporley, Cheshire, on 1st April 1908. It had not been recorded at that time from Australia or from New Zealand, as Iredale was at pains to point out. There appears to be no doubt that the specimen which was found near Tarporley " by a man who attends the weekly market at Chester " was examined in the flesh by Professor Newstead four days after it was stated to have been found. Its discovery was made known by Robert Newstead and T. A. Coward in *British Birds*, ii, 1908, p. 14, when a photograph was reproduced of the mounted bird, showing it to be one of the dark examples. The bird was reported to have been in an excellent state of preservation and to have shown no signs of having been in captivity. The mounted specimen was exhibited at a meeting in London of the British Ornithologists' Club, and according to Coward is now in the Chester Museum. In his contribution to the *Ibis*, 1914, Iredale entered judgement on all the species with which I have headed this article, and wrote :

In the " Hand-List of British Birds ". . . *Pterodroma neglecta* is admitted to the British List upon the strength of an occurrence of a bird found dead near Tarporley, Cheshire, April 1, 1908. Upon the same page *Pterodroma brevipes* Peale is also included, as a bird so identified was shot near Aberystwyth, Wales, in November or December 1889.

Neither of these two birds should figure in the British List as genuine wanderers to these shores. The first named, at my suggestion, has been re-examined and declared to be an authentic Kermadec specimen by Mr. W. R. Ogilvie-Grant of the British Museum. Though my own acquaintanceship with the Kermadec species is, as I have shown above [Iredale is here referring to the earlier part of his paper describing his ten-months stay on the Kermadec Is.], probably better than Mr. Grants,' I bow to his superior knowledge in the handling of bird-skins, and would therefore point out that it would be best, even if it be a Kermadec bird, to enter it in a footnote.

Iredale then continues :

Upon p. 155 of the " Hand List " Messrs. Hartert, Jourdain, Ticehurst, and Witherby write regarding *Daption capense*, which they do not admit to be a British bird : " Examples of this species, an inhabitant of the Southern Seas, have been recorded from the Dovey, 1879, near Dublin, 1881, and near Bournemouth in 1894, but former writers have excluded them as not being genuine wanderers with some reason ".

The extraordinary illogical argument that would admit *Oestrelata neglecta*

Schlegel to the British List and reject *Daption capense* Linné, I cannot uphold. The former has not yet been recorded from Australia or New Zealand, yet it can arrive half-way round the world in order to be admitted to the British List. Whilst, though *Daption capense* Linné has only to fly up the Atlantic Ocean, it must be rejected as unable to do so. Yet the powers of flight of the two species are exactly the converse, the *Daption* being a powerful sea-going bird, whilst the *Oestrelata* is hardly a wanderer at all.

The bird identified as *Pterodroma brevipes* Peale is now in the British Museum, and does not belong to that species.

Having made that terse statement (to which H. F. Witherby replied in a footnote under that species in *The Handbook of British Birds*) regarding the collared petrel,[1] Tom Iredale turned his guns upon F. Du Cane Godman, observing :

I have stated that Godman's acceptance of all the Kermadec forms as referable to one species [which he did in the *Monograph of the Petrels*], did not seem due to skilful judgement, as in the same place two species are admitted from South Trinidad Island, viz. *Oe. arminjoniana* Giglioli and Salvadori and *Oe. trinitatis* ibid. The only difference between these two species is that the latter is a uniform dark bird with wholly black legs, whilst the former is a variable coloured bird with sandalled legs. I have shown this character [of the coloration of the legs] to be absolutely valueless in connection with the Kermadec birds, and my examination of South Trinidad birds confirms me in the same conclusion.

As a matter of fact, the only difference apparent between the South Trinidad birds and the Kermadec ones, is that the former have slightly shorter toes and the latter have white shafts to the primaries, whilst the South Trinidad birds have dusky shafts. I might note that immature Kermadec birds also have dusky shafts. Mr. Grant lays great stress upon the latter character to decide the identity of the British specimen. I think that further investigation will show that white-shafted birds occur in the Atlantic. The British specimen is set up but it certainly seems to me to have the short toes of the South Trinidad form.

Under the circumstances I think I am perfectly justified in advising the non-inclusion of *Oestrelata neglecta* in the British List.

Mr. Iredale certainly infers in this article that the bird we have upheld as *Pterodroma neglecta* (which has changed its genus for the third time !) may prove to be *Pterodroma arminjoniana* (another variable species), which is much more likely to be capable of the journey to Tarporley than the Kermadec Islands' bird.

Or—noting the date of its capture—was it an April Fool ? If so it has been very successful.

Now to revert to the second species on the British List, *Pterodroma leucoptera brevipes*. In face of the statement by an Australian known to be well versed in the petrels, I made enquiries, in 1957, from the British Museum with the intention of having the specimen further examined. It

---

[1] Now figuring on the B.O.U. List as the white-winged petrel (no sillier name could have been chosen !) *Bulweria leucoptera brevipes*.

is a skin of considerable value as constituting the only British record. Godman in his *Monograph of the Petrels*, pt. 3, 1908, p. 210, states quite definitely that the specimen " shot in the British Isles between Borth and Aberystwith in the winter of 1899 . . . is now in the British Museum ", to which institution it was presented by Mr. Willis Bund, K.C. It was certainly there in 1914 about the time when Iredale wrote that it did not belong to *brevipes*. Moreover it is listed in the *Catalogue of Birds of the British Museum*. At my request a thorough search for this unique specimen has been made in the Bird Room and galleries and on 30th July 1957 a letter was received by the writer from Mr. R. W. Sims, who writes as follows : " We have searched everywhere for the specimen and there are now no more stones left to turn nor avenues to explore. According to the obsolete ' Guide to the Gallery of Birds ' by Ogilvie-Grant the specimen was No. 365 in the gallery. It was, presumably, there during the war when the gallery was shattered by the flying-bomb falling on the other side of Cromwell Road, and so was destroyed with the majority of exhibited specimens." The present writer was there on that fatal day when the bomb exploded and can vouch for the indescribable damage which was done—the gallery deep in plate glass from the shattered cases and heads, wings, and bodies of the mounted specimens strewn in all directions. If the British specimen of *Pterodroma brevipes* was in fact in the gallery at the time, it is not surprising that it cannot be found, but it seems an extraordinary thing that with other rare specimens it had not been evacuated to a safer retreat. Even more curious is the fact that a specimen with such a history attached to it should have been placed in the public galleries where birds are known to fade rapidly.

Its certain determination will always remain in doubt. That a petrel believed at the time to be the collared petrel was shot on the date and at the place named is not disputed. Its determination as *brevipes* was held in question by Tom Iredale, but it was evidently accepted as such by Gregory Mathews, who was in the chair at the List Committee meeting held on 18th February 1948 at which the decision was taken, with reference to the British occurrence, that *Pterodroma brevipes* (Peale) be placed as a race of *Pterodroma leucoptera* (Gould) and that it should appear in the British List as *Pterodroma leucoptera brevipes* (Peale). Had Mathews not concurred he must have raised the question of the specimen's identity at that meeting. So far as I know he did not. At the meeting held on 19th May 1948, the decision was taken to replace the genus *Pterodroma* by the genus *Bulweria* " as no important structural differences are to be found between the two genera " ! When our B.O.U. List is revised, which is badly needed already, it is to be hoped that some of the decisions reached in 1952 will be reconsidered. I believe that Mr. Mathews had been strongly influenced in his decision to accept the identification of the Welsh specimen by Mr. Witherby's statement published in *The Handbook of British Birds*, 1940, p. 66, where with reference to *Pterodroma leucoptera brevipes* he observes :

As the identification of this specimen has been questioned (see T. Iredale, *Ibis*, 1914, p. 435), it is as well to state that its underparts, except for the chin and throat, which are white, are darker than in other specimens I have seen and almost uniform, the feathers having such long grey-brown tips that the white bases are concealed, the axillaries and under tail-coverts are grey-brown with some fine white mottlings. The bird, however, is in full moult and the feathers of the underparts are newly grown and when worn would reveal more whitish. In all other respects, including the white shafts of its primaries and its measurements (wing worn about 210 mm., tail 96, tarsus 28, middle toe with claw 34, bill 23) the bird is like other examples of this species, and its identification has been confirmed by Mr. R. A. Falla, who has examined it. H. F. W.

In view of this very definite opinion expressed by two leading ornithologists, I do not feel justified in rejecting the species on my own responsibility, but agree that a specimen about which there has been so much dispute, and which is now apparently lost for ever, should appear in the British List *in square brackets*. I feel on surer ground in refusing to accept the Kermadec petrel as a genuine vagrant and on my determination to place the Cape pigeon on our list for the first time.

[COLLARED PETREL

Pterodroma leucoptera brevipes (Peale)]

Accidental Visitor which has occurred once *if properly determined as such*.
The specimen has been destroyed. See pp. 153-155.

IDENTIFICATION : The adult collared petrel has a slate-grey crown, and the upperparts rather darker grey with a tinge of brown on the scapulars, wing-coverts, and quills. The upper tail-coverts are grey and the tail-feathers blackish. The forehead and throat are white, with grey mottlings on the cheeks and a dark patch behind the eye. The breast and under-parts are either white with a grey pectoral band, or uniformly suffused with grey below the white throat. The under wing-coverts and axillaries are white. The bill is black. The tarsi and part of the toes are yellowish, the rest, including the outer toe, black. Its length is 10½ inches.

OCCURRENCE IN BRITAIN : A bird shot between Borth and Aberyst-with, Cardiganshire, at the end of November or beginning of December 1889 (see Discussion on p. 150) was determined as this species.

DISTRIBUTION ABROAD : The range as given by R. C. Murphy covers the islands of the New Hebrides and Fiji but nowhere else. Other races occur elsewhere in the Pacific. Under the circumstances I feel it is of little value to give any account of the habits of this small petrel. It is known to come within 200 miles of the Galapagos Islands but how the example, if correctly determined, crossed the Isthmus of Panama and the wide stretch of the Atlantic to reach our shores is a mystery we shall never solve.

[CAPE PETREL OR CAPE PIGEON

Daption capensis Linnaeus]

An Accidental Visitor

IDENTIFICATION : The Cape pigeon is very easily recognized by reason of its dark grey head, the mottled slate and white back, and the white patch in the middle of the outstretched wings. The underparts are white. It is 14 inches from bill to tail. The bill and feet are black. Dr. E. A. Wilson described the head and neck as all round dark plumbeous-grey inclining to blackish on the occiput and becoming white on the lower throat ; general colour above dark lead-grey chequered with white on the back, wings, and tail ; tail white with the apical portion blackish ; under-surface of body white with a few scattered spots of grey, particularly on the under tail-coverts and sides of body ; axillaries and under wing-coverts white. The primary quills are blackish along the outer web and at the tips, the inner webs are white ; the secondaries are white tipped with slate-grey.

OCCURRENCES IN BRITAIN : There have been three occasions in the past when the Cape pigeon has been taken in these islands but a doubt has existed as to whether they had reached this destination of their own account or had been released from a ship. The dates and localities where they appeared are as follows : estuary of the Dovey, Wales, 1879, recorded by Salter, *Zoologist*, 1895, p. 254 ; nr. Dublin, Eire, 30th October 1881, recorded by A. G. Moore, *Ibis*, 1882, p. 346 ; Bournemouth, recorded by M. A. Mathew, *Zoologist*, 1894, p. 396.

In *The Handbook of British Birds*, 1940, p. 80, Mr. Witherby says in a footnote that examples of this petrel have been known to be captured at sea and brought even as far as the Channel before being liberated. For this reason the occurrences had been considered by previous writers as not due to genuine wandering. Mr. Witherby, who gives it as his opinion that " its claims are probably at least as good as those of some other species ", excluded it from the list of vagrants to Britain on the strength of Captain Hutton's remark (*Ibis*, 1867, p. 188) that he was *informed* (itals. mine) by a sailor on board one of the Australian mail steamers that he once took half a dozen Cape pigeons alive (feeding them on salt pork) as far as the English Channel, but having a difference with the steward of the ship, who was part owner, he let them all fly away. This story is repeated by F. Du Cane Godman in his *Monograph of the Petrels*, p. 278.

The improbability of this fanciful story, which Hutton obtained at second hand from a sailor, does not appear to have been sufficiently realized by those who use it as an argument that *Daption capensis* did not, or could not, reach these islands of its own volition. The bird is one of the strongest fliers of the family to which it belongs, and as Iredale pointed out (*Ibis*, 1914, p. 434) it has only to fly up the Atlantic Ocean to be within British waters, a feat well within its capabilities. The Cape pigeon has reached France on more than one occasion (Hyères, Bercy) and even Holland. Within the last six years a black-browed albatross from the same home waters as the Cape pigeon has reached our shores and not for the first time either. In the Pacific *D. capensis* has reached the Marquesas Islands.

DISTRIBUTION ABROAD : The Cape pigeon ranges over the South Atlantic and South Pacific oceans, breeding, among many other places, in the South Orkney Islands, the South Shetland Islands, and Kerguelen Island. In the non-breeding season it is very commonly seen off the coasts of South Africa, where the writer first encountered it in July 1908 in latitude 28° S.; it occurs in great numbers in the Antarctic. During the two Antarctic voyages of the *Scotia* the Cape pigeon was one of the most abundant species observed. It was seen almost everywhere, both at sea and amid the ice as far south as 71° 50', though only in small numbers in this high latitude. In the late summer and autumn it occurs in great numbers in the Weddell Sea, far to the south of its breeding haunts, before it moves north to its oceanic winter quarters. Dr. Eagle Clarke suggested that this temporary excursion to the polar ice before migrating north might be explained by the superabundance of food to be found in the waters of the south at this time of year.

HABITS : Some excellent notes on the Cape petrel, as this species is more correctly named, were made by the members of the Scottish Antarctic Expedition to the South Orkney Islands. Extracts have already been quoted by Godman in his *Monograph of the Petrels* and by Gregory Mathews in his *Birds of Australia*, but as this species has not previously found more than the briefest notice in any book on British birds, it may not be out of place to give it some space here. In his reports [1] on the expedition Dr. Eagle Clarke paid much attention to *Daption capensis* for until the naturalists of the *Scotia* found its eggs on Laurie Island in December 1903 nothing was known of its breeding habits, though the bird itself had been known to voyagers since the days of Dampier in the closing years of the seventeenth century.

It was found to be a summer visitor to the South Orkneys and was entirely absent from May to September inclusive. The first of the spring

[1] W. Eagle Clarke, " Ornithological Results of the Scottish National Antarctic Expedition, Part i. The Birds of Gough Island ", in *Ibis*, 1905, pp. 247-268 ; " Part ii. On the Birds of the South Orkney Islands ", in *Ibis*, 1906, pp. 145-187 ; " Part iii. On the Birds of the Weddell and the adjacent Seas, Antarctic Ocean ", in *Ibis*, 1907, pp. 325-349.

immigrants was observed on 1st October, but it was not seen again until the 23rd, after which it became common.   No less than 20,000 were believed to nest on Laurie Island and they were to be found in hundreds all round the coasts.   In one cove over one hundred accessible nests were seen and many others out of reach.   They doubtless nest on several other islands in the South Orkneys which, as Dr. Clarke observed, may be regarded as the metropolis of the species.   They were never observed flying over the land but were to be seen on the wing in front of the cliffs, not wheeling over them like the snowy petrel, or sailing over the sea.   In the autumn they were only once seen after 21st April, on which date a flock was observed flying north.

Laurie Island, where the *Scotia* wintered, and which is the haunt of such vast numbers of Cape pigeons, may be briefly described for it was upon this island that the observations upon these petrels' breeding habits were carried out.   Twelve miles long by six at its broadest point, the island has an area of fully thirty square miles.

The interior is lofty, and several of the summits reach to an altitude of from 2000 to 3000 ft.   A number of deep bays run inland from north to south, separated by narrow rocky peninsulas or steep lofty mountain-ranges, and cause the island to have a very remarkable outline.   All the valleys are choked by glaciers, and what little exposed rock is visible is precipitous in the extreme.   Here and there on the lower slopes and at sea-level are a few acres of more or less level ground.   In winter the whole island, and even the faces of the precipitous cliffs, are covered with snow, which does not commence to disappear till October and November (the late spring and early summer months) ; but then many patches of moss-covered ground are laid bare, some of them bearing soil from six to ten inches deep.   Except this vegetable mould there is little soil anywhere.   The rocks, various kinds of graywacke, are mostly covered with lichens, especially *Usnea*, which, with various species of moss, form the entire terrestrial flora of the island.

The climate is essentially polar, a cold Antarctic current carrying streams of ice and numerous icebergs.   The most remarkable feature of the climate is the low, equable summer temperature which rarely rises above 37° or falls below 25°.   In winter, owing to the freezing up of the sea to the south, the islands are virtually on the edge of a continent.   Summer is characterized by almost continuously overcast skies, and the finest and clearest weather occurs in winter.   The snowfall is excessive, the sunshine very deficient, and strong gales are frequent.

The numerous nests of the Cape pigeon were placed either on ledges of cliffs, or in hollows in the earth and among small stones on steep scree-slopes, and all were quite open—a fact to which Eagle Clarke drew particular attention, for on Kerguelen Island young of this petrel had been found in burrows and grottoes.   It was noted on Laurie Island that before laying its eggs this petrel sat close on the nest for about a month and entirely disappeared from its nesting haunts for some ten days before the first eggs were laid. The eggs, which are white, were from oval to elongate-ovate in shape, the average size of " a large series " collected being 62·35 × 43·11 mm., showing a variation in length of 56·5-67·2 mm. and of width of 40·5-46·5 mm. Eggs were laid early in December.

The birds were found to be of a sociable nature, several frequently nesting near to each other on the same ledge, though isolated nests were not uncommon.

The collecting of eggs was a most unpleasant business as the birds have an objectionable manner of defence, ejecting an evil-smelling reddish fluid composed of what at that time was believed to be semi-digested remains. The birds were able to squirt this substance at an intruder with great precision from a distance of six or eight feet. They did not leave their nests readily and allowed themselves to be captured when sitting.

It was over twenty years after the visit of the *Scotia* to the South Orkneys that Dr. L. Harrison Matthews, F.R.S. (now the Director of the Zoological Society of London) put into Uruguay Cove on the north coast of Laurie Island in December 1925 and had his first sight of nesting Cape pigeons in the cliffs to the west of the Cove. This is what he saw : [1]

The cliffs above us were filled with hundreds of Cape pigeons sitting on their nests ; every ledge was crammed with them. They were as noisy as ever they are round a whaling factory, chattering and squabbling all the time, but here they had forgotten their usual habit and showed no fear at our approach, allowing us to touch them without flying away. . . .

The nests were made with chips of stone flaked off the cliff-face by the frost, and in a hollow at the top of each low pile there was a large white egg. While one bird incubated, its mate sat beside, chattering and cooing ; and though the eggs were already laid and well advanced in incubation, the birds' behaviour plainly showed that the love-making of the Cape pigeon is as noisy and demonstrative as that of any other petrel. There was still some beak- and head-nibbling going on, and it is probable that the general pattern of the nuptial display resembles that of other closely related species. I was surprised to find that none of the birds I touched tried to repulse me with a shot of stomach oil.

The origin of stomach oil in the petrels has been the subject of much speculation by naturalists, for this unpleasant habit of ejecting the fluid at will is not confined to the Cape pigeon but is common to many species of the Order. In 1949 Dr. Harrison Matthews, whose field notes I have already quoted, published in the *Ibis* the results of an investigation of this subject using four species—the fulmar, the storm petrel, the Manx shearwater, and the subject of this essay, the Cape petrel. All these birds were dissected and particular attention was paid to the structure of the glandular proventriculus. It is important to remember that the glandular

[1] Quoted from *Wandering Albatross*. Macgibbon and Kee, London 1951, pp. 71-72.

proventriculus is quite distinct from the crop, which is merely a receptacle for temporarily storing food, whereas the proventriculus is concerned with digestion. " At the lower end of the crop the gut is enlarged in diameter and has thickened walls lined with a glandular mucous membrane. This glandular part of the stomach, the proventriculus, is immediately followed by the gizzard, which is a very thick-walled muscular viscus in many species." Dr. Matthews found that in the petrels the proventriculus is much larger in proportion to the size of the bird than in other birds, and the ridges into which the mucous membrane is raised increase the surface area so that there is a much greater number of glands than would be possible were there no ridges as in most other birds. The secretions produced in the glands of the proventriculus are therefore likely to be relatively much larger in quantity in petrels than in other birds. Dr. Harrison Matthews propounds the theory that there is strong evidence (but not absolute proof) that the oil originates in the cells of the proventricular glands. He goes on to discuss the possible function of petrel oil. An ingenious theory was put forward by J. F. Green, writing in 1887 in *Ocean Birds*, that the oil is used to calm the surface of the sea during severe storms, an idea which Murphy pronounced as by no means ridiculous when one considers the " almost miraculous effect of a few drops of fish or seal oil upon the raging waters of the open ocean ". But Matthews has shown that stomach oil differs greatly in composition from seal and fish oils, pointing out that fulmar oil becomes waxy at $5°$ C. and sets solid at $0°$ C. The use of the oil for calming troubled waters is consequently improbable in high latitudes, whatever may happen in lower ones. Dr. Matthews concludes his instructive paper by saying that it appears likely that the petrel's habit of throwing oil has been developed from a simple escape reaction in which the bird empties its stomach in order to lighten itself for flying. The evolution of this into a defence reaction consists in directing the vomited matter towards the source of disturbance, even if the direction is merely incidental to the bird facing the intruder. If this occurs also when it is not necessary to lighten the body in order to fly, and if the stomach of the petrel normally contains a quantity of oil, the oil-squirting habit is the inevitable result. The suggestion sometimes put forward that the oil comes directly from the ingested food and is not a product of the bird's metabolism, is not favoured either by Dr. Matthews or by Dr. R. C. Murphy, the latter affirming that it is evidently a true secretion rather than a product of the digestion of fish, crustacea, or other marine organisms.

Godman in his *Monograph* points to the diversity in plumage exhibited by the series of specimens in the British Museum, which may no doubt he explained by the difference in season when the birds were obtained. Dr. Clarke, reporting on the voyage of the *Scotia* to the Antarctic, observes that in the autumn the specimens collected had the dark portions of their plumage of a fresh slate-black tint, instead of the faded brown presented by the examples obtained at the South Orkneys during the breeding season. He adds a note that whenever the *Scotia* stopped in the Weddell Sea for the purpose of taking soundings, these petrels settled on the water on the look-out for scraps of food. They were so tame that specimens were often captured by simply scooping them out of the water with a large landing-net. When in pursuit of food at or near the surface, the Cape petrels were seen to plunge downwards into the water after the manner of terns.

REFERENCES : Original Description : *Procellaria capensis* Linnaeus, *Syst. Nat.*, 10th ed., 1758, p. 132 : Cape of Good Hope.

Genus *BULWERIA* Bonaparte

BULWER'S PETREL   PLATE 8

Bulweria bulwerii (Jardine and Selby)

An Accidental Visitor

IDENTIFICATION : The entire upperparts of Bulwer's petrel are dark brown, the smaller wing-coverts, tail and quills almost black. The greater coverts are a light brown, forming a pale band down the wing. The chin is grey, the underparts sooty-brown with a tinge of grey. The bill is black, the eye dark hazel, the feet blackish and the tarsus pale flesh. It is 11 inches in length.

In the field, the body looks about the size of a fieldfare. The long pointed wings, the rather long wedge-shaped tail, and the dark brown colour throughout help to distinguish this petrel from all others in the Atlantic.

Petrels do not usually have pleasant voices, but in this Bulwer's is an exception. Ogilvie-Grant described it as consisting of four higher notes and a lower one, the latter more prolonged, the whole repeated several times and uttered in a loud cheerful strain, a pleasant contrast to the harsh voices of the large Atlantic shearwaters. Lockley described one call as a frog-like " whok " or " whow " like a very distant bark, as deep as a hound's.

OCCURRENCES IN THE BRITISH ISLES : The authentic instances of this petrel having been taken within our limits now number seven, but it has not been recognized since 1914 when the last example was obtained. The following are the dated occasions, all of which refer to England :

8th May 1837. One found dead on banks of river Ure, near Tanfield, Yorkshire.

3rd February 1903. One found dead near Beachy Head, Sussex.

4th February 1904. One found dead near St. Leonards, Sussex.

28th February 1908. One found dead near Scarborough, Yorkshire.

4th September 1908. One picked up near Winchelsea, Sussex.

24th October 1911. One picked up Pevensey, Sussex.

16th March 1914. One shot near Lydd, Kent.

DISTRIBUTION ABROAD : Bulwer's petrel is an inhabitant of the Western Atlantic islands, breeding regularly on the Madeira group, Porto Santo, the Salvage Islands, and the Canary Islands, and spasmodically on an island of the Azores and on one island in the Cape Verde archipelago. As a vagrant it has been recorded from a lightship between Corsica and Genoa on 3rd June 1898.

No distinction has been found between the Atlantic population of this petrel and those which breed in the Pacific, more especially on the Hawaiian Islands and the Marquesas. A race, very doubtfully distinguishable by its heavier bill, has been named *B. b. pacifica* from Japan and neighbouring islands.

HABITS : The Desertas, Porto Santo, and the Salvages are the islands most favoured by Bulwer's petrel in the Western Atlantic upon which to rear its young, but my own experiences with it have been mainly in the eastern Canary Islands where I found it nesting in some numbers on Montaña Clara, upon which uninhabited islet I lived amongst them for a week. Bulwer's petrel was originally described in 1828 by Jardine and Selby from one of the islands of the Madeira group, and the following year Heineken gave the name *anjinho* to the same bird in Brewster's *Edinburgh Journal*, in which he stated that the petrels arrived in the Madeira Islands in February and March but did not lay their egg until June. In point of fact, as Padre Schmitz has shown, the birds are seldom seen as early as February : in most seasons they appear towards the end of April and early in May, and do not lay until June. In the Canaries they come ashore about the same date as in Madeira, and I found many eggs in June, all of which were perfectly fresh. I was living on Montaña Clara from 7th to 14th June and breeding was then in full swing, birds sitting on their single egg in all the nest-holes.

Before giving a more general account of Bulwer's petrel in other groups, my personal experiences with it in the Canaries may be recounted. We had been on the look-out for it in all the islands of the eastern group which we had visited at the time when the birds should have been breeding, but it was not until I pitched my tents on Montaña Clara that we came across it. It is known in Tenerife as the " Tahoce negro ", but the fishermen who took me over to Montaña Clara called the bird " perrito ". This delightful bird is by far the most attractive in appearance of the Canary petrels. Montaña Clara is separated from the larger island, Graciosa, by a channel of turbulent water. It is heart-shaped, a mile and a quarter in length, three-quarters of a mile wide, and only half a square mile in area. It consists of a single large but imperfect crater, the walls of which rise to 700 ft. and fall from its highest point precipitously to the sea. On the south a steep ridge of lava, scoriae, and sandhills, intersected by narrow ravines, slopes to the south-east. On the low ground *Launœa*, *Suœda*, and *Mesembryanthemum* grow, but elsewhere the rocks are bare and jagged and the aspect is very barren. A single water-hole dependent on rain-water constitutes the only drinking supply. Landslides appeared to have taken place within recent times and in consequence the shore line is strewn with immense boulders under which Bulwer's petrels were breeding. Every available hole was occupied by one kind of petrel or shearwater or another : at least three and possibly four species were nesting at the same time in the caves and crevices of this very small islet, where competition for the suitable sites must be very great. We found that Bulwer's petrel nested mainly under the large boulders and as they are fairly small in comparison with the Atlantic shearwaters they could creep into holes or under boulders which the larger birds could not enter. They had their own particular breeding area and did not apparently encroach on the very similar terrain occupied by the Madeiran little shearwaters on the floor of the broken crater, one side of which was open to the sea. Many Bulwer's had their nest-holes just beyond the reach of the sea, but two pairs were forty feet up the side of the cliff and close together. We dug these holes out and found the birds sitting some two feet from the entrance. In no case where we could reach the bird was there any sign of a nest, the single white egg being laid on the bare stone. Two eggs brought to me from the same hole by my fisherman-companion may have been the products of two birds. Bulwer's petrel is almost entirely nocturnal in its habits and we never saw any flying in the vicinity of the island during the daylight hours. When pulled out of their holes they appeared dazed and crawled back under the stones as fast as they could. One bird placed on a rock in brilliant sunshine waddled to the edge and much to my surprise flew straight out to sea. We did not find that any egg had hatched by the time we left the island on 14th June : this is much later than the Madeiran little petrels whose young were almost ready to fly by that date.

In the Madeira group, where Bulwer's petrel is especially abundant, Ogilvie-Grant[1] secured a series of specimens from Deserta Grande, Lime Island (Porto Santo), and on Great Salvage ; but in none of these places had nesting commenced at the time of his visits. Godman had been more fortunate in 1871, and found it nesting in just such situations as I have described from Montaña Clara, *i.e.* at the foot of the cliffs under the fallen rocks. A great many years later—in 1925—Colonel and Mrs. Meinertzhagen landed on the Desertas on 18th May and spent three days examining the petrels and other birds which come to breed on these wave-lashed islets, close to Madeira (some 25 miles distant) but by no means easy to land upon. They camped on Deserta Grande, " the largest, precipitous, difficult of access and razor-backed ", and visited both the small islands, Bugio and Chão, but only on Deserta Grande did they find *Bulweria bulwerii*. At

---

[1] Ogilvie-Grant was in Madeira, Deserta Grande, and Porto Santo from 15th April for three weeks in 1890, and on Great Salvage from 23rd April for eight days in 1895 (cf. *Ibis*, 1896, p. 42).

dawn on 19th May a search was made for these birds among the holes around the camp and soon many were discovered to be at home. One typical nesting place in a hole in the rock, the entrance guarded by a cluster of white poppies, is the subject of an excellent plate in the *Ibis*, 1925, showing the sort of place beloved of this bird in the nesting season: 217 Bulwer's petrels were hauled out of their nesting-holes for examination, and twenty-seven were turned into museum specimens. It was found that fourteen were females and thirteen males, which shows that both sexes come and sit in their holes prior to egg-laying. Only one nesting-hole contained an egg at this early date. Colonel Meinertzhagen found that the nesting-holes were usually under rocks, sometimes among bare boulders, sometimes on the face of a steep slope, and sometimes in amongst dense bracken. On no occasion were two birds found in the same hole. Of the 217 petrels examined eleven had a leg severed at the junction of the tarsus and femur or slightly above it. The men from Madeira who had brought the Meinertzhagens to the Desertas had seen this before but could offer no explanation. Meinertzhagen suggested that the leg had been lost when the bird was snapped at by some large fish when "taxiing" along the surface of the ocean. Very few Bulwer's petrels were observed at sea by day—in fact I am surprised that any were seen near the island, for as I had discovered in the Canaries this bird is entirely nocturnal. If thrown into the air they fell in a heap and did not spread their wings as would a swallow, for instance, under similar circumstances. If placed on the ground they crawled into shade or the nearest hole. It was remarked that the local herring gulls were always on the look-out in case one of these petrels showed itself near the shore in daylight, and the men asserted that the gulls soon overhauled them and killed them. Meinertzhagen was unable to verify this statement—one that is difficult to credit as Bulwer's petrel is by no means a lazy or sluggish flier. Once on land, however, they would become an easy prey.

At certain times of the year Bulwer's petrel forsakes the islands where it rears its young and until the next breeding season comes round the birds are no more seen. Presumably the birds live far out at sea, sleeping on the water, but we know very little about them once they have left the islands. In the *Ibis* for 1914 I tabulated the daily life of Bulwer's petrel on the various islands where it nests. It is apparent that only exceptionally do they put in an appearance before the end of April, though odd birds may be recorded in March and I have a note that E. G. B. Meade-Waldo saw two or three at sea between Tenerife and Gomera on 6th February 1888. When Ogilvie-Grant visited the Salvages from 23rd to 28th April with his companions, Grönvold and Baring, the Bulwer's petrels which breed here later in the year had barely begun to arrive, and although they were seen and constantly heard the date was far too early for nesting.

In the Madeira group Padre Schmitz remarked their arrival " exceptionally early " on Porto Santo on 3rd May, but by 4th there were many on Deserta Grande. Schmitz states that May and the beginning of June are the most favourable months for finding the eggs but I would have said that one would be more certain of finding eggs in the last week of May and the whole of June. Meinertzhagen found only one Bulwer's petrel which had laid on the Desertas out of 217 examined between 18th and 20th May 1925. Early June would be my date to make certain of finding them. Down-covered young may be found from mid-July onwards and Schmitz records them on Porto Santo and on Madeira itself up to mid-September. Birds are all full-winged by the end of October and by November they have left the islands, not to be seen again on land until April and May of the following year.

No account of Bulwer's petrel would be complete without reference to Mr. R. M. Lockley's expedition to the Desertas, the Salvages, and Baixo Island, Porto Santo, in 1939. On the Desertas (10th-15th July) incubation was well advanced and some eggs were already hatching ; on Chão Deserta the species was found at all elevations from near sea-level to the top of both Desertas, using every kind of hole in rock debris, old walls, and cliffs, but apparently not excavating any burrows in the earth. On the Salvages (16th-17th July), these petrels were breeding exclusively in stone walls and rock crevices, eggs and newly hatched chicks were found ; while on Baixo (23rd-24th) they occupied most of the suitable small rock crevices, but were undergoing considerable persecution by Portuguese quarrymen temporarily on the island, who used them extensively for food. From a number of observations which Mr. Lockley made on Chão, it appears that Bulwer's petrel, like so many other petrels and shearwaters, incubates by shifts of two or more days and sometimes—as in one nest kept under observation—four days. He found, too, that the parent may stay with the chick during the day when it is first hatched. Mr. Lockley found—as I did on the Canaries—that it is strictly nocturnal in its activities on land. As soon as dusk had fallen the first Bulwers would fly over his camp site, behind which a flue-net had been erected. Sixteen adults were caught (and ringed) in this net within an hour, then the arrival flight seemed to cease, the pairs probably having settled on their nests. During the hour before and after midnight nothing came to the net. Later a number of ringed petrels which had been caught in the net and released were found again in their holes.

Evidence of courtship was witnessed on only one occasion when a pair in a hole without an egg attracted attention by a quickened version of the normal call which ran into a stream of " whok-whok-whok " non-stop for over a minute. It suggested great excitement and was not unlike the deep call of *Larus marinus* during coition, though, of course, very much fainter. A chick born during Mr. Lockley's visit dried rapidly and was covered profusely with black down about half an inch long, the head especially having a thick downy crop. There was no bald spot on the crown. The eyes were open and the chick was very precocious compared with the new-born nestling of the storm petrel. A nestling born on 13th July, when taken next day out of the crevice and placed on the rocks in sunlight, immediately began climbing towards cover, using its bill (still showing the egg-tooth) and white stumps to hook itself upwards and forwards.

Discussing the breeding competition between the petrels and shear-waters, Mr. Lockley remarked that there seemed to be pressure of population resulting from competition for nest-holes among all five species of petrels on Great Salvage. It was found that all the large rock-holes are occupied by (to use his nomenclature) *Puffinus kuhlii* during the summer, and the small rock crevices by *Bulweria bulwerii*. In one or two instances he found the latter incubating in a cranny within the larger cave of the large shearwater (*kuhlii*). On 16th-17th July the burrows in the soil were found to be occupied principally by *Pelagodroma marina* fledglings, by a few incubating adults of *Oceanodroma castro*, and still fewer unemployed *Puffinus assimilis*. Of these three petrels only the frigate petrel (*P. marina*) used the soil-burrows exclusively.

I have included two other groups of islands in the Western Atlantic where Bulwer's petrel has been recorded as breeding. Up to 1914 when I was working on this group there was no record from the Azores except the statement in 1855 of Dr. Bolle that the native land of *B. bulwerii* appeared to be the Azores. He was so far off the mark in this observation that no one ever recorded a nesting Bulwer's from the Azores, and I paid no more attention to that group. At last, however, in the spring of 1937 a man sent to the islet of Villa, near Santa Maria, returned with a live Bulwer's petrel and its egg which were identified by Colonel Agostinho,[1] to whom belongs the credit of this interesting discovery. Whether or not it was a spasmodic laying or whether larger numbers now revert to the Azores in the breeding season we shall not know until some ornithologist visits this group intent on solving the problem.

The other archipelago from which we had scant news of this petrel is the Cape Verde Islands. Neither Fea nor Boyd Alexander found it during their explorations and it was left to Correia to find it breeding for the first time. Twenty-five eggs and fifteen adults were collected on Raza from 17th to 26th May, 1922, and two adults and three downy young at Cima, one of the Rombos isles, between 22nd June and 2nd July. Mr. Correia's brief notes merely stated that Bulwer's petrel—the " João Preto " of the islanders—was found nesting among loose stones and that he seldom saw more than a pair, or at most four birds, in flight over the sea together. The twenty-five eggs which he obtained showed considerable

[1] Mayaud, *Alauda*, 1937, p. 314.

variation in dimensions. Dr. Murphy, who reported on this collection,[1] describes some of them as approaching conical shape. Measurements of six showed max. 31 × 45 mm. Min. 30 × 43 mm. and 31 × 41 mm. When Dr. W. R. P. Bourne made his ornithological survey of the Cape Verdes [2] in 1951 he failed to see Bulwer's petrel once he had passed the latitude of the Canaries, though the young should have been fledging in July in the Cape Verde Islands. It is difficult to account for this as Bourne was in various islands of the group from 13th July until 24th September. The erratic nesting times of the various petrels and shearwaters in the islands off the north-west African coast have been the subject of speculation by several naturalists [3] and various theories have been propounded to account for it. Interspecific competition for food and nesting-sites are the principal causes suggested; but neither of these seems to me to offer sufficient explanation, though in some cases the competition for nest-sites is doubtless of paramount importance. It does not, however, cover all the cases in which this " staggered " nesting takes place.

Before concluding this article I would refer to the egg-measurements of Bulwer's petrel as recorded by Jourdain, who gives the average of seventy-three eggs (including twenty-five by Schmitz) as 42·9 × 31·2 mm. Max. 47 × 30 mm. and 42 × 33 mm. Min. 39·6 × 30·4 mm. and 42 × 29·6 mm.

REFERENCES : Original Description : *Procellaria bulwerii* Jardine and Selby, *Illustr. Orn.*, vol. ii, 1828, p. 65 and text : Madeira or near by.

Genus *FULMARUS* Stephens

FULMAR

PLATE 11

Fulmarus glacialis glacialis (Linnaeus)

A Summer Resident which has spread tremendously within recent years
as a breeding species around our coasts

[*Author's Note* : It was my wish that this essay be entirely from the pen of James Fisher, who had undertaken to write it. He has made a life study of his subject and published a book of close on 500 pages on the fulmar's history and life. Owing to a sudden illness Mr. Fisher was obliged to abandon his task half completed, and the author of this book has finished the essay, drawing extensively from Mr. Fisher's volume for the facts, and on some other material. The

[1] Murphy, *Bull. U.S. Nat. Mus.*, l, 1924, pp. 211-278.
[2] Bourne, in *Ibis*, 1955, pp. 508-556.
[3] See R. M. Lockley, in *Ibis*, 1952, pp. 144-157, esp. p. 155 ; also W. R. P. Bourne, in *Ibis*, 1955, pp. 508-556, esp. p. 531.

paragraphs headed Local Distribution [1] and Populations and List of Colonies, General Distribution, Colour Phases, and the Atlantic fulmar at sea, were written by Mr. Fisher in 1958 especially for *The Birds of the British Isles*. The rest of the essay is a compilation by myself, mainly from Mr. Fisher's writings. Acknowledgment is made to Messrs. Collins (London) for permission to quote from *The Fulmar*, 1952.]

IDENTIFICATION : The fulmar is an unmistakable bird, combining features of appearance and flight which make for easy recognition whether at rest or at sea. It has been described as a large stocky petrel having light and dark colour phases with all degrees of intermediates between the extremes. Its length is 19-20 inches, the wing-spread 40-42 inches. The head, neck, and underparts of most Atlantic fulmars are white, often faintly—but never more than faintly—tinged with yellow. The head is large and round ; and when the fulmar flies or sits it seems to have no neck (or a very thick neck), for the head merges into the body to form a streamlined profile, scarcely relieved by any neck depression. In flight the fulmar appears to watch the observer with cold, dark eyes, as Eric Linklater once described to James Fisher ; an illusion produced not only by the dark brown iris but by a smallish triangular patch of bristly black-grey feathers immediately in front of the eye itself. Seen from above the fulmar is silvery-grey, of varying intensity, though about midsummer, when some of the grey barbules are shed from the back, the upper parts often look brown. The silvery-grey starts where the neck meets the back and is fairly uniform over the back and mantle, becoming lighter over the tail. The tail is pale grey, whitish at the edge. In flight the primary flight feathers, those on the outer half of the wing, look dark grey, clearly darker than the silvery-grey of the secondary feathers of the inner half of the wing. This dark grey is relieved by a pale patch not far from the wing-tip. The underside of the fulmar's wings is white, irregularly bordered with dark grey.

The colour of the fulmar's legs and feet varies very much from yellow through greens to bluish flesh-colour.

A special feature of the fulmar and one which arrests the eye immediately at close quarters is the deep, powerful, tube-nosed beak. The end of the upper mandible is roundly curved to fit over the bevelled end of the lower mandible, and forms a sharp hook. The two nostrils are completely enclosed in a horny tube on the top of the culmen and are separated by a thin septum or membrane. The colour of the bill is very variable ; the tip sections of both upper and lower mandible are usually

---

[1] The first full enquiry into the fulmar's distribution, and a census of the fulmar population in the British Isles, was begun in 1934 by James Fisher and George Waterston under the auspices of the British Trust for Ornithology. Their exhaustive report appeared in *The Journal of Animal Ecology*, x, No. 2, 1941, pp. 204-272.

yellow, but the rest of the bill may be anything from olive-green to bluish-grey. The tube is variably dark, sometimes grey-black, sometimes yellow-brown.

The flight is truly characteristic and, as Mr. Fisher has stressed, no novice need confuse the fulmar with a gull. Fulmars' wings have no angle but an almost straight leading edge.

LOCAL DISTRIBUTION[1] AND POPULATIONS : Until 1878 the only breeding colony of fulmars in the British Isles was distributed over the smallish steep archipelago of St. Kilda in the Hebrides—the westernmost islands of Scotland. As the consequence of a spread and increase of numbers which started about 120 years earlier in Iceland (and which continues until the present day) fulmars started to nest in Shetland in that year ; and in the subsequent eighty years have spread all round our coasts until by 1949 they were known to have laid eggs in at least 365 separate places, and to be " prospecting " an additional 212 suitable nesting-sites. Since 1949 further increases have taken place, and though the fulmar still prospects about twenty new potential colony-sites in the British Isles every year, there will soon be a shortage of new sites, and the increase, which is still (1959) geometric and only slowly slowing, will presumably show itself more by the increase of population at existing stations than through novel spread.

The fulmar population of St. Kilda appears—as far as the evidence goes—to have been fairly stable throughout history. The islands were deserted by their human natives in 1930, and in the previous century an average of about ten thousand young fulmars a year were taken for food by an average of under ninety (between 1855 and 1921 never more than eighty or less than seventy) inhabitants. In 1931 T. H. Harrisson roughly estimated about 25,500 breeding pairs in the archipelago ; in 1939 the writer counted about 21,000 occupied nests, in 1949 about 38,000. In 1956 A. Anderson counted almost exactly the same number of occupied nests (c. 19,400) on Hirta, the main island of St. Kilda, as the writer counted in 1949 (c. 19,900).

By 1949 the British fulmar population occupying nest-sites at breeding-stations outside St. Kilda was estimated (Fisher, 1952, p. 257) at just under 70,000 pairs : it is safe to say that since 1878, when the first new colony was established on Foula in Shetland, the British population has trebled. So fast has it increased that it is certain that our islands were continually colonized from outside, obviously from Iceland, and from the Faeroe Islands (first colonized from Iceland in or before 1839), until about 1915 ; since then the increase can theoretically be accounted for by the offspring of British stock, but it is very likely that colonization has continued until the present day.

[1] The sections on Local and General Distribution were received from Mr. James Fisher in August 1958 and can be relied upon as completely up to date.

The directions of the spread in Britain all point to a colonization from the Faeroe Islands ; the first Faeroe island to be colonized was Suðuroy, the southernmost, only 180 miles from Foula, the first British colony outside St. Kilda ; St. Kilda is 274 miles from Foula.

During the period of certain colonization from abroad fulmars were first proved to breed in the following places : 1878, Foula,* Shetland : 1887, North Rona and Sula Sgeir,* Hebrides : 1892, Papa Stour,* Shetland : 1896, Eshaness,* Shetland : 1897, Ramna Stacks, Hermaness and Saxa Vord, Shetland : 1898, Noss,* Shetland : 1900, the Kame of Hoy,* Orkney : 1901, Westray, Orkney ; Neap of Norby, Shetland : 1902, Berneray * and the Flannans, Hebrides ; Fetlar, Shetland : 1903, Handa,* Sutherland ; Fair Isle * and North Roe, Shetland : 1904, Cló Mór * and Strathy Point, Sutherland : 1905, Dunnet Head, Caithness ; Rousay, Orkney ; Fitful Head * and Horse of Burravoe, Shetland : 1906, Whalsay, Shetland : 1907, Sumburgh Head, Shetland : 1909, Face of Neeans, Shetland : 1910, Cape Wrath, Sutherland ; the Shiant Isles,* Hebrides ; Uyea and Wedder Holm, Shetland : 1911, Berriedale Ness, Caithness ; Brough of Birsay, Crustan, Costa Head, N. Deerness and Copinsay, Orkney ; Out Skerries, Shetland ; Portacloy and Stags of Broadhaven, Mayo : 1912, Grey Head and Burgh Head, Orkney ; Kame of Reawick, Uyeasound, Aithsness, S. Bressay, Shetland ; Horn Head, Donegal : 1913, Allar Head, Hebrides ; Papa Westray, Orkney ; Brindister and Mousa, Shetland ; Great Skellig, Kerry : 1914, Am Buachaille and Bulgach, Sutherland ; Marwick Head, Orkney ; Lingness, Shetland. Many of these, the older British colonies, are now very big after a quite steady increase in population ; besides St. Kilda, all those in the above list marked with an asterisk (*) had over a thousand occupied nest-sites by 1957, as did a few younger colonies.

The following list shows the dates upon which the British Watsonian vice-counties were colonized up to 1957. Under " first prospected " the year shown is ordinarily that in which fulmars were first seen actually landing upon a cliff or other potential breeding-place in the vice-county ; years in brackets with a question mark are those when fulmars were first seen flying around a suitable breeding-place in the vice-county without actually landing. The " first bred " years are strictly those in which an egg or young was first seen in the vice-county.

ENGLAND, WALES, AND SCOTLAND

No.	Watsonian Vice-County	First prospected	First bred
1	West Cornwall	1936	1944
2	East Cornwall	1937	1946
3	South Devon	1943	1949
4	North Devon	1935	1944
6	North Somerset	1951	—
9	Dorset	1943	1952

No.	Watsonian Vice-County	First prospected		First bred
10	Isle of Wight	(?1942)	1953	—
14	East Sussex		1946	—
15	East Kent	(?1944)		—
19	North Essex	(?1953)	1955	—
25	East Suffolk	(?1948)		—
27	East Norfolk		1939	1947
28	West Norfolk	(?1951)		—
41	Glamorgan	(?1944)	1953	1957
45	Pembroke		1930	1949
46	Cardigan		1944	1947
49	Caernarvon		1937	1945
52	Anglesey		1938	1947
61	South-east Yorkshire		1918	1922
62	North-east Yorkshire		1921	1927
66	Durham		1926	1927
67	South Northumberland		1928	1928
68	Cheviot		1919	1928
70	Cumberland		1938	1941
71	Isle of Man		1930	1936
73	Kirkcudbright		1942	1956
74	Wigtownshire		1928	1932
75	Ayrshire		1936	1939
81	Berwickshire		1914	1921
82	East Lothian		1923	1930
83	Midlothian	(?1940)	1947	—
84	West Lothian		1954	—
85	Fife (with Kinross)	(?1914)	1921	1931
90	Angus or Forfar		1920	1921
91	Kincardine		1914	1920
92	South Aberdeen	(?1956)		—
93	North Aberdeen		1913	1916
94	Banff		1914	1920
95	Moray		1919	1923
97	West Inverness (with N. Argyll)	(?1933)	1957	—
98	Argyll (Main)	(?1947)		—
100	Clyde Isles	(?1931)	1946	1948
101	Kintyre	(?1921)	1937	1940
102	South Inner Hebrides		1918	1924
103	Mid Inner Hebrides	(?1924)	1925	1929
104	North Inner Hebrides		1929	1930
105	West Ross	(?1931)	1933	1937
106	East Ross		1919	1924
107	East Sutherland		1936	1936
108	West Sutherland		1897	1903
109	Caithness		1900	1905
110	Outer Hebrides (excl. St. Kilda and Rockall)	(?1881)	1886	1887
111	Orkney	(?1889)	1896	1900
112	Shetland		1876	1878

IRELAND

No.	Watsonian Vice-County	First prospected		First bred
1	South Kerry	(?1889)	1913	1914
3	West Cork		1935	1938
4	Mid Cork		1945	—
5	East Cork		1945	—
6	Waterford		1930	1950
9	Clare		1924	1924
12	Wexford		1929	1930
16	West Galway		1931	1932
20	Wicklow		1946	1951
21	Dublin		1935	1936
27	West Mayo		1907	1911
28	Sligo		1939	1939
34	East Donegal	(?1913)	1915	1925
35	West Donegal		1907	1912
38	Down		1939	1954
39	Antrim		1921	1921
40	Londonderry		1934	1939

GENERAL DISTRIBUTION : *Fulmarus glacialoides*, the Antarctic fulmar, should be regarded as of the same superspecies as the northern fulmar (*Fulmarus glacialis*) and is probably its ancestor ; the two species differ principally in the shape and size of their bills. The Antarctic fulmar breeds on several mainland cliffs and offshore rocky islets around the Antarctic continent ; and in the South Shetlands, South Orkneys, South Sandwich Islands and Bouvet Island (with Lars Island) : altogether a couple of dozen stations are known at present. At sea it ranges into South Atlantic, Indian Ocean, and South Pacific, and has been recorded on the American Pacific coast north of the Equator.

Of the three generally recognized subspecies of the northern fulmar, *F. glacialis rodgersii* Cassin of the Pacific is closest to *F. glacialoides*, with a bill intermediate between those of the Antarctic and Atlantic fulmars. It nests for certain on at least six of the Kurile Islands ; on the two principal islands of the Commander Islands ; on at least four islands in the central and western Aleutian chain ; on the Pribilov archipelago, and St. Matthew and Hall Islands farther north in the Bering Sea ; in the Semidi Islands, south of Kodiak Island off the Alaska Peninsula. It probably also nests on islands by Afognak Island, north of Kodiak Island, and at Indian Point, near Cape Chaplina, Chukotskii Land, Siberia.

In spite of various statements in a somewhat confused literature there is no evidence that the Pacific fulmar nests on the Kamchatka Peninsula or St. Lawrence Island—or anywhere north of the Bering Strait, where the north coast of Chukotskii Land, Wrangel and Herald Islands, and Prince Albert Land (Victoria Island) have all been mentioned as the localities of breeding stations. However, non-breeders, and birds operating long distances from the nearest breeding places, operate through the year into the Polar Basin as far as Wrangel Island and Cape Barrow, when ice conditions permit. There is no evidence that the population meets any of the Atlantic subspecies in the Arctic. Southward the dispersed winterers and young or non-breeding birds operate to about 33° N. off the south-east of Japan, to an unknown distance in the open Pacific, and to San Diego, California—sometimes to Lower California, and Mexico.

The Atlantic-Arctic population of the northern fulmar is separated into two races, *F. g. minor* Kjærbølling and the typical race *F. g. glacialis* Linnaeus. The population breeding in the Canadian Arctic belongs to *minor*, a form smaller than *glacialis* with a bill intermediate in width between the slender bill of *rodgersii* and the broad heavy bill of *glacialis*, and shorter than that of either. The colonies in Canada have still to be investigated and the status of many is uncertain. The greatest colony in Baffin Island is probably that at Cape Searle on the east coast, where V. C. Wynne-Edwards estimated about 100,000 nests in 1950; besides this there are probably five, and possibly more, on the east coast, and certainly one, possibly two, in Admiralty Inlet, north Baffin Island. There is also certainly a colony at Cape Vera on Devon Island, and another on Smith Island off Ellesmere Island.

The fulmars of west Greenland are probably intermediate in measurements between the *minor* group of the Canadian Arctic and the typical *glacialis* of the Atlantic proper. Finn Salomonsen confirms that there are now colonies in the Thule area (one), the Upernavik area (one), the Umanaq Fjord area (four), and the Disko Bay area (three); the total breeding population is not likely to be less than 180,000 nests.

The rest of the fulmar population of the Atlantic-Arctic can be placed in the typical race *F. g. glacialis*, though the birds of Spitsbergen (and possibly other parts of the high Arctic) are smaller-billed than those of the Iceland-Britain population, the heaviest of all the fulmars. Four small colonies have been identified in northern East Greenland, about thirty-eight in the Spitsbergen archipelago, nine or ten in Franz Josef Land, and three in northern Novaya Zemlya. There are large breeding stations on the cliffs of Bear Island and Jan Mayen.

The fulmar is mentioned as a bird of Iceland in sagas of the early thirteenth century, and as a bird of the bird-cliffs in a treatise of *c.* 1640. The first bird-cliff to be particularized as the home of a fulmar colony was that of Grímsey, the northerly island which is one of the few points of Iceland (just) within the Arctic Circle. In 1713 the catching of young fulmars for human food on Grímsey was recorded. Grímsey seems to have occupied in Iceland a position similar to that of St. Kilda in Britain—with a native sea-bird fowler population and what may have been an unique outpost fulmar colony. It seems very likely, from a study of the literature by Finnur Guðmundsson, Pálmi Hannesson and other scholars of Iceland

(and by the writer) that Grímsey may have been the only fulmar colony in Iceland to begin with, unless the distant northerly sea-bird stack of Kolbeinsey, now much eroded, was also once a fulmar colony, which seems likely though formal proof is lacking.

In about 1753 the great spread of the fulmar—eventually to reach all around Britain and distant parts of Norway, began. It seems clear that at this time the Westmann Islands, in the south of Iceland, and Eldey, a great rock some distance off the south-west coast, were first colonized. Around 1800 the fulmars were quickly spreading in the Westmanns, and by 1821 as many as 30,000 young were being taken there yearly for human food. In this latter year fulmars colonized four mainland cliffs for the first time, one in the south near the Westmanns, two in the south-west near Eldey, and one at the western tip of the north-west peninsula. During the rest of the nineteenth century over twenty more colonies were founded on great headlands at the principal corners of Iceland. By 1909 there were at least 52 separate known fulmar colonies in Iceland ; by 1929, 79 ; by 1945, 155. Some of the recent colonies have been established on cliffs on inland mountains up to eleven miles from the south coast. Before the eating of young fulmars was forbidden in 1939, as the consequence of the discovery of psittacosis (ornithosis) virus in the population, up to 60,000 young ones were taken for human food every year. Although the known fulmar colonies of Iceland are fewer than those of Britain they are much larger, on average, and support a higher total population of fulmars.

In 1839 the fulmar was found breeding on the western cliffs of Suðuroy, the southernmost island of the Faeroes, distant 466 miles from the nearest headquarters of increasing fulmars at that time, the Westmann Islands. Suðuroy is nearer to St. Kilda ; but we can strongly presume that it was not colonized from here but from the nearest place where the fulmars were then increasing rapidly—south Iceland. It is possible that the fulmars may have come to the Faeroes rather earlier—one authority gives 1816. But experienced ornithologists who visited the Faeroes in 1828 and 1833 recorded that the fulmar definitely did not breed in the archipelago.

From Suðuroy the fulmars colonized every cliffy island of the Faeroes, mainly along the great cliffs of the west coast, then along the north coast to the north-easterly islands. They reached Stóra Dímun, Lítla Dímun, and Skúvoy in about 1845, Sandoy in about 1847, Trøllhøvdi and Mykines in about 1859, Vágar and the northern cliffs of Streymoy in about 1865, Viðoy and Fugloy in 1872, Nólsoy in about 1890, and the rest of the islands by about 1900. By the early nineteen-thirties no less than 80,000 young were being taken for human food annually in the archipelago—more than were ever taken in the whole of Iceland. Huge colonies now crowd every suitable cliff in the Faeroe Islands.

There can be no doubt that the Faeroes, and perhaps also Iceland, have provided the stock which has colonized Britain—and also Norway.

In the summer of 1920 fulmars were first noted on the cliffs of Rundøy, an island between Ålesund and Stadtland on the corner of Norway at the same latitude as the north end of the Faeroes. Breeding was first proved in 1924; by 1947 three or four hundred pairs were breeding, and by 1954 about 500. A little farther south another colony has possibly started since 1952 at or near the north of the island of Vågsøy. But more remarkably fulmars have now established breeding stations in the Lofoten Islands off the Arctic coast of Norway. They were first seen on some of the islands of the Røst group in about 1942, and in 1957 there were at least five nests with eggs on Vedøen, and possibly other birds prospecting or nesting on the neighbouring islands of Storfjellet and Trenyken. The nearest colonies to the Lofoten group are Rundøy, Bear Island, Jan Mayen, Shetland, and the Faeroes, in that order, and all between 400 and 650 miles away.

COLOUR PHASES : The populations of the Pacific and Arctic-Atlantic races of the fulmar are polymorphic, grading from birds with head, neck, and underparts white or yellowish-white to birds which are almost uniformly dark or very dark blue-grey. In the field observers can fairly easily divide what they see into " light " or " dark " birds by classifying intermediates as on the light side if their breasts are white and their underparts, necks and heads only lightly shaded or finely flecked with grey, apart from the crown, nape, and hind-neck which can be light grey ; and on the dark side if their heads, necks, and underparts are light grey and their breasts not truly white.

The distribution of the Arctic-Atlantic population at the breeding grounds is as follows : with a negligible percentage of exceptions the breeding birds of Britain, the Faeroes, Norway, Iceland, Jan Mayen and West Greenland are light. The small population at the mouth of Scoresby Sound, East Greenland, is mixed ; so is the large population on Bear Island—about 40 per cent. light. The birds of Spitsbergen, Franz Josef Land, north-east Greenland, and the Canadian Arctic are between 5 and 15 per cent. light. The colour-phase proportion in Novaya Zemlya is unknown. Birds breeding to the edge of the High Arctic are thus light ; birds breeding just over its threshold (Bear Island) mixed ; birds breeding well within it nearly all dark. The High Arctic is that part where the surface-temperature of sea-water is at or near freezing-point even in July and August ; it only touches the northern part of West Greenland.

The situation in the Pacific seems to be completely the reverse. On St. Matthew and Hall Islands, on or over the threshold of the High Arctic (though south of the Arctic Circle) all are light. All or nearly all the rest of the Pacific fulmars breed farther into the Low Arctic or outside the climatological Arctic altogether. In the Pribilov Islands nearly all are light ; in the eastern Aleutians more than half are dark ; in the Kodiak area and the western Aleutians nearly all are dark ; in the Kuriles only a negligible proportion are light.

At least the High Arctic correlation can be offered for the situation in the Atlantic-Arctic. No sensible correlation has yet been offered for the Pacific situation. Much work remains to be done before the distribution of the northern fulmar's colour-phases can be explained.

THE ATLANTIC FULMAR AT SEA : At sea there is considerable mixing of the colour-phases, and probably also of the two subspecies of the Atlantic fulmar. To the north its range extends far into the sea-ice in the regions where leads open in the summer. From the time of Nansen in the *Fram* to the days of Russian ice-floe stations in the neighbourhood of the Pole, fulmars have been seen at very high latitudes, on occasions within a few miles of the North Pole itself. Where sea-ice is thick in winter fulmars do not go ; for example, they wholly desert Davis Strait and Baffin Bay in the autumn and do not return until spring. The regular Atlantic boundary of the fulmar's range at sea lies almost wholly south of latitude 50° N. at all times of year. At most times a big salient is produced southwards, to 42° or 43° N., which embraces most of the eastern part of the Great Banks of Newfoundland. Fulmars are always rare and irregular west of the Banks. The salient is withdrawn to 47° N. in July and August, except for a few straggling birds. From November to February very few birds reach the Labrador coast and the fulmar's range is most limited ; though birds remain within sight of south Greenland, Jan Mayen, Spitsbergen and Bear Island they withdraw from most of the pack-ice and almost wholly from the Barents Sea.

Apart from the migrations that the young fulmars, and perhaps also some adults, may make to specially favoured feeding grounds—such as the Newfoundland Banks and the seas off the Varanger Fjord, north Norway —the picture of the fulmar's distribution at sea is that of a dispersive bird. It seems likely that fulmars may spend the first three or four years of their lives at sea with little or no attachment to breeding cliffs (they may not breed until they are seven years old).

[From this point to the end of the essay, the author of *The Birds of the British Isles* is responsible for the text.]

Before we consider the factors which influence the fulmar's dispersal over the ocean, mention must be made of the pioneer work of the late Professor James Ritchie on this bird, and his historical review of the fulmar population on St. Kilda nearly thirty years ago.

Writing in the *Scottish Naturalist*, 1930, Ritchie reminds us that for centuries St. Kilda was the only home of the fulmar in the British Isles and that, when looking for the reason for its spectacular spread, we have only to examine the change which took place in the human population of its island home. He pointed out, what of course is now well known, that prodigious numbers of fulmars and their eggs were taken annually by the islanders, who at the first government census numbered 180 persons. He estimated the slaughter even higher than that mentioned by Mr. Fisher earlier in this essay. It followed that as the human population decreased (the first sudden decrease took place when thirty-five individuals emigrated to Australia) the breeding stock of fulmars increased. Then in 1877, when the S.S. *Dunara Castle* began its regular visits to St. Kilda from the mainland, a significant change took place in the feeding habits of the St. Kildans themselves. It was remarked that the introduction to the islanders of the food of European civilisation affected to a high degree the number of breeding fulmars.

The final impetus which drove the fulmar to seek new breeding sites was—to use Ritchie's own words—" the lack of nesting accommodation on St. Kilda and its sister isles, due to the cumulative increase of the birds themselves, and that followed in the last instance from the sparing of thousands of birds annually because the St. Kildans turned from their own food to the new food brought within their knowledge and their reach."

Now let us turn to a more general matter—the part which its feeding habits have played in its wider dispersal.

From time immemorial the fulmar has followed the whalers—or rather since the days when whaling as a commercial enterprise began. Scoresby was one of the first to point out that the fulmar follows the living whale and this has been observed many times since, but to see the fulmar in its greatest numbers one must be present during the flensing process of a whale's carcass. Many are the accounts which have been written by eye-witnesses, to which reference is made in Mr. Fisher's volume. Dr. Koenig, the well-known ornithologist of Bonn and author of *Avifauna Spitzbergensis*, left a graphic description of many thousands of these petrels gathered round the carcasses of two harpooned whales in Safe Harbour, Spitsbergen, some fifty years ago. Fulmars feed not only on the whale's blubber but on the fat of other animals such as seals, walruses, and bears, and will not hesitate to fall upon their own kind or upon other birds when wounded.[1] They are very efficient scavengers. F. R. Allison,[2] who spent some time in 1952 on an ocean weather ship—the *Weather Explorer*—in the North Atlantic, reminds us that the fulmar's food as recorded is mainly planktonic and that most planktonic animals, " including jellyfish, ctenophores, nereids, chaetognaths, pteropods, copepods, mysids, cumaceans, isopods, amphipods, and euphausians ", recorded in the fulmar's diet by Fisher, Waterston, Salomonsen, and others have (as demonstrated by F. S. Russell (*Biol. Rev.*, ii, 1927, pp. 213-262) a vertical diurnal migration which brings them into surface waters at night. Murphy, in his *Oceanic Birds of South America*, also records the movement to the surface at night-time of cephalopods which, as Mr. Allison observes, are also preyed on by fulmars. Surprisingly few fish appear to have been

---

[1] See also Cottam and Hanson, *Zool. Ser. Field Mus. Nat. Hist.*, xx, No. 31, 1938, pp. 405-426 (part).

[2] F. R. Allison in *Scottish Naturalist*, lxiv, 1952, pp. 38-44.

specifically identified, but herring, sand-eel, and a fish the size of a pilchard are known to have figured in the fulmar's menu.

The fulmar is known to have two great feeding grounds : the Newfoundland Banks and the mouth of the Varanger Fjord. There birds are present all the year, feeding mainly on plankton. The Newfoundland Banks are possibly, Mr. Fisher suggests, the " nursery " for pre-breeding birds, mainly light-coloured ones but also a small proportion of dark ones, the latter probably from Baffin, Devon, and Ellesmere Islands. The Varanger Fjord in north-eastern Finmark may be the " nursery " for young dark birds of Bear Island, Spitsbergen, and Franz Josef Land. When Dr. H. M. S. Blair was investigating the bird life of Finmark he wrote that the fulmar winters in immense numbers on the Finmark coasts, departing for summer quarters farther north in early May. Fulmars still swarmed on 2nd May and outnumbered all other sea-birds on the open seas between the North Cape and Vardö, and many were seen on the Varanger Fjord as far west as Vadsö on 3rd May. The majority of those which passed close to the steamer on these dates were either " blue " or " dusky " fulmars or intermediates between that and the typical form.

INFORMATION OBTAINED FROM RINGING : Up to the year 1950 just over 1000 fulmars had been ringed, according to statistics obtained from *British Birds*, and of this number only a very few had been recaptured. Mr. Fisher mentions fifteen in an appendix in his book (1952), of which only eight had been ringed in the British Isles. Since 1950 the numbers have improved. The returns have been published annually in *British Birds* in reports for which Miss Elsie Leach or Mr. Robert Spencer have been responsible. These contain the ring-number of the bird and various other details. For the purpose of this book I have been content to reproduce the date and place of ringing and of recovery and the age of the bird (adult or young) at the time of ringing. Mr. Spencer has stated in his report for 1957 (*British Birds*, li, 1958, p. 453) that up to the end of 1957 the total number of fulmars ringed in Britain reached a grand total of 3567, of which 39 had been recovered.

	Date	*Where ringed and recovered*	*Age when ringed*
Ringed	4 Aug. 1925	Faeroe Is.	Nestling
Recovered	13 Aug. 1926	60° 30′ N., 12° W., east of Iceland	
Ringed	4 Sept. 1931	Bamburgh, Northumberland	Nestling
Recovered	5 Sept. 1931	Seahouses, Northumberland	
Ringed	16 July 1931	Mykines, Faeroe Is.	Nestling
Recovered	11 Oct. 1933	Mykines *c.* 13½ miles away	
Ringed	20 Oct. 1936	Vesterålen, N. Norway	Adult
Recovered	16 May 1937	Friesland, Holland	
Ringed	12 June 1938	South Iceland	Breeding adult
Recovered	4 June 1939	Where ringed	
Ringed	11 July 1945	Black Isle, Ross	Breeding adult
Recovered	10 July 1946	Where ringed	

Date		Where ringed and recovered	Age when ringed
Ringed	7 Aug. 1946	Giant's Causeway, Antrim	Nestling
Recovered	8 Sept. 1946	Where ringed, again released	
Ringed	26 Aug. 1946	Nr. Ramsey, Isle of Man	Nestling
Recovered	15 Sept. 1946	Saxilby, Lincs	
Ringed	9 Aug. 1946	Kyloe Crags, Northumberland	Nestling
Recovered	Sept. 1946	Found dead near nest	
Ringed	July 1943	Nólsoy, Faeroe	Nestling
Recovered	Apr. 1947	Where ringed	
Ringed	29 Aug. 1948	Umanaq, Greenland	Nestling
Recovered	27 Oct. 1948	St. Anthony, Newfoundland	
Ringed	17 July 1948	Dùn, St. Kilda	Nestling
Recovered	9 Nov. 1948	Newfoundland Banks, 47° 08′ N., 47° 40′ W.	
Ringed	10 July 1946	Black Isle, Ross	Breeding adult
Recovered	14 June 1949	Where ringed	
Ringed	17 July 1948	Dùn, St. Kilda	Nestling
Recovered	20 June 1949	Newfoundland Banks, 48° 30′ N., 50° 05′ W.	
Ringed	10 Aug. 1949	Sagdleq, Greenland	Nestling
Recovered	28 Oct. 1949	Rodgers Cove, Newfoundland	

Records above this line are taken from *The Fulmar*, Appendix v. Those which follow have been supplied to me by Mr. James Fisher and have come to hand since his volume was printed. The British records have all been published in the Reports of the Bird Ringing Committee.

Date		Where ringed and recovered	Age when ringed
Ringed	29 July 1951	Pentland Skerries, Orkney	Adult
Recovered	19 June 1952	Where ringed and again released	
Ringed	13 June 1952	Pentland Skerries, Orkney	Adult
Recovered	late June 1953	Where ringed and again released	
Ringed	31 July 1952	St. Kilda	Young
Recovered	22 Oct. 1954	Greenland, 64° 10′ N., 52° 10′ W.	
Ringed	26 Aug. 1954	Sula Sgeir, O. Hebrides	Young
Recovered	c. 31 Oct. 1954	Schleswig-Holstein	
Ringed	26 Aug. 1954	Sula Sgeir, O. Hebrides	Young
Recovered	9 Sept. 1954	Vaag Fjord, S. Faeroes	
Ringed	21 Aug. 1954	Sula Sgeir, O. Hebrides	Young
Recovered	5 Sept. 1954	Westray, Orkney (110 miles east)	
Ringed	24 Aug. 1954	Sula Sgeir, O. Hebrides	Young
Recovered	Apr. 1955	Les Sables d'Olonne, Vendée, France	
Ringed	26 Aug. 1954	Sula Sgeir, O. Hebrides	Young
Recovered	10 Dec. 1955	At sea off W. Ireland, 49° 30′ N., 11° 05′ W.	
Ringed	5 July 1951	Fair Isle	Adult on egg
Recovered	9 June 1952	Fair Isle	incubating same place
Ringed	26 July 1951	Gairsay, Orkney	Young
Recovered	9 Mar. 1952	Lowestoft, Suffolk, 495 miles S.S.E.	

Date	*Where ringed and recovered*	*Age when ringed*
Ringed 1 Aug. 1952	Rosemarkie, Ross	Young
Recovered 14 Oct. 1952	Frederickshaven, Jutland, Denmark	
Ringed 21 June 1952	Isle of May	
Recovered 4 Dec. 1952	Barents Sea, 73° 20′ N., 47° E.	
Ringed 16 Aug. 1952	Eynhallow, Orkney	Young
Recovered 13 July 1953	Off the Skaw, Jutland, Denmark	
Ringed 12 Aug. 1953	Eynhallow, Orkney	Adult
Recovered 27 Aug. 1953	Kallsoy, Faeroes	
Ringed 21 Aug. 1954	Sula Sgeir, O. Hebrides	Young
Recovered 27 Sept. 1954	Nr. Stromness, Orkney, 100 miles E.	
Ringed 22 Aug. 1954	Sula Sgeir, O. Hebrides	Young
Recovered 2 Oct. 1954	Woolacombe, N. Devon, 550 miles S.	
Ringed 24 Aug. 1954	Sula Sgeir, O. Hebrides	Young
Recovered 8 Sept. 1954	Suduroy, Faeroes	
Ringed 31 July 1952	St. Kilda	Young
Recovered 22 Oct. 1954	West Greenland, *c.* 64° 10′ N., 52° 10′ W.	
Ringed 9 Aug. 1953	Eynhallow, Orkney	Young
Recovered 10 Oct. 1954	At sea off Faeroes, *c.* 65° 50′ N., 30′ W.	
Ringed 21 June 1952	Isle of May	Adult
Recovered 2 Nov. 1954	Off Skagen, Denmark	
Ringed 21 Aug. 1954	Sula Sgeir, O. Hebrides	Young
Recovered 12 Jan. 1955	Bellvue, Newfoundland	
Ringed 15 Aug. 1955	Duncansby Head, Caithness	Young
Recovered 16 Sept. 1955	The Hague, Holland	
Ringed 25 Aug. 1954	Sula Sgeir, O. Hebrides	
Recovered 10 Apr. 1958	Western side of Sandoy, Faeroes, *c.* 61° 50′ N., 6° 54′ W.	
Ringed 21 Aug. 1954	Sula Sgeir, O. Hebrides	Young
Recovered 20 July 1955	At sea off Trondheim, Norway, 64° 08′ N., 8° 02′ E.	
Ringed 23 Aug. 1954	Sula Sgeir, O. Hebrides	Young
Recovered 10 Sept. 1954	At sea off Ireland, *c.* 52° 50′ N., 11° W.	
Ringed 15 Aug. 1955	Duncansby Head, Caithness	Young
Recovered 21 May 1956	Cabot Strait, Gulf of St. Lawrence	

The most spectacular journeys undertaken by British-ringed fulmars are those chronicled above from St. Kilda to the Newfoundland Banks (two), St. Kilda to Greenland (two), Sula Sgeir to Les Sables d'Olonne, Isle of May to Barents Sea, Sula Sgeir to Newfoundland, and Caithness to the Gulf of St. Lawrence.

The latest ringing report for 1957 (received too late to incorporate in the above list) records fulmars ringed St Kilda (4), Orkney (2), Caithness (1); recovered Norway (1), Newfoundland (3), Greenland (1), and off Ireland (2).

From the earliest days of Arctic exploration, navigators, whaling captains, and those whose business has taken them to the Greenland and Arctic seas, have been impressed by the superlative flying powers of the fulmar. William Scoresby junior, the early Arctic navigator, who gave

PLATE II

FULMAR
Fulmarus glacialis glacialis (Linnaeus)

his name to Scoresby Land, was loud in its praises, remarking that the fulmar could fly to windward in the highest storms and rest on the water, with great composure, in the most tremendous seas. Seen at sea, where they spend their entire life when not nesting, the evolutions performed by these birds are beyond comparison, especially if the waves are high and the wind at gale force. In really rough weather the birds are in their element. Dr. Salomonsen, in his fine volume *Grønlands Fugle*, describes the fulmar as a master of aerial navigation, displaying, especially in stormy weather, astonishing grace and skill. Watch it for a moment, as Finn Salomonsen has done, from the deck of a steamer battling against a storm in the Greenland seas. " In the heart of the gale it sweeps at tremendous speed over the turbulent sea with superb dexterity. It makes use of the power of the wind with great skill. On extended wings it glides against the wind for long distances without wing-beats, gradually losing height ; then it rises swiftly, borne upwards by the vertical currents which form on the windward side of the troughs. In calm weather it seems to fly with some effort, moving with rigid wing-beats just above the sea and almost touching the surface with its wing-tips." But no words can really convey the grace and ease with which its evolutions are executed.

Very different does it appear, as the writer has seen the fulmars this year on the fine cliffs at the Mull of Galloway, when the birds have come to land to lay their egg and rear their young. With stiffly outstretched wings the fulmars were gliding back and forth along the cliff top, following the contour of the land with extraordinary precision. When the cliffs skirted an inlet—be it ever so small—the bird did not take the short cut across its mouth to the land on the farther side but hugged the cliff edge of the indent all the way round. The presence of a human being on the brink of the cliff failed to deflect it from its course. Having reached the end of its patrol, it would turn about and come back on its tracks, faithfully following the cliff side as it did before. On the shelves below and in nooks and crannies, but well exposed to view, other fulmars were sitting—and sitting tightly on their single egg. I had hoped to see a patrolling bird settle by its mate but that was not to be.

The older naturalists, with the exception I believe of Edmund Selous, have been taken to task for not recognizing, or at any rate not reporting upon, the courtship behaviour of the fulmar when they saw it ; but that was in the days before every wag of a wagtail's tail was credited with some significance and accorded due notice in the biological columns of our journals ! Our forebears had some excuse in this instance, as modern opinion must allow, for, to quote from Mr. Fisher's text :

Describe it as we may, the fulmar produces but one display, a routine of head-waving (up and down, and from side to side), gaping (showing the lead, mauve or purple inside-mouth and throat pouch), nibbling, and stretching the head upwards and backwards on curved neck, cackling all the time. It has no wing-flirt, no swimming-game, no land-dance : on the water it displays with its head and neck, bobbing and bowing and shaking and cackling in just the same way as it does on the cliff ; it uses the same pattern of head movements in aggression, in courtship, and in social life. Only doubtfully can the circling of cliffs in July, noted by Perry and possibly associated with change-over, be regarded as display.

This change-over has been observed by very few scientists. Even Mr. Fisher acknowledges that he has never himself seen it, but he gives a brief account of the ceremony as witnessed by O. A. J. Lee, " a pioneer bird-photographer of great skill ", who at midnight on 20th June 1897 was engaged in watching the fulmars at Hermaness, and reported as follows : " Three or four fulmars sitting on their single eggs below me. The mate of one of these birds alighted beside it, and the sitting bird at once rose off the egg uttering a low crooning sort of note—' *coo-roo, coo-roo* ', rather like the murmuring notes of the ring-dove ; it then flew from the ledge, leaving the new-comer to sit on the nest."

Little has been said, save incidentally, concerning the voice of the fulmar. Usually when flying it is silent though occasionally " a quiet groan " may be heard (Fisher). It is more vocal when nesting and in display, as noted in *The Handbook*, it utters a series of guttural notes, variously described by H. Boase and others as " *ug-ug-ug* ", or by L. S. V. Venables as a long snarling guttural " *Kuh-kuh-kuh-kurr-r-r-r* ". Other naturalists have given their own interpretations of the sounds emitted, but as usual no one seems to hear or describe the sounds alike !

Though the fulmars breeding on the Mull of Galloway are few in number, the sight of them brought to mind Oliver Pike's account of his first visit to St. Kilda, where the numbers nesting on the vast precipices beggar description :

To see this cliff at its best it should be seen from the sea. It was one of the steepest cliffs I have ever seen. It towered above our small boat—a great frowning precipice, the lower part for three hundred feet composed of vast black rocks, washed bare and polished by the great waves of the winter storms. The higher portion for about one thousand feet was covered with grass and flowers. As we sailed slowly towards the gigantic cliff we noticed that high up on its grass-covered sides there were thousands of tiny white dots, like little specks of snow, while floating in a slow dreamy movement, thousands of the same white dots were passing and re-passing before the face of the cliff. Hardly a sound was there—just the lap, lap of the water as our boat pushed its way through, or the cry of a startled sea-bird as it hurriedly left its nest. This vast precipice that towered above us was the home of the fulmar petrel. . . .

About two hours later we were right amongst the birds. Thousands were flying about before me and going to or from their nests. The flight is distinct and unlike any other sea-bird I have seen. The bird gives three, four, and sometimes five rapid flaps of the wings, then floats on for about ten or twenty yards, then flaps again. Its flight is as noiseless as that of the owl and exceedingly graceful.

On such a precipice as that described above, the fulmar might reasonably expect to rear its young without interruption, save for the normal hazards of a sea bird's life. The cliffs of Conachair, Soay, and of Boreray have been described by James Fisher as " staggering ", but the precipices were scaled by the St. Kilda islanders, whose prowess as rock-climbers has become a legend. To appreciate what that means the reader should refer to Barrington's critical account of their skill, written from the viewpoint of a member of the Alpine Club. The numbers of young fulmars taken annually by the St. Kilda fowlers varied according to the human population on the island. To quote once more from Mr. Fisher's book, the approximate number of fulmars taken fell from an average of 12,000 per annum up to 1903, to 9,600 in 1911 and (with a corresponding decline in human inhabitants) to 4,000 in 1929. The average throughout the period was around 10,000 per annum. It is reported, too, that up to about the middle of the nineteenth century " many hundreds if not thousands " of fulmars were taken by the fishermen on the Grand Banks of Newfoundland and used for bait (Collins). In view of such figures it is apparent that man is by far the worst enemy with which the fulmar has to contend, for in many places where it breeds the fulmar is, or has been, used as an article of food, particularly the young which are not so unpalatable as the adults.

In the Faeroe Islands Salomonsen has recorded that by 1935 about 80,000 (and it may well have been a hundred thousand) young ones were taken every year—a slaughter that was ceased by legislation when it was discovered that psittacosis had made its appearance among the birds. Fulmars are taken for food in the Westmann Islands, in Iceland (until prohibited for the same reason as in the Faeroes), and to a small extent in west Greenland.

To what extent the fulmar is preyed upon by other birds is not so well known. In former days the white-tailed eagle no doubt took its toll, as the peregrine will do to-day. The greater black-backed gull is believed to take eggs and chicks just as the glaucous is suspected of doing in Greenland ; while in Iceland the gyr-falcon, and in the Aleutian Islands the bald eagle, must be reckoned amongst its worst enemies after man.

The oil obtained from the fulmar, both young and old, played an important part in the economy of the St. Kildans, as it does elsewhere, and the method by which this oil is—or was—obtained was ingenious. The captured bird was made to vomit the stomach oil into a receptacle carried by the fowler : at one time the dried gullet and stomach of a solan goose was used by the fowler for this purpose, as recorded by Macgillivray in 1852. The use to which this stomach oil is put by the fulmar during its life has often been discussed, for there is no doubt that the fulmar (and other petrels also) secretes much more in its stomach than other birds, and some use must be found for it. Mr. Fisher has shown that this oil may be used in at least four different ways : for ceremonial purposes, when oil passes from one bird to another in courtship display ; for feeding their young (when mixed with regurgitated food) ; probably also for preening ; and certainly as a means of defence.   A fifth use has been suggested—that petrels use stomach oil to calm the surface of the sea during severe storms ; but this seems very improbable for though oil so vomited on a turbulent sea would undoubtedly have a calming effect—a suggestion with which R. C. Murphy appears to agree—the fulmar at any rate has never shown any preference for calm water, indeed, the roughest of seas would appear to hold no terrors for this wholly pelagic species, ever associated, as Cleveland Bent has expressed, with drifting icebergs and floating pack-ice.

The use made by the fulmar of its stomach oil as a means of defence is only too well known by those who have climbed among the sitting birds. The oil has been shown by Dr. L. Harrison Matthews to be a secretion of the glands of the proventriculus ; it can be squirted in the direction of an intruder through the mouth to a distance of two or three feet, with a maximum, it is believed, of four feet.   That some of this strong-smelling oil may pass through the nostrils is also probable, but the assertion that the oil is forcibly ejected through the nasal apertures—a belief quoted by Macgillivray from earlier accounts and repeated since by other writers— is not borne out in practice, as those naturalists who have suffered from an annoyed fulmar have been able to prove.   The oil is normally a clear amber colour, but sometimes it is red, due to the birds having fed on planktonic crustaceans.   It is rich in Vitamin A and also contains Vitamin D ; it is not really a true oil but a wax ; as Mr. Fisher has said, it is very much like sperm oil found in the head cavity of sperm whales.   Its composition has been analyzed by Dr. L. Harrison Matthews, F.R.S., in a learned treatise to which reference has already been made.   The remarkable fact, ascertained by Rev. John Lees, that the fulmar chick is able to eject fluid before hatching and that, as found by Mr. Eric Duffey, it does so against parent and predator alike until its third week when—to use Mr. Armstrong's expression—it begins to use discrimination, produced another notable contribution to *Ibis*, 1951, pp. 245-251, in which Mr. E. A. Armstrong discusses its evolutionary origin.   See also *Ibis*, 1950, p. 152.

Mr. Eric Duffey (*Ibis*, 1951, p. 240) records that a chick only a few hours old, its down still wet, went through typical spitting behaviour when handled, though no oil was ejected.   The young chick, so Mr. Duffey assures us, recognizes no one as its friend—parent, strange fulmar or a bird of another species, all get the same reception.   The parent has to overcome this by a characteristic method of approach with which the chick gradually becomes familiar.

BREEDING HABITS : The fulmar's yearly cycle has been dealt with so exhaustively by Mr. Fisher in his standard work on this bird, where he draws a comparison between the bird's habits on the large and small British breeding colonies and those in the Faeroes, Iceland, Jan Mayen,

Bear Island, Franz Josef Land, Greenland, and the Canadian Arctic, that I can but advise the reader to obtain and read his book which contains a mine of information to be found nowhere else. Here, as this essay has already exceeded my normal allowance of space, I must be content to quote from Mr. Fisher's opening remarks, reminding the reader that but for an unfortunate illness this section of the essay would have been written by the author of *The Fulmar* especially for this book. If new facts have arisen and would then have been incorporated, they cannot add much to what he wrote only six years ago : words which may now be repeated and which describe in succinct language the breeding cycle of a fulmar's year.

On a still morning in early November some fulmars come back to their ocean-facing cliff. In ones and twos they fly silently up and down the rock-face, occasionally gliding over the cliff-top and making an overland excursion of a few yards. A group of twenty settles on the calm sea a hundred yards from the cliff-foot ; they growl and cackle. From time to time a fulmar leaves the water-group and flies up to the cliff face, to tour up and down. In the evening the wind gets up, and with it the sea ; next morning the fulmars have gone. A week later it is calm again and they are back ; this time one settles on a ledge for a few minutes. All through December the number of visitors increases, though all disappear whenever the weather is stormy ; many now land on ledges, and visit each other, display and cackle on them ; on a fine day the cliff is decorated with fulmars alone, fulmars in twos and fulmars (commonly) in threes. And so the situation continues ; not long after Christmas, on a fine day when the temperature is nevertheless well below freezing-point, an observer may see some hundreds of fulmars on the cliffs, perhaps as many as half or two-thirds of (and sometimes actually more than) the population at the peak of the previous breeding season.

The fulmars continue to visit the cliff and occupy it in fine weather throughout February and March, with some further increase of number. In April the numbers increase more rapidly, and the amount of display and visiting becomes very great. By the end of April the population is at its highest, and all nest-sites have been claimed ; the cliff is alive with busy birds.

At the beginning of May the non-breeders begin to drop out of the population. On (but never before) 5 May the first egg [1] is laid, and most of the birds lay their eggs between 20 and 29 May ; a few delay laying until about 7 June or even later.

During May and June the birds of the pair share in the incubation of their egg.[2] Some lose their egg, lay no replacement, hang about the colony for a week or a fortnight " incubating " an empty nest, and then begin to moult their flight feathers (primaries) and tail and go away to sea. The population of adult fulmars in occupation of the colony thus continues to drop. The first young hatch on about 24 June,

---

[1] [The white egg is described by Jourdain as a pointed oval but variable in shape. The average of 100 British eggs is 74×50·6 mm. Max. 81·5×50·5 and 72·5×54·1 mm. Min. 65·5×45·5 and 66·5×44·3 mm.]

[2] In their joint paper (*Journal of Animal Ecology*, x, No. 2, 1941, p. 255, on the " Breeding Distribution, History and Population of the Fulmar in the British Isles ") James Fisher and George Waterston concluded that the normal incubation period is 47 or 48 days, occasionally a week less or a week more, *i.e.* generally from 6 to 8 weeks.

though as late as 31 July some eggs may still be found. The young is tended continually by one or both parents until it is about a fortnight old.[1] As time goes on
it is left alone for longer and longer periods. The population of adults visible at any
one visit to the colony continues to decline ; after mid-July it is quite usual to find
more young on the ledges than adults occupying nest-sites or flying around. Adults
that lose their young soon go into moult, go to sea, and do not return in that season.

The young fulmars begin to fly from the ledges in the last ten days of August.
They continue to fly in early September, most leaving the ledges in the first week
of that month. Some are occasionally still on the ledges in mid-September, the
latest date being 22nd September. Though the adults have nearly all disappeared
by the end of August, and though hardly any are found still tending young in
September, a few may outstay the young on the ledges ; on large British colonies
what were believed to be adults have been seen until 1 October, and at St. Kilda
until 8 October. But a young or an adult fulmar at a British colony after mid-
September is quite unusual. Such is a general description of the cycle of the year
at a largish British fulmar colony.

The suggestion put forward in some quarters that the young are
ever purposely deserted by their parents is considered by Mr. Fisher to
be probably untrue. He tells me that new evidence shows that most, if
not all, are fed until they fly.

The fulmar's annual cycle appears to be very much the same in the
different parts of its range. Outside the Arctic the impression formed
from a study of the breeding colonies is that it is tied to laying in mid-
May. " If a fulmar harvest on St. Kilda was a few days late it was because
the weather delayed the harvesters ; not because they had to wait for the
harvested." Only in the Arctic is there evidence that the fulmar can be at
the mercy of the season. Outside the realm of ice it keeps its appointments
punctually. If it is later in the Arctic it is later by only a week or two.

It is clear from the investigations of Mr. Fisher and his many helpers [2]
that the fledging period is about the same as the incubation period and,
like it, is subject to a considerable fluctuation. It has never been directly
observed to be longer than fifty-seven days or less than forty-one, and
seems to be on an average forty-six. When the time comes for the young
fulmars to depart from the ledges most of them fly down to the sea. Some
scramble and fall down, but these are few in number. Sometimes they
take wing almost perfectly at once and then tour the ledges for some time,

[1] The relationship between chick and parent was the subject of an instructive review in
the *Ibis*, 1951, pp. 237-245, by Mr. Eric Duffey. He found that the brooding periods by the
individual parent birds are very irregular and do not amount to an equal share by male
and female. Mr. Duffey further proved that in the first two or three weeks of the chick's life
it does not recognise its parents and treats them as intruders to be repelled. The parent has a
characteristic method of approach with which the chick gradually becomes familiar.

[2] I have read with special interest notes on " The breeding of the Fulmar ", by W. J.
Eggeling (*Scottish Naturalist*, lxiv, 1952, pp. 148-150) and on " The incubation rhythm
of the Fulmar ", by Kenneth Williamson (*op. cit.*, pp. 138-147), which appeared after Mr.
Fisher's book had gone to press.

but the usual custom is for the heavy young fulmars, after their flight to the sea, to spend some days, and perhaps more than a week, afloat under the cliffs or at sea some miles away if the weather is calm.

Elsewhere in this essay I have quoted Mr. Fisher's tentative suggestion that the Varanger Fjord and the Newfoundland Banks may act as " nurseries " for young fulmars. In his book *The Fulmar* the author summarizes the Atlantic fulmar's seasonal and geographic distribution at sea as a whole—taking us month by month through the calendar. Some of the bird's movements have been mentioned here under the heading " The Fulmar at Sea ". We have learned how the bird's distribution is controlled by the distribution of its food supply. The actual suggestion of what is at present held to be the solution of the increase of the fulmar was thought of in two parts : trawling by R. M. Lockley, whaling by James Fisher. Mr. Fisher ends his chapter on this subject with the following paragraph. He believes that the picture he has given us of the fulmar is undoubtedly one of a dispersive rather than a migratory animal—apart from the tendency of its young to gather in certain specified areas. " It goes ", he writes, " where its food goes. It seeks leads in the polar ice hundreds of miles from base when there is summer light to hunt the abundant food to be found in such places. . . . It avoids the ice when it is dark and unprofitable. It hunts the plankton areas of the open Atlantic, and the plankton content of this ocean steeply declines as does the fulmar south of about 50° N." Fisher evidently shares with Finnur Guðmundsson and R. M. Lockley the view that the fulmar's life has been revolutionized to a remarkable degree by man : whaling and trawling in northern waters have completely changed its conditions of life in these regions by providing it with a constant and almost unlimited source of food. That these two factors—more especially the trawlers in more recent days—have had a tremendous influence on the spread of the fulmar is surely abundantly proved ?

REFERENCES : Original Description : *Procellaria glacialis* Linnaeus, *Fauna Sveica*, 2nd ed. 1761, p. 51 : Arctic Sea, restricted type locality : Spitsbergen.

Family DIOMEDEIDAE

Genus *DIOMEDEA* Linnaeus

PLATE 12

BLACK-BROWED ALBATROSS

Diomedea melanophrys melanophrys Temminck

Accidental Visitor

IDENTIFICATION : The back and wings of the black-browed albatross are brownish-black, the long scapulars being black at the end. The back shades to white at the base of the neck. The rump and upper tail-coverts are white, and the tail-feathers slate grey with white shafts. The head is white, but in front of the eye there is a dark line which shades into grey behind the eye on to the side of the head. The underparts are white, the feet fleshy grey (but see later for more detail) and the iris brown. The bill, which is yellowish-horn in younger birds, becomes gamboge yellow shaded with orange on the hook in the fully adult bird (Buller). It is 32 inches in length.

Dr. Murphy observes in his *Oceanic Birds* that the black-browed albatross is the only white-headed mollymauk in which the adult has a wholly yellow bill. This and the dark line over and through the eye are diagnostic. The wing-spread approaches a maximum of 2·5 m. The largest on record measured 246 cm., which is approximately 8 ft. 1 in.

Discussing the colour of the bill, which is of great importance when attempting to recognize albatrosses in life, Dr. Murphy describes it as yellow (sometimes as bright as gamboge yellow), becoming orange, pink, or even red on the hook of the maxilla, with a narrow ring of black skin around the base of the maxilla. According to Dr. Murphy the legs and feet are usually bluish-grey or greyish-flesh colour, darker blue or violet on the joints and webs ; but he adds that owing to wide individual variation the feet range from whitish to dark purplish-red among birds in the same region. The claws are horn-colour or whitish.

COMPARISON BETWEEN THE BLACK-BROWED AND YELLOW-NOSED ALBATROSS : There is but one other species of albatross with which the present species may be confused—that is the yellow-nosed albatross *Diomedia chlororhyncha*. It is important therefore to bear in mind the distinctions between these two birds, which were very clearly defined by Mr. H. F. I. Elliott in *British Birds*, xlvi, 1953, pp. 308-310. His letter was occasioned by the dispute over an albatross which had been captured in Derbyshire, photographed, and liberated before anyone qualified to determine its species had examined it. Having pointed out that the bird (shown in the photograph in *British Birds*, 1953, Plate 13) must " for good reasons of plumage, size, and geographical distribution " have been

PLATE 12

BLACK-BROWED ALBATROSS
Diomedia melanophrys melanophrys Temminck

either a black-browed albatross or a yellow-nosed albatross and not any other species, Mr. Elliott stated that its identity as one or the other of these two species turned on four points, namely size, colour of bill, colour of the under-surface of the wing, and colour of the feathering around the eye. He defined the distinctions between the two species of albatross under these headings :

1. *Size.* The black-browed albatross is on the average considerably the larger of the two species, its recorded weight varying from one and a half times to twice that of the yellow-nosed albatross. There is a considerable overlap in the wing measurements. Although there is virtually no difference between the two species in the length of bill, the depth of bill in *chlororhyncha* is usually noticeably less.

2. *Bill colour.* At all stages the greater part of the bill of *chlororhyncha* is black. In the juvenile about to leave the nest there is a very slight paleness on the apex of the culmen which develops gradually into the golden-yellow culminicorn of the adult, but at no stage would the casual observer describe the bill as anything but plain " black " (with more or less of a contrasting streak on the top of the culmen). On the other hand the bill of the fledged *melanophrys* is never darker than " greyish black " or black with an olive-brown wash.

3. *Under-wing pattern.* At all stages the pattern of the under-side of the wing of *chlororhyncha* has very much more white in it than that of *melanophrys*, in which, in the young bird, the white is reduced to a narrow axial streak. In particular the axillaries of *melanophrys* are grey and in *chlororhyncha* almost entirely white.

4. *Colour round the eye.* In all stages of *chlororhyncha* from nestlings near fledging to breeding adults there is a distinct supra-loral patch *in front of the eye*. This is a striking characteristic in the field. On the other hand the somewhat similar dark feathering near the eye of *melanophrys* is usually extended to form a brow, but though it is slightly more marked in front of, rather than behind the eye, it does not as in *chlororhyncha* nearly reach the bill and almost interrupt the white area between the eye and bill.

Mr. Elliott's conclusion that the Derbyshire specimen was unquestionably an example of the black-browed albatross confirmed Mr. J. D. Macdonald's opinion when the photograph of this specimen was submitted for his determination at the British Museum and refuted those critics who had formed the opposite view. Mr. Elliott's long experience of mollymauks in the field has enabled him to put his finger on the salient points for recognition of the various species.

OCCURRENCES IN GREAT BRITAIN : There are now two established records of this albatross in British waters, and most probably at least three others whose identification lay between the two species we have discussed and the grey-headed albatross but could not, through lack of detail available, be assigned to one species definitely. The first black-browed albatross to reach British shores and be identified as such was picked up exhausted near Linton, Cambridge, on 9th July 1897 (reported in the *Ibis*, 1897, p. 625, by E. A. Butler). The second, the bird over which the dispute arose in *British Birds*, xlvi, pp. 307-310, was found alive " a few days previous to 21st August " at Stavely, Derbyshire, where it had become entangled with telegraph wires without, however, sustaining serious injury. Inspector G. A. Lloyd of the R.S.P.C.A. took the sympathetic course—to quote J. D. Macdonald—of sending it by rail to Skegness, Lincolnshire, where it was released and presumably took to the sea once more. The bird was not examined by any competent ornithologist, but an excellent photograph was taken of it (reproduced as Plate 13 in Vol. xlvi of *British Birds*) from which it has been possible to identify the species to which it belonged. The editor of the *Derbyshire Times* sent the photograph to the British Museum and Mr. J. D. Macdonald reported this strange occurrence in *British Birds*, xlvi, p. 110, where a description taken from life by Mr. Morton H. Edwards was reproduced.

We now come to the *possible* occurrences which unfortunately can never be substantiated. On 18th July 1894 the late Dr. J. A. Harvie-Brown (joint author of the *Vertebrate Fauna of Scotland*) saw an albatross the size of the black-browed species about twenty miles off the Orkneys. The next was seen on 21st February 1895 by another competent ornithologist, Mr. George Bolam, who wrote in his book *The Birds of Northumberland and the Eastern Borders* :

Being down at low-water mark on the sands between Goswick and Holy Island, on 21st February, 1895—there a good mile from the nearest " land "—I saw the bird flying past, perhaps a quarter of a mile to sea, and both its flight and size precluded the idea that it could have been anything else than an albatross. It was pursuing a southward course, alternately rising perhaps thirty feet above the waves, and dipping down again to glide along their surface, thus enabling me to obtain a good view of both its upper and lower plumage ; whilst several mature great black-backed gulls which were upon the wing at the same time, and some of which it passed at no great distance, enabled a good estimate to be made of its dimensions and stretch of wing. . . . The weather, it may be added, had been of a very wintry description for some time previously, with frost, snow, and northerly winds.

Bolam remarked that he knew the occurrence would be looked at askance by ultra-sceptics as a very doubtful record, but improbable as it seemed for such a bird to be on our shores at such a date, he had no doubt at all that the bird was an albatross of some kind : " and as the black-browed species has more than once previously been recorded from the British Isles, and as the size and appearance of the bird seemed to agree generally with the description of that species, it is at least probable that to that it really belonged ". We can add our own opinion that Mr. Bolam was probably right in his deduction.

Finally we have a record from off Fair Isle, where on 14th May 1949 George Waterston, Commander G. Hughes Onslow, and Surgeon-Captain W. P. Vicary saw an undoubted albatross circling about in the vicinity of the Sheep Craig. The occurrence is reported in *Scottish Naturalist*, lxii, 1950, p. 23, under the initials of George Waterston : a close description is given but as the bird was not adult there must remain a doubt as to its determination. As the editors of the *Scottish Naturalist* point out, the yellow-nosed albatross *D. chlororhyncha* is recorded from Quebec and Maine, and the grey-headed albatross *D. chrysostoma* has occurred off Norway. It might, in fact, have been any of these three and the same must apply to the other two sight-records here enumerated. That all three may have been black-browed albatrosses is the most likely of the alternatives, but in no case was any truly diagnostic feature observed.

DISTRIBUTION : Although more than one race of this albatross has been described, the majority of writers, including Witherby in *The Handbook*, have not recognized more than the one species, described by Temminck from the Cape of Good Hope. Gregory Mathews, however, separated the birds from Australian seas under the name *impavida* with type locality Tasmania.[1] P. R. Lowe and N. B. Kinnear, when reporting on the birds obtained by the *Terra Nova* Expedition,[2] appear to accept this race and give details of measurements, while noting that there seems to be a considerable amount of individual variation in regard to the colour differences. R. C. Murphy, in *Oceanic Birds of South America* (1936), gives the general range of *D. melanophrys* as : " The Southern Oceans generally, from the tropic of Capricorn to latitude 60° S., and occasionally beyond. Breeds at Campbell and the Aukland Islands, and perhaps elsewhere in the New Zealand region ; at Kerguelen and the Prince Edward Islands, South Georgia, the Falklands, Staten Island and at the Ildefonso and Diego Ramirez islets near Cape Horn. Breeding records from Tristan da Cunha (Thomson 1878, Mathews 1932) are erroneous,[3] as are probably the references to nesting localities in Tierra del Fuego. Data are needed for Bouvet Island in the Atlantic, and for Heard Island in the Indian Ocean." Mathews believed that the typical subspecies (which is the one which ranges in the South Atlantic and has reached British waters in its wanderings) breeds in certain islands of the South Atlantic, but he produced no evidence that it did so on Tristan or Gough Island. In the *Terra Nova* report Lowe and Kinnear considered that Cape specimens agreed equally with the Kerguelen examples and with a Falkland Island skin, but, as they

[1] *Thalassarche melanophris impavida*, Mathews, *Birds of Australia*, vol. ii, 1912, p. 267 : Tasmania.

[2] British Antarctic (Terra Nova) Expedition 1910, *Zool.*, vol. iv, No. 5, p. 167.

[3] A Winter Visitor, March to September, c.f. Elliott, in *Ibis*, 1957, p. 572.

point out, before birds from South Georgia (with the longest bills of all) and specimens from Chile and Peru (which are hardly distinguishable from Kerguelen examples) can be assigned to their proper race, it will be necessary to compare a larger series including more specimens from the Falkland Islands.

In the meantime it seems best to unite the Falkland, Kerguelen, and Cape birds under the typical subspecies *Diomedia melanophrys melanophrys* and to recognize the Australian-New Zealand-Tasmanian birds as distinct under the name *D. m. impavida* Mathews. I have noted with interest that when reporting on the birds seen on their voyage in the South Atlantic and Southern Oceans in 1951-52, Professor G. J. van Oordt and Dr. J. P. Kruijt remark that:

This small albatross (*D. melanophrys*) was met with in two distinctly separated areas. . . . Our observations suggest that in the South Atlantic and in the Southern Ocean south of South Africa black-browed albatrosses occur which probably breed on South Georgia, on the Falkland Islands, or on Kerguelen, whereas the birds seen by us west of and in the Ross Sea may breed on Campbell and Aukland islands near New Zealand. *The birds belonging to these two populations are easily distinguishable in the field.* It was found that the New Zealand form, the subspecies *impavida* Mathews (not accepted by Peters 1931) extends its habitat well into the Antarctic Ocean near the pack ice, whereas the western form [*D. melanophrys melanophrys*] is a subtropical and subantarctic bird, which does not penetrate very far south.

I have italicized the words in Professor van Oordt's report which struck me as being most significant. There is, as these authors have emphasized, a break in distribution between the form breeding in Kerguelen, and the birds of the Australian area.

The above notes refer to the area in which the black-browed albatross breeds, mainly on lonely and inaccessible islets of the Southern Seas. Out of the breeding season the birds have a wider distribution which is not easily defined but which according to Murphy reaches to the Tropic of Capricorn. There have been many occasions when this mollymauk has been taken in the northern hemisphere but, so Murphy points out, the probability of transport by sailors must always be kept in mind. " The black-browed albatross takes a hook particularly freely and by no means all the captured birds find their way to the sea-cook's pots."

There is an example in the Peterhead Museum which was shot northwest of Spitsbergen in latitude 80° 11′ N., longitude 4° E. (Andersen 1894) ; as Murphy observes, this position is closer to the North Pole than the black-browed albatross has ever approached the South Pole, despite its antarctic affinities. Equally surprising is the record of a black-browed albatross from Greenland (published by Hørring and Salomonsen in 1941) [1]

[1] " Further records of rare or new Greenland birds ", *Medd. om Gronland*, cxxxi, 1941, No. 5, p. 59.

—the only occurrence so far north on the western side of the Atlantic. On the other side of the North Atlantic another mollymauk of this species, of which more will be said later in this account, lived for years among the gannets of the Faeroe Islands, and as already recounted, other examples presumed to have been of this species have been observed in British waters apart from the two which have been handled from Cambridgeshire and Derbyshire. It has also been reported to have been seen in the Baltic (Oesel Island), as mentioned by Jourdain in *The Handbook*. There does not appear to be a record of *Diomedia melanophrys* from off the North American Atlantic coast other than the Greenland example recorded above ; the only example which is reported to have reached the coasts of Maine and Labrador being one of the yellow-nosed albatrosses, *D. chlororhynchos*.

As a rule the black-browed albatross leaves the wake of vessels when pack-ice is encountered ; occasionally, however, it penetrates far south-wards, even beyond the Antarctic Circle. The more one studies the literature of these small albatrosses the more is one convinced how much care must be exercised in their recognition. Sight records in the North Atlantic can seldom be anything but guesswork, so closely do the various species resemble one another.

HABITS :[1] In his excellent account in *Oceanic Birds*, Dr. Cushman Murphy describes this mollymauk as " the commonest albatross in the southern hemisphere, the most sociable and the most fearless of man while at sea ". Gould in 1865 found that it ordinarily approaches much nearer a vessel than any other species, a fact which Dr. Murphy himself had abundant opportunities to confirm during the long cruise of the *Daisy* in the South Atlantic. My own experience in the South Atlantic is very slight, but even in my two voyages in the Cape seas I had opportunity to realize the truth of Gould's statement. It was the first albatross which I ever saw and it consequently left a lasting impression on my mind. Wandering albatrosses were also seen, and were observed to accompany the ship farther north than the black-browed mollymauks. The contrast in the size of these two magnificent birds was very noticeable.

To watch these birds to perfection one should be on board a sailing vessel, for the liners of to-day steam too fast to enable one to see, as Murphy has done, the birds at their best. On board the *Daisy* it was Murphy's custom to keep the legion of oceanic birds interested in the brig by trailing bits of fat pork or strips of loggerhead turtle-meat from the stern ; and the mollymauks proved to be even more inquisitive than the smaller petrels :

They would fly again and again across the quarter-deck, jerking up their heads like spirited steeds and showing curiosity and temptation in every action. Sometimes

---

[1] Dr. Murphy would himself have contributed this essay had he not been setting out on a voyage around the world at the time when I approached him to do so. He has, however, allowed me to quote freely from what he has already published.

they wiggled their feet in the air with an amusing running motion, or spread their translucent webs so that they looked blood-red against the sky. Sometimes they halted so abruptly in flight that it seemed they had struck an invisible barrier. During brisk breezes they zoomed across the stern close enough for me to see the colour of their eyes and to hear the humming swish of their stiff quills. To anyone properly equipped, they would then have offered a splendid opportunity for studying the fundamentals of aeronautics. Every movement revealed the constant, delicate reactions of the mechanism of balance—the gentle, almost unnoticeable rocking and see-sawing of the wings with the bird's body as a fulcrum. . . . After groups of mollymauks had followed the *Daisy* southwards for ten days or so, competition for food seemed to become more keen among them. They showed increased excitement when bait was trailed from lines, and would drop like fallen pillows from the height of the masthead, spreading wide their legs, throwing their bulging breasts forward and their heads far back. . . . Before alighting they stretched down the legs and turned the toes upward. Then the huge webs would strike the surface obliquely and the birds would skate forward several metres before they slowly settled into the buoyant swimming position, with their pinions held like those of angels high above their backs, to be folded later. . . . When the coveted pieces of turtle meat were not attached to lines the mollymauks would dive for them until only the tips of their long open wings showed above the surface of the sea.

The evidence was convincing that the same individual mollymauks followed our vessel for considerable periods, although the frequent presence of stray birds, singly or in small bands, altered the population about the brig from day to day. . . . Not infrequently flocks made up almost wholly of immature mollymauks of this species may be encountered. Members of one of the British Antarctic expeditions have noted this in low latitudes of the Atlantic and Indian Oceans. . . . At sea west of Cape Town, Dr. Wilson of Scott's expedition, once observed two black-browed albatrosses " billing one another exactly as though they were adult and young ". This is evidently another example of the year-round dance in which all albatrosses seem to indulge at sea as well as ashore.

Dr. Murphy stresses the great flying powers of the black-browed albatross—perhaps even greater than certain other members of a family well-nigh peerless in the air. That they can dive with ease when occasion requires is recorded by Commander Pennell. During the voyage of the *Terra Nova* from the Cape to Melbourne and south-east of the Cape of Good Hope, five of these birds were seen to settle in the water when objects were thrown overboard and then, from that position, to dive completely under water after them if necessary. On another occasion Pennell observed one dive into and under water with three-quarters expanded wings, coming up with the wings still half-open. Although not really ill-tempered they will peck at another of their kind should it approach too close when food is available : Pennell described them as " peevish " rather than quarrelsome at such times. He never saw two fighting.

When Dr. E. A. Wilson was voyaging between Cape Town and Australia on the *Corinthic* he particularly remarked one bird—a young of *D. melanophrys* which had a pure white head and pale yellow bill with a black tip. Adults of this albatross were seen every day from 12th September in 36° 26′ S., 22° 47′ E. until 29th September when the ship's position was 43° 48′ S., 146° 01′ E. All had yellow bills and orange tips. The white-headed bird mentioned must have been in very similar plumage to the one which was captured alive in Derbyshire.

In a short communication to the *Ibis*, 1931, the late Hugh Whistler published some notes which he had kept when returning to India on the S.S. *City of Exeter* via the Cape and Durban. Black-browed albatrosses appear to have been present in some numbers from 21st to 28th May after which they disappeared when the ship was in the latitude of Durban. One bird, recognized by having the inner tertials on one side white, was with the ship from 9 a.m. when first sighted, until dark, eight and a half hours later. As the ship was travelling at twelve knots it was reckoned that the bird had, at a moderate estimate, flown at least 300 miles in the day. C. B. Ticehurst, when *en route* for the Cape, met *D. melanophrys* for the first time on 19th August in latitude 20° S.

It has been remarked that Commander Pennell of the *Terra Nova* did not consider this albatross anything more than " peevish " : but that it can be unpleasantly aggressive at times is evident from an incident witnessed by P. W. Reynolds among the islands of Cape Horn. The black-browed albatross was found to be common in Nassau Bay and in the wider channels about Wollaston and Hermite Islands, and amazingly numerous about the Barnevelt Islands where Mr. Reynolds had hoped to find it breeding in December 1932. The Barnevelt Islands, at a distance of nine miles to the east of Deceit, are included by some authorities in the Hermite group. In this area on one occasion Reynolds watched the antics of a black-browed albatross which possessed something of the savageness of the giant petrel. A bird was clumsily emulating skuas and Dominican gulls in the persecution of an unfortunate cormorant (*P. atriceps*), which was repeatedly forced to dive beneath the combined attack without being permitted to swallow its catch. Reynolds considered that cold weather seems greatly to increase the ferocity and appetite of parasitic birds, but we can hardly place the albatross in that category because it joined in the fun on that occasion.

THE NESTING OF THE BLACK-BROWED ALBATROSS

L. Harrison Matthews, Sc.D., F.R.S.

Scientific Director, Zoological Society of London

The black-browed albatross nests on most of the sub-antarctic islands, from the Falklands and the islands off Cape Horn to Kerguelen and the islands south of New Zealand. Over thirty years ago I was able to make some study of this albatross, or white mollymauk as the sailors call it, on the island of South Georgia. The mollies come ashore in enormous numbers early in October to breed in rookeries in the cliffs, especially at the north-west of the island, although there are rookeries elsewhere, as for example near Cape Disappointment at the south-east end. The rookeries lie on the steep slopes at the top of the cliffs, and each contains several thousand nests ; they are often contiguous with those of the grey-headed albatross, or blue molly. The nests are built of mud and peaty moss on ledges among the tussac ; they are cylindrical, from one to one and a half feet high, with vertical sides and a depression on the top—a large rookery recalls the cheese room in an old-fashioned Somerset farm, with the cheeses stacked to mature in rows on the shelves. The birds collect the material for the nests from the nearby ledges ; the cock of one pair that I watched building was gathering beakfuls of peaty earth among the tussac and bringing them to the hen which stood on the half-finished nest. He put each beakful on the nest and, bowing his head down till his beak touched the ground, uttered a loud braying cry. The hen bowed back to him and brayed, then arranged the mud on the nest and trod it down with her large webbed feet. Before the cock went off for another load they nibbled each other's beaks and faces, bowed low and brayed.

When the mollies open the beak to bray, they bow the head forward and then shut the beak abruptly ; thereupon a parting at once appears in the feathers running back from the angle of the beak. The parting reveals the side of the mouth behind the beak, the gape that is bordered by soft lips. When the parting appears the lips of the gape are seen as a pink ridge of warty skin running back under the eye ; this is shown for a few moments only and then the feathers are allowed to fall back into place.

After every dozen loads or so brought to the nest that I watched being built the birds interrupted the building process with a more elaborate display. They stood facing each other, one on the nest and the other close beside, and started fencing with their beaks, delicately touching the sides and tips together, and finished by bowing to each other. Then each turned its head right round and nestled the tip of the beak in the feathers of the back between the wings. They held this attitude for a few moments and then both gave a low grunt, and turning their heads forward, started braying loudly with their beaks wide open, swaying their heads from side to side and spreading their tails. Then followed an interval during which the birds spent some minutes nibbling each other's beaks and the short feathers on the partner's face and chin ; and further braying displays intervened before they started work again.

This display might be labelled as mutual stimulation of the endocrine system, primarily through the pituitary, but apart from physiological considerations it seems obvious that the birds of a pair take the greatest delight in each other's company and in caressing each other, and " looking babies into each other's eyes ". I did not see an actual pairing on this occasion, so it is evident that a considerable amount of stimulation is required—or else they enjoy the display for its own sake, for they carry on like this for many days.

This sort of thing was going on all over the rookery and meanwhile streams of birds were arriving from the sea and others were going off to feed. Like all albatrosses, they cannot rise on to the wing from a level surface if there is no wind, but on these cliffs they had no difficulty—they just took one jump over the edge and away they soared. They were not very graceful when they came in to land ; they slowed down as much as they could, spreading out their great webbed feet as brakes, whereupon the light which shone through the greyish webs made them appear bright pink, and as soon as the birds touched down they nearly always capsized on to their breasts. They scrambled to their feet with an air of ruffled dignity and immediately brayed loudly several times before waddling away to their nests.

The eggs are gathered for food by the whalers and sealers from some of the more accessible rookeries ; the eggs are white and rather elongated, with a small sprinkling of red spots particularly towards the larger end, and weigh about ¾ lb. There is no need to turn the birds off their nests to get the eggs ; if you go gently you can put your hand beneath the sitting bird and take the egg from under her—she may nibble your sleeve as you do so, but she will not bite unless you make a sudden movement. When the egg is gone she settles down again on the nest as though nothing had happened, but after a minute or two she seems to realize that something is wrong. She rises up on to her " elbows ", not on to her feet, looks down into the nest beneath her breast, nibbles at the odd wisps of tussac lying in it, gives a few brays, and then sits down again and, shuffling round, goes on incubating nothing.

Later in the season, after most of the eggs had hatched, I had an opportunity of visiting another rookery at Cape Buller on one of those rare fine days that allow of landing in normally inaccessible places. I was able to get up the cliffs and steep slopes to a rookery of white mollies on less precipitous ground about four or five hundred feet above the sea. The tussac was rather short on this mountainside and the earth was trodden into ledges on which the nests were built. Most of the nests had half-grown youngsters in them, though a few had tiny chicks or even eggs. A considerable number of the old birds were sitting or sleeping on empty nests and some of them were going through their nuptial display with its usual braying noises.

I do not think that this rookery had been robbed of its eggs earlier in the season—it is too far from the sea and the landing is very difficult or impossible unless the weather is unusually smooth. Perhaps some of the nests had been robbed by the skuas, of which there were plenty always on the watch for any unprotected egg or chick, but I do not think they would account for all the empty nests or all those with late chicks or unhatched eggs. It seems very probable that although the majority of mollies start laying at about the same time, some of them are delayed, or even unable to produce an egg at all. All the albatrosses are slow breeders and hatch only a single egg each season ; if the physiology of the reproductive process is sluggish the importance of the complicated and long-drawn nuptial display in stimulating the production and laying of an egg is emphasized if in spite of it some birds are late or sterile.

The young are covered with fluffy greyish-white down and have dark, almost black, beaks. The smaller chicks were being guarded by one of the parents, and when they were exposed by the old bird standing up at my approach they uttered feeble pipings as they nestled farther under the protecting bodies ; but the half-grown young, many of which were quite alone and unguarded while their parents were away fishing, showed a disposition by no means retiring. Although the old birds show no fear of man, at least when they are in their rookeries, these youngsters were decidedly aggressive towards a stranger.

As I approached any one of them it sat up on its tail, raising itself to its fullest height, and shuffled round in the nest as I moved so that it was facing me all the time. If I went right up to one it appeared to get very agitated, and panted with emotion, and snapped its beak, all the while making a gulping noise deep down in its throat. The cause of the gulping noise was soon obvious for, with a few retchings, the young bird brought up a quantity of oil from its stomach and squirted it with considerable force at me. Unfortunately for the bird I was many times taller than it, and consequently it shot the oil upwards at me and much of it fell back upon the flustered creature. Nevertheless this aggressive behaviour and oil shooting evidently affords them good protection against the gulls and skuas which are their only possible enemies, for I found no signs of any of these larger youngsters having come to grief.

The oil is peculiar ; while it is hot as delivered it is quite clear and a bright tomato red, but as soon as it cools it sets to an opaque solid wax very much like spermaceti except that it is pink. Judging by its colour the red pigment is probably derived from the euphausian whale-food or " krill " caught by the old birds at sea and transferred to the young when they are fed. The oil itself is a secretion of the glands lining the first part of the stomach, the proventriculus, and is a product of the birds' metabolism. It is only the red colour that stains the oil which is directly derived from the food. Although the sun was shining brightly the air temperature was low, so that the oil set solid almost as soon as it fell on my clothes or on the down of the birds, whose warm fur coats are no mere ornaments even on a bright day such as this.

On another occasion I had an opportunity of seeing very large flocks of these albatrosses at sea feeding on a concentration of krill. At a spot about forty miles from the coast the birds were gathered in tens of thousands near a small iceberg, and the krill was so dense near the surface that it made the water quite soupy. Vast shoals of fish were also feeding on the krill and we could see them about two fathoms down, so closely packed that it looked like a solid bottom of huge pebbles just under the keel. Not only were the fish feeding on the krill from below, the birds were scooping it up from above. As far as we could see in every direction the sea was covered with birds, mostly white mollies sitting close together and all facing the breeze. Here and there among them were smaller flocks of blue mollies and wanderers, and the spaces were filled with immense numbers of smaller birds such as Cape pigeons and shoemakers, while over them all great flocks of little dove-grey whale birds skimmed, probably hundreds of thousands of them, their wings flashing as all the birds in a flock turned together like sandpipers over an autumn mudflat.

The mollies had evidently been gorging for some time and were fully fed, for most of them were not feeding very actively and merely gave a desultory peck now and again. Occasionally they reached down for some specially fat shrimp, stretching their heads as far as possible under the water ; here and there I saw birds going right below the surface—it could scarcely be called diving when they plunged rather awkwardly with half-open wings, and submerged for only a few inches or a foot at most. As each swell passed the crest was capped with a continuous line of white breasts as rank after rank of mollies poised at the top for a moment as it bore them up before they slipped down into the following trough.

REFERENCES : Original Description : *Diomedia melanophris* (*melanophrys* correct) Temminck, *Pl. Col. d'Ois.*, 1828, pl. 456 : Cape of Good Hope.

Order PODICIPEDIFORMES

Family PODICIPEDIDAE [1]

Genus *PODICEPS* Latham

PLATE 13

GREAT CRESTED GREBE

Podiceps cristatus cristatus Linnaeus

Resident. Most leave inland breeding areas in the autumn to pass three or four months around the coasts. British breeding birds are not known to migrate except locally. Overseas visitors may frequent our coasts in winter, but evidence is inconclusive.

IDENTIFICATION : This is the largest of the grebes which are found in these islands, its total length from the rather long pointed bill to the insignificant tail being nearly 20 inches, of which the actual body is about 12 inches. The neck is fairly long and slender, the head set at right angles. The wing is narrow but well able to support the bird's weight. Great crested grebes are unmistakable by reason of their size and—in the breeding season—by the extremely handsome tippet of chestnut feathers edged with black which can be expanded at will by both sexes, though it is less developed in the hen bird than in the male. At a distance the long tufts on each side of the black crown are clearly visible and assist in the identification. The cheeks and throat are glistening white, as are the underparts of the body. The upperparts are blackish tinged with brown. The diminutive tail consists of a tuft of soft brown feathers. The dagger-shaped bill is pinkish horn, the eye crimson, the legs and feet olive and greenish-yellow. The three forwardly directed toes have lobes on both sides, the very small hind toe being raised above the level of the others. The bill from the feathering measures about 2 inches.

In flight a considerable patch of white shows in the wing ; the neck is held straight out in front but with a decided dip, the head held below the horizontal axis of the body ; the legs project beyond the short tail. When rising from the surface these truly aquatic birds patter along the water but once launched they fly strongly and with direct purpose. When alighting on water grebes strike the surface with their breasts first, not with outstretched feet as do the duck family.

The remark in *The Handbook* under " Field Characters " that grebes fly but little, or comparatively little, except when migrating, is certainly not applicable to the present species in winter quarters. Anyone who has

---

[1] For the correct spelling of this family name as here used, see Newton's *Dictionary of Birds*, p. 381, note 1.

seen the great congregation of great crested grebes in the Bosphorus or in the harbour of Istanbul in winter, must be struck by the number of these birds to be seen on the wing as they fly from one point to another, often making long flights past the anchored vessels in the harbour. It may then be remarked how rapidly the wings are beaten and how inadequate the wings appear to be for the size of the body. For all that the grebes progress swiftly. Great numbers breed in the vicinity of the Black Sea and the birds are always to be seen in the harbours.

LOCAL DISTRIBUTION : The breeding population of the great crested grebe in the British Isles has increased out of all belief. Even some twenty-nine years ago Mr. Harry Witherby was able to announce that over 500 " breeding-waters " were occupied in England, Wales, and Scotland, with a total population of some 2825 adult birds[1]; and it is evident that the large figure quoted is greatly exceeded at the time when this paragraph is being written (April 1958). The census of the great crested grebe during the years 1931 to 1950 was restricted to twenty-one English counties, which are enumerated in the report.[2] Strict comparison with Mr. Witherby's total is not therefore possible. It is, however, significant that excluding Wales, Scotland, and Ireland the English grebes actually counted by a large number of observers in 1950—to take the last of the six counts for which figures are available—reached the figure 2039, due very largely to a considerable increase in certain southern counties and to the colonizing of new waters.

In the census report Mr. Hollom, who was responsible for collating the results, states : " this great shift of population since 1931 has mainly been on to waters which have only come into existence since that date and especially on to gravel pits in the Thames valley counties. In other areas too the increase can be associated with fresh waters, particularly when new reservoirs have come into being." It is further remarked that the attraction for grebes of relatively newly-filled waters must now be regarded as an established fact. The census emphasized the point that some counties now have about three times the number of grebes they held in 1931, while others have little over one-third of their former population. Certain counties even showed a definite decrease. Marked fluctuations were found to occur between one year and another in the grebe population suggestive, in Mr. Hollom's view, of site-shifting at a rate of about 2 per cent. of the total population each year. The weather appears to have an even more violent influence, the numbers dropping severely after a winter such as that of 1947. The southern English counties of Hertfordshire, Oxfordshire, Surrey, Essex, Buckinghamshire, Middlesex, and Berkshire, have shown a much greater increase in the great crested grebe population than elsewhere in the British Isles. In no other area have man-made habitats come

[1] *Handbook of British Birds*, 1940, p. 90.
[2] P. A. D. Hollom in *British Birds*, xliv, 1951, pp. 361-369.

into existence to the same extent. It is because of these new playgrounds that our great crested grebe has spread its wings with such success.

In an article published by Mr. Hollom in *Bird Notes and News*,[1] which covers a grebe census from 1946 to 1955, the statement appears that in the twenty-one counties already mentioned, extending from Surrey to Lancashire and holding between 600 and 700 grebe-frequented waters, some 2200 adult birds were located. It is pointed out that no census undertaken between 1931 and 1946 suggested a total of more than 1800 birds, so that an appreciable increase is apparent pointing to successful nesting on many waters.

The present writer has never been a great believer in a bird census as usually undertaken : too many annual fluctuations take place and the human element is by no means infallible, but with this reservation the figures arrived at by the British Trust for Ornithology are doubtless as near the mark as possible. Mr. Hollom, I am sure, will not agree with my opinion. He has written that the great crested grebe is " a conspicuous and easily identified bird, its possible breeding places, which are virtually limited to waters of five acres and upwards, could all be located on the ordnance survey maps and much of its past history and present numbers could be ascertained without difficulty from landowners and keepers ", etc., etc. Even so the counting of a bird of this nature is a formidable undertaking not to be despised. To arrive at even an approximate number of grebes nesting in sparsely populated country is a very different matter from making a count in Middlesex or East Anglia where bird watchers are legion. Wales is particularly badly served in this way and so far as I know no attempt has been made to cover that country. *The Handbook* (1940) records that the great crested grebe " had bred [at that date] in all counties except Monmouth, Pembroke, Cardigan, and Carmarthen ; not regular Caernarvon, Radnor, and perhaps other counties. Brecon has oldest established colony (1882 or earlier) and largest number of pairs, but density nowhere exceeds 4 pairs to 100,000 acres ".

Scotland has been much better served, and in their *Birds of Scotland* Dr. Evelyn Baxter and Miss Rintoul have given us the latest details available to them in 1953. Even so no census appears to have been made since 1931, when only 75 to 100 breeding pairs were located. The bird first colonized Scotland in 1877 and has increased considerably since that date. Attention may be drawn to a very wise remark which bears repetition. The authors, when discussing the number of breeding pairs, observe : " Their habit of prospecting lochs for a year or two before actually breeding on them makes it unsafe to assume that a pair of grebes in full adult plumage on a loch, necessarily means that they were nesting there. We, personally, would never record breeding of great crested grebes on a new water unless we had seen eggs or young." In Scotland the bird is mainly restricted

[1] Vol. xxvi, No. 1, 1953-54, pp. 22-25.

to the Lowlands or, as expressed in *The Birds of Scotland*, its breeding distribution is on the lochs south of the Grampians and round the north coast of Aberdeenshire into Moray. It has increased greatly in Perthshire and that county is now well colonized—it was in Perthshire that the first Scottish nest was found at the Loch of the Lowes above Dunkeld. On a loch between Perth and Angus this grebe has been recorded breeding at 700 feet above the sea. Miss Rintoul and Dr. Baxter name many Scottish lochs where they had personal knowledge of nesting. Their statement that the great crested grebe has never been proved to breed on the Islands came as a surprise to the present writer when first he read it, but that apparently is a fact. " There are [spring] records from Bute and the Inner Hebrides, the most interesting being of two pairs in breeding plumage on a loch in Tiree on 22nd May 1900. There is no record from the Outer Hebrides or St. Kilda, but they occur occasionally in Orkney and Shetland, and two or three were seen on Fair Isle in May 1940. . . ." In the winter months many of the birds move from the inland lochs to the sea coast and estuaries as they do from their breeding places south of the Border. When the lochs are not icebound a certain number of grebes remain on the breeding grounds throughout the winter, but the majority make their way to the sea.

The breeding range of this bird in Ireland is clearly indicated by Major Ruttledge who wrote in the new *Birds of Ireland* (1954) : " The great crested grebe has greatly increased in numbers and has extended its breeding range during the present century. It nests, often in very great numbers, in most suitable lakes throughout northern, central, and western Ireland. It is, however, absent as a breeding bird from most of the country lying south of a line drawn between Dundalk and Limerick. A few birds are present in winter on the larger inland waters.

That then is a summary of the great crested grebe's status in Great Britain at the present day, though we need to have more up-to-date knowledge as regards its spread in Scotland than is available at the time of writing.

It is stated in *The Handbook of British Birds* that " there is no evidence of British breeders beyond British waters or of immigration of Continental birds ". The " evidence "—presumably by ringing—is very difficult to get, for few great crested grebes are ringed in these islands and the chance of a ringed grebe being recovered abroad is infinitesimal. As regards immigration from the Continent I am far from sure that the statement quoted is correct. How else than by overseas visitors are we to explain the large gatherings which are from time to time seen off our coasts—such, for instance, as Dr. Evelyn Baxter and Miss Rintoul observed in the first week of February in the Firth of Culross when at least 500 birds were present,[1] far too many to be explained by local breeding birds gathering

[1] *The Birds of Scotland*, vol. ii, p. 499.

together. Moreover the weather at the time was mild. Again the very large numbers seen by the late Charles Oldham [1] off the coast of North Wales in early September (8th and 10th), too early to be accounted for by an exodus of British birds from their breeding haunts : the numbers again were too great to be accounted for by Scottish residents already on the move, and as Mr. Oldham remarked, the majority were in breeding dress. These are not isolated instances.

DISTRIBUTION ABROAD : The great crested grebe breeds throughout Europe from 60° N. in Norway and 66° N. in Finland, south to the Mediterranean. It ranges east far into Asia. In the Mediterranean islands it is reported to breed in Sardinia, Sicily, and Cyprus, but has long since ceased to do so in the last-named and was always scarce. There are also reports of nesting in Algeria and Morocco, but these old reports need substantiating. It used to breed on Lake Menzaleh in Egypt. The question of Palaearctic migrants breeding in northern Africa badly needs revision and fresh observations. Even *The Handbook of British Birds* (1940) quotes this species as breeding in Cyprus and Egypt as if it were an annual occurrence !

Another subspecies takes its place in tropical Africa.

Of the range of the great crested grebe in Russian territory Mme. E. Kozlova sent me the following note in July 1958 :

Distribution. In the European part of the U.S.S.R. the great crested grebe breeds north to the shores of Lake Ladoga and Lake Onega. Further east the northern boundary extends to about 60° N., then descends to the region of Perm. In Western Siberia it does not extend north beyond Jiumen, Ishim, the lakes of Barabinsky steppes, the regions of Atchinsk and Minussinsk. It nests in the region south-west of southern Baikal (Irkut River valley near the Mongolian frontier). It is common in Mongolia and China, but absent from Transbaikalia and from Amur Land. In the far east of the U.S.S.R. it appears again in Ussuri Land on Lake Hanka. In the south its range in the U.S.S.R. embraces the Ukraine, Transcaucasia and Turkestan.

Winter records from the U.S.S.R. : coasts of the Black Sea ; near the south-western shores of the Caspian Sea (Transcaucasia), south-eastern shores of the Caspian near Krasnovodsk (Transcaspia) and some lakes in Ferghana (Turkestan). Nowhere numerous.

Principal winter abodes in the Mediterranean countries, Iran, Baluchistan, India, S. China, Japan.

From northern Europe there is a marked migration southwards in the winter months, when many birds must reach northern Africa. Reports of the bird's abundance in Morocco in spring may perhaps be explained by the winter visitors gathering before returning to Europe. Irby, who visited the lakes of Ras el Doura at the end of April, recorded that the number of great crested grebes was " perfectly marvellous ". The lakes

[1] *Ibis*, 1931, pp. 87-89.

are still there, and just as difficult to " work " in the summer as when Irby was there eighty-five and more years ago ; but although he stated that " these grebes were in pairs but had not commenced laying " we still have no actual proof that they did so.   In the western end of the Mediterranean—and indeed over the whole extent of that sea—great crested grebes are not by any means numerous.   It is an uncommon visitor to the lagoons in the Balearic islands in winter, and some frequent the coasts.   It has been reported " in fair numbers " from Corsica, and I have found it myself in February off Sfax on the Tunisian coast but in no great numbers. Whitaker found it in Tunisia in winter and during the period of passage and suggested that it might breed in some of the lakes ; but he had no definite evidence to that effect.   It is rare in Egypt to-day.

Very different is its winter status in the Black Sea and the Sea of Marmara.   I write from personal experience in 1955, when the grebes in the Bosphorus and in the harbour of Istanbul were a feature of the busy scene.   The Caspian and Aral Sea are no doubt equally frequented in winter, though we are singularly ill-informed as regards this area at the present day.   The grebes certainly reach Cyprus in winter, where I have seen them in the harbours but never in the numbers seen farther north. It winters in small numbers in Iraq but is almost unknown in Arabia from which there are only two records.

Probably the great crested grebes in central and southern Europe only move from their breeding areas when driven to do so by stress of weather. Just as the British population takes to the adjoining coasts so the European birds only seek the nearest salt water when compelled by the freezing of their own lakes and marshes.   The northern breeding birds are those most likely to be driven south, but the numbers which reach the Mediterranean and northern Africa are not by any means so great as we might imagine from consulting the textbooks.

There have not been many recoveries of ringed grebes, but there is some evidence to support Count von Zedlitz's view that great crested grebes from northern Germany migrate in a south-easterly direction. Dr. Schüz quotes a case of a bird ringed on 10th April 1925 at Askania Nova, S. Taurida, Russia, which was recovered on 3rd October of the same year at Knacksee, Kr. Neustettin, but this is a very peculiar record. Another bird ringed in Mark Brandenburg, 21st June 1930, found its way to the Sea of Azov when it was recovered on the north coast on 8th November of that year.   This last record points to a fraction, at any rate, of the north German population having their winter quarters in the south-east.

Dr. Schüz, in a short article in *Vogelzug*, mentions that the case for a south-westerly or westerly migration of the great crested grebe—of which there is still little evidence—is supported by an unpublished record of the Vogelwarte Helgoland communicated to him privately by Dr. Drost. Schüz, writing in 1931, observed that this grebe had enlarged its territory considerably in Northern Europe during the previous few decades, colonizing Scandinavia, the British Isles, and even eastern Friesland; and he suggested that this encroachment into Western Europe has taken place from the east, where the great crested grebe is such an abundant bird. This, in Dr. Schüz's view, would be enough to explain a south-easterly trend in the birds' movements when they depart from a north-western breeding area.

The absence, or great scarcity, of the great crested grebe in Portugal and neighbouring seas in winter is remarked upon, but it may be asked from what country come the great crested grebes reported to be so numerous on the Atlantic seaboard of Morocco? If these are indeed winter visitors and not local birds there must be a considerable passage across the Straits of Gibraltar. Since Favier reported them going north from Tangier in March there have been no further references to this species from the area mentioned.

To show it is unsafe for the great crested grebe to remain too long in latitudes where severe frost sets in with little warning, an experience which befell Dr. Schüz in Germany may be instanced. Remarking that " when the ponds and rivers begin to freeze the great crested grebe have almost all left, presumably to pass the winter in southern Europe ", he recounts how he had seen " a young bird of this species on an open stretch of the Neckar near Tübingen. The bird did not leave the spot as frost set in and the ice closed round it. Finally it was no longer possible for it to get the necessary run for its flight, and on the following morning the crows had arrived and were pecking the corpse out of the ice "—a sad lesson to adolescent grebes who think they know better than their elders.

HABITS : With the exception of the dabchick or little grebe the subject of this essay is the best known of the five members of the family which figure on the British List ; while from the point of view of its habits and breeding biology it is one of the most discussed birds in the British Isles.[1] Easily recognized by reason of its large size and the ornamental head-dress which it acquires in the breeding season, it is now sufficiently numerous in these islands to have become a familiar sight to many. Anyone who has handled a great crested grebe will be struck by the beautiful texture of its plumage, more especially by the glistening white underparts, almost silky to the touch. Howard Saunders described its belly as " silver-white " and he was not far off the mark. The silkiness of its feathers nearly spelled its extinction in Great Britain, and had it not been saved by the Seabirds Protection Act of 1869, we should have lost one of our most beautiful and

---

[1] The most comprehensive review of this species ever undertaken is that by K. E. L. Simmons entitled " Studies on Great Crested Grebes ", illustrated by Robert Gillmor and published in *The Avicultural Magazine*, vol. lxi, 1955. I am fortunate that Mr. Simmons has consented to write the sections on courtship, pairing, and territory in this account. See pp. 215-223.

ornamental species. In the bad old days its skin was in great demand for muffs and stolls, a single skin fetching as much as 10s. when the craze was at its height somewhere about 1845. Birds were not then protected during the nesting season and its extermination was imminent.

Fortunately it is a species which can normally hold its own, laying usually three to five eggs but as many as six in a full clutch and being able to stand the severest weather, merely departing to the coast when conditions force it from the inland lakes and meres which are its favoured habitat. As it has thrived, so it has increased and spread to quite small sheets of water, occupying reservoirs as they are created and appearing even on brick and gravel-pits where one would scarcely have thought to look for them in days gone by. The extent of this spread to new waters,[1] particularly in southern England, is most remarkable and points to the conclusion that suitable inland water is the bird's chief requirement in these islands. Before I came to study this bird in detail I had imagined that it required a good-sized open sheet of water well supplied with reed-beds— and that is still, I believe, the ideal setting for its home. Such haunts as Fritton Lake in Suffolk and some of the Cheshire and Lancashire meres come nearest to my ideal for a great crested grebe sanctuary, but it is now evident that a pair or more will make their home amidst much less secluded surroundings than was formerly realized. Even more surprising is the fact that some of its old secluded haunts on lakes in country estates have been deserted, but for what cause it is difficult to guess, unless food has become scarce. One can hardly imagine a gravel-pit or reedless reservoir a good exchange even out of the nesting season.

In Britain it is not correct to state that all great crested grebes leave their chosen broad or loch for the coastal areas ; a few remain here and there. Writing of the bird in Suffolk, Claud Ticehurst remarked how after breeding, some birds, especially the young ones, disperse and are from time to time encountered on our tidal rivers " where no doubt winter visitors or passage migrants from elsewhere are met with ". He remarked how every winter from September to May great crested grebes may be seen on estuaries such as the Stour, and if severe weather sets in for long periods the birds are hard put to it to find food. That some are more hardy than others was the opinion of Miss Turner, for she found them on various meres all over the country between October and February, and observed that a few resort to Hickling Broad even when it is frozen over and are then to be seen swimming about in the " wakes " which are kept open for the sake of wildfowl. The Norfolk and Suffolk Broads are naturally a much favoured area, but even so the birds are particular in their choice and some broads which appear quite suitable in our eyes are left alone for some reason by the discerning birds. No one knew her Broadland better than the late Miss Emma Turner, and in one of her books [2] she has written

[1] *British Birds*, xliv, 1951, p. 365.   [2] *Broadland Birds*, Country Life Ltd., 1924.

an attractive account of the great crested grebes among which she lived for twenty years. Many of the facts which she discovered after hours of patient watching will find mention in this essay.

Of all its family the great crested grebe is the most aquatic. It spends its whole life on or in the water, and even when nesting it builds a floating platform of reeds from which at the least sign of danger it can take refuge by diving. On rare occasions a bird will come on to land. A description of one such instance has been sent to me by Mme. E. Kozlova, who witnessed it herself during one of her many expeditions.[1] She writes from Leningrad :

On 9th May I watched two grebes that were swimming among the small islets fringed with reeds in Lake Orok-nor. The birds would dive and obtain some kind of weed ; riding the water close one to another, almost breast to breast and holding the plant by the end, the birds would shake their heads and strike each other on the head with the free end of the plant, splashing themselves with silt.

The great crested grebe very rarely comes on shore. Only on one occasion during the first week after the arrival of these birds did I see one do so. The female was swimming close to a low swampy islet ; then slipping swiftly on to the shore she stood for a second and almost immediately dropped down on to her breast, stretching her head out on the ground. The male seemed to be greatly alarmed by the departure of his mate ; he swam all round the islet, twisting his head as if he were in search of something, and approached the female several times and withdrew again. A few minutes later the female jumped down into the water, and both birds swam away.

Of the diving Mme. Kozlova observes :

The great crested grebes arrived on Lake Orok-nor on 28th April and kept in pairs near the shore, spending their time either in diving for fish or in courtship performances. I timed them to see how long they stayed under water and found the time to be from 6 to 7 seconds in every case ; while swimming under water they covered a space of about 8 metres. When disturbed, this grebe rarely takes wing but in most cases dives, and can then swim under water for some 30 metres. Their harsh calls are heard uninterruptedly all through the spring.

In this connexion Mr. Simmons points out that dives of the great crested grebe usually last longer than the 6-7 seconds mentioned by the authority quoted. They may, in fact, last up to a maximum of 56 seconds and average about 25 seconds. Major H. M. Salmon and Mr. G. C. S. Ingram, in their instructive work on the diving habits of ducks and grebes (*Brit. Bds.* xxxv, 1941, pp. 22-26) wrote of *Podiceps c. cristatus* : " Diving pelagically ; 21 dives timed, maximum 45 seconds, mean 23·5 seconds, minimum 11 seconds." The average in this case worked out a little below that given in *The Handbook*, i.e. 12-50 seconds. Dewar is reported to have recorded diving to a maximum depth of 21 feet. The average appears to be 6-12 feet as recorded by B. W. Tucker in *The Handbook*.

[1] *Birds of Transbaikalia, N. Mongolia and Central Gobi.*

PLATE 13

GREAT CRESTED GREBE
Podiceps cristatus cristatus Linnaeus

PLATE 13

GREAT CRESTED GREBE

Mr. Simmons's figures given here for the duration of the dive are of course the latest from additional information in his possession.

Although naturally shy birds when nesting, I have often been astonished at their boldness in winter when meeting with them abroad. Earlier in this account I have mentioned their abundance in the harbour of Istanbul and there they may be seen swimming unconcernedly among the anchored ferry-boats close to the quay. The Lac de Tunis, past which ocean-going steamers make their way to the busy port, is another winter resort where these grebes can sometimes be observed with greater ease than when engaged in domestic matters, and there I have been able to approach them quite close. They seem impervious to weather but in rough water will sink their bodies low.

Fish are probably the main source of food supply, even though Collinge's analysis worked out at only 22·5 per cent. of the whole. It is generally believed that this was too low an estimate. Crustaceans, larvae, insects, and mollusca are also eaten, but when the birds are at sea insects and their larvae can be discounted. A smelt $5\frac{1}{2}$ inches in length was taken from a bird in Norfolk (Ticehurst), while another bird (of the African race *infuscatus*) was seen in the act of eating a frog. Professor M. F. M. Meiklejohn, who recorded the incident, observed that the frog, which was of a fair size, was held under the water for some time, shaken, and finally swallowed whole. This is unlikely to have been an exceptional episode. A case was reported [1] some years back of a great crested grebe continually stabbing at a swallow as the latter skimmed close by; the grebe was seen to raise itself out of the water in its attempts to strike the swallow, but without success. It is not suggested that the grebe would have swallowed the body had it been successful, though this is quite within the bounds of possibility. Of special interest are the quantities of feathers to be found in a grebe's stomach. This was referred to at some length in the Great Crested Grebe Enquiry of 1931,[2] but those who conducted the enquiry reached no definite conclusion as to the object of this feather-eating. The authors were inclined to believe that the cause is partly psychological, a development of preening and perhaps of the curious weed-presentation in display. Chicks a few days old have been seen to peck at and pluck out the breast feathers of an adult. It is a well-known fact that from an early age young grebes are fed on feathers and the curious fact has given rise to a good deal of discussion. Professor William Rowan suggested that the feather is a source of vitamin D needed by the young bird. P. Madon [3] rejected his own hypothesis that feathers help in the digestion of fish bones and other hard material and in the retention of certain *algae*; he believed that the explanation must be sought elsewhere than in the study of food.

[1] R. H. Winterbottom, in *British Birds*, xlviii, 1955, p. 229.
[2] *British Birds*, xxvi, 1932, pp. 149-150.
[3] *Revue française d'ornithologie*, 1926.

Dr. Alexander Wetmore is, however, inclined to the explanation that the feathers act as a strainer to prevent the passage of fish bones or large fragments of chitin into the intestine until they have been reduced to a proper size and condition by the process of digestion. This latter seems to the writer a most logical explanation if it were applicable to all diving birds and not only to the members of the grebe family. The problem has recently been discussed afresh by Kenneth Simmons,[1] and a connexion between feather-eating and pellet formation is suggested in the course of a thoughtful review of the evidence. In fact Mr. Simmons definitely states his opinion that grebes eat feathers for the main purpose of pellet-formation. In a summary of his paper he writes : " Adult great crested grebes eat feathers mainly when preening and also give them to the young. In the stomach these feathers break down into a special mush-like substance which envelopes fish-bone, etc., apparently to form ejectable pellets. As yet no one seems to have seen the actual ejection of such a pellet and the pellet itself is unknown."

In the Broad country the grebe returns to its nesting ground at the end of January or beginning of February, but some will arrive much later in the year and parties have been seen coming in to Hickling as late as mid-April, flying restlessly to and fro over the Broad all day, alighting at intervals in order to feed and go through a courting display. This display, of which more will be said later, will even take place at sea before the birds have come inland. Charles Oldham,[2] one of the finest naturalists of my younger days, watched birds off the north Welsh coast on 1st April indulging in " shaking bouts " and one couple in the " penguin dance ", from which he inferred that they were then on their way to their breeding grounds.[3] It would not surprise me to learn that these birds pair for life but that has not yet been ascertained with any certainty. Oldham lived at Tring and kept constant watch on the famous Tring reservoirs in Hertfordshire where many grebes nest every summer. He remarked how, except in backward seasons and when the waters are icebound, they return in force in February and the first half of March ; and at about the same time to the meres of Cheshire and Shropshire, although, as he states, more remain through the winter on the meres (unless they are icebound and vacated temporarily) than on the exposed reservoirs at Tring. In both Cheshire and Hertfordshire eggs are sometimes laid by the end of March and are not infrequent by mid-April and these districts, Oldham suggested, are perhaps typical of others south of the Scottish border. He should have added when water conditions and the season are normal, for Jourdain has shown [4] that in Britain the nesting period is dependent on more factors

[1] K. E. L. Simmons, in *British Birds*, xlix, 1956, pp. 432-435.
[2] One of the authors of *A Practical Handbook of British Birds*.
[3] *Ibis*, 1931, pp. 87-89.
[4] *The Handbook of British Birds*, 1940, p. 88.

than one and in consequence varies very much in different localities. Jourdain stressed first the presence of covert, nesting being delayed until the growth was sufficient to hide the nest. He found May a more usual month, " onward to July and at times August and September " ; and according to him full setts have only exceptionally been found in March. In Broadland the nests are generally placed amidst the densest cover and are inaccessible except by means of a duck-punt. Miss Turner [1] records one nest with six eggs—an exceptional number—in June, the young of which all hatched successfully. It has been mentioned already that the grebe builds a floating nest, but anyone who has had the opportunity to examine a number will soon appreciate how one nest may differ from another. This is well exemplified by Eric Hosking's photographs and Dr. Newberry's descriptive writing in *Birds of the Day*, which latter I have their permission to reproduce :

The most general form [of nest] is composed of dead reed stems bent over through the edges of the nest. The nest is built on a floating platform and a certain amount of vegetable growth is essential as a means of anchoring the nest, which would otherwise be at the mercy of wind and currents.

Another type of nest to be seen on the Norfolk broads is built on what is locally known as a " hover ", that is a piece of ground knit together by the tangled woody rootstocks of the reed, but broken away from the edge of a broad to form a semi-submerged, but floating, island. Built sometimes in shallow water, this nest has more support on submerged vegetation than the one described above. The structure, moreover, is more bulky and the nest itself, on the summit of the cone, higher out of the water. Additionally a plentiful soft lining of water-weed was present.

A third type differed in that a considerable number of sticks were used in its construction and the structure—which was rather exposed—was anchored in comparatively deep water enabling the bird to reach the nest by diving and springing up to it.

These experienced naturalists usually found the nests to contain eggs in May or June. Eggs are elongated ovals in shape, chalky-white when fresh laid but rapidly becoming stained. Jourdain measured 100 British-taken eggs and found an average of 54·8 × 36·7 mm. Max. 62·7 × 37·8 mm. and 46·5 × 39 mm. Min. 46·5 × 39 mm. and 55·3 × 34 mm. He gives the incubation period as twenty-seven to twenty-nine days, the young being independent of their parents at nine to ten weeks.

Territorial behaviour in the great crested grebe has been discussed by various authorities [2] and the latest conclusions drawn [3] seem to point

[1] *Broadland Birds*, p. 123.

[2] J. Huxley, *Proc. Zool. Soc.*, 1914, pp. 491-562 ; Venables and Lack, *British Birds*, 1934, pp. 191-198 ; 1936, pp. 60-69 ; and Miss McCartan and K. E. L. Simmons, *Ibis*, 1956, pp. 370-378.

[3] Mr. Simmons sums up the latest information on this subject in the special article he has written for this volume. See p. 215.

to each breeding pair defending at least the immediate nest-site, but the area of water adjoining that may be claimed by a breeding pair evidently varies considerably. In this connexion some notes made by the late Colonel R. F. Meiklejohn beyond the confines of the British Isles, and put at my disposal for inclusion in this account before his untimely death, may be repeated. Colonel Meiklejohn wrote :

Although it is claimed that each pair of grebes maintains a breeding area of considerable size, and this may be the case in Britain, I have found it nesting in colonies abroad. Presumably the extent of nesting areas is governed by food supply available for the young. On the reed-fringed islands in Hapsaal Bay, Estonia, I have found over a dozen nests in an area of some hundred yards long by ten to twenty yards wide. On two occasions high tides, with wind which produced waves, flooded many eggs out of the nests and several were to be seen floating on the surface or lying at the bottom in shallow water.

Similarly, in the extensive reed-bed near Villeneuve on the Lake of Geneva, where I found this species very abundant over a long period of years, there was an area of less than a hundred square yards in extent which contained, so we estimated, over thirty nests, some within a few yards of each other. Carrion crows took a heavy toll of the eggs, whilst the local fishermen destroyed any nests they found. Laying takes place from late May onwards and I have found fresh eggs at the end of June and even in early July, which indicates that this species is, sometimes at least, double brooded. . . . The nest is composed of reeds, grasses, and other vegetable matter, the cup sometimes being very shallow. The bird covers the eggs with grass, etc., when leaving them. The usual clutch is three to five.

Clutches of six eggs were found both in Switzerland on 26th June and in Estonia.

That colonial nesting is not unknown in Britain is apparent from a note sent to *British Birds* by Mr. J. N. Hobbs[1] who, in 1950, found eleven pairs of grebes in an area of submerged grass and rushes measuring not more than thirty yards square at Wilstone reservoir, Tring. Some of the nests were very close together. Attention was drawn to the fact that the grebe population at Wilstone is high and cover rather limited, but a dense reed-bed several hundred yards in length contained only ten nests ; so the colonial nesting described was not entirely due to the circumstances, which may account for it in other cases.

Incubation is by both sexes, the male taking a good share ; the nestlings are fed by both parents, and the young are taught to dive at an early age. Great crested grebe nestlings are extraordinarily attractive little creatures, clad in cinnamon-coloured down striped lengthwise from the crown of the head to the rump with black. There is a bare red patch in front of the eye and the bill is rose pink with two transverse black bands. In her studies of the great crested grebe on the Norfolk Broads Miss Turner describes[2]

[1] *British Birds*, xlv, 1952, p. 72.
[2] *Broadland Birds*, p. 125.

the early days of the chick's life and recounts how she watched these minute balls of fluff receiving their first instructions from their parents. She observed how just before the nestlings were hatched the adult grebe removed a considerable amount of material from the nest so that the chicks could easily slip to the water's edge and back again onto the nest when tired. It was the male bird that, with many encouraging cries, induced the chick to leave the nest and scramble on to its parent's back as the old bird backed up to the nest. The chick was seen to take hold of the soft down beneath the old bird's tail and by that means hoist itself up, keeping its balance by holding on to its parent's neck feathers. Thus the chick has his first ride. Later, as the little one gains confidence, the parent by a sudden turn tumbles it into the water, the chick seeming soon to recover from the fright its sudden fall must have given it. When, after much splashing, the little creature tires it is allowed to climb up again on to its parent's back and is then carried back to the nest. Another of the brood is then given similar instruction, or maybe two at a time. Young grebes do not hatch out simultaneously, and until the family is complete the chicks are carried to and fro in this manner—sometimes by the male, sometimes by the female. On their return to the nest they nestle beneath the brooding bird or clamber on to her back.

Miss Turner's account which I have quoted describes perhaps the usual method employed to give the chick its first swimming lessons, but that there may be some variation is indicated by the experience of Mr. A. N. Marriage of Taunton who, in a letter to *Country Life*,[1] described how he and his wife disturbed a great crested grebe on an exposed nest in a small patch of weed within less than fifty yards from the bank of a good-sized lake. No reeds surrounded this nest and a clear view was possible through binoculars. The adult bird was sitting at the time but was induced to leave the nest, and on doing so revealed little striped newly-hatched young and not eggs as had been anticipated. The parent bird swam to and fro uttering a low call note, and at last persuaded one of the young ones— which may, of course, have been in the water previously—to leave the nest, venture into the water and swim out to what was presumed to be the mother. Watching through glasses both observers were able to note the method by which, in this instance, the young birds mounted on to the back of the parent. Even though a grebe will often sink her body low in the water the difficulty of climbing on to her back can readily be appreciated, more particularly if the parent is alarmed. Mr. Marriage described how " as the little grebe, swimming lustily, approached the parent bird, she turned her back towards them, and extended behind her one foot spread out horizontally, and almost on a level with the surface of the water. On to this the young birds [presumably the whole family had followed the example of the first chick] first mounted and from this stepping stone quickly

[1] 6th April 1945.

scrambled to their final perch on their living raft, and, all being safely aboard, the old bird quietly sailed away towards the other end of the lake." This struck me as an amazing performance, the truth of which is now corroborated by Kenneth Simmons, who tells me he has seen it himself.

The young grebe's most dangerous enemies are pike and otters, and they may be attacked from the air by the marsh harrier. There are some localities in Broadland which appear quite suitable to human eyes which are always avoided by the great crested grebe; and these, so Ticehurst, has recorded, are where pike are known to swarm. The habit of riding on their parent's back just beyond where the wings join the body no doubt protects the little creatures from attack. Mme. Kozlova has drawn my attention to an experience of the Russian naturalist Shnitnikov and sends me the translation of a note taken from his *Birds of Semiretchje*, where he wrote :

I was rowing a boat in a bay of Lake Balkhash, passing near a reed-bed. At a distance of about ten paces I suddenly perceived a grebe that was swimming out of the reeds. The appearance of the bird seemed unusual. All its feathers were in disorder, the wings half open and slightly uplifted. The next moment I noticed a head and neck peeping out between each wing and the back of the bird. The grebe, having caught sight of the boat, dived at once together with her two chicks. Some moments later she appeared alone in the midst of the nearest reeds and swam out on the open water, having left her chicks evidently under cover of the reed-bed.

The voice of the adult grebe—to quote Miss Turner once more— entirely lacks musical quality. The call note is a harsh honking sound, while the sonorous crooning note of the breeding season is suggestive of utter content. On the other hand the dulcet notes of the young grebes are likened to the jingling of far away silver bells, a sound which may be heard far into the night.

By the middle of February returning birds may be seen on fresh water, but the exodus from the sea and the estuaries is gradual and continues for at least a month before the breeding population has settled down to the urgent business of rearing a family. Some are obviously paired when they arrive on fresh water, others are single and must search for a mate. Huxley[1] has shown that courtship ceremonies of various types may start very soon after arrival.

As the display and courtship of the great crested grebe is of such exceptional interest and is such a marked feature in its breeding biology I have judged it to be worthy of a special article. I am greatly indebted to Mr. Kenneth Simmons for having undertaken to write the account which follows. Mr. Simmons's " Studies on Great Crested Grebes " brought

[1] Sir Julian Huxley has made many important contributions to this subject. Cf. *Proc. Zool. Soc.*, 1914, pp. 491-562 ; *Auk*, xxxiii, pp. 152, 256 ; *Journ. Linn. Soc. Zool.*, xxxv, p. 253 ; *British Birds*, 1924, pp. 129-134 ; *Bird Watching and Bird Behaviour*, 1930 ; *Proc. 8th Internat. Orn. Congress*, 1938, pp. 430-455.

the author into the front rank of those who have devoted their time to this subject. In the essay which follows he has included information as yet unpublished elsewhere.

BREEDING BEHAVIOUR IN THE GREAT CRESTED GREBE

K. E. L. Simmons

A brief summary and discussion of certain aspects of the breeding cycle based on an eleven-year study in the south of England, 1948-58

I am honoured to write this essay for Dr. Bannerman's eighth volume of *The Birds of the British Isles* ; it is intended to give the reader a general summary of some aspects of the great crested grebe's breeding behaviour as these appear to a modern student of bird-life.

The great crested grebe has often attracted the serious attention and elicited the admiration of naturalists. Many years ago, Julian Huxley [1] watched and marvelled at the intriguing and beautiful courtship of the species, while the contributions [2] of another pioneer student of bird behaviour, Edmund Selous, should certainly not be overlooked. Then the grebe was also the subject of one of the first co-operative investigations [3] that have since become such a characteristic feature of British ornithology —an enquiry which told us a great deal about its general habits as well as about its numbers. Again, during the great period of amateur field work on behaviour between the wars, the grebe's territorial set-up was studied by L. S. V. Venables and David Lack. [4] More recently, I have in turn been absorbed in grebe watching and it has been my privilege to discover new facts as well as to amplify existing information. As a result of all this work—and it is impossible to mention here all the other papers and notes which have appeared—the great crested grebe, " one of our loveliest and most interesting birds," [5] is now also one of the better known of our British birds.

Before going on to outline the breeding cycle, I would first like to make one point of particular interest in grebe biology : this is the striking phenomenon of the " reversal of the sexes," as Huxley termed it, or the complete interchange of the breeding roles between male and female.

The identically adorned male and female grebe each performs the activities and duties associated with courtship, mating, nesting, and territory. There is no behaviour confined to one sex, the absolute sexual

[1] *Proc. Zool. Soc. London*, 1914, pp. 491-562.
[2] *Zoologist*, 1901, pp. 161-183 (and following) ; *Naturalist*, 1920, pp. 97-102, etc.
[3] *British Birds*, xxvi, 1932, pp. 62-92 (and following).
[4] *British Birds*, xxviii, 1934, pp. 191-198 and xxx, 1936, pp. 60-69.
[5] James Fisher in *Birds in Britain*, No. 51, 1957, B.B.C. Home Service (broadcast).

functions of fertilization and egg-laying excluded of course. The secondary sexual characters, both of habit and structure, have been reduced to a minimum. It is impossible for us to say that this form of behaviour (*e.g.* mounting) is exclusively masculine or that that form of behaviour (say soliciting) is exclusively feminine. As much as can be said is that certain habits are more characteristic of one sex than the other. For example, territorial skirmishing is more intensely conducted by the males though all females indulge to a lesser degree, while the occasional " masculine " female behaves just like a typical male in this respect. Then, while advertising " trumpeting " is much more usual in females, normal males perform this occasionally and some " feminine " ones quite commonly. All this complication makes observation the more interesting, interpretation the more fascinating and years of work the more necessary in unravelling it all.

At some flooded and partly overgrown gravel-pits in Berkshire, the sites where most of my work has been done, a substantial nucleus of great crested grebes stays each winter, leaving only when the waters are ice-bound and soon returning with the thaw. The " display plumage "— erectile tippets and crest—is often assumed (and used) during the winter. It is no uncommon sight to see birds in so-called " summer " plumage courting and threatening from December onwards, weather permitting. As a result, breeding gets under way quite early in the year—certainly much earlier than many ornithological textbooks would have us believe— with the first full clutches of eggs appearing regularly by the third week in March, for there is always adequate cover for the nests in the willows and *Typha*. The earliest ever local record was in 1957, when one pair successfully raised three youngsters from eggs laid in the first half of February ; the latest was in 1955 when chicks hatched out from an early September clutch. Had these been reared, they would not have become independent until the end of the year. In any case, young are still regularly being attended in October and even November from normal late broods.

Courtship dominates the first part of the cycle until the laying of the eggs. Very elaborate in form, with peculiar ritualistic movements evolved from the past history of the species, the grebe's courtship is full of variety, few species having so many different displays and postures at their disposal to express their conflicting emotions and indicate their intentions. Further, many of these activities are combined into formal, set courtship ceremonies in which both male and female participate. " The grebes . . . have wonderful mutual ceremonies . . . their courtship is as strange and fantastic as that of any gaudy tropical creature." [1] Before describing these ceremonies, special mention must be made of three individual displays.

The first of these " trumpeting," never appears in the fixed ceremonies and remained undiscovered long after the other displays were well known. Unlike the latter, which are mainly visual displays, at best only accompanied

[1] Julian Huxley, *Bird Watching and Bird Behaviour*, 1930.

by calls, trumpeting is essentially vocal. It is always performed by a bird separated from others with which it would like to associate. This lone grebe swims slowly about with its neck stretched in look-out while it projects a peculiar, far-carrying and throaty note. I previously [1] termed this behaviour " advertising " because the caller is clearly trying to attract the attention of another. Usually this bird is known to it, often it is the mate ; but in the case of unpaired birds a potential partner is the objective. The same behaviour is shown by parent birds when out of touch with the young. All my early records clearly indicated that this trumpeting was a habit confined to the female, but since 1955 I have recorded it from males also. Grebes so often give one the lie !

The second important display is " head-shaking." The bird, with neck stretched up and head ornaments spread, waggles its head from side to side at another. Birds already paired together frequently head-shake together, but unpaired birds will also display thus when looking for a mate and a paired bird will sometimes " flirt " with strange grebes when its partner is out of the way.

The third display worth special mention is what Huxley called the " cat attitude." In this cat-display, the grebe floats, spreads open the wings and bends them forward, upper surface showing towards the bird at which the posturing is directed. The conspicuous dark and white pattern is thus vividly exposed, while the tippets are spread and the neck lowered back on the shoulders. Outside the two ceremonies in which it appears, the cat-display is often performed by unmated females when they are confronted by strange males which have sometimes been attracted by the trumpeting of these birds and with which they may attempt to head-shake.

Returning to the ceremonies themselves, the main one is the *head-shaking ceremony* which is a mutual performance. When displaying typically, male and female face one another in the attitude described above, neck straight and thin, the vestigial tail tuft cocked and often uttering a ticking call. Between the faster shaking movements of the head come slower, swaying ones, the birds sometimes acting in rhythm, and this is often accompanied by the curiously formal " habit-preening " as each grebe in turn stiffly dips its head back and down to lift—just lightly—the scapular feathers before assuming the original position and continuing as before. The other three ceremonies are either preceded or followed by this common head-shaking. The most spectacular of these is the mutual *penguin-dance ceremony* which is relatively rare. Both birds dive and search for weed underwater, then rise to the surface and swim towards one another, tippets fully spread. Then follows the almost breath-taking " dance " which few ornithologists have seen. The two grebes unite and simultaneously rear up out of the water, treading it to maintain the unnatural position, to meet breast to breast, weed dangling in the bills and the crest curiously flattened.

[1] *Bird Study*, vol. i, 1954, pp. 53-56 ; *Studies on Great Crested Grebes*, 1955.

After a very few moments they subside and, having dropped the weed, head-shake. The other two ceremonies, both of which involve the cat-display, are reciprocal, the roles of male and female differing though interchangeable. In the more elaborate *discovery ceremony*, one of the pair, often the one rejoining its mate after a separation, swims towards the latter in a shallow " travelling dive " just under the surface of the water, with a marked ripple indicating its progress. The second grebe watches this tell-tale ripple coming towards it and assumes the cat-display, facing its mate as it emerges from the water near by in a weird " ghostly penguin " display with body and neck vertical, bill pointing down. Again head-shaking follows. In the less complicated *retreat ceremony* one bird, suddenly stopping while head-shaking, patters away from its mate over the water with much splashing, subsides and turns round in the cat-display. The mate rejoins it and the head-shaking continues. (The retreat ceremony was originally called the *display ceremony* by Huxley. However, he has recently [1] pointed out the inaptness of this so I have coined the new name here used for the first time.)

A notable feature of this courtship is its " self-exhausting " nature, as Huxley put it, for the ceremonies often lead to nothing, as it were, with the birds ceasing their activities to pass on into some routine behaviour, such as preening or hunting. The ceremonies are not " pre-coitional " in that they do not lead immediately to mating, which occurs on the nest and not in the water. However, courtship is not as absolutely " self-exhausting " as the earlier work suggested, for any ceremony, after starting in the water away from the nest, may sometimes be followed by the birds' swimming to the nest in order to build or even to perform the mating ceremony there. Nevertheless, courtship is not conducted at the very nest itself with the exception of head-shaking, a special form of which, for instance, is the last phase of the full mating ceremony. I would like to stress, because it has been disputed, that the term " courtship," as applied to these ceremonials of the grebe, is perfectly justified. In human society, we understand by courtship certain activities which serve to form a tie between male and female especially before marriage but also in the period of adjustment afterwards. And so it is in the grebe. With the exception of head-shaking, the courtship ceremonies are entirely confined to the pre-incubation stage, being most intense at the time of pairing and just after, especially in the case of birds pairing together for the first time. Head-shaking occurs after egg-laying, but mainly in special circumstances and not nearly so frequently as previously. Thus, the courtship does not last right through the cycle as has often been erroneously stated in the literature. Courtship serves principally to establish a bond between male and female grebe by helping to overcome certain very marked inhibitions and, as it were, prejudices that tend to disrupt and break up the union of the pair. Feelings of

[1] *British Birds*, l, 1957, pp. 81-83.

aggressiveness and fear are largely eliminated and the way paved for the successful consummation of the marriage on the nest-platform, and for later co-operation in rearing the family.

Much of the first outbreak of courting may take place in open, " communal " water and then continue later to the same or a lesser degree in the territory. The male and female together seek out and investigate likely places, often returning to the same nesting area that they occupied in the previous season. A certain amount of antagonism may already have occurred in the open water due to sexual rivalry but, now, this is often intensified as the birds dispute the breeding territories if necessary.

When a suitable site is found, a nest-platform is built, sometimes two or more. In normal conditions, that is when the grebe pair is not prevented from settling down by other already established couples, by lack of sites, etc., the mating ceremony will occur as soon as the floating platform is strong enough to bear the weight. Either sex may initiate this and take what would normally, in many other species, be considered the female role by jumping aboard the platform and " inviting " with neck stretched out along the nest. When more worked up, the soliciting bird will also suddenly perform " rearing," a grotesque display in which it quickly raises itself to a standing position, quivers the wings, thus flashing the white markings, and bends the head right down to point the bill at the nest. However, while both sexes will commonly solicit, in the vast majority of cases it is the male only who mounts to copulate. After mating, the pair head-shakes, the female still sitting on the weed-pile and the male floating with his back to her at first before he turns round to face her.

It is often given as definite fact in ornithological works that the female great crested grebe sometimes takes on the full " male " role in copulation. In fact the published evidence for this is extremely meagre and uncertain. However, on 4th July 1957 and twice subsequently I finally obtained full proof that reversed mounting does in fact occur, though obviously rarely for I had looked out for it unsuccessfully for many years. I was closely studying the pair concerned, and could easily distinguish the sexes ; in any case, *both* birds were seen to mount—fifty-six years after Selous first suggested the possibility of such a happening.

It is during the time of the mating ceremonies on the nest that penguin-dancing is likely to be seen in the water off the platform site. From rather incomplete evidence I would suggest that this extraordinary courtship ceremony is more of a feature of birds paired together for the first time because it seems extremely rare in old-established couples. While the latter do most of their courting in the territory, new pairs are almost invariably formed in the open " free " water. Unattached females drift about " trumpeting " to attract males to them. Some of the males that come are already paired but they pause at times to indulge in head-shaking flirtation. Other males that are unpaired also approach to head-shake and will also attempt to shake with females that are not advertising themselves. However, in either case, the female involved often cat-displays when a male is encountered and mutual head-shaking may follow, and also discovery and retreat ceremonies. The penguin-dancing only happens much later when relationships are more definite.

Before the eggs are laid, perhaps as much as a week before, the birds may start to sit on the empty nest, very irregularly at first but normal incubation routine has usually developed by the time that the second egg appears. The sexes share the duties of incubation more or less equally, with the female doing just a little more than the male—though there is not much in it. They alternate on the clutch, shifts lasting from just under half an hour to over four hours, with an average of a little over two hours.

The great crested grebe is wonderfully adapted to its breeding environment. For instance, there are several habits which guard the eggs and young against misfortune and danger. The eggs, cradled as they often are in damp sodden weed, have a protective chalky layer over the blue shell, and they become stained to blend, hidden, with the nest surrounds. During the month-long incubation period, if the sitting grebe is frightened off by an enemy, so often man, it covers over the eggs with weed and leaves them concealed from any hunting gull, crow, or harrier passing over. If these aerial predators themselves approach the nest closely when the grebe is not otherwise disturbed (I have myself only seen carrion crows do this), then they are confronted by the parent, fierce and determined with spread wings and ready bill. The young grebes do not hatch out all at the same time because incubation always starts well before the clutch is complete. Such staggered hatching is aimed, apparently, at reducing too severe a loss of chicks in case of bad weather and lack of suitable food at the critical time of emergence. The young are very susceptible to chilling at birth. Each hatches extremely quickly, within a very few hours of the first cracking of the shell, and must be kept dry and fed for some days mainly on aquatic insects and feathers, with only a few minute fish, until a reservoir of feathers has had time to collect in the stomach for whatever purpose this serves.[1] The parents would seem to find it difficult to manage adequately at first, often bringing fish too large and unacceptable ; it is some advantage for them not to have the whole new hatched brood to deal with at once.

Young grebes [2] are delightful, tiger-striped little creatures, tame and active. Though they are entirely dependent on the adults and do not feed themselves for many weeks, they can swim and dive almost at hatching. They can preen, too, and take the offerings that their parents bring. However, the one overriding inclination is to climb upwards and this results in getting the delicate young grebe out of the water—high, dry, and safe on

[1] " Feather-eating and pellet-formation in the Great Crested Grebe ", *British Birds*, xlix, 1956, pp. 432-435.

[2] Adapted from the script of a B.B.C. broadcast, 8th December 1957.

the adult's back where it is carried for the first two to three weeks of its life, under the " tent " formed by arched wings and long scapular feathers. During the time it is transported thus, the youngster waterproofs its short coat of down and gets more hardy for the almost entirely aquatic life it will lead. It is also protected from enemies, chiefly carnivorous pike from under-water. During the first ten days or so, the parents carry the young very willingly, even assisting them to climb aboard by placing a foot along the surface of the water, as Dr. Bannerman records in his own text, but during the third week they may start to discourage the young from boarding by shaking them off, manœuvring out of the way, and so on. The young persist at first and may still manage to " steal " a ride even when fully three weeks old, when so large that they seem almost to sink the parent. Soon, however, in the face of continued discouragement, the young grebes, still very keen to board, only go through the motions of so doing without actually making the final scramble up. Such " mock-boarding " behaviour may continue for several weeks and develops into a ritual. Later, many parents start to get positively hostile towards their own young. This is especially likely to happen with larger broods, of more than two young, when they become " divided," the male becoming solely responsible for some chicks, the female for the others. Each adult refuses to feed the other group of young and may even attack them viciously. In such circumstances, the " stripe-heads " develop a pitiful, cringing " appeasing " attitude towards the parents. My wife and I actually observed a case of this during the preparation of this article, near our home on 19th July 1958, in a family of four, three-month-old juveniles. I used to wonder what possible purpose such brood-division could serve until some observations in 1957 threw considerable light on the problem. One pair of grebes had three youngsters, and in most dramatic circumstances one of the two young dependent on the female starved to death when she became sick and ceased to feed it. The male refused to give food to the female's chicks though he reared his own single charge successfully. The second stripe-head survived, first by " pirating " fish destined for the male's and then by becoming prematurely independent when just over eight weeks of age. From this case (and other evidence not given) I deduce that this brood-division is an insurance in larger families that, in the event of sickness or death, or even neglect by one parent, only those young dependent on that parent suffer and not the whole brood. If a single working parent had to feed them all, then all might be lost.

The young grebes remain with their parents many weeks. They start to hunt after a fashion, and without success, as soon as they start to spend most of their time in the water. Although they can dive well—and do so when alarmed, for example—it is interesting to note that they hunt, not by typical diving, but mainly by submerging the head and peering below the water, " up-ending " on seeing something and then submerging clumsily thus. They do not dive in exploration, and keep largely to the shallows and vegetation such as water-crowfoot beds. They only dive normally for food when nearly at the age of first being able to fend fully for themselves if necessary, that is ten to eleven weeks after hatching.[1] They often remain with the adults longer than this, however, unless there is a second brood under way. Broods sometimes overlap, with the second clutch appearing when the first brood is about six weeks old.

I have left the question of territory until last. Few species show such a variety of territorial practice as does the great crested grebe,[2] though this has often been overstressed by observers who just have not had sufficient precise information upon which to base an opinion. Nevertheless, the size of the nesting area claimed by individual pairs of grebes does vary quite considerably from one water to another and even on the same water. The length of time that the territory is occupied and actively " defended " also differs from couple to couple. Each lake and the like occupied by great crested grebes has its own particular social structure, much depending not only on the actual density and status of the birds and the degree of personal aggressiveness, but on the amount and type of cover available and, importantly, on the topography. Because the nesting habitat is so very variable, the grebe has developed a " plastic " form of territorial structure, unlike species living in a relatively more uniform environment.

The one stable, all-important feature of a great crested grebe territory is the nest-site, and the first establishment of the territory is intimately linked with the selection of this site. In some pairs, the territory may be no more than a few square yards around the nest, the owners feeding entirely elsewhere in " free " water, perhaps having to dive under occupied water to reach it, male and female taking turns to leave while the other remains in charge. Colonies have been reported, as Dr. Bannerman records in his own text, but no one has adequately studied their social structure. At the other extreme one finds large territories, as extensive as several acres, kept clear of all other grebes by the owners and in which the latter spend the whole breeding cycle and even the moulting, flightless period afterwards. As in the case of the courtship, the territorial " defence and offence " behaviour of the grebe is essentially visual and dynamic, vocalism playing a relatively small part compared with the behaviour of some other grebe species (the dabchick for instance). I shall not detail the various activities here, but encounters include a forward threat-display, " mock " attack across the surface and from under water, barking calls and quite fierce and frequent fighting with bill-stabbing and apparent attempts at drowning.

[1] The figure of six weeks given in my *Studies on Great Crested Grebes* is incorrect ; detailed observation since has shown that I previously underestimated the age of young grebes.

[2] The reader is referred to McCartan and Simmons, in *Ibis*, xcviii, 1956, pp. 370-378, for a recent account.

In conclusion I would like to express the hope that the fascination of the facts given in this article, selected and incomplete as they necessarily are, will both make up a little for the absence of that grand style of writing which made the accounts of the old naturalists so appealing and make new friends for the science of animal behaviour, so much out of favour among amateur ornithologists in Britain to-day. Those readers who would like to know more about the great crested grebe's life are referred to my booklet *Studies on the Great Crested Grebe* (1955), which this essay brings up to date on certain points, and to a forthcoming book in preparation.

REFERENCES : Original Description. *Colymbus cristatus* Linnaeus, *Syst. Nat.*, 10th ed., 1758, p. 135 : Europe ; restricted type locality Sweden.

RED-NECKED GREBE

Podiceps griseigena (Boddaert)

1. Red-necked Grebe   PLATE 14

Podiceps griseigena griseigena (Boddaert)

A Winter Visitor, mainly to the east coast between the Firth of Tay and the Wash ; rare in the west but of annual occurrence in Northern Ireland, Orkneys, and Shetland. Probably also Passage Migrant in small numbers

2. Holboell's Grebe

Podiceps griseigena holböllii Reinhardt

An Accidental Visitor, obtained once only in Britain

DISTINGUISHING CHARACTER OF THE TWO RACES : This is only a matter of size, the latter (American) bird being larger. Comparative measurements as given in *The Handbook*, measured by Witherby :

Twelve European Red-necked Grebes		*Nine Holboell's Grebes*
♂ bill from feathers	35-45 mm.	47-55 mm.
♀ bill from feathers	35-40 mm.	45-54 mm.
♂ wing	160-180 (one 190) mm.	188-202 (one 210) mm.
♀ wing	155-176 mm.	176-196 mm.
♂ tarsus	50-58 mm.	58-65 mm.

IDENTIFICATION : Of the five grebes on the British list, this one comes next in size to the species dealt with last. In total length the European red-necked grebe measures about 18 inches. It is usually described as stockier and less slender in build than the great crested, with a stout short neck carried well erect. A broad white border to the wing is very conspicuous, and the shape of the head is also a character to observe—less angular than that of its relative the great crested. In winter dress, when it is most likely to be seen off our coasts, the red-necked grebe loses all trace of the rich chestnut on its neck, which is then brown like the lower part of the throat ; the upper parts of the body are brown, the sides of the head greyish, the chin and upper throat white, the crown greyish-brown. The underparts are silky white marbled or spotted on the sides of the body and flanks with dark brown.

T. A. Coward has pointed out how black and white the head looks in winter. An important character to note is that the black cap extends *right down to the eye* : there is no heavy white line over the eye as there is in *P. cristatus*, and if a side view is obtained through glasses the bill of the red-necked grebe appears stout and short in comparison, lacking the dagger-like appearance of the larger bird's appendage.

In summer (breeding) plumage the red-necked grebe is a handsome bird indeed, with its rich chestnut neck and grey cheeks bordered above with white. The back of the neck is black like the top of the head ; black ear-tufts are prominent but much less so than in the great crested. Unlike the latter species there is no tippet or ruff. The upperparts of the body are greyish-brown, the sides of the breast rich chestnut and the underparts below the breast silky white with underlying grey mottling on the sides. The soft parts of this grebe have had most varied descriptions. I prefer to rely on that careful recorder C. B. Ticehurst who, when discussing the colours of the iris, bill, and legs wrote : " The iris is said in many works to be whitish ; fresh specimens [presumably winter-killed adults] examined by me had the iris brown with a pale yellow line toward the peripheral edge and outside this blue-grey. The tarsi and toes on the inner side were a lovely pale salmon colour, the rest blackish with a greeny tinge ; bill yellow at the base of both mandibles shading off to horny green along the sides dark horn on the upper and greenish on the lower mandible." Witherby gives the bill black, and the base of the lower mandible and the cutting edge of the upper at the base lemon-yellow.

Mr. D. D. Harber has shown that in an occasional living example the bill may be entirely yellow : a bird seen on 24th September " still in almost complete summer plumage " had this feature, while another seen at the end of October in winter plumage had a completely yellow bill except for a narrow darkish line where the mandibles met. Since then other similar examples have been reported.

DISTRIBUTION IN BRITAIN : Of the two races which have been recognized in Britain, the European-Asiatic bird is mainly a winter visitor as already described, whereas the American representative, or Holboell's grebe, has only once been taken on our shores—an unsexed example shot by Mr. J. MacGregor of Aultbea in Ross-shire. It was no doubt a male, as the wing measured 200 mm. and the bill (exposed culmen) 55 mm. The actual date is not recorded, but was presumably some time in September

PLATE 14

RED-NECKED GREBE

Podiceps griseigena griseigena (Boddaert)

1925 (as given by Mr. Witherby in *British Birds*).   The specimen was recorded by Dr. Percy Lowe in the *Bulletin of the British Ornithologists' Club*[1] and was examined by the present writer who was at the meeting when the bird was exhibited.   It had been killed in the wild state and was accepted as the first—and still the only—British record.

The European-Asiatic race of the red-necked grebe may be met with in our islands regularly from October to March inclusive.   On occasions early arrivals have been recorded in August and September, while others have lingered until April before leaving for their northern breeding grounds. There are few truly summer instances of their being seen but there have been isolated records in May, June, and July.   There has never been any question of breeding.   It cannot be termed numerous and its distribution is local.   On the east coast of Britain this grebe may be reckoned as almost an annual visitor from autumn to spring in very small numbers, but occasionally an exceptional influx is reported.   Such was the case in Norfolk in February and March 1865, when no less than thirty-five were brought into Norwich market alone, the majority shot between 18th and 28th February.[2]   A second invasion took place into the same county in January and February 1922.[3]   Even more remarkable was the influx of grebes and divers into many counties of Britain on the last day of January 1937,[4] when many examples reached inland waters.   All three of our rarer grebes were represented and curiously enough in greater numbers than the other two.   Reporting this occurrence, Mr. Harry Witherby observes that of these the red-necked grebe was the most remarkable because, although as a rule the rarest of the three on inland waters, it appeared on this occasion in greater numbers than the other species.   The numbers were not, however, very large and a feature of the influx was its widespread character and the fact that most waters (even small ponds in some parts) had one or two grebes.   Only in Norfolk near the sea were any considerable numbers observed.   The cause of this exceptional invasion was never really ascertained, though it was ascribed to the weather ; but what caused the birds to go to inland waters was obscure at the time.   It was of interest to note that for several days before 31st January the temperature in the region of Denmark had been down to 20° F. and in the Baltic to 10°, falling to 7° on the 30th.   In Britain only a few degrees of frost were recorded at the same time.   A point of interest at the time was that all five species of grebes on the British List could be seen at once, both on the Tring reservoirs in Hertfordshire and at Salthouse in Norfolk.   During the 1865 and 1922 abnormal immigrations only *one* bird was apparently recognized in Ireland and that at the end of February 1865.   From

[1] Vol. xlviii, 1927, p. 53 ; 1928, p. 70.
[2] Stevenson, in *Zoologist*, 1865, p. 9574.
[3] Gurney, in *Trans. Norfolk Nat. Soc.*, xi, 1922, pp. 299-300.
[4] Witherby, in *British Birds*, xxx, 1937, pp. 370-374.

Scotland again one bird alone was reported in February 1922 but the 1937 immigration was well marked in Scotland, records coming in from both east and west coasts, and from inland lochs [1] in considerable numbers. Lesser immigrations were reported in north-east England in 1891 and from the Forth area in 1895.

The red-necked grebe is an uncommon bird in the west of Britain, while off the south coast it is very rare and irregular in the English Channel. In an investigation undertaken by Mr. F. D. Hamilton as to the respective winter status of the three rarer grebes on the east and south coast of Britain, which is discussed more fully under the black-necked grebe (see p. 252), it will be observed how much more scarce the red-necked grebe is than the other two. Of the 3624 records analyzed over six years, covering all three species (red-necked, black-necked, and Slavonian), the red-necked grebe only formed 3 per cent. on the south coast ; 14 per cent. from Essex to the Wash ; 34 per cent. from Lincolnshire to Northumberland ; and 10 per cent. from Berwickshire to the Forth area between 1st October and 30th April inclusive. The figures relating to the other two rarer grebes are given in tabular form on p. 252. North of the Forth Mr. Hamilton had not sufficient records sent in to enable him to form a comprehensive picture of their numbers in relation to the other two and the same applies to the western coast of Britain where this grebe is undoubtedly scarce.

Its status in Scotland and Ireland must be briefly mentioned. To the former country it is an occasional visitor, very rarely seen on the west coast but in the north more often observed in Orkney. To the Shetlands [2] it is a regular passage migrant and winter visitor, mainly on salt water, extreme dates being 22nd September to 20th April (Venables). On the eastern seaboard of Scotland the major proportion of the records come from the Firths of Forth and Tay, and neighbouring counties. A few inland records are mentioned by Miss Rintoul and Dr. Baxter.

In *Birds of Ireland* (1954, p. 6) Major Ruttledge states that the red-necked is the rarest of the visiting grebes, only some fifteen occurrences in all having been substantiated up to the date of publication. Since that date it has, curiously enough, been seen quite commonly, the increase probably being due to the interest in the birds of Ireland aroused by the publication of a new standard work on that country. The Irish Bird Report for 1955 records for that year six birds (3, 2, and 1), the single bird on 30th October, the other five in January ; while the Report for 1956 enumerates thirteen birds seen, the largest number (6) occurring on Strangford Lough on 29th December. We can hardly suppose that the red-necked grebe has suddenly taken to visiting Belfast Lough in numbers, but would suggest that prior to 1954 it had been very generally overlooked

[1] *The Birds of Scotland*, 1953, p. 501.
[2] *Birds and Mammals of Shetland*, 1955, p. 255.

or confused with *P. cristatus.* Up to 1956, therefore, we have a total of thirty-four birds having been recorded, nineteen in the last two years !

DISTRIBUTION ABROAD : This is a breeding species in the Holarctic Region, the typical subspecies nesting in northern Europe from Sweden (to 65° N.), Finland, and Denmark and in Russia eastwards to at least the River Ob. In south-east Europe it breeds from Yugoslavia and Bulgaria to the mouth of the Dniester, ranging eastwards to the Aral and Caspian seas. This is but a very rough sketch of its breeding habitat in Europe.[1] Mr. Thomasson has shown that the greatest nesting density occurs in Denmark and Finland.[2] It appears that the red-necked grebe was rare during the seventeenth and eighteenth centuries, but from the middle of the last century it became increasingly common in north-west Europe. Mr. Thomasson assumes that there is no evident tendency towards expansion in the distribution of this grebe to-day as is apparent in other species of this group. He considers that its present fluctuations in north-west Europe can only be considered small and of a local character. In the recent work on the birds of the Soviet Union, Professor Dementiev states that the typical race breeds sporadically and unevenly over its range in the U.S.S.R., but it is numerous in the areas of the lower Dniester and the lower Volga and in north-west Kazakhstan. From Lake Balkash eastwards the typical *P. griseigena griseigena* gives way to the larger subspecies *P. griseigena holböllii*, which ranges intermittently over eastern Siberia to Kamchatka and (apparently) Sakhalin. (The race *P. g. bergmani* Lönnberg described from Kamchatka has not been recognized by Professor Dementiev but is apparently considered valid by Dr. Kuno Thomasson in his review of the red-necked grebe to which reference has already been made.)

DISTRIBUTION IN THE U.S.S.R. of *P. g. griseigena* and *P. g. holböllii*, as defined by Elizabeth Kozlova (Academy of Sciences, Leningrad).

Podiceps griseigena griseigena. Within the European part of the U.S.S.R. it ranges north to Imandra Lake, to Arkhangelsk, extending in the east only to Ufa. Thus it is absent from the Petchora river basin, as also from the upper and middle course of the Kama River. It breeds in the northern Caucasus and in Transcaucasia. In western Siberia the exact northern limit of its range is not determined. There are breeding records from Irtysh River, south of the mouth of the Jobol River. Portenkv found it on the Sosva River, but does not know whether it bred there.

The southern limit of its range crosses the lower course of the Ural River and the mouth of the Irghiz River. The eastern boundary passes through the region of Barabinsky and Kulundinsky steppes (western Siberia). It is found breeding on

---

[1] The detailed distribution of the red-necked grebe in the Soviet Union has been compiled for me by Mme. E. Kozlova and is given below just as she wrote it. I have retained her own spellings for place-names.

[2] For a detailed description of its breeding range in N.W. Europe see the review by Mr. K. Thomasson (Uppsala) in *Zoologiska Bidrag Från Uppsala*, xxx, 1953, pp. 157-166.

the lower reaches of the Syr-Darya River. There are winter records from the coasts of the Black Sea (Crimea), from Transcaucasus and the southern parts of the Caspian Sea.

Podiceps griseigen holbölli. Ranges from the basin of the Vilinj River (Yakut Land = Yakutia, a tributary of the Lena River) and the upper reaches of Amur in the west, to Ussuri Land, Kamchatka and the Anadyr basin in the east ; it has also been found breeding on the Eravninsky lakes in Transbaikalia (52°-53·5° N., 112·5° E.), and in the region of Lake Balkhash (Kazachstan). Both the last regions (particularly the region of Lake Balkhash) are separated by vast areas from the continuous range of the race.

The northern limit of the range may be traced by finds near Viluisk town, near the mouth of the Aldan River (Yakut Land) and near Vezkhne-Kolymsk on the Kolyma River. Along the Kolyma River it extends up to its mouth. It is absent from the Indigirka and Yana rivers, and from the lower Lena, as also from the Khatanga River (Taimyr Peninsula). It breeds in the basin of Anadyr, in Kamchatka, and in the basin of the Amur. The southern boundary of the range crosses northern Manchuria and runs along the southern limit of Ussuri Land.

In the Canadian Arctic *P. g. holböllii*, which has only once been recognized in Britain, ranges from north-western Alaska through the North-West Territories, the districts of Mackenzie and Keewatin to Hudson's Straits and the Ungava peninsula. In the south of its American range it is reported to breed to northern Washington, North Dakota, and New Brunswick. In winter it passes the cold months mainly in the coastal waters of the Atlantic and Pacific to southern California and North Carolina.

WINTER DISTRIBUTION OF *P. griseigena griseigena* : There are records of the red-necked grebe having been taken in the Mediterranean at this season from Tangier to Tunisia : in the latter country Whitaker recorded it as " sometimes fairly abundant on the Lake of Tunis and other lakes in the north of the Regency ". He was writing in 1905 ! There are old records of many being present on the Ras el Doura lakes in Morocco, where Irby saw birds so young " that they must have been bred in the country ", but we have no recent records to substantiate his report made so long ago. To Tunis it is but a winter migrant. The same is true of the Balearic Islands where Captain Munn notes that it sometimes occurs in small numbers. Jourdain was doubtful if the Corsican record held good but Giglioli records it from Elba—but very late in the spring ! Recently it has been reported from an estuary near Venice by Moltoni. It may be more frequent in winter in the western Mediterranean than the records show, for in its off-season dress it is not easily recognized at sea unless by an expert ornithologist. Jourdain in *The Handbook* reported it from the Balkan peninsula, northern Asia Minor, northern Persia, Turkestan, and Semipalatinsk, observing too that it was casual in Egypt ; but it is not mentioned in Meinertzhagen's *Birds of Egypt* and Jourdain does not give the source of his information. In the eastern Mediterranean it can only be considered an accidental visitor. To what extent this grebe is found on fresh-water lakes in winter, and by what route these aquatic northern breeding birds arrive, as they evidently do in small numbers in the western Mediterranean, I am unable to state. When thoroughly airborne they are no doubt just as able to cross over land and mountainous areas as are great crested grebes or black-necked grebes, and they are reputed to fly at a considerable height when occasion demands.

Just as the American race has once been taken in Britain so has the European bird been recorded once from the other side of the Atlantic, when a specimen was secured in western Greenland—the first record of *P. griseigena griseigena* from the Nearctic. It was recorded by Dr. Finn Salomonsen.[1]

HABITS : When adorned in its breeding dress the red-necked grebe is a very ornamental species, but unfortunately at that season it has to be sought beyond the shores of the British Isles. In America and Canada, where it goes by the name of Holboell's grebe, it is considered one of the shyest of its shy family—the statement in *The Handbook of British Birds* that it is not so skulking as the little grebe or black-necked grebe being open to contradiction.

On its breeding ground in America, so Arthur Bent has recorded,

Holboell's grebe is often seen swimming about in pairs in marshy ponds or on lakes. When undisturbed it swims quite buoyantly with its head drawn down on its folded neck, much as a duck swims, occasionally rolling over on its side to wash and preen its plumage or pointing its bill up in the air to give its loud weird call. But on the slightest scent of danger it sinks until its tail is below the surface, its back is awash, and its head is stretched up to watch and listen as it swims rapidly away. Should a human being approach within a hundred yards of the shy creature, it is gone for good ; if on a large lake, it swims quickly away under water and appears again only in the dim distance ; if near a marsh, it seeks shelter in the reeds and does not show itself again. Human intimacy is not encouraged by this vanishing water sprite.

T. Gilbert Pearson remarked that they are unusually wary birds. Even in summer on their breeding grounds they are extremely shy, and ornithologists have reported that it was an easier task to find the nest than the bird itself. It is difficult to believe there is any difference in this character between the American and European bird which differ from one another only in their proportions. Its hearing is reported to be exceptional and only on rare occasions can it be surprised in the marshes by anyone entering its domain.

All grebes have the reputation of having remarkable voices and the red-necked grebe is no exception. The " song " is really a love song and will be described when we come to discuss the breeding habits. The ordinary note resembles that of the great crested's " keck keck " but is pitched in a higher tone. Its food consists of small fish and frogs, molluscs

[1] *Medd. Grønland*, xciii, No. 6, 1935, p. 15.

and insects, some vegetable matter and " quantities of feathers ". The American race *holbölli* is reported to be able to live quite happily in lakes where there are no fish at all. In some lakes of Manitoba it largely eats crawfish, aquatic worms, larvae, small crustaceans, tadpoles, etc. In fact it seems to have a varied menu which normally includes insects of many kinds.

It is reported to fly strongly once launched, but it cannot rise from ice or from the ground and if surprised on either can be easily captured. On the water it rises with much pattering along the surface, beating the water with wings and feet not unlike the commotion made by a suddenly alarmed coot. With its neck held out in front and its feet sticking out beyond the apology of a tail, it presents a diver-like appearance on the wing ; but it may be distinguished from these birds by the white area in the wings and its smaller size. In the water it is superb. Of the American bird Arthur Bent wrote :

It is a strong and rapid swimmer, and like all of its tribe a splendid diver. It usually prefers to escape by swimming rapidly away if the enemy is not too near, but in the latter case it dives like a flash, so quickly that it is useless to try and shoot one if it is watching. When undisturbed and not hurried it makes a graceful curving plunge, leaving the water entirely and going straight down with its wings closed ; probably it can dive to a greater depth in this way than any other. It can also sink gradually downward until only its head is above water, or go swimming off among the reeds with only its bill and eyes showing. When really alarmed it goes under water with astonishing rapidity, so quickly that we cannot see how it is done, but it is probably accomplished by a sudden kick and forward dive.

Naturalists who are familiar with it observe that in its habits it closely resembles the great crested grebe, frequenting much the same habitat, but is less often found on fresh water when in its winter quarters, preferring the sea-coast and lagoons adjoining the coast, as J. I. S. Whitaker has recorded in Tunisia. There it lives as a rule in small parties. Whitaker considered that its flight is lighter and more rapid than that of its larger cousin, and he remarked that it would take wing more readily.

Across the Straits of Gibraltar the red-necked grebe was said by Favier to migrate northwards in March, leaving some of its numbers behind to breed in Morocco. Confirmation of this migration, if a regular feature, would be of great interest to-day. There are not many cases of grebes—unless it be the great crested—being recorded actually on migration in Europe, and therefore the observations made during the autumns 1949 to 1953 on the Swedish coast by Mr. Tore Andersson are of special interest.[1] These observations were made at Rönnskärsudde on Väddö, where the Swedish coast faces the Åland islands and south-west Finland. Great crested grebes and red-necked grebes were seen here on passage in small numbers from August until October, and on one occasion a Slavonian

[1] *Vår Fågelvärld*, vol. xiii, 1954, pp. 133-142.

grebe was observed. All three figure on the British List. It was noted that whereas some grebes flew past on regular migration, some were swimming on the sea from directions between north and east and then following the coast southwards at a distance of 50-200 metres from the shore, *swimming* at a pace which was estimated to average two kilometres an hour. Evidence was obtained in one case that the greater part of the migration was performed by nocturnal over-sea flights, but that in the early morning the grebes settled on the sea and continued their journey by swimming, though naturally at a much slower pace. In no instance was any northward migration observed. The proportions between the birds seen flying and those swimming was only slightly in favour of the flying birds. Mr. Andersson points out that it is evident from a variety of observations that the Scandinavian grebe populations migrate almost exclusively by night, and he therefore suggests that diurnal migration by swimming is not just of casual occurrence but—in the case of the birds cited—part of the normal migratory rhythm.

If this theory holds good it is remarkable that similar movements among the grebes has not been observed in the United States. There we have definite evidence of day migration, but Bent in his great work on the *Life Histories of North American Diving Birds* is referring to his personal observations when he wrote: " When migrating along the Atlantic coast I have always seen it [Holboell's grebe] flying singly and not more than a few feet above the water ". Later in his essay he observes: " During the [fall] migrations I have always found this grebe to be a solitary species, but according to others it seems to be more or less gregarious at times. . . . On the Pacific coast it more often congregates in flocks on the migrations and during the winter, though I doubt if it actually flies in flocks." Of its winter habits he remarks that all through the fall, winter and spring these grebes are fairly common on the New England coast, where they may be seen riding the waves just offshore, feeding in the shoals just beyond the breakers. Large inland lakes attract Holboell's grebe, and when perchance one of these great lakes becomes frozen over, the unfortunate grebes are caught, for they cannot rise from an icy surface.

BREEDING HABITS: In western Europe the red-necked grebe begins its northward trek in April: 20th April is given as the latest date when winter visitors have been seen in the Shetlands. Eggs may be found in the Baltic States in the first week of June. Colonel R. F. Meiklejohn took first eggs which had just begun incubation on an extensive reedy stretch of water at Borchholme in Estonia. The usual clutch laid by this grebe is four to five, the chalky-white eggs becoming very stained as incubation proceeds. The nests in this case were built of aquatic plants placed on floating lumps of vegetation at the edge of reed-covered islets. On leaving the nest the grebes partly covered the eggs. According to F. C. R. Jourdain the breeding season of the red-necked grebe begins at the end of

April, but is usually in full swing in May and early June. He gives the average of one hundred eggs of the European bird as 50·6 × 33·99 mm. Max. 57 × 35·5 mm. and 55·4 × 36·5 mm. Min. 46·7 × 33·8 mm. and 50 × 30 mm. Incubation starts with the first egg and both birds take equal shares. The period of incubation is given by O. Heinroth as twenty-three days. This grebe is single-brooded unless its first clutch is robbed.

On the Atlantic coast of America Holboell's grebe starts northward in May, on the Pacific coast and through the interior late in April or early in May, and remains in its breeding area in the north until late in September or early October. The nesting season is said by Bent to extend from the last week in May throughout June : the average of sixty eggs is given as 53·7 × 34·5 mm., slightly larger than in the typical race as might be expected from a larger bird. The eggs showing the four extremes measure, max. 64·5 × 37·5 mm.; min. 49 × 33 mm. and 50·5 × 30 mm. The young grebes are said to be very precocious and to dive and swim instinctively almost as soon as they are hatched. So soon as they are able to feed and to swim about they may be seen riding in safety on their mother's back as she swims about the lake. Mr. Bent states in his very full account that the little grebes will cling to their mother's plumage as she dives and will come to the surface with her as if nothing had happened ! His description of the nestlings is so clear that I repeat it here with full acknowledgment to the author and to the Smithsonian Institute in whose *Bulletin* (No. 107) the life history of Holboell's grebe is given so attractively.

> The downy young show considerable variation in colour pattern, but in a general way they may be described as practically black above when first hatched, fading to blackish-brown or seal brown as the chick increases in size ; this colour includes the sides and crissum, leaving only the belly pure white ; the head and neck are broadly and clearly striped, longitudinally, with black and white ; the chin and throat are often spotted with black but are sometimes clear white. There is usually a distinct V on the top of the head, starting on the forehead, above a superciliary black stripe which usually includes the eyes, and terminating in broad white stripes in the sides of the neck ; there is also a median white stripe or spot on the crown, and the back is more or less distinctly marked with four long stripes of dull white or greyish. The lighter stripes, especially on the head and neck, are often tinged with buffy-pink. This downy covering is worn until the young bird is more than two-thirds grown, the colours becoming duller above and greyer below. The first real plumage is acquired early in September, dark above and white below, as in the adult, but signs of youth are retained in the head and neck, both of which are more or less striped with black and white on the sides ; the neck is also more or less rufous.

Remarking that the adult *autumn* plumage is characterized mainly by the absence of red, which entirely disappears from the neck and breast and is replaced by a white breast and dusky neck, Mr. Bent emphasizes how the pale grey of the chin, throat, and cheeks is then sharply defined against the dusky neck, just as it is against the red neck in the spring.

In Europe attention had mainly been focused on the remarkable courtship actions of the great crested grebe by the observations of Edmund Selous and later of Julian Huxley. The latter emphasized the necessity for naturalists to concentrate more on the courtship habits of other members of the same family. Little appears to have been done in Europe in this connexion, but American ornithologists have been more successful though we still have much to learn. A valued American correspondent of mine nearly fifty years ago—the late Dr. Joseph Grinnell—was one of the earliest to report the peculiar actions of a pair of Holboell's grebes which he chanced upon in the delta of an Alaskan river. He was startled by a series of most lugubrious cries and, advancing quietly, came upon a small lake almost surrounded by spruces, and margined on one side with willows. Suddenly the curious cries broke forth again and there, twenty yards away, were two grebes resting on the water. Both birds took part in the " song ", though the voice of one was notably weaker than that of the other. Grinnell then describes what occurred :

One of the birds would start with a long wail and then the other would chime in with a similar note, both winding up with a series of quavering cries, very much like the repeated whinnies of a horse. During these vocal demonstrations the neck would be thrown forward and the head and bill tilted upward at an angle of 45°. During the performance the birds were nearly facing each other, but at the conclusion one, presumably the male, would slowly swim around the other.

A slight movement on the part of the observer brought this scene to an end, when both birds instantly disappeared beneath the water leaving scarcely a ripple.

The nest consisted of a floating mass of sodden marsh grass, a foot in diameter. It was anchored among standing grass in about two feet of water. It lay twenty feet from the shore and about the same distance from the edge of the ice, which still existed in a large floe in the centre of the lake. The top of this raft of dead grass presented a saucer-shaped depression, which was two inches above the surface of the surrounding water. The eggs lay wholly uncovered and could be plainly seen from shore.

There is another grebe on the British List—the Slavonian or horned grebe which, though only a scarce resident in north Britain, is a numerous bird in North America, where there appears to be no love lost between it and the subject of this essay when they find themselves in competition. In Mr. Bent's account of *P. griseigena* he quotes Allan Brooks, the distinguished bird artist, to the effect that in British Columbia, where both species are abundant, Holboell's grebe wages incessant war on the horned grebe, the large birds diving and coming up beneath the smaller ones time and again to the terror of the latter, who often desert their nests in consequence.

Much of the information contained in this essay has been gained from observations made in the New World. We are fortunate that distinguished naturalists like A. C. Bent and Dr. Joseph Grinnell were able to watch these grebes at the breeding season and on passage and to leave such a pleasing account of their experiences of a very shy bird.

From reading the various accounts written about the European species and of the better-known Holboell's grebe it seems that no one had definitely proved whether the red-necked indulged in the so-called penguin-dance which forms part of the display of the great crested grebe. The late B. W. Tucker concluded from a statement made by the German ornithologist Naumann that it was common to both birds, but the reference to it in *The Handbook* leaves one uncertain and certainly there is no other reference to it in the English or American literature. That it has been witnessed by the Russian ornithologist Shulpin in Ussuri Land in 1936 had apparently been overlooked. Thanks to Mme. E. Kozlova, who has translated the few field notes available in the Russian language for use in my book, I am able to give Shulpin's observations which he made in the field—and with these brief, but interesting, notes I conclude this essay :

This bird lives on boggy lakes, overgrown with reeds and Typha, with only small pools of open water here and there. Its love antics are the same as those of *P. cristatus*. Mostly two birds meet breast to breast, standing up in the water with crests lifted and fanned out, croaking and yelling wildly. After a few seconds they drop down again and resume their feeding.

I found four nests at a distance of about 150 m. one from another. The birds used to leave their nests and hide long before we came near them. Then not a sound could be heard in the neighbourhood. The eggs were usually covered with a bunch of reeds, apparently drawn out of the water but a few seconds earlier. In one case the eggs under the cover were quite warm.

Evidently the bird, hearing someone approaching, leaves its nest immediately, dives for the reeds, covers its nest and swims away to hide in the jungle. The birds have certainly every reason to cover their eggs from enemies, but just at the time of incubation the nest itself is dark brown and so also is the surrounding broken and fallen rushes and other plants, whereas the freshly brought cover is bright green. Hence the nest is more conspicuous than ever. Indeed, I located nearly all nests guided by their green covering.

On 22nd June I observed on Lake Dorizeny an adult bird with downy young. The chicks would swim for a while, following their mother, but often climbed up on her back to warm their feet.

On one occasion I saw *P. griseigena* surfacing apparently alone. The bird looked cautiously around, remaining on the same spot. The next moment several chicks appeared from under her wings. They had evidently travelled with their mother under water.

REFERENCES : Original Descriptions. 1. *Colymbus grisegena*[1] Boddaert, *Tabl. Pl. Enlum.*, 1783, p. 55. Ex Daubenton *Pl. Enlum.*, 931. No locality given, later fixed as France. 2. *Podiceps holböllii* Reinhardt, *Videnskab Meddelelser*, 1853, p. 76 : Greenland.

---

[1] Corrected spelling *griseigena*.

SLAVONIAN or HORNED GREBE

PLATE 15

Podiceps auritus Linnaeus

Breeding and Resident in comparatively small numbers in the Scottish
Highlands, also a regular Winter Visitor to all British coasts in
varying numbers, and to estuaries and some inland lochs. Scarce in
Ireland. Also a Passage Migrant

IDENTIFICATION : In summer plumage when this grebe has donned its full
ornamental dress it is an extremely handsome species. The adult male
has the crown, forehead, chin, and the expandable tippet black. On each
side of the crown is a tuft of gold or golden-chestnut feathers variously
described in textbooks as pale chestnut (Eagle Clarke), yellow (Witherby),
chestnut (Coward). The upperparts are dark brown ; the breast and
flanks a warm chestnut and the belly white. The bill is black with a horn-
white tip, the eye ruby-red with a yellow or silvery inner ring, legs and
feet greenish-brown or greenish-grey, the toes edged yellowish. The female
is like the male in the breeding season but the head ornaments are not so
well developed. Its total length is rather more than 13 inches.

A complete moult takes place early in the autumn, when it is difficult
to distinguish this and the black-necked grebe ; both then have a black
and white appearance. In the Slavonian grebe the dark area on the crown
does not extend below the eye, the crest and tuft are absent and the underparts become almost entirely white, the flanks marbled with dark grey.
The main distinction, which can only be seen at close quarters, is in the
shape of the bill. That of the Slavonian is straight and stout, of the black-
necked more slender and with an upward tilt. This does not apply strictly
to young black-necked, and the up-tilted distinction can be deceptive.
In the Slavonian the black of the crown does not descend lower than the
eye and the very white cheeks meet on the nape giving it a capped appearance. In the black-necked grebe the cheeks are dusky below the eye and
the contrast less striking. The Slavonian and black-necked grebes are
much the same in size : both are intermediate between the little grebe
and the great crested.

LOCAL DISTRIBUTION : It is indeed remarkable that the Slavonian
grebe succeeded in establishing itself as a breeding species in Scotland,
considering the treatment it received in the past at the hands of collectors
and egg-thieves. The first known instance of its breeding on a loch in
the northern Highlands, of which more will be said later, was communicated
to the British Ornithologists' Club in 1910 by W. R. Ogilvie-Grant, the
nest having been discovered in Inverness-shire in June 1908 by Mr. Hugh
M. Warrand. Whether it had been established elsewhere in Scotland
before that date is problematical for a pair which had been shot on the
Loch of Killisport, Argyllshire, on 20th June 1860, a date which certainly

suggests a breeding pair, were exhibited at a meeting of the Royal Physical Society of Edinburgh. This grebe had been known as a *winter* visitor to Britain since 1796 when Montagu recorded a specimen obtained at Truro.

The history of the spread of this grebe as a breeding species in Scotland has been given by Dr. Evelyn Baxter and Miss Rintoul in their standard work on that country. It is only six years since their two volumes were published, but already changes have taken place and I have asked an acknowledged authority on Scottish birds to prepare the paragraph on the status and breeding distribution of the Slavonian grebe in Scotland in 1958. Dr. Ian D. Pennie of Golspie writes as follows :

" From being a regular winter visitor to the coasts of Britain the Slavonian grebe has in comparatively recent years become a regular, though still very restricted, breeding species. The possibility of its first breeding in Scotland was first suggested by the shooting of a pair, male and female, on the Loch of Killisport, Argyllshire, on 20th June 1860,[1] but it was not until 1908 that the first Scottish nest was actually found,[2] this on a loch in Inverness-shire, where, despite the shooting of the first pair and the subsequent ravages of egg-collectors, a thriving colony gradually became established on this and neighbouring lochs. Now, fifty years later, there are about fifteen pairs in Inverness-shire, and breeding has been recorded in Moray.

" In Ross-shire we have it on the authority of Dr. Frank Darling[3] that Slavonian grebes are established breeders on the western mainland, and although it is generally known to have bred in recent years in both Sutherland and Caithness it is unfortunate that establishment of this lovely bird has not been so secure as farther south. Breeding in Sutherland was first recorded in 1929,[4] four pairs on two adjacent lochs ; and although this strength was maintained for a few years there has been a gradual decrease. One pair only was known to nest in 1943 and there have been no positive records for the past three years. However, there may well be breeding pairs elsewhere in this vast county, as a bird in full breeding plumage was seen this year on a very suitable loch in another locality. The story is similar in Caithness. Breeding was recorded in 1932 and from then onwards pairs have been seen on three different lochs, certainly until 1945 ; but records have been much less frequent since then and it is doubtful whether any have bred this year, 1958."

Without mentioning specific localities for obvious reasons, Dr. Pennie's summary gives a good outline of the grebe's range north of the Border. Little account need be taken of suspected breeding on Benbecula in 1893,

[1] Gray, *Birds of the West of Scotland,* 1871.
[2] *Bull. B.O.C.,* xxv, p. 75.
[3] *Natural History in the Highlands and Islands,* 1947.
[4] Baxter and Rintoul, *The Birds of Scotland,* 1953.

or of the fact that birds in full summer plumage have been recorded from Barra and Orkney. Such records do not necessarily imply breeding. It will be remembered that in Orkney in spring J. G. Millais encountered birds in full summer plumage which lingered late into summer and were, in his opinion, almost common, presumably as passage migrants. In the Shetlands too in recent years Mr. and Mrs. Venables state that they have seen this grebe apparently in full summer plumage as early as 25th March ; and they draw attention to Saxby's statement that he saw occasional pairs lingering on until the end of May. They suggest that these late passage migrants were heading for Iceland, a locality where this grebe breeds commonly. As yet there is no nesting record from the Shetlands despite, or perhaps because of, the great numbers of ornithologists who regularly visit these islands in spring.

As a winter visitor the Slavonian grebe is known to many who have never seen it arrayed in all its nuptial beauty but, owing to its similarity when not in breeding plumage to the black-necked grebe it may easily pass unrecognized. Both are regular migrants, the Slavonian from April till June and from late August till November. The Slavonian is more often seen in winter, when it may be found round our coasts and in our estuaries in varying numbers, more commonly on the east coast, as is but natural, than in the west or south. It is to be seen singly or in very small flocks, and is stated by observers in north-east England and East Anglia to be more regular in its appearance than the red-necked grebe. There are no large immigrations of the Slavonian grebe recorded as in the case of the red-necked species. Severe weather will account for a temporary increase in its numbers on our shores. There are a number of inland records of wintering birds or of others on passage, but usually it prefers the salt water except when breeding. It is an annual but scarce visitor to the English Channel. Off the Norfolk and Suffolk coasts it is a familiar winter visitor as the late Claud Ticehurst recorded, remarking that " in contradistinction to the eared grebe . . . hardly a winter passes but that one or more, some-times flocks, are reported from somewhere in the Suffolk estuaries, and should hard weather supervene the chances of meeting this bird are enhanced ".

In a recent investigation undertaken by Mr. Frank D. Hamilton to discover the status of the three rarer British grebes along the south and up the east coasts of Britain during the winter months (1st October to 30th April inclusive) 3624 records were examined covering a period of six years 1949-55. Some interesting results were obtained and these will be discussed at greater length when we come to deal with the next species—the black-necked grebe—where the relative proportions of these three grebes in various areas of the south and east coasts of Britain are set out in tabular form. Ignoring for the moment the rare red-necked grebe, *Podiceps griseigena*, it is interesting to compare the relative numbers of the Slavonian grebe and black-necked grebe.

1. In the area embracing the Channel, Cornwall to Kent, the proportions were Slavonian 17 per cent., black-necked 80 per cent.
2. Essex to Norfolk (including the Wash), Slavonian 33 per cent., black-necked 53 per cent.
3. Lincolnshire to Northumberland, Slavonian 43 per cent., black-necked 23 per cent.
4. Berwickshire and Forth area, Slavonian 84 per cent., black-necked 6 per cent.

Mr. Hamilton inclines to the view that in area No. 4 the proportions may require some adjustments when further records can be accumulated. Even so it is of interest to note that the Slavonian reaches its greatest frequency (84 per cent.) on the north-east coast of Britain, while the black-necked has its main wintering area (80 per cent.) in the English Channel. It was found that the three grebes reached a very definite peak in different months —the red-necked in January, the black-necked in February, and the Slavonian in March. Records for the east of Scotland north of the Forth were too meagre to include in the summary but it was found that in the Dornoch Firth the only Grebe appearing in winter is the Slavonian— and that has been so over several seasons. It must be emphasized that the records which Mr. Hamilton analyzed were restricted to the south and east coasts of Britain. Lack of observers precluded the investigation being carried to the north and west coasts of England, Wales, and Scotland.

To Ireland this grebe comes regularly every winter to the bays of the north and north-west, as stated in the new *Birds of Ireland*, but it is always scarce, seldom more than half a dozen birds being seen at once, though it occurs in greater numbers, in some years more than others. It is to be met with in all maritime counties, but it avoids the bays which are too exposed on the south-west. It has occurred in six inland counties. From September onwards the occurrences increase, according to Major Ruttledge, reaching a maximum in February. I can endorse the author's statement that it is a matter of great difficulty to obtain sufficiently clear views of the distinguishing characters of bill and head plumage in order to differentiate between it and *Podiceps caspicus*.

DISTRIBUTION ABROAD: In the Old World the Slavonian grebe breeds in Iceland, northern Scotland, Faeroe Is.[1] (very rare : one pair), Scandinavia, formerly south to Denmark, Öland, Gotland and the Baltic States, Finland and Russia extending to 65° N. In the north of the Soviet Union its range is evidently restricted. In an extract translated[2] from Professor Dementiev's article on *P. auritus* in *Birds of the Soviet Union* it is stated that it is doubtful if the Slavonian grebe breeds in the White Sea-Archangel area, and it is pointed out that there is no mention of breeding

[1] K. Williamson in his book *The Atlantic Islands*, 1948, gives the status of this grebe in the Faeroes as rare passage migrant. One pair has bred for several years.

[2] By Mr. D. D. Harber in his review in *British Birds*, xlviii, p. 273.

on Sakhalin as given in *The Handbook of British Birds*. On the whole it is thought to be a rare bird although common in places, as for instance in the mountain lakes of the Altai and in the basins of the Ob and the lower Irtish rivers.

As the range of the Slavonian grebe in Russian territory has never been closely defined in the English language I have asked Mme. Kozlova to send me for inclusion here the following paragraph in which she has given the distribution in the U.S.S.R. as recognized by Russian ornithologists :

Podiceps auritus ranges north to the northern shores of Lake Onega, to the Vytchegda River and the region of Syktykvar town (Komy Province) ; breeds in western Siberia along the Obj River at least to Beriosov town. Along the Yenissei it goes north to about 57° N. ; and along the Lena, to the basin of the Viliuj River. It has been found breeding near Yakutsk town and probably nests in the southern portion of the Aldan River basin. It has been recorded in June from the mouth of the Uda River and Ajan town on the Sea of Okhotsk (or Okhotsky Sea) ; it is numerous on Sakhalin Island, in Kamtchatka and in Anadyr Land.

The southern boundary of its range passes in the regions of the towns of Minsk, Kalinin, Yaroslavl, Kasan, extending further south-east across Bashkiria, region of Orenburg. In Kazahstan it breeds north to Kustanai, Koktchetav. At Cassar and Akmolinsk regions, as also in the Kulundinsky steppe, on Tchany Lake (western Siberia), in Minussinsk Land. There are breeding records from the mountains of Altai and Tarbagatai, also from Balkhash Lake. It has been met with in the breeding season on the lakes of central Tian-shan, on Issyk-kul Lake. Further east the southernmost finds are : the mouth of the Asgun River, the mouth of the Kumara River (tributaries of the Amur), and the middle course of the Zeia River. It probably breeds on the lower Ussuri. It winters partly on the Aral and Caspian seas and on some lakes of the upper Amu-daria.

The Slavonian grebe is not happily named as it does not breed in " Slavonia "—the area lying to the south of the old Hungarian border bounded by the rivers Drave and Danube, now part of Yugoslavia. In North America this grebe has a wide breeding range across Arctic Canada to Alaska, extending south to British Columbia on the west and Minnesota in the east of that continent. Details of its range in U.S.A. are given in the new *Check List of American Birds*. It has also been taken in Greenland.

The winter range of this bird is a wide one. In America it occurs over nearly all territory of the United States south to southern California and Florida, while in Europe its winter range covers much of central and southern Europe and reaches the Mediterranean, though it is not common anywhere. It is recorded from various islands, more especially those west of Sicily and Malta. It wanders far afield and has been recorded from the Azores [1] and Bermuda and from Tunis in North Africa from which last locality there is a specimen in the British Museum. Irby examined one killed in the Straits of Gibraltar, but there are not many

[1] *Novitates Zoologicae*, xii, 1905, p. 96.

Mediterranean records of this species. The only record for Egypt (Heuglin) is believed to have been due to confusion with the black-necked grebe, though it is recorded as having bred !

HABITS : The subject of this essay is one which we are now privileged to term a British breeding bird, for it has now become firmly established in its Scottish haunts. None the less it is not a plentiful species, and any naturalist wishing to study it would be well advised to go farther afield for the purpose and to leave our own nesting birds to the peace of their Highland lochs. Our stock may perchance have reached us from Denmark, where a number of years ago the Slavonian grebe bred in small numbers in Jutland alongside the black-necked grebe, but more probably from Iceland in which island it is quite an abundant nesting species, though with a limited distribution in the breeding season. As there is little doubt that Iceland birds must pass the British Isles in winter, even if many do not remain around our shores at that season, I propose to devote some space to the habits of the Slavonian grebe in that country, and this I am able to do through the kindness of a friend—Dr. Finnur Gudmundsson of Reykjavik—who has allowed me to use the information contained in an article he wrote in 1952.[1] Discussing the bird's local distribution, he observes that in some parts of Iceland the Slavonian grebe is considered a fairly common breeding bird, whilst in other parts of the country it is completely lacking. Immediately to the east of the low hills on the eastern side of Hrútafjördur it is found breeding throughout the north and north-east of Iceland. Farther to the west it is again found nesting in considerable numbers in Medalland in the district of Vestur-Skaftafellssýsla, and from there throughout the south and the south-west as far as the Snaefellsnes peninsula it has a wide breeding distribution. In his article Dr. Gudmundsson is at pains to explain in some detail where this grebe does *not* nest in Iceland and for that information I would refer the reader to his paper, to which, following his excellent practice in all his writings, he adds a summary in English.

In the breeding season in Iceland the Slavonian grebe frequents lakes, ponds, and meres, and occasionally quiet reaches of slow-flowing rivers. It shows a marked preference for waters with fairly rich vegetation and rich and varied animal life. Dr. Gudmundsson believes that these habitat preferences partly explain its peculiar distribution in Iceland. As a nesting species it is mainly restricted to the lowlands and valleys, being most common below the 100-metre contour line. Lake Mývatn (227 metres above sea-level) is an exception to this rule. Nowhere in Iceland is it found breeding higher or as high above sea-level, and nowhere is it as abundant as there, the number of breeding pairs amounting to a few hundreds. Dr. Gudmundsson's description of its nesting will be included later in this account.

[1] *Náttúrufraedingurinn*, xxii, 1952, pp. 134-136.

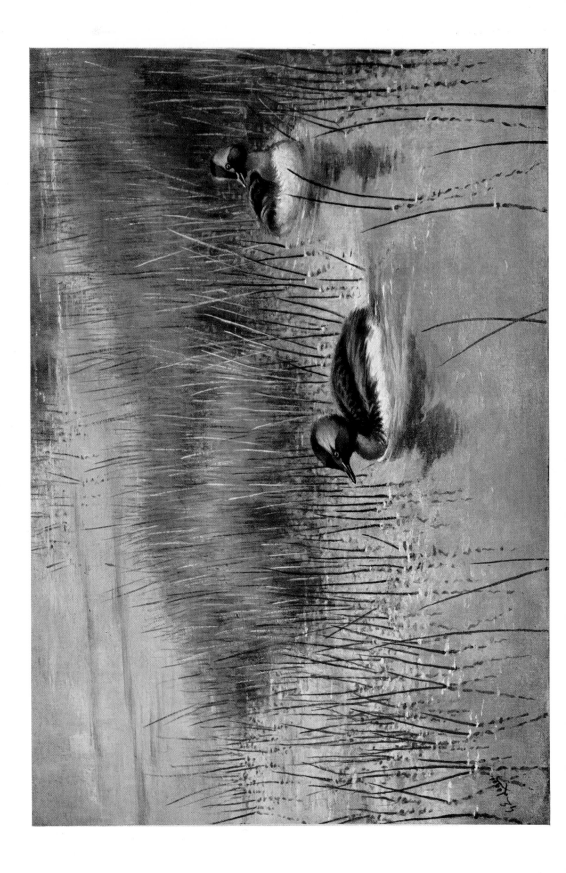

PLATE 15

SAVANNAH OR HORNED GREBE

Podiceps auritus Linnaeus

PLATE 15

SLAVONIAN OR HORNED GREBE
Podiceps auritus Linnaeus

In America, where the Slavonian grebe is widely and evenly distributed, though not abundant, considerable attention has been devoted to its feeding habits.[1] One of its favourite articles of food is said to be a small fish which the grebe is expert at chasing and catching ; the bird darts about swiftly and skilfully under water, catching the fish unawares and pursuing them at full speed. On inland waters it eats a large quantity of animal food, small frogs, tadpoles, aquatic lizards, water shrimps, leeches, beetles, and other insects, and feeds to some extent on grass and other vegetable diet. W. L. McAtee, who made an exhaustive report on the food of this grebe a number of years ago now, found that feathers constituted practically 66 per cent. of the contents of fifty-seven horned grebes' stomachs examined. Feathers are fed to the young and play some essential (though unknown)[2] part in the digestive economy. McAtee found that various beetles, chiefly aquatic, composed 23·3 per cent. of the food ; other insects, including aquatic bugs, caddis and cheronomid larvae, dragonfly, nymphs, etc., nearly 12 per cent. ; fishes 27·8 per cent. ; crawfish 20·7 per cent. ; and other crustaceans 13·8 per cent. Other animal matter taken in small quantities included snails and spiders. Little vegetable food was discovered in the series examined. When living on the coast its menu is very different, consisting of small fish, shrimps, and minute crustaceans.

Within its American range the Slavonian grebe performs its spring moult in April, sometimes a little earlier or later, but it is usually completed before the end of May. Birds in full nuptial plumage have been taken as far south as South Carolina, but as a rule the birds migrate north before the moult is complete. It is interesting to read in Dr. Gudmundsson's notes that this bird also arrives in Iceland in April, for in that island it is mainly a migratory species, leaving in late September and October to return to its breeding haunts in the spring. There is a spring movement past British coasts from early May to June, but to what place these rather late migrants are making it is not possible to say unless it is to the Baltic States and farther east.

From the little that has been published on our breeding birds one must presume that, unless driven from their Highland lochs by severe frost, when they would repair to coastal waters, they are properly described as residents ; but owing to the secrecy rightly maintained about their nesting places in Britain, it is not easy to follow their movements throughout the year. Mr. George Waterston, a leading authority on Highland birds, writes to me on 17th April 1958 in answer to my enquiry : " This species is undoubtedly maintaining its numbers in its traditional haunts on both sides of the Great Glen in Inverness-shire and has recently extended

[1] A. C. Bent, *Life Histories of North American Diving Birds*, p. 23.
[2] But see Mr. K. L. Simmon's explanation of this habit in the young of the great crested grebe, p. 210 above.

into Moray. I think it is still breeding in Caithness. The birds are summer visitors to these lochs. The type of habitat most favoured by Slavonian grebes are lochs surrounded with sedges—not reeds." Under a later heading, two separate accounts of its breeding habits and courtship in Scotland will be given from the observations of two leading authorities.

When migrating, the Slavonian grebe is reported usually to travel singly or in small scattered flocks. Sometimes in winter a flock of some size has been observed but when on the move the flock apparently breaks up. Mr. Bent has remarked how off the New England coast he has frequently seen horned grebes migrating, with the scoters, in October, a mile or two off shore, where several may be in sight at one time; he has never seen them in anything approaching a flock when passing along the coast but notes that throughout the interior of North America, where they are more numerous, they seem to fly in flocks. They are then reported to fly high in the air and to follow the course of streams. That is not a sight we are often likely to see in Britain, for migration, when it has come under notice, has been over the sea parallel with the coastline. Bent remarks that it is a curious looking bird in flight with its long neck and slender body stretched out in a straight line, with big feet dragging behind and small wings vibrating at high speed. It cannot easily be mistaken for anything else.

BREEDING HABITS : In an earlier paragraph some indication has been given of the type of habitat preferred by the Slavonian grebe more especially in the nesting season, though it should be stressed that in America a much wider choice lies open to it than for instance in our own islands. In that continent it will apparently be quite content with a little pond upon which to bring up a family (as instanced on the Magdalen Islands, Quebec), but often a more extensive area is preferred. Slavonian grebes have a preference for the more open type of sedges as opposed to thick reed-beds. Some idea of the nest situation can be obtained from Mr. Eric Hoskings's series of excellent photographs taken in Scotland and published in *British Birds*, xxxiii, or from those which accompanied the Rev. H. M. Stone's contribution on this subject which appeared in *Country Life*.[1] On one Highland loch described to me by a friend the birds have been established since 1947. This loch lies at an altitude of five hundred feet and is about half a mile long by a quarter wide. It is situated in an area of rather wet moorland, of the type frequented (when permitted to do so) by hen harriers. The loch is about three-quarters surrounded by an impenetrable swamp of rushes and sedges, in which there is a large nesting colony of black-headed gulls. There are swampy islands in the loch full of willow thicket.

It may be of interest to those readers who do not have access to the *Bulletin of the British Ornithologists' Club* to have repeated here the account of the first-known nesting in Scotland. The facts were communicated to the B.O.C. by W. R. Ogilvie-Grant, one time Keeper of the

[1] 1947, p. 623.

Bird Department of the British Museum, who had them from Mr. Hugh Warrand at first hand. Mr. Warrand had obtained permission for himself and a friend to fish on a small reedy sheet of water in the hills of Inverness-shire, but the day being very warm and bright few fish were rising and the fishermen therefore landed and lay down by a rock on the shore. While waiting there Mr. Warrand observed a bird moving among the reeds near by, and presently noticed that it was swimming round a pile of green reed-stalks like a coot's nest. The attention of his friend and of a keeper was called to the bird, which had a peculiar head with sweeping crests of buff, and all observed it for some time swimming restlessly about the nest among the reeds. Mr. Warrand's note continues : " I regret to say that the next time I saw this grebe it was lying dead in a bird-stuffer's shop, and I was told whence it had come and who had brought it—facts which have since been fully corroborated. I had hoped that it would have been left in peace to establish a family, and greatly deplored its death." Mr. Warrand was cheered, however, to learn the following year (1909) that one or two pairs had appeared on the same loch, but soon afterwards heard that the nests had been ruthlessly robbed by a private collector.

The Slavonian grebe has been studied in its Scottish home by Mrs. (Cecilia) Knowles who lived for many years at Dunlichity Lodge, by Inverness. I am particularly fortunate in having had all her notes sent to me with her permission to quote from them as I wish. Her observations were made chiefly on the Ruthven group of lochs, but her field-notes cover a wider area and numerous lochs, and her knowledge of *Podiceps auritus* in Inverness-shire and beyond is probably second to none. Although classed as a resident species in some textbooks this does not mean that the bird is resident on its breeding loch all the year round. Mrs. Knowles believes that some birds, possibly juveniles, winter in their breeding area but *only* if the winter is mild. At the first spell of frost they are gone. As very few winters in Inverness-shire can pass without some frosts— often indeed severe—it follows that it is the exception rather than the rule to find the grebes sedentary. Apart from the frost, which may drive them away to the estuaries or to some open water elsewhere, there are, in Mrs. Knowles's opinion, other causes which influence their departure. The date is governed to a great extent by the success or failure of breeding. If a pair lose their brood or eggs they may leave very early, in July or early August. Otherwise one parent usually stays with the juveniles till they are independent. Unless they intend to stay as long as the weather is mild they are gone at latest by the end of September, and only a few are left in the last days of August. Mrs. Knowles has noted that any that stay on after September are always in winter plumage very early, and in her opinion are therefore not adults in early moult but full-grown juveniles. The weather again takes charge when the time comes for them to return to their breeding loch—any time from the middle of March

to the first week of April.   On one particular loch the average date of
their return is 1st April, though Mrs. Knowles has known them to arrive
as early as 28th February (1953) and as late as 16th April (1952).   For
some reason the very severe spring of 1947 did not have such an effect
on their arrival as might have been expected, for they were back on their
favourite breeding loch by 12th April.   When first they arrive the female
is indistinguishable from the male, but certain individual characteristics
may be noted when a bird has been under observation for a little time.
The female at once begins gathering nest material, at first rather vaguely
as if she did not know what she was about.   The male soon proclaims his
sex by going off on expeditions of about twenty minutes' duration down
the loch, possibly, if not probably, to look for rival claimants to his territory.
Fights often occur at this time, in which the females take absolutely no part,
remaining aloof and rather disdainful ;   they are invariably over the possession of territory.   Once this is asserted it is vigorously maintained and a
wandering pair will at first be unmercifully chased around, though ultimately
they may settle down near by in the same reed-bed.   Slavonian grebes are
not communal nesting as a rule, but where breeding sites are limited they
may nest very close together.   As an instance of this Mrs. Knowles records
having found seven nests in one patch of reeds which measured about fifty
yards square.   On three of their well-known breeding lochs the numbers
should be much greater than they are.   On one loch in 1952, Mrs. Knowles
counted eleven nests in one bay and four in an adjoining bay with an average
of three eggs per nest.   By the end of August only three juveniles remained
alive.   The reason for this was a pair of lesser black-backed gulls, which
arrived some time in July and decimated the juveniles.   On another loch
by Dunlichity a pair tried to breed over three years and never got away
with young.   Pike are very numerous in that particular loch and were
believed to be the cause of the failure.

Nest building is undertaken by both sexes, and lasts some time according to the depth of the water at the site.   A large raft-like structure of
reeds is made on which a semi-floating nest is built.   Sometimes the raft
is more than three feet across.   The birds were seldom seen to breed before
June, though if they arrive early on the loch they may start building the
nest, which even in shallow water has to be built from the bottom of the
loch, as the winter storms always destroy any remnants of last year's nests.
Floods in early summer often destroy a nest when half built ;   or they may
cause it to rise above the top of the reeds, to the consternation of the owners.

On these Inverness-shire lochs Mrs. Knowles usually found eggs by
15th June ;   the earliest date when young were seen is 29th June.   The
possibility of this grebe rearing a second brood is suggested by an incident
which convinced her that such was the case.   One day in September she
saw a grebe swimming about with two chicks nearly out of down and with
them was one fully fledged juvenile who never left the parent duck, or, if

inadvertently left behind when feeding, made frantic efforts to catch up with her.   Bernard Tucker—then Editor of *British Birds*—to whom Mrs. Knowles communicated the facts, was not satisfied that this was sufficient proof of second breeding as he considered that the elder duckling might have been " adopted " and not the progeny of the duck with the chicks.   He does not appear to have convinced Mrs. Knowles, though she admits the possibility of his argument.   She found that the grebes in her area usually nest in " bottle sedge " and equisetum, but on another loch, when the water was at a very high level and may have submerged the usual breeding reeds, she found a nest with four eggs at the edge of the loch in submerged heather and lousewort.

Mrs. Knowles could point to many examples of the tameness of the Slavonian grebe during the nesting season   She has watched it preening and courting from fifteen yards and closer with only the sketchiest of cover, while on another occasion when with several other people she sat completely exposed to view on a grass bank, a grebe came back and settled down on its nest not ten yards away.

Grebes are all known to have an interesting and sometimes remarkable courtship—exemplified more especially in the great crested grebe, but found too in the other species.   It does not fall to many to witness this ceremony with the subject of this essay, owing to the remoteness of its breeding haunts and its comparative scarcity in our islands   Mrs. Knowles, living close to a breeding loch, had many such opportunities and made good use of her chances   So too, on one occasion, did that superlative bird-photographer Eric Hosking, and in the article[1] which accompanied his photographs he describes the courtship of a pair of grebes which he had under observation on a Highland loch.   This took place under rather strange circumstances, as the clutch of three eggs which were present on 7th June in the nest were gradually reduced to one, apparently through the attentions of a neighbouring gullery.   The grebes continued to brood the one remaining egg, but also continued to add material to the nest.   It is worthy of note that when only one egg remained in the nest the brooding bird failed to cover it on leaving the nest—a failing which has been noted in other species—but subsequently when a second egg was laid it was covered in the usual way before the sitting bird left it.   Nothing of an unusual nature was seen to take place until the evening of 18th June, when the hen swam to the nest carrying a small quantity of nesting material ; this she placed on the edge of the nest and carefully arranged.   Then she leaped from the water on to the nest and lowered herself as if to brood but instead fell into the water again and swam from sight.   Very soon after- wards the cock followed exactly the same procedure.   He had only just disappeared when the hen returned with more nesting material.   After placing this in position she paddled backward for a short distance, then

[1] *British Birds*, xxxiii, 1939, pp. 170-173.

rapidly forward before leaping on to the side of the nest. Then, to Mr. Hosking's surprise, she went through the motions of removing non-existent nesting material from the top of the single egg which had not been covered. She then settled down to brood. Shortly afterwards the display was witnessed—the hen, still brooding her single egg, began to call very excitedly and a moment later the cock emerged from the reeds just behind the nest. He also called excitedly and it was noted that he carried no nest material on this occasion. The excitement then became intense. The hen solicited by stretching out her head and neck, curving the latter in a snake-like manner, while her chin almost rested on the surface of the water. Both birds called excitedly. The cock swam rapidly and jerkily round the nest, spreading and displaying the gorgeous golden-yellow ear-tufts. His head was jerked from side to side and bowed up and down. He stopped in front of the hen and bowed until his bill rested on the water, the ear-tufts being brought right forward so that their vivid colouring showed to the best advantage. For some moments the cock remained in this attitude while the hen remained motionless, looking straight at the cock as though hypnotized. Next the cock swam round the nest twice, hesitating while at the rear of the hen. He proceeded to paddle backwards, then very rapidly forwards, and leaping out of the water jumped on the hen's back. With his large, white-lobed feet he smacked the shoulders of the hen alternately and very rapidly, after which coition took place. The hen remained prone all the time and the cock left immediately afterwards. On the following day Mr. Hosking again witnessed the same courtship display and mating. There was, however, a preliminary. Both birds were observed carrying rotting nesting material which they were seen to pull up from just beneath the surface of the water ; several journeys were made and while the hen was close to the nest the cock swam alongside the nest, but remained in the water, stretched out his neck, raised the golden-yellow ear-tufts and called, remaining in this attitude for some seconds. The hen took no notice of this display and had in fact continued building through it all. Mr. Hosking was fortunate indeed to be present at the right moment, and not only to secure a series of photographs of the display but to have left us such an excellent account of what he saw. Further displays were seen later in the week ; by 21st June a second egg was in the nest and on 25th there were three fresh eggs, by which time the courtship and display actions had naturally ceased. The original egg remained in the nest. Mr. Hosking was unable to remain long enough to see the eggs hatch, but ends his account with the following observation :

It is presumed that this particular pair of birds were unique in not recommencing the breeding cycle on being interrupted by the theft of most of their first clutch and in continuing to incubate the single egg during the courtship period. Although all grebes add nesting material during the whole of the stages of incubation, this pair brought much more than normal, so that it would seem that they went through a partial phase of nest-building concurrently with that of courtship and display ; but the fact remains that the single egg held them to the original nest.

The field-notes which Mrs. Knowles has now sent to me not only bear out very closely the observations quoted, but add some important features. She too noted how closely the nest-building and courtship were inter-related, the cock often swimming in with a piece of material which he offers most ceremoniously to the hen. " As nesting time draws on there is much twittering and squeaking in the reeds from both birds, and by the hen in particular to recall the cock from his roving expeditions. Then the note has a very peevish tone to it. This note and also the twittering goes on during the courtship."

I have heard it disputed that the Slavonian grebe indulges during courtship in what is commonly termed " the penguin dance ". Mrs. Knowles can vouch for it taking place. She writes :

Like the great crested grebe the Slavonians have a most charming ceremonial dance, similar to that of the penguins, both sexes rising on tails, facing each other and bending forward with rhythmic dabbings at the side of each other's neck, then to their own neck, then to each other again, keeping up usually the tittering note. Just before mating the hen bird will lie flat on the water at the appearance of the cock, her wings slightly spread and neck and beak stretched out on the surface of the water.

Mrs. Knowles then alludes to the remarkable repertoire of notes possessed by the Slavonian grebe—" a kind of ' uck, uck ' of conversation and chat, an ' ack, ack ' of alarm, rather sharply given, and when a rival is seen approaching a chattering ' cack-ack-a ' ". In addition they have a whole range of soft twitterings and a sort of trilling gurgle when alone together in the reeds, " a most cosy and domestic sound ". In his classic work on *North American Diving Birds* Cleveland Bent describes the " love song " of the Slavonian grebe to be heard in the spring as a wonderful combination of weird, loud, striking notes once heard never forgotten, and consisting of a series of croaking and chattering notes followed by several prolonged piercing shrieks. Bernard Tucker, commenting on this description in *The Handbook of British Birds*, observes that no European observer seems to have described such notes. He too remarks on the bewildering vocabulary which this grebe evidently possesses. In some notes on the breeding habits of this grebe made in the prairie region of the Rocky Mountains, Alexander Du Bois [1] found that the usual vocal performance of these grebes is a sort of " ko-wee, ko-wee " repeated at regular intervals. He compared the notes to the squeak of a dry wheelbarrow, producing one double squeak at each revolution of the wheel, but with a clearer quality than the simile might indicate. Each " ko-wee " has a

[1] *Auk*, xxxvi, pp. 170-180, an abridged account appearing in *British Birds*, xiv, 1920, pp. 2-10, with photographs.

rising inflection, its two syllables run closely together, with the accent on the last syllable.

Of the many observations which Mr. Du Bois made on the occasion cited, the birds' efforts to detract his attention must be mentioned. Whenever he appeared at the edge of the slough it was the custom of the two grebes to float about upon the area of open water with an air of supreme unconcern. " They busied themselves constantly with their toilets, preening the feathers of all parts of their bodies and very frequently tipping or rolling themselves in the water to reach their underparts with their bills. In this half-capsized posture they would float for several seconds, exposing to view the strikingly prominent white area that is normally below the water-line." This preening and floating in different positions, on the part of both birds, proceeded without interruption whenever Mr. Du Bois visited them and it became evident to him that it was practised as a ruse to hold his attention and thus divert him from the nest. The actual site of this nest was exceptionally open to view, as can be seen by a photograph reproduced in *British Birds*, xiv, p. 3. The birds had built in a temporary marsh after an extremely rainy spring and there was practically no cover. The nest, which consisted of a mass of coarse grasses, many of them fresh and green, was floating in about a foot of water, the body of the nest below the water-line being of such bulk as almost to touch the muddy bottom. So used to Mr. Du Bois and his tripod camera did these grebes become that eventually he was able to obtain a photograph of the sitting bird within arm's length of the lens. If he approached too close to the nest the female grebe made a dash at him " shooting entirely out of the water "— a show of force which was frequently repeated and sometimes ended with a violent splashing dive sending up a shower of spray.

Although this account is already long, I must conclude my notes on the breeding biology with a description by Dr. Finnur Gudmundsson of the Slavonian grebe's habit in Iceland. It will serve as a comparison with the account of our British breeding birds already given. Dr. Gudmundsson describes the nests on Lake Mývatn as composed entirely of wet decaying water weeds, and observes that it is usually floating on the water among growing vegetation of *Carex rostrata*, *Equisitum fluviatile*, *Scirpus palustris* or *Menyanthes trifoliata*. Nests may also be built on beds of submerged water-weeds such as *Myriophyllum spicatum*; on Lake Mývatn branches of willow (*Salix phylicifolia*) or birch (*Betula puhescens*) reaching into the water often serve as anchorage for the nest. In some cases the nest is built up from the bottom of shallow water with no cover at all. In other cases nests may be found on relatively dry banks of lakes or on sandy or gravelly shores of lakes, but such nests are most likely built, so Dr. Gudmundsson considers, at a time when the water-level is considerably higher. On Lake Mývatn the Slavonian grebe either breeds singly, each small bay or inlet in that case being occupied by one pair only, or in small colonies. The clutch consists (in Iceland) of four to five eggs, occasionally three or six. In favourable seasons the eggs are laid in the first half of June, but owing to the frequent destruction of nests and eggs through storms or changes in water-level, clutches of fresh eggs are not infrequently found in July and even in August. Both sexes build and both take turns in incubating.

Mr. Nethersole-Thomson, who has studied the breeding biology of this grebe in Scotland, says that the birds change places at four to five hours' interval. He found the incubating period in Scotland to be twenty-two to twenty-four days : in Iceland Hantsch gives twenty to twenty-four days while Du Bois found twenty-four to twenty-five days to be the period of incubation in Montana. It must be most unusual for breeding to commence as early as 12th May as recorded in *The Handbook of British Birds*. Late May to mid-June is the normal nesting (egg-laying) period in Inverness-shire, as Mrs. Knowles has stated, and these dates may be applied to Scotland generally, mid-June being the most likely time to find a clutch.

Describing the eggs as at first " chalk white ", Mrs. Knowles notes how soon they become yellow, deepening to orange, or even dark mahogany-red, with contact with the wet reeds of the nest and as a result of the action of the minerals deposited in the water. Jourdain gives the average measurement of thirty-seven British-taken eggs as 46·7 × 31·3 mm. Max. 50·5 × 32·4 mm. and 46·4 × 33 mm. Min. 42·4 × 30·6 mm. and 44 × 29·1 mm. One hundred foreign-taken eggs averaged 44·5 × 30·7 mm., which is appreciably smaller than the British series.

Nestling Slavonian grebes are charming but odd little creatures and have been well described in Mr. A. C. Bent's *Life Histories of North American Diving Birds* as almost black above, striped and spotted with greyish-white ; there is a median white stripe on the occiput and a white V on the forehead, extending down the sides of the neck in broad irregular stripes ; the sides of the head, neck, and throat are white tinged with salmon-pink and spotted with dusky.

It appeared to Mrs. Knowles that when first hatched the chicks remain in the nest for a day or two, but during that time they are frequently carried out from the reeds, if danger threatens, on the back of one of the parents—usually the cock. The chicks are frequently fed in this position. If upset in the water they can swim and dive in a feeble way when quite newly hatched, as Du Bois has observed. One day in Iceland Collingwood Ingram, the distinguished horticulturist, put this to the test. He recounts how, coming upon a family party paddling on a sheet of water, the three chicks riding comfortably on their parents' backs, he made a sudden movement to attract their attention. " In the twinkling of an eye both the old birds vanished." The sudden plunge left the surprised youngsters floating alone and disconsolately on the surface of the water, though not for long, for the next moment they too had dived out of sight. The young grebes develop fast and, as A. C. Bent tells us, soon acquire the juvenile or first plumage which is worn through the late summer and into the autumn. He describes it as similar to the first winter plumage but characterized by the dusky stripes and spots on the sides of the head and throat. These dusky markings disappear during the autumn and the young then become similar to the adults.

In the more northern latitudes where winter comes down with a bang the Slavonian grebes leave their nesting haunts and travel far afield. In Iceland Dr. Gudmundsson records how the birds leave in late September and October. At the famous Lake Mývatn, where it will be remembered some hundreds of pairs have their breeding quarters in countless little bays and in small colonies, the exodus in autumn begins in the second half of September and continues until the lake freezes over, which usually occurs some time in October. In the neighbouring coastal regions the Slavonian grebes are observed on the sea throughout October and the first week of November, while in south-west Iceland odd birds are met with on coastal waters throughout the winter : the others vanish. Dr. Gudmundsson states that a marked bird has been recovered in the Faeroes in November but that nothing is known for certain about the winter quarters of the Iceland population. Is it not reasonable to suppose that many find winter sanctuary round the shores and estuaries of the British Isles ?

REFERENCES : Original Description. *Colymbus auritus* Linnaeus, *Syst. Nat.*, 10th ed., 1758, p. 135 : Europe and America ; restricted type locality, Sweden.

PLATE 16   **BLACK-NECKED GREBE**

Podiceps caspicus caspicus Hablizl

[*Podiceps nigricollis* Brehm auctorum]

A Summer Resident which has bred locally but irregularly in England, Wales, and Scotland, usually in very small numbers. In Ireland it appears to be more regular and more numerous as a breeding bird. It is an irregular Winter Visitor in small numbers to the coasts of Britain and also a Passage Migrant, when it occurs on inland waters where it does not nest, but mainly on the south and east coasts.

IDENTIFICATION : The adult in breeding plumage has the entire head, neck, back, and scapulars dull black ; from behind the eye extend some narrow elongated feathers of an almost flaming gold, with considerable lustre. Bordering the black on the lower neck, and the sides of the breast and thighs, the feathers are intermixed black and chestnut. The wings are dark brown, the inner primaries and secondaries white ; the under-parts are silky-white. In winter plumage the golden " ears " are lost ; from the forehead to the rump the upperparts are very dark brown ; the chin, upper throat, the sides of the nape, the breast and abdomen silky-white ; the lower neck brown. The iris is orange-pink ; the bill blue-grey shading to pinkish at the base ; the legs greenish to bluish-grey. The lower mandible of this grebe is distinctly upturned at the tip and the upper mandible slightly so, giving the whole bill an upturned appearance, more so than it really is (after Meinertzhagen). In size the black-necked grebe measures about 12 inches. It has a characteristic high forehead and in winter dress the black of the crown extends below the eye and on to the ear-coverts. It is intermediate in size between the great crested and the little grebe but close to the Slavonian, with which it may easily be confused. The Slavonian grebe in comparison has a stouter straight bill which is not upturned at the tip and the dark cap, when in winter plumage, does not reach below the eye. The two birds have a similar black and white appearance at that season.

LOCAL DISTRIBUTION : Unlike the Slavonian grebe, which has a more northern distribution, the black-necked grebe is a lowland bird which does not select isolated highland lochans upon which to rear its family. In Scotland to-day (1958) there are probably two small colonies, one in the Central Highlands and the other in Renfrewshire ; the Midlothian summer haunt of the species was apparently forsaken before the outbreak of the Second World War. Dr. Fraser Darling in his book *Natural History in the Highlands and Islands* records (p. 251) that he saw a pair on a suitable loch in Sutherland but could not be sure that they were breeding.

In England it has bred spasmodically from Westmorland (1935) and Durham (1946) to Hertfordshire and Somerset (1932), while other counties in which it has bred on one or more occasions are Yorkshire, Cheshire, Cambridgeshire, and Norfolk. The most likely localities in which nesting may continue at intervals are in Hertfordshire (the Tring reservoirs), Buckinghamshire, and in Cheshire, but so long ago as 1930 Mr. Witherby believed that some conditions at Tring militate against the black-necked grebe becoming firmly established in that area. It was not until 1939, when a pair brought off two young, that A. W. Boyd definitely established it as a breeding bird in Cheshire, but as a winter visitor the species has been seen much more often since T. A. Coward classed it in 1910 as a rare winter visitor to the estuaries of the county.

Wales has been able to claim a small colony in Anglesey, first discovered in 1904 by Charles Oldham and S. G. Cummings, while there was reason to believe the birds were in the district twelve years before the date mentioned. Breeding appears to have continued until about 1928 but never more than four pairs were located.

Ireland is the country to which we may look with more confidence that the black-necked grebe will hold its own, though it is a vain hope that the very large colony found in 1929 and still flourishing in 1932 (when 155 nests were examined) will ever regain its past glory. We read in *The*

Birds of Ireland that in 1934 this lake was almost dry, and for at least two more years the conditions were unfavourable ; they have improved since 1937, since when " small numbers have bred in most years ". Elsewhere sporadic nesting has been reported, but despite pains taken to explore numerous waters, no colony larger than fifteen nests was discovered (in 1949) in the county where the big colony was located in 1930. Several pairs are reported as having bred in Galway in 1951, but soon afterwards the lake went dry. In 1955, after a wet winter, two broods were reared, but in 1956 three of the breeding places in Ireland, including the Galway site, were completely dry following exceptionally dry weather. The once famous resort in Roscommon fared no better than Galway. It is depressing to read in the *Irish Bird Report*, 1957, that " known breeding haunts were either dry or untenanted ". Two winter records are mentioned. The successful breeding of this grebe in Ireland seems to be very largely dependent on the rains. Either its haunts are almost dry or else, as in 1955, the very wet winter and spring kept water-weed submerged well into the breeding season, with disastrous results apparently at Roscommon.

As a winter visitor to the British coast its distribution is irregular. Major Ruttledge has affirmed that it continues to be a very uncommon visitor to Ireland, and perusal of the *Irish Bird Report* from 1953 onwards certainly bears out his contention. I am indebted to Mr. Frank D. Hamilton, who has been conducting an enquiry into occurrences of wintering grebes around the coasts of Britain, for the following details. Mr. Hamilton tells me that the main object of his investigation was concerned with the frequency of the *three rarer species* of grebes (Slavonian, black-necked, and red-necked) along the south coast and up the east coast of Britain, both in relation to the area and the time of their occurrence in winter. The published or unpublished notes in his possession cover the period 1949-55, " winter " being defined as the six months from 1st October to 30th April inclusive. The number of records analyzed during the period under review numbered 3624. For the purpose of his investigation the coast-line was divided up into four sections :

    1. South coast, Cornwall to Kent.
    2. Mid south coast, Essex to the Wash.
    3. Mid north coast, Lincolnshire to Northumberland.
    4. North coast, Berwickshire and Forth area.

The general status in winter of the three Grebes found in the areas specified worked out approximately as follows :

Area	SLAVONIAN per cent.	BLACK-NECKED per cent.	RED-NECKED per cent.
1	17	80	3
2	33	53	14
3	43	23	34
4	84	6	10

It is apparent from these figures that the majority of the three grebes seen in the winter on the south coast of Britain are black-necked grebes, more than 2000 records having come to hand, but it must be borne in mind that the great crested grebe and the little grebe are not included in these figures. It was found that on the south coast (Cornwall to Kent) there is a definite tendency for all three grebes to reach their highest numbers in December, with a gradual falling off afterwards. In the mid south area (Essex to the Wash), the black-necked and the red-necked species show very little fluctuation but the Slavonian tends to show its peak numbers in December. In the mid north area (Lincolnshire to Northumberland) only a small passage was observed in November and none in December. In the north coast area (Berwickshire and the Forth area) no passage was observed in the last three months of the year but the black-necked and the red-necked grebe have a very definite peak in February and the Slavonian grebe likewise in March. Mr. Hamilton was not able to obtain sufficiently regular records from north of the Forth area to make an analysis possible for north-east Scotland, but certain facts came to light : in the Dornoch Firth, for instance, the only visiting grebe is the Slavonian—and that over several winters. Several instances of grebes turning up in August and September in breeding plumage were reported, especially from " down south ". Records from Wales are very scarce. In the *Birds of Pembroke-shire* R. M. Lockley and his co-authors can only give three records between 1925 and 1949 and the bird must be considered a very rare visitor. In the *List of the Birds of Carmarthenshire* (1954) only one record is mentioned.

DISTRIBUTION ABROAD : As a breeding bird the black-necked grebe occurs throughout the greater part of the Palaearctic Region, but its northern range does not extend so far towards the Arctic as that of the Slavonian grebe. It extends to Denmark and southern Sweden (rare) and on about that latitude eastwards to Siberia, where it does not range north of 67°. In *The Birds of the Soviet Union* it is stated that *P. nigricollis* " apparently " breeds in Ussuria, Manchuria, and northern China. Its southern breeding range embraces the Aral-Caspian region and Trans-caucasia, west to the Mediterranean basin. It is resident in small numbers in the marshes of the Tigris and Euphrates. It has bred in Cyprus in the past but has ceased to do so now, since there is little if any suitable cover and it is much persecuted by Cypriot sportsmen. At the other end of the Mediterranean it almost certainly nests in the Balearic Islands (Munn) where some remain all the year round. Jourdain believed that it bred in Corsica but had no definite evidence. Its distribution is not confined to the Mediterranean islands, for we find it breeding in North Africa in Morocco and Algeria and almost certainly in the larger lakes of northern Tunisia. It does not breed in Egypt, but is found breeding in tropical Africa where, under the name *Proctopus caspicus* (Hablizl), it is reported [1]

[1] *African Handbook of Birds*, vol. i, p. 5.

to breed in Abyssinia and on Lakes Naivasha and Nakuru in Kenya. As a wanderer it has reached the Azores.[1] Other races take the place of the typical subspecies : in South Africa *P. c. gurneyi*, and in North America *P. c. californicus*.

The winter range of *P. c. caspicus* is a large one, the European population ranging to the Mediterranean where it has been reported from the Straits of Gibraltar to the Suez Canal. It wanders far afield, and while it is found in winter around the south and east coasts of Britain it is recorded also from such distant places as the Azores, Madeira, the Canary Islands, and Cyprus, as well as from most other islands in the Mediterranean Sea.

HABITS : It seems a pity not to stick to the colloquial name for this grebe which heads this essay, in preference to " eared grebe " employed by some of our distinguished naturalists. The black-necked is the much more distinctive name of the two, for although the neck is only black in summer plumage the " ears " are not restricted to this species, and the name " eared " has been applied with some force to the Slavonian grebe which was named *auritus* by Linnaeus.

The black-necked grebe is such a suspicious bird that there are not many places in England or Wales where conditions are likely to attract it, for its preference for thick reed-beds is well known. With more generous treatment it might eventually colonize some locality in East Anglia where former attempts have been frustrated by man. It is a colonial nester and, given protection, should increase in numbers in the few suitable spots we can offer. Unfortunately it has not made much headway in Scotland.

In its general habits it closely resembles the Slavonian grebe. It has been said that it is perhaps more given to diving than any of its family and prefers to elude its enemies in this way rather than by using its wings. That it can fly well and fast is proved by the distances which it travels in the winter months. The diving habit of grebes was discussed in an interesting contribution to *British Birds*[2] some years ago. Bernard Tucker evidently made use of the information it contained when writing in *The Handbook* on the recorded lengths of dives, where it is stated that 25-35 seconds seems most usual, though dives lasting 9-50 seconds are on record. In the paper cited in the footnote the authors had kept two birds under observation in water 15-17 feet in depth ; 38 dives were timed with maximum duration 40 seconds, mean 32·2 seconds and minimum 15 seconds. It was almost certain that the birds were going to the bottom as no fish were on this occasion brought to the surface.

It is suggested that perhaps this grebe is more of a bottom feeder than others, but that fish form a larger proportion of its diet than we should infer after consulting *The Handbook*, has been proved on a number of

[1] *Novitates Zoologicae*, xii, 1905, p. 96.
[2] G. C. S. Ingram and Major H. Morrey Salmon, " The diving habits of ducks and grebes ", in *British Birds*, xxxv, 1941, pp. 22-28, with comments by Dr. J. M. Dewar.

occasions. Mr. Ingram and Major Morrey Salmon stated that they had evidence that fish are by no means an uncommon item of food, and they observed that on one occasion in March they watched a black-necked grebe rise twice in fifteen minutes with a fairly large fish in its bill, which was not killed and swallowed without considerable trouble. On another occasion a number of fish were seen to be caught and brought to the surface, the successful fisher being constantly worried by its companion diving and coming up alongside in an attempt to snatch the fish from its bill. These grebes were making dives of 20-25 seconds. Beneath the surface the black-necked and little grebes were obviously competing, for every now and again a little grebe would shoot to the surface and scutter off over the water, the black-necked emerging close on its tail in hot pursuit. One little grebe definitely carried a fish in its bill, evidently the object of attraction. In this connexion attention may be drawn to a statement by Mr. G. W. Temperley[1] criticizing the remark in *The Handbook* that " Fish are only taken to a small extent ". Mr. Temperley had been watching a family of black-necked grebes in County Durham and observed that the parents appeared to be feeding themselves and their young solely upon fish of about the size of a small minnow or stickleback. The juveniles, when old enough to dive for themselves, invariably emerged with fish in their bills. Besides its usual method of feeding by diving or picking up food from the surface, a bird was seen by Ingram and Morrey Salmon to potter about in shallow water at the edge of a reservoir with its head and neck submerged, and to continue to do so for well over twenty minutes— the only time the observers saw a grebe so engaged. Jourdain has stated that insects of many genera are its main food, also mollusca and crustacea ; and, like others of its family, it swallows a considerable quantity of feathers. T. A. Coward noted that insects were captured on the surface " with the rapid right and left snatches of a phalarope ". A. W. Boyd has also described the actions of this grebe when feeding upon insects. Many were captured on the surface of the water and in the air ; the grebe would shoot its neck out at right angles and snap them in the air, or point its bill perpendicularly in the air and catch them with a little leap.

Superb diver that it is, this grebe may be seen swimming buoyantly and fairly high in the water ; but it can, like the other members of its family, sink its body so low that only its bill shows above the surface. It can progress in this way in open water : when it dives it does so without noise or splash. All grebes are out of their element on land, but the black-necked is said to be the least clumsy in this respect.

The voice of the black-necked grebe is not unattractive. In their standard work on the birds of Scotland, Dr. Evelyn Baxter and Miss Rintoul state that in their experience it is not as noisy as the Slavonian grebe. Its note has been rendered " bidder-vidder-vidder-vidder "—an

[1] *British Birds*, xl, 1947, pp. 21-22.

interpretation which met with the approval of Dr. Hugh Blair, who frequently heard a note of rippling character, very different from the trill of the little grebe, being louder and not so melodious. There are, of course, various accounts of its call notes. In Africa [1] observers have described it as " a soft pee-epi, pie-piep ", the breeding note " widderr-widderr " and an alarm note " whit-whit ".

My own experiences with this grebe have been on sea or lagoon in some distant land, and there it certainly prefers to keep its distance. That it may relax its vigilance to some extent in the nesting season is probable, for Dr. Baxter and Miss Rintoul " found it quite bold " and often watched the parents feeding their young on the open water. I once came upon a little party of these grebes on a saline lagoon in the Canary Islands : they kept well out in the middle of the lagoon, and had evidently made a long flight for they appeared very tired. On only one previous occasion had they been recorded from the group. The weather was boisterous and the seas stormy, but as we watched the grebes rose and flew over a dividing spit of land and out to sea.

When in the Canary Islands in 1959 I visited some of my old camping grounds of years ago, and on a freshly-made dam in the interior of Grand Canary encountered two grebes, almost certainly of this species, disporting themselves on 31st January.

How far afield those grebes which breed in the latitude of Scotland may go, it is impossible to say. The bird is found, as already stated, at least as far as the Mediterranean in considerable numbers ; but these may of course be local birds, for it breeds in Spain and also in Morocco. Irby wrote that in his day it was the most common of the grebes in the vicinity of Gibraltar, and in winter they are generally plentiful in Gibraltar Bay. Our Scottish birds are reported to leave their breeding haunts from August to October and not to appear again until April.[2] There is a very definite movement of the black-necked grebes which breed in America. There the autumn migration starts late in August and proceeds slowly. Mr. Bent has recorded that throughout the northern portion of their breeding range the birds linger until driven out of the lakes by freezing ; but they never wholly disappear from the southern portion of the range, although the individuals seen in winter were probably not bred in that vicinity. Mr. Bent adds that theirs is a coastwise movement as well as a southward migration in autumn. The species winters abundantly along the southern half of the Californian coast, as well as farther south and in the lakes of the interior. Probably much the same movements will apply to the birds in Europe and Asia. Some conception of its vast range will be obtained by reading Mr. G. D. Wilder's account [3] of the migrations of the black-necked grebe,

[1] *African Handbook of Birds*, vol. i, p. 6.
[2] *Birds of Scotland*, vol. ii, p. 504, under *Podiceps nigricollis*.
[3] *China Journ.*, Shanghai, xxxv, 1941, pp. 27-31, 68-71.

PLATE 16

BLACK-NECKED GREBE
Podiceps caspicus caspicus Hablizl

recorded under the typical race, which takes place annually down the coast of China—at the other end of the world !

It should be mentioned here that the American race of *P. caspicus* is confined roughly to the western half of the North American Continent from British Columbia and Manitoba to Mexico. It is of interest to note that this race *californicus* is not considered a shy species. It is seldom seen in flight, except on its migrations, and is reluctant to leave the water, preferring to escape by diving or merely swimming away at a moderate speed. It is stated to be able to rise from the water readily, and like the European bird can fly quite swiftly. It swims smoothly through the water with scarcely a ripple. When diving in deep water it often leaps into the air and plunges straight down, diving with wings closed. Mr. Bent states that it is less inclined to remain under water or skulk in the reeds than the other small grebes, but prefers to come to the surface and watch proceedings from a distance. Like all others of its family this unfortunate bird suffered greatly in the past from the millinery trade : thousands were shot every year during the breeding season when they were tame and easily killed. The breasts were stripped off, dried, and shipped to New York where they were much in demand for ladies' hats, capes, and muffs. Fortunately, as Mr. Bent tells us, this practice has been stopped by the establishment of protected reserves. Its habit of nesting in colonies led to thousands of its eggs being taken for the market, so that it is a wonder that the American race of the black-necked grebe managed to survive.

Breeding Habits : One of the best known of the grebes' haunts in England has been on the reservoirs at Tring, and it is there that the courting actions of various pairs have been watched and described so well by Oliver Pike,[1] Charles Oldham,[2] and other naturalists of my younger days. It was forty years ago that Oliver Pike visited Marsworth reservoir on 10th May 1919, by which date four birds had arrived on the water. By that same evening the males were fighting desperately, while the two females kept at a distance of about twenty yards and watched the fight. One male was very aggressive and followed the other. Mr. Pike watched the combat for about an hour, the battle waxing most violent, the birds falling over one another in the water, dashing at each other and diving. The following morning only one pair remained on the reservoir. The next day both birds spent the day diving for food, but on 12th May they were going through their courting exercises which are described as so pretty to watch : the two faced one another and one bird gave a curious snake-like twist to its neck, followed by a rapid shake of the head, very much like the courting action of the great crested grebe ; but altogether it made a greater show of it. The brief show being over, the birds swam side by side

[1] *British Birds*, **xiii**, 1919, pp. 146-154, from which the notes published here are taken with due acknowledgement.

[2] *Trans. Herts Nat. Hist. Soc.*, 1921, pp. 211-219.

across the reservoir and entered the reeds at the spot where a pair—probably the same pair—had nested the year previously. It was observed that the male kept close to his mate and if they passed a coot, or if another bird approached them, he placed himself between her and the possible enemy. Oliver Pike eventually found the nest and prepared to photograph it, but before this was accomplished the nest was robbed by egg-collectors. Having lost their first clutch, the pair decided to waste no time before building again and spent another week in courting, thus giving the observer further opportunity to see what transpires. At intervals throughout the day— 25th May—love-making took place :

In this, the male would often swim casually away from his mate for a distance of about thirty yards ; he would then dive and one could tell by the actions of the female that he was coming towards her under water ; just before he appeared, she would lay her neck full length on the water, and raise her wings over the back in the form of a shield and wait for him. With most unerring precision he always came up about a yard in front of her, and with head lowered swam rapidly to her. As they met both birds looked as if they were standing on their tails, and with necks extended, breasts and beaks almost touching, they faced one another. One would now shake its head, and the other immediately followed with exactly the same action. Both had the head feathers erected, and for about fifteen seconds they remained like this, but suddenly dropping to the water, they swam together rapidly side by side. . . . For ten or fifteen yards they would swim together like this, their bodies almost touching, then both dived simultaneously.

In April 1944 P. J. Askey and A. W. Boyd had an opportunity to watch the display of the black-necked grebe in Cheshire. This took place regularly from 22nd April until the end of the month. During this period there were always three birds present and finally a fourth. The third bird was evidently an intruder and was frequently attacked by one of the pair, which rushed along the surface with outstretched neck and on several occasions dived and torpedoed the intruder from below, causing it on one occasion to utter a " whitt-whitt " of alarm. These observers discuss [1] what they saw under the headings habit-preening, head-shaking, neck-stretching, billing, and weed-presentation : but apart from the preening habit, upon which they lay some stress, they do not appear to have seen much that Mr. Oliver Pike had not already described twenty-five years earlier. They make no allusion to what he then wrote. The unfortunate third party seems to have had a thin time of it. At the end of the month, on a number of occasions, it displayed to one of the pair by preening and head-shaking, but the bird to which these overtures were made did not respond and the other bird of the pair drove it off with some violence. A final attempt was made apparently by " the intruder " to win favour by presenting a small fish, only to have the gift refused and to be met with

[1] *British Birds*, xxxviii, 1944, pp. 136-137.

" a hissing noise ". The three birds were still present on 28th June but no young birds were seen that year.

The discovery that the black-necked grebe was actually nesting successfully in Scotland was made by Charles G. Connell (now Sir Charles) on 27th July 1930, when accompanied to a well-known Midlothian reservoir by Professor Ritchie. Two pairs each accompanied by young were seen. Sir Charles and Dr. Stenhouse had located these grebes two years earlier, but it was not until 1930 that breeding was definitely established. Connell published the account of his discovery in the *Scottish Naturalist*,[1] and the notes he made at the time of his visit are worth repetition here as they show close observation of his subject. The grebes were remarkably tame and evidently allowed themselves to be studied at leisure. In the water their attitude was normally upright with the neck carried much more erect than is usually shown in illustrations. Seen from behind the birds had a squat appearance. The high forehead gave a distinctive look to the head, while the most conspicuous feature at this season was the buff-coloured feathers on the face, in a fan-shape and spreading backwards from the region of the eye. The red mark at the base of the beak, and the upturned bill, could only be observed when the bird was fairly close. The flanks were noticeably rusty-brown, and the silky-white underparts were visible only when the bird rose in the water or rolled over to preen itself ; thus differing from certain illustrations in the books. It was noted that the grebes showed a disposition to fly from one part of the loch to another, flying rather slowly. Normally they dived quietly, but when chased by gulls, as they were on several occasions, they disappeared with a noisy splash.

It is sad to be informed by George Waterston that the black-necked grebes abandoned this site as a breeding place before the outbreak of the Second World War, and to learn how restricted are the birds' haunts to-day (1958), north of the Border.

In Ireland breeding was first established by the shooting of a young bird in 1915 and three years later, in June 1918, a pair in full breeding plumage with three young in down were procured. They now form a family group in the National Museum in Dublin. The most remarkable colony of black-necked grebes in the British Isles was that which C. V. Stoney and G. R. Humphreys discovered on a secluded lough in Ireland.[2] Humphreys made the initial discovery on 26th April 1929, but it was not until the first days of June that the colony could be explored by the two naturalists, and not until the following year, on 22nd May 1930, that their numbers could be approximately assessed.

A very large breeding colony of black-necked grebes was found at the head of the lough in a dense reed-bed several acres in extent, with reeds eight feet in height,

---

[1] *Scottish Naturalist*, 1930, pp. 105-109.
[2] *Bull. Brit. Oological Assoc.*, No. 24, 1929. See also for 1931, pp. 45-46.

and protected on all sides by a mass of floating vegetation. In addition there were several separate groups of nests in isolated clumps of sedge, etc., growing out of the water not far from the main reed-bed now referred to ; these were the clumps examined in 1929. In these various groups it was estimated that about two hundred and fifty *pairs* of black-necked grebes were nesting. In the dense reed-bed the nests were only a few feet apart, while some of those in the isolated clumps touched each other.[1] A certain definite section of this huge reed-bed was densely occupied. . . . The nests were large untidy structures, more than half submerged, and never looked so finished as those of the little grebe. The usual sett of eggs was three, but many nests held four, and one with five eggs was seen. The eggs are distinguished at a glance from those of the little grebe as they are usually longer and invariably wider. At this date [2] most of the eggs seemed to be incubated, but a few young were to be seen, beautiful little objects, their backs striated with black and grey. Some were to be seen riding on the backs of their parents. In the dense reed-beds the sitting birds disappeared completely at the approach of an intruder, but in the other clumps dozens of black-necked grebes might be seen at close quarters issuing from their shelter and " taxi-ing " over the surface of the water.

Mr. Humphreys and Mr. Stoney considered it a strong probability that this was not an isolated breeding ground in Ireland. They state that these grebes appear to prefer loughs which have grassy bottoms and to avoid those that are bare and rocky. The drying up of this lough in Roscommon with its huge colony of grebes has already been referred to in an earlier paragraph (p. 251) when discussing local distribution, and under the same heading will be found an account of the bird's present status in Ireland. It is indeed a tragedy that this huge colony was unable to survive owing to climatic conditions, and as we must infer from the new *Birds of Ireland* (1954)—in which Mr. G. R. Humphreys assisted— no other large colony comparable to that described was ever discovered, despite continued searching on many loughs.

The nests which were examined in Ireland held the normal complement of eggs—three, four, and sometimes five—but in Germany larger numbers up to eight are recorded by Henrici. Chalky-white when fresh, and quickly stained, they are described by Jourdain as ovate or elliptical ovate in shape: 100 British-taken eggs averaged 43·08 × 29·74 mm. in size, max. 50·2 × 28·7 mm. and 44 × 31·8 mm., min. 39·8 × 28·3 mm. and 39·9 and 27·7 mm. Oliver Pike stated that the incubation period lasts twenty to twenty-one days. The downy young are very different in appearance from the young of the little grebe, grey in colour with pure white breast and throat : their striking appearance excites the admiration of all who see them for the first time.

In their graphic account of the Roscommon breeding haunt Humphreys and Stoney make no mention of the number of gulls which breed there too. Other grebes, great crested and little grebes, were there in numbers,

[1] *British Birds*, xxiv, 1930, pp. 170-173.
[2] 22nd May 1930.

PLATE 17

LITTLE GREBE
Podiceps ruficollis ruficollis Pallas

as well as coots and doubtless moorhens, but gulls are not brought into the picture. It is, however, a striking fact that on the continent of Europe, of the several species known to nest in colonies of gulls and terns, the black-necked grebe is probably the best known. In a contribution to *Ornis Fennica*[1] Sigfrid Durango discusses the problem and suggests that there is evidence to prove that gulls and terns are a defence against egg-robbing birds. He cites instances in which the black-necked grebe is an inhabitant of gull or tern colonies in Sweden, Denmark, Germany, France, Macedonia, Algeria and North America, and quotes Swanberg that in different years the black-headed gulls nested in different parts of Lake Krankesjön in Scania. Every year the grebes followed the gulls to their new nesting ground. He further states that in North Africa the black-necked grebe mostly associates with the black tern and the black-headed gull and in North America with Franklin's gull. The inference is surely that the black-headed gulls—themselves robbers of no mean order—recognize and respect those grebes which nest in their midst, while they would not hesitate to attack a nest with eggs left uncovered, or undefended chicks, beyond the territory of their own colony. How does Conrad Lorenz, the widely-known bird psychologist, explain that ?

REFERENCES : Original Description. *Podiceps caspicus* Hablizl, *Neue Nord. Beytr.*, 4, 1783, p. 9 : type locality Gilan, Persia. Synonym *Podiceps nigricollis* Brehm, *Handb. Naturg. Vög. Deutschl.*, 1831, p. 963 : Eastern Germany.

LITTLE GREBE

PLATE 17

Podiceps ruficollis ruficollis Pallas

[*Podiceps fluviatilis* Tunstall of earlier authors]

Resident ; also Winter Visitor from overseas. A certain amount of local migration and wandering takes place but no direct evidence (admittedly difficult to obtain) of Passage Migration beyond the British Isles

IDENTIFICATION : This is much the smallest (10½ inches in total length) and far the most common of the five grebes on the British List, and differs from all the others in one striking particular. It is the only one which does not develop a head-ornament of any kind in the breeding season. In its summer plumage the whole of the upperparts are blackish-brown from the crown to the rump, with reddish-chestnut (or bright rufous) cheeks, throat, and forepart of the neck. The chin is blackish, often freckled with white. The upper part of the breast is dusky, the rest of the underside silvery-grey, becoming dark and tending to dusky blackish on the flanks and thighs. The wings blend with the back and in flight show some white, but not a great deal when it is remembered that the inner webs of the outer

[1] Vol. xxx, No. 1, 1954, p. 18.

secondaries are largely white, the white area increasing on the inner secondaries. The eye is reddish-brown, brighter red in the breeding season than at other times ; the bill black with white tip and apple green at the base ; the feet greenish-olive to lead grey. The bill is comparatively stout and stumpy, measuring 16-21 mm. from the feathering.

A complete moult begins in August and is continued up to December, the wing feathers being shed simultaneously and rapidly. In its winter dress the little grebe is more drab in appearance, losing the rufous cheeks, throat, and neck—which become brownish-buff—and being generally paler on the upperparts and whiter below, the lower part of the breast and belly becoming silky-white.

LOCAL DISTRIBUTION : This very numerous resident species is widely distributed throughout the whole of the British Isles, breeding in every mainland county of Scotland, England, Wales, and Ireland ; but it is least numerous in Northern Scotland. It is not recorded from Shetland as a breeding bird ; Mr. and Mrs. Venables considered it a winter visitor between October and April. It was therefore with interest that I read in the *Scottish Naturalist*, vol. lxix, 1957, p. 52, a note from Mr. Alex Tewnion that he had watched a pair continually diving in a small reedy arm of Loch Cliff in the island of Unst on 12th July 1955 : but the recorder was unable to remain long enough in the vicinity to substantiate whether or not this pair were breeding. The little grebe breeds commonly in lochs of the Outer Hebrides and in some of the Orkney Islands. David Lack found several pairs on Mainland in 1941, five or more on Sanday, two or three pairs on Stronsay, and one pair on Westray. It nests on many islands in the Inner Hebrides. On the Scottish mainland it breeds up to 2000 feet in altitude.

In England and Wales it is found nesting on countless lakes and ponds as well as on ornamental waters. Lord Hurcomb tells me that it used to breed in St. James's Park before the 1914-18 War when the lake was drained. It does not appear to have nested again until 1939 and 1940 ; it also nested there in 1945 but apparently not since. It is believed, so Lord Hurcomb writes, that the periodical draining of the lake removes the small fish (including sticklebacks) and larvae on which it feeds, but it has bred very successfully more recently on the lake in the grounds of Buckingham Palace. For example, in August 1948 Lord Hurcomb saw four broods on that piece of water. In the same month of the following year he saw twelve adult or well-grown birds there and three chicks. There is little doubt that it has continued to nest successfully in that sanctuary. Lord Hurcomb suggests that the constant appearance of little grebes in autumn in St. James's Park is probably partly a dispersal of these broods. In Richmond Park and in Kew Gardens it nests regularly.[1]

[1] It has also been reported to nest in a park in Amsterdam (P. L. Steenhuizen in *Ardea*, 1934).

In Ireland the little grebe breeds on quiet waters everywhere and is not confined to the mainland, nesting as it does on Rathlin Island and on Achill. It is to be found even in small reed-beds in western Donegal and its range extends in Galway to the western seaboard (Ruttledge). With so common a bird it is unnecessary to be more exact regarding its many haunts, but in *The Birds of Scotland* and the new *Birds of Ireland* the authors concerned give more detailed distribution which should be consulted by those interested.

In very severe winters there is a considerable movement of the resident stock to the coast and estuaries—especially in Scotland—but on larger waters many remain so long as the water is free from ice. There is a certain type of loch which the little grebe appears to shun, and such lochs are frequent in north-west Scotland, to which area it is not much attracted. It is recorded in Dr. Baxter's and Miss Rintoul's book that " if not frozen out the little grebe seems to cling more closely to its breeding lochs than our other grebes. If the lochs be not ice-bound a certain number remain throughout the winter, but even in open waters there is a considerable movement down the rivers to the shores, and to lochs and rivers where they do not breed." They are to be seen in harbours diving unconcernedly among the trawlers.[1]

South of the Border the smaller patches of water freeze over first, and these are usually deserted in winter for larger lakes and reservoirs or, as observed already, the sea coast and estuaries. There are many winter visitors from overseas to swell the numbers at this time of year : more will be said of these in a later paragraph.

DISTRIBUTION ABROAD : The typical race of the little grebe has a large range, from the British Isles in the west to the Ural Mountains in the east. Its northern limit is in south Sweden where it breeds sparingly, as it does also on the southern shores of the Baltic, and in Estonia. It ranges throughout eastern Europe and is common in the Low Countries. In the south its range covers southern Russia, Asia Minor, and the Mediterranean with its larger islands. It is reported to have bred in the Balearic Islands (Majorca and Minorca), Corsica, Sardinia, Sicily, Crete (once, Mihan 1943), and Cyprus (intermittent). It does *not* breed in Malta, the lack of water in summer being enough to account for its absence. South of the Mediterranean we find the little grebe (still the typical subspecies) breeding in Morocco, Algeria, and Tunisia. It is a rare visitor to the Canary Islands and this is probably as far south as the European race ever ventures. Birds seen in that archipelago may originate from breeding places in Spain or Morocco where in certain localities it is abundant. The little grebe is also migratory in this area and numbers are reported as wintering in the neighbourhood of Gibraltar.

Another subspecies, *P. r. capensis*, which has the base of the primaries

[1] Dr. Evelyn Baxter and L. J. Rintoul, *A Vertebrate Fauna of Forth*, 1935.

white, takes the place of the typical bird in Egypt, and we find this African race ranging south to the Cape, from which it derives its Latin name, and widely in West and Central Africa south of the Sahara. It also has an Asiatic range from Transcaucasia to Burma.

One other race may be mentioned—that from Iraq named *Podiceps iraquensis*, smaller and darker than the others and with the white at the base of the primaries intermediate in extent between *ruficollis* and *capensis*. As a species the little grebe has a huge range reaching China and Japan, India, and Australia.

HABITS : The little grebe—more commonly named the dabchick—has been unlucky in having had its Latin name changed from *Podiceps fluviatilis* Tunstall 1771 to *Podiceps ruficollis* Pallas 1764, so the time-honoured *fluviatilis* goes and the older name takes precedence. It will be found listed under the former name in many not very old works, including the third edition of Howard Saunders's *Manual*, revised by Eagle-Clarke, incidentally one of the best single books on Britain's birds ever written.

In its mode of life the little grebe does not differ much from the other grebes we have been describing in these pages. Like them it is a marvellous diver, the average length of its dive varying from 15 seconds (Hollom) to 25 seconds (Coward). It can submerge as quietly as any of its family, barely leaving a ripple. Meinertzhagen has recorded (*Birds of Arabia*) that it can remain submerged for " well over a minute ". It feeds much on insects and on small fish, fresh water molluscs, and crustaceans ; but it is said to be less addicted to swallowing feathers than its other close relations.

Although it is a shy bird, seeking cover at the slightest suspicion of danger, it is not fussy in its choice of a habitat. Almost any small pond (or even good-sized ditch) where there are reeds or where the banks are overhung with vegetation will suffice to hold a pair, and they manage to find water, if any exists, in the dryest localities. One of the last my wife and I saw was in a small reservoir hidden in the foothills of the Troödos range in Cyprus, which could only have been spotted by a bird flying over the island—an island, moreover, noted for the paucity of its water supply.

Little grebes can fly very fast and are more given to doing so than the others we have been discussing. It is curious that in flight the white area on the secondaries shows practically not at all, but the feet, which stick out behind like paddles, are prominent enough. T. A. Coward wrote of the " quick flutter of short rounded wings "—a very apt description.

Textbooks—including *The Handbook*—state that there is no evidence of migration beyond British waters, but evidence is not easily obtained, and the little grebe is definitely a migratory species over much of its Continental range, so why not through the British Isles ? It is known that many visit us in winter from the Continent, and what is to prevent some of them continuing to France or even farther without our knowing. In

Suffolk C. B. Ticehurst remarked seeing small flocks of migrants early in April, presumably wending their way north. There are also numerous records of little grebes striking lighthouse lanterns at night on various parts of the coast, including Ireland. Ticehurst records one bird which was taken on a boat forty miles out from Lowestoft on 12th October, and observes, in his *History of the Birds of Suffolk*, that the little grebe is " a very marked migrant and numbers of these with us during winter are but visitors which disappear again in the spring ". Many, moreover, are seen in winter in localities where they do not breed, and this statement refers equally to the whole of the British Isles. In severe weather, as Ticehurst reminds us, little grebes, like other divers, must migrate in order to find food, but one bird at Fritton lake solved the difficulty by consorting with the barnyard fowls, coming up with them to be fed.

Ringing of little grebes in Great Britain certainly points to our local birds being mostly resident, but there have been few ringed and fewer recoveries. In *British Birds*, xliv, 1951, it is stated that only thirty little grebes had then been ringed in these islands and the first Continental recovery for the species is there recorded : a bird ringed at Colchester, Essex, on 1st November 1950 by General Wainwright, was recovered on 23rd March 1951 at Gravelines (Nord), France. Subsequently there have been other recoveries in Britain : a bird ringed in Essex on 15th August 1952 was recovered on 4th December 1952 at the same place as it was ringed ; and two birds ringed as full grown at Colchester on 12th August 1953 and 2nd July 1953 were recovered respectively on 8th November 1953 eleven miles away, and in December 1953 at Grimsby, Lincolnshire, 130 miles from where ringed. A little grebe ringed at Abberton, Essex, on 2nd November 1952, was found dead at Castricum, N. Holland, on 7th June 1956. Such meagre returns give us little to go upon beyond emphasizing the fact that most of our little grebes *appear* to be sedentary. The record showing a journey from Colchester to the north of France and the Dutch one above are all the more intriguing in consequence. By the time that the Report for 1953 was issued the total number of little grebes ringed in Britain had reached the number of seventy-two. By 1957 the grand total ringed had reached one hundred and twelve, of which only six had been recovered up to 31st December of that year.

The returns from the ringing of little grebes in Switzerland have been analyzed by M. Michel Desfayes.[1] He found that for the most part they were faithful to their winter quarters, a number which had been ringed the previous year having returned to the same place. There were, however, some remarkable exceptions. M. Desfayes instances a bird ringed at Saillon in the Rhône Valley on 23rd January 1949 which was recaptured near Florence, Italy, on 21st December 1950, a distance of 410 kilometres south-east. A grebe ringed at the same time and place, and bearing the

[1] *Nos Oiseaux*, xxi, 1951, pp. 93-94.

next ring number to the one which accomplished that journey, was killed on 6th February 1951 in the same watercourse at Saillon where it was ringed. M. Desfayes asks where these Swiss wintering grebes nest, and suggests that two little grebes which had been ringed at Saillon in the winter may provide the answer: one ringed on 19th October 1947 was recovered at Oberkirch, Sempach, on 28th March 1948; the other, ringed on 17th January 1948, was recovered at Zwett, Lower Austria, a distance of 640 kilometres east-north-east. Commenting on his ringing experiments he observes that of the sixty-odd little grebes which he captured and ringed on the waterways of the Rhône Valley he had never once seen one fly and remarks that it is only before their departure in spring that the little grebes are seen to use their wings on these waterways. On the other hand, it is not uncommon to see grebes flying in winter on the Lake of Geneva.

The writer has met with the little grebe abroad in a good many countries beyond the British Isles. It is to be found sometimes abundantly on the Lac de Tunis where, in company with the great crested, red-necked, and black-necked, it occurs in winter, more particularly when severe weather holds Europe in its grip. I have seen it in a muddy looking stream in a southern Tunisian oasis, and it not infrequently occurs in isolated localities in Algeria. Admiral Lynes found it in secluded lakes in the Middle Atlas, and Riggenbach came across it at Mogador in November. It has turned up in a lagoon in the eastern Canary Islands—the same lagoon from which I recorded a flock of black-necked grebes many years ago, and, as stated in an earlier paragraph, it is a common bird in the vicinity of Gibraltar. At the other end of the Mediterranean it visits Cyprus and is also a breeding bird in that island. In the Mediterranean countries it is certainly a well-known migratory species and it is difficult to believe that it is not so throughout its range, though partly sedentary in many lands where it is not frozen out. In Tangier, where they are likewise partly resident, they are reported to pass north in April and to return from October to December. We hear, too, of little grebes migrating from Hungary to central Italy, as recently recorded by Moltoni.

BREEDING HABITS: Since Sir Julian Huxley was the first to discuss [1] the sexual habits of the little grebe, with particular reference to the self-exhausting ceremonies performed by both birds of the pair after pairing, the breeding biology of the species has been studied in this country by George Bird [2] and especially by the Rev. P. H. T. Hartley,[3] resulting in a series of communications to *British Birds*. It is to these three naturalists, and to Mr. Hartley more than anyone, that I am indebted for the information contained in this section of my essay. Mr. Guy Mountfort followed

[1] *British Birds*, xiii, 1919, pp. 155-158.
[2] *British Birds*, xxvii, 1933, pp. 34-37.
[3] *British Birds*, xxvii, 1933, pp. 82-86, and xxx, 1937, pp. 266-275.

these publications with an article in *L'Oiseau*[1] shortly after Mr. Hartley's exhaustive paper was published.

Julian Huxley puts his finger at once on the most arresting feature of the courting ceremony when he observes :

The dabchick shows a seasonal change of plumage, the colours and patterns of the head becoming more striking for the nesting season. It differs, however, from all the other species of the family in never possessing any tufts, crests, or frills on the head. It is therefore interesting to find that the common form of mutual ceremony in this species depends, not on visual stimulation as in *Podiceps cristatus*, but on an auditory stimulation. It is in fact a duet, performed together by both birds of the pair.

Huxley then goes on to describe the note which, he states,

is very startling, consisting of a long shrill peal, somewhat like the neigh of a horse transposed into a very high region of the scale, and mixed with some wildness and a certain quality of laughter. This note may be given by a single bird, but it is more often heard as a duet. It varies considerably in length and quality. Sometimes it is fairly short, and consists only of a single phrase. At other times it is pitched higher and oscillates up and down in a series of very short phrases. In this case it almost always lasts a much longer time. . . . The duet in its most typical form is given by the two birds of a pair close together, more or less facing each other, with their necks stretched straight up. It is thus accompanied by an attitude somewhat different from the ordinary, a little stiff and ceremonial in character. It may issue from among the reeds, or from a pair on the open water. As far as my observations go, it is not preceded by any special action. The birds may be resting, fishing, or swimming steadily. Frequently the birds will come up after a number of fishing dives, give a duet, and at once start fishing again. If not very close together at the start, they almost always swim towards each other during the performance. Neither does the ceremony lead to other sexual actions. Like the head-shaking of the great crested grebe, it is self-exhausting, and after it is over the birds resume their previous activities. . . . When the call is begun by a single bird from among the reeds (i.e. when the birds of a pair are very likely not within view of each other) there is often not a true duet, but after the lapse of a few seconds another bird, which we cannot be positive is the mate of the first, takes up the call, and prolongs it for some time after the other has stopped.

Huxley was not able to distinguish differences in the quality of the sound emitted by male and female, although there may be a difference. He remarked, however, that the difference in size between the members of a pair is always clear and is more marked than in pairs of the great crested grebe. A slight difference in brilliance of coloration was also remarked. Duets are known to take place in other species in genera far removed from the grebe : Huxley instances the barred owl of Texas. According to the negroes this bird says : " Who who who, who cooks for you all ", the

[1] *L'Oiseau*, 1934, pp. 554-558.

phrase being often heard as a duet between the two. This duet is remarkable in being accurately timed ; the notes of one bird alternate with those of the other so as to produce the effect of an echo. There are of course other interpretations of the vocal sounds made by the little grebe but that quoted struck the writer as a particularly clear exposition of what actually takes place. Discussing their habit of calling in duet, Mr. Hartley observes that if this habit is any criterion—and he believes it is—some birds pair for life, for in November and January it is quite usual. He remarked that these winter birds not only frequently " titter " together, but that they do so in certain fixed places, keeping an undefended territory throughout the winter. Duets from birds within the flocks in winter are fairly frequent but far more often two birds will leave a fleet of dabchicks and " titter " when they reach their own marches.

I have already quoted Huxley's suggestion that the common form of mutual ceremony in this species does not depend on visual stimulation as in the great crested grebe. That is certainly true, but to a very small extent visual stimulation may play some part in the ceremony also. Hartley has emphasized that when two little grebes are floating breast to breast during part of their sexual display, in what he terms " the tittering position ", each must see the little patches of lemon-yellow skin at the base of the mandibles of the other, strikingly distinct against the rufous cheeks and dark throat. In this way a visual stimulus may be added to the vocal. Hartley sees in the little grebe a species which has evolved a vocal expression of its emotions, an inter-sexual display of sound rather than of action. He considers that its slight antic displays are probably like those of the ancestors of the genus, so that in its small gestures may be seen the beginnings from which the elaborate and beautiful displays of the great crested grebe have grown. The only formal sexual behaviour which was noted is the marked " invitation pose " adopted by the female, who crouches low on the mating platform with her neck sharply angled and beak almost touching the weeds. If the male is slow to respond she will break her pose to fiddle with the materials of the nest. The platform on which mating takes place is not always used for the reception of eggs. The male dabchick may react to its mate's invitation in one of four ways, which Hartley describes [1] as follows : (1) it may ignore the invitation ; (2) it may pile weeds around its mate ; (3) it may climb onto the nest beside the inviting bird, and itself assume the crouching pose ; or (4) copulation may be effected.

Naturalists who have studied it agree that the mated dabchick is a passionately territorial bird. The actual territories are strictly protected, both sexes defending their borders. These territories may be quite small in extent or may be as much as a quarter of an acre, as on the pond near Leatherhead where Hartley made his observations. He found that where

[1] *British Birds*, xxx, 1937, p. 271.

several territories border on an open space, free from weeds, this constitutes a neutral area where paired birds can meet and associate with others without fighting. He describes how territorial demonstrations—which far more often than not fail to end in actual fighting—take place many times daily between pairs whose marches adjoin.

One bird makes a series of short rushes towards his neighbour's territory, flapping his raised wings, and keeping his head and neck outstretched, uttering at the same time his tittering call. The owner of the territory advances in the same style; between each rush both birds float with heads drawn in, flank feathers fluffed out, and wings slightly raised. So they approach each other until they float about a foot apart, and strictly on the territorial border. . . . Both birds then dive at the same moment, or one very quickly after the other. . . . After one or two plunges honour is satisfied and as an almost invariable finish to the demonstration, each bird swims back to float close beside its mate and to utter several long " titters " in duet.

At other times the demonstrations do not end so peaceably; furious submarine scrimmages take place, or fights upon the surface when the birds strike with wings and feet and seem, as Mr. Hartley states, to try to drive each other under water. Territories may be taken up very early in the year. On Fetcham pond the birds began to defend their own territory in the middle of February. Before this date the dabchicks would spend their time in fairly close flocks; in this circumstance mass evolutions have been observed, when twenty or twenty-five grebes will dive simultaneously as one bird, several times in quick succession. Again the movement of a fleet in any direction may start with all the birds making a simultaneous pattering rush along the surface.

Nest-building begins exceptionally in March but more generally in April onwards, egg-laying continuing to July or later as the little grebe is normally double brooded and sometimes rears three broods in a season. Hartley has stated that up to four clutches may be laid in a season, but the proportion of chicks to eggs is small, many nests being destroyed by flooding. During the last war, when the Thames was used as a highway by high-speed army launches, a great many little grebes had their nests swamped. Previous to the outbreak of war the little grebe was common near Pangbourne, twelve breeding pairs having been counted by Meinertzhagen between Goring and Reading.[1] From 1940 to 1945 not a single pair bred on that stretch of the river and the moorhens only saved themselves from a like fate by sensibly building their nests " for the duration of the war " in bushes and trees overhanging the water. When peace returned the moorhens reverted to water-level nests, but we are not told whether the little grebes returned to their old haunts. Both sexes take their share in building the nest, and, as George Bird records in the paper

[1] *Bull. Br. Orn. Club*, lxix, 1949, p. 108.

cited earlier, the nest consists of floating semi-decayed water-weeds and similar material brought up from the bottom of the lake by both birds (see *British Birds*, xxvii, pl. 1 facing p. 34). He was able to watch the pair he had under observation from a distance of six feet :

> Both birds took part in incubating and were always extremely alert. The sitting bird would leave the nest at the first sign of danger, quickly covering the eggs before doing so. There seemed to be periods for each bird to sit . . . the changeover was accompanied by an interesting ceremony, the approaching bird making a delicate and scarcely perceptible whistle, and bringing pieces of *green* vegetation to assist the further building up of the nest. The fresh green material is interspersed with the more decayed portion and sets up fermentation, which possibly may assist incubation. Each bird regularly brought material before taking over its period of sitting.

The nest described here contained five eggs on 30th April. Mr. Bird estimated that the clutch had been complete not more than two or three days. Four ducklings hatched on 13th May, which, as he himself pointed out, was abnormally early if his estimate of time was correct. Jourdain in *The Handbook* gives the normal incubation period as nineteen to twenty days for each egg. Mr. Hartley was unable himself to ascertain the exact incubation period : his statement that "it is about twenty-five days" probably includes the period from the beginning of incubation to the hatching of the last egg as Jourdain has already indicated. In his account of the incubation period Mr. Hartley wrote : " The first egg laid is brooded at intervals. At this time the birds relieve each other every five to six minutes, whereas when the full clutch is laid, changes take place about three times in two hours. If a bird be frightened off a clutch of incubated eggs, it covers them carefully with nest materials before leaving, but the first egg is only sometimes hidden." Unlike the great crested grebe which, when covering her eggs, picks up strands of weed and actually lays them across the eggs, the dabchick is content to " rake some of the material lying on the rim of the cup over the eggs ". Four to six is the usual clutch, exceptionally seven. The statement in *The Handbook of British Birds* (without comment) that *ten* eggs have been recorded in England infers that these were the product of one bird. Mr. John Walpole-Bond,[1] who inspected these eggs, was convinced they were the product of two hens which had each laid five—a much more likely explanation. That authority never knew a sett of eggs exceed six in number. The eggs are white or creamy when first laid, quickly becoming stained. Jourdain gives the average measurement of 100 British eggs as $37 \cdot 8 \times 26 \cdot 2$ mm. Max. $43 \times 27 \cdot 4$ mm. and $39 \cdot 2 \times 28 \cdot 3$ mm. Min. $32 \cdot 8 \times 23 \cdot 7$ mm.

When first hatched, the young seem to have very little power of using their legs and feet, and shuffle along with extended wing and body rather than use their feet (G. Bird). When they leave the nest they either

[1] *History of the Birds of Sussex*, vol. iii pp. 86-87.

glide off and swim away or dive right in.   Bird noted that they raise themselves and plunge head foremost.   Sometimes they were seen to dive with scarcely a ripple.   I fully endorse Mr. Bird's concluding remark, that no more pleasing sight can be imagined than a happy family of dabchicks gliding over the surface of the water with their plumage puffed out like balls of feathers, bobbing about amongst the water-lilies.

The poor mites have enemies to contend with from their earliest days. On water where pike are prevalent these voracious fish take toll of any young birds which come within their reach and many are the little grebe ducklings—and their parents—which fall victim to them.   On Fritton lake in Suffolk, where the pike take a heavy toll, Ticehurst has recorded how a little grebe has been taken whole from the belly of one of these fish. Gulls swoop down upon them and it is little wonder that the ducklings seek refuge on their parents' backs, chancing a sudden plunge if the parent becomes alarmed.   Hartley remarked that little grebes seem to be afraid of birds flying over them ; a party of black-headed gulls wheeling overhead will cause a grebe to " crash dive ", throwing up flashes of water and only exposing the head and neck when it emerges.   Even a low-flying peewit has occasioned a splashing dive and one is left to imagine the state of terror into which a grebe family would be thrown should a harrier come by.   Without any such emergency George Bird recollects seeing adult birds dive with chicks under their wings and surface some distance away, returning to the nest later in the same manner.   Hartley has observed that the practice of carrying young birds about upon the back is not so common as among the great crested grebe, though on the nest the chicks always sit beneath their parents' scapulars.

REFERENCES : Original Description. *Colymbus ruficollis* Pallas, Vroegs *Cat. Adumbratiuncula*, 1764, p. 6 : Holland. *Colymbus fluviatilis* Tunstall, *Orn. Brit.*, 1771, p. 3 : Great Britain, based on Brisson's " Grebe de la rivière ".

Order GAVIIFORMES

Family GAVIIDAE

Genus *GAVIA* Forster

PLATE 18

GREAT NORTHERN DIVER

Gavia [1] *immer* (Brünnich)

A Winter Visitor to all coasts of Britain and Ireland, including the English Channel to which it is an annual visitor, occasionally in some numbers ; more numerous in Scotland, especially the north. A regular Passage Migrant in spring and autumn through Shetland and Orkney Islands. On Scottish mainland also visits deep inland lochs. It has never been *proved* to breed, though regularly seen in summer in full breeding dress in Scotland and there are good grounds for believing that it nests sporadically in the Shetlands. [2]

IDENTIFICATION : This is a truly magnificent bird and in breeding dress is unsurpassed in beauty. The whole head and neck are black, glossed with purple on the upper part of the throat and with green on the lower neck. On each side of the black neck is a band of white, caused by twelve or fourteen white vertical streaks close together ; there are also a few white streaks or spots on the centre of the lower throat, barely noticeable unless at close quarters. The breast is glistening white, the belly whitish. The back is black heavily spotted with white, the spots on the scapulars in the shape of squares or oblongs. The sides of the breast are vertically streaked with black. The eye is crimson and very arresting ; the bill is black in summer and greyish-horn in winter, with the ridge of the upper mandible slate coloured. Some examples acquire full breeding plumage before the bill has changed colour. The tarsus is black externally and whitish internally. In summer plumage there is, as Collingwood Ingram [3] remarked when watching a fine male in Iceland, " a plush-like quality about the neck plumage of these divers that seems to give that part a peculiar matt surface which greatly intensifies its rich black colour ". Its total length is 30-33 inches, the male being larger than the female. In winter after the autumn moult the striking white streaks on the sides of the neck are lost, the rich black of the head and neck is replaced by brown, and the

---

[1] The generic name *Gavia* Forster is now to be used for the divers in place of *Colymbus* Linnaeus by a decision of the International Commission of Zoological Nomenclature Opinion 401.

[2] The evidence is clearly set out by L. S. M. and U. M. Venables in *Birds and Mammals of Shetland*, 1955, pp. 257-258.

[3] " Field notes on the Birds of Iceland ", in *Ibis*, 1942, p. 492.

PLATE 18

GREAT NORTHERN DIVER
Gavia immer (Brünnich)

throat and lower part of the neck become white. The rest of the upper-parts are grey-brown. The heavy bill and large size is probably the only sure character by which the great northern diver may be distinguished from the black-throated diver at this season. Dr. Salomonsen has had many opportunities of comparing the great northern diver with the red-throated diver in the field and in his *Grønlands Fugle* wrote :

This striking bird [*G. immer*], of the same genus as the red-throated diver, is much the larger bird of the two and has a stronger bill and a noticeably thicker and heavier head and neck. At a reasonable distance the adult birds in summer plumage can easily be distinguished by their coloration, the dark head with the white patch on the sides of the neck and the white-spangled pattern of the upperparts, which at some distance look pale grey or even whitish both in flight and on the water. In winter plumage and in juvenile dress the upperparts are brownish with distinct light greyish feather edges, the characteristic white dots [on the upperparts] of the red-throated diver thus being absent. Here again the shape and size of the bill is a character to note, the tip-tilted finer bill of the red-throated diver being in marked contrast to the massive straight bill of the larger bird.

LOCAL DISTRIBUTION : September is the month when this diver may be expected to put in an appearance, though in the north of Scotland and the Outer Hebrides groups of birds may be observed swimming off shore as early as August. Dr. Baxter and Miss Rintoul state in *The Birds of Scotland*, that it is quite common around the Scottish coast, more particularly in the north and west. Moreover, it is a well-known visitor to all the island groups and has been recorded repeatedly in summer from both the Outer Hebrides and Shetland. When Robert Gray wrote the *Birds of the West of Scotland*[1] he described it as very common in that area, being widely distributed from the Mull of Galloway to Cape Wrath in the north of Sutherland. He mentioned its abundance in the Outer Hebrides and the fact that it is found there at all seasons of the year except the month of July. There is unlikely to be much change in its status at the present day. We have Mr. and Mrs. Venables' recent volume on the Shetlands to inform us that great northern divers can be seen on inshore Shetland waters all the year round ; but they very seldom come on to freshwater lochs, except Loch Spiggie which they visit not infrequently. The Venables found that these fine divers are most abundant during autumn and spring, when flocks run into double figures ; they add that some birds move on in early winter though many are left behind. During the summer immature birds were found to be well distributed throughout the voes and sheltered bays, and adults in full plumage were invariably seen. There are good grounds for considering that the bird has bred in the Shetland Islands and these have been ably discussed by Mr. and Mrs. Venables. Within recent years the testimony of G. Johnson of Aith in 1932, and of G. T. Kay in 1933, is certainly an indication of local breeding,

[1] Published in 1871 in Glasgow by Thomas Murray and Son.

and presumably Mr. and Mrs. Venables consider their evidence reliable, while their own experience of seeing (on 26th August 1946) from a yacht in Basta Voe, Yell, an adult in summer plumage accompanied by one young bird, which could hardly have weathered 500 miles of open sea, is equally suggestive. In all three instances the young birds seen were accompanied by adults "as if the family association were still intact". I shall not refer to this evidence again in this essay as the details are given in Mr. and Mrs. Venables' book.

It must not be thought that the great northern diver occurs only in Scottish waters: it is to be found off the east, west, and south coasts of England. Gales are usually responsible for driving the birds within sight of shore and quite a number are reported from inland waters by Ralph Chislett.[1] Claud Ticehurst [2] probably sums up its status for East Anglia most accurately when he states that it is not very rare in winter though years pass without one being recorded. In the adjoining county of Norfolk B. B. Riviere considered it the rarest of the British divers, and the inference is that those that pass south to winter in the English Channel probably do so out of sight of land. It is usually seen in East Anglia in the young plumage, and in that dress has been recorded from some of the rivers and broads. Mid-November is the most usual time for it to appear. That a fair number winter in the English Channel seems obvious. Booth, in his many peregrinations in those waters after sea fowl, records [3] meeting with "immense numbers", while John Walpole-Bond [4] states that between November (rarely October) and the end of May the bird is and always has been of annual, and fairly common, occurrence off Sussex. Finally we may quote Colonel Ryves's opinion that the great northern diver is the commonest (of our three common species) visitor to Cornwall [5] and is frequently recorded in Mounts Bay and on the Helford river, the Fal estuary off Loe Pool, and the Land's End. On the Pembrokeshire coast of Wales the great northern diver is a regular winter visitor, sometimes numerous in Milford Haven, most of the birds seen being immature. In *The Birds of Pembrokeshire* (1949) Mr. Lockley and his collaborators state that it is frequently seen near the islands and on the open coast, occasionally remaining late in spring.

In Ireland it is a numerous visitor to certain bays around the coast, especially, so Major Ruttledge has recorded, those of the north and west and Dublin Bay. It is less plentiful on the south coast but is not infrequently found on inland waters. It is reported to arrive usually in October and from then until April and May the great northern diver is plentiful. A large proportion of the birds are in immature plumage.

The statements quoted give a fairly comprehensive picture of the

---

[1] *Yorkshire Birds*, pp. 219-220.   [2] *History of the Birds of Suffolk*, p. 445.
[3] *Rough Notes*, vol. iii.   [4] *A History of Sussex Birds*, vol. iii, pp. 87-89.
[5] *Bird Life in Cornwall*, p. 183.

diver's status around these coasts without searching further literature. As usual the information from the Bristol and Irish Channels is of the scantiest. It would seem that the great northern divers which visit us in winter come from two or three main breeding grounds, Greenland, Iceland, and Norway.

DISTRIBUTION ABROAD : This is a Nearctic species with a considerable breeding range in North America, its place being taken in the northern Palaearctic and in Siberia by the white-billed northern diver to be discussed later. Dr. Salomonsen has defined the breeding range of *Colymbus immer* as north-eastern North America northwards to the middle part of Baffin Island (Nettilling area, on the authority of Bray and Manning [1]), Frozen Strait, Repulse Bay (R. Horring, *5th Thule Expedit.*, ii, 1937, p. 36), and the Mackenzie Delta.[2] From these areas it ranges southwards to the northern parts of the United States. He considers that it has its centre of distribution in the low-Arctic and Hudsonian zones but penetrates to a certain extent into the high-Arctic region and spreads to the south even beyond the Canadian zone. A subspecies was described from the south-western breeding area and named *C. i. elasson*, but it is not generally recognized as a valid race. Beyond this breeding range the great northern diver breeds also in Greenland,[3] Iceland,[4] and Bear Island,[5] but not apparently on Spitsbergen which it seldom seems to visit (cf. Jourdain, *Ibis*, 1922, p. 169, for records up to that year). Nor has it been proved to breed on Jan Mayen though G. C. and E. G. Bird,[6] who remained on the island from 8th July to 28th August 1934, reported a non-breeding pair and saw another small party at sea during a fairly exhaustive survey of the bird life of the island. Despite the fact that the Faeroe Islands is the type locality of the great northern diver, the birds do not breed there. They are reported to be common winter visitors, and often to spend the summer, but no nest has ever been found (K. Williamson).

The winter range of the great northern diver in the Palaearctic region extends regularly to the English Channel (see Local Distribution), but farther south it becomes increasingly rare and can only be regarded as a rare straggler to the western Mediterranean. It has been obtained once in the Balearic Islands [7] (Minorca, January 1917) and is reported to be seen occasionally in winter in the Straits of Gibraltar (Irby). That it wanders far on occasions is proved by its casual appearance in the Azores,[8] where it has been collected several times and is said to be " not very rare in winter ", and even in Madeira.

[1] *Auk*, lx, 1943, p. 505.
[2] A. E. Porsild, in *The Canadian Field-Nat.*, lvii, 1943, p. 20.
[3] Salomonsen, *Grønlands Fugle*, Copenhagen, 1950, pp. 24-30.
[4] Gudmundsson, in *Nátturufraedingurinn*, xxii, 1952, pp. 44-45.
[5] Bertram and Lack, in *Ibis*, 1933, p. 294.
[6] *Ibis*, 1935, p. 847.
[7] Munn, in *Novitates Zoologicae*, 1931, p. 129.
[8] *Novitates Zoologicae*, xii, p. 96, record under *Gavia imber* Gunn.

That it will travel overland in Europe is proved by a recent appearance on Lake Maggiore (Moltoni), but the assertion in *The Handbook of British Birds* that it is "casual on waters in Europe to the *Black Sea*" (italics mine), has always seemed to me to require verification when we take its breeding range into consideration. Professor Dementiev has now corrected[1] this error, writing that the great northern diver is very rare in the Soviet Union; statements that it has occurred at Odessa and off the Crimea are undoubtedly erroneous.

The American population, to quote Arthur C. Bent, winters mainly within the United States especially along both coasts; east to Maine and the Atlantic coast states, south to Florida and the Gulf coast. West to the Pacific coast (lower California to British Columbia), and north to the northern United States and the Great Lakes. As already remarked, the population which nests from northern California and northern Wisconsin to British Columbia and is found in winter on the coast of California, received the dubious honour of being distinguished under the subspecific title *G. i. elasson*, only to be later incorporated in the synonymy of the typical bird.

HABITS : Ornithologists of my generation who remember Dr. T. Gilbert Pearson, President Emeritus of the National Association of Audubon Societies, will recollect the interest which that great American bird-lover took in the protection of bird life in the United States. The loon, as United States citizens name our great northern diver, once a greatly persecuted bird, came under the watchful eye of Gilbert Pearson and was obviously one of his favourite birds about which he wrote with much charm. In a short article which he contributed to *The Book of Birds* he bewailed the cruelty of man who used the loons as moving targets, plundered their nests without eating the eggs, and never left the birds alone. He draws a picture of their summer haunts :

To one whose duties or pleasures have taken him into the northern wilderness, the sound of the word "loon" brings to memory visions of quiet lakes, with shores bordered by firs, spruces, and the gleaming white trunks of clustered birch trees.

To the voyager in these regions, whether in quest of trout or salmon or merely seeking the enjoyment of being where Nature has been unmarred by man, the weird, mournful cry of the loon is an inseparable part of the world about him. The far-reaching trembling wail comes across the lake with a quality of unutterable melancholy. One may hear it at dawn, at evening, at any hour, day or night, and rare is the person who does not pause to listen when this cry comes down the wind.

At the end of his account, of which the above are but the opening paragraphs, Gilbert Pearson was able to record that since the Audubon laws were enacted to protect them, and civilized man acquired more interest in the living bird, the loons have not been persecuted in America so extensively as formerly. No doubt there is still room for improvement.

[1] *Birds of the Soviet Union*, vol. ii, pp. 252-253.

One of its most extensive breeding grounds is situated in Greenland, and from there we have an up-to-date account of its habitat from the pen of Dr. Finn Salomonsen in his major work on Greenland birds.[1] The great northern diver arrives in south-west Greenland about the second week of May, but does not reach Scoresby Sound until mid-June. At first after its arrival it keeps to the sea, but it soon moves to the lakes in the interior when these have thawed, and there it stays until the lakes freeze again in October. It never frequents the small shallow pools beloved of the red-throated diver, but resorts to large and deep lakes. Rare as a breeding bird on the outer coast and islands, it is on the whole, so Dr. Salomonsen states, restricted to the fjord country. Here it haunts the broad, low valleys and extensive rolling lowland so rich in lakes ; but it shuns alpine landscapes and narrow glens. Salomonsen doubts that it breeds at any great altitude where the lakes thaw very late in normal years. Only one pair is usually to be found on each lake, but very large expanses of water may be occupied by two or three pairs. Dr. Salomonsen states that although this diver prefers lakes rich in fish, it is very dependent on the sea or fjords for food ; most pairs undertake regular food-flights and in the breeding season these flights are made at night. On the larger lakes in Greenland the birds practically always nest on islands in the lakes ; the nests are most difficult to reach and in consequence little is known as to dates of egg-laying, which probably takes place in June. In eastern Greenland the main departure for the south takes place in September, but in south-west Greenland the birds do not leave until the latter part of October. The great majority travel on to the south to winter from Maine to Florida but a very small number winter regularly off the coasts and in the fjords of south-west Greenland. The Greenlanders who live in the south-west of their country still hunt the great northern diver for the sake of its plumage, with which they make beautiful ornamental wall-carpets. It requires fifty specimens to make a single good-sized carpet, as only the head and neck are used in its manufacture. Formerly it was a flourishing industry but Dr. Salomonsen assures us that in many centres it has died out, though it flourishes still in Qagssimiut in the northern Iulianehåb district ; during Dr. Salomonsen's visit in 1949 at least four carpets were on sale.[2]

The great northern diver shares with the other members of its family the useful ability to sink its body below the surface of the water [3] leaving only the head and part of its neck exposed. In this manner it apparently hopes to avoid detection. Should a pair be disturbed they do not take refuge in flight, as does the red-throated diver on similar occasions, but

[1] *Grønlands Fugle*, pp. 24-30.
[2] *Grønlands Fugle*, p. 30.
[3] A photograph of a bird " swimming low " near its nest was reproduced in *British Birds*, ix, p. 144, illustrating Mr. Eric Dunlop's field-notes on this species, pp. 142-147.

remain swimming on the surface at a respectful distance, keeping a watchful eye upon the intruder and relying, as Dr. Salomonsen has remarked, on their ability to dive at the slightest sign of danger. That naturalist has observed that when searching for food before diving the bird will regularly dip its bill and the forepart of its head under water. It dives silently and remains below the surface usually for nearly half a minute, only on rare occasions, in Salomonsen's opinion, remaining submerged for more than sixty seconds. Holbøll's assertion that he has recorded dives up to eight minutes is surely based on some miscalculation. In this connexion I have been interested to read Major R. F. Ruttledge's discussion of the length of dive of this species in *Birds of Ireland*. He states that dives are normally of about forty-five seconds' duration, but one that was timed lasted two minutes and twenty seconds, and another two minutes. Ruttledge remarks that such lengthy dives must be exceptional. It will be remembered, however, that T. A. Coward has recorded a dive of three minutes which Mr. Witherby concluded was probably the maximum under normal circumstances.

Great northern divers spend much time in preening their plumage, during which operation they exhibit a variety of attitudes. Mr. E. B. Dunlop observed a bird frequently lying on one side in the water with one leg out, and remarked another which, when swimming on an even keel, lifted one leg out of the water and waved it in the air behind it, both opening and closing the web as it did so.

Not a great deal has been ascertained about this diver's feeding habits. Salomonsen considered it mainly a fish-eater and watched a pair eagerly diving in a lake full of sticklebacks. In Scoresby Sound, Greenland, E. Bay examined stomach contents of five birds and found only vegetable matter in large quantities, including, in one, green willow shoots. When fishing off the English coast in winter, herrings and sprats are likely to be its standby as C. B. Ticehurst suggests ; but roach, plaice, and viviparous blennies have also been recorded. In Jan Mayen Island C. G. and E. G. Bird[1] shot a diver in August in a lagoon full of Arctic char, but no fish remains were found in the bird's stomach which contained thirteen spherical pebbles ($8\frac{1}{2} \times 6$ mm. approx.), one feather 44 mm. long, and a great quantity of semi-digested moss of which only a *Rhacomitriun* was identifiable. The members of the British Greenland expedition constantly saw this diver carrying fish from the fjord in late June or early July to the inland lake where breeding was taking place, and the point is again emphasized that both this and the red-throated diver depend much upon the fjords for their food supply.[2] Dr. Finnur Gudmundsson states that in the breeding season in Iceland the great northern diver frequents the deeper and larger fresh-water lakes rich in trout (*Salmo trutta*) or char (*Salvelinus alpinus*), which constitute its main food supply at that time of year.

[1] *Ibis*, 1935, p. 847.   [2] *Ibis*, 1930, pp. 399-401.

BREEDING HABITS : The earliest date in the year when any form of display appears to have been recorded in Great Britain is 17th February, when Major R. F. Ruttledge watched numerous great northern divers in Greatman's Bay, off the Galway coast of Ireland. This took the form of " speed-boating " on the surface, the performers leaving behind them a considerable wake. Two birds in particular were involved. It was observed that as one bird travelled in large arcs with body half submerged and wings beating, the other remained submerged. Upon the submerged bird surfacing the other would " taxi " towards it, meanwhile moving the head slowly from side to side. Both birds on meeting would raise the chest and neck and stab the water violently. Major Ruttledge considered the spectacle remarkable in that the divers repeated the performance time after time, and a number of other pairs were seen to be performing in a somewhat similar manner.

June is the month when this diver sets about nesting in earnest in Greenland, as has been remarked earlier in this essay, and it is in that month too that the birds lay their eggs in Iceland,[1] though clutches may sometimes be found in late May. The weather again is the important factor, for in Iceland they return to their breeding lakes as soon as these become ice-free, which usually occurs in May. The bird's preference for deep freshwater lakes for breeding has already been stated, but where there is a concentration of lakes, Dr. Gudmundsson has found that it may also occur on smaller lakes in the vicinity of larger lakes abounding in fish. In Iceland it is found breeding both in the lowlands and in the highlands, where its upper limit of distribution lies about 600 metres above sea-level. This habitat it shares with the whooper swan, often with the long-tailed duck, and up to a certain altitude also with the scaup duck. Owing to its preference for the environment described it is more common in the highlands than in the lowlands. Even so it has been known to breed on lowland lakes in many parts of the country and in a few cases even on lagoons. As George Yeates tells us in his book,[2] the nesting season varies with the earliness or tardiness of the Icelandic spring. On his first visit to Iceland eggs were discovered which must have been laid in mid-May. In 1949, when the lakes of north Iceland were still ice-bound in mid-June, incubation had just started by 2nd June.

As a rule only one pair occupies each lake in the breeding season, the nest being placed either on the bank of the lake or on a tiny island. Dr. Gudmundsson writes that it is invariably so close to the water that the sitting bird can slide directly from the nest into the water, a distinct pathway worn by the birds often leading from the nest to the water. In his field-notes on Greenland birds E. M. Nicholson describes[3] finding a nest

[1] Finnur Gudmundsson, *Náttúrufraedingurinn*, xxii, 1952, pp. 44-45.
[2] *The Land of the Loon*, 1951.
[3] *Ibis*, 1930, pp. 399-401.

on an islet in a considerable lake which, although placed on the very brink, was situated in so shallow a part that the sitting bird had to heave herself ponderously over the side and flop four or five feet through the water before reaching diving depth. In this case the nest consisted of an earthen platform six inches or so above the water, containing a saucer-shaped hollow over a foot across. Around this were roughly laid some *Empetrum* and *Vaccinium* plants torn up from the bank behind, which had been broken down wholesale within a radius of about eighteen inches, leaving a conspicuous peaty scar on the shore. On this occasion the pair kept close together and were silent and cautious but enquiring in their behaviour. When Nicholson appeared they swam right towards him but with bodies very low, ready to dive at the least alarm. As he sat still they came and regarded him within a few feet. Nests which Dr. Gudmundsson describes in his account of this bird in Iceland were large, shallow, circular depressions in the marshy ground 37-47 cm. in diameter and 4-10 cm. in depth, mostly lined with some moss, sedges, or other vegetable matter which the birds collect in the immediate surroundings of the nest. The nest hollow and the nest material is commonly, but not always, wet. The two eggs laid by the great northern diver resemble in colour those of the red-throated diver, but are larger. Jourdain's description of the eggs is as follows : elliptical or elongated oval in shape ; ground colour varies from some shade of olive-green to olive-brown or dark amber-brown, occasionally quite unmarked but usually with small spots of dark brown ; sometimes with a few bold blackish blotches : slight gloss. He gives the average measurement of 100 eggs as 89·8 × 57·6 mm. Max. 101·5 × 62·5 mm. Min. 85 × 54·5 mm. and 86·1 × 54·3 mm. In comparison 100 of the red-throated divers' eggs average 74·96 × 48·32 mm. Dunlop ascertained that eggs were laid at intervals of two days at least, the incubation period lasting from twenty-nine to thirty days.

Naturalists who have been so fortunate as to observe this bird during the nesting season have been struck by the very close bond which exists between the male and female, resulting in many mutual displays and display flights. George Yeates emphasizes that these displays take place not only in the early days of courtship but throughout at least the incubation period. It was noticed that when a foreign pair of loons alighted on a nesting loch, the female immediately slipped off her nest and joined her mate ; the two pairs then " danced " and raced with necks low outstretched on the water, an action on the part of the rightful owners of the loch which was interpreted as a threat display. The most remarkable ceremony witnessed was a prolonged flight by both birds begun by a race over the water. The birds would drift out into the lake uttering indescribable yells as an overture ; when well out from the land both birds became silent and "taxied" heavily over the water until air-borne when a fresh uncanny chorus echoed round the hills—a long protracted wailing of tremendous carrying power. This extraordinary duet was kept up for the whole flight which was often a wide circuit and must on occasions have approached five miles. As the birds reached their home waters once more they ceased to call and on stiff wings swung in neck to neck to cut a furrow in the water as they finally alighted. Readers who are familiar with the literature on Greenland birds may remember that E. M. Nicholson witnessed a post-nuptial display flight on 19th July in which four great northern divers took part. The four birds were seen flying over repeatedly uttering an excited whinnying cry. Two began to glide with wings raised at as steep a V angle as would sustain them in the air without losing height. After an interval of slow-beating flight by all four the ceremony was repeated, but whether by the same two birds was impossible to determine. Finally a single bird began to glide again, apparently trying to induce another—possibly its mate—to follow northward, but now the other three swung off south-west and the party apparently broke up.

One other feature in the display must be mentioned—that witnessed by G. K. Yeates in Iceland when he approached the birds' nest. Then the sitting bird after leaving the nest and surfacing from the first dive was frequently seen to dip its bill in the water as though drinking. At other times it would preen itself in a curious and characteristic manner. Rolling on its side, so that the gleaming white underparts were exposed, it rotated round and round one spot with one foot paddling. On some of Yeates's visits to the nest an imposing threat display was carried out. Rearing up, wings pressed to its sides until it appeared to be sitting on its tail on the water, the bird thrashed the surface with its paddles, making the water fly and creating not only considerable commotion but also much noise. In this attitude, erect and upright, the bird looked very like a penguin. Yeates's visits to the nesting islet evoked this display on frequent occasions but once the birds were seen to perform in exactly the same manner when a third loon appeared in the home bay.

Mr. Yeates's description of the " cacophonous duets and devilish calls " of the great northern diver leaves one in no doubt that what appears to be exaggerated descriptions of the loon's vocal powers are in reality only too true but defy expression. There is, however, one call which in Mr. Yeates's view can be set to syllables—a high-pitched *hoo-hoo-hoo* frequently uttered when the bird is in flight, but which can also be given by an excited bird on the nest.

The loon's chick when first hatched is covered with soft, thick, short down. The entire upperparts are dark in colour, described by A. C. Bent as " fuscous black " on crown and back, " fuscous " on throat and sides ; only the central portion of the belly is white, tinged laterally with greyish. They are carried about at first on their parents' backs, and should the old bird dive and the chicks be thrown into the water they are well able to care for themselves until the old bird surfaces again, when the youngsters scramble back to their position under the scapulars. More than a hundred years ago Audubon gave a description of the development of the young loon which certainly cannot be bettered to-day. After describing their appearance he observed :

They swim and dive extremely well even at this early stage of their existence, and after being fed by regurgitation for about a fortnight, receive portions of fish, aquatic insects, and small reptiles, until they are able to maintain themselves. . . . They are generally very fat and so clumsy as to be easily caught on land, if their retreat to the water is cut off. But should you miss your opportunity and the birds succeed in gaining the liquid element, into which they drop like so many terrapins, you will be astonished to see them as it were run over the water with extreme celerity, leaving behind them a distinct furrow. When the young are well able to fly the mother entices them to remove from the pond or lake on which they have been bred, and leads them on the wing to the nearest part of the sea, after which she leaves them to shift for themselves. Now and then after this period, the end of August or beginning of September, I have still seen the young of a brood, two or three in number, continuing together until they were induced to travel southward, when they generally set out singly.

A. C. Bent, who quoted this note of Audubon's, remarks that August seems rather early for young loons to be flying, as they are usually not strong on the wing until the middle or end of September. Writing from his own experiences Bent discusses the autumn migration of the loon in America, and observes that the young birds precede the adults by about three weeks and go much farther south. On the Atlantic coast the principal flight is along the coast-line, where they are at times very common, flying with the scoters and generally crossing headlands or long capes. They usually fly high in the air, singly, or in small groups widely scattered, but large numbers have been seen at one time. Migrating loons keep in touch with one another on foggy mornings by their laughing calls. Sometimes they halt to rest and then congregate in large numbers on the water several miles off shore, when the constant murmur of their voices in soft conversational tones may be heard on a still morning. Winter finds them far to the south of their breeding range. By far the greater number spend the winter on the sea coast, where they are usually seen singly or in small parties, but occasionally in larger gatherings : others resort to inland lakes and streams throughout their winter range, which extends as far north as they can find plenty of water. Some, unfortunately, starve to death, or fall victim to some sportsman if the pond or lake on which they have taken up their abode freezes over, for they need plenty of water to be able to rise from the surface.

Most of the great northern divers which visit the shores of Great Britain in the winter months are suspected of having travelled from Iceland or perhaps even from Greenland, for there is a considerable exodus from both these lands. Divers are capable of making tremendous journeys to reach their winter habitat, as witness the black-throated diver, some of which have been proved by Russian ornithologists to travel up to 6000 kilometres to winter in the Baltic. There is nothing, therefore, to prevent some at any rate of the Greenland great northern divers from reaching the shores of Britain. As yet actual proof that this happens is wanting. We know that in late August and in September the great northern divers leave the lakes of Iceland and return to the sea. During the winter months they are frequently observed along the shores of the climatically favourable south-west, especially in the area from Vestmannaeyjàr to Snaefellsnes, but they are never seen on the north-east coast. Gudmundsson believes that a considerable part of the Icelandic population leaves Iceland entirely, and presumably—in the absence of recoveries from ringed birds—spends the winter along the shores of the British Isles and perhaps also along those of Continental western Europe. We have seen already how far south these birds will travel.

REFERENCES : Original Description. *Colymbus immer* Brünnich, *Orn. Borealis*, 1764, p. 38 : Faeroe Islands.

WHITE-BILLED NORTHERN DIVER   PLATE 19

Gavia adamsii (Gray)
[The Yellow-billed Loon of the American Check List]

A Scarce Visitor to north and east Britain ; probably of regular but rare occurrence in the seas around the Shetland Islands

IDENTIFICATION : In the colour of its plumage this large diver closely resembles the great northern diver, *G. immer*, the birds being sufficiently alike for confusion to occur in their identification unless both are in breeding plumage. The safest character rests in the shape of the bill, for as Colonel R. Meinertzhagen observed [1] in Arctic Lapland " the upward tilt of the lower mandible gives a remarkable and very retroussé effect to the whole bill, an illusion which is noticeable with the naked eye ". The difference in the two birds was first pointed out by Professor Collett [2] and was later clearly enunciated by Harry Witherby [3] when examining specimens to be included or rejected in the British List. Giving credit to Professor Collett for pointing out the distinctions Mr. Witherby then wrote :

In summer plumage *C. adamsii* [4] is quite easy to distinguish owing to the white spots on the upperparts being much larger and the white streaks on the throat and neck broader and fewer than in *C. immer*, besides the head and neck being

---

[1] " Winter in Arctic Lapland ", in *Ibis*, 1938, pp. 754-759 ; see p. 759.
[2] *Ibis*, 1894, pp. 269-283.
[3] *British Birds*, xvi, 1922, pp. 9-12.
[4] The divers were then placed in the genus *Colymbus*.

glossed purple rather than green. At all seasons and ages the shafts of the primaries in *C. immer* are dark brown, while in *C. adamsii* they are whitish (except at the tip), but this character, though useful is not invariable. . . . Otherwise in juvenile and immature plumage the two birds are alike. The shape of the bill is, however, always diagnostic, and is much more important than its colour or size. [See illustration in *British Birds*, xlv, 1952, Plate 83.] The upper line of the upper mandible in *C. adamsii* is remarkably straight and does not descend towards the tip as in *C. immer*, while its sides are flatter and not so rounded ; also the upward slope of the gonys is more abrupt than in *C. immer* and this gives the tip of the lower mandible a slightly upturned appearance.

The bill in adult examples of the white-billed diver is yellowish-white tinged with horn colour at the base, also pale in the young bird. In the great northern diver the adult has a blackish bill in summer while in winter it becomes pale grey. In winter plumage, therefore, the colour of the bill is not diagnostic in the field as it is in the adult summer dress. It has been pointed out by T. A. Coward that the green and purple gloss on the head of the white-billed northern diver varies individually and the number of neck streaks is not constant. In its measurements and massive bill the white-billed species is appreciably the larger of the two.

In his " Notes on the Yellow-billed Loon " in south-eastern Alaska the American naturalist Professor A. M. Bailey [1] wrote that in flight they can be identified by their size : " if the light is at one's back, these great, heavy-bodied birds stand out with startling clearness—the long, arrow-like neck is thrust outward and the wings drive forward at tremendous speed. Outlined against the fleecy clouds, with snow-topped mountain ranges serrating the horizon, and ice-bergs of wonderful blueness in the channel ahead, these wanderers from the Arctic regions complete Nature's composition of an otherwise unfinished work of art." It has been remarked by J. Dixon that in the water the discrepancy in size between the great northern diver and the present species is not apparent, the latter appearing much smaller than is actually the case.

OCCURRENCES IN BRITAIN : Until Mr. Witherby re-examined the specimens which had been assigned to this species from Britain, when engaged upon *The Practical Handbook of British Birds*, a good deal of confusion existed and it was found that at least two which had been recorded as *G. adamsii* were in point of fact *G. immer*. Three others could not be traced and Mr. Witherby [2] discarded any records where, in his opinion, a doubt as to the correct identification could remain. The result of these investigations allowed only two certain records : since then there have been a number of others.

The first was obtained in December 1829, near Embleton, Northumberland (now in the Hancock Museum).

The second in the spring of 1852 at Pakefield, near Lowestoft, Suffolk

---

[1] *The Condor*, 1922, pp. 204-205.   [2] *British Birds*, xvi, 1922, pp. 9-12.

(in the collection of the late J. H. Gurney of Keswick Hall). This bird is mainly in winter plumage but on the back some feathers of the breeding dress are beginning to show—the bill is ivory-white.[1]

The third example was disallowed by Witherby, on the grounds, presumably that he was unable to examine the specimen. It was shot from Filey Brigg, Yorkshire, in January 1897, and was examined in the flesh by John Cordeaux.[2] He was an ornithologist of repute and I see no reason to reject his identification. See Ralph Chislett, *Yorkshire Birds*, p. 220.

The fourth, apparently overlooked by Witherby, was seen clearly in Scarborough harbour on 29th February 1916 by W. J. Clarke.[3] Full details are given by A. J. Wallis in *British Birds*, xlv, 1952, p. 422. This record is now accepted by the editors of *British Birds*, loc. cit., p. 423.

The fifth was found dead on 21st January 1946 at Whiteness Voe, Shetland, by Mr. and Mrs. Venables;[4] it was immature.

The sixth was seen on 8th June 1947 at Weisdale Voe, Shetland, also by Mr. and Mrs. Venables; this bird was not obtained but swam close in. It was an adult in full breeding plumage.

The seventh was recorded off White Hill, Yell, Shetland, early in May 1950 by W. Sinclair: an adult.

The eighth in Spiggie Voe, Shetland, on 21st May 1950 by Venables: an immature.

The ninth in the Bay of Scousburgh, Shetland, on 24th April 1951 by Venables: an immature.

The tenth was found dead on the sands at Scarborough, Yorkshire, on 30th January 1952 by Mr. Eric Sigston; it was recorded by Mr. A. J. Wallis in *British Birds*, xlv, p. 421.

The eleventh was found alive on the shore at Sandsend, near Whitby, Yorkshire, on 10th February 1952. It was recorded by A. B. Walker in *British Birds*, xlv, p. 422: an adult female.

The twelfth was found dead at Monifieth, Angus, on 24th February 1952 by Mr. G. B. Corbet:[5] an adult.

The thirteenth was seen off-shore at Dirleton, East Lothian, on 24th February 1952 by Mr. Russell G. Thin.[6]

The fourteenth was seen off Levenwick, Shetland, on 8th June 1952 by Mr. T. Henderson, and is the last of six Shetland Islands' records listed in Mr. and Mrs. Venables's book.[7]

[1] C. B. Ticehurst, *History of the Birds of Suffolk*, p. 446.
[2] *List of British Birds belonging to the Humber District*.
[3] *The Naturalist*, 1916, pp. 217-219.
[4] This and the other Shetland records which follow are given in sequence by L. S. V. and U. M. Venables in their *Birds and Mammals of Shetland* (1955).
[5] *Scottish Naturalist*, lxiv, 1952, p. 119.
[6] *Scottish Naturalist*, lxiv, 1952, p. 120.
[7] *Birds and Mammals of Shetland*, p. 259.

The fifteenth was found exhausted in East Yorkshire near the mouth of
Hedon Haven, Paull, on 18th February 1953 by Messrs. Bunting and
Stathers of Paull, and was submitted to Mr. K. Fenton [1] for identification. If the third and fourth record here listed are accepted this makes
the fifth record from the Yorkshire coast to date.

The sixteenth was first seen off Broughty Ferry Castle, Angus, on 21st
January 1954, in the river, by Mr. Alexander Cross.[2] What appears
to have been the same bird was seen again by Mr. Cross, Mr. Corbet,
and two other observers on 14th February close to the same place,
and yet again on 28th February at the Stannergate, Dundee, by
Mr. Cross. Mr. J. Grierson [3] also saw this diver at Broughty Ferry
and reported the fact to the Editors of the *Scottish Naturalist*. There
is no reason to believe that more than one bird was involved.

The seventeenth was seen from the Kilspindie side of Aberlady Bay on
12th November 1955 by Mr. F. D. Hamilton [4] and Miss Kathleen
Hogarth ; this bird remained in the neighbourhood until at least
17th November when it was seen in Gosford Bay by Mr. Ian Hay.

The eighteenth and nineteenth were seen together near Avoch Harbour,
Inverness Firth, East Ross-shire on 4th February 1959 by Mr. John
Lees [5] and others.

A white-billed diver was again seen [6] on the Gosford-Aberlady coast, East
Lothian, from 19th February until 29th April 1956 in the same area as
the bird reported as the seventeenth in this list. It was seen at close range
by, among others, F. D. Hamilton and Miss Hogarth ; but it was impossible to say whether or not it was the same bird which they observed in
November 1955 or another.

It will be remarked that thirty years elapsed between the fourth
record in 1916 and the fifth in 1946 and that in the next six years no less
than nine birds were recorded, of which the majority appeared in the Shetland Islands. I am doubtful whether Mr. and Mrs. Venables are correct
when they state that the white-billed diver has been occurring in the Shetlands more regularly in recent years. I would put these records down very
largely to the vigilance and knowledge of Mr. and Mrs. Venables themselves
and to the sharper look-out now being kept for such rarities around our
coasts. Since Mr. Venables and his wife completed their work in the
Shetlands and left the islands there have been no more records of the white-
billed diver from that group to date (May 1958) when this essay is being
prepared, which seems to me significant. On the other hand, there have
been several records from the well-patrolled East Lothian coast.

DISTRIBUTION ABROAD : The white-billed northern diver breeds in the

[1] *British Birds*, xlvi, 1953, p. 214.   [2] *Scottish Naturalist*, lxv, 1954, p. 37.
[3] *Edinburgh Bird Bull.*, iv, p. 49.   [4] *Scottish Naturalist*, lxviii, 1956, p. 57.
[5] *Scottish Birds*, i, 1959, p. 91.   [6] *Scottish Naturalist*, lxix, 1957, p. 61.

Arctic, both in the Palaearctic and Nearctic Regions. It is in fact essentially an inhabitant of the Arctic coast concerning which all too little is known. Its breeding range extends in the Old World from what was formerly known as the Murman coast and the White Sea to the Chukchen (Tchuktchen) Peninsula in eastern Siberia ; and in the New World in north-western Alaska between Cape Prince of Wales and Point Hope and the Mackenzie River delta. Fuller details of the range in these two vast areas follow.

In the Old World, which naturally concerns us most, the white-billed northern diver (or yellow-billed loon as the Americans and Russians prefer to describe it) does not appear to nest in Finmark, and it is rare in the spring and summer months off the Norwegian coast. There are two records, however, which should be mentioned. Dr. E. S. Steward saw a white-billed diver off the estuary of the Storelv in the Varanger peninsula on 26th May 1932, and Dr. H. M. S. Blair an adult in full summer plumage in Revsbotn, north of Hammerfest, on 4th June 1934. Jourdain's statement in *The Handbook of British Birds* that it " breeds probably occasionally in Finland " no doubt rests on the record from Petsamo, which in those days was situated in Finnish Lapland but is now in Russian territory. He may also have had in mind the expedition made to northern Lapland in June 1931 by Dr. Ivar Hortling, E. C. Stuart Baker, and General Betham. A male white-billed northern diver " with testes the size of pigeons' eggs " was brought to them near Pummanki on the Fisher Peninsula on 12th June, having been caught in the salmon-nets on that day. The bird was in perfect plumage and a typical example of *G. adamsii*. These naturalists stated in the report of their expedition [1] that the bird is seen every year at Henö and other places in the extreme north, as well as on the Varanger Fjord during the summer, though there is no notice of its breeding so far west.

Dr. Hugh Blair has kindly supplied the following notes on its Scandinavian distribution :

Locally-killed white-billed divers were finding their way into Norwegian museums in the sixties of the last century, if not before ; but these were all at first referred to the better-known great northern diver. The species was eventually added to the Norwegian avifauna in 1877, when Collett identified an example shot in Flekkefjord two years previously. By 1921 this diver had been recorded in Norwegian waters often enough to allow of Collett describing it as a regular visitor, most frequently seen in autumn and winter, and in some years quite common. While undoubted white-billed divers have penetrated into nearly every inlet, including the Oslo Fjord, the majority of those wintering around Norway keep to the more northerly coasts. There is only one freshwater record. As so often happens with Arctic birds, the number of these divers visiting the country varies from season to season. Of some sixty sent in to museums in the period 1893-1910, no fewer than twenty-four were killed in the former year. On the other hand, the three years 1899-1901 passed without the curator of Tromsö Museum receiving, or even hearing

---

[1] " Bird notes on a trip to Lapland ", in *Ibis*, 1932, pp. 100-127 (p. 115).

of, a solitary specimen. Of those recorded for 1893 seven were birds of the year, as many immature individuals in the plumage of the second winter, and the remainder adults. Collett noted that the different plumages were represented in about the same proportions amongst the specimens obtained in later years.

Some of the white-billed divers recorded for Norway were drowned in fishing-nets or on lines. One big male found on a line had been caught at between ten and fifteen fathoms.

It is hardly surprising to find such a bird of the open sea much rarer in Sweden than in Norway. Here again most of the few recorded have been obtained in coastal waters, the exception being a young bird killed on Gellivara. Herr R. Kreuger informs us that the white-billed diver has been seen " a number of times " off the northern coast of Finland. It has also appeared, though only " sporadically " along the south coast, and on one or two occasions in the interior of the country. To Danish waters this bird seems to be no more than an accidental visitor.

To Sweden it is evidently a rare visitor. In *Fauna and Flora*, 1922, pp. 108-111, Lönnberg wrote about a specimen which Dr. O. Holm observed lying on the snow at Bjurön, in Lövånger, Prov. Hälsingland, Sweden, at the beginning of May 1922. Dr. Holm sent the head, legs and wings to the State Museum where these parts are still kept. The bird in question had been killed when lying on the snow. Concerning this bird Count Gyldenstolpe writes to me (June 1958) from the Royal Natural History Museum, Stockholm :

There does not seem to be any question that the example found is a young *adamsii*, and the claws are pale horn-coloured, the bill yellowish-white, somewhat brownish on the basal portion of the culminal ridge, as well as with a narrow dark band on both mandibles near the edge of the feathering.

Besides the example thus mentioned by Lönnberg, we have two more specimens in our collections from Swedish waters, one collected at Sandskär, Hälsingland, on 18th January 1923, and a young male (?) obtained at Gotska Sandön in the Baltic on 19th May 1948.

Observations from the territory of the U.S.S.R. are naturally more numerous, but even so field notes are more scanty than should be the case considering the bird's status in that vast expanse bordering the Arctic Sea. Pleske, in his *Birds of the Eurasian Tundra* (p. 353), states that the white-billed northern diver is of regular occurrence in the open sea off the Murman coast, while it breeds east of the White Sea to the north of the Chuckchen Peninsula everywhere along the edge of the forest region. Dr. Hortling had two eggs of this diver in his collection, but whether they were taken in Lapland or farther east (as seems more probable) is not stated. In consequence especially of the work of Russian ornithologists the breeding area of *Gavia adamsii* must be stated in greater detail than was possible thirty years ago. I am indebted to Mme. E. Kozlova for her translation of Professor Dementiev's definition of the range of this diver in the territory of the Soviet Republic in 1951, and also to her summary of its status in

WHITE-BILLED NORTHERN DIVER

(Gavia immer)

Charles Whymper

PLATE 19

WHITE-BILLED NORTHERN DIVER
Gavia adamsii (Gray)

Novaya Zemlya, the region of the Indigirka River and in Anadyr Land. Throughout I have retained the spelling of place names as used by Mme. Kozlova and have not attempted to correlate these with the spelling used on recent British-compiled maps of the U.S.S.R. In the following notes from Russian sources the white-billed northern diver is referred to as the " yellow-billed loon "—the name by which *Gavia adamsii* is known in the United States. Professor Dementiev gives the distribution as follows :

Breeds on Ainov Islands near Petchenga [Petsamo]. Observed on 5th June on Solovetzky Islands in the White Sea. Certainly breeds on Kolguev Island and on the southern island of Novaia Zemlia. Occurs on the lower reaches of the Obj, but its breeding here is not proved. Met with in summer in the tundra of Gydansky Peninsula and on the lower Enisei. Undoubtedly breeds on Taimyr Peninsula (on the tundra near the sea shore and further inland). No certain information from the lower reaches of Lena or Yana rivers. Mikhel (1935) found it on the lower Indigirka, south to Uiandina (68° 30′ N.). Found in the basin of Kolyma River, south to Sredne-Violymsk (67° 30′ N.), where a downy young was captured on 26th July 1905. Breeds also on the Pacific coast of Tchuktchen Peninsula ; has been obtained near Pitlekai (just east of Koliutchin Bay, northern shores of Tchuktchen Peninsula), where a nest with one egg near a lake has been discovered on 10th July.

Portenko (1939) records it breeding in the basin of the Anadyr River, where it nests in the delta and in mountain regions on the upper reaches of a number of rivers, being absent from the middle course of the Anadyr River.

Obtained in May 1941 and on 20th July 1946 on the north-western shores of Ochotsky Sea near Magadan (Jauyi Bay, 150° E.) and Nogaev Bay.

Obtained once (14th May 1940) on Liachov Island (south of New Siberian Arkhipelago).

Winter records from Behring Sea, from the Pacific off the shores of Kamtchatka, from the vicinity of the Commandos and Kuril Islands, also from the Barenz Sea off the Murman coast (Lappland).

The arrival and departure of the yellow-billed loon seems to depend on the time of the freezing of water basins. On Novaia Zemlia the last loons were observed at the beginning of October, on the Anadyr River at the end of September. In spring the first loons were obtained in the north of the U.S.S.R. in the second half of May and in the beginning of June ; once on 14th May on the New Siberian islands.

Habitat. Lakes in the tundra, not far from the sea shore, also (in north-east Siberia) in mountainous regions near rivers and lakes.

In addition to the above distribution notes Mme. Kozlova has kindly translated extracts referring to this diver in three important Russian publications. The authors' names are given first, the subject of their notes follows :

Gorbunov, 1929 : *Contributions to the fauna of Novaia Zemlia.* I observed *C. adamsi* only twice : on 13th September 1923 in Puhovi Bay (north-west shores of the Southern Island) and on a lake in Malij Karmakula Bay (western shores of the Southern Island). The loon breeds on a small island of a lake, where it was observed every day. Golytzin in the summer of 1896 saw *C. adamsi* on the same lake.

Mikhel, 1935 : *Notes on the birds of Indigirka River. C. adamsi* is common on the lower Indigirka where it is to be met with on large lakes in the tundra and forest zones, south to Uiandina. More often seen on tundra lakes than in the forest zone, but nowhere numerous. The authors observed four loons on 22nd September on a lake. They were very cautious ; after having caught sight of the intruder they all dived and came to the surface a long way off. This loon sometimes gets entangled in fishing nets, and being very strong usually tears the nets or comes out on shore, dragging the net behind.

Portenko, 1939 : *Fauna of Anadyr Land.* In the estuary of the Anadyr River the yellow-billed loon is common during the summer. On 21st July 1931 I saw on the water near the sea-shore about fifteen individuals. On 28th July a few birds flew above me on the upper reaches of Kozatchka River (a tributary of the Anadyr). One specimen, caught in a net, was brought to me by fishermen in the beginning of August. This loon breeds near lakes in the tundra zone of the mountains and travels each day to the estuary of the Anadyr to feed.

Before discussing its distribution in north-western America and the Canadian Arctic, some mention must be made of the bird's winter quarters in the Old World. This has undoubtedly set a problem. We know little more to-day of its winter quarters in European waters than when Professor Collett [1] wrote in 1894 that it " visits the coasts of Norway annually, especially during the autumn and winter, in some years even in considerable numbers ". A. C. Bent [2] commented that this suggested the possibility that its main migration route may be westward along the Arctic coasts of Asia and Europe to its principal winter home in the vicinity of Norway. Collett observed that during their visits to the Norwegian coasts these birds, on some occasions, penetrate to the interior of the southernmost fjords, as for instance, the Oslo Fjord, but most of them appear to stop on the northern shores. They disappear from Norwegian waters as a rule during the spring and summer, although, as Professor Collett suggests, stray individuals may pass the summer on the shores of Norway without breeding. We have observed in the British Isles that a few will reach our shores mainly in the winter months, more particularly the seas around Shetland. Others visit the Baltic, Sweden,[3] and Finland. H. Gechter [4] records the first German occurrence from the mouth of the Elbe ; G. C. A. Yunge [5] a similar occurrence (in 1935) in Holland ; in the same year one was reported by J. Musílek from Czechoslovakia ; and in 1936 Graf J. Seilern recorded a bird from Austria — all no doubt of accidental occurrence.

In a very recent number of the *Anzeiger der Ornith. Gesch. in Bayern,*

[1] " On the occurrence of *Colymbus adamsi* in Norway ", in *Ibis*, vi, 1894, p. 269.
[2] *Life Histories of North American Diving Birds*, p. 64.
[3] Lönnberg, *Fauna och Flora*, 1922, pp. 85-92.
[4] *Orn. Monatsberichte*, xli, 1933, p. 150.
[5] *Ardea*, 1935, p. 47.

Band v, Nr. 1, pp. 43-44, Herr W. Rathmayer mentions having seen a juvenile of *Gavia immer adamsii* " on the Isar near Altheim below Landshut, Lower Bavaria. The bird was swimming entirely tamely about thirty metres from the bank, sometimes right beside a black-throated diver (*Gavia arctica*), so that my companion Dr. Rothemberger and I had good opportunity to compare them."

To this short list of European records Jourdain, in *The Handbook*, adds Denmark, Poland, Slavonia, and Italy, from which countries stragglers have been reported. It has also been recorded somewhat doubtfully from Spitsbergen [1] and from Greenland (once).[2] It is very remarkable that it is not mentioned in Mr. Kenneth Williamson's list of the birds of the Faeroe Islands.[3] Surely as it visits the Shetlands more or less regularly it must occur in winter within Faeroe Islands' territorial waters? The breeding of this diver near Petsamo is noted by Professor Stresemann in *Ornithologische Monatsberichte*.[4]

On the other side of the Atlantic Ocean the white-billed diver has a considerable range as has been stated earlier in this section. In the new *Check List of North American Birds* the authors, under the chairmanship of Dr. Alexander Wetmore, define its range in the New World as follows : Breeds from Cape Prince of Wales, Point Hope, Point Barrow, and the Salmon river of Alaska to the Mackenzie River delta and western Keewatin north of the timber line. In summer the New World birds are found north to Banks, Victoria and Somerset Islands and Boothia Peninsula, east to Melville Peninsula and south to Great Slave, Yathkyed, and Baker Lakes. In winter to south-eastern Alaska (Alexander Archipelago) and rarely Vancouver Island. It is accidental in Greenland, Long Island, and Colorado.

HABITS : We have only to turn to A. C. Bent's *Life Histories of North American Diving Birds* to realize how little was known about the white-billed northern diver when that volume was published in 1919. In his very first paragraph he writes : " Few naturalists have ever seen it and very little is known of its habits. It is one of the rare species about which I have hoped to learn something new, but I regret to say that I have been unable to add much to its life history beyond what has already been published and that is meagre enough." Since these words were penned some progress in our knowledge of this species has been made but nothing like what I had hoped to be able to present in this essay to complete its life history.

---

[1] Graf Zedlitz, *J.f.O.*, 1911, p. 300, saw off Amsterdam Island what he believed to be this species in a rough sea at 150 yards on 5th August 1910.

[2] Helms, *Vidensk. Medd. fra Naturhist. Forening i. Kjøbenhavn*, 1899, p. 234 ; also recorded by Salomonsen, *Grønlands Fugle*, p. 562.

[3] *The Atlantic Islands*, 1948, Order *Colymbiformes*, p. 322.

[4] *Orn. Monatsber.*, xlviii, 1940, pp. 188-189.

The migration route of this diver was for years a source of perplexity to American ornithologists. One of the first to point to the truth was Professor W. W. Cooke,[1] who tentatively outlined the spring migration route of this Arctic bird as extending from Siberia to the Bering Strait, thence to the Arctic coast of Alaska and via Point Hope and Cape Lisburne to Point Barrow ; swinging wide from this point the birds turn south-eastward along the Arctic coast and head for the mouth of the Mackenzie River. Cooke's suggestion received corroboration from Joseph Dixon,[2] when a member of the Harvard Alaska-Siberia Expedition of 1913-14. Owing to unfavourable ice conditions the explorers were forced to spend a considerable time in what, according to the A.O.U. *Check List* of that day, was supposed to be the centre of the breeding range of *Gavia adamsii*, i.e. the Arctic coast of Alaska between Point Barrow and the mouth of the Mackenzie River. Particular attention was consequently paid to the yellow-billed loon in the hope of finding an authentic nest, but not only did the members of the expedition fail to find any trace of a nest but none of the fourteen specimens collected between 3rd June and 16th July showed any signs of breeding. In the report of the expedition Dixon proved to his satisfaction that the spring route of the loon was as suggested by Cooke. Either birds were actually seen or, as at Point Hope and Cape Lisburne (some 200 miles north of Bering Strait on the Alaska side), evidence of the birds' presence was secured in the shape of cartridge-bags or tool-bags belonging to the Eskimos and made from the necks of the yellow-billed loon. These bags were of recent origin and could not well have been trade goods from farther north. At Humphrey Point in Arctic Alaska, i.e. two-thirds of the distance from Point Barrow to the Mackenzie River, these loons were seen commonly on most days between 3rd June and 16th July, from three to twenty being recorded within the twenty-four hours. After 20th June several were seen paired in large ponds a few miles inland, but they did not [so Dixon believed] breed there. The expedition left the area on 16th July, but they had seen enough to realize that *in the spring* the yellow-billed loon uses this route extensively. It had been reported to have been found by whalers in great numbers in a lagoon on the south end of Bank's Land during the last days of August and the first of September.

The exploring party spent the period from 24th July to 3rd September between Point Barrow and Demarcation Point, many excursions being made ashore. Dixon's ship spent the winter frozen in about seven miles off Humphrey Point, Alaska. From the winter camp ashore a continual watch was kept for the loons but not one was seen and, as Dixon observed in his report, " one of the strangest features of our experience was our absolute failure to gain information as to the fall migration ". Observations were continued until the ship reached Nome on 19th September 1914,

1 " A problem in migration ", in *Condor*, xvii, 1915, pp. 213-214.
2 " Migration of the Yellow-billed Loon ", in *Auk*, xxxiii, 1916, pp. 370-376.

despite various stops at Wainwright Islet, Point Hope, and Kotzebue
Sound, where a week was spent but no sign of fall migration was secured.
Nor was there any trace of the bird in Siberia where the expedition collected
on Chuckchen Peninsula for three weeks until 22nd June.   Dixon's experiences on this expedition settled four points in his mind which may be
briefly summarized :

1. Corroboration that Cooke was correct about the route of the spring
   migration.
2. The improbability that the yellow-billed loon bred on the Arctic coast
   of Alaska and Canada which coast it traverses on migration. (He was
   later proved to be wrong in this assumption.)
3. The probability that the loon does not leave its supposed breeding
   ground in the fall through the region visited, which is only the highway
   in the spring.
4. That from evidence accumulated (and cited in his report) the coast of
   south-eastern Alaska might still be profitably scrutinized for information
   regarding the migratory movements of the yellow-billed loon.

Dixon came very near the truth in his last point as will be seen hereafter.   He pointed out that the fact that loons were seen in the breeding
season in the area between Point Barrow and the Mackenzie was no criterion
that they bred there ; and he emphasized the fact that along the whole
coast of Alaska non-breeding water-birds occur in numbers throughout
the summer, in places far outside their breeding range.   He justifiably
concluded that under these conditions something more than identification
of a species is necessary to establish its status as a breeding bird, and
adds that " nothing short of the capture of the parent bird together with
the sett of eggs by some responsible party ", would constitute a dependable
record.   Dixon draws a picture of the yellow-billed loon in this frozen
land with which we may close the account of his own experiences :

    The flight of the yellow-billed loon in migration was one of the most impressive
sights of our Arctic trip.   A dim speck low over the frozen tundra or glaring ice-
fields suddenly develops wings which beat rapidly with the rhythm and energy of a
steam engine.   The huge bill and neck seem to be extended slightly upwards, and the
bird glides swiftly forward in a straight line with none of the undulating movements
of the brant and eider ducks.   The rapid " swish, swish " of the huge wings dies
away in the Arctic silence, and the next moment one is gazing in the distance where
a rapidly diminishing dark object seems to be boring a hole in the low clouds in the
east.   There was no variation in speed or direction, and the birds travelled at least
forty miles an hour over a measured distance.   Most of these secured were " through
travellers " in full flight, and all were exceedingly fat.   A bird weighed twelve
pounds before skinning.

    A few years later—in 1920—Alfred M. Bailey, when on field-work
for the Biological Survey in South-eastern Alaska, was afforded exceptional

opportunities for observing the water-birds and was the first to prove the correctness of Dixon's suggestion that this area of Alaska would prove worthy of more attention in connexion with the movements of the yellow-billed loon. In a short article published in *The Condor*,[1] Dr. Bailey describes meeting with it throughout the year except during the months of July and August. His survey took him to Admiralty Island, Kuiu and Kupreanoff Islands, Keku Straits, Wrangell Island, Marmon Island, Douglas Island, Gastineau Channel, and Stephens Passage (thirty seen), between 6th February and 11th June. Fall (autumn) records were made in Seymour Canal (Admiralty Island), Youngs Bay in Stephen's Passage, Point Couverton, Icy Straits, Chatham Straits and finally at Killisnoo, these all between the end of September and the end of October. These were practically all new records, substantiating a much earlier one from Admiralty Island made by Joseph Dixon in the spring of 1907,[2] and as such were of particular interest. Further, no autumn records of this loon had previously been obtained. Dr. Bailey stated that in the area he was working in 1920 the yellow-billed loons could not be considered rare. He described how they are extremely wary and give boats a wide berth so that they are apt to be overlooked. On one occasion when he was going up Icy Straits the birds started for the shadows of the shore or the centre of the channel to avoid his boat when it was quite five hundred yards away. With average light it was quite impossible to identify the yellow-bills at much more than gun-shot distance without the aid of binoculars; and for that reason he believed collectors had overlooked their presence. " When a specimen is in the hand," he remarks, " the large size and coloured bill seem so apparent that one could not fail to notice them; but in the water, especially in bad light, their size shrinks remarkably and then they do not look different from common loons."

That was the state of our knowledge in 1920, when Dr. Bailey returned from south-eastern Alaska. Two points in the life history of this rare bird had been cleared up : the area where many birds wintered in south-east Alaska had been located, and the direction of its migration on its north-ward flight from Bering Strait up the Arctic coast as well as along the Siberian side—Bailey had already proved that they occur regularly along the south-eastern Alaskan coast and on their northward journey skirt the sea-coast practically the entire distance. It is possible, as he himself suggested,[3] that these loons " following off shore along Bering Sea, instead of rounding Cape Prince of Wales, make the short cut-off across Seaward Peninsula, exactly as do the black brant and the cackling and white-fronted geese ". It fell to the same explorer to prove at least one breeding

[1] " Notes on the Yellow-billed Loon ", in *Condor*, xxiv, 1922, pp. 204-205.

[2] See Grinnell, *Univ. Calif. Publ. Zool.*, vol. v, 1909, p. 182.

[3] " A Report on the birds of north-western Alaska and regions adjacent to Bering Strait," in *Condor*, xxvii, 1925, p. 29.

locality of the yellow-billed loon in north-western Alaska by personally taking an egg at Mint River on 11th July 1922, and subsequently receiving others in the two following seasons from the same locality obtained by his native assistant at Mint River and the near vicinity on 5th July 1923 and 3rd July 1924 (two clutches), each of two eggs. Bailey describes the eggs as having a warm brown ground colour, the surface being mottled with dark-brown spots; in one sett, however, the ground colour is yellowish-olive, both eggs being dotted with blackish. He gives the measurements of these seven eggs as follows: 93 × 55 mm.; 90 × 50 and 91 × 57 mm.; 90 × 59 and 88 × 58 mm.; 85 × 53 and 83 × 53 mm. Two clutches of eggs in Herr Kreuger's collection have the following measurements: one taken at Kolguev on 27th July 1906 measured 95·4 × 58·5 and 96·1 × 59·7 mm.; the other from Togora, Alaska, on 21st June 1917, measured 91·1 × 55·9 mm. The expedition to north-western Alaska, organised by the Colorado Museum of Natural History in 1921, planned to remain in the field for a year in the region of Wainwright and Cape Prince of Wales. The former place, an Eskimo village and trading post, was reached on 22nd August and became the headquarters of the explorers. It is situated within two miles of Wainwright Inlet, "a bay-like arm which extends inland for many miles and into which empty the icy waters of several tundra rivers". In the spring migration the yellow-billed loons were fairly common at Wainwright from 22nd May onwards. The height of the migration was during the period 2nd to 19th June. Most birds were flying singly, and after that time single birds or pairs were seen regularly throughout the summer, but never on the freshwater ponds or tundra lagoons: they were either seen flying over the land or in the water at the mouth of the inlet. Natives claimed that they nest occasionally but it was not until Dr. Bailey had reached Wales at the extreme north of Seaward Peninsula and from there worked the tundra for nesting birds, that he was able to discover the loons at their nests. The birds proved quite common along Loop Lagoon in July, only about twenty miles up the coast from Wales, and especially on the lakes a few miles inland. Mint River and the nearby vicinity proved a good place for them during the second week in July. Dr. Bailey's account of his discovery shall be told in his own words : [1]

On the 11th [July 1922] . . . the Eskimos reported birds on the lakes at the foot of Potato Mountains. We were camped on a gravel bar of the Mint River and all night I could hear the then distant calls [of the yellow-billed loons], a more mournful and lonely sound than the weird cry of the common loon.

The next day was stormy with alternate rain and snow squalls but we were early afield. We first investigated the larger lake where Nagozruk had seen the birds the previous day. . . . Although we saw them rise from a little grass-grown

[1] With acknowledgement to the author and the editor of *The Condor*, in vol. xxvii of which (pp. 20-32) " A report on the birds of north-western Alaska and regions adjacent to Bering Strait " was published.

pond back of the lagoon, we found nothing but a crude nest of grass, and empty. I worked pond after pond that day and every one of any size had its pair of yellow-billed loons and usually from one to three empty nests along the shore—but all recently built. They looked as though the loons had cut out turf and overturned it to make mud platforms. After nearly all day afield I determined on one more lake, so crawling carefully to the summit of a ridge which separated this chain of lagoons, I surveyed the broad expanse with my binoculars. About four hundred yards away was a yellow-billed loon sitting upon the bank of a little grass-grown peninsula. I stood up and again looked for the bird. It was gone. Hurrying around the pond I came to the vicinity where the bird had been and there was a nest, but empty. I walked on for about ten feet and found a mud mound with a scant lining of grass and a single egg. Beyond this nest at intervals of about ten feet were two other fresh mounds.

Bailey's expedition settled the point which Dixon disputed—that the yellow-billed loon bred on the Arctic coast of Alaska, at any rate in the area between Point Barrow and Cape Prince of Wales. Observing that he believed Mr. Dixon to have been mistaken in denying the bird's breeding in this area, he points out that the yellow-billed loon seems to be later in nesting than other water-birds. On his dog-sled journey between Barrow and Prince of Wales he talked with many natives who informed him that the " King Loon " nested along the lakes back from the coast. Eggs were collected by the Rev. Mr. Hoare who was formerly at Point Hope, and Bailey talked with men who had helped him to secure the eggs.

The latest information regarding this loon in northern Alaska is of more recent date and was obtained during the study of the mammals and birds by scientists from the Kansas University Museum [1]. The area worked was the treeless tundra delimited by the crest of the Brooks Range to the south, the international boundary to the east and the Arctic Ocean to the north and west. Field headquarters were at the Arctic Research Laboratory at Point Barrow. The expedition was in the field in the summers of 1951 and 1952, all the observations on the yellow-billed loon being made in July and August. Birds were located at Topagaruk, at Koalak River, Porcupine Lake, Lake Peters, Lake Schrader (where it was known to have young), and Wahoo Lake (nest and eggs found). The party arrived at Wahoo Lake on 3rd July 1952 and found two yellow-billed loons swimming on the lake side by side. Their nest was located on 4th July and held two fresh eggs. Not till three days later was the first call heard, from a bird 4000 feet from the nest at the other end of the lake. The nest was visited on 19th July. The incubating male bird remained on the nest with neck held low and extended until the boat was twenty-five feet away, when he plunged into the lake. His feet and wings beat the water increasing his

[1] James W. Bee, " Birds found on the Arctic slope of Northern Alaska " in *Univ. of Kansas Publications, Museum of Nat. Hist.*, vol. x, No. 5, pp. 163-211, March 12, 1958. I am indebted to Dr. Alex. Wetmore for sending me this report from Washington.

speed as he made off. The nest, approximately 60 cm. in diameter, of sedges, grasses, and an assortment of plant debris, was on a mound of soil 23 cm. above, and 40 cm. from, the open water. The cup of the nest measured 37 mm. in depth. The site of the nest in the south-east corner of the lake was near the area supporting the most lake trout. Between the open water of the lake and the shore, twenty feet of sedges and grasses deterred wolves, red foxes, and caribou from molesting the nest ; tracks of these mammals were numerous on contiguous shore areas. It was remarked by the naturalists that the early run-off entering the lake created a variable water level : the overflow decreased 60 per cent. in the period 2nd to 11th July. The loons lay their eggs when the lake's level is fairly well stabilized. The cotton grass (*Eriophorum*) at the latter date was developing white flowers and the sedges, growing in dense stands, were showing springtime green.

It appears from the field-notes obtained that when first these birds arrive on their breeding ground they do not at once start calling. For instance, on Porcupine Lake a yellow-billed loon was seen every day in 1952 from 13th to 18th July, but it was not heard until 8 p.m. on 17th July. Thereafter its long-drawn-out wail or raucous hilarious call was uttered at intervals in the evening and well towards midnight. Mr. Bee observes in his report that of the three species of loons seen on the Arctic Slope (*G. arctica pacifica*, *G. stellata*, and *G. adamsii*), the yellow-billed loon is the least numerous. Owing to its large size it is more often taken than either of the others, while Eskimos consider its dark fine-grained flesh a delicacy. A female was found to weigh 5897 grammes. It measured 870 mm. in total length and had a wing-spread of 1600 mm. Mr. James Bee considers that on the more isolated areas of the Arctic Slope the yellow-billed loon remains common ; elsewhere it needs protection. He points out that its relationship to the great northern diver, *G. immer*, cannot be defined until additional specimens are obtained, especially from the contact zone between the areas of their geographical distribution. In the meantime he very rightly treats the yellow-billed loon as a distinct species.

American expeditions sponsored by leading museums in that country have proved without doubt that one of the main breeding areas of the white-billed diver (as we in Britain prefer to call it) is in the treeless tundra zone of northern Alaska. How far east within Canadian territory it actually breeds I do not know, but it will be remembered that Professor Bailey believed it nested along the entire coast from Cape Prince of Wales to the Mackenzie River delta and beyond.

REFERENCES : Original Description. *Colymbus adamsii* Gray, *Proc. Zool. Soc. London*, 1859, p. 167 : Alaska.

PLATE 20   # BLACK-THROATED DIVER

Gavia arctica arctica (Linnaeus)

(*Colymbus arcticus* auctorum)

Resident and breeding locally north Scottish mainland, also Winter
Visitor. It has *not* been proved to have ever nested in Ireland, but
is a rare Winter Visitor to the coast, exceptionally inland. Especially
rare on west coast of England but more frequent on east coast though
cannot be classed as of regular occurrence. Breeding in Shetland is
" extremely doubtful " (Venables) and the same must apply to the
Orkneys, no properly authenticated case having been recorded. It
nests sparingly in the Outer Hebrides

IDENTIFICATION : The black-throated diver must be reckoned one of the
most handsome birds which we can claim as a breeding species in the British
Isles, if not the most beautiful of all.   The writer has met with it in its
breeding plumage in the Highlands of his own country and in Sweden,
and apart from the great northern diver can think of nothing comparably
beautiful at that season of the year.   It is, in consequence, a great favourite
among bird-photographers of the eminence of Eric Hosking and Niall
Rankin, who have each provided us with outstanding photographs of these
birds at their nests, thus making them known to a wide circle of men and
women who have probably never seen the birds in their native haunts—
haunts which are to-day not easily discovered, or even reached especially
in the nesting season.   I have read all that these authorities—and many
others besides—have written about the black-throats, and will begin this
essay with Niall Rankin's description of the birds as he saw them on a
Highland loch : [1]

The finely contrasted colouring of the divers' plumage is one to be marvelled
at.   The top of the head, cheeks and back of the neck are of softest dove-grey.
The whole of the upperparts of the body and the wings are black save for four
patches of white barring, one on either side of the back at the base of the neck and
one large patch on each wing.   Both wings carry a few white flecks as well.   But it
is the head-on view of the bird which is the most impressive.   Below the eyes the
grey fades into black which is continued down the whole of the front of the neck,
except for a narrow broken band of white feathers just below the chin—like a
miniature pearl necklace—until it ends in a sharply divided line above the pure
white of the breast.   Separating the black panel of the front of the neck from the
grey on the back of it is a series of delicate stripes, alternating black and white,
which run vertically down the side of the neck, then curve sharply backwards to be
lost in the grey.   The whole of the underparts are white.   Below the black of the
throat a second series of similar stripes starts on either side of the upper breast,
part of which sweeps round to join the black of the upperparts, while the remainder

---

[1] Niall Rankin, *Haunts of British Divers*, Collins, 1947, to the author and publishers of
which I am indebted for their permission to quote extracts from the work.

PLATE 20

BLACK-THROATED DIVER
Gavia arctica arctica (Linnaeus)

ends abruptly against the white of the breast. There is no difference in plumage between the sexes.

Its total length is 22-27 inches (Tucker). The soft parts are : iris wine-red ; bill blackish-slate above, the tip horn, in winter greyish ; legs and feet blackish, webs with flesh-coloured centres.

As a diver the black-throated species can compare with any of its relatives, and, as Colonel Rankin has observed, its form is perfectly stream-lined for its underwater activities. " A long narrow head gently tapering to the pointed beak, carried on a strongly built neck and the body also tapered from back to front." On the wing it appears cigar-shaped, to use a description employed by T. A. Coward. It is an inhabitant of the larger lochs and is less often found on the dhu-lochans which attract the red-throated diver more especially ; more will be said of its preferences in a later paragraph, but it is by no means to be found on all such large sheets of water however suitable they may appear at first sight. The bill is an excellent guide to identification—not so massive as in the great northern diver and lacking the perceptible up-tilt of the mandibles so characteristic of the red-throated diver.

DISTRIBUTION IN THE BRITISH ISLES : The true home of the black-throated diver in our islands is in the northern counties of Scotland—in Inverness-shire, Ross and Cromarty, Sutherland, and Caithness. South of northern Perthshire and Argyll it does not breed. It has bred in Angus and has been found in at least three different localities in Argyll. In the Inner Hebrides it nests or has nested in a few of the islands—Coll, Jura, Mull, and perhaps Skye. It has now bred on Arran,[1] first recorded in 1951. The distribution of this diver in the northern islands is curious. It breeds in the Outer Hebrides. In 1932 it was found to be commoner in North Uist than in the other islands.[2] There does not appear to be a single well-authenticated case of nesting in the Orkneys or Shetlands within recent times. Millais reported two eggs taken on a small loch in Hoy in the former group, but no trace of the birds could be found in 1941 when Dr. Lack and G. T. Arthur visited every loch in the breeding season. In 1948 Dr. Evelyn Baxter received a report that the species was breeding on a loch on Rousay, but the record does not appear to have been verified. Shetland records are even more uncertain, despite the statement in *The Handbook*. In their recent prolonged investigation in these islands L. S. V. and U. M. Venables consider breeding in Shetland to be extremely doubt-ful ;[3] moreover, they successfully dispose of earlier statements upon which the nesting of the black-throated diver in Shetland appears to have rested. They list all records of the bird's occurrence in the Shetlands from which

[1] J. A. Gibson, *The Birds of the Island of Arran*, 1956.
[2] *The Birds of Scotland*, vol. ii, p. 511.
[3] *Birds and Mammals of Shetland*, 1955, p. 260.

it is apparent how seldom it has been seen—only on nine occasions between 1919 and 1952. This diver does not breed anywhere south of the Scottish border.

In Ireland it is a sparse winter visitor and has never been proved to breed. In the new *Birds of Ireland* (1954) the author of the section which includes the divers, Major R. T. Ruttledge, has drawn attention to the statement in *The Handbook of British Birds* that a black-throated diver with half-grown young was seen in August 1933 in north-west Ireland, and that birds were seen in subsequent seasons and breeding was thought to continue (!). Major Ruttledge then adds : " From a very careful examination of all the evidence and information available it is clear that some misunderstanding took place and that the validity of this breeding record must be discounted ". Major Ruttledge had already given [1] details as to how this error arose and in a footnote to his statement in *British Birds*, Bernard Tucker adds that he is in full agreement with Major Ruttledge that the breeding record included on the evidence of Eliot Howard (who was not aware at the time of the importance of the supposed occurrence) should not now be accepted. Although this matter has been well ventilated in the standard works cited, it is important that in *The Birds of the British Isles* the true facts should be repeated. Errors in *The Handbook*, whatever their origin, are apt to be repeated and great credit is due to Major Ruttledge for his clear exposition as to how this one in particular arose.

Scotland therefore remains the only breeding place of the black-throated diver in the British Isles.

As a winter visitor this diver is much more generally seen around our coasts, more especially the area washed by the North Sea, for then overseas migrants come in with stormy weather. Curiously they are uncommon in the northern Isles, quite remarkably so in Shetland, nor are they found on the west coast except sparingly. Dr. Evelyn Baxter and Miss Rintoul have summed up the Scottish distribution of the black-throat during the winter months in the following sentences : [2]

After the breeding season, these divers and their young appear on the salt water, being sometimes seen in August in family parties ; they return to their breeding lochs about April. Though as a rule not very plentiful black-throated divers may be seen in late autumn and winter almost anywhere round our coasts, and in our neighbourhood [the coast of Fife] we consider them to have become commoner of recent years. The largest number we have ever seen together was when we were crossing in the ferry from Newport to Dundee on 21st January 1933, when we saw quite fifty divers, mostly black-throats, though a few were red-throats. The main autumn movement takes place in September and October.

These authors record big arrivals off Lunan on 27th September 1935 believed to have come from overseas, many more on 23rd November off

[1] *British Birds*, xliii, 1950, p. 167.   [2] *The Birds of Scotland*, vol. ii, 1953.

the East Neuk, and not uncommonly in winter off the Forth islands. On one occasion in September my wife herself came upon a gathering of these divers, which she estimated as quite fifty birds, in Inverpolly Bay, presumably massing after the breeding season before departure farther south.

There is a considerable movement of divers of one species or another down the east coast of England, but they are not easily distinguished at a distance and most recorders believe the black-throat to be the rarest of the three which may be seen off shore. G. W. Temperley considers it an infrequent visitor to the Durham coast in winter and still rarer to inland waters. Bolam in Northumberland considered it not rare, but more numerous in some years than in others and always much scarcer than the red-throat. Probably its status has undergone little change since he wrote in 1932. Its status in East Anglia was summed up by C. B. Ticehurst— also in 1932—in his *History of the Birds of Suffolk* in the following words: " The older writers considered this bird to be rarer than the great northern diver and perhaps that may be so, but owing to its preference for estuaries the records, at least of late years, show that the black-throated diver is the commoner of the two. It is not, however, quite a regular winter visitor, though hardly a severe spell of weather passes but that one or more turn up in our tidal waters. The occurrence of this species does not, however, depend entirely on severe weather conditions, since many have been obtained during mild winters."

Claud Ticehurst—one of the most accurate and knowledgeable of naturalists of my day—looked for its arrival off the East Anglian coast about mid-November and had records of examples seen in March and April, when the birds would be on their way north once more. A few have penetrated some distance up the rivers and have been observed on the Broads as well as in the tidal estuaries. Ticehurst issues a timely warning against the shooting of these divers by shore gunners " as no doubt some of them are our Scottish breeding stock ". On inland waters in winter it is of course a vagrant, and very rare outside the breeding season. There are, however, a number of instances when this diver has been driven inland. Mr. Chislett gives a number of examples in *Yorkshire Birds*, adding that inland occurrences are often associated with stormy weather. T. H. Nelson went so far as to write that the black-throated diver was rarer on the coast than the great northern diver but " more frequently observed inland ". Chislett comments that this has not been so in recent years. During the south-westerly gales of early February 1950 black-throated divers were reported from inland localities in Warwickshire, Worcestershire, and Berkshire.

If Mr. John Walpole-Bond's experiences off the Sussex coast are applicable to all our south coast counties the black-throated diver must be of annual occurrence in the English Channel. He alone knew of about fifty cases of capture apart from sight-records, pointing to the bird being a tolerably frequent visitor. Considering that Continental examples move south from breeding grounds in north-west Europe in some numbers, wandering at least as far as the Portuguese coast if not beyond, it is not surprising to find it recorded from the English Channel counties. A record of more than passing interest is that mentioned by Colonel B. H. Ryves,[1] of a score or more black-throated divers—some in breeding plumage —in Gerrans Bay, Cornwall, between 26th March and 20th April 1938.

Although the black-throated diver appears from reports to be more numerous on the east coast of Britain than the west during the winter months, it is stated by R. M. Lockley [2] to be seen off the Pembrokeshire coast of Wales almost as frequently as the great northern diver, especially in Milford Haven and near the islands on the open coast ; the latter bird is a regular winter visitor and sometimes numerous.

DISTRIBUTION ABROAD : *Gavia arctica*, to treat of the species as a whole, has a wide range in the sub-arctic regions of the Old and New World, but it seems to the writer that to define its status as " a Holarctic species " [3] is apt to mislead, for the black-throated diver is certainly not so widely distributed as that term implies—including as it does the Palae-arctic and Nearctic zoological divisions of the earth's surface.

In this vast area three races have been generally accepted. *Gavia arctica arctica* has a breeding range which, in addition to Scotland, embraces Norway, Sweden and Finland, Kolguev, Waigatz and Novaya Zemlya, northern Germany and the Baltic States, and European Russia eastwards to the Olenek River—the most easterly limit as yet established by ringing. East of the Lena River (if I read the distribution map correctly in *Birds of the Soviet Union*, vol. ii, 1951, p. 254) occurs the eastern Siberian race, *Gavia arctica viridigularis* with a green rather than a purple throat, which, according to Professor Dementiev, extends as far as Anadyr Land and Kamchatka, but *not* beyond the Bering Strait. From Point Barrow in Alaska eastwards along the whole Arctic coast to Hudson Bay we find the Pacific black-throated diver *Gavia arctica pacifica*—a rather smaller species which has a paler back and is less prominently streaked on the sides of the neck.

These divers are all highly migratory. The Pacific race passes south in the winter to southern California ; the eastern Siberian race ranges down the coast in a southerly and south-easterly direction evidently through the Kurile Islands, while the typical subspecies *Gavia arctica arctica*, with which we are mainly concerned, winters—to quote Dementiev as translated by Mr. D. D. Harber [4]—" in small numbers on lakes in the interior of European Russia. Ringing has established that birds of the typical form, from even its most easterly limit (the Olenek) winter in the

[1] *Bird Life in Cornwall*, p. 183.   [2] *Birds of Pembrokeshire*, 1949.
[3] See *Handbook of British Birds*, vol. iv, p. 121.
[4] *British Birds*, xlviii, 1955, p. 272, review of *Birds of the Soviet Union*, vol. ii.

Baltic, thus making a journey of more than 6000 kilometres." The birds from the tundra first move north and then west along the coast on autumn migration, while those from European Russia migrate in winter partly to the Baltic and partly to the Black Sea, sometimes reaching the Mediterranean. The Russian authorities who edited this volume on the U.S.S.R., Professors Dementiev and Gladkov, have rejected the west Siberian race *suschkini* as unrecognizable.

The winter range of the European black-throated diver extends down the North Sea and English Channel, down the Atlantic coasts of France, Spain, and Portugal as far at any rate as the Straits of Gibraltar, where Irby[1] recorded that it is occasionally seen in winter. It seems probable that it passes through the Straits, assuming that it has not passed overland, as it has been reported on several occasions by Philip Munn from the Balearic Islands.[2] Two were shot in the Bay of Alcudia, Majorca, on 21st December 1928 and others seen at the same time. It is also reported from Formentera in spring.[3] More will be said of the somewhat complicated migrations of this bird under the next heading.

HABITS : The presence of the black-throated diver as a breeding species in Scotland to-day must be attributed to the bird's love of inland waters which are not too easily accessible. Otherwise there is small doubt that it would have to be added to the list of vanishing birds, so far as our own islands are concerned. Writing on the changes which have taken place in the status of our avifauna during the last hundred years, David Lack and W. B. Alexander observed that this diver has " somewhat decreased " through human persecution. Shore gunners have certainly taken their toll of our dwindling breeding stock, others have been caught in fishing nets, but worst of all are those thoughtless and selfish fishermen, mercifully not over-numerous, who stamp on the diver's eggs when they come across a nest in the remoter parts of the Scottish Highlands, a beastly habit to which Niall Rankin draws attention in his *Haunts of British Divers*. I am a keen trout fisherman myself and remember with what a thrill I first encountered a black-throated diver when fishing in the vicinity of Lake Assynt. To stamp on its eggs, and thus help to deprive others of the pleasure with which I watched that bird, and to contribute to its growing scarcity—must surely strike all but the imbecile as senseless vandalism. No protection laws will deter such fools, but luckily most fishermen are good sportsmen and often keen naturalists, though one black sheep among them can do a lot of harm, and gain the " fraternity " a rotten name.

It has been observed earlier in this essay that the black-throated diver —at any rate in Scotland—almost invariably selects a large sheet of water, preferably one dotted with islands, rather than the smaller hill lochs so

[1] *Ornithology of the Straits of Gibraltar*, 2nd ed., 1895, p. 305.
[2] *Novitates Zoologicae*, 1931, p. 130.
[3] *Beitr. zur Fortpflanzungsb. der Vögel*, 1927, p. 102.

appreciated by its relative the red-throated diver. Colonel Rankin, with his wide experience of these birds, considers the reason to lie principally in their method of feeding : " the black-throat does most of its fishing in fresh water, so prefers to have a large area around its actual nesting site, while the red-throat, being principally a sea-fisherman, likes to find a secluded stretch of water within easy reach of the coast ; thus the hill-lochs, which usually become smaller with increasing altitude, most nearly meet its requirements ". In his account of this diver he stresses the fact that not only is it restricted in Scotland to a comparatively out-of-the-way area but also within that area it is confined to certain lochs which conform to its special needs. Many a loch which would appear ideal for these divers in every other respect, is ignored owing to its tendency to rise rapidly with a sudden spate on its tributary burns, and swamp the diver's nest which is invariably—and of necessity—placed within a few yards of high-water mark. The black-throated diver chooses as its breeding place only those lochs whose depth seldom varies to any degree. Colonel Rankin makes this abundantly clear in the passage from which I have quoted. Where these conditions obtain in the wilds of Ross and Sutherland one may be reasonably sure of finding a pair of black-throats in possession.

It was on a day towards the end of May that Niall Rankin set out with a keeper in just such country as has been described, to search for a black-throat's nest, and the picture he so skilfully brings before our eyes is typical of the diver's habitat. With his permission, I quote from his *Haunts of British Divers* [1] with grateful acknowledgement :

The loch of the divers stands far removed from any human habitation. A little under two miles long and about half a mile wide, it is surrounded on all sides by a wide strip of boggy " flow " ground, so common in this part of Scotland. Covered with a variety of mosses and a prolific growth of the cotton grass (*Eriphorum*), this type of ground knows no drainage and holds every drop of moisture that ever falls upon it, so that walking is by no means a pleasure, and to cross it with a heavy load is tedious. Beyond this strip the ground rises steadily on three sides to form a high ridge all along the skyline. The fourth, or western side, is dominated by the great peaks of Canisp, Suilven, Cul Mhor and Cul Bheag, four isolated hills which, rising steeply from the low ground around them, form the western panarama for so many viewpoints in Sutherland. In this loch are several islands of varying size, heather-covered, with a few stunted birch trees. . . .

The flow ground is the summer home of many pairs of golden plover, whose plaintive whistle can be heard on all sides the whole day long ; here, too, many pairs of dunlin build their nests in the dry grassy tussocks. These come down to the shore to feed, making their presence known by electrifying the air with their unmistakable and penetrating trill. Whilst busily feeding along the beach or amongst the rocks a dunlin will suddenly perch himself on a large stone, open wide his bill

---

[1] Published by Collins, London, 1947, to whom my acknowledgements are likewise due and herewith accorded.

and let forth this piercing note, his whole body and feathers vibrating with the tremendous effort, as if the future of his little universe depended on it.

Sandpipers, too, add their lively notes to the general medley of sound. Green plover rear their young on the grassy knolls and several pairs of oyster-catchers lay their eggs on the shingle strands of scattered bays. Ravens pass to and fro across the loch, journeying to their homes amongst the rocks of the higher ridges, while an occasional greater black-backed gull will come inland to maraud any unguarded eggs or young. Curlew seek the lower level of the hills, their rich, liquid song being heard throughout the day, though they seldom seem to visit the shores of the loch.

Such is the nesting haunt of the black-throated diver whose nest Rankin was soon to discover on one of the islands in the loch. More will be said of its nesting in the appropriate place. Lonely and seldom visited the diver's loch may be, but whatever the weather—and it can be pretty severe at times even in June—the birds live among surroundings of incomparable beauty, to which they contribute in no small measure by their own presence. Long may they nest in peace.

Sixty-five years before Niall Rankin's book was published, the Moray naturalist, Charles St. John, drew attention in his *Natural History and Sport in Moray* (1882) to the danger besetting this species " owing to the value placed on both the skin and eggs by collectors ", which resulted in its becoming scarcer every year. A ruthless collector himself, St. John had a rare knowledge of the birds and beasts of the Scottish Highlands, and his account of the black-throated diver is as readable in 1960 as if it was penned but yesterday. After recording that " it breeds on Lochindorb, but on no other loch in the district ", St. John writes pleasingly of its status and habits in the days when its haunts were much less accessible than they are to-day :

On the northern lochs they breed very commonly, though generally only one pair frequents the same loch. Their eggs are two in number and invariably placed on some small low island and close to the water edge. During the month of May, on a fine calm evening, I have seen great numbers of these birds in the Bay of Tongue, in Sutherland. The rocks and hill-sides resound with their singular and wild cry, as they seem to be holding a noisy consultation as to their future movements. The cry is most peculiar and startling. I could scarcely persuade my companion, who was not used to these birds, that the sounds did not arise from a number of people shouting and laughing—till I pointed out to him the birds splashing and playing on the calm surface of the beautiful bay. As the evening advanced the divers gradually dispersed, going in pairs, after a few circles in the air over the bay, in a direct and rapid course, and at a great height over the surrounding mountains, each pair evidently wending their way to some well-known mountain loch, where their breeding quarters were decided upon. As each pair left the bay, the remaining birds seemed with one accord to salute their retiring companions with a universal shout of mingled laughter, howling, and every other earthly and unearthly cry. During their flight they frequently uttered a short, shrill bark-like cry. On a quiet day this bird seems to rise with some difficulty from a small lake but when the wind is high and the water rough they take flight with great readiness. Once on wing they fly very rapidly. When in the water they swim with great part of the body immersed, showing little more than the head and neck. If hemmed into a corner of the loch, or wounded, they will frequently dive, and on rising to the surface show little more than the top of the bill till they fancy that the danger is past. The only food that I ever saw in their stomachs when dead, has been a small fresh-water leech and other similar animals. I do not think that fish forms any part of their food ; [1] indeed though their bill is powerful and strong, it is rather adapted for catching shell-fish, aquatic snails, etc., than for holding fish.

St. John then goes on to describe the nest and eggs and ends with the statement about its growing scarcity which I have already quoted. His opinion that it was no enemy to trout is of particular interest, but Rankin and others have proved that it will take trout up to four inches in length. An analysis of stomach contents made by W. E. Collinge and quoted in *The Handbook* worked out as follows : fish 59·45 per cent., crustacea and annelids 23·4 per cent., marine mollusca 15·46 per cent., unidentifiable matter 1·69 per cent. Sea fish were small species of goby, sand-smelt, herring, sprat, etc. ; freshwater species were trout, perch, and roach ; crustacea included large numbers of crabs and prawns ; frogs, leeches and sea-slugs have also been recorded. No recent analysis has been made in this country and before the black-throated diver is condemned as injurious to trout, an investigation to that end should be undertaken when the diver is in its *summer* haunts, but *not* in Britain.

St. John wrote of the birds gathering in the Bay of Tongue preparatory to seeking their favourite lochs upon which to rear their small family. He made that observation in May, and although he does not mention the date it must have been early in the month, for by the end of May many pairs already have eggs. Jourdain has stated that eggs may often be found in the first half of May and occasionally in the first week. Eagle Clarke states that it is known to have arrived at its nesting haunts as early as 1st March but that surely must be an exceptional date.

In the last edition (1940) of *The Handbook* it was remarked that the display of the black-throated diver had not been recorded. Two years later it was witnessed on a sea-loch in Wester Ross by Ian D. Pennie, whose attention was attracted by four divers splashing and calling on the loch on the evening of 26th April. The four divers were seen chasing each other in a circle on the water with necks outstretched and making repeated cries which sounded like " kraa-wook " or " kraa-o wa-o ". On 29th April, on a calm bright evening some three-quarters of an hour before sunset, a pair of divers on the loch began calling—a mournful wail uttered three times and then a loud " kraa-wook " repeated six or seven times.

[1] In that supposition St. John was unfortunately wrong but it is significant that if they fed upon trout to any appreciable extent he would have been the first to note it.

After a minute's silence a second pair of birds appeared and settled on the water beside the first. The divers then " skated " (in a similar manner to mergansers but more slowly) in line four abreast along the water, with necks extended forwards and wings half raised and held stiffly arched away from the body; the birds repeated the call " kraa-wook " several times. The two pairs were then seen to swim quietly for about two hundred yards when the performance was repeated. One pair then rose and flew out of sight and nothing more was heard except a few wailing calls from the remaining pair, which were answered from the distance, presumably by the others.

BREEDING HABITS : Some reference to the breeding biology of the black-throated diver has been made in earlier paragraphs but it may now be discussed in more detail. St. John has stated that the bird invariably nests on islands in lochs but that is not the case; nests may be found on the shores of lochs as well as on islets in the middle. In Estonia Colonel Meiklejohn, whose field note-books I have in my possession, records finding nests on 27th and 28th May in different years, both of which were on small grassy headlands running out into the lakes. The nests in this case were depressions in flattened vegetation, close to the water's edge. The nest found by Rankin in one of the northern Scottish counties was on a small islet in the loch and to quote his own words :

The place where the eggs lay was hardly worthy of the title " nest ". Two yards from the water's edge was a clump of rushes, not the common bur-reed (*Sparganium ramosum*) . . . but the thin circular *Juncus communis*, which can be seen in any undrained meadow. The divers had flattened out the centre of the clump and lined this platform with moss and rush-stems. That was all there was to it, and there the hen had laid her two dark, olive-green eggs. . . . Behind the nest was a narrow belt of the giant woodrush (*Luzula sylvatica*) and then the ground rose steeply to the crown of the island, covered with boulders and woody heather.

The nest described appears to be typical of nests found in Scotland but other types of nest have been recorded—notably from Norway and Sweden. Dr. Blair writes :

" The paragraph on the breeding habits of this diver in *The Handbook* is badly worded, as it suggests that built-up nests of aquatic vegetation are frequent in Scandinavia. It should be corrected to read : ' In Scandinavia nests are frequently in shallow water as much as five to ten yards from land, and have been recorded as built up of aquatic vegetation '. Some of those ' five to ten yards from land ' were on hummocks, and could not be regarded as built up. Undoubted ' built-up ' nests do occur, however, and came under our notice on three occasions. One of these, examined by the late George Bolam on a Pasvik backwater, lay some five yards out from the land, in a dense, yard-high thicket of willows rooted in the shallows. It consisted of a large mass of weed and peat-mud—the latter perhaps dragged up with the weed—built solidly up from the river-bed in water some eight inches deep, and firmly attached to the nearby willows, on some decumbent branches of which it rested.   This grebe-like structure rose fully ten inches above the water-level, and was well protected against storm by the bushes that grew between it and the open water of the river.   The whole nest was naturally very damp ; but the slight depression on which the eggs lay was drier than might have been expected." A rather similar nest seen by Dr. Blair proved to be inaccessible.   It was well out from the shore, on the water-side fringe of a tangle of willows and birches, through which Dr. Blair found it impossible to force a way.   From the opposite shore, however, the nest could be studied through binoculars, and it had every appearance of being a built-up structure.   Another nest could also be regarded as " built-up ", though much less elaborate than either of the two just described.   Here the birds had added a " top-dressing " of water-plants to a hummock of peaty-mud which barely rose above the shallows a few paces from the swampy margin of the lake.   Excellent photographs of an unusual nest, taken in Sweden by Mr. M. D. England, have been published in *British Birds*.[1]   He describes the finding of a nest in June 1954 " built up on small rocks in the centre of a large lake where the water was shallow enough for a few reeds and two stunted trees to grow ".   In 1955 the black-throats nested again on the same tiny islet [2] within six feet of the previous nest.   " It was built, as before, of reeds and grasses, but instead of being more or less in the water was high above it on the completely dry part of the island.   In addition it was deeply cupped, and the bird must have had considerable difficulty in climbing into it." Mr. England considers it reasonable to conclude that at least one of the birds was the same as the 1954 pair.   As these divers are believed to remain constant to one another there is no reason to infer that they were not the identical pair which built the first nest.

Sweden abounds in the sort of lakes which the black-throated diver revels in and there I have been privileged to see them on some private waters [3] where they live completely undisturbed, and can be studied at leisure.   An authority on this bird in Sweden was the late Count Zedlitz, whose notes on the breeding biology of *Gavia (Colymbus) arctica* contains some highly interesting matter.   I am indebted to Miss P. M. Thomas of Tring Museum for the following translation of Count Zedlitz's work entitled " Nesting and other habits of the black-throated diver in Sweden ".[4]   He wrote as follows :

This beautiful large diver lives as a breeding bird on all the larger lakes of Sweden, it is only to be found on the coastal waters in the non-breeding season.   I

[1] *British Birds*, xlviii, 1955, p. 276 and Plate 40 facing p. 265.
[2] *British Birds*, l, 1957, p. 439, and Plate 63.
[3] On the estate belonging to Count Hamilton, Ovistrum, Falerum.
[4] *Beitr. Fortpfl. biol.*, 1924, pp. 4-6.

know of only one case where a pair bred on one of the rock islands off the east coast, that forming the game preserve of the noted animal painter Bruno Liljefors. But the reason for this exception is clear ! One of the old birds had been lamed by a shot during the migration season, its partner had remained faithful to him, and so they set up their nursery on a " Schär " surrounded by the salt sea. Inland the " Lummen ", as they are called here, infallibly appear within twenty-four hours of the ice melting on " their " lake, i.e. mostly in April, sometimes later, e.g. this spring on 6th May. Previous to this, they can be seen now and again in the sky looking out for open water. My breeding birds always arrive together and from the first day form as a matter of course a pair, which firmly convinces me that they like other large birds pair for life. My view, which as far as I know is new, is supported by the above-mentioned observations on the " Schär ".

The call-note of the male can be heard a kilometre away, mostly during the morning and evening, but sometimes during the day. Each pair has its own territory in which no other member of its species is tolerated during the breeding season. During the late summer, on the other hand, small companies of old and young of both sexes can regularly be seen. A certain percentage of birds are not breeding in any given year, but pass the summer in small groups or solitary. These are young birds of the preceding year. Between arrival and the commencement of the breeding season there is usually an interval of three to four weeks, sometimes more. The clutch always consists of two eggs. They are laid on the sand, mostly without any underlayer of any kind, if on rocky ground then there is sometimes a thin mat of twigs from the surrounding bushes ; I have never seen a nest built of material brought from any distance, though I have heard of nests made from reeds and rushes in places where such plants are plentiful. The breeding-place lies at first only a few metres from the edge of the water, as the bird is extremely helpless on land, it does not run but slides ! If the water level falls later in the spring, the distance naturally increases. I have never seen pairing in the water, as mentioned in old literature, and believe that to be an error in observation : courtship games take place in the water, during which the female swims in front now on her side, now almost on her back, turning somersaults in between, the male naturally becoming excited also, but the act of pairing I am convinced takes place on land just as in the case of *Colymbus stellatus* Pont.

About two days elapse between the laying of the first and second egg, during which one of the old birds sits on the single egg to guard it against crows and ravens. If the birds are robbed of their eggs during the first days, they sometimes lay again, but I have never observed this procedure when the eggs have already been incubated. Incubation of an egg lasts about twenty-nine days, and as the second egg is about forty-eight hours behind the first, the whole period would be about thirty-one days. If the old birds suffer much disturbance during the incubation period, they as a rule only hatch out the first chick and leave the spot ; the embryo in the second egg being deserted dies off. For this reason one frequently sees one chick rather than two with a pair of adult birds.

The parent birds sit alternately, the unoccupied one remaining near the nest and hastening to it as soon as danger threatens. During the first days the sitting bird will leave the nest and dive skilfully into the water on the approach of a boat, but as soon as the eggs are incubated, it sits firmly and will, if driven off the nest, encircle the intruder amid cries and splashings in an endeavour to entice him away. When the chicks are hatched out and danger approaches, the old birds will take them on their backs and swim away so swiftly that a rowing boat cannot keep pace with them.   The chicks are first of all slaty-black, including the bare skin portions, the centre of the underside alone is lighter, more smoky-grey.   Both parents are untiring in their watchfulness and care of their young.   Growth is fairly slow, and I have found young not fully fledged as late as September.

Immediately the young are hatched, the male can be heard calling, if not so continuously as in spring.   This I take to be an expression of relief and pleasure, understandable enough after thirty-one days of unremitting anxiety.   If one has ever seen the fear of the old birds at the discovery of their nest, one can appreciate the joy of the paterfamilias as soon as he has won liberty for himself and his family on the broad lake.   A new proof that " song " has not for its origin sex stimulus alone !

Weird as are the usual cries of this diver, the late Maud Haviland (Mrs. Grindley) once heard it utter a beautiful modulated whistle which she took to be a love-call.

In the above account, Count Zedlitz mentions the efforts of the parents to entice an intruder from the vicinity of the nest by cries and splashings. To judge from records, an incubating black-throated diver rarely feigns injury, and that perhaps only if surprised.   Dr. H. M. S. Blair took one bird unawares, his approach being masked by the dense, tall scrub that grew nearly to the water's edge.   As he came unexpectedly into view hardly five yards from the nest, the diver flapped off, trailing her wings as if wounded, and occasionally rising half out of the water.   About twenty yards out, she stopped, and then floated with half-open wings, to all appearances completely helpless.   Although her actions suggested that she had been brooding for some time, her eggs proved to be only slightly incubated. A diver surprised on the nest by Abel Chapman also " performed a singular feat ", which is best described in Chapman's own words : [1]   " After flying thirty yards she suddenly collapsed, though I had not fired, and fell heavily on the water, to all appearance wing-broken.   There, for several seconds, she lay flapping helplessly on her side, and swimming round, as though paralyzed, in narrow circles."

The Seebohm collection of eggs in the British Museum contains a good series of Scottish-taken eggs, with others from Sweden, Lapland, and the Petchora River.   These eggs are well described [2] by Oates as follows :

Eggs of the divers are coarse in texture, but have a fair amount of gloss.   They are typically of a narrow oval shape, but long cylindrical and biconical specimens with both ends quite alike, are not uncommon.   The eggs of all *Colymbidae* resemble each other very closely, and size is the only character of any assistance in discriminating them.

---

[1] *Wild Norway*, p. 110.
[2] E. W. Oates, *Catalogue of Birds Eggs in the British Museum*, vol. i.

The ground colour varies considerably, ranging through dark olive-brown, umber brown and russet brown, to dark stone-colour or dull greenish-grey. The eggs are double spotted. The underlying or shell markings are inconspicuous small spots of purplish-grey or pale brown. The surface markings, consisting of spots and blotches, are inky-purple, purplish-brown, or even black. These are not usually of any great size, nor are they very thickly spread over the shell. They are, in most cases, distinct and well-defined and they are often more numerous round the larger end than elsewhere. On a few examples the markings at the larger end have a streaky appearance.

Oates gives measurements as 2·95 to 3·55 in. in length, and from 1·9 to 2·16 in. in breadth, presumably of the forty-three eggs which are catalogued, thirteen of which were taken overseas, the rest in Scotland. Jourdain's measurements of a hundred British eggs average 83·7 × 52·6 mm. Max. 90·6 × 50 and 89·1 × 56 mm. Min. 75·1 × 50·3 and 77·7 × 48·2 mm.

After nesting, family parties gather in the sea lochs and elsewhere round our coasts as has already been stated, but to what extent the Scottish breeding birds are migratory it is not easy to say ; for there is a decided movement southwards from the Continent, many more black-throated divers being seen on the move in the North Sea than we can claim as our own stock even if the whole Scottish population migrated, which they do not. Great Britain lies on the southern fringe of the breeding range and our lochs are seldom frozen like the inland waters of northern Europe. It must be from western Scandinavian countries that the birds which pass down the North Sea originate. Breeding is late in the far north of Norway. Dr. Blair records that the first black-throated divers to come inshore near Vadsö in 1926 was on 7th May. In that latitude nests rarely contained eggs before the middle of June and some clutches were not laid until the end of that month. These birds would not be ready to move south with their families before September at the earliest. In east Finmark this diver is very common and widely distributed ; Dr. Blair found it nesting on nearly every lake of any size and on the more sheltered bays of some of the wider reaches of the Pasvic such as Sundvand.

Ornithologists on the Continent are not agreed as to the route which the divers take when they leave the frozen lakes of northern Russia and western Siberia. Professor Dementiev held the view that they passed westwards along the shores of the Arctic Ocean to Scandinavia, while Dr. E. Schüz holds that their route in autumn is in a south-westerly direction, the birds flying *overland* towards the Black Sea and possibly the Caspian, the autumn passage following a clockwise path. Dr. Schüz draws attention to the large passage of black-throated divers past Rossitten in May, and records that well over a thousand have been caught in fishing nets and ringed. The recovery of seventy-three of these birds has enabled Dr. Schüz to come to the conclusions stated above. He believes that the birds which winter in the Black Sea area migrate northwards in spring to reach the Baltic whence they mainly turn eastwards to reach their breeding grounds in Siberia, while some remain to breed in Scandinavia. If Dr. Schüz's view is correct, then these black-throated divers which appear in severe weather off the east coast of Britain must be of Norwegian origin. The Heligoland naturalist Gätke saw it " pretty often " during the winter months off that once famous bird observatory, but he does not mention any migratory movements of note past the island. Its movements in Western Europe are still somewhat of a mystery but Dr. Schüz's investigations have thrown much light on its movements east of Rossitten and account for its rather surprising presence in the Black Sea area by a mass migration overland.

REFERENCES : Original Description : *Colymbus arcticus* Linnaeus, *Syst. Nat.*, 10th ed., 1758, p. 135 : Europe, restricted type locality Sweden.

PLATE 21   **RED-THROATED DIVER**

Gavia stellata (Pontoppidan)

Resident, breeding in Scotland on mainland and in many of the islands. Resident also in very small numbers in Ireland (Donegal). A Winter Visitor from overseas to all British coasts and estuaries and to some lochs ; also a Passage Migrant, especially down east coast of Britain, less so on west, in spring and autumn.

IDENTIFICATION : It should not be difficult to recognize this diver if a sufficiently clear view is obtained. 21 to 23 inches in total length, it is appreciably smaller than the great northern diver, and in winter dress it is easily identified by the white spots over the entire upper surface. It is approximately the same size as the black-throated diver, but its back is greyer and its neck is more slender. It has an elongated body of flattened shape, and being practically tailless, with the legs placed far back on the trunk, has a very characteristic appearance both on the water and when launched in the air. Its most marked character is the bill, which is noticeably uptilted, finer than in the black-throated diver and sharply pointed like all its family. In summer plumage its grey head and triangular red throat-patch (which may look black at a distance or in certain lights) save confusion with any of the other British divers.

Juvenile red-throated divers are spotted like the adults in winter but the spots are more grey than white.

In flight the wings are beaten rapidly, and the flight is direct and quite powerful. There is no white patch in the wing, which is such a conspicuous feature in the great crested grebe. The neck is carried outstretched as in the grebes and the feet are extended beyond the tail. A point usually emphasized in textbooks is the manner of carrying the head and neck during flight below the contour of the body, but this does not distinguish the divers from the grebes and in particular from the great crested, in which the head and neck are held at a similar angle to the body. Divers strike the water in the same manner as grebes, that is breast first and with considerable power. They do not break their impact with their feet as do the ducks; consequently they require plenty of space in which to land. The red-throated diver is able to descend on to a much smaller sheet of water than the other British divers are wont to frequent.

LOCAL DISTRIBUTION: The summer range in the British Isles is restricted to Scotland and a small area in Ireland. In the former country it does not breed on the mainland south of Argyll and the Mull of Kintyre on the west, but it nests regularly on Arran,[1] a few pairs frequenting some of the small hill-lochans, one of which lies over 1000 feet above the sea. It is reported to nest sparingly in Perthshire, but does not, so far as I know, breed anywhere in the Lowlands. Its stronghold on the Scottish mainland is in the county of Sutherland and there it is described as numerous, frequenting especially the more northern districts. It is of interest to read that Harvie-Brown and Macpherson considered the districts of Durness, Edderachyllis, and Assynt to be its headquarters. As it is perfectly satisfied with quite small lochs—" small dhu lochs where there are no fish ", to quote Dr. Kennedy—on which to breed, it has a better chance than the black-throated diver to increase its numbers, provided the foxes, which take such a toll of their numbers, are kept in check. It nests commonly in the Outer Hebrides. In the Shetlands it was maintaining its numbers well when *The Birds of Scotland* was published in 1953, and we learn from Mr. and Mrs. Venables [2] that the bird has increased in many districts —in fact the species now nests on over half the inhabited islands of Shetland and on a few of the smaller uninhabited ones. It is most numerous, according to the authorities named, in Unst, Yell, and North and West Mainland, but still rare south of Lerwick. In Orkney both Mainland and Hoy support a number of pairs, while odd pairs occur on three other islands of that group.[3] It nests on many of the islands of the Inner Hebrides.

The red-throated diver does not breed in England or Wales though it is the commonest of the divers off the coasts in winter and is a regular passage migrant in spring and autumn. More will be said on this point later in this essay. Its only breeding place in the British Isles outside Scotland is in Ireland and there, oddly enough, the bird has a most restricted range. My information comes from Major R. F. Ruttledge who wrote of the red-throated diver in the new *Birds of Ireland*: " This diver has bred, or attempted to breed (for its eggs were frequently robbed) in one district in Donegal since 1884. The place where it was originally found

---

[1] J. A. Gibson, *The Birds of the Island of Arran*, 1956.
[2] *Birds and Mammals of Shetland*, 1955.
[3] David Lack in *Ibis*, 1943, p. 12.

nesting continued in use, though alternative sites on nearby lochans have been chosen at times. In 1886 two pairs were nesting, and in 1948 at least two pairs in widely separated localities." As a winter visitor to Ireland the birds are found all round the coasts, though usually greatly outnumbered by the great northern, so Major Ruttledge states. Outside the breeding season it seldom wanders inland.

DISTRIBUTION ABROAD : Breeding both in the Nearctic and Palae-arctic Regions, the red-throated diver has a wide range in northern Europe which includes the British Isles, Franz Josef Land, Spitsbergen, Iceland, the Faeroe Islands, Bear Island, and Norway, Sweden, and Finland. In European Russia and in Asia it has an immense breeding area as shown on the small-scale map in the *Birds of the Soviet Union* (vol. ii, p. 245). The advisability of recognizing a distinct race (*squamata*) from Franz Josef Land and Spitsbergen is considered by Professor Dementiev to be doubtful and is left in abeyance. In Arctic North America the breeding range extends from northern Greenland westwards to Alaska, the Aleutian and Commander Islands, and the Bering Sea. Farther south in Canada we find it breeding in Newfoundland, Labrador, and Central Quebec, and in the west to British Columbia.

The winter range in Western Europe extends down the Atlantic coast of France, Spain, and Portugal certainly to the Straits of Gibraltar, where it has been reported to be common. I am less sure of its status in the Mediterranean despite what has been written without comment in our textbooks. When we survey the evidence there is very little. It is more likely to occur in the Adriatic and in the Black and Caspian Seas. There are specimens, it is true, from Algerian waters preserved in Paris and Milan Museums, and stragglers have been reported from Malta and Gozo. It has been observed off the coast of Minorca, Balearic Islands, in severe winters but only very rarely ; and at the other end of the Mediterranean it has been reported from " the lagoons of Lower Egypt " (von Heuglin) but that has never been substantiated and no specimen exists. My own opinion, after many winter voyages in the Mediterranean, is that it is exceedingly scarce in that latitude and can only be expected to occur so far south in exceptionally severe weather. Mr. Anthony Lambert includes it in his check-list of the birds of Greece as very rare and irregular. It figures in Dr. Kasparyan's Turkish list without qualification.

The Asiatic population of this diver reaches the Seas of China, Formosa and Japan in its winter range, while the birds from Canada, Arctic America, and Greenland migrate south along the whole Atlantic coast to reach the northern part of Florida and the Gulf of Mexico. On the Pacific side the divers reach, and winter, along the entire coast of California. A. C. Bent has stated [1] that the inland migration route of the red-throated diver includes the Great Lakes and follows the valleys of the large rivers, but

[1] *Life Histories of North American Diving Birds.*

it is eventually coastwise. The birds winter occasionally in the interior, where they can find large sheets of open water ; but the principal winter home of the species is at sea and it extends along practically the whole of both coasts of the United States during the cold weather.

HABITS : The decrease of the red-throated diver in the nineteenth century through constant persecution, when its eggs were plundered and its plumage sought for millinery purposes, was fortunately arrested in time, and its numbers have increased again since that shameful period in our history. Whether it has regained the status which it enjoyed prior to those days may be doubted, but in 1871 Robert Gray [1] was able to proclaim this diver as " a very common bird in the West of Scotland . . . found at all seasons of the year and permanently resident throughout the Hebrides ". A few years later, in 1885, William Yarrell and Howard Saunders wrote of its abundance in Scotland, " especially on the western side, at all seasons of the year, breeding in Sutherlandshire, and in a few other counties, as far south as the island of Arran ; and also in the Hebrides, Orkneys and Shetlands ".

Macgillivray, too, recorded the " great numbers " to be seen during the breeding season in Lewis, North Uist, and Benbecula " which are singularly intersected by arms of the sea and covered with pools and lakes ". In the Orkneys its headquarters were on Hoy, but it now nests on other islands of the group.

There is a distinct difference in the choice of breeding place between the red-throated and the black-throated divers. The latter choose small low islands on deep inland lochs, and for preference those with flat open shores rather than such as are precipitous or rock-bound.[2] The red-throated species for the most part shuns these big open lochs, selecting rather the margins of small tarns or even quite small pools, often at a considerable elevation, preferring, as Eagle-Clarke expressed it many years ago, more desolate spots than the black-throated diver.

Much the same description of its habitat in Iceland has been sent me by Dr. Gudmundsson who speaks of the red-throat as a fairly common and widely distributed bird in his country, mainly confined to the lowlands and valleys, where it occupies the smaller lakes and tarns and very occasionally calm rivers or river mouths. Even so, it is known to breed in a few places in the Central Highlands of Iceland including one locality in the very centre of the island 500 to 600 metres above sea-level. Here in Iceland it prefers lakes or tarns with some marginal vegetation, " even if these may contain no fish ". As a rule there is only one pair occupying a lake or tarn, but in a few places several pairs may breed together, forming small colonies.

Now cross the Atlantic and view the home of the red-throated diver

[1] *Birds of the West of Scotland.*
[2] As described by James Wilson in notes to Robert Gray.

as described by Cleveland Bent—a naturalist who has an eye for beauty as well as birds and a facile pen to describe it :

> The rugged coast of Labrador, with its chain of rocky islands, ice-bound for nine months of the year and enveloped in fog or swept by chilling blasts from drifting icebergs during most of the other three, seems bleak and forbidding enough, as we pick our way through the narrow channels back of the outer islands. But in the interior it is different. Though the summer is short, the sun is high in the heavens and the days are long ; the abundant moisture in the air stimulates the growth of vegetation ; the snow disappears rapidly and the verdure of spring follows quickly in the wake of retreating winter. . . . Back from the rocky coast only a short distance the rolling hills are softly carpeted with deep mosses, covered with fresh verdure and dotted with blooming wild flowers in great variety and profusion. Here among the thousands of small lakes and ponds in the sheltered hollows, fed with the water from melting snow and studded with little islands, the red-throated loons find a congenial summer home and hither they come as soon as the fetters of winter are unlocked. We saw them everywhere along both the south and north almost daily flying inland to the lakes or even about the little ponds on the islands.

In its daily behaviour there is not much difference between this and our other resident diver, which has been discussed already at some length. It far outnumbers the black-throated species in our islands, both as a breeding bird and as a winter visitor. Owing to its preponderance in numbers it is the much better known of the two and is connected with sundry superstitions. Its cry is said to portend rain, and in certain parts the bird is known as the rain goose. Robert Gray has recorded that these cries are so full of melancholy, when heard echoing in the midst of the rock-bound Hebridean lakes, that few persons hearing them once would ever desire their repetition. He added that " should the eggs be taken, the poor creatures seem to feel the deprivation with unusual keenness and give expression to their grief—for sorrow I really believe it to be—in loud lamentations ". For that reason many of the natives would never think of robbing the birds. That the rain superstition is not entirely groundless may be gathered from an incident which befell Gray one evening in the Outer Hebrides which he relates as follows :

> On the 1st of August 1870, I witnessed a curious scene at Lochmaddy, in the island of North Uist, about nine o'clock in the evening. The air was remarkably still and sultry, and frequent peals of thunder in the distance were the only sounds that for a time broke upon the irksome quiet that otherwise prevailed. At length the thunder, on becoming louder, seemed to waken up the divers on various lochs within sight of where I stood, and first one pair, then another, rose high into the air, and flew round in circles, until there must have been twenty or thirty in all. After a time they settled in one of the creeks about half a mile to the eastward, and then there arose a wild and unearthly noise from the birds, which I cannot describe. It is, in fact, a sound which no one can ever forget after once hearing it, especially in these Hebridean solitudes where it acquires its full emphasis. Next morning about four o'clock, while bowling along towards the sound of Benbecula in the face of a

PLATE 21

RED-THROATED DIVER
Gavia stellata (Pontoppidan)

rain-cloud such as I wish never to see again, several of the birds passed us overhead at a considerable height, uttering the same cries, which might be likened to a person in despair making a last shout for help when no help is near.

Those who have read E. W. Nelson's *Report upon Natural History Collections in Alaska* (1887) may recollect that he refers to the red-throated diver's capacity in spring of foretelling (with cranes) an approaching storm by the increased repetition and vehemence of their cries. Nelson interpreted the ordinary call of this diver as " gr-r-ga, gr-r, gr-r-ga, ga, gr-r "; the harsh notes, rising everywhere from the marshes during the entire twenty-four hours, are one of the most characteristic sounds to greet the ear in spring in the northern wilds.

In an earlier statement I have mentioned that there is not much difference in the general behaviour of this diver and the black-throated species, but that certainly needs qualifying in some respects. Within the last few years there has been some correspondence in *British Birds* relating instances when the red-throated diver has been seen to take off from the ground—a feat of which the black-throated species is surely incapable. As this must be a very unusual occurrence I quote the instances as they were recorded. On 13th January 1951 at the estuary of the river Stour in Kent, Mr. Dennis Harle[1] came upon a red-throated diver sitting about ten yards from the water's edge and level with it. On his closer approach the bird took off from the sand with little difficulty. It first raised itself and then with rapidly beating wings and flailing feet, it pattered over the sand, becoming airborne within the space of six yards. It flew strongly out to sea and returned to the exact spot it had vacated. Mr. Harle observed that on landing the legs were trailing and held stiffly out from its tail, the breast hitting the ground in the same way as when landing on water. No less than four times was this repeated, the bird returning within eighty yards of where it was first flushed before it finally flew out to sea. In each case it rose from the ground. The second instance occurred on 25th February of the same year, 1951, and was reported by Mr. D. B. Peakall,[2] who disturbed a red-throated diver apparently sleeping on a bank at Hornsea Mere, Yorkshire. On being approached the bird took a few clumsy steps forward and then flew up from the ground although within ten feet of the water's edge.

On those occasions when the water recedes before the eggs are hatched, the red-throated diver is less at a disadvantage than the other divers would be in similar circumstances, for of the several species already discussed *Gavia stellata* is the least clumsy on land. Even so it cannot normally walk in the usually accepted manner, but, as Bernard Tucker has described, " usually progresses by heaving itself forward in a succession of jerks by strokes of legs and may aid itself with wings if alarmed ". A rather contrary

[1] *British Birds*, xlv, 1952, p. 331.   [2] *Op. cit.*, xlvi, 1953, p. 110.

opinion was expressed by George Bolam in his book *The Birds of Northumberland and the Eastern Borders*. Coming one day upon a red-throated diver which had evidently been resting on the shore, the tide having receded, he was surprised to see it rise from some seaweed on the rocks several yards from the water " and scuttle towards that element in a tolerably upright attitude, at a very fair pace, and with a very grebe-like gait ". There are other known instances when this diver has been seen to " walk ", notably by that well-known naturalist Caton Haig whose diaries I have seen at the British Museum. Sir Julian Huxley [1] made some interesting observations on this subject in Spitsbergen when with the Oxford University Expedition in 1921.

BREEDING HABITS : Although May is far advanced in the northern wilds of Alaska before the divers return to their breeding haunts, and fresh eggs are found in July, we can expect their arrival on our Scottish lochs in the month of April or thereabouts. At the same time these birds which have wintered around our own coasts from overseas take their departure, the return passage north having been noted between March and May, though some even linger till June. In the absence of ringed birds to prove the point, it is generally believed that the considerable Iceland population of red-throated divers spend the winter along the coasts of Britain and farther south, and no doubt these are the birds which have been observed passing up the East Anglian coast in spring. Ticehurst records in his *History of the Birds of Suffolk* that F. M. Ogilvie [2] saw large numbers moving north on 2nd May 1892, " at least forty birds flying high, in flocks of three or four individuals, and again on 5th May twenty more ; most had white throats but some were in breeding dress ". Recent confirmation comes from Dr. Evelyn Baxter and Miss Rintoul who frequently watched for whole days at the East Neuk of Fife divers going north in spring and south in autumn. " They fly past in ones and twos, some passing on, others alighting in the sea for a short time, until there is a considerable gathering when they are up and off ". The same passage has been remarked in Ayrshire and past the island of Tiree among many similar observations.

Those birds which breed in colder climates than the British Isles—the population of Iceland and Greenland may be taken as examples—reach their home waters in April and May respectively. At first they frequent the fjords and estuaries, if such exist, returning to their breeding lakes as soon as they become free from ice. Not until late May, or more commonly in early June, are eggs laid in Iceland. In Greenland Dr. Salomonsen tells us there is a difference of three to four weeks between their arrival dates in the south and in the area from Scoresby Sound northward to Peary Land. " When the divers arrive in the High Arctic the sea

[1] *British Birds*, xvi, 1922, pp. 34-45 (esp. pp. 44-45).
[2] Author of *Field Observations on British Birds*.

is still covered with ice and the freshwater lakes are still frozen over. In the first period after their arrival in these regions the divers resort to the clearings between the ice-fields, the crevices in the tidal zone just off the ice-foot and the open water at the outlets of glacier streams. When the lakes thaw they gradually disappear from the coast."

Our own divers have no such severe conditions with which to contend, but even so it is usually late in May when eggs may be found. Jourdain has recorded 9th May as an exceptional date in Scotland, while in Iceland, Finmark, and Finland they rarely lay before the end of the first week of June, continuing sometimes into July. In the Vadsö district of East Finmark Dr. Blair records finding fresh eggs between 7th June and 4th July and the first young birds were not seen before the 12th. E. C. Stuart Baker and Dr. I. Hortling record finding the first clutch of eggs in the north of Finnish Lapland on 14th June. On one of the larger islands Hortling, Baker, and General Beetham [1] found a colony of between fifty and sixty pairs, of which fully thirty pairs were breeding on one small lake, certainly not two hundred yards long. In the MS. notes which he left me Colonel R. F. Meiklejohn mentions finding eggs on Karlö Island in Finland on 16th June " on a small islet in an inland lake ", and another nest with two eggs on a grassy headland running out into Lake Onega, U.S.S.R., on 9th June. In Spitsbergen D. B. Keith found what appears to be an early egg on 20th June. The egg was taken by skuas and another nest constructed which contained two eggs on 10th July. One egg hatched on 5th August. These dates are mentioned to show how protracted the breeding season of the red-throated diver can be, and that in Western Europe alone.

The birds in the High Arctic must await the thawing of the lakes and ponds before egg-laying is possible, but contrary to expectations—in Greenland at any rate—there is no essential difference in the breeding season from south to north unless the lakes thaw out particularly late. A newly laid clutch has been found in Peary Land on 28th June, two days later than the date on which Seebohm and Harvie-Brown took a clutch on the Petchora River (68° N.). It is of interest to compare these dates with those, varying between 7th and 20th July, when Henry Seebohm took eggs of the red-throated diver on the Yenesei River (71° 30′ N.), as instanced by his series in the British Museum egg-collection at Cromwell Road.

In his report on the birds collected in northern Alaska [2] in 1951-52, James W. Bee records finding three pairs of red-throated loons nesting among sedges along the edges of small lakes—some as small as 100 × 40 ft. —in the vicinity of Kaolak River, south-west of Point Barrow. On 13th July two nests each held two eggs approximately half incubated. One

---

[1] " Bird notes on a trip to Lapland ", in *Ibis*. 1932, p. 116.
[2] *University of Kansas Publications, Museum of Nat. Hist.*, vol. x, No. 5, pp. 163-211, March 12, 1958.

nest and that of an Arctic tern were about thirty feet apart on an island in the centre of the lake. The loons arrived and departed from the lake without molestation by the terns, but whenever a human being approached the lake a tern would fly 300 feet out on the lake to meet him. On another small lake 200 × 40 ft. wide, bordered by exceptionally high sedges, a pair of loons had young on 29th July. Attention was called to the birds by their guttural notes and by a sound resembling the meowing of a cat. If approached the loons dived with a splash " suggesting the sound made by a beaver as it strikes its tail against the water before submerging ". A loud high-pitched shriek-like call was given just before diving. They remained under water for about twenty seconds, came to the surface and repeated the behaviour.

The normal clutch of this diver consists of two eggs, very rarely three. They are smaller than the eggs of the black-throated diver, and have more gloss on the surface. The ground colour varies considerably in both species. In fact all the divers lay very similar eggs which, as Eugene W. Oates declared in vol. i of the *Catalogue of the Collection of Birds' Eggs in the British Museum*, can only be certainly distinguished by their size. He observes that the ground colour varies considerably, ranging through dark olive brown, umber brown, and russet brown, to dark stone colour or dull greenish-grey. The eggs he describes as " double-spotted ". The underlying or shell markings are inconspicuous small spots of a purplish-grey or pale brown. The surface markings, consisting of spots and blotches, are inky-purple, purplish brown, or even black. These are not usually of any great size, nor are they very thickly spread over the shell. They are, in most cases, distinct and well defined, and they are often more numerous round the larger end than elsewhere. On a few examples the markings at the larger end have a streaky appearance : 100 eggs of the red-throated diver taken in Britain and measured by F. C. R. Jourdain averaged 74·96 × 48·32 mm. Max. 82·5 × 45 and 80·4 × 48·7 mm. Min. 66·7 × 43·7 and 65 × 42 mm. The measurements (by A. C. Bent) of fifty-eight eggs in the United States National Museum average 72·5 × 45 mm. The period of incubation varies to some extent, apparently between twenty-four and twenty-nine days. Twenty-six days as ascertained by D. B. Keith in North East Land seems to have been based on very close observation.

We have seen that the nest of this diver may be placed in different situations. The bird is not dependent, as is the black-throated diver, on small islands in large lakes, but prefers throughout its range to breed on small tarns or even on small sedge-choked pools such as Dr. Blair has described in Finmark—though an area " no more than three yards in diameter " must surely be a record. Gudmundsson in Iceland considers the nest very similar to that of the great northern diver but smaller (diameter 27-28 cm., depth 4-5·5 cm.) and often lined with somewhat larger quantities of wet moss or other vegetable matter. It is always placed near to the edge of the water and the worn pathway leading from the nest to the water is usually very conspicuous. Colonel Meiklejohn found nests which he described as " sometimes a mere depression in grass or vegetation, at others just a heap of aquatic vegetable matter ".

Dr. Finn Salomonsen has given an excellent account of the red-throated diver's nesting habits in Greenland, and after describing its preferences in habitat continues :

The breeding-pond constitutes the territory of the pair and no other pair is permitted to breed there. I have never observed colonial nesting in Greenland. Many pairs may however congregate at the feeding-places in the sea and fjords. Other species of water birds are tolerated on the breeding place of the diver and very often a red-necked phalarope keeps it company. Sometimes even a mallard or a long-tailed duck nests at the pool besides the phalarope. In lakes of larger size I have occasionally found two pairs of red-throated divers, one breeding at either end of the lake. The pair does not restrict itself to the breeding-pond but often visits other ponds and lakes in the vicinity, no doubt in order to feed. The majority appear to be dependent on the sea for food. There is a considerable traffic in the air between the breeding-places and the fjords. Here the divers feed either in quiet bays or near the shore, often many in company. These movements are most pronounced at night. In the fertile Maligiak at the head of Ikertôk fjord I noticed during one night in early August more than a hundred birds heading towards the fjord either singly or in flocks of six to eight individuals.

Dr. Salomonsen [1] then gives a brief résumé of the courtship display,[2] which usually takes place on the water at the breeding pool or at a quiet beach, and is very often carried out at night. He describes it as a spectacular performance, " most elaborate and varied ". The following phases can as a rule be distinguished : An introductory pursuit of the partner on the water, with the body and neck partly submerged while the bill points obliquely upward and the bird utters peculiar long-drawn-out plaintive shrieks, like *ooh-eeh*. Subsequently a splash-dive followed by a loud outburst of growls and snarls mixed with the ordinary notes (*kruck*) and the mewing shrieks mentioned above. Finally a phase in which a normal swimming position is adopted by both birds but with their necks extended and held stiff and vertical. Dr. Salomonsen states that up to five birds may take place in this display, some of them only as passive spectators. The display continues during the whole summer and was witnessed as late as 5th August. The well-known naturalist Alw. Pedersen has observed a special courtship flight so high up in the air as to be almost invisible, with strong cackling notes uttered simultaneously. It ceases when brooding

[1] *Grønlands Fugle*, pp. 19-20.

[2] The sexual behaviour of the red-throated diver has been investigated in Spitsbergen in 1921 by Dr. Julian Huxley and Professor G. J. van Oordt (*British Birds*, xvi, 1922, pp. 34-46) and later by Mr. D. B. Keith in North East Land, the second largest island of the Spitsbergen Archipelago (*British Birds*, 1937, pp. 66-81). The subject was developed by Sir Julian Huxley in a lengthy review in the *Journal of the Linnaean Society*, 1923, pp. 253-292.

commences. A first-hand account of the courtship display, as observed in Finnish Lapland in June 1931 by Dr. Ivar Hortling, E. C. Stuart Baker,[1] and General R. M. Betham, was published in the *Ibis* in the year following. It will be remembered that these ornithologists had discovered a colony of red-throated divers which numbered between fifty and sixty pairs which gave an exceptional opportunity for the observers to see what happens. They thus describe the ceremony :

The courtship displays of these birds are really very extraordinary, the more so in a colony, as the impulse to display seems to seize almost every bird in unison. The males—and in some cases the females too—arise as high out of the water as they can, keeping in an upright position and pointing the head down close to the breast. Whilst in this position the birds—generally two males, but occasionally a female and male—keep within a few inches of one another, both bowing energetically and at intervals uttering a short croak which seems to be made in unison with each bow. Gradually the bowing and croaking get faster and faster until finally the bowing ceases and the heads are held perfectly vertical, whilst a long, roaring chorus of loud notes is emitted by the birds in rapid succession. These courtship displays and choruses seem to take place every two or three hours, though occasionally odd displays may be indulged in by individual birds. After the upright positions and choruses are abandoned, the birds race round on the top of the water, whipping it with their wings as they progress, but never actually leaving it. Whilst they thus race round each other in circles, a few short croaks are uttered, with an occasional very loud high note, but there is no concerted chorus, as when several birds are occupied in the upright courtship position. On one occasion we woke just about midnight because of an exceptionally loud chorus of these birds, the lake being distant from our sleeping hut less than a quarter of a mile.

The young red-throated diver when first hatched is completely covered with short, thick, dark-brown down. As it advances in age and size these colours become paler, particularly on the underparts. According to A. C. Bent their development is very slow. The plumage of the juvenile bird is not attractive as in the grebes ; the head and neck are mottled with mouse grey and a dirty shade of white, the grey predominating on the crown and throat ; the upperparts are dusky mottled with " drab-grey " spots or V-shaped markings. In this dress the young diver remains with little decided change throughout the winter, except for individual variation in the size and shape of the markings described. The V-shaped markings are, in Bent's opinion, characteristic of the first winter plumage ; they are never seen in any subsequent winter plumage and may be regarded as a sign of immaturity. In Alaska Edward Nelson observed that the young are led to the streams, large lakes, or sea coast as soon as they are able to follow the parents. In that northern land August sees all upon the wing except an occasional late bird, and from 15th September to the end of the month they gradually become more and more scarce until only a very few can be found on 1st October.

[1] At the time Hon. Secretary and Treasurer of the B.O.U.

It is very difficult to say how far from their home lochs the British breeding birds go in winter. There are red-throated divers in numbers around our coast and we hear of them often on inland waters where they certainly do not breed, as on Loch Skene, 1700 feet above the Grey Mare's Tail in Dumfriesshire, and on St. Mary's Loch near Selkirk. They are very common in the big estuaries and in particular in the Firth of Tay and the Forth, but to what extent these are our own stock it is impossible to define, with so many " foreigners " from Iceland, Spitsbergen, and beyond to swell the numbers. Young of the year are likely to go farther afield than their parents, judging by the habits of some other species ; but it is not an easy bird to ring and the returns would be exceedingly rare if the results of ringing other diving birds are anything to go by. Fortunately the traffic in their skins has practically ceased to exist and it has certainly increased of recent years in its breeding haunts in Britain. How strange that it is so rare in Ireland—the latitude being perhaps just too far south.

REFERENCES : Original Description. *Colymbus stellatus* Pontoppidan, *Danske Atlas*, vol. i, 1763, p. 621, pl. 62 : Denmark.

Order COLUMBIFORMES

Sub-order COLUMBAE

Family COLUMBIDAE

Genus *COLUMBA* Linnaeus

PLATE 22 **WOOD-PIGEON**

Columba palumbus palumbus

A Resident throughout Britain excluding the Shetland Islands ; a
Winter Visitor and Passage Migrant. The origin of the winter flocks
into England is still not satisfactorily settled (though the writer has
his own opinions) nor that of the Irish winter immigrant.

IDENTIFICATION : The wood-pigeon, or ring-dove, requires little introduction, so familiar is it both to country and town folk in these islands. As
Mr. Lodge's painting shows it is rather heavily built and gives the impression of being plump and well fed. The head is bluish-grey and the
general colour is slate-grey, the neck glossed with violet and green and a
small but conspicuous white patch on either side. The mantle is more
brownish ; the wing-coverts grey broadly edged with white, forming a
very conspicuous bar when the wing is open. The tail is blackish and the
rump slate-grey. The underparts are rich vinous purple merging into pale
ash-grey on the belly ; the flanks and ventral region are bluish ash-grey ;
the bill is pink basally, yellow towards the tip which is horn colour ; the
legs and feet are coral-red tinged with mauve. The eye is pale straw
colour. Its total length is 16-17 inches ; the male is rather larger than the
female.

Immature birds, much duller in their plumage than their parents,
have no white patch on the sides of the neck and care must be taken not to
confuse them with stock doves, though the latter is a much smaller bird.
After the first moult the young wood-pigeon assumes the plumage of the
adult bird, but the moult takes place very late in the year.

The five-note coo-ing of the wood-pigeon is a very familiar sound in
our woods, and must be familiar even to those who dwell in towns.

LOCAL DISTRIBUTION : Throughout the whole of England and Wales
the wood-pigeon is an abundant breeding species wherever there are woodlands, its numbers being greatly augmented during the winter months by
immigrants, whether or not from overseas has been disputed.

In Scotland the position of the wood-pigeon to-day was well summed
up by Dr. Baxter and Miss Rintoul in 1953 when they wrote that as a

PLATE 22

WOOD-PIGEON
Columba palumbus palumbus Linnaeus

PLATE 22

WOOD-PIGEON
Columba palumbus palumbus Linnaeus

result of the increase of plantations which provides more nesting places, the improvement in agriculture which furnishes more food, and the destruction of raptorial birds which removes a natural check to its increase, the wood-pigeon has become very much more plentiful as a breeding bird in the last 140 years. This pigeon's increase in southern Scotland has been especially marked and though it is naturally more scarce in the north-west Highlands and Islands it breeds on many of the Inner Hebrides. Within recent years it has been reported as common on Bute, Arran, Islay, Jura, and Gigha ; and nesting, though not commonly, on Mull and Skye, to specify some of its haunts in that area. In the north-east of Scotland the wood-pigeon is a common breeding bird, especially in Caithness in all suitable localities. In the Outer Hebrides it breeds in Lewis ; in the Shetlands it has been recorded as nesting " of late years " about Kergord.[1] In Orkney it breeds abundantly in the woods of Mainland and Rousay and to some extent in two other islands recently colonized.

Its distribution in Ireland [2] also appears to be on the increase according to Major R. F. Ruttledge, who considers it one of Ireland's most common and widespread birds. Wherever there are woods of any size it is to be found, and to-day it is resident on Achill Island in very small numbers. Large flocks of immigrant wood-pigeons, we are told, come to Ireland for the winter, their numbers varying from year to year ; the majority are believed to be of Continental origin.

DISTRIBUTION ABROAD : The Continental range of the wood-pigeon is wide, extending as it does in Northern Europe to about 64° N. in Norway and Sweden and to 61° N. in Finland and Russia. In the whole of Central and Southern Europe it is widespread, reaching the Mediterranean and many of its islands in the typical form. Thus we find no distinctions apparent between European continental specimens and those from the Balearic Islands, where it is mainly a summer visitor, a few remaining throughout the year, the Italian islands of Sicily and Sardinia, Corsica, Crete, and Cyprus, in the last two of which it is restricted to the mountain forests. In *The Handbook of British Birds* Malta is included in the breeding range. Anyone familiar with that island—or the Maltese—will realize that no wood-pigeon would have a chance to nest in Malta. I have been unable to trace the origin of that statement. North and east of Cyprus the wood-pigeon breeds in Syria and Iraq as well as in Asia Minor.

A number of recognized subspecies have been described from the following localities or areas : *C. p. maderensis* : Madeira, *C. p. azorica* : Azores, *C. p. excelsa* Morocco, Algeria, and Tunisia, *C. p. casiotis* : from western Himalayas—Pakistan, Afghanistan, and Kashmir, and *C. p. iranica* : Persia as recognized by Russian ornithologists. It is simply *nonsense* to consider the two fine pigeons of the Canary archipelago,

[1] *The Birds of Scotland*, vol. ii, p. 518.
[2] *Birds of Ireland*, p. 279.

C. bollii and *C. junoniae*, or the large laurel pigeon of Madeira *C. trocaz* as subspecies of *C. palumbus*.

In the *Birds of the Soviet Union* it is difficult to make out the range of *C. p. casiotis* and the eastern extent of *C. palumbus palumbus* from the small-scale map in Vol. ii, p. 34 ; but apparently the typical subspecies is considered to range at least as far east as the Ural Mountains and Trans-caspia. The author of the section dealing with Columbiformes in the Russian volumes—R. N. Meklenburtsev—states that the wood-pigeon has declined in numbers in the Soviet Union owing to timber felling and perhaps over-shooting, and that flocks of hundreds are no longer to be seen as in former days.

The typical race of wood-pigeon is said to be an irregular but not infrequent passage migrant to the Faeroe Islands,[1] and it is reported to have wandered to Iceland [2] rarely and Spitsbergen.[3]

Habits : The wood-pigeon has become so abundant in Great Britain that it is now a serious menace to agriculture and various steps, of which more will be said later, have been taken by the Agricultural Research Council to keep its numbers in control. Normally dependent on wooded country, it colonizes plantations almost as soon as they spring up, feeding largely on cultivated fields and taking a heavy toll of cereals.

In earlier days the writer spent a great many months shooting on the Norfolk and Suffolk borders and the hordes of wood-pigeons which appeared in the woods in January or earlier, reputed to have come in from overseas, beggared description. Writing of the bird in Suffolk from many years' experience the late Claud Ticehurst stated [4] that " late in the autumn or winter foreign birds arrive from overseas and increase the pigeon population everywhere—usually it is not before the latter part of October that these foreign flocks arrive and often not before the end of November, while sometimes masses herald in, or accompany, hard weather and snow ". He emphasized the damage done by these " blue clouds of pigeons which, unable to get food in the woods, take to these agricultural fields where green crops are grown " and instances a seven-acre field of Brussels sprouts " completely eaten up in a week or two—the whole crop ruined ". Organized shoots to combat this pest have little result and certainly to-day, with the price of cartridges what it is, would not be an economic proposition. These overseas pigeons—if indeed they *do* come from overseas—are clever at eluding the guns and soon become extremely wary, but when they fall to the gun and their crops are examined, there is ample proof of the damage they can do. Ticehurst quite sensibly wrote that with so omnivorous a

---

[1] K. Williamson, *The Atlantic Islands*, p. 322.

[2] Eagle Clarke in Howard Saunders's *Manual* (3rd edition), p. 785.

[3] F. C. R. Jourdain in *The Handbook of British Birds*, but not mentioned in his list of birds of Spitsbergen in *Ibis*, 1922, pp. 161-179.

[4] C. B. Ticehurst, *History of the Birds of Suffolk*, p. 468.

feeder as the wood-pigeon a list of foods which the bird eats is hardly worth providing [1]—but to show the damage that they can do, he records extracting 117 beans out of one bird's crop! Collinge in his analysis of 428 cases found that 96·5 per cent. was vegetable food, 3·5 animal—the latter made up of earth-worms, slugs, snails, and insects. In its favour it should be noted that a great many seeds of injurious weeds and plants are consumed, including, as W. H. Hudson reminds us, an immense quantity of seeds of charlock, a most harmful weed ; but this is not likely to weigh much with the farmer who sees his peas and beans disappearing at an alarming rate. Beech-nuts, hazel-nuts, and acorns are consumed in vast quantities when available ; and to some extent they influence the duration of the pigeons' sojourn in a given area. When there is a poor crop of beech-mast or of acorns the pigeons take their departure from the district earlier than would otherwise be the case.

Shooting men in East Anglia—and no doubt in other parts of the country—used often to state that they could distinguish between the winter flocks which invaded the counties in hard weather and the breeding stock, and so prevalent was the idea that two different pigeons were involved that both H. F. Witherby [2] and B. B. Rivière [3] took up the challenge and were able to prove that much of the confusion arose owing to some observers mistaking birds which had not fully moulted into first winter plumage and were in consequence in various stages of moult. The lack of white on the neck is a sign of *youth*. The myth that continental birds are larger and heavier can also be easily exploded. Quite apart from the question of moult, there is an individual variation in wood-pigeons which cannot be explained by their distribution, nor are these oversea visitors darker in plumage as some would maintain. The birds which we can see any day in the London parks, so tame that when feeding with the sparrows they just run out of one's path, will often appear to be very large when compared with their country cousins, but that is in truth but an optical delusion, for when food is plentiful, as it is in the vicinity of our farmhouse in Scotland, the wood-pigeons fare well and most certainly show it in their ample figures.

In many authoritative books on British birds the name wood-pigeon is sunk in favour of ring-dove. T. A. Coward's little book is a case in point in which that author points out the correctness of the term as applied to the subject of this essay, rather than to the domesticated dove with a black ring on its neck which occasionally usurps it. Our ring-dove is a very portly bird which, as Coward affirms, " walks, perches and bows with

[1] This has now been done in great detail for the Oxford area and been published by M. K. Colquhoun in the Agricultural Research Council's Report, Series No. 10, H.M. Stationary Office, 1951. See Tables 23 and 24 facing p. 32.

[2] *British Birds*, x, 1917, p. 273.

[3] *Field*, 17th Feb. 1917, p. 263.

swelled neck and fanned tail like a dovecot bird but has certain characters and habits of its own ". As I write this essay, at the end of May, a pair are nesting in a thick rhododendron beneath my study window, where they may be watched at leisure. Their display flight is particularly arresting at this time of year, as the bird rises some fifty feet and then glides down to rise again in undulating motion with stiff pinions and fanned tail.

The noise made by the wings at the summit of the ascent, described as a " vigorous clap " in *The Handbook*, elicited a footnote from B. W. Tucker that the wing-clapping of the wood-pigeon has been widely ascribed to the striking of the wings over the back, a theory which has been disputed by Coward and others, who consider that the sound is due to the particularly forcible down-stroke of the wing analogous to the crack of a whip.

In summer dress the wood-pigeon is astonishingly beautiful, the patch on the sides of the neck glistening white, the head more blue than grey and the breast a delicate vinous, while the iridescent violet and green feathers of the neck add immeasurably to its charm. As the bird spreads its wings the white patches on the coverts appear like magic, only to disappear completely when the wings are folded again. That observant naturalist W. H. Hudson drew attention to its graceful dignity, its deliberate motions on the ground contrasting with the hurried, eager manner of the stock-dove and rock-dove; and he remarked how its voice gains greatly in beauty in the breeding season, though it may be heard in favourable weather throughout the year, " the love song of the ring-dove being one of the woodland sounds that never fail to delight the ear ". He charmingly describes its " love dance ", to which brief reference is made above, observing that all doves have performances of this kind and that of the wood-pigeon is not the least graceful :

On the ground, or on a branch, he makes his curious display before the female, approaching her with lowered head, and with throat and neck puffed out, in a succession of little hops, spreading his tail fanwise, and flirting his wings so as to display their white bars. All at once he quits his stand, and rising in the air to a height of thirty or forty yards, turns and glides downwards in a smooth and graceful curve. This mounting aloft and circling descent is very beautiful to see, and produces the idea that the bird has been suddenly carried away by an access of glad emotion.

The song period of the ring-dove, among other species, was the subject of an enquiry by the British Trust for Ornithology in 1939-40, the results of the investigation being summarized by H. G. Alexander. In the case of the ring-dove the song period or cooing did not begin till late February or March and in some areas not before April, but it continued right through the summer till late September or early October. Mr. Alexander observes in his report that even during the months of regular cooing, the incidence of the song shows great variation, some pigeons being liable to strange silent days, as remarked especially by P. H. T. Hartley, A. J. Harthan, and my friend Helen Rait Kerr, in their several districts. The returns sent in from Scotland were not numerous and the foregoing remarks do not necessarily apply to the birds which have their habitat north of the Border. Indeed Mr. and Mrs. Venables in their *Birds and Mammals of Shetland* have a very different tale to tell. In the small population in those islands irregular song began in the first week of April, regular song extended from late April or early May to late June, and irregular song finished in the first week of July—an astonishing contrast, as they point out, with what occurs in England. In a note sent to *British Birds* the same authors remark on the short period of song they heard in Flintshire, North Wales, during four years' residence, compared with what appears to take place over much of England, upon which Mr. Alexander mainly based his report. Major Ruttledge tells us that in Ireland in March the wood-pigeon is frequently heard cooing more than an hour before sunrise, and as late as five hours after the sun has set the notes are sometimes heard.

BREEDING HABITS : The breeding season of the wood-pigeon is protracted. In southern England it normally commences in April, sometimes even in March ; H. Walpole-Bond states in his *History of Sussex Birds* that he had nesting records for every month of the year. He considered that three broods are always reared in a season and sometimes even more. Jourdain gives the nesting season as usually from April till September. Colonel R. F. Meiklejohn took eggs in Aberdeen in October. All manner of sites are chosen for the nest, usually fifteen to twenty-five feet from the ground. It is made of fine sticks producing a wickerwork effect through which the eggs are plainly visible from beneath. The whole structure is absurdly small for the size of the bird. When not in a tree, bush, or hedge, the nest may be placed in ivy climbing up a tree, occasionally on top of a crow's or magpie's nest or a squirrel's drey, more rarely on rock ledges and buildings, and exceptionally on the ground.[1] The inadequacy of the frail platform must surely end in disaster for the young birds if, as very occasionally happens, three eggs are laid instead of the normal clutch of two or (not uncommonly) one. Pure white, the eggs are elliptical ovate in shape and slightly glossy : 100 British-taken eggs measured by Jourdain averaged 41·1 × 29·8 mm. Max. 47·8 × 33 mm. Min. 36·6 × 28 and 42·2 × 26·6 mm.

Both sexes take turns at incubation, which begins with the first egg ; the male is stated by Colonel B. H. Ryves to sit chiefly by day, the female during the night. The same naturalist states in his *Bird Life in Cornwall* that the nest is built entirely by the hen but the male does all the foraging and carrying of the sticks. He says " some nests become quite large as

[1] Eagle Clarke in 3rd ed. of Howard Saunders's *Manual*, p. 786.

the same nest is often used for all broods for two or three years in succession ". This experience differs from that of Walpole-Bond in Sussex, who states emphatically that he has never known the same nest used for two broods. This is proof that it is no use making dogmatic statements as to what birds will do and what they will not. This author has learned to avoid that dangerous word " never ". Incubation lasts seventeen or eighteen days (Walpole-Bond) and the squabs (i.e. chicks) are fed by both parents on pigeon's milk, which is produced in the crop of the parents, the young thrusting their bills into their parent's throat.

On rare occasions the wood-pigeon has been seen to feign injury in realistic fashion. On the first recorded instance Mr. H. A. Booth[1] found that on every occasion when he flushed a wood-pigeon from its nest containing two eggs in a hawthorn, some ten feet from the ground, the bird fluttered down to the ground and then hopped along with flapping wings " just like a winged pigeon attempts to escape ". It continued to do this for about a hundred yards from the nest when it flew close to the ground for another hundred yards or so before settling in a tree. A similar experience befel A. W. Boyd[2] in Cheshire, who after climbing to a nest in a copper beech saw the old bird drop to the road beneath and flap along on its breast for many yards before flying away. C. F. Tebbutt[3] records yet another case and suggests that as the situation and growth of the tree selected for the nest made it impossible for the parent bird to fly off with the usual clatter and commotion, it had recourse to injury feigning to detract attention away from the nest to itself. In all these cases the pigeon seems to have feigned injury from the moment it fell to the ground, but more remarkable was the case recorded by H. Walpole-Bond[4] when he, R. H. Deane, and P. W. Boughton-Leigh put a bird off its nest which contained one squab. Instead of attempting the injury-feigning ruse at once, the pigeon flew about sixty yards apparently normally, alighted in a field " and there and then alternately grovelled with wings widely expanded, and flapped and shuffled along as though terribly hurt ".

At the end of the long nesting season, when the young of the year are fully grown, they disperse over the country ; but they do not, so far as we know, travel very far as a rule. The number of returns from ringing wood-pigeons in the British Isles has been surprisingly low considering the numbers of these birds which are annually shot or destroyed in other ways. In the Report on Bird-Ringing for 1955, Table ii, the grand total of pigeons ringed in Britain since the commencement of the scheme is stated to be 5891, of which 337 have been recovered. In the Report on Bird-Ringing for 1957 (*British Birds*, vol. li) the grand total of wood-pigeons

[1] *British Birds*, xiii, p. 165. See also vol. xxxvi, p. 162, for other cases recorded.
[2] *British Birds*, xxvii, p. 166.
[3] *British Birds*, xxxvi, p. 115.
[4] *A History of Sussex Birds*, vol. iii, p. 360.

ringed in Britain had reached 6448, of which 413 had been recovered. The only returns from overseas are as follows :

Ringed as nestling [1]		Recovered	
Lower Culham, Berks .	7.6.31	Conflans, Sarthe, France .	15.11.32
Cookham, Berks .	17.7.55	Goulien, Finistère, France.	31.12.55
Nr. Sidlesham, Sussex .	9.7.57	St. Malon-sur-mel, Ille-et-Vilaine, France .	17.12.57
Sidlesham, Sussex .	26.7.57	St. Ouen la Rouerie, Ille-et-Vilaine, France .	22.12.57

The movement from England and Scotland to Ireland seems to be negligible if judged alone by the recovery of ringed birds, for although large flocks are said to arrive in Ireland from overseas,[2] the only return from England is a bird ringed in Northumberland in 1944, recovered in Tipperary in November 1955—ten years later ! It is worth noting that none bearing a local ring have found their way to Ireland from Scotland, but the proportion of birds ringed in the Highlands to the total population of Scottish birds must be very small indeed. I still lean to the view that many Scottish wood-pigeons reach Ireland in winter.

IMMIGRATION : We must now turn to a subject which has been hotly debated among ornithologists for a good many years and has recently received fresh impetus by the views expressed in the Agricultural Research Council's Report on the status of the wood-pigeon in the British Isles, issued in 1951. The point at variance is, from what country of origin do the large flocks of wood-pigeons come which pour into East Anglia and some of the southern counties of England during the early winter months ? The subject was set out most clearly by my valued friend W. B. Alexander when Director of the Edward Grey Institute of Ornithology.[3] Discussing the evidence for or against the theory that an immigration takes place from the Continent, Alexander states :

The various migration inquiries have hitherto yielded very little evidence of the migration of wood-pigeons across the North Sea. In the British Association inquiry, when particulars of observations made at lighthouses and light-vessels were collected, records of pigeons were extremely few in comparison with those of most other species, and chiefly refer to single birds : the few records of flocks mostly seem to relate to parties travelling along the coast. On Heligoland and on Fair Isle, the two chief islands in western Europe where migration can be observed, the wood-pigeon is a scarce visitor in spring and autumn, usually seen only singly and never in flocks of any size.

Alexander concluded from the evidence at his disposal that the great

[1] I am indebted to Mr. J. W. Pavslow of the Bird-ringing Secretariat, British Museum, for sending me these four records—the only ones to date, June 1958.

[2] Major R. F. Ruttledge, *Birds of Ireland*, 1954, p. 280.

[3] " Report on the Wood-pigeon ", in *Journal of the Roy. Agric. Soc. of England*, vol. c, Part iii, 1940, pp. 1-9.

flights which arrived on the coasts of south-east Scotland and north-east England between 1860 and 1901 came from the Highlands of Scotland ; that the arrivals which occur on the east coasts of Norfolk and Suffolk in autumn are migrants from Scandinavia ; and that during winter, flocks of non-migratory birds on both sides of the Channel make flights dependent on food and weather conditions, and may cross the Channel in either direction. He believed that, at the date of writing his report, the numbers of pigeons arriving from the Continent were not large and it seemed that continental birds never formed any large proportion of the winter flocks in the British Isles.

In that last statement I believe Mr. Alexander to have been mistaken. In any case the problem was not allowed to rest there.

In 1951 the Agricultural Research Council issued a lengthy report running to sixty-seven pages devoted to the wood-pigeon in Britain, compiled by M. K. Colquhoun. This report deals mainly with the bird from an economic point of view and as a " pest " to agriculture, but in the course of his review Mr. Colquhoun devotes a section to what he terms " foreign " wood-pigeons. After mentioning the work of Witherby and of C. B. Ticehurst and referring to the historical review of W. B. Alexander (to which I have already devoted some space), Mr. Colquhoun shows the trend of his opinion in his last sentence, writing : " To sum up, the so-called ' foreign ' wood-pigeons are really juveniles. Flocks of wood-pigeons are seen in winter in East Anglia and elsewhere which seem too large for the resident breeding stock, but no proof has been offered that such birds come from abroad ". By " proof " Mr. Colquhoun apparently means ringed examples—but surely we have proof enough without that. The immigration into Britain from the Continent of several species of *Corvidae*, chaffinches, skylarks, starlings, and lapwings was an undisputed fact long before the ringing of birds came into fashion, so why doubt the origin of the wood-pigeons which swarm into East Anglia and other parts of eastern England and Scotland, just because no ringed examples have so far been recovered with a Finno-Scandinavian or German ring attached to their legs ? Pigeons move in search of food, and when their food supply is no longer procurable in northern Europe they migrate to where it can be found. Gunnar Svärdson [1] has emphasized that the Finno-Scandinavian climate has changed in the last few decades, being now on the whole milder. Severe winters have become rarer and the spring and autumn have become warmer as well. Thus the food situation in winter has improved for a number of species and the number of wintering birds has greatly increased. Svärdson points out that in the southernmost parts of the region song-thrushes and wood-pigeons can now be found in winter fairly regularly. Formerly this was not the case. That fact may influence the overseas migration very considerably.

[1] " Visible migration within Fenno-Scandia ", in *Ibis*, 1953, pp. 181-211.

In the April 1953 number of the *Ibis* appeared several valuable papers dealing with various aspects of migration. The autumn movement on the east coast is discussed by Dr. D. W. Snow, who stresses the great autumn immigration from the east, mainly to East Anglia, specifying among other regular immigrants the subject of this essay. He draws attention to the papers published in the same number of the *Ibis* by Van Dobhen and Svärdson, who deal with the movement as it is seen passing down the north-west coasts of Europe and *striking out to sea in westerly directions, bound for this country* (the italics are mine). Dr. Snow then goes on to discuss what has been seen on our own coasts, quoting Ticehurst and Rivière and other authoritative workers in East Anglia.

To the facts which he has been able to marshal may be added some sight records by observers of wide reputation. Thus Lord Templewood in his book *The Unbroken Thread* writes of seeing flocks of wood-pigeons crossing the Norfolk coast in daylight for hours on end during the autumn migration. Again, Douglas Carruthers watched on one winter's afternoon in west Norfolk (twenty miles from the coast inland from Wells) a mass movement of wood-pigeons, far too large to be a local one, involving thousands, perhaps five thousand birds, flying N.N.E., which almost certainly had come in from the sea, though proof was wanting. Still more significant was the experience of Colonel R. Meinertzhagen, who, when returning by sea from Sweden between 2 and 3 p.m. on 29th October 1946, about ninety miles east of Newcastle, with a slight westerly wind blowing, records many flocks of wood-pigeons passing his ship, mainly in flocks of thirty but one huge pack amounting to over a thousand birds. The birds were flying S.W. and at about 500 feet above sea-level. That wood-pigeons will fly at much greater heights far beyond eyesight from the ground, is recorded by the same observer who, when flying over southern Greece on 16th March 1952, encountered 200 wood-pigeons flying north. The aircraft was flying at 12,000 feet in clear sky and with no land visible. The pigeons paid not the slightest attention to the aircraft and the pilot was forced to bank steeply to avoid them.[1] Flying-Officer Carr-Lewtry has also recorded meeting with wood-pigeons at 3100 feet. In *The Times* newspaper of 18th February 1956 an article from a correspondent,[2] who obviously knew what he was about, describes a huge flight of pigeons coming in, in waves, from the mouth of the Moray Firth—" there must have been thousands of the birds ". Where else could these birds have come from unless from Scandinavia or even from farther east ?

The instances quoted are but a few of those which have come to my knowledge in the course of my reading, but surely they alone serve to prove the point at issue. In this essay I have not touched upon the immigration into Kent and Sussex from across the Channel, as recorded by

[1] *Birds of Arabia*, pp. 41-42.
[2] A shooting man on the mystery of the wood-pigeon.

A. D. Wilkinson,[1] nor on the huge numbers seen passing over specified localities in southern England. Oxford is a case in point, the movements around which centre have been discussed by David Lack in a recent contribution to *British Birds*.[2] In the same contribution M. G. Ridpath records his observations in Kent and Sussex in 1952-53-54, when the tendency of wood-pigeon flocks to fly out to sea in a southerly direction, sometimes beyond vision, and then to return was noted by a team of observers. Coastwise movements of wood-pigeons—a pack of 4200 was seen in the early morning at Beachy Head, closely packed and flying high as if on set migration—was observed by Dr. Lack in October 1952[3] and although the movement was along the coast there was a tendency for flocks to turn to sea southwards and continue out till hardly visible *and then turn back to the land* and resume their coasting. In this connexion the observations of Mr. A. D. Wilkinson[4] with special reference to the pigeon immigration on the Sussex coast should be consulted. Summing up their joint observations Lack and Ridpath remark that large flights of wood-pigeons southwards in the early mornings in late autumn have been seen in various places in England. These birds, they state, are definitely coming from roosts but normally fly south, not in some other direction, so it seemed to the observers that the movements are connected in some way with migration.

In view of the various conflicting opinions expressed I wrote to Dr. Lack at the Edward Grey Institute of Field Ornithology for his final conclusions and received the following reply dated 12th June 1958 :

Since Ridpath and I wrote in *British Birds*, the wood-pigeon's migration story has become increasingly complicated, and is still not solved. There is no question that the roosts increase enormously in size in early November, but it is still quite uncertain whether these birds are purely local in origin. Repeated watches in Kent and Norfolk have shown no signs of wood-pigeons arriving from overseas, and in a watch carried out this April there was no sign of them departing. At the same time, wood-pigeons in early November do set off out to sea from the south coast, but many of them return after a mile or two and it is very possible that the rest do so a little further out, when out of sight of the observer. It looks as though the bird has an urge to migrate at this time of year which is never fulfilled.

It will be seen from this essay that I am firmly convinced of migratory movements across the North Sea, and that the packs of wood-pigeons which so greatly swell the usual population in Norfolk in the winter months, especially in the severe weather so often encountered after Christmas, are of Continental, *not* Scottish, origin. But if proof by ringing is the only proof to be accepted, we could surely make an all-out effort to ring in a

[1] *British Birds*, xliii, 1950, pp. 233-238.
[2] " Do English wood-pigeons migrate ? ", in *British Birds*, xlviii, 1955, pp. 289-290.
[3] " Visible migration in S.E. England, 1952 ", in *British Birds*, xlvii, pp. 1-15.
[4] " The annual immigration of the wood-pigeon and stock-dove on the coast of East Sussex ", in *British Birds*, xliii, 1950, pp. 233-238.

given season a really large number of Scottish-bred birds and advertise the fact widely in England and Ireland. The ringing stations on the Continent could be asked to make a similar effort in their own countries and with this international collaboration we might at last learn whence our winter flocks come. This suggestion is not my own, but was put forward by Lord William Percy (who lives in Norfolk) in private correspondence with Douglas Carruthers [1] after reading Mr. Colquhoun's official report to which allusion has been made.

It is a fact, as Mr. Colquhoun has stated, that a great many wood-pigeons breed in the Highland valleys where there are both young conifer plantations suitable for breeding and arable land suitable for food. These birds doubtless hang on as long as they can until forced by weather conditions to move south, and it is these birds which some authorities insist are the " foreign visitors " into East Anglia. But why should they fly so far south if they can find conditions to their liking nearer home ; and even supposing they do reach the latitude of Norfolk why should these birds, bred in a Highland glen, fly out to sea and then come in again over the Norfolk coast ?

Here in Kirkcudbrightshire and in Dumfriesshire we constantly receive huge packs of wood-pigeons in winter which are certainly not lowland bred. Governed by the food supply in this mild corner of Scotland the flocks move from one district to another and no doubt much farther afield. I have never doubted that these are Scottish-bred birds from farther north in search of better feeding, though foreigners coming in temporarily and on passage may swell their ranks.

In *Birds of Ireland* (1954) we are informed by Major Ruttledge that most immigrants to Ireland are of Continental origin, a conclusion at which he arrived after perusal of *The Handbook of British Birds* with its somewhat dogmatic statements. Ruttledge further remarks that " in February and March the winter visitors depart at a time when our [Irish] resident birds are already paired ". Miss Elsie Leach (British Museum Bird-ringing Section) informs me that up to June 1958 there has never been more than one wood-pigeon ringed abroad and recovered in the British Isles. That one was ringed at Viborg, Denmark, in 1925 and recovered in Leix (Queen's County) in 1934—nine years later. The authors of *Birds of Ireland*, so I am informed, had no other corroboration upon which to base their conclusions, but the single case of a wood-pigeon ringed in Northumberland in 1944 and found in Tipperary in November 1945, supports the contention that *English*-bred pigeons do not, except on the rarest occasions, cross to Ireland. But what of the Scottish-bred birds ? I am convinced in my own mind, with no proof to offer, that it is the Scottish wood-pigeon population which crosses the narrow seas to Ireland. Major Ruttledge, writing to me in June 1958,

[1] Another distinguished Norfolk naturalist living near King's Lynn.

assures me that " hordes of wood-pigeons " come to Ireland " far more than can be bred in the country and especially in some years—and if English birds are sedentary [as *The Handbook* states] what is their origin ? " I would reply Scotland, and in severe weather Continental birds as well which have crossed the North Sea. We shall see who is right.

CONTINENTAL MIGRATION : With a view to having the very latest reports from ringing stations in Norway, Sweden, Denmark, Holland, and Finland I wrote to the directors of twelve institutes or museums engaged in this work on the Continent and received most courteous replies from all five countries, including maps with the direction taken by their migrating wood-pigeons as established by ringing.

NORWAY : The Director of the Stavanger station, Dr. Holger Holgersen, writes : " We do not have many recoveries of ringed pigeons but the few we possess indicate a migration from Norway through Jutland (Oct.) to S.W. France, where we have recoveries from the months of Oct.-Nov. in Basses Pyrénées and Hautes Pyrénées. No recoveries have so far been reported from the true winter months, except near Stavanger (January), confirming what we already know from observation, that the wood-pigeon winters in parts of this country. In and near Stavanger it is rather common in winter, as well as in summer. The species breeds as far north as Mosjöen (66° N.) and it is extending its range northwards as well as along the west coast, where it was rare until the end of last century." Dr. Yngvar Hagen, Director of the Norwegian State Game Research, informs me that very few recoveries have been reported, Visible migration from the eastern side of Oslo Fjord shows them mainly going south with little deviation ; such observations having been made 1-2 miles inland. After they reach the Skagerak (or Kattegat) coast, the direction the birds take is unknown.

SWEDEN : As Professor E. Lönnberg reported[1] in his book on Swedish birds and in a later work *Svenska fåglars flyttning*, wood-pigeons ringed as chicks in Sweden take a south-westerly course, but only a few have been recovered in Portugal (Verdas Novas), S.W. France (Bordeaux), Central France (Dept. Altier). Three of these recoveries were in late winter and spring. Dr. B. Danielsson of Farsta tells me that only a few wood-pigeons have been ringed by the Swedish bird station at Ottenby. The direction of their flight is south-westerly as shown in Professor Lönnberg's map.

Records of wood-pigeons ringed in Sweden by the Naturhistoriska Museum, Stockholm, have been kindly supplied to me by Miss Greta Vestergren. Wood-pigeons have been recovered in the autumn in the following countries : Denmark, 1 ; France, 35 ; Spain, 4 ;

[1] Lönnberg in his *Introduction to Swedish Birds* (1929).

Portugal, 1. Besides these the following were recovered between January and April : from Denmark, 1 (at the end of April) ; Belgium, 2 ; France, 22 ; Germany, 1 (in the middle of April) ; Spain, 1 ; Portugal, 3. Wood-pigeons ringed by the Riksmuseum never reach very high figures : thus in 1954, 77 ; in 1955, 61 ; in 1956, 34 ; and 1957, 90 examples were ringed. Under these circumstances it is remarkable that so many have been recovered.

DENMARK : In reply to my enquiry Dr. Hans Johansen, of the Copenhagen University Zoological Museum, informs me that most of the local wood-pigeons leave Denmark at the beginning of October to winter in the western parts of middle Europe, especially in France but some-times in Spain. The rest of the Danish wood-pigeons stay in their home country in winter. These last are mostly the town-nesting birds ; only rarely do they remain in the country districts. The passage migrants from Scandinavia pass through Denmark mainly in October, flying in a south-westerly direction but, as these birds are not ringed on their way through Denmark, there is no information from Danish sources to confirm how far they travel. Dr. Johansen adds that in warm winters with good feeding conditions—especially in rape fields—*big flocks* remain in Denmark in November and December, sometimes even remaining the whole winter. Many Swedish wood-pigeons stay in Denmark every year and in cold winters many of them die.

Dr. P. Skovgaard, writing from Viborg, informs me that Danish wood-pigeons ringed as nestlings in his country have mainly been recovered in France (9 recoveries), Belgium (1 recovery), Holland (1 recovery), and Germany (3 recoveries, Heide Holstein, Oldenburg, Hanover). The French returns came mostly from the Pyrénées on the Spanish border as shown in a map published in *Alauda*, ser. ii, No. 4, 1931. Dr. Skovgaard writes that if the Norwegian pigeons depart in a narrow " lane " as do those in Denmark and take the same direction in their flight " they must pass the eastern part of England " —but he has no data to confirm this. Danish wood-pigeons returning in early spring are much more spread. He states that the bird can be seen in Denmark during all months in mild winters more than in severe winters—most of the winter in Denmark being mild until January. At the end of September and beginning of October the harvested fields are blue with wood-pigeons, but whether these are Danish-bred birds, as he supposes, or birds from farther north, he cannot be certain.

HOLLAND : Dr. J. Taapken writes from Leiden that Dutch-ringed birds show recoveries mainly from north-west Germany, Belgium, and the north of France.

CONTROL OF NUMBERS : A statement regarding measures taken to control the numbers of wood-pigeons in England and Scotland in particular was given by Mr. Edwin Cohen to the International Committee for Bird Protection and published in their Annual Report for 1957. Mr. Cohen remarked that practical experience and the findings of the Wood-Pigeon Enquiry conducted by the British Trust for Ornithology on behalf of the Agricultural Research Council seem to have shown conclusively that wood-pigeons at their present strength in Britain are a serious economic pest. It was pointed out that for many years war has been waged against the wood-pigeon with the gun by sportsmen, and shooting on a much wider scale has been practised by farmers directed by County Pest Officers. Mr. Cohen further stated that although tens of thousands of birds are destroyed in this way each year, it does not appear to have reduced the wood-pigeon population.

If that is a fact, and there is no reason to doubt the statement, does it not prove conclusively that our own population of wood-pigeons is some-how increased from overseas ?

In all this hullabaloo about the damage to crops done by our wood-pigeons do not let us forget that a great deal of their feeding is done on grassland and that they destroy the seeds of countless billions of noxious weeds. Another point to be reckoned in their favour is that their flesh is excellent and when these islands were at war Londoners were very thankful if kind friends sent them a fat brace of pigeons with which to vary a monotonous war-time diet. Its " economic value " was then reversed.

REFERENCES : Original Description. *Columba palumbus* Linnaeus, *Syst. Nat.*, 10th ed., 1758, p. 163 : " Europa Asia ". Restricted type locality Sweden.

PLATE 23   **STOCK-DOVE**

Columba oenas Linnaeus

Resident in all four countries ; widely but locally distributed as a nesting species. Winter Visitors are believed to come to Britain from overseas but only slight evidence to date except apparent increase in population. Similarly our own stock is believed rarely to emigrate.

IDENTIFICATION : The predominating colour of the stock-dove is blue-grey which pales on the rump and darkens on the tail which shades from lavender-grey at the base to blackish at the tip. The grey wings, with slate-coloured quills, are crossed by two imperfect black bars caused by interrupted black spots on the inner secondaries and wing-coverts. The breast is vinaceous, below which the body is pale blue-grey, while on each side of the neck is a patch of metallic green shot with purple. The underside of the wing (axillaries and under wing-coverts) is grey. The iris is brown, the skin

PLATE 23

STOCK-DOVE
Columba oenas Linnaeus

surrounding the eye pink ; the bill is horn at tip, red towards the base, the fleshy portion white. The legs and feet are pink tinged with mauve.

The stock-dove should not be confused with the ring-dove, not even with first-year birds. Its smaller size, less bulky body, and quicker motions should save it from confusion with its commoner relative. The absence of a white wing-patch distinguishes the stock-dove from an adult wood-pigeon in flight, and when at rest the absence of white along the carpal joint. The stock-dove is also distinctive in having no white patch on the sides of the neck. C. B. Ticehurst has drawn attention to its " very quick dashing flight, turning on alarm with extraordinary rapidity ", and to its relatively shorter tail as an aid to distinguish the bird in the field.

It is much more readily confused with the rock-dove by those who are not familiar with it. Minor points of distinction are to be found in the colour of the eye—stock-dove dark brown, rock-dove yellow, and in the colour beneath the wing—stock-dove grey, rock-dove white. Mr. Derek Goodwin writes : " On the wing the stock-dove is easily confused with a rock or domestic pigeon. . . . It appears, however, to carry its head with the bill pointing more downward, and thus presents a slightly different outline. At a little distance the stock-dove's wing shows a pale grey area between the black edging and the darker blue-grey of the lesser and median coverts. This demarcation is often strikingly noticeable when it is in flight some way off, although if the bird is held in the hand and its wing spread it is scarcely discernible ".[1] Personally I look first at the rump, for although it is a variable character, in nine cases out of ten a rock-dove has a very conspicuous white or whitish rump, whereas in the stock-dove the rump is grey-blue. In flight, too, the heavy black bars across the wing of the rock dove are diagnostic, whereas in the stock-dove the narrow interrupted black spots on the wing are barely noticeable.

Another distinction is to be found in the voice. The note of the stock-dove is very different from the coo of the larger bird : in *The Handbook* it is described as a deep, gruff " ooo-woo ", the second syllable short, clipped, and emphatic, repeated some four or five to, more often, a dozen or more times. Coward terms it a " short, deep, grunting call ", quite distinct from the modulated notes of the wood-pigeon.

LOCAL DISTRIBUTION : In Britain as a whole the stock-dove is a widespread species but it is still rather fickle in its selection of habitat. It requires an environment suited to its tastes and favours parklands where old timber exists, being especially plentiful on large English estates. Wooded crags and cliffs such as we often find inland, abounding in nooks and crannies, are the stock-dove's delight but it will be found as well on maritime cliffs where no trees exist. It is partial too to ruins, among the ivy-clad walls of which it finds ideal nesting places.

The versatility which it exhibits in the selection of nesting sites gives

[1] *Bird Notes and News*, xxvi, 1953, 4, p. 4.

it a fairly wide choice of habitat, and it is of interest to note how much it has increased in certain areas in the last hundred years. Discussing this topic W. B. Alexander and David Lack [1] point out that at the beginning of the nineteenth century the stock-dove was confined to south and eastern England, but by the end of the century it had increased and spread rapidly and had colonized south-west England, Wales, northern England, south and east Scotland, north-east Ireland, and the Isle of Man. The increase was maintained and though in the extreme south-west of England it is resident in Cornwall, it is reported by Colonel Ryves to be not common as a whole, breeding sparsely on the coastal cliffs and chiefly in the Wade-bridge area. In East Anglia it finds much suitable country wherever there are large woods and parkland, while all over the warren country of Norfolk and Suffolk it is common and resident. Its most spectacular change of status is to be found in northern England. When Nelson wrote his *Birds of Yorkshire* (1907) he drew attention to the remarkable increase of the bird since 1844, where it was considered a rarity, and to the numbers which twenty years later had taken to the old warren grounds. To-day Mr. Chislett can point to its being plentiful in some areas wherever it can find suitable nesting holes. In Durham George Temperley, writing in 1951, calls it a common resident though local, " more plentiful in winter when flocks arrive from overseas ". The bird was unknown in Durham ninety years earlier. In Lancashire, though less numerous than the wood-pigeon, it outnumbers that species in many south-eastern districts. [2]

That will give some idea of the bird's spread over England. Its status in Scotland and Ireland shall be borrowed from the two recently issued standard works, with full acknowledgement to the authors. [3]

The history of the stock-dove's spread in Scotland since it was first found nesting in 1866 on Luffness and Gullane Links has been traced by Dr. Evelyn Baxter and Miss Rintoul. In 1874 it was discovered nesting at Dalkeith in Midlothian and two years later in Kirkcudbright. In 1878 it began to colonize Fife and was found nesting at Duns Castle in Berwick-shire ; in 1882 it nested in Roxburgh, in 1883 in Stirlingshire and in the same year its first nesting was recorded from Dumfriesshire. In 1895 Peebles was added to the list of breeding counties, and four years later Selkirk. And so its colonization went on. Very remarkable was its arrival about 1883 in the Laigh of Moray, where it was discovered breeding among sandy hillocks. Within ten years they " simply swarmed " in the Moray Basin, as Harvie-Brown recorded. It had reached east Sutherland in 1889. It spread up the west coast to Argyll but not beyond. The authors

---

[1] " Changes in status among British breeding birds ", in *British Birds*, xxxviii, 1944, pp. 67-68.

[2] Clifford Oakes, *The Birds of Lancashire*, 1953.

[3] *The Birds of Scotland* (1953), and *Birds of Ireland* (1954), were both published by Messrs. Oliver and Boyd of Edinburgh.

of *The Birds of Scotland* wrote in 1953 that " stock-doves are still unknown as breeding on the west side north of Argyll ; in Caithness, in the Hebrides and the Northern Isles ". They point to the general trend of colonization which appears to be from the south and from the coastal regions inland, up the glens and river valleys. Those which have been reported from the Inner Hebrides have usually been winter or autumn visitors ; more rarely in spring. The same applies to records from the Orkneys, Shetlands, and Fair Isle, indicating a probable influx from Scandinavia.

While the stock-dove was spreading in Scotland it was making slower progress in Ireland. Major Ruttledge tells us (*Birds of Ireland*) that the first stock-doves definitely detected in Ireland appeared in Co. Down in 1875 but it was not until 1896 that it bred west of the river Shannon, though in the intervening years there had been an increase in many of the central counties. In 1954 it had still not established itself in Leitrim and Tyrone and there was no indication at that date of breeding in Kerry but it has since bred near Tralee. Major Ruttledge considers that winter visitors from overseas probably arrive in Ireland, but to date there is no definite evidence and little information has been forthcoming about its migrations. Two birds have been killed at lighthouses (Tuskar Rock, Wexford, in mid-October and Maidens Light, Antrim, in November). The breeding population, which was much reduced in the war years as the result of extensive shooting and trapping, is considered to be resident and we may hope it has by now regained its former numbers. In the *Irish Bird Report*, 1957, it is said to be now well established at Crossmolina, Mayo, in the breeding season.

DISTRIBUTION ABROAD : This is a European and western Asiatic species which nests as far north as central Norway and Sweden, the southern area of Finland and Russia to 61° N. in the west and 58° N. in the east. Its status in the Soviet Union will be given later in this section. Its eastern breeding range certainly extends to the Ural Mountains, while to the south it occurs in the Mediterranean and in north-west Africa. It is found all over central Europe. It nests in Morocco in the Great and Middle Atlas, and evidently in the wooded parts of Algeria. As a winter visitor it occurs widely in the Mediterranean area. We met with it ourselves in Cyprus. Immense flocks are reported to visit Sinai,[1] and it is a winter visitor to Iraq and south Persia. To the Nile Delta it is but an occasional straggler. It has been reported from several of the Mediterranean islands : it is an occasional straggler to the Balearic islands during migration ; to Corsica occasionally in winter. It breeds in Sicily but not in Malta. In Greece it is said to be a partial migrant breeding locally in the north ; also a passage migrant and winter visitor. It figures in the latest list of Turkish birds but its status is not mentioned.

Several races of the stock-dove have been described from north Persia

---

[1] Meinertzhagen, *Birds of Arabia*, p. 445.

Tianshan and Yarkand, but all are believed to be doubtfully distinct from the typical race.

The status of the stock-dove in the Soviet Union is said by R. N. Meklenburtsev [1] (*Birds of the Soviet Union*) to have undergone considerable change owing to the catastrophic effect the improvement of the forests, with consequent removal of decayed timber and thus of its nesting places, has had upon it. It is said to be relatively rare everywhere. Even in its winter quarters in Transcaucasia it is only seen in flocks of thirty or forty birds, though possibly packs of a few hundred individuals may still be seen in the western Ukraine during the autumn migration. The race which has been named *yarkandensis* from Turkestan is not numerous but has not declined in numbers like other pigeons in that area, probably because it does not nest near human habitations.

Habits : It has already been remarked earlier in this essay that the stock-doves which breed in the British Isles are believed to be resident all the year round, but that sometimes the young birds in their first year will make oversea journeys. There has not been much evidence to support this latter assertion, but it was well summed up by Dr. Norman Ticehurst in *The Handbook* some years ago. He gave as an instance of long-distance travel by young birds the recovery of one which had flown from Stirling to Cambridgeshire, and of another which had journeyed from Worcester to the south-west of France " suggesting that at this age the bird may be partly migratory ". The old birds evidently do *not* move about very much, if the recovery of ringed examples near their nesting place in succeeding years is any indication. In Yorkshire, where a number of ringed birds have been recovered in subsequent years close to the place where they were ringed, we learn from Mr. Ralph Chislett [2] that no proof has been obtained that any Yorkshire birds leave the *county*, much less the country ! Two pairs of birds were proved by Mr. C. Wontner-Smith to have remained mated together for at least two years.

Suitable nesting sites and suitable feeding grounds appear to be the two essentials in the stock-dove's life. These islands of ours can offer both in abundance, and that no doubt is the main reason of its increase over the last hundred years. Being much more a bird of the open country than the ring-dove, and less dependent on trees, alternative nesting sites play a large part in influencing its local distribution. It seems just as content to breed on sea cliffs or among sand-dunes, as in places where trees and climbing shrubs predominate. Rabbit holes have always been favoured by this dove in certain localities and one is tempted to believe that in districts where the rabbit has been exterminated and the warrens have fallen in, the stock-doves will depart from the neighbourhood. So well known was its tendency to nest in rabbit holes that the old warreners of Norfolk

[1] Translation and summary by D. D. Harber in *British Birds*, xlviii, 1955, p. 269.

[2] *Yorkshire Birds*, p. 225.

and Suffolk [1] habitually placed crossed sticks across the entrance of the burrow through which the old birds could feed the young while the young themselves were prevented from escaping.

Although stock-doves are not nearly so numerous in the countryside as wood-pigeons they very often consort together and may be seen feeding in company. They have the reputation of destroying vast numbers of weeds which is certainly true, charlock seeds being particular favourites; but grain is also consumed. Their menu, so far as vegetable matter is concerned, is highly varied, but they cannot be accused of doing as much harm as the huge flocks of wood-pigeons; in any case much of the grain eaten is already lying waste on the stubbles. On the shore the birds will feed on the seeds growing on salt marshes including that of the sea-pea. The late C. B. Ticehurst found they had been eating snails, two species of which *Hyallina nitidulus* and *H. crystallina* were identified from their crops. Berries of many kinds, mast, and small acorns constitute a considerable part of their food supply when these are available. Usually in small flocks, stock-doves are none the less gregarious and, as T. A. Coward has remarked, are of a sociable nature, a fact which is borne out by several pairs often nesting in close proximity. Mr. B. J. Ringrose was, I believe, one of the first to draw attention [2] to large gatherings of stock-doves which he saw in Wiltshire in the month of May, one hundred doves in company with a few turtle-doves being seen on a newly harrowed and sown field. His communication was followed by others [3] recording similar observations. Mr. L. S. V. Venables remarked that in both the coniferous and the deciduous woods of south-west Surrey flocks of stock-doves are quite regular right through the year. He found that during the spring and summer the flocks rarely contained more than twenty birds but in the autumn and winter many more, though by then they were usually joined up with wood-pigeons. These statements brought a note from Mr. K. B. Rooke [4] that on 3rd and 4th May 1934 he saw fully two hundred stock-doves feeding on a newly-sown field in north Somerset, with a few wood-pigeons. Single birds and pairs were often observed to fly between the flock and the adjacent woods in which they were nesting. Mr. Rooke suggests that breeding stock-doves do sometimes flock in numbers on suitable communal feeding grounds, and it is difficult not to agree with his conclusion.

Earlier in this essay I remarked that our British stock-doves are considered to be sedentary, nearly all the evidence from ringing pointing to that conclusion. On the other hand it is equally certain that the population which breeds in latitudes (between 58° and 61°) north of the British Isles is migratory. When their food supply gives out they are forced to travel south. Stock-doves have been reported by several writers as immigrants

---

[1] C. B. Ticehurst in *History of the Birds of Suffolk*.
[2] *British Birds*, xxxiii, p. 140.
[3] *British Birds*, xxxiii, pp. 165, 196.   [4] *British Birds*, xxxvi, p. 19.

to Britain during the autumn migration and as passage migrants off the east coast of England in spring and autumn. Dr. Eagle Clarke was the first to record its presence at Fair Isle [1] in September and October 1911, on the authority of the Duchess of Bedford. On the main Shetland islands it is reported by Mr. and Mrs. Venables [2] to be an uncommon and probably irregular autumn migrant at the present day, the extreme dates being 11th September and 24th October. A single bird on 9th May is their only spring record. There are island records from South Uist in November, from the Orkneys and from Hyskeir in the Inner Hebrides—the latter a spring record on 6th March. On the east coast of Scotland Miss Rintoul and Dr. Evelyn Baxter have seen occasional birds, presumably on passage, on the Isle of May in the Forth ; the bird has also been recorded from this islet in April.

There is evidently a regular movement in eastern England during the months when migrants are passing. This is mentioned by Dr. Norman Ticehurst in *The Handbook*, where he observes that there is some evidence that small numbers immigrate in autumn with the migrant wood-pigeons between the Firth of Forth and the Humber and also in north-east Kent, though more observations are required. We can echo that to-day. Dr. Ticehurst draws our attention to the fact that the stock-dove is often found in considerably greater numbers than the local breeding population ; perhaps he had in mind Richard Paton's experience in Ayrshire ; the latter recorded many joining the resident birds in winter, probably from the more northern counties. Writing of the stock-dove in Yorkshire, Mr. Chislett comments on the difficulty of distinguishing immigrants when a bird is also resident—as is the stock-dove—along the coast. He states, however, that in some years stock-doves have been seen coming in from the sea in the autumn along the Yorkshire coast.

Finally we have the quite definite evidence of Sussex ornithologists of an autumn immigration of stock-doves and wood-pigeons into that county. The observations were made in a coastal district of east Sussex— with Pett Leval at the centre of the area—and were collated by Mr. A. D. Wilkinson, who published his report, covering four successive years 1945-1949, in *British Birds*.[3] The word " immigrant " is stated in the report to refer to birds " coming in directly from the sea, the line of flight being such that they appear to the observer to have come across the Channel from France : the direction and frequently the manner of flight being quite different from that of the many species passing across the district in spring and autumn flying parallel to the coast ". The arrival of the pigeons— both ring-doves and stock-doves were involved, the former in greater numbers—was a fact well known to the sporting fraternity of the area, and

[1] *Studies in Bird Migration*, vol. ii, p. 164.
[2] *Birds and Mammals of Shetland* (1955), p. 264.
[3] xliii, 1950, pp. 233-238.

every October and November guns used to lie in wait for the incoming birds. Mr. Wilkinson found that there was great variation in numbers from year to year—very light in 1945 and 1946, much heavier and more widespread in 1947, light in 1948 with a narrow front of entry and very heavy and more widespread in 1949. The stock-dove flocks varied in size from 15-20 individual birds to a flock of 150 (seen by D. D. Harber) on 18th December. Some flocks flew straight on inland while others came down. Both high-flying and low-flying flocks were observed, the former usually continuing on their course. In the last year of the investigation considerable numbers came in between 30th October and 28th November. On the latter date a thousand birds (both wood-pigeons and stock-doves) were counted between early morning and 2 p.m., the passage being so marked that it was reported in the *Hastings and East Sussex Naturalist*, Vol. vii, No. 5, p. 193. The chief movements took place in November, but during the four years instanced immigration was recorded between the extreme dates 10th October as earliest, 18th December as latest. Any increase of birds in the surrounding woods was always preceded by immigration and as no migratory movements from overland were reported, it followed that the pigeon population reflected the amount of immigration from overseas to that area.

In a contribution to *British Birds* in 1955 [1] Mr. M. G. Ridpath argues against this immigration, pointing to the tendency of pigeons to fly out to sea in a southerly direction, sometimes beyond vision, and then to return. He is referring in the main to the wood-pigeon when he makes this assertion, but refers specifically to the " apparent arrivals in autumn on the south-east coast, those for instance at Pett Level (Wilkinson 1950) and at the Seven Sisters (South Eastern Bird Report 1947) ". On the evidence produced on both sides I am more inclined to agree with Mr. Wilkinson that the movements seen in November in east Sussex reflect a genuine case of immigration from the other side of the Channel. It would need a whole army of watchers on both sides of the Channel to convince me to the contrary. On the other hand the evidence Mr. Ridpath has produced in his report should be carefully studied.

Stock-doves are not very frequently ringed, and perhaps because of this, and because they are not shot to anything like the same extent as wood-pigeons, only two have been obtained in this country which have been ringed abroad. The first was ringed at Utrecht in Holland on 26th June 1936 and recovered in Buckinghamshire in February 1940; the second was ringed as a nestling at Tyrväntö, Finland, on 23rd July 1954 and recovered at Ormesby, Norfolk, in March 1955. The latter was recorded in *British Birds* [2] by Miss Elsie Leach of the Bird Ringing

[1] *British Birds*, xlviii, 1955, pp. 290-292.

[2] *British Birds*, li, 1958, p. 69. See also vol. xli, p. 205, where the Dutch example was recorded.

Section at the British Museum, who drew attention to the rarity of such an occurrence in this species.

In northern countries the stock-dove is not nearly as plentiful as the wood-pigeon, and this no doubt would account for the difference in numbers which have been recorded in Heligoland in past years. Gätke wrote in his *Birds of Heligoland* that the autumn migration of the ring-dove commences in the latter half of September and lasts throughout October until after the middle of November, but only rarely are flights of twenty or thirty individuals observed. It is, however, a regular and fairly common passage migrant through Heligoland. The stock-dove, on the contrary, is only met with in solitary instances, never in companies like the ring-dove, only one or two birds being seen in the course of each spring and autumn.

BREEDING HABITS: Under the heading of Local Distribution the favourite haunts of the stock-dove in the British Isles are mentioned, and as these are also its choice for nesting sites little more need be said on the subject. I would list holes in old trees in open parkland as the most likely spot of all in which to find the bird breeding, where, as in much of England, such parkland exists; but elsewhere it is probably on the sea cliffs that we can expect to find it making its nest in some hole or cranny. It has already been indicated that rabbit holes are often favoured, and that is particularly the case in parts of East Anglia and in the dunes at Bundoran, Co. Cork, among other localities on record. It has the same habit in Belgium as Comte Léon Lippens has mentioned.

In Scotland, where open parklands with old timber are not prevalent as in England, the stock-doves have to seek other sites in which to build. Rabbit-burrows are favourite nesting places and, as recorded in *The Birds of Scotland*, birds have been known to nest in the debris at the base of cliffs, in ruined castles, in ivy on occupied buildings, in pigeon-houses, and in nesting boxes. In Banffshire they are recorded as breeding among the heather on the steep face of Bochel. As Dr. Baxter and Miss Rintoul point out in that volume, the altitudinal range of the stock-dove is considerable, breeding as it does on golf links at sea-level and right up among the hills and mountains to 2600 feet. In the west of Ireland they show a preference for dense growth on lime trees, ivy-covered walls, and holes in trees. The instance of these doves nesting under furze bushes at the height of 800 feet on the steep slopes of the Mourne Mountains is believed by Major Ruttledge [1] to be unique. Another odd nesting place is mentioned by C. B. Ticehurst, who states that on the heaths and warrens of Suffolk eggs are laid not only in deserted rabbit-burrows but also under gorse bushes which have been so nibbled down by rabbits as to resemble large green pin-cushions; many of these have a hole through the side where rabbits have entered and are in turn used by the stock-doves.

R. F. Meiklejohn, who found a great many nests in various lands,

[1] *Birds of Ireland*, p. 277.

states that the amount of material used in the construction varies a great deal. Sometimes it is a slight platform of twigs, but in rabbit-burrows a few stalks and a little grass suffice for the nest. Occasionally a more substantial platform is built to which bits of root or straw, leaves, etc. are added. Less well known is the fact, as stated by J. Walpole-Bond, that every now and again substantial layers of freshly plucked leaves, such as those of the laurel and horse-chestnut, form a flooring for the eggs of the stock-dove (*History of Sussex Birds*, vol. iii, p. 97).

The stock-dove is an early nester. In some years, as Ticehurst discovered, eggs are laid by the end of February and pretty generally by the end of March. Not infrequently eggs may be found up to the end of September and so several broods must be reared in the year. J. Walpole-Bond, with a wider experience of nesting birds than most people, states that breeding normally begins in March but most stock-doves are not sitting until between 6th and 16th April. He gives the approximate date for second layings as mid-June, and third setts (as they may occur) are prevalent in August and early September. A very extraordinary case was reported by Edwin Cohen.[1] In his garden at Sway, Hants, is an ash with a large hole sixteen feet up. This is a favourite nesting site for tawny owls and stock-doves. In 1949 he found a tawny owl sitting on three eggs on 28th February, an exceptionally early date. When he revisited the nest on 22nd March the owl had deserted and stock-dove material had been laid over the owl's eggs. Five broods of stock-doves, two young in each, were reared in that hole in that season, of which four broods certainly, and the other probably, flew safely. Young of broods 1 and 3 overlapped in the nest with the incubation of clutches 2 and 4, in the latter case by at least nine days. The young of brood 5 flew on 5th and 6th October.

Mr. Walpole-Bond[2] considers the stock-dove a light sitter. Both sexes take part in incubation which lasts from seventeen to twenty-one days, the fledging period being about a month. Eggs are two, very rarely three, smooth-shelled and white with a little gloss. Jourdain gives the average measurement of 100 British-taken eggs as 39·3 × 29·1 mm. Max. 43 × 29·3 and 41·3 × 31·5 mm. Min. 35·4 × 27·4 and 39·5 × 26·5 mm.

Of the stock-dove's display Walpole-Bond observes that in February and March particularly, though also between April and August inclusive, the birds indulge in their courting flight display. He describes the exhibition as at variance with that of the ring-dove for, instead of preceding it, as does the latter, by a succession of switchbacks, the stock-dove flies round in wide irregular circles, generally progressing with normal flight though occasionally elevating its wings and floating along for a few moments in that position. Often several birds fly round together as described. Now and again one will smack its wings above its back, but this is only a feeble

---

[1] *British Birds*, xliii, 1950, p. 292.
[2] *A History of Sussex Birds*, vol. iii, pp. 95-98.

effort in comparison with the similar action of the ring-dove. As several stock-doves pass a tree in their aerial fling they will often make as if to alight—usually near the summit—and then, suddenly changing direction, dash ahead with renewed and almost frenzied vigour. Stock-doves never crash through the branches in the manner so often indulged in by the wood-pigeon, but slip adroitly through even thick belts of trees without touching a twig. It is, as Walpole-Bond has remarked, by far the more graceful of the two pigeons we have now discussed. The stock-dove shares with the ring-dove the usual bowing display, accompanied by swollen throat and fanned tail, as the bird pirouettes round the object of its attentions, accompanying its movements with its deep note.

One of the earliest ornithologists to discuss the bowing and other courtship displays of the stock-dove was the late Edmund Selous in his book *Bird Watching*,[1] published nearly sixty years ago. Describing what he terms the " most interesting aerial nuptial evolutions of the male and female stock-dove ", he continues :

They navigate the air together, following each other in the closest manner one being, almost all the while, just above the other. . . . Now they rise, now sink, making a wide irregular circle. Both seem to wish, yet not to wish, to touch, almost, yet not quite, doing so, till when very close the upper one drops lightly towards the one beneath him, who sinks too ; yet for a moment you hear the wings clap against each other. . . . Every now and again the wings will cease to vibrate, and the two birds sweep through the air on spread pinions, but otherwise in the manner that has been described.

Another pair rise from the ground in this manner, one directly above the other, quiver up still higher with hardly an inch between them, then suddenly . . . sweep apart and float in lovely circles, now upwards now downwards. As they do this another bird rushes through the air to join them, he circles too, all three are circling, the light glinting on one, falling from another, thrown and caught and thrown again as if they played at ball with light.

Selous himself, after watching these antics, first believed the birds to be indulging in simple nuptial flight ; but later he came to believe that " angry passions were at the root of all this loveliness ", the flight as described being but a continuation in the air of stand-up combats on the ground. Of two stock-doves fighting he writes :

This is very interesting and peculiar. They fight with continual blows of the wings, these being used both as sword—or, rather, partisan—and shield. The peculiarity, however, is this, that every now and again there is a pause in the combat, when both birds make the low bow, with tail raised in air, as in courting. Sometimes both will bow together, and, as it would seem, to each other—facing towards each other at any rate—but at other times they will both stand in a line, and bow, so that one bows only to the tail of the other, who bows to the empty air. Or two will bow

[1] Published by J. M. Dent and Co., Aldine House, 1901, to whom my acknowledgments are due for their permission to quote some passages from the text.

at different times, each seeming more concerned in making his bow than in the direction of bestowal of it. It is like a little interlude, and when it is over the combatants advance again against each other, still they stand front to front and quite close. Both then make a little jump, and battle vigorously with their wings, striking and parrying. . . . There were four or five birds when this fight broke out, but I could not feel quite sure whether the non-fighting ones watched the fighting of the other two. . . . Also the fighting birds may sometimes, when they bowed, have done so to the birds that stood near, but it never seemed to me that this was the case and it certainly was not so in most instances.

Referring to Selous's opinion that when two hostile stock-doves go through a slow ceremonial of bowings and other attitudes, this represents a " ritualization " of fighting—the conversion of a true combat into a tourney —Sir Julian Huxley expressed the view, in a paper read to the International Ornithological Congress at Oxford,[1] that the attitude adopted by the male bird is a genuine threat action and has its biological significance as a sign of readiness to fight, although it may in addition be ritualized, as frequently occurs in bird behaviour.

The stock-dove is one of our resident birds which will well repay further study, especially as regards its behaviour during the long breeding period. In *Bird Watching*, by a pioneer of that art, we have been shown the way. There is much more in the full account than I have space to quote, but two things stand out prominently : the difficulty which we mortals have in interpreting bird behaviour and—when one has read his whole chapter—the exceptionally acute powers of one of the most observant naturalists this country has produced : Edmund Selous.

REFERENCES : Original Description. *Columba oenas* Linnaeus, *Syst. Nat.*, 10th ed., 1758, p. 162 : Europe. Restricted type locality Sweden.

ROCK-DOVE

PLATE 24

Columba livia livia Gmelin

Resident and abundant in certain areas in Scotland and Ireland. Decreased greatly in Southern England and has ceased to breed in many places

IDENTIFICATION : In size the rock-dove and the stock-dove are much the same, and as both are mainly grey in colour there is an excuse for confusion between them. The rock-dove may always be recognized by the two prominent black bars across the pale-grey wings and by the white rump, although this latter is a variable character in other parts of the world. As the rock-dove crosses with the domestic pigeon there are not many parts of Britain where the pure strain still exists. Another point of distinction is the white under the wing (axillaries and under wing-coverts) in the rock-dove,

[1] *Proc. VIIIth Internat. Orn. Congress*, 1938, p. 434.

whereas these parts are grey in the stock-dove. Yet another difference, more easily seen at close quarters, is the grey breast of the rock-dove while that of the stock-dove is vinaceous. When the rock-dove spreads its tail, the outer feathers show a little white at the base. The lovely metallic green and purple sheen on the feathers of the breast and sides of the neck are well depicted in Mr. Lodge's picture, to which reference must be made for any details which I have omitted. It will be noticed that the terminal portion of the grey tail is broadly tipped with blackish. The eye is orange-red with a yellow inner rim, the bill lead colour, the fleshy base whitish ; the legs and feet are red. In flight the white under wing-coverts can be clearly seen from below ; while the white rump, if the viewer is looking down on the bird, is equally diagnostic. The two black wing-bars clinch the identification.

LOCAL DISTRIBUTION : This dove is said to be on the decrease, markedly so in parts of southern England where it has ceased to breed in many places where it was formerly common. Dr. Lack and Mr. W. B. Alexander, reviewing the changes in its status in the last hundred years, emphasize its scarcity or extinction in certain localities in the south, but could find no explanation to account for the decrease, which in view of the marked increase in other doves—the stock-dove in particular—is very curious.

Sea-cliffs are the acknowledged home of the rock-dove in Britain and it follows that on the coast of England there are huge stretches of shore-line where it never did occur. In former years it bred in England in Devon, Cornwall, and Yorkshire, and certainly on the rocky Welsh coast and in the Isle of Man. To-day the true wild bird appears to be practically extinct and, as Mr. Witherby wrote in 1940, " it is now very doubtful if any pure wild birds now breed anywhere in England or Wales, though in many places feral domestic pigeons breed and some are much like wild birds. . . ." Colonel B. H. Ryves wrote in his *Bird Life in Cornwall* (1948) : " I believe this pigeon to be extinct in Cornwall ". I recollect with what astonishment I read that sentence when his little book was published. G. W. Temperley, in *A History of the Birds of Durham* (1951), considered it a doubtful resident, probably now extinct in its original form, though doubtless at one time breeding in the caves along the shore. He adds that even in 1874 Hancock wrote that it was impossible to say positively whether the birds which then bred occasionally on the cliffs at Marsden and in other localities on the sea-coast were really of the wild form.

The Farne Islands were probably the last stronghold of the rock-dove on the Northumberland coast. Discussing the bird in her book *The Farne Islands* (1951), Mrs. Hickling (then Grace Watt) wrote that George Bolam believed that some of the birds which he had occasionally seen at the Farnes were genuine rock-doves, but she adds that the species has not been observed of recent years. Bolam in *The Birds of Northumberland*

PLATE 24

ROCK-DOVE
Columba livia livia Gmelin

(1932) wrote that in strict accuracy the rock-dove could not be included in his list : although some of the rock-building pigeons on the coast were true enough to colour, yet all suspicion of a taint of domestic origin could not be ruled out. Those which he thought might have been genuinely wild rock-doves on the Farne Islands, to which Grace Watt refers in her book, he deduced as such solely on account of their shyness—" the severest test that can be applied ". One day early in June 1958 the writer of this book was standing on Flamborough Head idly watching the flocks of guillemots and occasional razorbills passing out at sea, and the fulmars which, following closely the contour of the cliffs, passed within a stone's-throw away, when a couple of rock-doves flew out from a hidden cave below. I had imagined them to be genuine wild birds in one of their last English strongholds, but Mr. Chislett in his *Yorkshire Birds* is more cautious, writing : " the fact that doves are breeding in caves and crevices in cliffs is no proof of specific purity even on the coast. . . . Feral and wild doves intermingled may be seen along most of the Yorkshire coast, and in winter associate with domestic pigeons at farms nearby. . . . Whether any have maintained a pure strain through the ages is very doubtful, if not impossible." No doubt Mr. Chislett is right.

No finer setting could surely be found for the rock-dove than the towering cliffs and stacks of the Welsh coast, especially those of Pembrokeshire. An enquiry of R. M. Lockley for his views on the bird's present status has brought the following reply dated 16th June 1958 : " There are still quite a few left in a wild state along the coast of Wales ; but they are much interbred with gone-wild homing pigeons, so that the pure blue rock is much less seldom seen than the hybrid of many colours ". In *The Birds of Pembrokeshire* (1949) there is a statement that a small colony of six pairs with typical pure plumage were breeding in rocks near St. David's Head in 1947, in which year records were obtained of other typical " blue rocks " at Newport Head, the Strumble area, St. David's, Marloes, Linney Head, and Stackpole Quay. It came as a surprise to me to discover that *Columba livia* has long since vanished from its once tenanted haunts on the coast of Carmarthenshire,[1] and is no longer included in the list of the birds of that county.

It is to Scotland and to Ireland that we must go if we are to see the genuine wild rock-dove, and even in those more favoured countries there is strong evidence that the domestic strain is making itself increasingly felt among wild flocks.

In Ireland the bird is found breeding in all the maritime counties, and in Major Ruttledge's opinion the very great decrease which has taken place in England and Wales does not seem to be paralleled in Ireland. He writes in *Birds of Ireland* (1954) : " As far back as 1912 its numbers were thought

[1] G. C. S. Ingram and H. M. Salmon, *A Hand List of the Birds of Carmarthenshire*, 1954.

to be declining in Mayo and yet this decrease does not appear to have continued, for the bird is definitely holding its own in that county as a breeding species ". He reports that it is plentiful on the Clare coast, the Dingle peninsula, and on the southern coast of Kerry. In Sligo there is no scarcity of breeding stock, while in Donegal and the islands off that coast the bird breeds numerously. Major Ruttledge adds that observers in north-east Ireland have not noticed any decrease and the same holds good for the Waterford coast. Although in many wild areas in Ireland the bird has become mixed with feral birds and the influence of domestic blood is noticeable, Major Ruttledge believes that in Clare, Kerry, and Sligo the birds remain very true to type.

There are still areas in the north and west of Scotland where purebred rock-doves are holding their own. Dr. Baxter and Miss Rintoul, in their comprehensive survey of breeding haunts for their *The Birds of Scotland* (1953), acknowledge that, although much diminished in numbers and indeed extinct at some of its old breeding places, it is still a common bird in many parts of the west and north. In the south and east of Scotland the appearance of the flocks is sadly spoiled by the many birds with mixed blood. In Kirkcudbright few if any pure-breds remain, but there are perhaps still some about the Mull of Galloway, which the writer visited in June 1958 for the express purpose of ascertaining the truth. Very few rock-doves were seen, but a pair of racing pigeons gone wild told their own tale. On some of the islands of the Inner Hebrides the rock-dove is still abundant and that perhaps is its ancestral home in the Highlands. In Tiree it is especially numerous, the authors of *The Birds of Scotland* recording hundreds breeding and roosting in 1950 at Kennivara. The rock-dove is known to have been breeding in Tiree before 1794 and in Coll before 1843. In the last report on this island it was still abundant in 1949-55.[1] It is common and numerous in the Outer Hebrides, and equally abundant in Orkney. It was known to nest in Shetland in 1794 but it is not so abundant as in the Orkney Islands at the present day. Apparently extinct on Fair Isle in 1912, though formerly numerous, it has re-colonized the island—a flock of over 100 being present in 1943. Normally the rock-dove is a sedentary bird merely wandering in search of food. Its reappearance on Fair Isle after its earlier disappearance is a point of more than ordinary interest. In the very full statistical account of this bird in *The Birds of Scotland* any details which I have omitted here can be found.

DISTRIBUTION ABROAD : So many races of the rock-dove have been described, many of which are perfectly recognizable, that it would be safer to restrict the range of the typical race—the one that occurs in Great Britain. This ranges from the coastal districts of Western Europe and the western Mediterranean, southwards down the Atlantic coast of Morocco as far as Mogador. In the north of its range it is found breeding in the

[1] J. Morton Boyd, " The Birds of Tiree and Coll ", in *British Birds*, li, 1958, p. 105.

Faeroe Islands, the extreme south of Norway, the Baltic States, and the U.S.S.R. to at least the Ural Mountains, east of which there is considerable mixture with *C. l. neglecta*.

The range of the rock-dove in the U.S.S.R. has been dealt with recently in *The Birds of the Soviet Union*,[1] vol. ii, by R. N. Meklenburtsev where it is stated there that the typical species *C. livia livia* has only a relatively limited distribution in a truly wild state in that huge area. It is to be found in the Crimea and around the sea of Azov and a few are reported to have occurred in the past in the areas of the Lower Dnieper and the Don. Whether that is so to-day is open to question. It is stated to breed in the north Caucasus, but that too is from an ancient record and is better discounted. It is said possibly to breed on the Volga, Oka, and Sura, and certainly does so on the Sviaga. Some also breed between the Volga and the Urals. It is reported to be rare in the area of the Upper Tobol, and in 1908 was to be found in the Upper Irgiz area. A few years later it was recorded from the north shore of the Aral Sea. How reliable these old records are when computing the rock-dove's distribution in 1958 is a moot point. In Tarbagatai there are said to be considerable colonies but here, as in the whole area east of the Ural Chain, interbreeding with *neglecta* has taken place. Meklenburtsev mentions that the typical race was found in 1938 nesting in the Altai and earlier, in 1914, in the area of the upper Yenesei. North of these places the rock-dove has only spread in a semi-domesticated form—that is up to 66° N. on the Petchora. Nowhere is it numerous. In European Russia there are often only isolated pairs breeding, though occasionally small colonies of several pairs occur. In the eastern half of their Asiatic range colonies of up to several dozen pairs are found where sixty years earlier flocks of fifty thousand birds were being recorded. The same diminution in numbers has occurred in the Asiatic race *C. l. neglecta*—a paler form found in Transcaucasia and Central Asia. Thirty years ago this pigeon was found in those areas in tens of thousands in every Central Asian town; to-day it has disappeared completely from the towns and villages and is only to be seen in uninhabited places.

In Western Europe rock-doves breed in suitable localities as far south as Portugal and Spain. It is common on both sides of the Straits of Gibraltar and ranges in the Mediterranean islands as far east as Sicily and Malta. It is also recorded from Asia Minor but in Cyprus we find the Persian race *C. l. gaddi*,[2] and in the Jordan Valley *C. l. palestinae*. Cretan rock-doves are assigned by Meinertzhagen[3] to *C. l. gaddi* as I would have expected, but Professor Stresemann[4] allies Cretan birds with the typical race.

---

[1] Reviewed in *British Birds*, xlviii, by D. D. Harber who has given a useful translation of the bird's range and status from which I have quoted at length.

[2] D. A. and W. M. Bannerman, *Birds of Cyprus*, 1958, p. 279.

[3] *Birds of Egypt*, vol. ii, p. 503.　　　　　　[4] Stresemann in *J.f.O.*, 1956, p. 52.

From the European coastal area of the Mediterranean the typical race ranges to Asia Minor, the Black Sea, and the Caspian-Aral area. In Egypt *C. l. schimperi* is the race which occurs. In Tunisia, where I have collected rock-doves, we referred the specimens to *C. l. gaddi*. We met with them in ancient buildings in central Tunisia, again in the Tell Atlas and in the desert area of Gafsa.[1] They swarmed in the amphitheatre at El Djem, but the probability of mixture with domestic birds so near a village deterred us from collecting specimens at that place. Races of the rock-dove occur in island groups far out in the Atlantic. Two of these subspecies I have named myself; *canariensis* from the Canary Islands, and *atlantis* from the Azores and Cape Verde Islands. In the central Sahara we have *C. l. targia*, in the French Sudan *C. l. lividior*. Rock-doves occur in the great and middle Atlas Mountains and appear very pale in the brilliant sun, possibly through bleaching. We have seen them there in huge flocks but did not collect specimens. The Moroccan birds are usually considered to be typical and certainly appear a very pure-blooded strain.

HABITS : This splendid sporting pigeon will be a great loss to the rock-bound coasts of Britain if it continues to decrease as it has done in England within the last century. Fortunately there are wild areas in Ireland and Scotland where it will long survive and even perhaps spread once more to the Welsh and English cliffs. There are naturalists—Harry Witherby was one of them—who doubted that a pure-bred rock-dove existed, even ten years ago, south of the Scottish Border. The endless intermingling of domestic feral birds has had a disastrous effect on the purity of the strain. Even in quite remote places this mixture of blood is all too apparent.

My own experience of the rock-dove covers many countries, and wherever I have seen them their powerful flight has given me a thrill, more especially when they drop from the clouds to their roosting place in some precipitous sea-cliff. It takes a quick eye and a steady hand to bring any to the bag on such occasions. I have in mind a certain cliff in Grand Canary, where the precipices drop sheer to the sea. In such surroundings the rock-doves were in their element, passing daily to the cultivated land to feed, and returning in the evening, their crops well filled, to roost and later rear their young in the countless caves, from any one of which they would pour like an avalanche at the discharge of a gun.

There are some rock-dove communities which never come within sight or sound of the sea. Such are the large flocks which inhabit the precipices and caves of the Great Atlas of Morocco. On the occasions when I have crossed these mountains I have delighted in watching these pigeons descending from their fastnesses in the snow-capped range to feed on the scanty crops around the Arab villages, their white rumps shining and the bars on

[1] Bannerman in *Ibis*, 1927, pp. 202-204.

their pale wings betraying the species while still a long way away. As they settle in a cloud, maybe on the banks of a bone-dry wadi, the rays of the sun catch the iridescent purple and green on their necks as they bend to the important task of searching for seeds. Now and again very large flocks were encountered in this setting, all beautifully pure-bred *Columba livia*—stressing, if that be needed, the hybrid nature of our birds at home.

In places like southern Morocco, where a relentless sun beats down from a cloudless sky, the rock-doves may strike the observer as being exceptionally pale in colour, tempting the naturalist to think he may have stumbled upon an undescribed race. Comparison with specimens from nearer home probably dispels the illusion, for brilliant light can play strange tricks with a bird's appearance in the field. Even so a number of "good" races have been described, fourteen of which, so I note with interest, are recognized as valid by Russian systematists.[1] For two of those races I was responsible in years gone by. Throughout the extensive range of this species there is no apparent difference in their habits. Many never go far from the coast, roosting and nesting, preening and resting within sound of the roar of the waves.

It is a far cry from the Great Atlas to Cyprus, but in the latter island I have this year, 1958, been watching the rock-doves on their daily journeys from the Kyrenia range of mountains to feed under the carob trees on the coastal plains. They come down in the early morning as regular as clock-work and there they would fly round in a compact flock, before deciding where to settle, their grey plumage looking almost white in the clear atmosphere against the dark foliage of the carobs and the blue of the sea. Hunger appeased, the flocks would return to their mountain cliffs, where they shared the crevices and fissures with jackdaws, house martins, and kestrels, to pass the hot hours of the day in the cooler atmosphere of the hills. Maybe a Bonelli's eagle would have its eyrie on the same cliff-face but the pigeons showed less fear of it than of the dreaded goshawks which appeared to strike terror whenever they sailed overhead. When flying on these daily foraging expeditions the birds would keep in close order in their flock, and with steady wing-beats and set purpose would cover the distance in a very short time. It has been remarked how quick it is normally on the wing, but to appreciate its power of flight to perfection, it should be seen as I saw it one day, from the heights of an uninhabited islet of the Canaries, spotted by a Barbary falcon. As two pigeons flew out from their cave to cross an arm of the sea, the falcon, until that moment hidden from view, went off in hot pursuit. Never have I seen rock-pigeons accelerate in their flight as did those birds, and although as the peregrine made his stoop I thought their number was up, a swerve at the last fraction of a second and the falcon had missed, passing swiftly below them and barely saving himself from a ducking in the waves.

[1] *Birds of the Soviet Union*, vol. ii, p. 7.

Never even in the most remote parts of Scotland or Ireland can we hope to see such numbers as have been described from the Continent. In Spain, where most of the big Sierras have a large population of these doves, the late Howard Saunders recorded seeing immense flocks in the Sierra Nevada pouring forth from the deep cavernous gorges on the way to their feeding grounds. He estimated that within a short time fully seven thousand birds passed in his immediate vicinity—each flock being led by a pied and doubtless half-bred bird, of which there were generally a few individuals in every band.

I have digressed to give a picture of the rock-dove in other lands ; but it is not necessary to go far afield to see this bird in its most perfect setting—the coast of the Highlands and Islands in our own country. In some of our Western Isles the rock-doves must have their work cut out to find a living—a fact upon which Robert Gray remarked many years ago. He instanced the large flocks which inhabited the Haskar rocks, making their daily journey to Long Island to feed, and how they frequented the flat cultivated lands of Benbecula, North and South Uist, and Barra. Gray considered it probable that the St. Kilda birds also made daily flights to distant places in search of food. On South Uist and Benbecula he used to watch the flocks diligently clearing the ground of small shells such as *Helix ericetorum* which is present in extraordinary abundance. In the Shetland Isles Mr. and Mrs. L. M. Venables found that the feeding area of the rock-doves included sea beaches and especially washed-up banks of seaweed, marram dunes, grassland, and agricultural land, especially stubble. Flocks of up to 250 birds are considered large in the Shetlands and these only occur during the winter months. There, as in most other districts in Scotland, it is widely distributed wherever there are suitable cliffs with deep fissures and caves, practically all nests being placed in such places. It is good to read in their book that except in Lerwick the majority of Shetland birds are pure bred. We do not in Britain have colonies of rock-doves on inland cliffs ; the so-called " rock-doves " of such places are, as described by Witherby, either *stock*-doves (!) or rock-doves which have crossed with feral dovecot pigeons and taken to a nomadic life. Some of these latter closely resemble the wild rock-doves of the sea-cliffs and are therefore often mistaken for the pure-bred bird.

Throughout the whole of its range it is a rock-frequenting bird, never perching on trees. It has, however, been known under special circumstances to alight upon water.

To end this account of the rock-dove's most favoured habitat I will quote from the picturesque description sent to his friend Robert Gray by the naturalist of Iona, the late Henry D. Graham. The language employed is old-fashioned but the scenes he depicts are none the less satisfying :

The granite cliffs in the south of Mull, the basaltic crags of Staffa, and lofty precipices of trap rock upon the adjacent islands, are all perforated by innumerable caverns of every imaginable size and shape ; from the well-known majestic hall of Fingal, resounding with the sullen booming of ever-rolling waves, down to the fairy little grotto whose cool white shell-sand is scarce dimpled by the sparking ripples of the sheltered sea. Some of these caves are grand and of lofty dimensions, with no floor but the deep blue water which heaves to and fro through their huge frowning portals ; others are romantic and picturesque, their rocks covered with many coloured lichens, and their dark apertures fringed with shaggy heather and ivy, amongst which is browsing a wild mountain goat with huge horns and beard. But many more of these caverns are horribly gloomy and forbidding—deep black dens extending far beyond the reach of the light of day, stretching into the very bowels of the adamantine cliff ; the air smells dank and foul, and the walls are dripping with unwholesome slime. Such caves generally have legends attached to them—of a fugitive clansman hiding from the pursuit of the avenger of blood, of wholesale deeds of murder, or of wild scenes of diablerie ; and the names of the *Cave of Death*, the *Pit of Slaughter*, and the *Hobgoblin's Den* are often met with, showing their grim character. These haunts of bygone murderers, smugglers, and outlaws, are now tenanted by doves, the emblem of innocence. They may be seen perpetually flitting in and out, some parties going off to feed, others returning to rest ; a few birds sitting about the entrance, pluming themselves in the sunshine, or quietly dozing upon a sheltered ledge of rock. Upon a nearer approach the cooing of the old birds may be heard, together with the querulous *peep-peeping* of the young demanding food, and the occasional stir of wings ; but, upon any alarm being given, the clang and whirr of wings reverberate from the profundity of the cavern, and out pours a long stream of snowy white bosoms and silver wings, which swiftly skim along the surface of the sea and disappear round the next headland. In Iona alone (though but a small island) we have as many as nine or ten caves frequented by pigeons, and in nearly every island of the Hebrides there is sure to be one cave called *par excellence*—" Ua' Caloman "—the pigeon cave.[1]

BREEDING HABITS : From the foregoing pages it will be appreciated that in the British Isles the rock-dove's life is closely bound up with caves and precipices, the majority of which are within sight and sound of the waves. It is in such an environment—as Henry Graham has left on record—that the young are born and brought to maturity and although the Sierras of Spain and the great mountain ranges of Europe, Asia, and Africa may shelter their tens of thousands in ravines and caverns far from the coastal areas, the rock-doves in Great Britain and Ireland are essentially maritime birds. The same may be said of those which have made their homes in distant islands, such as the Azores, the Canaries, Cyprus, or the Balearics, and the many islands of the Grecian archipelago to instance some of their sea-girt haunts, where they live very much the same life as their relatives in the British Isles.

Less has been written of the courtship and love-making of the rock-dove than of any of our pigeons, no doubt owing to the scenes taking place for the most part in the hidden recesses of deep caves, for it is in these

[1] *Birds of the West of Scotland*, 1871, pp. 221-222.

" deep caverns moist with the spray from the thundering surge "[1] that the rock-dove lays its eggs in the dark recesses which such places have to offer. We can observe the normal antics almost any day in our domestic pigeons, the direct and very close descendants of *Columba livia*, and if one is lucky the wild rock-dove may be observed paying court to the lady of his choice on the same ledges as are occupied by razorbills and guillemots. The male will extend his neck to its fullest extent and bow low to the female, puffing out the feathers of his neck to exhibit the lustre on the green and violet feathers to the best advantage. Fanning the tail and sweeping it on the ground, the bird will pirouette in a half-circle, cooing loudly at the same time, turning this way and that, as may be witnessed so often in the domestic bird displaying before his intended. The bows and turning about may be repeated several times. When displaying in the air the bird will fly in slow motion, then with wings raised will glide for a space before once more beating its wings. Nodding of the head, accompanying the display on the ground, is also a common feature noticed in domestic pigeons. The object of all these attentions may or may not respond as desired, and if not stimulated by the actions of the male bird is likely to seek peace by flying away, to be pursued by her relentless suitor, unless perchance he has become discouraged and gives up his quest until a more propitious moment presents itself, or his ardour is freshly aroused. Naumann, the German ornithologist, as quoted in *The Handbook*, has recorded the male, in intervals of bowing and turning round in half-circles, hopping or running round the female with spread tail depressed on the ground. I have witnessed all the other motions described above but have yet to see a rock-dove hop.

The favourite place for a nest is on a ledge in the deep recesses of a cave, though I have seen the birds entering fissures in the cliffs where there was no sign of a cave. In some countries I have watched them entering crevices in which jackdaws and Alpine swifts were obviously nesting, but I have never succeeded in reaching one of these communal breeding places —or what appears to be so—for they are usually in most inaccessible spots. When the nest is on a cave ledge, as are so many in Great Britain, it is but a slight structure of a few twigs, stalks, roots, etc. If the same nest is used more than once, if not " for years ", it becomes much more substantial. Such nests were examined on the island of Coll by the late R. F. Meiklejohn whose MS. notes are now in my possession. That well-known naturalist took the eggs of the rock-dove in many lands and in the interior of Algeria —at El Outaya—a locality which I know well myself—found it breeding both on ledges of rocks in the mountains and also in the shaft of wells. I have myself seen these pigeons come *out* of wells in desert country, but have never been successful in finding their eggs there, generally at some depth in the walls. Colonel Meinertzhagen also remarks on this habit of breeding in wells in Arabia, in which country the nest is more often placed on a rock ledge

---

[1] To quote from the 4th edition of Yarrell's *History of British Birds*, vol. iii, p. 17.

or in a ruined building and consists of a mere pad of vegetable matter. In the caves around our British coasts sea-weed is not uncommonly found as nesting material, but more often—in Scotland at any rate—heather stems are used. The rock-dove has a habit of nesting in deep holes in the roof of caves, where it is usually quite inaccessible. It is of course well known that *stock*-doves will often utilize the holes of rabbits in which to lay their eggs. I have never heard of such a site being used by the rock-dove.

The eggs are smooth-shelled and white with some gloss. Two is the normal clutch, occasionally only one. The 100 eggs measured by F. C. R. Jourdain gave an average of 39·3 × 29·1 mm. Max. 43 × 29·3 and 41·3 × 31·5 mm. Min. 35·4 × 27·4 and 39·5 × 26·5 mm.

The laying dates of the rock-dove have been a matter for some discussion. Referring to Jourdain (as the prince of oologists of our time) we find that he states in *The Handbook* that most eggs are laid from April to July, but they have been recorded as early as March and as late as September. There are, however, some caves around the Scottish coasts where the time of year does not appear to be taken into account by the rock-dove inhabitants. Thus the Rev. John Lees discovered birds breeding on 15th January 1944 [1] in a group of caves on the Eathie shore by Cromarty, and upon investigating the matter further he was able to substantiate nesting in these caves *all the year round*. The fact is recorded in the *Birds of Scotland* by Dr. Baxter and the late Miss Rintoul but was evidently not generally known. For instance, Howard Saunders in the fourth edition of Yarrell's *History of British Birds* wrote that the first clutch of eggs is generally laid early in April, and the second early in June ; even a third laying is not infrequent for birds just hatched have been found as late as 18th October, so that even a fourth brood is possible " although the young probably succumb to the approach of winter ". That this last supposition is not necessarily the case has now been established by Mr. Lees, who painstakingly investigated nesting operations in four separate caves in the area specified—north-east of Rosemarkie. It should be emphasized that the rock-doves in these caves were found to be as near pure bred as British rock-pigeons on the mainland can hope to be ; only occasionally does an intruder creep in. The results of this remarkable survey may be told in Mr. Lees's own words when summing up the evidence in his paper.[2]

Breeding activity goes on more or less all the year round. There is a marked maximum in April, coinciding with the general nesting season for resident birds. The minimum occurs in July—only few doves anywhere on the coast are found breeding then. This may be coincident with the moulting of the body feathers ; but moulting certainly proceeds during the autumn months, when the caves are strewn with moulted feathers from nesting birds.

Nesting usually takes place simultaneously by small groups of pairs (2-10) occupying adjacent sites in one cave.

---

[1] *British Birds*, xxxvii, p. 237.   [2] *British Birds*, xxxix, pp. 136-144.

In each cave there are alternate periods of nesting, and quiescence. The latter are usually quite short, and sometimes non-existent, through the overlapping of active periods. Breaks of a month or two, however, may occur in summer, or after some disturbance of one of the nests.

The active periods fall into four groups. There is the main period of spring nesting, where hatching takes place about April. This is followed, after a break, by a summer activity, young birds appearing in August. After this come autumn and winter periods with hatchings about November and January.

Mr. Lees concludes that it is doubtless an exaggeration to say that all rock-doves breed nearly the full round of the calendar and have four families a year ; it may be, he suggests, that in the caves he examined a second party of birds use the nests after the first have flown, but that one nest should be used by a cycle of different pairs during the year appears unlikely. It was found that severe weather did not interfere greatly with nesting, for deep snow covered the ground almost continuously from 1st January to 6th February, the temperature on 25th January being about 2° F. In spite of this, there were young birds in two caves not included in Mr. Lees's survey.

The period of incubation was found to be eighteen days. Heinroth gives seventeen to seventeen and a half and J. L. Bonhote nineteen days, both recorded from birds in captivity. Mr. Lees found that the fledging period varied from thirty-five to thirty-seven days. During this investigation proof was forthcoming that rock-doves require little excuse to desert a cave. In one case the experiment of interchanging an egg with that of a jackdaw not only forced the dove whose egg was removed to desert her nest, but all others in the cave followed suit. In another cave the destruction of a single dove's nest led to desertion by the whole colony.

In one cave examined—as in several others—the floor was strewn with wings of the small tortoiseshell butterfly *Aglais urticae* : there were literally hundreds of such wings all nipped off close to the body, the inference being that the doves were responsible, although actual proof was wanting. No other lepidopterine wings were found. *The Handbook* records that in partial absence of cultivation the rock-dove feeds on seeds and mollusca in larger proportions than the wood-pigeon or the stock-dove. To this list, if Mr. Lees is correct in his surmise, we must now add " lepidoptera in season ".

To what extent we can conclude that the breeding of the rock-doves in this part of Scotland is typical of other colonies it is difficult to say. I cannot recollect ever having remarked winter breeding in other parts of the rock-dove's range beyond our islands, but admittedly one took it for granted that the birds would not nest at the height of the winter even in North Africa. That they may do so in view of Mr. Lees's experience at Eathie shore, by Cromarty, cannot be dismissed. Colonel Meinertzhagen gives the breeding time of *C. livia palestinae* in Arabia where eggs are laid as early March to late April. Certainly the rock-doves breeding in the north of Scotland and in the northern islands appear to have an exceptionally extended nesting season. It seems that if food is plentiful, then breeding continues. Saxby believed that "incubation is constantly in progress from the end of February to the end of October" in Shetland,[1] and found a well-developed egg in the ovary of a bird on 21st January. That the same nest may be used by a pair on at least several occasions is vouched for by Saxby, and we now have the evidence of Mr. and Mrs. Venables [2] that a nest containing eggs which they found in a North Havra cave on 17th May consisted of generation upon generation of heather twigs with a slight new cup of oat straw, which had obviously been used many times. There is evidently room for more investigation as regards the breeding season of the rock-dove—not only in Britain but in other parts of its extensive range.

REFERENCES : Original Description. *Columba livia* Gmelin, *Syst. Nat.*, vol. i, 1789, p. 769. No locality stated. Southern Europe accepted as type locality.

Genus *STREPTOPELIA* Bonaparte

TURTLE-DOVE

PLATE 25

Streptopelia turtur turtur (Linnaeus)

A Summer Visitor to breed in England and Wales, but locally distributed, mainly in the east and south. In Scotland has nested in Berwickshire ; in Ireland has bred very sparingly. As a Passage Migrant it is recorded from all countries.

NOTE : The eastern turtle-dove (*Streptopelia orientalis*) is considered a distinct species notwithstanding the views of some modern naturalists and at least one of the Old Brigade. It will be the next bird discussed.

IDENTIFICATION : This is a small slenderly-built dove not more than $10\frac{1}{2}$ inches in total length. The upperparts, mantle, and wing-coverts are rust-coloured with black middles to the feathers, the back browner. The forehead is pale grey, becoming ashy on the crown and brownish on the nape. The neck, throat, and breast are pinkish-vinous, and on each side of the neck is a patch of black and white feathers, the black feathers being tipped with white and bluish-grey. The inner coverts, secondaries, and scapulars are black broadly margined with rufous cinnamon, the outer coverts mostly blue-grey. The primaries are dark brown. Very conspicuous when spread is the tail, the central feathers dark brown, the

[1] *Birds of Shetland*, 1874, pp. 151-152.
[2] *Birds and Mammals of Shetland*, 1955, pp. 265-266.

remainder black washed with grey and broadly tipped with white : the outer tail-feather is white on the entire outer web. The sides of the body are dark blue-grey with a vinaceous wash ; the middle of the belly and the under tail-coverts are white. The eye is yellowish-brown, the eyelids red, the bill blackish, and the feet and legs claret colour.

Immature birds are browner above, particularly on the crown, nape, and mantle : the breast is also much browner than in the adult.

LOCAL DISTRIBUTION : This dove is a summer visitor to the British Isles, but though expanding its breeding range it is by no means universally distributed. When Alexander and Lack summed up its status in 1944 [1] they wrote that at the beginning of the nineteenth century it was confined to southern, eastern, and central England, but rapidly increased and extended its range to Wales, Cheshire, and Yorkshire before 1865. It has continued to increase since those days and has nested occasionally in the northern counties of England. In his *History of the Birds of Durham* [2] G. W. Temperley wrote in 1951 that although the turtle-dove breeds sparingly in the north-east of north Northumberland, and has done so for some years, it has not yet been proved to do so either in south Northumberland or in Durham, though it has occasionally been reported in the middle of the breeding season. It breeds spasmodically in Cumberland. Much more encouraging has been its spread in Yorkshire. Mr. Chislett writes [3] that more than forty years ago he knew it as a fairly numerous breeder in south Yorkshire as far north as the Barnsley area, beyond which it straggled occasionally. To-day it is generally distributed over the countryside where woods and coppices occur and is numerous in the valleys of the East Riding. In the north-east it now breeds in woods at altitudes of 800 feet, which were avoided until very recent years. Mr. Chislett gives many other areas in this large county to which it has spread as a breeding species in his valuable history of Yorkshire birds to which reference should be made. Its spread westwards into Wales is mentioned in *The Handbook*, where it is reported to have increased in Flintshire, Denbighshire, Merioneth, and Caernarvonshire and to some extent in Monmouth and Glamorgan. Since then we have Ingram and Salmon's *Birds of Carmarthenshire*, [4] in which the statement is made that the turtle-dove comes annually to the county in very limited numbers and breeds only in extremely few localities. In Pembrokeshire it has only bred on one occasion for certain, at Orielton, although Major Congreve believed eggs had been taken elsewhere. Apart from being a regular passage migrant in small numbers to Pembrokeshire and its islands it is extremely seldom seen. North of the Welsh coast, it is

[1] *British Birds*, xxxviii, 1944, p. 68.

[2] *Trans. Nat. Hist. Soc. Northumb., Durham and Newcastle upon Tyne*, vol. ix, 1951, p. 210.

[3] *Yorkshire Birds*, p. 226.

[4] G. C. S. Ingram and H. M. Salmon, *A Hand List of the Birds of Carmarthenshire*.

reported to have much increased in Cheshire, and in Lancashire [1] Clifford Oakes writes that it has become well established in south Lancashire and is a common summer resident ; but the breeding range is restricted to the south of the county, its failure to spread farther north being surprising.

Besides the breeding birds there are the passage migrants which wend their way up our coasts, mainly on the eastern side of Britain. This may be conveniently witnessed in East Anglia where, off Lowestoft, C. B. Ticehurst records having seen turtle-doves " on a good many occasions during May . . . passing north along the coast in twos and threes early in the morning ". As Witherby once remarked, these are probably the birds which account for the non-breeding records in our northern counties and islands.

Considering that the turtle-dove has spread northwards so rapidly on the eastern side of England it was not surprising to learn of the first breeding record from Scotland. A pair nested in the garden of The Hirsel (the seat of the Earl of Home in Berwickshire) in July 1946, and the occurrence was reported by Major the Hon. Henry Douglas-Home in *British Birds*.[2] In answer to my enquiry as to the status of the turtle-dove in the south-east of Scotland Henry Douglas-Home has sent me the following notes on the breeding of the bird on the Hirsel estate and neighbouring areas. He writes —in July 1958—that he *believes* the turtle-doves are spread fairly well through Berwickshire, Roxburghshire, and East Lothian, but he can only vouch for the following for certain :

BREEDING AT THE HIRSEL

1946   10th July building in big rhododendron bush at The Hirsel.
        13th July, dove sitting all day, sexes probably sharing incubation. One very tame and one very temperamental. This nest was disturbed and the doves deserted. The fact was reported to *British Birds* as already noted.

1947 1948 1949   Several pairs of turtle-doves spent all the summer on The Hirsel, but owing to military duties Major Douglas-Home was unable to search for the nests.

1950   Turtle-doves greatly increased this year, 9-10 pairs at least on the Hirsel estate. One pair successfully reared two young from nest in wild currant bush five yards from stable wall. The nestlings flew 22nd July.

1951   20th May, doves nesting in same bush by stables, old nest cleared away, new nest in same fork. The dove sitting on 1st June ; two young reared and flew on 29th June.
        At least 10-12 other pairs in the Hirsel woods.

1952   Major Douglas-Home away most of summer and no nests therefore recorded.

1953   Doves again built in same bush, which contained two eggs on 20th June. Both chicks successfully reared. A second nest in same bush contained a sucked egg.

Since 1953 the turtle-doves have increased yearly on the Hirsel estate and this year (1958) there are 12-15 pairs at least, perhaps more.

---

[1] Clifford Oakes, *The Birds of Lancashire*, 1953.
[2] *British Birds*, xxxix, 1946, p. 283.

Other records from elsewhere than The Hirsel are, on Major Douglas-Home's authority, as follows :

1957   Hendesyde, Roxburghshire : a fair colony 8-10 pairs in a young wood. Three nests were located.

        Bonkyl estate, north of Duns, Berwickshire, held several pairs.

1958   Easter Langlee, Galashiels, Selkirk : one pair present, but the nest not found.

Finally a letter from Lord Malise Graham records his having seen a single turtle-dove at Connel, Argyll, in mid-June.

In their history of the birds of Scotland Dr. Baxter and Miss Rintoul have recorded that the turtle-dove occurs in Scotland not uncommonly on migration, the greater number having been noticed in May and June. The bird has now been recognized in all but seven of the mainland counties : moreover it has been recorded from a number of localities in the Inner Hebrides as well. In the *Scottish Naturalist* for 1951 the Editors, commenting on the appearance of turtle-doves in Argyll (Skipness 1st November 1950 and Kilberry 26th September 1951) as recorded on p. 194 of their journal, remark that the turtle-dove has been reported as an occasional visitor to many west coast areas, including Ardnamurchan in western Argyll, but that few records relate to the south of that county and only one to Kintyre where a bird was seen at Carradale on 11th June 1923. The flock of fifteen seen by M. Campbell at Kilberry on the Sound of Jura on 27th September—the day after the record mentioned above—is therefore of particular interest to Scottish historians who are watching the spread of this dove in their country with great interest.

Although the records from Western Scotland as yet are only spasmodic its appearance in the extreme north has been observed on many occasions. Certainly to Orkney it can only be classed as an occasional visitor, but to Fair Isle and Shetland its visits are so regular that it ranks as a passage migrant. Mr. and Mrs. Venables saw single birds on various dates from 6th June to 17th July and from 3rd September to 27th October during their several years' survey of the islands' birds. They considered it an " almost regular spring and autumn migrant in small numbers and by no means confined to trees but often seen feeding under the lee of stone walls ". It is remarkable that it should come so regularly in summer to the Shetlands where it is not a breeding bird. There are isolated records of turtle-doves having been seen on such distant islands as the Flannans, North Rona, and St. Kilda. Even more remarkable is its fairly regular appearance in autumn in the Faeroe Islands.[1] It is at the same time of year that it wanders occasionally to the Outer Hebrides, from which group it has been recorded on several occasions from North Uist. The last of these records is of a bird seen by Collingwood Ingram on 8th September 1950 sheltering in the sand-dunes from the strong southerly wind.

[1] K. Williamson, *The Atlantic Islands.*

PLATE 25

TURTLE-DOVE
Streptopelia turtur turtur (Linnaeus)

In Ireland the turtle-dove was unknown as a breeding bird until 1939, when it was discovered to have bred in the woods of St. Anne's, Co. Dublin, and the fact was reported [1] by E. O'Mahony. The authors of *Birds of Ireland* have now stated that they have reliable information that a small colony has been established elsewhere in a restricted area which they do not divulge. They stated further that reports of odd pairs breeding in Kerry and Co. Down had come to hand. Major Ruttledge considers it probable that diligent research would prove that the bird breeds more often than is generally supposed. Once it has gained a fairly strong footing in that country it is likely to increase as it has done elsewhere. In reply to an enquiry as to what progress it has made in that direction since *Birds of Ireland* was published Major Ruttledge writes in July 1958 that he would not feel justified in saying that the turtle-dove has increased as a breeding bird since 1954. " Breeding has been taking place each year in a comparatively limited area and by a few pairs only. On the whole it shows no increase." No further breeding at St. Anne's has come to his knowledge, but that is probably owing to the district changing character, trees being cut, etc. Major Ruttledge believes that breeding in Co. Cork and other southern counties will be duly substantiated. The lack of reliable *resident* naturalists probably accounts for the paucity of breeding records, and Major Ruttledge believes that more pairs may be breeding in Ireland than are generally known.

DISTRIBUTION ABROAD : The turtle-dove breeds throughout the whole of Western Europe except in Norway and Sweden (though it has been recorded to have nested in the south of Sweden) and Finland, occurring from Great Britain and Denmark eastwards through the Baltic States and Russia where it breeds up to 60° N. In Asia it ranges to the Kirghiz Steppes and the Aral-Caspian region, and it breeds in Asia Minor and the Crimea. Its southern range in Europe reaches the Mediterranean and it breeds in many of the Mediterranean islands, including Cyprus. In the Balearic archipelago it is a common summer visitor, as it is also in Corsica, Sardinia, Sicily, Crete, and several other islands. Vast numbers pass through Malta, but there the bird is given little opportunity to breed owing to human persecution ; for the same reason comparatively few remain to nest in Cyprus. Colonel R. F. Meiklejohn's notebooks record that it passes through Crete in spring, " sometimes in very large numbers ", when many are shot for food. On none of the inhabited islands does it find anything but a hostile reception.

East of the Aral-Caspian region and the Persian Gulf we find another subspecies *S. t. arenicola*, and this same race, or birds indistinguishable from it, inhabits north-west Africa from Tunisia westwards to Morocco. Yet in Madeira and the Canary Islands the breeding bird is the European form *S. turtur turtur*. Still another race *S. t. isabellinus*, distinguished by

[1] *British Birds*, xxxiii, 1939, p. 140.

its pale " isabelline " plumage, inhabits Egypt. Meinertzhagen would unite all the turtle-doves in both the *turtur* and *orientalis* groups (which I keep separate) and consequently recognizes twelve subspecies of *Streptopelia turtur*, going so far as to include in his group such tropical forms as *hypopyrrus* from the Benue River and *lugens* from the Abyssinian Highlands.

HABITS AND MIGRATIONS : The typical race of the turtle-dove is such a pronounced migrant wherever it occurs that even in Mediterranean countries and in islands as far south as the Canaries it cannot be considered a resident bird any more than is the case in Great Britain. I have watched its passage movements in many lands from the Canary Islands and Tangier to Tunis and Cyprus, and have met with it on many occasions at sea far from the sight of land—for the turtle-dove, for some reason, is one of the most conspicuous migrants throughout the whole of the Mediterranean when the birds are passing to or from their winter quarters.

When I was writing in 1930 the second volume of *The Birds of Tropical West Africa*, we had very little knowledge how far the European turtle-dove penetrated south of the Atlas ranges, but the discovery of the typical European race just north of Burrem on the Niger [1] at an isolated well in the desert (just south of 18° N.) pointed to its crossing the Sahara, while the large flights consisting of many hundreds of birds seen by Golding in the vicinity of Lake Chad [2] were much more likely to have been the European migrant than the race (*hoggara*) which is probably confined to the Air Massif. The birds were flying N.N.E. on 20th March. We know to-day that the European turtle-dove must cross the desert area on a wide front, but it is more common in East Africa than it is in the west (Gambia) and reaches the Sudan, Abyssinia, and the north-eastern Belgian Congo during the non-breeding season. To the northern Sudan it is an abundant visitor from October to March.[3] Curiously enough it is only a summer visitor to the Canary Islands [4] to breed and does not winter there.

It is not surprising that so many cross the Mediterranean. This passage has been summarized by R. E. Moreau (in *Ibis*, 1953, p. 351), who observes that the records from that sea are as widely distributed as they could be ; vast numbers pass over Valencia in both spring and autumn and another marked migration occurs in the area of Cape Trafalgar where we have seen them on various occasions in the early spring. In former days—and perhaps in our own time—great flocks arrived in Tangier in late April and May to cross the Straits to Europe, and we have Irby's statement that it is to be seen in extreme abundance in Andalucía. The birds arrive on the Spanish coast from Africa during the first week in May, " more coming in that week than during all the rest of the migration ".

[1] Bates, in *Ibis*, 1934, p. 217.
[2] *The Birds of Tropical West Africa*, vol. ii, 1931, p. 333 ; vol. viii, 1951, p. 242.
[3] Cave and Macdonald, *Birds of the Sudan*, 1955, p. 167.
[4] Bannerman, in *Ibis*, 1920, p. 124.

The lateness of their arrival in Tangier no doubt accounts for our not having seen this passage for ourselves when we were watching the migration in recent years in the vicinity of the lighthouse at Cape Spartel, and on the (then) International boundary. Farther to the east, in the central Mediterranean, the passage through Malta towards the end of April is very large indeed. W. H. Payn learned that one man had netted 700 in a single spring—which spells doom to thousands as they pass through that island. The same slaughter goes on in Cyprus, where huge numbers are shot or caught on lime-sticks in spring and autumn, especially the latter. Even so, the numbers probably pale in comparison with the mass migration through Syria and the Jebel Druze. Specimens collected in these countries by Colonel Meinertzhagen belonged to the typical race. In his recently published *Birds of Arabia* that author writes of the abundant passage of the turtle-dove through Palestine, Transjordan, and Egypt from the end of March to late April and again from mid-August to October.

Most of the birds using the routes specified spread over Europe during the breeding season, but to what countries those which have bred or been bred in the British Isles travel we have little indication other than the certainty that they must winter in Africa, ranging to the Sudan and Abyssinia. Many turtle-doves have been ringed in Britain and recovered abroad, but we have yet to have a recovery from south of the Mediterranean. The majority bearing British rings have been taken in France, Portugal, and Spain, some having reached Estremadura, Cordoba, Huelva, and Seville, obviously *not* at their journey's end.

The passage through Portugal is the most spectacular of all, and was well described by an old friend of my early days, William Tait, author of *The Birds of Portugal*. In that volume he told how the doves arrive at Oporto in the beginning of April—sometimes a little earlier—and leave again from the latter part of August till the third week of September, exceptionally passing until November. He wrote :

In the autumn immense numbers migrate south along the coast of Portugal, preferring an east or south-east wind, and travelling in large and also small flocks, from 500 to 1000 yards from the sea. Should the wind be mild they fly very high but if strong they barely skim the tops of the Indian-corn stalks. . . . As soon as the anti-cyclone dry east wind begins to blow, numbers of gunners collect in the early morning along the sea-coast to intercept the unfortunate travellers, and near the mouth of the river Douro a continuous fusillade may be heard from shortly after sunrise until about 10 o'clock in the morning.

Mr. Tait was satisfied that some of the flock flew by night, some birds striking the lantern at the entrance to the river. These birds seemed to be unwilling or unable to deviate from their route and from time immemorial huge bags have been taken. It was remarked that when the migrating bands reached the mouth of the Douro, if the wind was strong they did not strike across to the opposite side of the river but followed the right bank for a short distance before crossing to the south side. Only if there was no wind and the birds were flying high would they cross towards the mouth. The same thing occurs at the mouth of the Tagus, a much broader river entrance; and there the doves are reported to fly many miles up the right bank, as far as Villa Franca de Xira, before crossing to the south side. Sometimes the turtle-doves are not alone, but accompanying the flock are swallows, tree pipits and meadow pipits, skylarks, and other species passing in a stream with perhaps a few hoopoes, shrikes, cuckoos, woodchats, and an odd wood-pigeon, forerunners of the great procession wending their way to warmer climes. When the doves reach Andalucía— and doubtless before as well—they are the object of pursuit by anyone with a gun, and many are shot at the drinking pools to which the birds come down to quench their thirst : three or four in a row are the minimum shot at one discharge. When we realize that this is going on through the length and breadth of the Mediterranean the wonder is that there are any doves left. The late Joseph Whitaker recorded how considerable numbers are obtained in Sicily in the olive groves and among the carob trees when the wind is favourable to their passage. The hundreds if not thousands which are shot in Southern Europe during the autumn passage will account for the comparatively large number of birds bearing British rings which are reported annually. Once the birds have travelled beyond the Latin countries and have perchance gained the southern shores of the Mediterranean (where sportsmen are less prevalent) they have more chance to survive until another year.

And this unfortunate little bird is—to quote Alfred Newton in his *Dictionary of Birds*—the time-honoured emblem of tenderness and conjugal love. What a way we treat it !

We may expect the turtle-doves to arrive in Great Britain from the end of April to the third week of May ; but reference to the B.O.C. migration reports shows that some arrive much earlier on the Hampshire, Sussex, and Kent coasts, and though the forerunners are never numerous they may be seen from the first week of April onwards, the main body putting in appearance around 19th April and the succeeding fortnight. By the end of the first week of May they have reached roughly a line drawn from the Wash to the Mersey—but here again very much depends on the weather which the birds encounter on their journey north.

BREEDING HABITS AND COURTSHIP: In a justly renowned picturebook [1] of British birds, with illustrations from life by Eric Hosking and text by Cyril Newberry, is a superb photograph of a turtle-dove on its nest—the caption reading : " The smallest and loveliest of the British Pigeons ", a description which does not fall short of the mark. Then Dr. Newberry introduces us to the subject of the picture in these words :

In the stillness of a summer evening there are few sounds more enchanting than

---

[1] *Birds of the Day*, 1944, p. 116.

the soft coo-ing of the turtle-dove. The very mention of it takes our memories back to a lowland waste of sandy heath, with scrub and thorn-bushes dotted here and there, for it was in such country that we first encountered this bird. Since then we have found it in spruce plantations ; in mixed copses and thin woodlands ; and in large hawthorns in the hedgerow.

We picture now the male dove on his favourite perch high up near the top of a hawthorn, his shapely figure outlined against an ethereal sky and his haunting notes swelling on the balmy air.

To the writer the soft notes of the turtle-dove recall a very different scene : a camp pitched under the shade of date-palms in a dry parched land—the desert island of Fuerteventura [1]—the cooing of the doves mingling with the even softer notes of the hoopoes as we woke to a blazing hot day in the middle of May. Not far from our tents lay the sheltered *barranco*—a dry ravine or nullah leading inland from the sea, its bed thickly clothed with tamarisk in which the doves had made their flimsy nests, and from which these pleasant sounds were coming to herald another day. In the crowns of the palm-trees several pairs of kestrels were also breeding, but, living as they did on lizards and insects, the other feathered inmates of this little oasis in the eastern Canaries had little to fear from these neighbours. Here, where there were no lurking sportsmen and no lime-sticks, the turtle-doves could breed in peace, but in a setting far removed from that which inspired Dr. Newberry to write of its love-flight from the top of a hawthorn tree, or which furnished the pioneer bird-watcher Edmund Selous with material for a fascinating chapter.

The courtship of the turtle-dove was described by Selous in his book *Bird Watching* [2] long before ornithologists of his day had paid particular attention to the emotions expressed by birds during the mating season. Drawing the attention of his readers to the courting actions of the wood-pigeon, the author then observes :

The turtle-dove bows too, in courtship, but it is a series of quick little bows or, rather bobs, which he makes to his fiancée instead of one or more slower and much more imposing ones : the pace has been quickened and the interval lessened, and the bow itself is shorn of much of its pomp and circumstance. . . . All the time he is thus bowing or bobbing the turtle-dove utters a deep, rolling, musical note which is continuous (or sounds so) and does not cease until he has got back into his more everyday attitude. . . . This is in tree-land ; but I have seen the turtle-dove court on the ground, and he then, between his bobbings, made a curious dancing step towards the female, who retired and gave her final answer by flying away.

But besides this, these birds have another and most charming nuptial disport-ment. Sitting *à deux* in some high tree, one of them will every now and again fly out of it, mount upwards, make one or two circling sweeps around and above it, then,

---

[1] The largest of the eastern Canaries explored by the writer in 1913. Cf. *Ibis*, 1914, pp. 38-90.

[2] Published in 1901 by J. M. Dent Ltd., from whom I have permission to quote an extract.

after remaining poised for some seconds, descend on spread wings in the most graceful manner, alighting on the same branch beside the waiting partner. This is a beautiful thing to see, and especially in the early fresh morning of a clear, lovely day. It seems then as if the bird kept flying up to greet " the early rising sun ", or as rejoicing in the beauty of all things.

Many years after these words were written the subject of display and song in the turtle-dove was reviewed [1] by M. K. Colquhoun, who drew a comparison between this species and the wood-pigeon. Mr. Colquhoun rightly points out that of the two types of display—the bowing or bobbing, and aerial—the former is best known, and is essentially, on the male's part, a prelude to coition. It was noted that during bowing the neck is contracted, the breast slightly " pouted " and the bill pointed directly downwards : the bird does not therefore look openly at his mate. Mr. Colquhoun remarked that aerial display consisted of two components, the vertical or steep climb and the glide. In the vertical climb the bird soars steeply with rapidly beating wings and widely stretched tail for some thirty yards or less, after which it glides down, usually in a circular movement, sometimes landing in the same tree and resuming its song. Colquhoun noticed that from directly beneath the bird as it mounts skywards the white disc of its belly gleams with an astonishingly brilliant effect, particularly with the sun low in the sky. It was observed that the climb is always made in the presence of a mate. While the wood-pigeon makes from one to three undulations in flight with a wing-clap for each, the turtle-dove rarely makes more than one, with apparently less effort. The display note of the turtle-dove may be written *rur-rur-rur*. It is finally suggested in this account that the bowing display is invariably accompanied by the quick throbbing notes and also that while display, including aerial, may take place at any time of day, it is at its maximum early in the morning when, under favourable conditions such as a bright sunny morning towards the end of a warm period, the quick throbbing notes may be uttered four times in one hour before 8 a.m. Colquhoun disputes the suggestion made by Selous that the display note is continuous : a note accompanies each bow. Mr. Colquhoun hesitated to deny that the turtle-dove ever gives a wing-clap, but observed that it is certainly rare and seldom audible. On occasions it certainly does act in this way ; the performance has been witnessed and the sound clearly heard by Miss E. M. Barraud,[2] who published a note on the subject. Her attention was drawn to the birds by a noise which she describes as " a vigorous clapping ". One bird was perched on an electric cable, the other was in mid-air making a short climb " at the peak of which it clapped its wings twice ".

There is nothing new to write about the turtle-dove's nesting habits to which we must now give some attention. In European countries where

[1] *British Birds*, xxxiii, 1940, pp. 222-224.
[2] *British Birds*, xxxix, 1946, p. 284.

it breeds it is a bird of open woodland rather than forest, and for a nest situation it has a wide choice.   The late John Walpole-Bond, who had considerable experience of its nesting in Wales and England, wrote of it in his *History of Sussex Birds* : " Perhaps most frequently the nest is placed in a tall straggling quickset or in one of those scattered thorns so prevalent in woods and plantations.   All the same quite a number of turtle-doves breed in conifers (though very seldom in larch), elders, birches, hollies, and hazels.   Occasionally . . . pear and apple in orchards and certain bushes . . . though twice only have I known nests in gorse ".   Mr. Walpole-Bond had several instances when the nest was built on top of a blackbird's or song-thrush's nest.   He describes the nest itself as only about five inches across and so flimsily constructed of fine twigs that portions of the eggs are visible from beneath, though it often remains empty for several days.   In Suffolk, Ticehurst has told us that although almost any bush or small tree is selected for the nest, especially hawthorn, the favourite site on the heathlands is the taller whins.

It is usually the third week of May [1] before the first eggs are laid, and some are in early June.   Second layings take place during July and both eggs and young are to be found in the nest in August—the probable result of a third laying.   The clutch consists normally of two white, slightly glossy, eggs, occasionally three, while a single egg is not unknown.   Both parents incubate, the incubation period lasting fourteen to fifteen days (Bond).   Jourdain in *The Handbook* gives the period as thirteen to fourteen days, but that was from birds in confinement, not always an accurate guide.   He gives the average measurement of 100 British-taken eggs as 30.7×22.98 mm.   Max. 33.4×23.8 and 31.5×24.7 mm.   Min. 27.7×22 and 30×21 mm.   The young remain eighteen days in the nest, and according to G. C. Ingram and H. M. Salmon fly two or three days later.

Both wood-pigeons and turtle-doves have been known to feign injury when the young are in the nest, but in the case of the latter there are very few published records.   Witherby, in an editorial note in *British Birds*, xiii, to a communication describing a wood-pigeon which had fluttered down to the ground and then " hopped along with flapping wings ", observed that he had seen a turtle-dove behave in much the same manner. Further references will be found in *British Birds*, xxvii, where both A. W. Boyd and R. M. Garnett published notes on the subject.   The latter saw a bird fly down to open ploughed land and then scuffle about on the ground, a proceeding which it repeated when it flew on to a sandy lane on a different occasion.   This habit cannot be general, as more often than not the bird when alarmed will fly straight away without recourse to any diverting ruse.

When the young leave the nest they may be seen in family parties in the vicinity, but they begin to take their departure from our shores as early

[1] It struck me as remarkable that I found fresh eggs in the Canary Islands approximately at the same time.

as mid-August. From then on flocks may be seen on open ground, and later when the grain is garnered they may be encountered in the stack-yards. Writing[1] of its feeding habits Derek Goodwin remarks how it eats wheat readily, but as it only gleans such grain as is going to waste on the ground it does no harm thereby. It varies its diet like other pigeons with occasional greenstuffs and, as Goodwin observes, probably takes its toll of invertebrate animal life, especially when feeding young. In late summer turtle-doves have been known to gather into considerable flocks before departure, several observers having recorded such gatherings from time to time. For instance Mr. I. Lemon[2] counted about 200 on 2nd August 1951 on telegraph wires in Northamptonshire, and believed that many more were feeding in corn below. Occasionally a member of this flock was heard to sing; another sixty were seen on 16th September by Mr. C. F. Tebbutt in Huntingdonshire.[3] Other large flocks are mentioned by the editors of *British Birds* when publishing a record of 154 birds counted in Norfolk by Mr. M. J. Seago. They draw attention to similar reports in other periodicals where flocks of 100[4] and 200[5] turtle-doves had been seen at once.

The turtle-dove is so attractive in appearance and is the cause of so little damage—if any—that it should surely be encouraged to make its home in these islands at the time when it is rearing its young. It consumes the seeds of countless injurious weeds and if perchance it helps itself to some peas now and again, we must remember—to quote the late Lord Passfield, O.M.—that " what they take from the crops is usually only a fair wage for valuable work performed ". In the case of the turtle-dove the damage it does is practically *nil*.

As the September days shorten the flocks make their way to the coasts and before October is upon us the majority of our turtle-doves are on their way south once more—running the gauntlet of the innumerable sportsmen who lie in wait for them in Portugal and beyond. It is indeed remarkable considering the risks they run that so many return, as has been proved by ringing, to the nests of the previous season. I have no late information as to the status and numbers of the bird in Portugal to-day but when Tait wrote his chapter on Migration around 1924, he quoted some of the older sportsmen who lamented that turtle-doves were not then so numerous as they had been. We can take some comfort from Tait's exclamation that the profusion of turtle-doves all over Portugal was (at that date) *so great* during the summer months, " where their pleasing coo-ing can be heard almost wherever one goes, that much powder and shot and much perseverance . . . will be required before their numbers are reduced to any appreciable extent ". We must hope that this forecast holds true to-day. We can

---

[1] *Bird Notes and News*, vol. 26, 1953-54, p. 5.
[2] Both gatherings reported in *British Birds*, xlv, p. 424.
[3] *British Birds*, xlvi, p. 113.   [4] *Bedfordshire Naturalist*, 1951, p. 33.
[5] *Sussex Bird Report* for 1951, p. 16.

at least give the turtle-doves a welcome and a summer refuge in the British Isles, where birds are appreciated for their beauty rather than their culinary excellence, except by a very few.

REFERENCES : Original Description. *Columba turtur* Linnaeus, *Syst. Nat.*, 10th ed., 1758, p. 164 : " Habitat in India " *errore*. Correct type locality England.

RUFOUS TURTLE-DOVE

Streptopelia orientalis [1] (Latham)

An Accidental Visitor

IDENTIFICATION : The late Hugh Whistler described this dove as a rather large vinous-brown dove, 13 inches in total length, with the sexes alike, having conspicuous rufous scale markings on the wings and a patch of black and blue-grey scale markings on the sides of the neck. A dark graduated tail edged with white or slate-grey is conspicuous in flight. The tail is rather long and graduated. A more detailed description by the same authority reads as follows :

Head, neck, and back brown tinged with vinous ; on each side of the neck a patch of black feathers tipped with bluish-grey ; sides of the wings blackish with broad ferruginous borders giving a scaled appearance ; quills brown with pale edges ; lower back and rump slate-grey ; upper tail-coverts brown ; tail blackish-brown, all except the central pair of feathers, tipped with slaty-grey ; lower plumage vinous, paler on the chin and throat ; wing-lining and a patch under the tail slaty-grey. Iris orange ; eyelids pale blue with red edges ; bill brown, vinous at base ; legs vinous-red, claws black.

As Mr. Whistler points out, the rufous turtle-dove is so closely allied to the common turtle-dove of Europe that its races are sometimes considered as races of the western bird. It is—in my view unfortunately—a fact that modern systematists tend to lump together under one specific term anything which can be remotely allied. There is possibly a better case for uniting *orientalis* as a subspecies of *turtur* (as Meinertzhagen has done in his *Birds of Arabia*), but the result is a somewhat unwieldy group of doves covering the greater part of the Palaearctic Region which can be much more conveniently dealt with as two distinct species. I am far from being alone in preferring this course. Whistler and Kinnear in India kept them distinct, so did Smythies in Burma, Hartert in the Palaearctic Region, and Witherby in the British *Handbook*. Even Russian systematists prefer to keep the two species apart in the *Birds of the Soviet Union*, but

[1] Although this bird has been universally recorded as the typical subspecies, it seems far safer to refer to it henceforth under the binomial term, and very little is gained by attempting to nail it down subspecifically. There are at least three races which have been recognized in India alone.

the other school will probably have its way in the end ! Modern tendencies point that way—but it is not progress.

OCCURRENCES IN BRITAIN : The first example of this eastern species was obtained near Scarborough, Yorkshire, on 23rd October 1889 and was recorded by Seebohm in the *Proceedings of the Zoological Society of London*, 1890, p. 361. It was described as being a young bird. The second to be obtained was shot at Castle Rising, Norfolk, during a pheasant shoot on 29th January 1946, and was identified at the Norwich Castle Museum by Mr. E. A. Ellis. It was recorded in *British Birds*, xxxix, p. 184, by Mr. B. B. Rivière, who wrote that a bird such as this must always be under suspicion as an " escape ", but a letter to the *Eastern Daily Press* asking for information about any known to have been kept in aviaries in Norfolk elicited no reply. The distinguishing features of this bird were the large size (wing 190, tail 120, tarsus 27, bill to feathers 17 mm.), the dark slate-blue rump, and grey instead of white under tail-coverts ; the tips of the neck-patch feathers and the ends of the tail-feathers were also grey.

DISTRIBUTION : The typical subspecies is said to be a breeding bird in China and Japan north to Korea, Mongolia, and middle eastern Siberia, ranging in the south to eastern Tibet and the Himalayas. In his *Handbook of Indian Birds* (4th edition edited and revised by Sir Norman Kinnear), Whistler observes that the rufous turtle-dove extends in several races from eastern Siberia, China, Japan, and Tibet to the greater part of India, Ceylon, and Burma ; also western Central Asia, Turkestan, and Afghanistan.

HABITS : As Mr. B. W. Tucker observes when recording this species in *The Handbook*, its behaviour does not appear to differ in any essential respect from that of the European turtle-dove. Mr. Whistler wrote of this bird in India that when breeding it is found usually in thick forest but is otherwise mostly observed in the more open and cultivated areas where large trees, groves, and gardens provide shelter within easy reach of the stubbles where it likes to feed on fallen grain and seeds. He describes it as very active on the ground, running and walking freely, and when disturbed invariably taking refuge in trees.

In winter and on migration numbers may be found in company, but they can hardly be said to gather into flocks, as the birds do not keep together, but fly off in all directions when disturbed. Whistler records that this dove drinks very frequently. The note he describes as " a dull sleepy drone, *cooo-cooo-kakour*." The breeding display of the rufous dove consists of flying into the air and volplaning down again with wings and tail stiffly spread out. It breeds more or less during the whole year according to locality, making the usual scanty platform of twigs and bents through which the eggs can be seen. The nest is placed in a tree or bush at no great height from the ground, with little effort at concealment. Two pure white and very glossy eggs form the clutch. F. C. R. Jourdain has recorded the average measurement of twenty-eight eggs as 33·6 × 24·7 mm.

In Burma, where it is mostly seen in the more open and cultivated areas round forest villages, it feeds largely on fallen rice grains after the harvest and is to be found where large trees and patches of scrub-jungle provide it with shelter within reach of the paddy stubble. Mr. B. E. Smythies, who provided these field-notes, observed that it will fly considerable distances to feed : one bird shot with its crop full of paddy was six miles from the nearest paddy field across hills and thickly wooded country. It spends the heat of the day in the forest and flies out to forage in the afternoon, returning at dusk. It is a resident bird throughout the forests of Burma, ascending to 5500 feet, while in north-east Burma the race *orientalis* is found on the Yunnan frontier up to an altitude of 7000 feet.

REFERENCES : Original Description. *Columba orientalis* Latham, *Ind. Orn.*, vol. ii, 1790, p. 606 : China.

COLLARED TURTLE-DOVE [1]

Streptopelia decaocto decaocto (Frivaldsky)

A recent addition to British avifauna. First seen in Lincolnshire in 1952 but origin doubtful. Breeding of another pair substantiated in Norfolk in 1955. Now definitely established in several areas ; apparently Resident

IDENTIFICATION : The whole upperparts of this dove are uniform pale earth-brown, the head and neck grey tinged with lilac, the forehead pale mauve. A black collar narrowly bordered with white surrounds the hind neck forming a half-necklet. The wing-coverts are pale blue-grey, the flight feathers very dark brown. The middle pair of tail-feathers are light brown, the remainder grey and blackish-brown with broad white tips. The breast is pale lilac or pinkish-mauve, becoming ashy-grey on the belly and more slate-grey under the tail. The underside of the tail is very conspicuous, the whole of the underside of the rectrices having broad white tips while the base is black. The quill lining is white. This combination of black and white makes a striking character as the bird rises. The eye is crimson, the eyelids whitish ; the bill black ; the legs and feet pinkish-red.

In *British Birds*, l, p. 242, three correspondents [2] describe succinctly the field characters which impressed them when watching the birds in England ; and of what they term " general habits " they write as follows : " A sandy grey dove, somewhat larger than turtle-dove, with a narrow black

[1] I am greatly indebted to Professor E. Stresemann, D.Sc., for having read this essay in manuscript and for his advice on many points. Professor Stresemann and Dr. E. Nowak have made a meticulous study of the spread of this dove and have published their conclusions in the *Journal für Ornithologie*, xcix, 1958, No. 3.

[2] R. A. Richardson, M. J. Seago, and A. C. Church.

half-collar, edged white, round back of neck; dark primaries and black and white under-tail surface, particularly striking in flight ". The juvenile plumage, described from young hatched in Norfolk, is apparently subject to some variation, for one bird was distinctly washed with cinnamon while another, of the same parentage, is described as almost mousy fawn-coloured. A dark ring is present though incomplete and usually very faint. Newly-fledged nestlings have no collar. The fawn body plumage and wing-coverts have narrow pale fringes and blue-grey bases, giving a two-tone appearance and a faintly patterned effect. The primaries and tail-feathers are similar to those of the adult bird. The iris is olive-brown ; the feet lead-grey.

The adult birds, though wary, were tolerably approachable but were alarmed by unaccustomed movements. They fed on the ground but were seen to spend long periods preening or dosing in trees. They were fond of perching on vantage points, such as dead branches, power cables, telephone poles, and so on. They gave the impression of being typical pigeons with swift and powerful flight ; on the ground they moved with the usual waddling walk of the family. The song of the male—the female was not heard to utter a note—is described as a pleasant tri-syllabic *coo, coo-co* with emphasis on the middle syllable, uttered up to a dozen times in succession. More will be said on this subject when we come to discuss the habits, for the bird is known to the author of this book in the Middle East and to many other ornithologists.

HISTORY OF ITS ARRIVAL IN BRITAIN AND LOCAL DISTRIBUTION AT PRESENT DAY : An event of such moment as the spread of this dove across Europe finally to reach the British Isles—not only as a vagrant but evidently a bird that has come to stay—naturally aroused much excitement in the ornithological world, and consequently the new arrivals were studied by a band of ornithologists almost from the start of their life in England, and their every movement was chronicled—fortunately by responsible individuals. The literature on the subject is already extensive and I am left with little to do but express my indebtedness to those ornithologists from whose writings I have compiled this account, and to the editors of those journals, *British Birds* in particular, in whose pages the early history of *S. decaocto* in England was recorded. Mr. I. J. Ferguson-Lees in particular has enabled me to keep this section up to date and is responsible for the " history " during 1957 and 1958 which he has kindly prepared for this volume.

It is possible that the first wild collared dove to be seen in Britain was the one identified by Mr. R. May at Manton, north Lincolnshire, on 24th July 1952 and duly recorded,[1] though some uncertainty as to whether the bird was a genuine wild example was felt at the time. The uncertainty arose owing to the fact that a dealer at Pontefract, Yorkshire—less than

[1] R. May and J. Fisher in *British Birds*, xlvi, 1953, p. 51.

an hour's flight from Manton—had recently sold several of these doves in the district. The fact that a pair bred at Manton in 1957 does not really affect the issue : they would presumably have been attracted to the area by the calls of the bird already there, whether it was an escape or not. Mr. Ferguson-Lees tells me that it was not the lone male which paired and nested in 1957 : it has remained the outsider all the time, and it is perhaps significant, as Mr. Ferguson-Lees points out later in this essay, that it was left there by itself in 1958. When first this bird arrived in the cottage garden of Mr. and Mrs. Hampshire in the first or second week of May 1952 (which is the usual date for the taking up of territories on the Continent) it constantly displayed, but never succeeded in finding a mate. Finally it disappeared but reappeared at Middle Manton on 21st April 1953 after an absence of seven or eight months. I understand that it has reappeared in the district every year since. When first recording this bird Messrs. May and Fisher pointed out that the nearest place in Europe reached by the collared dove in its westward extension by 1952 was Amersfoort on the south-east side of the Zuider Zee in Holland.

We now come to the first undisputed breeding of an apparently wild pair in another county—Norfolk.[1] This took place in a small garden in north Norfolk, two young being reared. At least two pairs were present in the area but only one pair bred in 1955. Two doves wintered in 1955-56.

In 1956 three different sites were occupied :

Site A. A large walled garden near the sea with extensive lawn and shrubberies. Three nests were discovered (in July, August, and September respectively) in the season and five young were reared in them by this pair of doves.

Site B. In a garden on the outskirts of the town ; nest found early April ; shells of hatched eggs later picked up beneath a pine tree. Two young were reared before the site was deserted.

Site C. A pair bred in the same place as the 1955 nesting record, this time in an umbrella-shaped ilex, and reared at least one young one. An egg near hatching was found beneath the tree after an August gale.

It was ascertained that during 1956 sixteen individual doves, including young birds, were known to be in the area, twelve of which were present in February 1957. Single birds which were seen at Cley in the early autumn may have been wandering Norfolk-bred juveniles. The history of this immigration and of the first definite nesting in Britain is published in *British Birds*, l, by Messrs. Richardson, Seago, and Church, where very full details are given of their discovery. There have been reports published of birds having been identified unquestionably as collared doves

---

[1] *British Birds*, l, 1957, pp. 239-242.

from other English counties, in addition to those mentioned from Lincoln-shire and Norfolk. On 15th April Mr. G. H. Forster recorded [1] a collared dove from Gomshall, Surrey, and the spread was continued in 1957.

From this point Mr. I. J. Ferguson-Lees will take up the tale. I would here express my thanks to him for the report he has specially pre-pared to cover the seasons 1957 and 1958, thus bringing the spread of the collared dove in Britain right up to date. He writes as follows :

Quick and sudden spread has been the essential feature of the collared dove's extension of range across Europe, and so it was expected that the discovery of new breeding areas would rapidly follow the colonization of part of Norfolk in 1955 and 1956. Sure enough, in 1957 collared doves were found nesting in three new counties —in Kent and Lincolnshire, and in Moray right up in Scotland. Their appearance in the last of these counties, which represented a straight jump of some 375 miles from the Norfolk colony, was not as surprising as it might seem at first sight, for " hops " of 300-400 miles have all along been a striking characteristic of the collared dove's advance and this one was in the standard north-westerly direction. Such " hops " have been particularly commented on by most of the several writers who in recent years have summarized the collared dove's spread (the most complete account in English is that written by James Fisher in 1953, in *British Birds*, xlvi, pp. 153-181 ; and the most recent, which came out in 1958, is that by E. Stresemann and E. Nowak in *Journal für Ornithologie*, xcix, pp. 243-296).

The Moray pair was discovered on a farm at Covesea in June and the nest was found in a *Cupressus macrocarpa* bordering the garden wall : it contained one infertile egg and one young bird which was successfully reared. The events were reported in *The Scottish Naturalist*, lxix, pp. 188-189, by several observers including Mr. Alistair Adam, on whose farm the nesting took place. In Lincolnshire, at Manton, where a single male collared dove was found in 1952 and in each successive summer (though it is still impossible to be certain that this one was not an escape from captivity, see *British Birds*, xlvi, p. 55), a further pair arrived in May 1957, and on 30th June Mr. Reg May flushed the female from a completed but empty nest that had been built on top of an old song thrush nest in rhododendrons. Later that same day he was to watch her lay the first of two eggs and on 31st July two young left the nest. In Kent, the third and last county to be colonized for the first time in 1957, a pair was located on 30th May in an area of farmland and mixed woods in an eastern district. They bred in a pine at the edge of a copse and two young were seen in the nest on 28th June, but on the next day the nest was found to be empty and on the 30th the wing of one of the juveniles was picked up about thirty yards away. The second young bird was safely reared, and on 9th July one of the adults was found to be incubating on a second nest in another pine about forty yards from the first : two young were successfully reared in August.

Meanwhile, in Norfolk the 1956 position was consolidated in 1957. At Site A there were at least two breeding pairs present, and four separate males were calling on 15th June (but one of the breeding females was found dead on 13th June and the bereaved male did not find a new mate for nearly six weeks) ; two juveniles

---

[1] *British Birds*, l, 1957, pp. 270-271. It cannot be absolutely *certain* that this was a wild bird.

were seen in May and a nest with one youngster was found on 13th June. At Site B, where there were as many as twelve birds on 5th February, one pair was present in the summer and almost certainly bred nearby. A pair at Site C moved to a mixed wood 150 yards away (Site D) after a nesting failure ; there they reared one youngster and were later incubating a third clutch of eggs.

During the summer of 1957, too, there were reports of collared doves from other parts of Norfolk and Kent and from several other counties. Most of these reports came from the south-eastern quarter of England (though one bird reached St. Agnes in the Scilly Isles on 30th August) and most referred to single birds that stayed only a day or two. However, a male arrived at a locality not far from the Essex coast in late May and, after passing the breeding season unmated, was joined by a second male on or before 22nd September ; three birds were present on 13th October, four by the end of that month, five on 9th November, and six from 24th November onwards.

So much for 1957. The 1958 picture is not absolutely complete at the time of writing (early September 1958) and in some cases the full information has still to come in.[1] However, there is enough evidence to show that there has been surprisingly little increase over 1957 : two of the four 1957 breeding counties (Norfolk and Moray) show virtually no change and only one (Kent) seems to have had an increase ; no nesting was proved in Lincolnshire and, although breeding probably took place in Essex, a new county, there have been so few reports from outside the colonized counties that one is left with a general impression of no progress during 1958.

In most of the breeding-areas the majority of the collared doves spend the winter somewhere in the district and it seems probable that, even where they appear to leave at the end of the summer and return in the spring, they do in fact only move out of the immediate neighbourhood. At any rate the pair in Moray wintered at Covesea despite the comparatively severe weather at the beginning of the year, and it was found that there was a third adult with them (the young bird reared in 1957 was thought to have been taken by a cat) : in the summer of 1958 they reared two broods of two young each, the second leaving the nest on 10th August, and at the end of that month there were seven birds present in the area. In Lincolnshire, where nesting was not proved in 1958, only the original male was to be seen for most of the summer except on one day, 13th July, when there were four birds displaying and fighting. In Norfolk it is probable that no more than four pairs spent the summer in the breeding area ; no nests were found, but several young were reared. Precise information for Kent is not yet to hand, but nesting spread to a second area in the east of the county ; here at least one young was reared and a second pair was present. In Essex the flock wintered and then split up ; the area is a difficult one and, though it is believed that one young bird was reared, nesting could not be proved.

---

[1] Since these notes have been printed Mr. Ferguson-Lees has been able to complete the picture for 1958, from which it is plain that progress was, after all, made in the spread of the collared dove to other areas. In a note which he and Mr. Williamson published in *British Birds*, lii, p. 104, it is announced that a nest with two nearly fledged young was found in a pine on 6th July in Hertfordshire and at least one adult was still in the area in early August. In Northumberland four birds were located in September, two of them probably juveniles, and three, if not four, were present until at least 9th February 1959. News has just reached me that in 1959 *S. decaocto* nested in Ayrshire, the most westerly record to date.

Chicken-runs and farm surroundings, long regarded as the typical habitat of the collared dove, are a significant feature of almost all the British nesting areas, and it is in such places that the species may particularly be looked for (though beware of confusion with the rather similar, semi-domesticated Barbary dove, *Streptopelia risoria*). For the most part they are fairly bold in the presence of man and readily become accustomed to the routine activities of the locality, but they are by no means tame and do not usually allow a very close approach.

This summary of the British status could not have been written without much assistance from R. A. Richardson and M. J. Seago (Norfolk), R. May and R. K. Cornwallis (Lincolnshire), W. Crawford and R. Richter (Moray), E. H. Gillham and R. G. Williams (Kent), and G. A. Pyman (Essex). To all of them we are greatly indebted for the information they have provided.

DISTRIBUTION ABROAD : The collared turtle-dove, with its type locality in south-east Europe, has a huge range at the present day, for this is the same dove which Whistler described as " by far the commonest dove in India ", in his *Handbook of Indian Birds* (4th edition), where it is listed on p. 400 as *Streptopelia risoria* [1] Linnaeus, a name which I had understood to be indeterminable. From Hungary and the Balkan peninsula we can trace its range eastwards through Asia Minor, Iraq, Persia, India, and Ceylon. In Burma it is represented by another subspecies, *S. d. xanthocycla*, said to have yellow skin round the eye.

The southern range of *S. decaocto decaocto* in the Middle East includes Cyprus (if not almost exterminated as a resident species) and Palestine, where it ranges to the southern end of the Dead Sea ; but it does not occur

---

[1] Regarding the correct name of the collared turtle-dove and the use of the name *risoria* as applied by Whistler (and Sir Norman Kinnear who edited and revised the 4th edition of Whistler's book after the author's death), I wrote to the British Museum for an explanation, and received the following reply from Mr. R. W. Sims of the Bird Section :

" The name *decaocto* was brought into use in 1920 by Hartert (see the *Vögel der paläarktischen Fauna*, Bd. II, 5-6, p. 1496 n.) because the earlier name *risoria* Linnaeus referred to the introduced Barbary dove of Sweden, which Hartert believed was a domesticated variety, derived from the African form *Streptopelia roseogrisea*. Since that date most workers have followed Hartert. (The recent A.O.U. 1957 Check-list supported Hartert and named the resident Barbary (ring) dove of western America as *Streptopelia risoria* (Linnaeus), noting its genetic affinity with *S. roseogrisea* of Africa.) Whistler, in using *S. risoria* for the Indian collared (ring) dove, presumably did not agree with Hartert, nevertheless ' *C. risoria* Linnaeus ' as used by Whistler is the same as *Streptopelia decaocto* Frivaldsky of Hartert, Peters, and recent authors. Thus, the name of the collared (ring) dove is *S. decaocto* (Frivaldsky), while that of the introduced and domesticated Barbary dove is *S. risoria* (Linnaeus), the new British dove being the former.

" Fisher in his review of the collared turtle-dove (*British Birds*, 1953) was probably correct in restricting the type locality of *decaocto* to Philippopolis in Bulgaria, because although Frivaldsky did not give a type locality under the actual description of *decaocto* he was, nevertheless, in that section of the book describing animals and plants from Philippopolis. At that time Philippopolis formed part of the Ottoman Empire ; however, after 1918 it became part of Bulgaria when its name was changed to Plovdiv. To-day Plovdiv (42° 10' N., 24° 43' E.), with a population of 125,000, is the second largest city in Bulgaria."

in Sinai or Arabia proper, where the closely allied *S. roseogrisea* takes its place.[1]

The westward spread of the collared turtle-dove from the Balkans through Europe to the North Sea, and now to Britain, has been spectacular. James Fisher has chronicled its remarkable extension in an exhaustive paper contributed to *British Birds*,[2] which should be read by all interested in distributional problems. I have made considerable use of it in this essay. In the course of his analysis Fisher observes that the main phase of the spread has occupied a singularly short time, for it cannot have got under way until the early 1930's. In the last thirty years (reckoning from the publication of his paper in 1953) this dove, he writes, has been observed in at least 468 places in Europe in which it had never been seen before, including places in Scandinavia about 1200 miles from Belgrade, the point where the spread can be said to have started.[3] Fisher suggests that the spread originated primarily in the great plain of the Danube north of Belgrade. The first record of the bird in Italy is given as 1944, and it first appeared in the Po valley in 1949. Austria began to be colonized in 1938; by 1948 collared turtle-doves were in towns and villages all along the course of the Danube in Austria. By 1946 some had crossed the border into Germany, reaching Augsburg in 1947 and the neighbourhood of Munich, Aalen (Württenberg), and near Stuttgart in 1948. By 1949 the bird had reached the Upper Rhine and had appeared in south-west Czechoslovakia. In 1950 it was recorded from canton Zürich and Basel in Switzerland and the same year penetrated to the Vosges, France. Two years later (1952) a bird was picked up in the Ardennes, which had been ringed the previous year in Saxony. Individual birds made some spectacular " leaps ", as Fisher terms them, in 1948 and 1949. In the former year a dove was seen—and others since—at the very north tip of Jutland in Denmark; the following year the Kattegat was crossed and a dove appeared in Halland, south Sweden. By 1952 the bird was reported from Fjärås in that country. Colonies were formed in Holland in 1949, 1950, and 1952, and in 1952 the first collared dove appeared in the British Isles, though *not* necessarily from Holland. The above is a very general indication of how the collared turtle-dove has raced westwards, colonizing place after place and country after country. It has not yet reached Ireland but that is surely a matter of time only, for the bird has an obvious desire to extend its range, and since it is a prolific species, and one which

[1] Some modern authors, Meinertzhagen, Grant, and Praed, would unite *roseogrisea* and *decaocto*, making the former, and its races *arabica* and *bornuensis*, all subspecies of *decaocto*. I am not in agreement with that course.

[2] James Fisher, " The collared turtle-dove in Europe ", in *British Birds*, xlvi, 1953, pp. 152-181, with maps and bibliography.

[3] Professor E. Stresemann of Berlin informs me that the spread from Belgrade seems not to have begun earlier than about 1928.

is likely to be a welcome guest, there is no knowing where its travels will end.

Fisher's paper was published in 1953 and brought the distribution of this dove up to the year 1952. Since then it has continued its remarkable expansion and I am indebted to Professor Erwin Stresemann, the distinguished zoologist from Berlin, for the following brief account of the position at the time of going to press. Writing under date 22nd July 1958, Dr. Stresemann observes :

To the east, *Streptopelia decaocto* has now reached (and is nesting in) Kiev, Lublin, Warsaw, Danzig, and even the district of Tallinn (=Reval) in Estonia ! In 1958 it has successfully nested in Stavanger (Norway). In the west, it now nests at several places in Alsace, Luxembourg, and Belgium. In 1958, it nested in almost every part of Germany, but very unevenly distributed, locally common, rare or absent in other large districts. The first settlement was in Nürnberg (about 1944) where *Streptopelia decaocto* is very common now (more than 100 breeding pairs).

For details see : E. Stresemann and E. Nowak, " Die Ausbreitung der Türkentaube in Asien und Europa ", in *J. f. Orn.*, xcix (1958), No. 3.

HABITS : My first meeting with this delightful dove was in the port of Salonika when the cargo boat upon which I was a passenger, bound for the Black Sea, was tied up against the quay. Grain had been loaded here and spilled around to the advantage of the collared turtle-doves which were clustered on the roofs of the nearby sheds. My experience of edible—and inedible—birds in the Middle East is that they are all scared stiff of human beings, and it was refreshing to see these doves so free from fear, sunning themselves and preening amidst such a busy scene. The winter was still with us and the doves were less active and forthcoming than would have been the case in the early spring.

In his very excellent summary of the habitat of this turtle-dove, compiled from a voluminous literature, James Fisher writes :

In its spread across Europe the collared turtle-dove has shown certain pronounced habitat preferences which have been widely commented upon. The literature is full of evidence that what it likes for food and shelter resembles very closely that which it enjoys in India, which can be assumed to be its ancestral home. It is a graminivorous bird of parks, gardens, and cultivated land, typically where cultivated land abuts on marginal scrubland, and it has become a pronounced parasite, or at least symbiote, of man, having little fear of him (at least in much of its range), nesting freely in his gardens, frequently feeding with his chickens and other domestic animals and raiding his ripened corn and stackyards. Of the birds of Turkestan, the collared turtle-dove, according to Gladkov,[1] is among those most rigidly confined to the cultivated parts, and his investigation suggests that it has spread into central Asia relatively recently after the rise of cultivation. Keve-Kleiner's very fine analysis [2]

---

[1] N. A. Gladkov, " Notes sur la faune ornithologique des terrains cultivés du Turkestan ", in *Bull. Soc. Nat. Moscou, Sec. Biol.* (N. Ser.), xlvii, 1938, pp. 360-373.

[2] " Die Ausbreitung der orientalischen Lachtaube in Ungarn im letzten Dezennium ", in *Aquila*, l, 1944, pp. 281-298.

of the literature shows how closely the establishment of the collared turtle-dove is associated with villages and small holdings. The first record of a collared turtle-dove at a village is, of course, not always followed by the arrival of a mate and successful breeding. Several of the Continental records are winter ones, often of wandering flocks, some of up to a hundred members, obviously in search of food. But from May to September the pioneers appear to become mostly resident and territorial, and, if they find mates, may frequently rear three broods or more in a year. . . . Perhaps the greatest amount of movement, and certainly the greatest crop of desultory records, takes place in autumn, as might be expected with new-fledged young birds seeking their fortunes.

In its extensive distribution in India and Ceylon the collared turtle-dove covers many types of country except forest areas, and in the Himalayas is to be found at elevations up to 11,000 feet. All over Asia Minor and Iraq the bird is a resident, except for some of the progeny which disappear and probably make distant flights as in Central Europe. In Palestine it is a common resident north of the line Gaza-Hebron, and Colonel Meinertzhagen found that it appeared to be an abundant winter visitor to southern Palestine.[1] He observed large flocks passing north at Ramleh from 19th March to the end of April. None were seen in the Judaean highlands in winter, but it is common at that season in the Jordan valley, when it breeds from the last few days of April. Whether any of these migrants reach Cyprus on their northern flight I am doubtful. Its status in that island to-day is puzzling. In two winters searching for it in the towns and in the country we never saw a sign of it before May and then only near Nicosia. Forty-five years ago it must have been a numerous bird. Sir John Bucknill frequently met with it in the secluded Turkish gardens within the old walls of Nicosia and was struck by its tameness and familiarity. As recently as 1928-30 it was commonly seen and found nesting by Sir Charles Belcher when Chief Justice. Now the bird is practically extinct in Cyprus or very very rare. The same fate has overtaken it in the island of Rhodes, where, Professor Stresemann informs me, it was abundant in 1876 ; but soon after the island became an Italian possession (in 1912) the collared turtle-dove *vanished completely*, apparently due to lack of protection by the government. A few are still to be seen in captivity in Cyprus. Several lived in an aviary in Lady Loch's garden at Ayios Epiktitos. In the early days of 1958 they would wake up and call at the slightest sound in the middle of the night, and when the moon was full their dreamy *coo-coo-co* could be heard at any hour of the night until dawn. Such a tame bird will naturally have but a small chance of survival in an island where the Greek-speaking Cypriots have such a scant respect for bird life.

BREEDING HABITS : James Fisher remarked in his study of the collared turtle-dove that the species seems emphatically disposed to nest in conifers, particularly cypresses, but also cedars, larches, and pines. That may well

[1] *Ibis*, 1920, p. 248.

be its choice as it spreads westwards in Europe; cypresses will remind it of the homelands from which it emigrated, but in much of its Middle East range it must be content with a thorn-bush in which to build its fairly solid platform. Thorny bushes are also its preference in India. In that land the nest is always placed on trees or bushes, in most cases at heights between five and twenty feet from the ground. It does not use sites on buildings. Whistler describes the nest as the usual dove platform, of small sticks, dry grass stems, and fine roots, sometimes fairly solid in construction, with a saucer-like cavity for the eggs. The clutch consists of two and the eggs are described by the same authority as broad and perfect ovals, hard in texture and somewhat glossy. The colour is white with a slight ivory tinge. They average $1·16 \times 0·90$ in. according to Whistler, while Hartert in his *Vögel der Paläarktischen Fauna* quotes four measurements by Jourdain of eggs in the British Museum as $32 \times 24·5$, 32×24, $28·2 \times 22$, and 27×22 mm. In India most nests will be found in April and May but as most pairs rear more than one brood the season is protracted.

Those doves which have recently colonized the British Isles have shown a partiality for certain trees. All known nesting sites in Norfolk were between twenty-five and fifty feet up in pines or *Cupressus macrocarpo*. The Scottish pair which nested in Moray also selected the last-mentioned tree, building their nest in the densest part, fifteen feet from the ground. This nest was solidly built of sticks and lined with thick brown roots. Messrs. Richardson, Seago, and Church, who kept observation on the Norfolk arrivals, wrote of the courting behaviour as follows:

Display-flight resembles that of *S. turtur* during which the black and white lower surface of fanned tail is very conspicuous. Immediately before coition and when greeting female returning after long absence—e.g. incubation duties—the male faces her with swelled neck, coos and bows in unison several times. The tail or wings are not spread or dropped but carried normally. In the presence of a rival the male chivvies his mate in the opposite direction using the threat note described above, and while in sexual pursuit he follows her with a rather weak, draggling flight.

After describing the song they remark that the male also coos when displaying to the female, though in rather quicker tempo than normally. In territorial pursuit and threat-display a forceful angry-sounding note is used which may be interpreted " kwurr-kwurr-kwurr ". Young birds were heard to appeal for food with a shrill and feeble " weep ".

The Moray birds which nested on Mr. Alistair Adam's property were also kept under constant notice, and it was remarked that the juvenile from the first brood, which was able to fly strongly on 30th July, was still with its parents on 10th September though becoming more independent in the latter part of the month. These birds were rarely seen away from the farm, usually feeding within its precincts or in the cottage gardens around, and not in the fields. They were quite tame and approachable within a few yards, uttering their " coo-cooo-cu " from some favoured post or telephone pole.

Ornithologists in the British Isles have not had the opportunity as yet to make a close study of this recent accession to our avifauna, and I have therefore turned to the very full investigation of a breeding colony in Germany by Herr Fritz-Bernhard Hofstetter, the results of which he published a few years ago in the *Journal für Ornithologie* [1] under the title " Studies on a population of Collared Turtle Doves "—the word population being used in the same sense as colony. The article is a very long one in the German language, and I am indebted to Miss P. M. Thomas, late of the Zoological Museum, Tring, for having made a précis-translation of the contents for my use here. The investigation was made at Soest in Westphalia, and by the year it took place the collared turtle-dove population within the town environs had increased greatly, both as regards area and numbers. It must be clearly understood that the study is entirely the work of Herr Hofstetter of Schleswig-Holstein who has kindly permitted the following summary of the results he obtained [2] to appear in my volume. These I have arranged under the appropriate headings :

Food. This consists chiefly of all kinds of grain, especially poultry food, though fresh food (young green, berries, cherries) is also eaten.

Roosting Places. The communal sleeping-places lie as a rule outside the environs of the town. During the winter months they are visited by the large majority of the population, and occasionally spontaneously changed.

Habitat by Day. Their daytime resort was found to be the Plange mill, which from its central position offered especially favourable feeding opportunities. This spot, however, is more than merely a favourite feeding ground. It is also visited by collared turtle-doves during the breeding season, although there are ample opportunities for feeding closer to their breeding places over 1 km. away. Any member of the species may move freely in this communal territory, which all possess.

Breeding Habitat. In the breeding places the individual dove will suffer no other member of the species, other than the female, during the breeding season. In fact, conditions in the area resemble those of a giant dovecot. The dimensions of the breeding grounds vary between 1·5 and 10·6 hectares. They extend far beyond the environs of the town, without other ecological environment than houses, hen-houses, and trees of medium height, as well as large and small garden plots. In general, these breeding places are permanent. However, any great disturbance may occasion a change of place, at least in the case of younger birds.

Territorial Rights and Sex Relationships. These are acquired either by inter-marriage or by a young pair moving into an uninhabited one. Because of the short time allowed for observation it was not possible to prove definitely that the sexes remained together for more than one breeding season, but in view of their general biological behaviour this is likely to be the case. Deviations from monogamy

---

[1] *J. f. O.*, xcv, 1954, pp. 348-410.

[2] Herr Hofstetter reminds me that some of his observations are typical of the Soestian colony only and are not applicable to the species throughout its breeding range.

(courtship of a strange female, copulation with a strange female, desertion of the female partner for a stranger, polygamy) occurred. The link with the territory seems in general stronger than the link with the female.

Call-notes. Calls may be divided into two groups : the coo, which is merely the expression of general emotion, and the responsive, which has certain definite functions. The second group is divided into three variations, but with the same motive, namely defence, challenge (including courtship), and the nesting call, heard during the nest-building and care of the young.

Display and Courtship Behaviour. The display can be interpreted in several ways, namely defence of territory, preliminary to courtship and pairing. The calls and display of the collared turtle-dove have their parallels in those of the turtle-dove, which, biologically speaking, resembles almost exactly the collared turtle-dove. The modes of behaviour described probably spring more or less from the same basic emotion. Their intensity is conditioned by the level of the basic emotion and also by its reciprocal effect. If the latter is lacking in one of the participants, this may cause " recessive " behaviour in the partner, which in individual cases is sometimes not quite in keeping with the situation. This behaviour is common to both sexes— with the exception, of course, of the display, which is never observed in adult females.

Nest-seeking. The search for a nest, which precedes the building of it, has a special significance. Nest-seeking does not form part of the behaviour of the rock-dove. On the other hand the collared turtle-dove does not chase the female as does the rock dove. Presumably, nest-seeking (collared turtle-dove) and chasing (rock-dove) are designed to excite proper conditions for the breeding season ahead, i.e. to synchronize the readiness of the partners to propagate.

Nest-building. Nest-seeking ends in nest-building. During the latter the pair often revert to their behaviour during the actual nest-seeking. The building of the nest is carried out by the female, while the male brings the material. Wire is a very frequently used nesting material. Choice is conditioned more by thickness and length than material suitability. The male tests it with his beak. Trees of all kinds are chosen for nest-building, though pear trees, except for early broods, are obviously preferred. Only one pair nested on buildings, but with very poor breeding results. Old nests are frequently re-used for an immediately following brood.

Breeding. Copulation was most frequently observed nine to ten days before egg-laying. Like the rock-dove, the female shows her readiness by ducking. When the initiative comes from the female, this is the only preliminary to pairing. If the male is the active partner, he excites the female by the usual display.

Nest Relief. The birds do not appear to observe any fixed times of relief from sitting. But as is the case with other species of doves, the female is usually free from duty at midday. Apart from this, there appear to be shorter periods of relief in the morning and late afternoon. When relief is taking place the nesting call is the signal.

Sequence of Broods and Care of Young. Broods follow one another without interval. In normal cases the nest is ready for the next brood one day before to one day after the previous brood have quitted it. If some disaster has overtaken a brood, preparations for a new one (nest-seeking) commences on an average some two to three days later. Guardianship of the young of the first brood is still exercised for a time by the female, even when the young of the following brood are hatched and in contrast to their elder brothers and sisters must be fed on crop milk. This does not injure them in any way. On the contrary, a change over from crop milk to corn can be fatal, if the stage of development of a backward chick still necessitates crop milk.

Breeding Period. The breeding period may extend from the first days of March to the third week in October. The average number of broods is about five.

Chick Rearing and Mortality of Young. About 100 chicks are reared out of 100 broods. Therefore one pair rears on a yearly average about five chicks. Conditions in the case of broods commenced before 15th April are considerably more unfavourable. Of fifteen early broods observed only five were successful ; only seven young were brought off. The mortality of the young collared turtle-doves is considerably less than that of the nearly related species of dove. At the commencement of the breeding season 1953 there were present in the territory percentages of young ringed birds as follows : 60 per cent. of the 1952 birds and 46 per cent. of the 1951 birds.

Unfortunately the collared turtle-dove had not gained a place on the British List in time for my artist-collaborator to paint its portrait. George Lodge died in February 1954, and although a single example had arrived in Lincolnshire in April 1953, it was under suspicion as a possible escape until 1955, when the first breeding records were substantiated and the collared turtle-dove was recognized as a true addition to our avifauna. There is a very charming plate of the species in colour, drawn from life from a Norfolk family, by Mr. R. A. Richardson, published in *British Birds*, 50, Plate 1, where the colours and pose of adult and two young birds have been faithfully depicted.

REFERENCES : Original Description. *Columba risoria* L. var. *decaocto*. A. M. Frivaldsky, *Társaság Evkönyvei* (*Ungarische Akademieschriften*), 1834-36, iii kötet (Bd. iii), osztály (Teil) 3, pp. 183, 184, Taf. viii, 1838 : Philippopolis, Bulgaria, formerly Turkey in Europe=Plovdiv.

Order[1] PTEROCLETIFORMES

Family PTEROCLIDIDAE

Genus *SYRRHAPTES* Illiger

PLATE 26   **PALLAS'S SANDGROUSE**

Syrrhaptes paradoxus (Pallas)

An Irregular Visitor at wide intervals. During an invasion odd pairs may be
expected to nest sparingly as in the past

IDENTIFICATION : All the members of the sandgrouse family have a very
complex colour-pattern which is difficult to describe, and the present species
is no exception. The relationship to the pigeons can be seen quite clearly
in the shape and the pose of the head. There is, however, no soft membrane
at the base of the bill as in the *Columbidae* and in other respects they differ
very markedly from that group. In earlier works of mine I followed P. R.
Lowe in placing the sandgrouse as a sub-order of the Columbiformes but I
did so with reserve, feeling that they deserve Ordinal rank.

The only member of the group which figures on the British List is the
one which Mr. Lodge has skilfully depicted on Plate 26. The main features
to observe are the long pointed wings and the long central feathers of the
tail, a combination of grey and sandy-buff, the inner webs being barred
and the elongated portion black. The general colour of the upperparts is
sandy-buff with black barring. The crown and nape are grey, tinged with
yellowish, the rest of the head and neck orange-buff and grey. The chin
is whitish, passing into rust colour on the throat and greyish-buff on the
breast ; a grey streak passes from behind the eye down the cheeks. Across
the breast is a mottled band, and a patch of black is a conspicuous feature
on the belly. The legs are feathered to the toes : these feathers are dull
white as are those of the ventral region. Very noticeable are the pale-grey
flight-feathers ; the coverts are sandy with dark centres. The eye is dark
brown, the bill grey-blue. The tarsus is feathered.

The female is duller than the male, the crown, nape, and sides of the
neck being striped and spotted with black as is the entire upper surface
including the wing-coverts. The colours of the head and throat are paler,
and the throat is divided from the grey breast by a narrow crescent of
black. The female also has elongated central tail-feathers but they are
shorter than in the male.

---

[1] There is much to be said in favour of the Russian view that the sandgrouse should be
elevated to Ordinal rank. This has been done by Professor Dementiev in the *Birds of the
Soviet Union*, vol. ii, 1951, and by Colonel Meinertzhagen in *Birds of Arabia*, 1954.

PLATE 26

PALLAS'S SANDGROUSE
Syrrhaptes paradoxus (Pallas)

On the wing a flock has been mistaken, on good authority, for golden plovers. The sandgrouse's wing is more curved and it keeps stroke with far more regularity.

OCCURRENCES IN BRITAIN : The early history of Pallas's sandgrouse in these islands is given very clearly in the third and last edition (1927) of Howard Saunders's *Manual*, edited and revised by the late Dr. W. Eagle-Clarke[1] of the Royal Scottish Museum. It shows careful research and tallies with movements recorded on the Continent. I cannot do better than repeat it here. It takes the history of the bird up to 1909, since which date there has been an extraordinary cessation of occurrences so far as this country is concerned. The account,[2] approved, if not entirely written as I suspect, by Eagle-Clarke, reads as follows :

Few events in the annals of ornithology have excited more interest than the irruptions of Pallas's sand-grouse. These, as regards the British Isles, were first brought to notice by a few appearances in Norfolk,[3] Caernarvonshire,[4] and Kent,[5] in July and November 1859 ; while several examples were obtained on the Continent during the same year. In 1863 the ripples of a far larger wave of invasion spread westward over Europe, Heligoland being reached by 21st May, the date on which our first visitors of that year were shot in Northumberland, out of a flock of fourteen.[6] Next day about twenty reached Staffordshire, and numbers were subsequently found in many parts of the British Isles, the majority on the eastern side, from Kent to Caithness, and a few alighted in the Shetlands. Inland, as well as in the south of England, occurrences were not wanting, and while they were less plentiful in the west, it was in Pembrokeshire that the last survivor was shot, in February 1864. One bird even wandered to Benbecula in the Outer Hebrides [this was on 13th October 1863], and several were killed in Ireland, some of them as far west as County Donegal. All these, however, were merely detachments from a larger army which arrived in Galizia and Moravia on 6th May, and rolled westward to the Atlantic, spreading

---

[1] Howard Saunders's own account of this species will be found in the 4th edition of Yarrell's *History of British Birds* which he completed.

[2] Reproduced by kind permission of the publishers Messrs. Oliver and Boyd.

[3] The earliest date on record of the appearance of the sandgrouse in Britain was about the beginning of July 1859 at Walpole St. Peter's, about two miles from the Wash ; the example, a fine male, being secured for the Lynn Museum (Yarrell, *History of British Birds*, vol. iii, p. 33).

[4] On 9th July 1859 another male was shot from a flock of three, near Tremadoc at the north end of Cardigan Bay . . . and presented to the Derby Museum at Liverpool (Yarrell, vol. iii, p. 33).

[5] In November 1859 a certain George Jell of Lydd, in Kent, preserved a specimen for a Mr. Simmons of East Peckham, near Tunbridge (Yarrell, vol. iii, p. 33). Although Yarrell does not state where the specimen was obtained, we find it recorded in Ticehurst's *History of the Birds of Kent*, 1909, as having been killed at New Romney ; cf. Newton, in *Ibis*, 1864, p. 186. The specimen is preserved in the Maidstone Museum.

[6] The details of the 1863 invasion were gathered with extreme care by Professor Alfred Newton and communicated to the *Ibis*, 1864, pp. 185-222 ; the invasion is also dealt with—and some additional particulars added—in Newton's account of the sandgrouse in his *Dictionary of Birds*, pp. 805-810.

southward as far as Rimini in Italy and the Pyrénées.   Northward the birds reached the Faeroes, Sweden, and about Lat. 62° in Norway, while a few eggs were taken among the sandhills of Denmark and Holland.   In 1872 small flocks were observed in Northumberland and Ayrshire ; in 1876 a pack was seen in May near Winterton in Norfolk, and in October two birds were shot in County Kildare, Ireland. Incidentally it may be mentioned that the year 1876 saw the establishment of an important colony on the Kirghiz Steppes east of the Volga.

In 1888, from the end of February onwards, it was noticed that flocks of sand-grouse were in movement on the steppes of Orenburg in eastern Russia ; next flocks were observed passing over Poland, the Austrian Empire, and various parts of Germany ; while by May the invasion had reached the British Islands.   The eastern districts were, naturally, the most favoured, and two clutches of eggs were taken on the wolds above Beverley in Yorkshire by Mr. Swailes ; but the birds were widely spread over the country, even to the extreme west.   In Scotland, where the late Mr. W. Evans estimated that the sojourners were from 1500 to 2000 in number, a young bird was found in the Culbin Sands, Moray, about the end of June 1888 by Mr. Alexander Scott, gamekeeper, who further succeeded in finding, on 8th August 1889, another nestling which could not have been more than two or three days old. This was sent in the flesh to Professor Newton, and its portrait, with full description, appeared in the *Ibis*, 1890, pl. vii, pp. 207-214.   As on the former occasion visitors found their way to the Outer Hebrides, and some also alighted in the Orkneys and Shetlands ; a pack of forty visited Fair Isle.   In Ireland a considerable number were captured or observed, the migration extending on this occasion as far west as Clare and Mayo.   A special Act of Parliament was passed for the protection of sand-grouse in 1888, but very great destruction had already taken place during the summer of their arrival, and the Act did not take effect until February 1889, by which time most of the survivors of the " warm reception " given to the newcomers had succumbed to the moisture of our climate, or had departed for more congenial regions.

On the Continent the irruption of 1888 reached southward to Valencia in Spain and northward to the Faeroes and to Lat. 62° 24′ in Norway.

Since the great invasion of 1888, there have been several arrivals of small numbers, and one of some magnitude in 1908.   In 1890 a few appeared in Yorks, Lincs, Norfolk and Suffolk ; in 1891 Yorks, and the north of Scotland ; in 1899 Yorks, Lincs, and possibly Holy Island ; in 1904 Yorks ; in 1906 Yorks, Norfolk, and possibly East Lothian.   In May 1908 considerable numbers appeared in Yorks, Lincs, Norfolk, Essex, Kent, Hants, Surrey, Berks, Herts, and Cheshire ; and lastly in Yorks in 1909.

The above very lucid account from Eagle-Clarke's pen brings the history of the species in Britain up to 1909.   In *The Birds of Scotland* Dr. Baxter and Miss Rintoul add a little more detail, remarking that though numerous in many places in Scotland, in 1888, they were specially abundant in Aberdeenshire and along the shores of the Moray Firth, where, as recorded above, they even bred.   Some birds penetrated right into the interior as on the Moor of Rannoch, and Ben Rinnes, Banffshire.   During these immigrations the sandgrouse has visited every county of Scotland except Lanark, Peebles, Selkirk, Roxburgh, Kinross, and Dunbarton.

Not surprisingly smaller numbers were seen in Ireland in the years 1863, 1876, and 1888—the last-mentioned by far the largest, when records came from Clare, Cork, Wexford, Offaly, Dublin, Meath, Galway, Roscommon, Mayo, Down, Tyrone, Derry, and Fermanagh. To these records which appeared in Ussher and Warren's *Birds of Ireland* (1900), Major Ruttledge has been able to add nothing in the new *Birds of Ireland* (1954). Surprisingly, however, there is a record for the very year when that volume was issued which is published in the *Irish Bird Report* 1955, recording a couple of sandgrouse, presumed to be Pallas's, which frequented the sand-hills by the entrance to Wexford harbour in May 1954 and were present for a week or more. The description of the birds taken down by the observer leave little doubt that the identification was correct, and the record has been accepted by the authorities—Major Ruttledge among them —for keeping *Birds of Ireland* up to date.

There has been no other mention of Pallas's sandgrouse arriving in this country with the exception of the Yorkshire record in October 1912 of 160 birds seen on a moor at Lockton. These birds are reported to have flown past the observer " near the ground within twenty yards of him ". Sandgrouse when flying in packs do not fly " near the ground " nor is October a date when such a visitation might be expected, and Mr. Witherby rightly refused to accept the identification (cf. *British Birds*, vi, p. 318). The supposed occurrence is also mentioned by Mr. Ralph Chislett, quite rightly, in his *Yorkshire Birds* (1952), p. 228.

DISTRIBUTION ABROAD AND PERIODIC WANDERINGS : The home of Pallas's sandgrouse is behind the Iron Curtain, from the Aral-Caspian region eastwards to China. The late Hermann Grote, a skilled and very careful German ornithologist of our time, worked out from current literature and private reports what he considered to be its range in 1936, and published his opinion in a valuable contribution to a German scientific periodical [1] which I have had translated for use in this book. Grote considered that although in 1936 the sandgrouse was apparently extending its breeding area to the west (and perhaps also to the north), it did not then belong to the regular, *i.e.* annual, breeding birds in the extreme south-eastern corner of Europe. He pointed out that to the east of Astrakhan sandgrouse will nest for a number of years and then cease to do so for another period of years, and that it is exceptional—if not improbable—to find *Syrrhaptes* breeding west of the Volga. Defining its range more exactly, he stated that in the Kirghiz Steppes to the east of the Ural River its northern breeding area does not extend beyond 40° N. ; it does not even breed annually in the given areas. As regular breeding places only those regions abutting on the Emba (and to the south of it) can really be regarded as authentic. These records in our literature of breeding areas far to the

[1] *Sonderdruck aus Beiträge zur Fortpflanzungsbiologie der Vögel*, Jahrgang 12, 1936, pp. 14-15. English translation by Miss P. M. Thomas of the Zoological Museum, Tring.

north (*e.g.* in the Ufa province) can only be regarded as isolated attempts at breeding or the chance breeding of a temporary invasion of sandgrouse. There can be no question of normal nesting. Grote confirms that small sandgrouse invasions have often been noticed in eastern Russia and suggests that in almost every year isolated companies of this sandgrouse may wander into the eastern steppes of Russia.

In the second volume of *The Birds of the Soviet Union* there is on p. 84 a small line-map of Asia roughly defining the area in which *Syrrhaptes paradoxus* occurs in the view of Professor Dementiev, who wrote the section on the sandgrouse. No doubt the author consulted Herr Grote's paper from which I have quoted, and it is noteworthy that these two authorities agree as to the western limits. When reviewing this volume, written of course in Russian, Mr. D. D. Harber [1] quotes Dementiev as stating that the regular nesting place of Pallas's sandgrouse in the area of the lower Volga and in the Volga-Ural Steppes is considered doubtful. The area of certain breeding begins only in the Aral-Caspian region and extends to western Manchuria. The reason for the irregular movements of this sandgrouse—a question so often asked by European students—is answered by Professor Dementiev and will be discussed under the next heading.

The early invasions of Pallas's sandgrouse into Europe were recounted by Alfred Newton in the *Dictionary of Birds*, notably that of 1863, when " a horde computed to consist of at least 700 birds [2] overran Europe " in May and June, reaching Sweden, Norway, the Faeroes, Ireland, the Adriatic, and the Bay of Biscay, some of the wanderers actually breeding on the sand-hills of Jutland and Holland ; and the second great invasion of 1888 which—to quote Professor Newton—repeated most of the features of the 1863 incursion. The event, however, took place a month earlier in the year and the passage across Europe soon expanded more widely. " In the north-east the Gulf of Finland was crossed to Helsingfors but the most northerly (Roraas in Norway) and westerly (Belmullet in Ireland) points reached were only a little farther than the limits of 1863. Southward a great extension was shown, not only in Italy (Santa Severa not far from Rome) but in Spain (Albufera of Valencia), that country being now invaded for the first time." In an earlier paragraph the results of these two invasions as they affected Britain have already been indicated. Newton reminds us in his account that prior to 1848, when a single example was obtained at Sarepta on the Volga in the winter months, Pallas's sandgrouse had been known only as an inhabitant of the Tartar Steppes, and not until 1859 was the bird seen in western Europe.

HABITS : Of all the sandgrouse species inhabiting the desert spaces

---

[1] *British Birds*, xlviii, pp. 268-276. *Syrrhaptes* on p. 269.

[2] From the numbers involved in this invasion in Europe we should have put the figure much higher than 700 and wonder if a " o " has been accidentally omitted ?

of the earth, the subject of this essay is the most enigmatic. There has been much speculation as to the course of its periodic migrations right up to the present day, though it is now fifty years since its presence has been recognized in Britain. In the recently issued *Birds of the Soviet Union*, Professor Dementiev ascribes this species' irregular movements to food difficulties due to heavy snow, or the formation of a crust on the snow. In his opinion the movements are not due to over-population. He points out that they take place not only in a westerly but also in an easterly direction, though the latter have been less studied. There is no synchronization between westerly and easterly movements, which shows that only the populations of certain areas are affected by local conditions.

There are few European ornithologists alive to-day who can have seen Pallas's sandgrouse in its native haunts, for travel in the fascinating lands beyond the Caspian is no longer tolerated, much less encouraged, and many years may pass before one of our countrymen has again the opportunities which came the way of Douglas Carruthers when, as a young man, he explored the country between Turkestan and Mongolia and passed through the heart of the country where Pallas's sandgrouse has its headquarters. Even so it is possible, as he found, to travel far without seeing it. It was the middle of March when Carruthers moved out of the oasis of Kara Kul:

Other birds were moving south—the sandgrouse—for, like the shepherds, they knew that the spring grass would flourish earliest on the banks of the Oxus, and thither they hurried in countless thousands for a quick feed before going north to their breeding grounds. They did not stay long for within a week (23rd March), they almost darkened the sky with their legions as they passed over me heading in the opposite direction. They were mostly pin-tailed (*Pterocles alchata* Linn.), with a few black-bellied (*Pterocles orientalis* Linn.) amongst them and they moved as only sandgrouse can, with direct, arrow-like flight, accelerated to sixty miles per hour. Curiously enough there were no members of that capricious species Pallas's sandgrouse (*Syrrhaptes paradoxus* Pallas) whose strange unreliable habits are so well commemorated in its name—*paradoxus*. This is its true home, but I came across it only once during my year's work in Russian Turkestan. However, I was treated to a rare sight some years later, when I found myself underneath its main mass-migration from Central Siberia to its winter quarters. On that memorable occasion in October, for two whole days, from dawn to dusk, the sky was full of moving hosts of Pallas's sandgrouse. As far as the eye could see, and in every direction, there were large packs and small parties passing south, and as the country was the open Dzungarian plain, and the weather very clear, and we were on the move, the numbers necessary to make up the whole kaleidoscope, and to keep it running for that period of time, must have been very great indeed.[1]

Douglas Carruthers refers again to this chance meeting with the mass-migration of sandgrouse in his classical volumes *Unknown Mongolia*. It

---

[1] *Beyond the Caspian*, Edinburgh, Oliver and Boyd, 1949, pp. 56-57.

was on 10th and 11th October that the scene met his eyes ; as he moved across the Emil Steppes. With a strong west wind behind them the packs were hurrying towards the south-east, the large packs flying high, but small flocks of half-dozens flying quite low. With the vast hosts of Pallas's sandgrouse were also many large black-bellied sandgrouse and Carruthers believed he was watching the great autumn migration of all the birds of the Sergiopol and Semipalatinsk Steppes to their winter quarters in the plain of Dzungaria.[1] The clear map which accompanies Mr. Carruthers's *Beyond the Caspian* will help the reader to appreciate the lie of the land where sandgrouse are wont to wander. In the following paragraphs quoted from his book Mr. Carruthers describes the area through which part of his journey took him :

Immediately after crossing the Zarafshan to the north, one meets the desert ; in fact in some places the sand-dunes appear to be encroaching upon and actually altering the course of the river. . . . But the so-called desert is of a very varied type. There are sand-dunes, it is true, but they mostly grow a phenomenal amount of herbage. There is hard steppe, but it is covered with tamarisk, and at certain seasons with good grazing. The vast region called vaguely, Kizil Kum, which fills the void between the Oxus and the Syr, is of much greater variety than is indicated by the map. It is neither a Rub al Khali nor a Sahara of virulent type. We know of at least one Russian expedition which made light of crossing it at its widest extent with a cumbersome caravan of 500 camels, 230 cossacks, and as many infantrymen plus two cannons ! It is not all sand-dune and steppe by any means ; there are outcrops of hills and many " lows " growing dense reed-beds and poplar thickets. For it must be remembered that this land has seen many changes. The Oxus and the Syr have not always flowed as they do now and there are many indications of old river beds which once carried water and supported cultivation, but are now jungles. All the way from the Oxus to the Syr and to the Aral Sea this type of country holds good. . . . It is without permanent habitation.

In the introduction to the book in which this account appears Carruthers observes that these regions have stood beyond the range of even the ubiquitous Englishman and no-one else to his knowledge has been privileged to live openly, and travel freely, as long as he was allowed to do under Russian rule *north* of the Oxus. This is the land—once again a *terra incognita*—where Pallas's sandgrouse has its nearest home to the western world. It will be remembered that the Kirghiz Steppes were colonized by this sandgrouse in 1876. A request to Douglas Carruthers to define the position of this area, which is never clearly shown on modern maps, has elicited the following reply : " The Kirghiz Steppes = the void to the north of Aral and Balkash, from the Ural river to the Irtish at its widest on my map.[2] It is an illogical name (there are no Kirghiz [living] there) and out

---

[1] *Unknown Mongolia*, vol. ii, pp. 407-408.

[2] This is an excellent layered map entitled " Central Asia and Adjacent Regions," printed by Stanford, London, bound in at the end of *Beyond the Caspian*.

of date. It is covered by the Provinces of Turgi and Akmolinsk of present-day Kazakstan, not applicable to my own or any modern map." Mr. Carruthers adds " *Syrrhaptes paradoxus* never showed up in the Kizil-Kum either in summer or winter : its name is sufficient to account for this ".

I have found only one other reference to the passage of Pallas's sandgrouse—that by Mme. E. V. Kozlova in her account of the birds of northern Mongolia. During one of her expeditions she witnessed a very large migration on 4th March 1926, when on the upper reaches of the Onghiin-gol River in Khangai. Flock after flock appeared from the south-east and proceeded north-west, flying high above the forest. Thirty-five flocks passed in one and a half hours and the migration lasted from early morning until 4 p.m. Mme. Kozlova observes that these sandgrouse keep in flocks during the whole summer and breed in colonies.

It was, I believe, Alfred Newton who remarked that anyone familiar with a sandgrouse of any species would have no difficulty in recognizing any of the others belonging to the family should he meet with them in his travels. That is perfectly true. In their plumage, which matches so exactly the ground upon which they live, in their direct so-called arrow-like flight, in the regular beat of their wings in unison, in their habit of flying in flocks or packs, and in their outline when seen against a cloudless sky, there is no mistaking a sandgrouse. It has been my good fortune to know four species in the Canary Islands, in the Sahara, and in Cyprus, but the subject of this article I have never seen alive in Europe or Asia. It is, as Hermann Grote recorded, a characteristic bird of the wormwood steppes and semi-desert region. The clay soil of the steppes, sparsely covered with wormwood and interspersed with barren saltings, affords an especially favourable dwelling place ; the coloration of the bird being wonderfully adapted to the tones of the soil, scorched by the hot sun.

The various species of sandgrouse that I have known in Africa come to drink at specified hours. Some species drink but once a day in the early morning, others every morning and evening as punctually as clockwork. Both the chestnut-bellied (*exustus*) and the coronetted (*coronatus*) come into the latter category ; Lichtenstein's (*lichtensteinii*) never drinks till the sun is set and often arrives long after dusk, remaining in the vicinity of the water all night. The four-banded (*quadricinctus*) drinks but once a day and that in the evening. It was interesting, therefore, to read how Pallas's sandgrouse is reported by Sushkin to leave the eggs during the nesting season for long periods when they fly to the drinking pools. He has observed them at their drinking places during the daytime from 10 to 4 o'clock ; they seek their food in the neighbourhood of the pools, bath in the sand or just lie quietly in the sunshine, flying at intervals to the water. Sushkin remarked how they always used the same drinking places, flying several kilometres for the purpose. Another Russian observer, Bostanjoglo, reported somewhat differently, stating that the sandgrouse

flew to their drinking places at sunrise and sunset and passed the daylight
hours in the steppe. It may be that during the period when they have
eggs and nestlings they vary their habits, but as a rule sandgrouse, wherever
they may be, are remarkably punctual drinkers and can be relied upon to
turn up at the expected time.

BREEDING HABITS : The literature on Pallas's sandgrouse contains
very little on its breeding biology and, as Herr Grote observed in the
paper I have quoted, our knowledge of its nesting—apart from Raddes'
detailed description—rests for the most part on observations made in
Europe on birds which have nested when invading countries other than
their own. Observations made by Russian authors in the real breeding-
places of Pallas's sandgrouse are consequently of particular value.

A sandgrouse is a very difficult bird to watch on the nest, for often
there is no cover of any sort and as it lays its eggs in a depression on the
ground on the desert floor, with which the eggs and the bird's plumage
harmonize so closely, it is far from easy to watch the bird back onto its eggs.
In the Aral-Caspian region Dementiev has recorded [1] that the male may
be seen in mid-April displaying to the female when any intruding male is
driven away. The " display " if the performance deserves such a grand
title, consists of the male " running round the female in a pigeon-like
manner, but without puffing out his neck and without bowing. Sometimes
he flies in circles round the female." Then, to quote once more from
Grote's account :

During the middle of April companies of sandgrouse arrive in the Kirghiz
breeding places, but pairing does not take place until the first half of May. All
through the breeding period the birds keep together in loose-knit bands, for *Syrrhaptes* nests in small colonies and flies in companies to the drinking pools.

In the Kirghiz Steppes the eggs are not laid before the last days of May. The
clutch, which almost always consists of three, rarely of four eggs, lies in a depression
in the ground. Apparently both sexes incubate the eggs for males shot during the
breeding season showed incubation marks. While the female is sitting the male
remains close by ; the birds interrupt their brooding for many hours daily.

Sushkin's opinion is then quoted that the development of the embryo
is activated to a considerable degree by the warmth of the sun, for the
sandgrouse leave their eggs for long periods when they visit the drinking
pools.

As a rule this sandgrouse breeds twice in a season and the chicks, like the eggs,
are left to themselves for hours during the day.

Moulting is a slow process. According to Sushkin the feathers of the lower back
are moulted towards the middle of June and two weeks later those of the head.
Moult of the soft plumage reaches its height at the end of July. Most of the tail
and wing feathers are renewed about the middle of July.

Very few eggs of this sandgrouse were in the British Museum collection

[1] Translated by D. D. Harber in his review in *British Birds*, xlviii, p. 269.

when the first volume of *The Catalogue of Birds' Eggs* was written by Oates. A pair from the Altai obtained in May by C. A. Tancré are described as having a pale stone-coloured ground, the surface markings consisting of specks, spots, and blotches of yellowish-brown evenly distributed over the shell. F. C. R. Jourdain had examined a much larger series and pointed out that the clutch is usually three, sometimes two only, and occasionally four : the last must surely be exceptional and may be given solely on the authority of Radde. Jourdain described them [1] as elongated ellipse in shape, with blunt ends, stone-buff or greyish-stone to warm yellow-brown in ground colour, spotted and blotched with purplish-brown and numerous ashy shell-marks : the shell slightly glossy. The average of 100 eggs was 42·1 × 29·6 mm. Max. 46·5 × 29·9 and 42·5 × 32·4 mm. Min. 39·2 × 28·5 and 40·3 × 27 mm. From literature he gave the breeding season in Turkestan from mid-April to June and in Mongolia from mid-May to June.

Herr G. Radde [2] found Pallas's sandgrouse breeding on the salt-impregnated soil of the Tarei-nor, the basin of which is situated, so he states, in 50° N. 116° E. He described the nest as very simple, resembling those of the other sandgrouse, a shallow hollow about five inches in diameter being scratched out in the soil which has been dry for years. The edge is lined with a few salsola shoots and grasses, but the latter are frequently absent. Radde goes on to describe the dates when he found eggs and young birds, and observes that they are fond of the young juicy shoots of the *Salicorniae* upon which they regularly graze. In the spring he found the crop and stomach full of the seeds of the salsola. It will be observed on reading Radde's account carefully that he says " eggs go up to four " (*i.e.* do not exceed four), but in the instances he quotes where he found eggs himself there is no mention of a clutch of this size, and if he obtained his information from local sources it may well have been due to two hens.

Reliable individual records of the nesting of Pallas's sandgrouse in Central Asia are rare but several were published by Mme E. Kozlova in the *Ibis*, 1932, p. 586. She writes : " I have reliable records of the breeding of this sandgrouse in the following regions : in Central Gobi, in Northern Gobi and in south-east Khangai. Kozlov noted a nest with three eggs on 16th May 1909 in Central Gobi ; the same explorer obtained another nest with eggs on 27th May north of Gurbun-Saikhan. On 6th June 1926, in Kholt (south-east Khangai), two downy young were found on the steppe, with a flock of adult birds ".

REFERENCES : Original Description. *Tetrao paradoxa* Pallas, *Reise d. versch. Prov. d. Russ. Reichs*, vol. ii, 1773, p. 712, pl. F. Type locality Tartary desert.

---

[1] *The Handbook of British Birds.*
[2] *Reisen im Süden von Ost-Siberien*, vol. ii, pp. 292-294. Translation in Yarrell's *History of British Birds*, vol. iii, pp. 40-43.

INDEX

	PAGE
adamsii, Gavia	283
ALBATROSS, BLACK-BROWED	188
ctica, Gavia arctica	298
otelis, Phalacrocorax	13
a s, Podiceps	235
barol ffinus, and races	101
bassana la	21
borealis, nus diomedia	123
boydi, Puf baroli	101
brevipes, Pte oma leucoptera	155
Bulweria bulw	161
bulwerii, Bulwer	161
capensis, Daption	156
carbo, Phalacrocorax, races	1
caspicus, Podiceps caspi	250
castro, Oceanodroma	60
Columba livia livia	349
Columba oenas	338
Columba palumbus palumbus	324
Columbidae	324
Colymbus	272
CORMORANT	1
CORMORANT, Green	13
CORMORANT, SOUTHERN	1
cristatus, Podiceps cristatus	2
Daption capensis	156
decaocto, Streptopelia decaocto	375
Diomedea melanophrys melanophrys	188
diomedia, Puffinus, and races	123
DIVER, BLACK-THROATED	298
DIVER, GREAT NORTHERN	272
DIVER, RED-THROATED	312
DIVER, WHITE-BILLED NORTHERN	283
DOVE, COLLARED TURTLE-	375
DOVE, ROCK-	349
DOVE, RUFOUS TURTLE-	373
DOVE, STOCK-	338
DOVE, TURTLE-	361
Fregata magnificens rothschildi	35
Fregatidae	35
FRIGATE BIRD, MAGNIFICENT	35

	PAGE
FRIGATE PETREL	78
FULMAR	167
Fulmarus glacialis glacialis	167
GANNET	21
Gavia adamsii	283
Gavia arctica arctica	298
Gavia immer	272
Gavia stellata	312
Gaviidae	272
glacialis, Fulmarus glacialis	167
gravis, Puffinus	111
GREBE, BLACK-NECKED	250
GREBE, GREAT CRESTED	200
GREBE, HOLBOELL'S	223
GREBE, HORNED	235
GREBE, LITTLE	261
GREBE, RED-NECKED	223
GREBE, SLAVONIAN	235
griseigena, Podiceps, and races	223
griseus, Puffinus	135
hasitata, Pterodroma	146
holboellii, Podiceps griseigena	223
Hydrobates pelagicus	39
hypoleuca, Pelagodroma marina	78
immer, Gavia	272
uhlii, Puffinus	123
leu ptera brevipes, Pterodroma	155
leuc hoa, Oceanodroma leucorrhoa	48
l'herm eri, Puffinus l'herminieri	108
livia, Co mba livia	349
magnificens othschildi, Fregata	35
marina hypole ca, Pelagodroma	78
mauretanicus, F ffinus puffinus	86
melanophrys, Dio edea melanophrys	188
neglecta, Pterodroma	150
oceanicus, Oceanites	68
Oceanites oceanicus	68
Oceanodroma castro	60

	PAGE
Oceanodroma leucorrhoa leucorrhoa	48
oenas, Columba	338
orientalis, Streptopelia	373
palumbus, Columba palumbus	324
paradoxus, Syrrhaptes	388
pelagicus, Hydrobates	39
Pelagodroma marina hypoleuca	78
PETREL, BLACK-CAPPED	146
PETREL, BULWER'S	161
PETREL, CAPE	156
PETREL, COLLARED	155
PETREL, FRIGATE	78
PETREL, HARCOURT'S	60
PETREL, KERMADEC	146, 150
PETREL, LEACH'S FORK-TAILED	48
PETREL, MADEIRAN	60
PETREL, STORMY	39
PETREL, WHITE-FACED	78
PETREL, WILSON'S	68
Phalacrocoracidae	1
Phalacrocorax aristotelis	13
Phalacrocorax carbo, and races	1
PIGEON, CAPE	156
PIGEON, WOOD-	324
Podiceps auritus	235
Podiceps caspicus caspicus	250
Podiceps cristatus cristatus	200
Podiceps griseigena, and races	223
Podiceps ruficollis ruficollis	261
Podicipedidae	200
Procellariidae	39
Pteroclididae	388
Pterodroma hasitata	146
Pterodroma leucoptera brevipes	155

	PAGE
Pterodroma neglecta	150
Puffinus baroli, and races	101
Puffinus diomedia, and races	123
Puffinus gravis	111
Puffinus griseus	135
Puffinus kuhlii	123
Puffinus l'herminieri l'herminieri	108
Puffinus puffinus, and races	86
rothschildi, Fregata magnificens	35
ruficollis, Podiceps ruficollis	261
SANDGROUSE, PALLAS'S	388
SHAG	13
SHEARWATER, ALEXANDER'S LITTLE	101
SHEARWATER, ATLANTIC	123
SHEARWATER, AUDUBON'S	108
SHEARWATER, BALEARIC	86
SHEARWATER, CAPE VERDE LITTLE	101
SHEARWATER, CORY'S	123
SHEARWATER, GREAT	111
SHEARWATER, MADEIRAN LITTLE	101
SHEARWATER, MANX	86
SHEARWATER, MEDITERRANEAN	123
SHEARWATER, SOOTY	135
sinensis, Phalacrocorax carbo	1
stellata, Gavia	312
Streptopelia decaocto decaocto	375
Streptopelia orientalis	373
Streptopelia turtur turtur	361
Sula bassana	21
Sulidae	21
Syrrhaptes paradoxus	388
turtur, Streptopelia turtur	361